READINGS IN
AMERICAN FOREIGN POLICY

Readings in
AMERICAN
FOREIGN POLICY

Edited by
ROBERT A. GOLDWIN
St. John's College

SECOND EDITION
Revised by
HARRY M. CLOR
Kenyon College

New York
OXFORD UNIVERSITY PRESS
London   1971   Toronto

PREFACE TO THE SECOND EDITION

This revision of *Readings in American Foreign Policy* is designed to bring the volume up to date by introducing readings which deal with the crucial issues emerging in the 1960's. The revised edition preserves the basic structure and is intended to serve the same educational purposes as the original text. As in the original, the aim is to present opposing viewpoints and diverse perspectives on major controversial issues, and to raise fundamental questions about the ends and means of foreign policy.

In nine of the volume's ten sections the reader is presented with both an historical treatment of the subject and an exploration of contemporary or recent problems. Some of the new materials in this edition are addressed to issues arising out of United States involvement in Vietnam and to the current debate over the direction of American foreign policy after Vietnam. This volume of readings is not designed to reflect any particular political viewpoint. It is based, however, upon an educational viewpoint—one which regards confrontation with basic controversial issues as vital to political learning.

Although final responsibility for the selection of articles rests with me, I am greatly indebted to my colleague, Professor Lewis Dunn of Kenyon College, for his invaluable advice and suggestions.

HARRY M. CLOR

Kenyon College
Gambier, Ohio
August 20, 1970

PREFACE TO THE FIRST EDITION

The purpose of this volume of readings is threefold: to serve the college and university student as primary or supplementary course material, to offer the general reader an opportunity to acquaint himself systematcially with the best thought on a wide range of the fundamental problems, and to function as the basic reading material for organized programs of adult education discussion groups.

Several unique features distinguish this book from other books of readings and affect the ways in which it can best be used. Its main characteristic is the plan of selection and editing. The articles are grouped in sections, each about 50 to 75 pages long, intended to be read as a unit. The selections have the continuity of a debate; opposing views are deliberately juxtaposed and the reader must judge the merits of each argument. The articles within each unit will be most instructive, therefore, if they are read in the order in which they appear. The sections are also best taken up in order, for the materials in later sections assume knowledge of the issues discussed in earlier sections.

This book has no index; although it contains a great deal of historical information, it is not a book for "looking up" isolated facts or events. It is a book of political argument. Although the readings present clear and forceful statements of a variety of positions—some quite partisan, others more detached and analytical—the collection as a whole is not meant to represent or support any particular viewpoint. Readers should not assume that any author in these pages is the spokesman of the editors. Nor is this volume intended to be comprehensive. The aim is rather to provoke thought on a limited number of highly significant problems and to provide a sound basis for further study.

CONTENTS

X.   WHAT PRINCIPLES GUIDE AMERICAN
FOREIGN POLCY?

APPENDIX

A NOTE ON THE AMERICAN FOUNDATION
FOR CONTINUING EDUCATION

This book was originally sponsored by the American Foundation for Political Education for use in discussion programs for the education of adults. During the years 1947–1958, the AFPE organized and conducted discussion groups in hundreds of communities, in cooperation with local educational institutions and civic agencies. Many of these programs continue, but in 1958 the AFPE ceased its practice of directly subsidizing the costs of local programs and has changed the nature of its activities. It now concentrates on the development of reading materials in many fields. To conform to the changed focus of the work, the organization's name was changed to the American Foundation for Continuing Education.

In 1969 the active direction of the AFCE was taken over by Syracuse University.

Alexander N. Charters, President
Doris S. Chertow, Editor
American Foundation for Continuing Education
Syracuse University Publications in Continuing Education

105 Roney Lane
Syracuse, New York

I

FOREIGN AFFAIRS IN THE AMERICAN DEMOCRACY

A Selection from

DEMOCRACY IN AMERICA*

BY

ALEXIS DE TOCQUEVILLE

[1835]

CONDUCT OF FOREIGN AFFAIRS BY THE AMERICAN DEMOCRACY

We have seen that the Federal Constitution entrusts the permanent direction of the external interests of the nation to the President and the Senate,[1] which tends in some degree to detach the general foreign policy of the Union from the control of the people. It cannot therefore be asserted with truth that the external affairs of State are conducted by the democracy.

The policy of America owes its rise to Washington, and after him to Jefferson, who established those principles which it observes at the present day. Washington said in the admirable letter which he addressed to his fellow-citizens, and which may be looked upon as his political bequest to the country: "The great rule of conduct for us, in regard to foreign nations, is, in extending our commercial relations, to have with them as little political connection as possible. So far as we have already formed engagements, let them be fulfilled with perfect good faith. Here let us stop. Europe has a set of primary interests which to us have none, or a very remote relation. Hence, she must be engaged in frequent controversies, the causes of which are essentially foreign to our concerns. Hence, therefore, it must be unwise in us to implicate ourselves, by artificial ties, in the ordinary vicissitudes of her politics, or the ordinary combinations and collisions of her friendships or enmities.

---

* Alexis de Tocqueville (1805–1859), French nobleman and political thinker and Foreign Minister of France in 1849, spent nine months in America, 1831–1832. His *Democracy in America*, the most famous commentary on this country by a foreigner, was written as a result of this visit.

[1] "The President," says the Constitution, Art. II, sect. 2, §2, "shall have power, by and with the advice and consent of the Senate, to make treaties, provided two-thirds of the senators present concur." The reader is reminded that the senators are returned for a term of six years.

Our detached and distant situation invites and enables us to pursue a different course. If we remain one people, under an efficient government, the period is not far off when we may defy material injury from external annoyance; when we may take such an attitude as will cause the neutrality we may at any time resolve upon to be scrupulously respected; when belligerent nations, under the impossibility of making acquisitions upon us, will not lightly hazard the giving us provocation; when we may choose peace or war, as our interest, guided by justice, shall counsel. Why forego the advantages of so peculiar a situation? Why quit our own to stand upon foreign ground? Why, by interweaving our destiny with that of any part of Europe, entangle our peace and prosperity in the toils of European ambition, rivalship, interest, humor, or caprice? 'Tis our true policy to steer clear of permanent alliances with any portion of the foreign world; so far, I mean, as we are now at liberty to do it; for let me not be understood as capable of patronizing infidelity to existing engagements. I hold the maxim no less applicable to public than to private affairs, that honesty is always the best policy. I repeat it, therefore, let those engagements be observed in their genuine sense. But, in my opinion, it is unnecessary, and would be unwise, to extend them. Taking care always to keep ourselves, by suitable establishments, in a respectable defensive posture, we may safely trust to temporary alliances for extraordinary emergencies." In a previous part of the same letter Washington makes the following admirable and just remark: "The nation, which indulges toward another an habitual hatred, or an habitual fondness, is in some degree a slave. It is a slave to its animosity or to its affection, either of which is sufficient to lead it astray from its duty and its interest."

The political conduct of Washington was always guided by these maxims. He succeeded in maintaining his country in a state of peace whilst all the other nations of the globe were at war; and he laid it down as a fundamental doctrine, that the true interest of the Americans consisted in a perfect neutrality with regard to the internal dissensions of the European Powers.

Jefferson went still further, and he introduced a maxim into the policy of the Union, which affirms that "the Americans ought never to solicit any privileges from foreign nations, in order not to be obliged to grant similar privileges themselves."

These two principles, which were so plain and so just as to be adapted to the capacity of the populace, have greatly simplified the foreign policy of the United States. As the Union takes no part in the affairs of Europe, it has, properly speaking, no foreign interests to discuss, since it has at present no powerful neighbors on the American continent. The country is as much removed from the passions of the Old World by its position as by the line of policy which it has chosen, and it is neither called upon to repudiate nor to espouse the conflicting interests of Europe; whilst the dissensions of the New World are still concealed within the bosom of the future.

The Union is free from all pre-existing obligations, and it is consequently enabled to profit by the experience of the old nations of Europe, without being obliged, as they are, to make the best of the past, and to adapt it to their present circumstances; or to accept that immense inheritance which they derive from their forefathers —an inheritance of glory mingled with calamities, and of alliances conflicting with national antipathies. The foreign policy of the United States is reduced by its very nature to await the chances of the future history of the nation, and for the present it consists more in abstaining from interference than in exerting its activity.

It is therefore very difficult to ascertain, at present, what degree of sagacity the American democracy will display in the conduct of the foreign policy of the country; and upon this point its adversaries, as well as its advocates, must suspend their judgment. As for myself I have no hesitation in avowing my conviction, that it is most especially in the conduct of foreign relations that democratic governments appear to me to be decidedly inferior to governments carried on upon different principles. Experience, instruction, and habit may almost always succeed in creating a species of practical discretion in democracies, and that science of the daily occurrences of life which is called good sense. Good sense may suffice to direct the ordinary course of society; and amongst a people whose education has been provided for, the advantages of democratic liberty in the internal affairs of the country may more than compensate for the evils inherent in a democratic government. But such is not always the case in the mutual relations of foreign nations.

Foreign politics demand scarcely any of those qualities which a democracy possesses; and they require, on the contrary, the perfect use of almost all those faculties in which it is deficient. Democracy is favorable to the increase of the internal resources of the State; it tends to diffuse a moderate independence; it promotes the growth of public spirit, and fortifies the respect which is entertained for law in all classes of society; and these are advantages which only exercise an indirect influence over the relations which one people bears to another. But a democracy is unable to regulate the details of an important undertaking, to persevere in a design, and to work out its execution in the presence of serious obstacles. It cannot combine its measures with secrecy, and it will not await their consequences with patience. These are qualities which more especially belong to an individual or to an aristocracy; and they are precisely the means by which an individual people attains to a predominant position.

If, on the contrary, we observe the natural defects of aristocracy, we shall find that their influence is comparatively innoxious in the direction of the external affairs of a State. The capital fault of which aristocratic bodies may be accused is that they are more apt to contrive their own advantage than that of the mass of the people. In foreign politics it is rare for the interest of the aristocracy to be in any way distinct from that of the people.

The propensity which democracies have to obey the impulse of passion rather than the suggestions of prudence, and to abandon a mature design for the gratification of a momentary caprice, was very clearly seen in America on the breaking out of the French Revolution. It was then as evident to the simplest capacity as it is at the present time that the interest of the Americans forbade them to take any part in the contest which was about to deluge Europe with blood, but which could by no means injure the welfare of their own country. Nevertheless the sympathies of the people declared themselves with so much violence in behalf of France that nothing but the inflexible character of Washington, and the immense popularity which he enjoyed, could have prevented the Americans from declaring war against England. And even then, the exertions which the austere reason of that great man made to repress the generous but imprudent passions of his fellow-citizens, very nearly deprived him of the sole recompense which he had ever claimed—that of his country's love. The majority then reprobated the line of policy which he adopted, and which has since been unanimously approved by the nation.[2] If the Constitution and the favor of the public had not entrusted the direction of the foreign affairs of the country to Washington, it is certain that the American nation would at that time have taken the very measures which it now condemns.

Almost all the nations which have ever exercised a powerful influence upon the destinies of the world by conceiving, following up, and executing vast designs—from the Romans to the English —have been governed by aristocratic institutions. Nor will this be a subject of wonder when we recollect that nothing in the world has so absolute a fixity of purpose as an aristocracy. The mass of the people may be led astray by ignorance or passion; the mind of a king may be biased, and his perseverance in his designs may be shaken—besides which a king is not immortal—but an aristocratic body is too numerous to be led astray by the blandishments of intrigue, and yet not numerous enough to yield readily to the intoxicating influence of unreflecting passion: it has the energy of a firm and enlightened individual, added to the power which it derives from perpetuity.

---

[2] See the fifth volume of Marshall's "Life of Washington." "In a government constituted like that of the United States," he says, "it is impossible for the chief magistrate, however firm he may be, to oppose for any length of time the torrent of popular opinion; and the prevalent opinion of that day seemed to incline to war. In fact, in the session of Congress held at the time, it was frequently seen that Washington had lost the majority in the House of Representatives." The violence of the language used against him in public was extreme, and in a political meeting they did not scruple to compare him indirectly to the treacherous Arnold. "By the opposition," says Marshall, "the friends of the administration were declared to be an aristocratic and corrupt faction, who, from a desire to introduce monarchy, were hostile to France and under the influence of Britain; that they were a paper nobility, whose extreme sensibility at every measure which threatened the funds, induced a tame submission to injuries and insults, which the interests and honor of the nation required them to resist."

DEMOCRACY AND FOREIGN POLICY*

BY

JAMES BRYCE

[1920]

Statesmen, political philosophers, and historians have been wont to regard the conduct of foreign relations as the reproach of democratic government. The management of international relations needs—so they insist—knowledge, consistency, and secrecy, whereas democracies are ignorant and inconstant, being moreover obliged, by the law of their being, to discuss in public matters unfit to be disclosed. That this has been perceived by the people themselves appears from the fact that modern legislatures have left this department to officials, because it was felt that in this one department democracies cannot safely be democratic.

Per contra, popular leaders in some countries have, with an increasing volume of support, denounced Foreign Offices as having erred both in aims and in methods. They allege that the diplomacy of European States is condemned by the suspicion which it has constantly engendered and that the brand of failure is stamped upon it by the frequent recurrence of war, the evil which diplomacy was created to prevent.

These views, apparently opposite, are not incompatible. Oligarchies, and the small official class which in many democracies has had the handling of foreign affairs, may have managed them ill, and yet it may be that the whole people will manage them no better. The fault may lie in the conditions of the matter itself and in those tendencies of human nature which no form of government can overcome. What we want to know is not whether oligarchic and secret methods have failed—that may be admitted—but whether democratic and open-air methods will succeed any better. What light does history throw on the question?

---

*From *Modern Democracies* by James Bryce (Viscount Bryce). Copyright 1921 by Macmillan and Co. Reprinted by permission. James Bryce (1838–1922), British statesman and historian, Professor of Law at Oxford, was British Ambassador to the United States, 1907–1913.

Here at starting let a distinction be drawn between Ends and Means in the sphere of foreign policy. . . . The relations of States to one another, varying from day to day as the circumstances which govern them vary, cannot be handled by large assemblies in a large country, but must be determined by administrators who are incessantly watching the foreign sky. Modern legislatures accordingly, though they sometimes pass resolutions indicating a course to be followed, or condemning a course which has been followed, by a Ministry, have recognized that in foreign affairs the choice of Means must belong to a small body of experts, and have accordingly left to these persons all details, and the methods which diplomacy must employ in particular cases, allowing them a wide, possibly a too wide, discretion.

But while Foreign Offices and diplomatic envoys may be the proper persons to choose and apply Means, the general principles which should guide and the spirit which should inspire a nation's foreign policy are a different matter, too wide in scope, too grave in consequences, to be determined by any authority lower than that of the people. . . .

About one aim there can be no divergence. The State must preserve its independence. It must be safe from attack, able to secure fair opportunities for its citizens to trade and to travel abroad unmolested; and these legitimate aims can be pursued in a spirit of justice and friendliness to other States. All States, however, whatever their form of government, have pursued other aims also, and pursued them in a way frequently at variance with justice and honor. . . . Most States have, in pursuing these objects, been a law unto themselves. When strong, they have abused their strength, justifying all means by the plea of State advantage. They have disregarded good faith from the days when democratic Athens wantonly attacked the isle of Melos, killing and enslaving its inhabitants, down to the days of Louis XI and Caesar Borgia, and from the days of Borgia's contemporary Machiavelli down to those of Frederick the Second of Prussia, who began his literary career with a book designed to refute the maxims of the Florentine statesman. Though in considering how popular governments have succeeded in the sphere of foreign policy, regard must be had to the moral quality of that policy both in Ends and in Means, the moral aspect may be in the first instance reserved, and the enquiry may go only to the question whether a democracy is in that sphere more or less efficient than other forms of government. Supposing "success" to mean the maximum of power a State can attain in the world arena, what kind of government will best attain it? We can thereafter return to the moral side and enquire what sort of government will be most likely to observe justice and good faith, doing its duty by its neighbor States as a good citizen does his duty by his fellows.

Does Ignorance forbid success to a democracy? Let us hear the case which professional diplomatists make.

A monarch is free to select his ministers and ambassadors from among the best informed and most skilful of his subjects, and in an oligarchy the mind of the ruling class busies itself with foreign relations, and knows which of its members understand and are fitted to handle them. The multitude has not the same advantage. It is ill qualified to judge this kind of capacity, usually choosing its ministers by their powers of speech. If, instead of leaving foreign affairs to skilled men it attempts to direct them either by its own votes, as did the Greek cities, or by instructing those who represent it in the legislature, how is it to acquire the requisite knowledge? Few of the voters know more than the most elementary facts regarding the conditions and the policy of foreign countries, and to appreciate the significance of these facts, there is needed some acquaintance with the history of the countries and the characters of the leading men. Not much of that acquaintance can be expected even from the legislature. One of the strongest arguments for democratic government is that the masses of the people, whatever else they may not know, do know where the shoe pinches, and are best entitled to specify the reforms they need. In foreign affairs this argument does not apply, for they lie out of the normal citizen's range. All he can do at an election is to convey by his vote his view of general principles, and, in the case of a conflict between two foreign nations, to indicate his sympathies.

If the masses of the people have been inconstant in their views of foreign relations, this is due to their ignorance, which disables them from following intelligently the course of events abroad, so that their interest in these is quickened only at intervals, and when that happens the want of knowledge of what has preceded makes a sound judgment unlikely. They are at the mercy of their party leaders or of the press, guides not trustworthy, because the politicians will be influenced by the wish to make political capital out of any successes scored or errors committed by a Ministry, while the newspapers may play up to and exaggerate the prevailing sentiment of the moment, claiming everything for their own country, misrepresenting and disparaging the foreign antagonist. Consistency cannot be expected from a popular government which acts under a succession of impulses, giving no steady attention to that department in which continuity of policy is most needed.

Secrecy in the conduct of diplomacy is vital in a world where each great nation is suspicious of its neighbors, and obliged by its fears to try to discover their plans while concealing its own. Suppose the ministry of a country to have ascertained privately that a foreign Power meditates an attack upon it or is forming a combination against it, or suppose it to be itself negotiating a treaty of alliance for protection against such a combination. How can it proclaim either the intentions of the suspected Power or its own counter-schemes without precipitating a rupture or frustrating its own plans? A minister too honorable to deceive the legislature may feel himself debarred from telling it the facts, some of which may have been communicated under the seal of confidence. It is all very well to say that an open and straightforward policy best befits a free and high-minded people. But if such a people should stand alone in a naughty world, it will have to suffer for its virtues. As a democracy cannot do business secretly, it must therefore leave much, and perhaps much of grave import, to its ministers. Herein the superiority for foreign affairs of a monarchy or an oligarchy is most evident. . . .

To test the capacity of a popular government in this branch of its action, let us see how far such governments have shown wisdom in following sound aims and have succeeded in applying the means needed to attain them. . . .

(1) The case of France is peculiar in this respect, that the general lines of its policy have during the whole life of the Third Republic (1871-1920) been determined by its position towards Germany, the one enemy from whom hostility was always to be feared, and from whom it was hoped to recover territory lost in war. This fact colored all France's foreign relations, forcing her to husband her strength and to seek for allies. As all parties felt alike on this supreme issue, all were agreed in keeping it out of party controversy. The incessant changes of Ministers scarcely affected the continuity of policy. Democracy was on its good behavior; fickleness as well as partisanship was held in check. Some friction arose between Ministers and Committees of the legislature, yet secrets were generally kept and the people acquiesced in a silence felt to be necessary. It goes without saying that errors were now and then committed, but these taken all together were less grave than the two which marked the later part of Louis Napoleon's reign—the expedition to Mexico and the war with Prussia. And, as the result has shown, they were incomparably less than those which brought ruin on the three great monarchies which entrusted their foreign relations to militaristic bureaucracies— Germany, Austria, and Russia. . . .

(2) As the rule [of public opinion] is in the United States more complete than elsewhere, it furnishes the best index to the tendencies and capacities of a democracy.

The Republic has been engaged in three wars within the last hundred years. That against Mexico in 1846 was the work of the slave-holding party which then controlled the Executive and the Senate, and whose leaders brought it on for the sake of creating Slave States and strengthening the grip of slavery on the Union. It was widely disapproved by public opinion, especially in the northern States, but the acquisition, by the treaty which closed it, of vast and rich territories on the Pacific Coast did much to silence the voice of criticism.

The war against Spain in 1898 might probably have been avoided, for Spain had been driven to the verge of consenting to withdraw from Cuba when the breach came. But the nation, already wearied by the incessant troubles to which Spanish misgovernment had given rise during many years, had been inflamed

by the highly colored accounts which the newspapers published of
the severities practiced on the insurgents by Spanish generals, and
the President, though inclined to continue negotiations, is believed
to have been forced into war by the leaders of his own party who
did not wish their opponents to have the credit of compelling a
declaration.   In obtaining, by the peace which followed a short
campaign, the cession to the United States of Puerto Rico and the
Philippine Islands, the President believed that he was carrying out
the wishes of the people.   This may have been so, for they were
flushed with victory, and were moved not merely by the feeling
that victory ought to bring some tangible gain, but also by a sort
of philanthropic sentiment which was unwilling to hand back the
conquered territories to Spanish maladministration.   This war,
therefore, though it shows that a popular government may yield to
excitement and gratify its ambition for enlarged territory, cannot
be deemed a case of mere aggression for the sake of conquest.

The war of 1917 against Germany and Austria is too fresh in
our memories to need comment.   There was certainly nothing
selfish or aggressive in the spirit that prompted America's entrance
into it.   The sinking of the *Lusitania* and other passenger vessels
supplied a definite *casus belli;* the mind of the nation had been
stirred to its depths by the sense that far-reaching moral issues
were involved.

Not wars only, but also the general diplomatic relations of the
United States with its neighbors . . . deserve to be considered. . . .

When in 1912 the long dictatorship of Porfirio Diaz vanished
like melting snow, Mexico relapsed into anarchy.   The property
and lives of American citizens were frequently endangered.   Some
murders and many robberies were perpetrated by rebel bands which
the nominal rulers at the capital could not suppress.   Had the government of the United States wished to make these outrages a
ground for occupying Mexican territory, it could have found justification for doing so.   But the public opinion of the American
people steadily resisted all temptations, perceiving that annexation
would involve either rule over the Mexicans as a subject race, or
their incorporation with the United States as full citizens.   As both
of these courses were equally fraught with danger, they determined
to leave Mexico alone.   A like disinterestedness had been shown

in the case of Cuba, from which they had withdrawn their troops once (in 1903) after expelling Spain, and again a few years later when troubles in the island had compelled a second occupation. All these cases gave evidence not only of the authority which popular opinion exerts over the main lines of foreign policy, but also of the growth in it of a spirit of good sense and self-restraint such as was not always seen in earlier years. The nation, when it came to full manhood, laid aside the spirit of self-assertion and the desire for conquest, and gave proof of a sincere desire to apply methods of arbitration and show its respect for the rights of other nations. . . . With this higher sense of justice there has also come a stronger aversion to war. No great people in the world is equally pervaded by the wish to see peace maintained everywhere over the world.

(3) In Great Britain . . . from 1848 onwards the opinion of the masses of the people, as distinct from that of the richer or more educated classes, became a factor to be reckoned with in foreign policy, though the conduct of diplomatic relations was left, and has indeed been left till now, in the hands of the Ministry of the day. . . .

The American Civil War of 1861-1865 was the first occasion on which a marked divergence between the sentiment of the [British] masses and that of the so-called "classes" disclosed itself. "Society," *i.e.* the large majority of the rich and many among the professional classes, sided with the Southern States, while nearly the whole of the working class and at least half of the middle class, together with many men of intellectual distinction, especially in the Universities, stood for the Northern. Feeling was bitter, and the partisans of each side held numerous meetings, but it was remarked that whereas the meetings which were called by the friends of the North were open to the general public, admission to those summoned to advocate the cause of the Seceding States was confined to the holders of tickets, because it was feared that in an open meeting resolutions of sympathy with the South could not be carried. These and other evidences, showing that the great bulk of the nation favored the cause of the North as being the cause of human freedom, as soon as President Lincoln's Proclamation had made it clear that slavery would disappear, confirmed the Cabinet

in its refusal to accede to Louis Napoleon's suggestion that England and France should join in recognizing the Seceding States as
independent.

. . . If we may take the prevalent opinion of the nation to-day
(1920) as a final judgment, *i.e.,* as being likely to be the judgment
of posterity, it is interesting to note that . . . the "classes" would
appear to have been less wise than the "masses." Everybody now
admits that it was a gain for the world that in the American Civil
War the Northern States prevailed and slavery vanished. . . .

Summing up the results of this examination of the foreign policy
followed by three great democratic countries during the last fifty
years, we find that the case of France proves that it was possible
for a democracy to follow a consistent policy, the conduct of the
details whereof was left in the hands of successive administrations,
and safely left because the nation was substantially agreed as to the
general lines to be followed. The case of the United States proves
that public opinion, which is there omnipotent, is generally right
in its aims, and has tended to become wiser and more moderate
with the march of years. The case of Britain shows that the
opinion of the bulk of the nation was more . . . approved by results
than was the attitude of the comparatively small class in whose
hands the conduct of affairs had been usually left. . . .

In these last few pages Ends rather than Means have been considered, though it is hard to draw a distinction, for most Ends are
Means to a larger End; and the facts examined seem to show that
in determining Ends the voice of the people must have authority.
But what is to be said as to the details of diplomacy in which, assuming the main ends to be determined by the people, a wide
choice of means remains open? It has been deemed impossible for
the people to know either which means are best suited to the purpose aimed at or, if the people is kept informed of them, to apply
those means successfully, for in our days what is told to any people
is told to the whole world. So long as each nation strives to secure
some gains for itself as against other nations by anticipating its
rivals in enterprises, or by forming profitable alliances, or otherwise driving bargains for its own benefit, those who manage the

nation's business cannot disclose their action without damaging their chances of success.   Hence even the countries that have gone furthest in recognizing popular control have left a wide discretion in the hands of their Ministers or envoys and have set bounds to the curiosity of parliamentary representatives.   Must this continue? If it does continue, what security have the people against unwise action or the adoption of dishonorable methods?

One expedient used to overcome this difficulty has been that of a committee of the legislature which can receive confidential communications from a Minister and can bind its members to keep them secret.   This is done in the United States, where the Foreign Relations Committee of the Senate, though it cannot dictate to the President (or his Secretary of State), can through its power of inducing the Senate to refuse assent to a treaty exercise a constant and potent influence. . . . The committee plan has its defects.   No secret known to more than three men remains for long a secret; and a Minister can, if he likes, go a long way towards committing his country before he tells the committee what he is doing, taking of course the chance that he may be disavowed.   Sometimes, moreover, action cannot await the approval of a committee, for to be effective it must be immediate.

The voices which in European countries demand the abolition of secret diplomacy and the control by the people of all foreign relations appeal to an incontestable principle, because a nation has every right to deliver its opinion on matters of such supreme importance as the issues of peace and war.   The difficulty lies in applying a sound principle to the facts as they have hitherto stood in Europe.   If publicity in the conduct of negotiations is to be required, and the mind of the people to be expressed before any commitment is made by its Ministers, there must be a renunciation of such advantages as have been heretofore obtained by international combinations or bargains secretly made with other nations. If, on the other hand, these advantages are to be sought, secrecy must be permitted and discretion granted to Ministers.   The risk that secrecy and discretion will be abused will be gradually lessened the more public opinion becomes better instructed on foreign affairs, and the more that legislatures learn to give unremitting attention to foreign policy.   In England as well as in America few are the representatives who possess the knowledge needed, or take the trouble to acquire it.   It is this, as well as party spirit, which has led Parliamentary majorities to endeavor to support their party chiefs, even when it was beginning to be seen that public opinion was turning against them.   If ministries were to become more and more anxious to keep as close a touch with the feeling of the nation in foreign as they seek to do in domestic affairs, the risk that any nation will be irrevocably entangled in a pernicious course would diminish.   So too if there should be hereafter less of a desire to get the better of other nations in acquiring territory or concessions abroad, if a less grasping and selfish spirit should rule foreign policy, fewer occasions will arise in which secret agreements will be needed.   The thing now most needed by the people and its representatives is more knowledge of the facts of the outside world with a more sympathetic comprehension of the minds of other peoples.   The first step to this is a fuller acquaintance with the history, the economic and social conditions, and the characters of other peoples.

The conclusions to which the considerations here set forth point are the following:

In a democracy the People are entitled to determine the Ends or general aims of foreign policy.

History shows that they do this at least as wisely as monarchs or oligarchies, or the small groups to whom, in democratic countries, the conduct of foreign relations has been left, and that they have evinced more respect for moral principles.

The Means to be used for attaining the Ends sought cannot be adequately determined by legislatures so long as international relations continue to be what they have heretofore been, because secrecy is sometimes, and expert knowledge is always required.

Nevertheless some improvement on the present system is needed, and the experiment of a Committee deserves to be tried.

Whatever faults modern democracies may have committed in this field of administration, the faults chargeable on monarchs and oligarchies have been less pardonable and more harmful to the peace and progress of mankind. . . .

THE REPUBLICAN PRINCIPLE*

BY

ALEXANDER HAMILTON

[1788]

There are some who would be inclined to regard the servile pliancy of the Executive to a prevailing current, either in the community or in the legislature, as its best recommendation. But such men entertain very crude notions, as well of the purposes for which government was instituted, as of the true means by which the public happiness may be promoted. The republican principle demands that the deliberate sense of the community should govern the conduct of those to whom they intrust the management of their affairs; but it does not require an unqualified complaisance to every sudden breeze of passion, or to every transient impulse which the people may receive from the arts of men, who flatter their prejudices to betray their interests. It is a just observation, that the people commonly *intend* the PUBLIC GOOD. This often applies to their very errors. But their good sense would despise the adulator who should pretend that they always *reason right* about the *means* of promoting it. They know from experience that they sometimes err; and the wonder is that they so seldom err as they do, beset, as they continually are, by the wiles of parasites and sycophants, by the snares of the ambitious, the avaricious, the desperate, by the artifices of men who possess their confidence more than they deserve it, and of those who seek to possess rather than to deserve it. When occasions present themselves, in which the interests of the people are at variance with their inclinations, it is the duty of the persons whom they have appointed to be the guardians of those interests, to withstand the temporary delusion, in order to give them time and opportunity for more cool and sedate reflection. Instances might be cited in which a conduct of this kind has saved the people from very fatal consequences of their own mistakes, and has procured lasting monuments of their gratitude to the men who had courage and magnanimity enough to serve them at the peril of their displeasure.

---

*From *The Federalist*, No. 71. Alexander Hamilton (1755–1804), American statesman and economist, Secretary of the Treasury under Washington, was co-author (with Madison and Jay) of *The Federalist*.

LEADERSHIP AND DEMOCRACY*

BY

WALTER LIPPMANN

[1943]

The example of Monroe, Jefferson, and Madison [in formulating the Monroe Doctrine] teaches us that while a true policy will win the assent of the people, the policy will not be formulated if the responsible statesmen shirk the responsibility of making the initial decision. Monroe announced to Congress the policy which he and Madison and Jefferson had decided upon. He did what he conceived to be right and necessary. The correspondence of the three Virginia Presidents is concerned not with what the Gallup poll might show about the opinions of the people, but with what the vital interests of the country required in the situation as it presented itself. They did not ask whether the people, who were divided, could be induced to support a sound policy. They formulated a sound policy which the divided people came, because of its inherent virtue, to unite in supporting. This was that leadership by statesmen without which democracy is nothing but the vain attempt of men to lift themselves by their own bootstraps.

In our age, to be sure, a great policy cannot be adopted, as it was in 1823, by private consultation among a few leading men. But the essential principle is not changed: the measure of a policy is its soundness; if it is sound, it will prove acceptable. The policy must be examined on its merits and not with respect to its immediate popularity.

*From *U. S. Foreign Policy*, copyright 1943 by Walter Lippmann. Reprinted by permission of Little, Brown and Co., Atlantic Monthly Press. Walter Lippmann (b. 1889) is an American columnist and author of many books on political subjects. His most recent book is *The Public Philosophy*.

CAN FOREIGN POLICY BE DEMOCRATIC?*

BY

MULFORD Q. SIBLEY

[1948]

DEMOCRACY AND PUBLIC POLICY

Democracy signifies that public policy shall be *made* by the community as a whole and not by any segment of the community and that policy shall be in the *interest* of the whole community rather than of any particular part. Both these elements are essential if we are to term a society or a policy "democratic." Thus, policy determined by the community but having as its substance arbitrary and special privileges for a class is not democratic. Policies determined by an individual or a class, although for the benefit of the entire community, are also undemocratic. Conceivably a despot or an aristocracy might govern *for* the people—many have claimed to do so—but that would not be a democracy.

In this discussion of foreign policy we are primarily concerned with democracy as method or means, since this would seem to be the crucial problem. In a sense, democracy is primarily a method; the democrat would argue that once a policy is molded by methods which are genuinely democratic, the substance of the decisions is more likely to be for the benefit of the whole community. What, then, in more specific terms, does democracy as means imply? It implies at least that:

(1) Leaders must be under the effective control of the community. There must be some mechanism or mechanisms whereby the community can select and depose those who are called upon to speak in its name. Those who assume the function of proposing alternative courses of action—the central function of leadership in democratic policy-making—should be under such effective control of their constituents that any suggested public policy could become definite and binding only after the community had given its free

*From a symposium entitled "Can Foreign Policy Be Democratic?" in *American Perspective,* September 1948. Reprinted by permission. Mulford Q. Sibley (b. 1912), Professor of Political Science, University of Minnesota, is the author of works on the political theories of modern pacifism.

consent. In a democracy leaders suggest, advise, propose and advocate. It is the community which debates, selects, consents to and makes final a given course of action.

(2) Leaders should speak only truthfully. One of the most important points of distinction between democratic and non-democratic leadership is in their respective attitudes to the problem of the political lie. At one end of the scale stand the leaders who make it a conscious principle to utilize the political lie as a method of leadership; in the middle are those who deliberately use political lies only in situations which they define as "crises"; while at the other end are those leaders who steadfastly refuse to use the political lie, even in times which they may judge to be crises. Only the latter of the three classes, according to the framework of this discussion, could be called in any sense "democratic." They alone see that democracy is more than the achievement of a supposedly "democratic" goal: it is, above all, a method for making public decisions. Deception, even if used honestly for what the leader regards as the long-run welfare of society, in effect shifts the making of decisions from the community to the leader, and contradicts the central canon of democracy.

(3) All the relevant information available on a given issue must be before the public when it is called upon to make a decision, if the decision is to be intelligent and rational. One of the functions of true political leadership is to provide this information, withholding nothing of relevance and presenting it in such a form that it can serve as the basis for intelligent discussion. No leader, even though he be a high executive in government, has the moral right to withhold any *public* (as contrasted with purely private) information which comes into his possession and which has any relation to the subject under discussion.

(4) Decisions will be made only after thorough discussion, for only through discussion can a community will be discovered. A community will is not a mere aggregate of individual wills, uninformed and undisciplined by the social process which we call discussion; rather is it a new phenomenon which arises in the process of discussion.

(5) Factors which make for irrational decisions will be mini-

mized. Such factors include lack of education, great disparities in individual incomes and any system of communications which does not adequately reflect or express all points of view. A democratic discussion must consist in deliberation on conflicting positions by citizens who are sufficiently freed from immediate concern for physical needs to make rational deliberation possible. If conflicting interpretations of public policy are not given widespread publicity, if some approaches to an issue of policy are excluded (through monopolistic controls of press and radio, for example), there will be little about which to deliberate. If, on the other hand, the community is adequately informed, but includes large numbers of over-fed and under-fed citizens, the rationality of the decision reached is also impaired.

APPLICATION OF PRINCIPLES TO FOREIGN POLICY

The specific application of these principles to the conduct of foreign policy suggests, as a minimum, that:

(1) No foreign commitment whatsoever could be made until, after thorough and public discussion under conditions required for a democratic decision, it is approved by a representative body. This principle would not exclude the representative body's delegating power to the executive, under specific limitations, to make agreements like those of the reciprocal trade program. It would, however, exclude any agreements not specifically authorized by Congress and any agreements not customarily submitted for senatorial approval—the so-called executive agreements.

(2) An executive making what purported to be secret commitments, of any kind and under any conditions, would on their discovery be subject to immediate impeachment. Likewise, a President who on the plea of "international crisis" disregards the conditions essential for a democratic decision, who uses deception for what *he* regards as the public good, should be removed forthwith from office.

(3) No executive would have the power to withhold information demanded by Congress or a congressional committee for any reason, except that the information was purely private in character. Even in this case, Congress or its committees should have the final right to decide whether the information was purely private or not.

The present arrangement, whereby the President is held to have the power to withhold information whose release he deems contrary to the public interest, would be changed and Congress alone have the right of decision. It is absurd to speak of democratic processes so long as one man has the power to decide whether publication of requested information is detrimental to the public welfare. If giving the information to a congressional body would in effect make it public immediately (as many argue), then it is better, from the democratic point of view, to undergo whatever risks might be involved than to rely on procedures which are the antithesis of democracy.

(4) All relevant information regarding progress in international negotiations should be made public immediately so that agreements can be formulated and molded in the full light of public debate. It is sometimes argued that such publicity might hamper negotiations and that democratic procedures are satisfied if the final agreement alone is submitted for public approbation or disapproval. But if the public has to wait until the final formulation of the proposal, collective wisdom, which democrats rightly value so highly elsewhere, would have no opportunity to develop and operate. Such procedure would be analogous to the formulation of ordinary statutes in secret and their approval or disapproval by public vote, the community not being consulted in their formulation. Democracy involves much more than a plebiscite; it implies continuous and public discussion of a principle from its embryonic form to its final statement, and the final statement might well differ widely from the initial proposal.

OBJECTIONS AND COMMENTS

It may be objected that a line of argument of this kind smacks of purism, neglects the realities of political life and exalts an abstraction. Specific objections might take and have taken these forms:

(1) It is urged that political deception is permissible in time of crisis. The leader, it is said, being farsighted and compelled to take into account a public opinion which is shortsighted, has to accept the short-run vision of the people and lead the community to disaster. Refusing to do so, he must resign his office or delib-

erately deceive the people into believing that he is leading where they wish to go, while in actuality taking them in the opposite direction. Thus Thomas A. Bailey in his recent book, *The Man in the Street*, admits that "Franklin Roosevelt repeatedly deceived the American people during the period before Pearl Harbor" (p. 11), and then goes on to justify those deceptions on the ground that the people were too shortsighted to see their own interests. Bailey frankly concedes, moreover, that Roosevelt's methods were undemocratic: "A President who cannot entrust the people with the truth betrays a certain lack of faith in democracy" (p. 13).

To the advocate of democracy, this "certain lack of faith" is really a total absence of faith. If the people are not to be entrusted with their destiny in times of crisis, then *when* should they make decisions? According to those who uphold deception, it is to be used only in a crisis when there is not time to "educate" the community as to the true situation. But who determines when the crisis exists and when deception is necessary? The leader, of course. The final decision is his and not the community's. No theory could be a sharper thrust at the heart of democratic faith. Democracy, its defenders would reply, does not hold that it is the function of leaders to guarantee the safety of the nation at the expense of truth.

This controversy turns on the question of values. Bailey argues in effect that Roosevelt's policy was the only one which would preserve the United States and that the only way he could get the policy adopted was by deception. To which the democrat would reply: "Admitting for the moment that Roosevelt's policy was the only one which would preserve the nation, there are greater values than the preservation of the nation. If the choice is actually between the absence of deception, with destruction of the nation on the one hand, and deception with preservation of the nation on the other, the democrat would choose the former. The existence of democracy is not bound up with the preservation of any given Nation State. Deception used in the supposed defense of the nation means in the long run the destruction of democracy." But the democrat would also question whether deception is ever necessary to preserve a nation which aspires to democracy: if it is, then that nation would seem well on the way to a repudiation of the democratic faith.

(2) Another objection to a democratically controlled foreign policy would assert that the "masses" are not well-informed. Bailey calls them the "apathetic and ill-informed masses." No democrat would argue that the people are technically well-informed in foreign affairs, but he would contend that with communications adequate and relevant information available (today it is *not*, due to less than democratic attitudes in high places), leaders could present genuine alternatives and the community could make a competent final decision after hearing all the alternatives weighed. No democrat would argue that all the decisions made democratically will be "right" decisions; but he will contend that in the long run they are more likely to be "right" than decisions made undemocratically, and that the risk is far less than that involved in discarding democratic methods on the plea of public necessity.

The community is certainly as competent to make final decisions of policy as Franklin Roosevelt was. Perhaps it would have been better for the cause of democracy had the United States remained out of the war (as Bailey implies it would have done had not Roosevelt "rightly" deceived it). The contrary proposition is at least not self-evident. Most persons now agree that the ignorant English mill-workers were right when they opposed British recognition of the southern Confederacy and that the British Cabinet, including the brilliant Gladstone, was wrong in advocating recognition. Likewise, contemporary and future events may show that the American people were right before their deception by Roosevelt and that Roosevelt was wrong in deceiving them into war, wrong in being less than honest with them from the election of 1940 through the many deceptions down to his death, wrong in making secret commitments at Yalta and deliberately denying that he had made them, wrong not only because of his methods but in the substance of his decisions.

(3) It might be argued that deception or withholding of relevant information is justified because all elements of a democratic

society are not present. If communications *were* free, if all sides of a question *were* fairly presented through press and radio, if money *did not* shackle opinion, it will be argued, it might be right to insist on publication of all relevant information and on the evil of deception. But since no society is more than a semi-democracy, at best, for the leader to be perfectly truthful and to release all information would result only in the distortion of that information by press and radio. Rational decisions by the community would still not be possible.

This is a specious argument. Granted that no society is more than a semi-democracy at best, and that information would be twisted to serve the interests of special groups, still the publication of all relevant information would at least make more possible the intelligent discussion of alternative courses of action. There are likely to be a few minority organs of press and radio which would take issue with predominant interpretations. Moreover, if the bulk of the press and radio are opposed to the President, surely the latter through his prestige and prerogatives can combat what he might regard as distorted interpretations on at least equal terms.

(4) Finally, it may be urged that the nature of modern war makes democratic processes in foreign affairs increasingly impracticable. Bailey argues that in the "days of the atomic bomb" we may have to move "more rapidly" than a "lumbering public opinion" will allow, yielding a large part of our democratic control of foreign affairs.

There is some force to this argument. As war becomes total, as ostensible "democracies" invent and use the atomic bomb, democratic methods tend to be destroyed not only in formulating foreign policy, but in domestic as well. Hence we are told that we cannot permit democratic control: we must surrender it as gracefully as possible. The atomic bomb puts a premium on surprise attacks, making the congressional power to declare war even more of a mockery than it is today. Without secrecy and deception, modern war is impossible; therefore, delegate more authority to the President so that he can keep more information secret and decide more issues without reference to community consent. This would seem to be clearly implied in statements like those of Bailey. That is one solution. But it is not a democratic solution. The democrat, it seems to me, will take the same set of circumstances and infer that if modern war and democracy are incompatible, the solution is to refuse to use war as a method and to adopt other more effective realistic means to oppose tyranny. What possible logic is there in using methods to preserve democracy which by their very nature destroy the democratic process?

I do not think that at this point the democrat will be interested only in such long-run goals as the abolition of war by world organization. The problem is one of immediate strategy. Specifically, that national State which first renounces and abandons reliance on armaments and war as methods is the community most likely to preserve and extend democracy and to defeat tyranny, not merely specific tyrants. There is only one basic alternative to war as a technique, and that is the late Mr. Gandhi's method. Subconsciously, many seem to recognize this, as when the leaders of the western world paid lip-service to Gandhi's achievements at the time of the Mahatma's death. Actually, however, we have not been converted. We continue to construct the weapons of mass destruction whose effective use is incompatible with the democratic process, and to profess at the same time that we are using these means to preserve democracy. We cannot have it both ways at once. Until we choose clearly and definitely preparation for war and destruction of democracy, on the one hand, or elimination of war preparation and an adaptation of Mr. Gandhi's methods, on the other, the problem of democratic control of foreign policy will remain in its present ambiguous, confused and unsatisfactory state. Leaders will continue to deceive us, ostensibly to preserve us, and the basic right of the community to damn itself if it so chooses will be ignored.

THE CURTISS-WRIGHT CASE

United States v. *Curtiss-Wright Export Corp.* ET AL.

(299 U. S. 304)

[1936]

MR. JUSTICE SUTHERLAND delivered the opinion of the Court.

On January 27, 1936, an indictment was returned in the court below, the first count of which charges that appellees, beginning with the 29th day of May, 1934, conspired to sell in the United States certain arms of war, namely fifteen machine guns, to Bolivia, a country then engaged in armed conflict in the Chaco, in violation of the Joint Resolution of Congress approved May 28, 1934, and the provisions of a proclamation issued on the same day by the President of the United States pursuant to authority conferred by § 1 of the resolution. In pursuance of the conspiracy, the commission of certain overt acts was alleged, details of which need not be stated. The Joint Resolution follows:

"Resolved by the Senate and House of Representatives of the United States of America in Congress assembled, That if the President finds that the prohibition of the sale of arms and munitions of war in the United States to those countries now engaged in armed conflict in the Chaco may contribute to the re-establishment of peace between those countries, and if after consultation with the governments of other American Republics and with their co-operation, as well as that of such other governments as he may deem necessary, he makes proclamation to that effect, it shall be unlawful to sell, except under such limitations and exceptions as the President prescribes, any arms or munitions of war in any place in the United States to the countries now engaged in that armed conflict, or to any person, company, or association acting in the interest of either country until otherwise ordered by the President or by Congress.

"Sec. 2. Whoever sells any arms or munitions of war in

violation of section 1, shall, on conviction, be punished by a fine
not exceeding $10,000 or by imprisonment not exceeding two
years, or both."

The President's proclamation, after reciting the terms of the
Joint Resolution, declares:

"Now, therefore, I, Franklin D. Roosevelt, President of the
United States of America, acting under and by virtue of the authority conferred in me by the said joint resolution of Congress,
do hereby declare and proclaim that I have found that the prohibition of the sale of arms and munitions of war in the United States
to those countries now engaged in armed conflict in the Chaco
may contribute to the re-establishment of peace between those
countries, and that I have consulted with the governments of other
American Republics and have been assured of the co-operation of
such governments as I have deemed necessary as contemplated by
the said joint resolution; and I do hereby admonish all citizens of
the United States and every person to abstain from every violation
of the provisions of the joint resolution above set forth, hereby,
made applicable to Bolivia and Paraguay, and I do hereby warn
them that all violations of such provisions will be rigorously
prosecuted . . . . "

On November 14, 1935, this proclamation was revoked. . . .

Appellees severally demurred to the first count of the indictment on the grounds (1) that it did not charge facts sufficient to
show the commission by appellees of any offense against any law
of the United States. . . .

The court below sustained the demurrers upon the first point
. . . . The government appealed to this court under the provisions
of the Criminal Appeals Act of March 2, 1907 . . . .

First. It is contended that by the Joint Resolution, the going
into effect and continued operation of the resolution was conditioned (a) upon the President's judgment as to its beneficial effect
upon the re-establishment of peace between the countries engaged
in armed conflict in the Chaco; (b) upon the making of a proclamation, which was left to his unfettered discretion, thus constituting an attempted substitution of the President's will for that of

Congress; (c) upon the making of a proclamation putting an end to the operation of the resolution, which again was left to the President's unfettered discretion; and (d) further, that the extent of its operation in particular cases was subject to limitation and exception by the President, controlled by no standard. In each of these particulars, appellees urge that Congress abdicated its essential functions and delegated them to the Executive.

Whether, if the Joint Resolution had related solely to internal affairs it would be open to the challenge that it constituted an unlawful delegation of legislative power to the Executive, we find it unnecessary to determine. The whole aim of the resolution is to affect a situation entirely external to the United States, and falling within the category of foreign affairs. The determination which we are called to make, therefore, is whether the Joint Resolution, as applied to that situation, is vulnerable to attack under the rule that forbids a delegation of the law-making power. In other words, assuming (but not deciding) that the challenged delegation, if it were confined to internal affairs, would be invalid, may it nevertheless be sustained on the ground that its exclusive aim is to afford a remedy for a hurtful condition within foreign territory?

It will contribute to the elucidation of the question if we first consider the differences between the powers of the federal government in respect to foreign or external affairs and those in respect of domestic or internal affairs. That there are differences between them, and that these differences are fundamental, may not be doubted.

The two classes of powers are different, both in respect of their origin and their nature. The broad statement that the federal government can exercise no powers except those specifically enumerated in the Constitution, and such implied powers as are necessary and proper to carry into effect the enumerated powers, is categorically true only in respect of our internal affairs. In that field, the primary purpose of the Constitution was to carve from the general mass of legislative powers *then possessed by the states* such portions as it was thought desirable to vest in the federal government, leaving those not included in the enumeration still in the states. That this doctrine applies only to powers which the states had, is self-evident. And since the states severally never possessed international powers, such powers could not have been carved from the mass of state powers but obviously were transmitted to the United States from some other source. During the colonial period, those powers were possessed exclusively by and were entirely under the control of the Crown. By the Declaration of Independence, "the Representatives of the United States of America" declared the United [not the several] Colonies to be free and independent states, and as such to have "full Power to levy War, conclude Peace, contract Alliances, establish Commerce and do all other Acts and Things which Independent States may of right do."

As a result of the separation from Great Britain by the colonies acting as a unit, the powers of external sovereignty passed from the Crown not to the colonies severally, but to the colonies in their collective and corporate capacity as the United States of America. Even before the Declaration, the colonies were a unit in foreign affairs, acting through a common agency—namely the Continental Congress, composed of delegates from the thirteen colonies. That agency exercised the powers of war and peace, raised an army, created a navy, and finally adopted the Declaration of Independence. Rulers come and go; governments end and forms of government change; but sovereignty survives. A political society cannot endure without a supreme will somewhere. Sovereignty is never held in suspense. When, therefore, the external sovereignty of Great Britain in respect of the colonies ceased, it immediately passed to the Union. That fact was given practical application almost at once. The treaty of peace, made on September 23, 1783, was concluded between his Britannic Majesty and the "United States of America."

The union existed before the Constitution, which was ordained and established among other things to form "a more perfect Union." Prior to that event, it is clear that the Union, declared by the Articles of Confederation to be "perpetual," was the sole possessor of external sovereignty and in the Union it remained without change save in so far as the Constitution in express terms qualified its exercise. The framers' Convention was called and exerted its powers upon the irrefutable postulate that though the states were several their people in respect of foreign affairs were one . . . .

It results that the investment of the federal government with the powers of external sovereignty did not depend upon the affirmative grants of the Constitution. The powers to declare and wage war, to conclude peace, to make treaties, to maintain diplomatic relations with other sovereignties, if they had never been mentioned in the Constitution, would have vested in the federal government as necessary concomitants of nationality. Neither the Constitution nor the laws passed in pursuance of it have any force in foreign territory unless in respect of our own citizens (see *American Banana Co.* v. *United Fruit Co.*, 213 U. S. 347, 356); and operations of the nation in such territory must be governed by treaties, international understandings and compacts, and the principles of international law. As a member of the family of nations, the right and power of the United States in that field are equal to the right and power of the other members of the international family. Otherwise, the United States is not completely sovereign. The power to acquire territory by discovery and occupation (*Jones* v. *United States,* 137 U. S. 202, 212), the power to expel undesirable aliens (*Fong Yue Ting* v. *United States,* 149 U. S. 698, 705 *et seq.*), the power to make such international agreements as do not constitute treaties in the constitutional sense (*Altman & Co.* v. *United States,* 224 U. S. 583, 600–601), none of which is expressly affirmed by the Constitution, nevertheless exist as inherently inseparable from the conception of nationality. This the court recognized, and in each of the cases cited found the warrant for its conclusions not in the provisions of the Constitution, but in the law of nations. . . .

Not only, as we have shown, is the federal power over external affairs in origin and essential character different from that over internal affairs, but participation in the exercise of the power is significantly limited. In this vast external realm, with its important, complicated, delicate and manifold problems, the President alone has the power to speak or listen as a representative of the nation. He *makes* treaties with the advice and consent of the

Senate; but he alone negotiates. Into the field of negotiation the Senate cannot intrude; and Congress itself is powerless to invade it. As Marshall said in his great argument of March 7, 1800, in the House of Representatives, "The President is the sole organ of the nation in its external relations, and its sole representative with foreign nations." The Senate Committee on Foreign Relations at a very early day in our history (February 15, 1816), reported to the Senate, among other things, as follows:

"The President is the constitutional representative of the United States with regard to foreign nations. He manages our concerns with foreign nations and must necessarily be most competent to determine when, how, and upon what subjects negotiation may be urged with the greatest prospect of success. For his conduct he is responsible to the Constitution. The committee considers this responsibility the surest pledge for the faithful discharge of his duty. They think the interference of the Senate in the direction of foreign negotiations calculated to diminish that responsibility and thereby to impair the best security for the national safety. The nature of transactions with foreign nations, moreover, requires caution and unity of design, and their success frequently depends on secrecy and dispatch."

It is important to bear in mind that we are here dealing not alone with an authority vested in the President by an exertion of legislative power, but with such an authority plus the very delicate, plenary and exclusive power of the President as the sole organ of the federal government in the field of international relations—a power which does not require as a basis for its exercise an act of Congress, but which, of course, like every other governmental power, must be exercised in subordination to the applicable provisions of the Constitution. It is quite apparent that if, in the maintenance of our international relations, embarrassment—perhaps serious embarrassment—is to be avoided and success for our aims achieved, congressional legislation which is to be made effective through negotiation and inquiry within the international field must often accord to the President a degree of discretion and freedom from statutory restriction which would not be admissible were domestic affairs alone involved. Moreover, he, not Congress, has the better opportunity of knowing the conditions which prevail in foreign countries, and especially is this true in time of war. He has his confidential sources of information. He has his agents in the form of diplomatic, consular and other officials. Secrecy in respect of information gathered by them may be highly necessary, and the premature disclosure of it productive of harmful results. Indeed, so clearly is this true that the first President refused to accede to a request to lay before the House of Representatives the instructions, correspondence and documents relating to the negotiation of the Jay Treaty—a refusal the wisdom of which was recognized by the House itself and has never since been doubted. In his reply to the request, President Washington said:

"The nature of foreign negotiations requires caution, and their success must often depend on secrecy; and even when brought to a conclusion a full disclosure of all the measures, demands, or eventual concessions which may have been proposed or contemplated would be extremely impolitic; for this might have a pernicious influence on future negotiations, or produce immediate inconveniences, perhaps danger and mischief, in relation to other powers. The necessity of such caution and secrecy was one cogent reason for vesting the power of making treaties in the President, with the advice and consent of the Senate, the principle on which that body was formed confining it to a small number of members. To admit, then, a right in the House of Representatives to demand and to have as a matter of course all the papers respecting a negotiation with a foreign power would be to establish a dangerous precedent."

The marked difference between foreign affairs and domestic affairs in this respect is recognized by both Houses of Congress in the very form of their requisitions for information from the executive departments. In the case of every department except the Department of State, the resolution *directs* the official to furnish the information. In the case of the State Department, dealing with foreign affairs, the President is *requested* to furnish the information "if not incompatible with the public interest." A statement that to furnish the information is not compatible with the public interest rarely, if ever, is questioned.

When the President is to be authorized by legislation to act in respect of a matter intended to affect a situation in foreign territory, the legislator properly bears in mind the important consideration that the form of the President's action—or, indeed, whether he shall act at all—may well depend, among other things, upon the nature of the confidential information which he has or may thereafter receive, or upon the effect which his action may have upon our foreign relations.   This consideration, in connection with what we have already said on the subject discloses the unwisdom of requiring Congress in this field of governmental power to lay down narrowly definite standards by which the President is to be governed.   As this court said in *Mackenzie* v. *Hare,* 239 U.S. 299, 311, "As a government, the United States is invested with all the attributes of sovereignty.   As it has the character of nationality it has the powers of nationality, especially those which concern its relations and intercourse with other countries.   *We should hesitate long before limiting or embarrassing such powers."* (Italics supplied.)

In the light of the foregoing observations, it is evident that this court should not be in haste to apply a general rule which will have the effect of condemning legislation like that under review as constituting an unlawful delegation of legislative power.   The principles which justify such legislation find overwhelming support in the unbroken legislative practice which has prevailed almost from the inception of the national government to the present day.

*　*　*

The judgment of the court below must be reversed and the cause remanded for further proceedings in accordance with the foregoing opinion.

Reversed.

PRESIDENTIAL SUPREMACY IN FOREIGN POLICY *

BY

NICHOLAS deB. KATZENBACH

[1967]

. . . The framers of the Constitution recognized the impossibility of compressing the idea of the separation of powers into a simple formula. They did not attempt to engrave clear lines of demarcation.

With respect to diplomacy, they recognized the complexity of foreign affairs even in the far calmer climate of our Nation's childhood—a time when we took as our watchword Washington's declaration that, "It is our true policy to steer clear of permanent alliances, with any portion of the foreign world."

Hence the Constitution contains relatively few details about how foreign policy decisions shall be made and foreign relations conducted. It recognized that the voice of the United States in foreign affairs was, of necessity, the voice of the President. Consistent with that basic necessity, it also provided for the participation of Congress in a number of ways, direct and indirect.

John Jay observed in The Federalist that the Presidency possesses great inherent strengths in the direction of foreign affairs: The unity of the office, its capacity for secrecy and speed, and its superior sources of information.

But, as Professor Corwin has said:

(D)espite all this, actual practice under the Constitution has shown that while the President is usually in a position to propose, the Senate and Congress are often in a technical position at least to dispose. The verdict of history, in short, is that the power to deter-

---

* Testimony before the United States Senate, Committee on Foreign Relations, *Hearings, U.S. Commitments to Foreign Powers,* 1967. Nicholas deB. Katzenbach (b. 1922) is a former Undersecretary of State (1966–1968) and the author (with Morton Kaplan) of *The Political Foundations of International Law.*

mine the substantive content of American foreign policy is a divided power, with the lion's share falling usually to the President, though by no means always.

The Constitution left to the judgment and wisdom of the Executive and the Congress the task of working out the details of their relationships. Disagreements susceptible of decision by the Supreme Court have been rare. As a result, controversies over the line of demarcation in foreign affairs have been settled, in the end, by the instinct of the Nation and its leaders for political responsibility.

This has not been an easy formula to apply, even early in our history. President John Adams' use of troops in the Mediterranean, President Monroe's announcement of his renowned doctrine, President Jefferson's Louisiana Purchase, all were criticized at the time as exceeding the power of the Executive acting without the support of a congressional vote.

Similarly, Presidents have frequently criticized actions by Congress as invasions of their responsibility for the conduct of our foreign affairs.

But if the constitutional formula of flexibility was not an easy one, it has surely proved to be a practical and useful one. It has always seemed to me that the genius of our Constitution rests on the recognition of its drafters that they could not provide precise resolution for all future problems, foreseen and unforeseen. And I think that the conduct of foreign affairs demonstrates the validity of this approach.

Despite occasional differences and debates, history has surely vindicated the wisdom of this flexibility—of this essentially political approach to the conduct of our foreign affairs.

In the world we now live in, answers have not become easier. And yet the constitutional allocation of powers continues to work well today.

Let me turn to the nature of our foreign policy and the role of the United States in the world today—to the commitments of this Nation in foreign affairs.

The basic objective of our foreign policy is the security of the United States and the preservation of our freedoms. How this objective is achieved obviously depends upon the kind of world in which we live and the extent to which we can bring American power and influence to bear upon it.

For most of our history, we had only spasmodic foreign business. We lived in relative isolation, content to allow the European powers to maintain the balance of power on which, in fact, our national security depended.

In recent years, there has been a revolutionary change in the political structure of the world—and of the relative importance of foreign affairs to the United States. What has been perceived by all—by Presidents, by the Congress, and by the people—is that our independence and our security can no longer be assured by default. They depend in large measure on our capacity to lead in the achievement of a system of assured world peace. Within the broad horizons of such a framework—and only within such horizons—can American democracy and American society be safe.

This framework, I believe, rests on three propositions. The first is that events elsewhere can have critical effects on this country; hence our security is bound up with that of other countries.

The second is that we must heed more than power politics. For if we are true to our domestic ideals and are concerned for our domestic security, we cannot ignore the conditions in which people around the world must live—conditions which can and do fuel reverberating political explosions.

The third is that we cannot and should not meet these first two needs alone, any more than we could or should seek unilaterally to establish a pax Americana. We must develop international instrumentalities to help provide collective security and to help create social progress and eliminate the flammable conditions of misery that embrace so much of the world's population.

The United States has made serious, substantial, and enduring efforts to act on all three of these propositions. I do not think it is susceptible of proof, but I firmly believe that the crises we have avoided as a result of imaginative military and political action are at least as important as the crises we have survived.

The progress in our efforts has been substantial—and it has been the result of a national commitment. And this has been possible in large measure because of two factors.

This commitment has not been one of administration or of party, but of bipartisanship. One of the remarkable aspects of American foreign policy in the past 20 years is that it has become bipartisan. Partisan politics have, in fact, stopped at the water's edge.

The second factor is the consistent, coordinate action of the Executive and Legislative branches, each in their proper sphere, to propose and dispose, to create and carry out a national commitment. . . .

There is a long series of examples:

The resolution to support Greece and Turkey was passed by the Congress. . . .

The Marshall plan was the result both of congressional and executive action. . . .

The NATO treaty was approved by the Senate. . . .

Important to President Eisenhower's decision to use the U.S. fleet in the Straits of Taiwan and his decision to send marines to Lebanon in 1958 were congressional resolutions expressing the security interests of the United States in those areas.

President Kennedy's decision to call up reserve and National Guard units at the time of the Berlin crisis accorded not only with our NATO obligations, but also a series of congressional actions in support of the security of Western Europe.

*   *   *

Let me emphasize the constitutional quality of these commitments. By their nature, they set only the boundaries within which the United States will act. They cannot and do not spell out the precise action which the United States would take in a variety of contingencies. That is left for further decision by the President and the Congress.

In short, none of these incur automatic response. But they do make clear our pledge to take actions we regard as appropriate in the light of all the circumstances—our view that we are not indifferent to the actions of others which disturb the peace of the world and threaten the security of the United States.

Congress has been a full partner, as well, in the great national effort to accelerate the pace of economic and social progress elsewhere in the world. . . .

In all of these actions, the various committees of Congress and the Congress as a whole have participated fully in a variety of ways. In each, there has been express approval and authorization for executive action.

Frequently, in adopting legislation related to the conduct of foreign affairs, the Congress makes findings and declarations of policy, which express its views on broad policy issues and offer guidance to the executive branch.

On several occasions the Congress has adopted joint or concurrent resolutions declaring U.S. defense and foreign policy in relation to particular troubled areas of the world.

The Congress also has a key role in international agreements. In the case of treaties, the Senate's advice and consent is required. In the case of legislation to implement treaty commitments, or to authorize subsequent executive agreements, both Houses give approval.

Finally, there is the central fiscal power. In the exercise of its annual appropriations functions, the Congress reviews and debates the foreign policies of the administration.

Beyond these formal methods of congressional participation in foreign policy, there is the process of informal consultation between the Executive and the Congress. There are literally thousands of contacts each year between officers of the Executive branch and Members of Congress.

Not only do the Secretary and other high officials of the Department of State consult regularly and frequently with congressional leaders and committees; the President has often conducted such consultations personally and extensively.

As I noted at the outset, the drafters of the Constitution recognized that the voice of the United States in foreign affairs was that of the President. Throughout our history the focus has always been upon the Presidency, and it is difficult to imagine how it could be otherwise. Jefferson put it succinctly: "The transaction of business with foreign nations is Executive altogether."

I think it is fair to say, as virtually every commentator has in fact said throughout our history, that under our constitutional system the source of an effective foreign policy is Presidential power. His is the sole authority to communicate formally with foreign nations;

to negotiate treaties; to command the armed forces of the United States. His is a responsibility born of the need for speed and decisiveness in an emergency. His is the responsibility for controlling and directing all the external aspects of the Nation's power. To him flow all of the vast intelligence and information connected with national security. The President, of necessity, has a preeminent responsibility in this field.

But to say this is not to denigrate the role of Congress. Whatever the powers of the President to act alone on his own authority —and I doubt that any President has ever acted to the full limits of that authority—there can be no question that he acts most effectively when he acts with the support and authority of the Congress.

And so it is that every President seeks in various ways—formal and informal—the support of Congress for the policies which the United States pursues in its foreign relations.

In part, the Constitution compels such support. It gives the President the responsibilities for leadership. It also gives the Congress specific powers which can on the one hand frustrate and distort and on the other hand support and implement.

Obviously, then, there are great advantages to the Nation in the conduct of its foreign policy when circumstances permit the President and the Congress to act together. The commitments of this Nation to the United Nations Charter and to our allies are more than a matter of constitutional process. It is essential that these basic commitments should be clear, both to our friends and to our potential adversaries. Fitfulness of policy and unpredictability of action make for serious international instability, disorder, and danger.

In short, our safety and our success depend in large measure on the confidence of other nations that they can rely on our conduct and our assurances.

It is, therefore, as important that the Congress fill its constitutional role as it is that the President fill his. The Congress is and must be a participant in formulating the broad outlines of our foreign policy, in supporting those fundamental and enduring commitments on which the conduct of day-to-day diplomacy depend.

But to say this is not to say that the Congress can or should seek to substitute itself for the President or even to share in those decisions which are his to make.

As I have said, the Constitution relies not on express delineation to set the powers of the Executive and the Congress in this field, but depends instead on the practical interaction between the two branches. Today, these considerations require that the President fill the preeminent role:

He alone has the support of the administrative machinery required to deal with the sheer volume of our foreign affairs problems.

He alone is the focus of diplomatic communciations, intelligence sources and other information that are the tools for the conduct of foreign affairs.

He alone can act, when necessary, with the speed and decisiveness required to protect our national security.

I see no need to revise the experience of our history, or to seek to alter the boundaries of Presidential or congressional prerogative regarding foreign affairs. The need, as always, is to make the constitutional scheme and the experience of history continue to work.

*   *   *

The CHAIRMAN. I think the Constitution contemplated that the Congress should make the decision of whether or not we should engage in war. Don't you agree to that?

Mr. KATZENBACH. Yes, Mr. Chairman. I agree that the Congress should, except in the case of emergencies, participate in major decisions of that kind. . . .

The point is this. The use of the phrase "to declare war" as it was used in the Constitution of the United States had a particular meaning in terms of the events and the practices which existed at the time it was adopted and which existed really until the United Nations was organized. The phrase came from a context that recognized "war" to be an instrument of implementing the acceptable policy, but which is not acceptable in the climate today, which rejects the idea of aggression, which rejects the idea of conquest. . . .

Now, it came for a function. As you rightly say, it was recognized by the Founding Fathers that the President might have to take emergency action to protect the security of the United States, but that if there was going to be another use of the armed forces of the United States, that was a decision which Congress should check the Executive on, which Congress should support. It was for that reason that the phrase was inserted in the Constitution.

Now, over a long period of time . . . there have been many uses of the military forces of the United States for a variety of purposes without a congressional declaration of war. But it would be fair to say that most of these were relatively minor uses of force, although indeed in one case a landing of the Marines to protect property, I think, led the Marines to remain in a foreign country really in effect as an American Government, for some 20 years, which I would scarcely call minor. The reason for this was that there was a reluctance to describe these as acts of war and to use a formulation of declaring war, when war even in those days had the context of the use of military forces in another country in pursuit of national policy to acquire territory or to do various other things as an instrument of national policy.

And so there were several acts, they were called acts less than war, and called by a variety of other names. They were not submitted to the Congress to declare war because of the feeling for many, many years, that this would immediately mislead people with respect to what the objectives of the United States in these limited instances were.

Now, with the abolition of the use of force for all but a small number of purposes, by the commitment expressed in the U.N. Charter with respect to aggression, the question arises as to how the Congress can and should participate in the decision to use force; (1) where there is an emergency, and (2) beyond that, in a matter such as Korea where I think there was a genuine need for speed, or in the current instance in Vietnam?

A declaration of war would not, I think, correctly reflect the very limited objectives of the United States with respect to Vietnam. It would not correctly reflect our efforts there, what we are trying to do, the reasons why we are there, to use an outmoded phraseology, to declare war.

The CHAIRMAN. You think it is outmoded to declare war?

Mr. KATZENBACH. In this kind of a context I think the expression of declaring a war is one that has become outmoded in the international arena.

But I think there is, Mr. Chairman, an obligation on the part of the Executive to give Congress the opportunity, which that language was meant to reflect in the Constitution of the United States, to express its views with respect to this. In this instance, in the instance, if you will, of Vietnam, Congress had an opportunity to participate in these decisions. Congress ratified the SEATO treaty. . . .

As the situation there deteriorated, as American ships were attacked in the Tonkin Gulf, the President of the United States came back to Congress to seek the views of Congress with respect to what should be done in that area and with respect to the use of the military of the United States in that area, and on those resolutions Congress had the opportunity to participate and did participate, as you well remember, Mr. Chairman. The views of the Congress I think were very clearly expressed. That resolution authorized the President of the United States, by an overwhelming vote, with only two dissents in both Houses of Congress, two together, to use the force of the United States in that situation. The combination of the two, it seems to me, fully fulfill the obligation of the Executive in a situation of this kind to participate with the Congress to give the Congress a full and effective voice, the functional equivalent of the constitutional obligation expressed in the provision of the Constitution with respect to declaring war. . . .

Senator LAUSCHE. Does the Chief Executive, without the advice and consent of the Congress, have a right to involve our troops in military strife, and if so, when? . . .

Mr. KATZENBACH. In strife, military strife, military combat. I think it can be done certainly where they are attacked themselves directly. I think it can be done for the purpose of protection of American citizens, American shipping, that kind of obligation of which there is an abundant historical precedent, and I think that he can do it in an emergency if circumstances require rapid action and if he is acting pursuant to what has been a declared and supported public policy of the United States, or he can do it with a prior authorization of the Congress to do it in these circumstances. . . .

The CHAIRMAN. Does it not seem to you that sometimes there is need for caution and deliberation in making a foreign policy decision—that sometimes there is a tendency to exaggerate the extent of the emergency.

Mr. KATZENBACH. I think situations can be urgent. The fact that they are urgent does not necessarily justify intervention if a better policy is not to intervene. That doesn't stop the urgency of the situation. It has nothing to do with the urgency of the situation. But it has something to do with who makes the decision, because the President either makes the decision to intervene or not to intervene in the kind of situations such as South Korea, the point that we were discussing. Now, it seems to me that he is taking a position on that of the importance to the Nation and to the country, whether he acts or doesn't act. The urgency is in the situation, and where the situation is not urgent, if you believe the situation is not urgent, then certainly it should not be put in the category of urgent situations. But where they are, action or inaction can amount to the same thing.

OF PRESIDENTS AND CAESARS *

BY

FRANK CHURCH

[1969]

Mr. CHURCH. Mr. President, the Roman Caesars did not spring full blown from the brow of Zeus. Subtly and insidiously, they stole their powers away from an unsuspecting Senate. They strangled the Republic with skillful hands. Gibbon describes their method in this stately passage from the "Decline and Fall":

> It was on the dignity of the Senate that Augustus and his successors founded their new empire . . . In the administration of their own powers, they frequently consulted the great national council, and *seemed* to refer to its decision the most important concerns of peace and war . . . The masters of the Roman world surrounded their throne with darkness, concealed their irresistible strength, and humbly professed themselves the accountable ministers of the Senate, whose supreme decrees they dictated and obeyed . . . Augustus was sensible that mankind is governed by names; nor was he deceived in his expectation, that the Senate and the people would submit to slavery, provided they were respectfully assured that they still enjoyed their ancient freedom.

Senators of the United States may still enjoy their ancient freedom to debate and legislate, but through our own neglect, we have come to deal increasingly more with the form than with the substance of power. Again and again, the Senate has acquiesced, while American Presidents have steadily drawn to themselves much of the power delegated to Congress by the Constitution. In the process, especially in the field of foreign commitments and the crucial matter of our military involvement abroad, Congress as a whole—and the Senate in particular—has permitted a pervasive

---

* From the Senate debate on the national commitments resolution, June 20, 1969. *Congressional Record,* Vol. 115, No. 102. Frank Church (b. 1924), Democrat, is United States Senator from Idaho (1957–   ) and a member of the Committee on Foreign Relations.

erosion of the bedrock principle on which our political system was founded, the separation of powers.

For this reason, the national commitments resolution—Senate Resolution 85—may be the most significant measure that the Senate will consider during the current session of Congress. It seeks to set in motion a process pointing toward the restoration of the vital balance in our system prescribed by the Founding Fathers. The erosion of congressional power in the field of foreign policy has gone so far that a full return of the pendulum cannot be expected with passage of a single sense-of-the-Senate resolution. But here we must make our start.

The resolution, as reported with but one dissenting vote by the Committee on Foreign Relations, speaks for itself:

> Whereas accurate definition of the term "national commitment" in recent years has become obscured: Now, therefore, be it
>
> *Resolved,* That it is the sense of the Senate that a national commitment by the United States to a foreign power necessarily and exclusively results from affirmative action taken by the executive and legislative branches of the United States Government through means of a treaty, convention, or other legislative instrumentality specifically intended to give effect to such a commitment.

THE CONSTITUTIONAL ISSUE

As crisis has followed upon crisis in these last 30 years, the concentration of power in the hands of the President has grown ever more rapidly, while the Congress has been reduced to virtual impotence in the making of foreign policy. The cause of this change has been the climate of crisis itself, each one of which necessitated —or seemed to necessitate—decisive and immediate action. As each crisis arose, the President assumed, and the Congress usually agreed, that the Executive alone was capable of acting with the requisite speed. No one thought very much about the constitutional consequences of Presidential dominance in foreign policy; we tended to think only of the crisis we were dealing with, of the assumed need for speedy action, and of the importance of national unity in a time of emergency.

Now, however, we must think about constitutional problems, because nothing less than the survival of constitutional government is at stake. Our democratic processes, our system of separated powers, checked and balanced against each other, are being undermined by the very methods we have chosen to defend these processes against real or fancied foreign dangers. There is no end in sight of the era of crisis which began some 30 years ago. We cannot safely wait for quieter times to think about restoring the constitutional balance in our own Government. For as we delay, the fact of prolonged crisis, itself, will further erode our constitutional principles. The extended crisis of our own time was measured by President Nixon in the unsettling remark he made in his speech at the Air Force Academy. He said the United States, since 1941, "has paid for 14 years of peace with 14 years of war."

The corrosive impact that such an exorbitant payment invariably imposes upon democratic systems was described long ago by Alexis de Tocqueville, who wrote:

> No protracted war can fail to endanger the freedom of a democratic country. War does not always give over democratic communities to military government, but it must invariably and immeasurably increase the powers of civil government; it must also compulsorily concentrate the direction of all men and the management of all things in the hands of the administration. If it leads not to despotism by sudden violence, it prepares men for it more gently by their habits.[1]

Committing Our Country Abroad

Our protracted engagement in warfare has produced, first of all, a striking discrepancy between the ways in which many of our foreign commitments have been made in recent years and the treaty process through which they were meant to be made. Article II, section 2 of the Constitution states that the President "shall have power, by and with the advice and consent of the Senate, to make treaties, provided two-thirds of the Senators present concur."

---

[1] Alexis de Tocqueville, *Democracy in America,* London. Oxford University Press, 1946. Translated by Henry Reeve, p. 533.

Keeping this clear language of the Constitution in mind, consider the following:

On August 25, 1966, Secretary of State Rusk told the Senate Preparedness Subcommittee:

> No would-be aggressor should suppose that the absence of a defense treaty, Congressional declaration or U.S. military presence grants immunity to aggression.

The statement was meant to convey a stern warning to potential aggressors. It did that, and that was all to the good, but it also put Congress on notice that, with or without its consent, treaty or no treaty, the Executive will act as it sees fit against anyone whom it judges to be an aggressor, and that is not to the good. It is indeed nothing less than a statement of intention on the part of the Executive to usurp the treaty power of the Senate.

The denigration of treaties goes back at least to 1940, when the current era of world crisis began. In the summer of that year, when France had fallen and Britain was in imminent danger of German invasion, Presidet Roosevelt made an agreement with Great Britain under which 50 overaged American destroyers were given to her in exchange for certain naval bases on British territory in the Western Hemisphere. The arrangement was made by executive agreement despite the fact that it was a commitment of the greatest significance, an act which, according to Churchill, gave Germany legal grounds for declaring war on the United States. . . .

The destroyer deal was the first of a long series of significant foreign commitments made by executive agreement, each one of which has constituted an added precedent for the taking over by the President of the treaty powers meant to be exercised by the Senate. So far have things gone that treaties are now widely regarded, at least within the executive branch, as no more than one of a number of available methods of committing our country to some action abroad.

Indeed, executive branch officials have at times sought by simple statement to create "commitments" going far beyond those agreed to under normal treaty processes. Thailand is a case in point. . . .

In 1962, Secretary of State Rusk and the Thai Foreign Minister, Thanat Khoman, issued a joint statement in which Secretary Rusk expressed "the firm intention of the United States to aid Thailand, its ally and historic friend, in resisting Communist aggression and subversion"—a commitment going far beyond that contained in the SEATO Treaty to "consult" in case of subversion.

One of the newest devices used to circumvent the treaty power of the Senate is the congressional resolution, framed in such sweeping language as to give advance consent to unspecified future action by the President. . . .

THE WAR POWER

Unlike the treaty power, the Constitution did not divide the war power equally between the two branches of Government but vested it predominantly in Congress. Article I, section 8 of the Constitution states that—

> Congress shall have the power to declare war; to raise and support armies; to provide and maintain a navy; to make rules for the Government and regulation of the Armed Forces; to provide for calling forth the militia to execute the laws, suppress insurrections, and repel invasions; to provide for organizing, arming, and disciplining the militia; and to make all laws necessary and proper for executing the foregoing powers.

Article II, section 2 of the Constitution states that the President shall be Commander in Chief of the Army and Navy.

The language of the Constitution is clear and the intent of the framers beyond question: the war power is vested almost entirely in the Congress, the only important exception being the necessary authority of the President to repel a sudden attack on the United States. Only in recent years have Presidents claimed the right to commit the country to foreign wars, under a sweeping and, in my opinion, wholly unwarranted interpretation of their power as Commander in Chief.

The framers of the Constitution very deliberately placed the war power in the hands of the legislature, and did so for excellent reasons. All too frequently, the American Colonies had been drawn, by royal decree, into England's wars. The leaders of the newly independent Republic resolved to make certain that their new country would never again be drawn into war at the direction of a single man; for this reason they transferred the war power to the legislative branch of the newly created Government. In so doing, they recognized that the President might sometimes have to take defensive action to repel a sudden attack on the United States, but that was the extent of the war-making power they were willing for him to exercise. . . .

During the first century of American history most of our Presidents were scrupulously respectful of Congress' authority to initiate war. . . .

The Monroe Doctrine is often cited by proponents of unrestricted Presidential power as a precedent for executive authority to commit the country to military action abroad. In fact, President Monroe himself regarded his declaration as no more than a policy statement. . . .

In 1846, President Polk sent American forces into disputed territory in Texas, precipitating the clash which began the Mexican war. Abraham Lincoln, then a Republican Member of the House of Representatives from Illinois, was certain that the President had acted unconstitutionally, and he wrote:

> Allow the President to invade a neighboring nation whenever *he* shall deem it necessary to repeal an invasion, and you allow him to do so, *whenever he may choose to say* he deems it necessary for such purpose—and you allow him to make war at pleasure. Study to see if you can fix *any limit* to his power in this respect, after you have given him so much as you propose. . . .[2]

Nonetheless, by the end of the 19th century, precedents had been established for Presidential use of the Armed Forces abroad for certain limited purposes, such as suppressing piracy and the slave trade, "hot pursuit" of criminals across frontiers, and protecting American lives and property, as well as for repelling sudden attack. But in the early 20th century, Presidential power over the commitment of the Armed Forces abroad was greatly expanded. Presidents Theodore Roosevelt, Taft, and Wilson, acting without

---

[2] Letter to William H. Herndon, Feb. 15, 1848, in *The Collected Works of Abraham Lincoln*, 9 vols. (New Brunswick: Rutgers University Press, 1953,) vol. 1, pp. 451–452.

authority from Congress, repeatedly intervened militarily in Mexico, Central America, and the Caribbean. The Congresses of that period, most unwisely, failed to resist these Presidential incursions on their constitutional authority, with the result that they became corrosive precedents for the further and much greater incursions that were to follow during and after World War II.

I have already noted how President Franklin Roosevelt usurped the treaty power of the Senate in making his famous destroyer deal with Great Britain; he also went further than any previous President in expanding Executive power over the Armed Forces. In the course of the year 1941, he committed American forces to the defense of Greenland and Iceland, authorized American warships to escort, as far as Iceland, convoys which were bound for Britain, and ordered American naval vessels to "shoot on sight" against German and Italian ships in the western Atlantic. Well before Congress declared war on the Axis Powers, President Roosevelt had already taken the country into an undeclared naval war in the Atlantic. Few would deny that he did these things in an excellent cause, that of assisting Britain in those desperate days when she stood alone against the tide of Nazi aggression. But in doing what he did for a good cause, President Roosevelt enabled his successors to claim the same authority in the furtherance of causes much more dubious.

After World War II, the trend toward Presidential dominance accelerated greatly and the real power to commit the country to war is now exercised by the President alone. . . .

In other words, the intent of the Constitution has been virtually negated.

In 1950, President Truman committed the Armed Forces of the United States to the Korean war without any form of Congressional authorization. The President himself made no public explanation of his action, but an article in the Department of State Bulletin, which is the official record of State Department policy, asserted:

> The President, as Commander in Chief of the Armed Forces of the United States, has full control over the use thereof.[3]

---

[3] *Department of State Bulletin,* vol. 23, No. 578, July 31, 1950, pp. 173–177.

No one in Congress protested at the time, but some months later, in January 1951, Senator Taft asserted that the President had "simply usurped authority" in sending troops to Korea.[4]

When the Korean war went badly, President Truman's political opponents, who had supported him at the outset, charged him with responsibility for the war and accused him of exceeding his authority. In order to protect themselves from this kind of accusation, subsequent Presidents have adopted the practice of asking Congress for joint resolutions when they contemplate taking military action in some foreign country. Presidents Eisenhower, Kennedy, and Johnson all have requested such resolutions and Congress has readily complied. . . .

Couched in the broadest of terms, these resolutions have generally expressed Congress' advance approval of any military action the President might see fit to take in the area concerned.

The most important and fateful of all these was the Gulf of Tonkin resolution adopted in August 1964, after only 2 days of hearings and debate. The resolution expressed congressional approval of any measures the President might choose to take to prevent aggression in Southeast Asia and further stated that the United States was prepared to take any action the President might judge to be necessary to assist a number of Southeast Asian states, including Vietnam.

The Gulf of Tonkin resolution has been cited, again and again, as proof of Congress' approval of the war in Vietnam. It was later said by Under Secretary of State Katzenbach to be the "functional equivalent" of a congressional declaration of war. In my opinion, Congress neither expected nor even considered at the time of the debate on the resolution that the President would later commit more than half a million American soldiers to a full-scale war in Vietnam.

WHY CONGRESS ABDICATED

How did it come about that Congress permitted itself to be so totally and disastrously misunderstood? And why has Congress

---

[4] *Congressional Record,* 82nd Cong., 1st Sess., vol. 97, January 5, 1951, p. 57.

tamely yielded to the President powers that, beyond any doubt, were intended by the Constitution to be exercised by Congress?

As to the first question, Congress failed to state its intentions clearly in the case of the Gulf of Tonkin resolution, because it assumed that those intentions were generally understood. . . . In adopting a resolution supporting the President on Vietnam, the great majority in Congress believed that they were upholding the position of moderation which President Johnson was expressing in his campaign. The failure of Congress to make its purpose clear was nonetheless a grave error.

With respect to the second question, the abdication of Congress in the field of foreign policy, the reasons are varied and several. To begin with, the politics of crisis is that of anxiety in which Congress, like the country, tends to unite behind the President. Because the United States has exercised its role as a world power for only a short time, we have not really gotten used to dealing with foreign emergencies and, more important still, to discriminating between genuine emergencies and situations that only seem to to require urgent action. Lacking experience in dealing with such flaps as the Gulf of Tonkin incident in 1964, we have tended to act hastily with insufficient regard for the requirements of constitutional procedure, assuming, quite wrongly, that it would somehow be unpatriotic to question the President's judgment in a moment of assumed emergency.

Then there is the way our history has been taught since the end of the First World War. It is now part of the conventional wisdom that the Senate's refusal to ratily the Versailles Treaty not only destroyed Woodrow Wilson's dream of world order, but actually accounted for the failure of the League of Nations to prevent World War II. . . .

But even if the Senate blundered in 1919, it does not follow that the President must, therefore, be regarded as infallible. The myth that the Senate's refusal to ratify the Versailles Treaty not only affairs today lies shattered on the shoals of Vietnam. The lesson to be learned may well be found in the observation of James Bryce, the British statesman, who said:

> In a democracy the people are entitled to determine the ends or
> general aims of foreign policy. History shows that they do this at

least as wisely as monarchs or oligarchies, or the small groups to whom, in democratic countries, the conduct of foreign relations has been left, and that they have evinced more respect for moral principles.[5]

The "small groups" to whom Bryce refers have themselves induced Congress to underrate its own competence in foreign affairs. . . .

Now, modesty and self-effacement are not characteristics usually associated with politicians but, curiously enough, many Members of Congress seem to have accepted the view that foreign policy is best left to the experts. This view is patently false: Clemenceau said that war was too important to be left to the generals; similarly, the basic decisions of foreign policy are too important to be left to the diplomats. . . .

No discussion of congressional abdication in the realm of foreign policy would be complete, however, without mention of the great impetus given the growth of Presidential prerogative by the general acceptance, following World War II, of the doctrine of bipartisanship in the conduct of our foreign relations. The lure of that beguiling slogan, "politics stops at the water's edge," led us to the erroneous conclusion that any action taken by the President abroad demanded bipartisan backing at home. . . .

Far from removing foreign policy from the arena of partisan politics, the doctrine of bipartisanship has simply gathered more power into the hands of the President by eliminating, between elections, any semblance of organized opposition in Congress. When the duty to oppose no longer rests, as it normally must, upon the "loyal opposition" in Congress, the day-to-day responsibility for holding the President to account, for the timely questioning of his chosen course, and for the posing of alternatives, falls much less effectually to the scatterfire of individual Members expressing their personal dissent. . . .

THE CONSEQUENCES OF ABDICATION

As a result of the passing of the war power out of the hands

---

[5] James Bryce, "Democracy and Foreign Policy," *Readings in Foreign Policy,* edited by Robert A. Goldwin, New York, Oxford University Press, 1959, p. 17.

of Congress, perhaps the most important of our constitutional checks and balances has been overturned. For the first time in our history, there has come into view the possibility of our President becoming a Caesar, because, as Gibbon wrote in "The Decline and Fall":

> The principles of a free constitution are irrevocably lost, when the legislative power is nominated by the executive.[6]

It is no exaggeration to say that the President of the United States now holds the power of life and death for 200 million Americans and, indeed, for most of the human race. That power is vividly described by the brilliant columnist, James Reston, who wrote of the ascendancy of the Presidency in these words:

> On the great acts of foreign policy, especially those involving the risk or even the act of war, he is more powerful in this age than in any other, freer to follow his own bent than any other single political leader in the world—and the larger and more fateful the issue, the greater is his authority to follow his own will.[7]

No human being can safely be entrusted with such enormous powers. . . .

Even the wisest and most competent of Presidents is still a human being, susceptible to human flaws and human failures of judgment. The greatest insight of our Founding Fathers was their recognition of the dangers of unlimited power exercised by a single man or institution; their greatest achievement was the safeguards against absolute power which they wrote into our Constitution. . . .

What, one may ask, could be expected to come of a new congressional attitude toward foreign policy? First, one may hope that it would encourage Congress to show the same healthy skepticism toward Presidential requests pertaining to foreign relations that it shows toward Presidential recommendations in the domestic field.

---

[6] Edward Gibbon, *The History of the Decline and Fall of the Roman Empire,* 3 vols. (New York: Random House, Modern Library Edition), vol. 1, p. 54.

[7] James Reston, *The Artillery of the Press; Its Influence on American Foreign Policy,* New York, Harper & Row, 1967, p. 45.

One may hope that Congress hereafter would exercise its own judgment as to when haste is necessary and when it is not. One may hope that, in considering a resolution such as the Gulf of Tonkin resolution, Congress would hereafter state as explicitly as possible the nature and purpose of any military action to be taken and, more important still, that it would make it absolutely clear that the resolution was an act of authorization, granting the President specific powers which he would not otherwise possess. One may hope, finally, that Congress would never again forget that its responsibility for upholding the Constitution includes the obligation to preserve its own constitutional authority.

One hears it argued these days—by high officials in the executive branch, by foreign policy experts, and by some political scientists— that certain of our constitutional procedures, including the power of Congress to declare war, are obsolete in the nuclear age. This contention, in my opinion, is without merit. Nothing in the Constitution prevents—and no one in Congress would ever try to prevent the President from acting in a genuine national emergency. What is at issue is his authority to order our military forces into action in foreign lands whenever and wherever he judges a genuine national emergency. What is at issue is his right to alter constitutional processes at his option, even in the name of defending those processes.

I do not believe that the Constitution is obsolete; I do not believe that Congress is incapable of discharging its responsibilities for war and peace; but, if either of these conditions ever should arise, the remedy would lie in the amendment process of the Constitution itself. As George Washington said in his Farewell Address:

> Let there be no change in usurpation; for though this in one instance may be the instrument of good, it is the customary weapon by which free governments are destroyed.

II

GROWTH AND EXPANSION

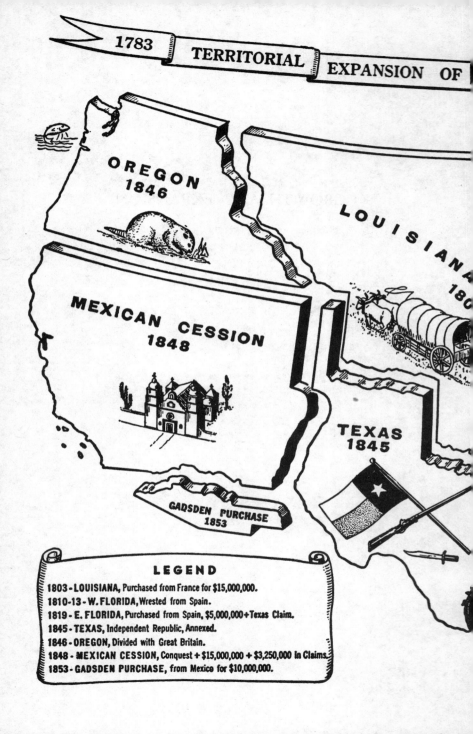

OREGON
1846

LOUISIANA
180

MEXICAN CESSION
1848

TEXAS
1845

GADSDEN PURCHASE
1853

LEGEND

1803 - LOUISIANA, Purchased from France for $15,000,000.

1810-13 - W. FLORIDA, Wrested from Spain.

1819 - E. FLORIDA, Purchased from Spain, $5,000,000 + Texas Claim.

1845 - TEXAS, Independent Republic, Annexed.

1846 - OREGON, Divided with Great Britain.

1848 - MEXICAN CESSION, Conquest + $15,000,000 + $3,250,000 in Claims.

1853 - GADSDEN PURCHASE, from Mexico for $10,000,000.

CONTINENTAL UNITED STATES 1853

N
W E
S

PURCHASE

ORIGINAL
UNITED STATES
1783

1810-13
FLORIDA 1819

This map copyright 1950 by
Appleton-Century-Crofts, Inc.
Reproduced from Thomas A.
Bailey, *Diplomatic History of
the American People.*

SELECTED READINGS ON AMERICAN EXPANSION, 1802-1881

1. THOMAS JEFFERSON TO ROBERT R. LIVINGSTON
Washington, April 18, 1802

The cession of Louisiana and the Floridas by Spain to France, works most sorely on the United States. On this subject the Secretary of State has written to you fully, yet I cannot forbear recurring to it personally, so deep is the impression it makes on my mind. It completely reverses all the political relations of the United States, and will form a new epoch in our political course. Of all nations of any consideration, France is the one which, hitherto, has offered the fewest points on which we could have any conflict of right, and the most points of a communion of interests. From these causes, we have ever looked to her as our *natural friend*, as one with which we never could have an occasion of difference. Her growth, therefore, we viewed as our own, her misfortunes ours. There is on the globe one single spot, the possessor of which is our natural and habitual enemy. It is New Orleans, through which the produce of three-eighths of our territory must pass to market, and from its fertility it will ere long yield more than half of our whole produce, and contain more than half of our inhabitants. France, placing herself in that door, assumes to us the attitude of defiance. Spain might have retained it quietly for years. Her pacific dispositions, her feeble state, would induce her to increase our facilities there, so that her possession of the place would be hardly felt by us, and it would not, perhaps, be very long before some circumstance might arise, which might make the cession of it to us the price of something of more worth to her. Not so can it ever be in the hands of France: the impetuosity of her temper, the energy and restlessness of her character, placed in a point of eternal friction with us, and our character, which, though quiet and loving peace and the pursuit of wealth, is high-minded, despising wealth in competition with insult or injury, enterprising and energetic as any nation on earth; these circumstances render it impossible that France and the United States can continue long friends, when they meet in so irritable a position. They, as well as we, must be blind if they do

63

not see this; and we must be very improvident if we do not begin to make arrangements on that hypothesis. The day that France takes possession of New Orleans, fixes the sentence which is to restrain her forever within her low-water mark. It seals the union of two nations, who, in conjunction, can maintain exclusive possession of the ocean. From that moment, we must marry ourselves to the British fleet and nation. We must turn all our attention to a maritime force, for which our resources place us on very high ground; and having formed and connected together a power which may render reinforcement of her settlements here impossible to France, make the first cannon which shall be fired in Europe the signal for the tearing up any settlement she may have made, and for holding the two continents of America in sequestration for the common purposes of the United British and American nations. This is not a state of things we seek or desire. It is one which this measure, if adopted by France, forces on us as necessarily, as any other cause, by the laws of nature, brings on its necessary effect. It is not from a fear of France that we deprecate this measure proposed by her. For however greater her force is than ours, compared in the abstract, it is nothing in comparison of ours, when to be exerted on our soil. But it is from a sincere love of peace, and a firm persuasion, that bound to France by the interests and the strong sympathies still existing in the minds of our citizens, and holding relative positions which insure their continuance, we are secure of a long course of peace. Whereas, the change of friends, which will be rendered necessary if France changes that position, embarks us necessarily as a belligerent power in the first war of Europe. In that case, France will have held possession of New Orleans during the interval of peace, long or short, at the end of which it will be wrested from her. Will this short-lived possession have been an equivalent to her for the transfer of such a weight into the scale of her enemy? Will not the amalgamation of a young, thriving nation, continue to that enemy the health and force which are at present so evidently on the decline? And will a few years' possession of New Orleans add equally to the strength of France? She may say she needs Louisiana for the supply of her West Indies. She does not need it in time of peace, and in war she could not depend on them, because they would be so easily intercepted. I should suppose that all these considerations might, in some proper form, be brought into view of the Government of France. Though stated by us, it ought not to give offence; because we do not bring them forward as a menace, but as consequences not controllable by us, but inevitable from the course of things. We mention them, not as things which we desire by any means, but as things we deprecate; and we beseech a friend to look forward and to prevent them for our common interest.

If France considers Louisiana, however, as indispensable for her views, she might perhaps be willing to look about for arrangements which might reconcile to it our interests. If anything could do this, it would be the ceding to us the island of New Orleans and the Floridas. This would certainly, in a great degree, remove the causes of jarring and irritation between us, and perhaps for such a length of time, as might produce other means of making the measure permanently conciliatory to our interests and friendships. It would, at any rate, relieve us from the necessity of taking immediate measures for countervailing such an operation by arrangements in another quarter. But still we should consider New Orleans and the Floridas as no equivalent for the risk of a quarrel with France, produced by her vicinage. . . .

2. TREATY BETWEEN THE UNITED STATES AND FRANCE FOR THE CESSION OF LOUISIANA, Concluded April 30, 1803

. . . *ARTICLE I.* Whereas by the Article the third of the Treaty concluded at St. Ildefonso the 9th Vendémiaire and 9/1st October 1800 between the First Consul of the French Republic and his Catholic Majesty it was agreed as follows.

"His Catholic Majesty promises and engages on his part to cede to the French Republic six months after the full and entire execution of the conditions and Stipulations herein relative to his Royal Highness the Duke of Parma, the Colony or Province of Louisiana with the Same extent that it now has in the hands of Spain, & that it had when France possessed it; and Such as it

Should be after the Treaties subsequently entered into between Spain and other States."

And whereas in pursuance of the Treaty and particularly of the third article the French Republic has an incontestible title to the domain and to the possession of the said Territory—The First Consul of the French Republic desiring to give to the United States a strong proof of his friendship doth hereby cede to the said United States in the name of the French Republic forever and in full Sovereignty the said Territory with all its rights and appurtenances as fully and in the Same manner as they have been acquired by the French Republic in virtue of the above mentioned Treaty concluded with his Catholic Majesty. . . .

Article III. The inhabitants of the ceded territory shall be incorporated in the Union of the United States and admitted as soon as possible according to the principles of the federal Constitution to the enjoyment of all the rights, advantages and immunities of citizens of the United States, and in the mean time they shall be maintained and protected in the free enjoyment of their liberty, property and the Religion which they profess. . . .

3. ROBERT R. LIVINGSTON TO JAMES MADISON

Paris, May 20, 1803

The subject of this letter is too important to admit of delay, in case the treaties should have been any time in your hands; but, as it has not yet been fully considered by Mr. Monroe, he thinks he can not make it that of a joint letter till we have more fully discussed it, which we propose to do to-morrow or the next day. . . .

I informed you long since, that, on inquiring whether the Floridas were within the cession of Spain, I was told by M. Marbois he was sure that Mobile was, but could not answer further. I believed his information incorrect, because I understood that Louisiana, as it then was, made the object of the cession; and that since the possession of the Floridas by Britain, they had changed their names. But the moment I saw the words of the Treaty of Madrid I had no doubt but it included all the country that France possessed by the name of Louisiana, previous to their cession to Spain, except what had been conveyed by subsequent treaties. I accordingly insisted, with M. Marbois, at the time we negotiated, that this would be considered as within our purchase. He neither assented nor denied, but said that all they received from Spain was intended to be conveyed to us. That my construction was right, is fairly to be inferred from the words of the treaties, and from a comment upon them contained in the Spanish Minister's letter to Mr. Pinckney, in which he expressly says that France had recovered Louisiana as it formerly belonged to her, saving the rights of other Powers. This leaves no doubt upon the subject of the intention of the contracting parties. Now, it is well known that Louisiana, as possessed by France, was bounded by the river Perdido, and that Mobile was the metropolis. For the facts relative to this I refer you to Reynal and to his maps. I have also seen maps here which put the matter out of dispute.

I called this morning upon M. Marbois for a further explanation on this subject and to remind him of his having told me that Mobile made a part of the cession. He told me that he had no precise idea on the subject, but that he knew it to be an historical fact, and that on that only he had formed his opinion. I asked him what orders had been given to the prefect, who was to take possession, or what orders had been given by Spain as to the boundary, in ceding it? He assured me that he did not know; but that he would make the inquiry, and let me know. At 4 o'clock I called for Mr. Monroe to take him to the Minister of Foreign Affairs; but he was prevented from accompanying me. I asked the Minister what were the east bounds of the territory ceded to us? He said he did not know; we must take it as they had received it. I asked him how Spain meant to give them possession? He said, according to the words of the treaty. But what did you mean to take? I do not know. Then you mean that we shall construe it our own way? I can give you no direction; you have made a noble bargain for yourselves, and I suppose you will make the most of it.

Now, sir, the sum of this business is, to recommend to you, in the strongest terms, after having obtained the possession, that the French Commissary will give you, to insist upon this as a part of

your right; and to take possession, at all events, to the river Perdido. I pledge myself that your right is good; and, after the explanations that have been given here, you need apprehend nothing
from a decisive measure. Your Ministers here and at Madrid,
can support your claim; and the time is peculiarly favorable to
enable you to do it without the smallest risk at home. It may also
be important to anticipate any designs that Britain may have upon
that country. Should she possess herself of it, and the war terminate favorably for her, she will not readily relinquish it. With
this in your hand, East Florida will be of little moment, and may
be yours whenever you please. At all events, proclaim your rights
and take possession.

4. THOMAS JEFFERSON TO J. B. COLVIN*

Monticello, September 20, 1810

Sir,—Your favor of the 14th has been duly received, and I have
to thank you for the many obliging things respecting myself which
are said in it. If I have left in the breasts of my fellow citizens a
sentiment of satisfaction with my conduct in the transaction of
their business, it will soften the pillow of my repose through the
residue of life.

The question you propose, whether circumstances do not sometimes occur, which make it a duty in officers of high trust, to assume
authorities beyond the law, is easy of solution in principle, but
sometimes embarrassing in practice. A strict observance of the
written laws is doubtless *one* of the high duties of a good citizen,
but it is not *the highest*. The laws of necessity, of self-
preservation, of saving our country when in danger, are of higher
obligation. To lose our country by a scrupulous adherence to
written law, would be to lose the law itself, with life, liberty,
property and all those who are enjoying them with us; thus
absurdly sacrificing the end to the means. When, in the battle of
Germantown, General Washington's army was annoyed from
Chew's house, he did not hesitate to plant his cannon against it,

---

*From *Writings of Thomas Jefferson,* ed. Andrew A. Lipscomb, issued in
1905 by the Thomas Jefferson Memorial Association of the United States,
Washington, D. C.

although the property of a citizen. When he besieged Yorktown, he leveled the suburbs, feeling that the laws of property must be postponed to the safety of the nation. While the army was before York, the Governor of Virginia took horses, carriages, provisions and even men by force, to enable that army to stay together till it could master the public enemy; and he was justified. A ship at sea in distress for provisions, meets another having abundance, yet refusing a supply; the law of self-preservation authorizes the distressed to take a supply by force. In all these cases, the unwritten laws of necessity, of self-preservation, and of the public safety, control the written laws of *meum* and *tuum*.

Further to exemplify the principle, I will state an hypothetical case. Suppose it had been made known to the Executive of the Union in the autumn of 1805, that we might have the Floridas for a reasonable sum, that that sum had not indeed been so appropriated by law, but that Congress were to meet within three weeks, and might appropriate it on the first or second day of their session. Ought he, for so great an advantage to his country, to have risked himself by transcending the law and making the purchase? The public advantage offered, in this supposed case, was indeed immense; but a reverence for law, and the probability that the advantage might still be *legally* accomplished by a delay of only three weeks, were powerful reasons against hazarding the act. But suppose it foreseen that a John Randolph would find means to protract the proceeding on it by Congress, until the ensuing spring, by which time new circumstances would change the mind of the other party. Ought the Executive, in that case, and with that foreknowledge, to have secured the good to his country, and to have trusted to their justice for the transgression of the law? I think he ought, and that the act would have been approved. . . .

From these examples and principles you may see what I think on the question proposed. They do not go to the case of persons charged with petty duties, where consequences are trifling, and time allowed for a legal course, nor to authorize them to take such cases out of the written law. In these, the example of overleaping the law is of greater evil than a strict adherence to its imperfect provisions. It is incumbent on those only who accept of great charges, to risk themselves on great occasions, when the safety of the nation, or some of its very high interests are at stake. An officer is bound to obey orders; yet he would be a bad one who should do it in cases for which they were not intended, and which involved the most important consequences. The line of discrimination between cases may be difficult; but the good officer is bound to draw it at his own peril, and throw himself on the justice of his country and the rectitude of his motives.

I have indulged freer views on this question, on your assurances that they are for your own eye only, and that they will not get into the hands of newswriters. I met their scurrilities without concern, while in pursuit of the great interests with which I was charged. But in my present retirement, no duty forbids my wish for quiet.

5. CABINET DISCUSSION OF THE FUTURE OF THE UNITED STATES, 1819*

. . . He [Mr. Crawford] said he had been conversing with Mr. Lowndes, who told him that, both in England and France, everybody with whom he had conversed appeared to be profoundly impressed with the idea that we were an ambitious and encroaching people, and he thought we ought to be very guarded and moderate in our policy, to remove this impression.

I said I doubted whether we ought to give ourselves any concern about it. Great Britain, after vilifying us twenty years as a mean, low-minded, peddling nation, having no generous ambitions and no God but gold, had now changed her tone, and was endeavoring to alarm the world at the gigantic grasp of our ambition. Spain was doing the same; and Europe, who, even since the commencement of our Government under the present Constitution, had seen those nations intriguing with the Indians and negotiating to bound us by the Ohio, had first been startled by our acquisition of Louisiana, and now by our pretension to extend to the South Sea, and readily gave credit to the envious and jealous clamor of Spain and England against our ambition. Nothing that we could

---

*From *Memoirs of John Quincy Adams,* ed. Charles Francis Adams, published 1875 by J. B. Lippincott & Co. This excerpt covers part of a discussion between President Monroe and some members of his cabinet on Nov. 16, 1819. William H. Crawford was then Secretary of the Treasury.

say or do would remove this impression until the world shall be familiarized with the idea of considering our proper dominion to be the continent of North America. From the time when we became an independent people it was as much a law of nature that this should become our pretension as that the Mississippi should flow to the sea. Spain had possessions upon our southern and Great Britain upon our northern border. It was impossible that centuries should elapse without finding them annexed to the United States; not that any spirit of encroachment or ambition on our part renders it necessary, but because it is a physical, moral, and political absurdity that such fragments of territory, with sovereigns at fifteen hundred miles beyond sea, worthless and burdensome to their owners, should exist permanently contiguous to a great, powerful, enterprising, and rapidly-growing nation. Most of the Spanish territory which had been in our neighborhood had already become our own by the most unexceptionable of all acquisitions—fair purchase for a valuable consideration. This rendered it still more unavoidable that the remainder of the continent should ultimately be ours. But it is very lately that we have distinctly seen this ourselves; very lately that we have avowed the pretension of extending to the South Sea; and until Europe shall find it a settled geographical element that the United States and North America are identical, any effort on our part to reason the world out of a belief that we are ambitious will have no other effect than to convince them that we add to our ambition hypocrisy. . . .

6. JOHN C. CALHOUN TO RICHARD PAKENHAM*

Washington, September 3, 1844

. . . Our claims to the portion of the territory drained by the Columbia River may be divided into those we have in our own proper right and those we have derived from France and Spain. We ground the former, as against Great Britain, on priority of discovery and priority of exploration and settlement. We rest our

---

*At the time of this letter, Calhoun was Secretary of State and Pakenham was British Minister to the United States.

claim to discovery, as against her, on that of Captain Gray, a citizen of the United States, who, in the ship Columbia, of Boston, passed its bar and anchored in the river, ten miles above its mouth, on the 11th of May, 1792; and who, afterwards, sailed up the river 12 or 15 miles, and left it on the 20th of the same month, calling it *"Columbia,"* after his ship; which name it still retains. . . .

Nor is the evidence of the priority of our discovery of the head branches of the river and its exploration less conclusive. Before the treaty was ratified by which we acquired Louisiana, in 1803, an expedition was planned, at the head of which were placed Meriwether Lewis and William Clarke, to explore the river Missouri and its principal branches to their sources, and then to seek and trace to its termination in the Pacific some stream, *"whether the Columbia, the Oregon, the Colorado, or any other which might offer the most direct and practicable water communication across the continent for the purpose of commerce."* The party began to ascend the Missouri in May, 1804, and in· the summer of 1805 reached the head waters of the Columbia river. . . .

It took place many years before it was visited and explored by any subject of Great Britain, or of any other civilized nation, so far as we are informed. It as clearly entitles us to the claim of priority of discovery as to its head branches and the exploration of the river and region through which it passes, as the voyages of Captain Gray and the Spanish navigator, Heceta, entitle us to priority in reference to its mouth and the entrance into its channel.

Nor is our priority of settlement less certain. Establishments were formed by American citizens on the Columbia as early as 1809 and 1810. . . .

Such are the facts on which we rest our claims to priority of discovery and priority of exploration and settlement, as against Great Britain, to the region drained by the Columbia river. So much for the claims we have in our own proper right to that region.

To these we have added the claims of France and Spain. The former we obtained by the treaty of Louisiana, ratified in 1803;

and the latter by the treaty of Florida, ratified in 1819. By the former, we acquired all the rights which France had to Louisiana *"to the extent it now has (1803) in the hands of Spain, and that it had when France possessed it, and as it should be after the treaties subsequently entered into by Spain and other States."* By the latter, his Catholic majesty *"ceded to the United States all his rights, claims, and pretensions"* to the country lying west of the Rocky Mountains and north of a line drawn on the 42nd parallel of latitude, from a point on the south bank of the Arkansas, in that parallel, to the South Sea; that is, to the whole region claimed by Spain west of those mountains, and north of that line. . . .

When the first convention was concluded, in 1818, our whole population did not exceed nine millions of people. . . . Now, our population may be safely estimated at not less than nineteen millions, of which at least eight millions inhabit the States and territories in the valley of the Mississippi. .. . .

To this great increase of population. . . may be added the increased facility of reaching the Oregon territory. . . . These joint causes have had the effect of turning the current of our population towards the territory. . . . There can, then, be no doubt now that the operation of the same causes which impelled our population westward from the shores of the Atlantic. . . to the valley of the Mississippi, will impel them onward. . . into the valley of the Columbia, and that the whole region drained by it is destined to be peopled by us. . . .

7. EDITORIAL BY JOHN L. O'SULLIVAN, 1845*

Why, were other reasoning wanting, in favor of now elevating this question of the reception of Texas into the Union, out of the lower region of our past party dissensions, up to its proper level of a high and broad nationality, it surely is to be found, found abundantly, in the manner in which other nations have undertaken to intrude themselves into it, between us and the proper parties to the case, in a spirit of hostile interference against us, for the

*From the *Democratic Review,* July-August, 1845. It is believed that the phrase "manifest destiny" appeared for the first time in this article.

avowed object of thwarting our policy and hampering our power, limiting our greatness and checking the fulfilment of our manifest destiny to overspread the continent allotted by Providence for the free development of our yearly multiplying millions. This we have seen done by England, our old rival and enemy; and by France, strangely coupled with her against us, under the influence of the Anglicism strongly tinging the policy of her present prime minister, Guizot. The zealous activity with which this effort to defeat us was pushed by the representatives of those governments, together with the character of intrigue accompanying it, fully constituted that case of foreign interference, which Mr. Clay himself declared should, and would unite us all in maintaining the common cause of our country against the foreigner and the foe. We are only astonished that this effect has not been more fully and strongly produced, and that the burst of indignation against this unauthorized, insolent and hostile interference against us, has not been more general even among the party before opposed to Annexation, and has not rallied the national spirit and national pride unanimously upon that policy. We are very sure that if Mr. Clay himself were now to add another letter to his former Texas correspondence, he would express this sentiment, and carry out the idea already strongly stated in one of them, in a manner which would tax all the powers of blushing belonging to some of his party adherents.

It is wholly untrue, and unjust to ourselves, the pretence that the Annexation has been a measure of spoliation, unrightful and unrighteous—of military conquest under forms of peace and law —of territorial aggrandizement at the expense of justice, and justice due by a double sanctity to the weak. This view of the question is wholly unfounded, and has been before so amply refuted in these pages, as well as in a thousand other modes, that we shall not again dwell upon it. The independence of Texas was complete and absolute. It was an independence, not only in fact but of right. No obligation of duty towards Mexico tended in the least degree to restrain our right to effect the desired recovery of the fair province once our own—whatever motives of policy might have prompted a more deferential consideration of her feelings and her pride, as involved in the question. If Texas became peopled with an American population, it was by no contrivance of our government, but on the express invitation of that of Mexico herself; accompanied with such guaranties of State independence, and the maintenance of a federal system analogous to our own, as constituted a compact fully justifying the strongest measures of redress on the part of those afterwards deceived in this guaranty, and sought to be enslaved under the yoke imposed by its violation. She was released, rightfully and absolutely released, from all Mexican allegiance, or duty of cohesion to the Mexican political body, by the acts and fault of Mexico herself, and Mexico alone. There never was a clearer case. It was not revolution; it was resistance to revolution; and resistance under such circumstances as left independence the necessary resulting state, caused by the abandonment of those with whom her former federal association had existed. What then can be more preposterous than all this clamor by Mexico and the Mexican interest, against Annexation, as a violation of any rights of hers, any duties of ours? . . .

California will, probably, next fall away from the loose adhesion which, in such a country as Mexico, holds a remote province in a slight equivocal kind of dependence on the metropolis. Imbecile and distracted, Mexico never can exert any real governmental authority over such a country. The impotence of the one and the distance of the other, must make the relation one of virtual independence; unless, by stunting the province of all natural growth, and forbidding that immigration which can alone develop its capabilities and fulfill the purposes of its creation, tyranny may retain a military dominion which is no government in the legitimate sense of the term. In the case of California this is now impossible. The Anglo-Saxon foot is already on its borders. Already the advance guard of the irresistible army of Anglo-Saxon emigration has begun to pour down upon it, armed with the plough and the rifle, and marking its trail with schools and colleges, courts and representative halls, mills and meeting-houses. A population will soon be in actual occupation of California, over which it will be idle for Mexico to dream of dominion. They will necessarily become independent. All this without agency of

our government, without responsibility of our people—in the
natural flow of events, the spontaneous working of principles, and
the adaptation of the tendencies and wants of the human race to
the elemental circumstances in the midst of which they find themselves placed. And they will have a right to independence—to
self-government—to the possession of the homes conquered from
the wilderness by their own labors and dangers, sufferings and
sacrifices—a better and a truer right than the artificial title of sovereignty in Mexico a thousand miles distant, inheriting from Spain
a title good only against those who have none better. Their right
to independence will be the natural right of self-government
belonging to any community strong enough to maintain it—distinct in position, origin and character, and free from any mutual
obligations of membership of a common political body, binding it
to others by the duty of loyalty and compact of public faith. This
will be their title to independence; and by this title, there can be
no doubt that the population now fast streaming down upon California will both assert and maintain that independence. Whether
they will then attach themselves to our Union or not, is not to be
predicted with any certainty. Unless the projected railroad across
the continent to the Pacific be carried into effect, perhaps they may
not; though even in that case, the day is not distant when the
Empires of the Atlantic and Pacific would again flow together
into one, as soon as their inland borders should approach each
other. But that great work, colossal as appears the plan on its
first suggestion, cannot remain long unbuilt. Its necessity for this
very purpose of binding and holding together in its iron clasp our
fast settling Pacific region with that of the Mississippi valley—the
natural facility of the route—the ease with which any amount of
labor for the construction can be drawn in from the overcrowded
populations of Europe, to be paid in the lands made valuable by
the progress of the work itself—and its immense utility to the
commerce of the world with the whole eastern coast of Asia, alone
almost sufficient for the support of such a road—these considerations give assurance that the day cannot be distant which shall
witness the conveyance of the representatives from Oregon and
California to Washington within less time than a few years ago

was devoted to a similar journey by those from Ohio; while the magnetic telegraph will enable the editors of the "San Francisco Union," the "Astoria Evening Post," or the "Nootka Morning News" to set up in type the first half of the President's Inaugural, before the echoes of the latter half shall have died away beneath the lofty porch of the Capitol, as spoken from his lips.

Away, then, with all idle French talk of *balances of power* on the American Continent. There is no growth in Spanish America! Whatever progress of population there may be in the British Canadas, is only for their own early severance of their present colonial relation to the little island three thousand miles across the Atlantic; soon to be followed by Annexation, and destined to swell the still accumulating momentum of our progress. And whosoever may hold the balance, though they should cast into the opposite scale all the bayonets and cannon, not only of France and England, but of Europe entire, how would it kick the beam against the simple solid weight of the two hundred and fifty or three hundred millions—and American millions—destined to gather beneath the flutter of the stripes and stars, in the fast hastening year of the Lord 1945!

8. THE OSTEND MANIFESTO*

James Buchanan, John Y. Mason, and Pierre Soulé, to William L. Marcy

Aix La Chapelle, October 18, 1854

The undersigned, in compliance with the wish expressed by the President in the several confidential despatches you have addressed to us, respectively, to that effect, have met in conference, first at Ostend, in Belgium, on the 9th, 10th, and 11th instant, and then at Aix la Chapelle, in Prussia, on the days next following, up to the date hereof. . . .

---

*Buchanan was Minister to England, Mason Minister to France, and Soulé Minister to Spain. They met in Ostend, Belgium, at the suggestion of Secretary of State Marcy, to discuss relations with Spain with regard to Cuba. This report was a confidential dispatch, sent in secrecy, and never given official cognizance.

We have arrived at the conclusion, and are thoroughly convinced, that an immediate and earnest effort ought to be made by the government of the United States to purchase Cuba from Spain. . . .

It can scarcely be apprehended that foreign powers, in violation of international law, would interpose their influence with Spain to prevent our acquisition of the island. Its inhabitants are now suffering under the worst of all possible governments, that of absolute despotism, delegated by a distant power to irresponsible agents, who are changed at short intervals, and who are tempted to improve the brief opportunity thus afforded to accumulate fortunes by the basest means.

As long as this system shall endure, humanity may in vain demand the suppression of the African slave trade in the island. This is rendered impossible whilst that infamous traffic remains an irresistible temptation and a source of immense profit to needy and avaricious officials, who, to attain their ends, scruple not to trample the most sacred principles under foot. . . .

Under no probable circumstances can Cuba ever yield to Spain one per cent. on the large amount which the United States are willing to pay for its acquisition. But Spain is in imminent danger of losing Cuba, without remuneration.

Extreme oppression, it is now universally admitted, justifies any people in endeavoring to relieve themselves from the yoke of their oppressors. The sufferings which the corrupt, arbitrary, and unrelenting local administration necessarily entails upon the inhabitants of Cuba, cannot fail to stimulate and keep alive that spirit of resistance and revolution against Spain, which has, of late years, been so often manifested. In this condition of affairs it is vain to expect that the sympathies of the people of the United States will not be warmly enlisted in favor of their oppressed neighbors.

But if Spain, dead to the voice of her own interest, and actuated by stubborn pride and a false sense of honor, should refuse to sell Cuba to the United States, then the question will arise, What ought to be the course of the American government under such circumstances?

Self-preservation is the first law of nature, with States as well as with individuals. All nations have, at different periods, acted upon this maxim. Although it has been made the pretext for committing flagrant injustice, as in the partition of Poland and other similar cases which history records, yet the principle itself, though often abused, has always been recognized. . . .

After we shall have offered Spain a price for Cuba far beyond its present value, and this shall have been refused, it will then be time to consider the question, does Cuba, in the possession of Spain, seriously endanger our internal peace and the existence of our cherished Union?

Should this question be answered in the affirmative, then, by every law, human and divine, we shall be justified in wresting it from Spain if we possess the power; and this upon the very same principle that would justify an individual in tearing down the burning house of his neighbor if there were no other means of preventing the flames from destroying his own home.

Under such circumstances we ought neither to count the cost nor regard the odds which Spain might enlist against us. We forbear to enter into the question, whether the present condition of the island would justify such a measure? We should, however, be recreant to our duty, be unworthy of our gallant forefathers, and commit base treason against our posterity, should we permit Cuba to be Africanized and become a second St. Domingo, with all its attendant horrors to the white race, and suffer the flames to extend to our own neighboring shores, seriously to endanger or actually to consume the fair fabric of our Union. . . .

9. JAMES G. BLAINE TO JAMES M. COMLY*

Washington, December 1, 1881

. . . I have had recent occasion to set forth the vitally integral importance of our Pacific possessions, in a circular letter addressed on the 24th of June last to our representatives in Europe, touching

*Blaine was Secretary of State, Comly Minister to Hawaii, when this letter was written.

the necessary guarantees of the proposed Panama Canal as a purely American waterway to be treated as part of our own coast line. The extension of commercial empire westward from those states is no less vitally important to their development than is their communication with the Eastern coast by the Isthmian channel. And when we survey the stupendous progress made by the western coast during the thirty years of its national life as a part of our dominion, its enormous increase of population, its vast resources of agriculture and mines, and its boundless enterprise, it is not easy to set a limit to its commercial activity or forsee a check to its maritime supremacy in the waters of the Orient, so long as those waters afford, as now, a free and neutral scope for our peaceful trade.

In thirty years the United States has acquired a legitimately dominant influence in the North Pacific, which it can never consent to see decreased by the intrusion therein of any element of influence hostile to its own. The situation of the Hawaiian Islands, giving them the strategic control of the North Pacific, brings their possession within the range of questions of purely American policy, as much so as that of the Isthmus itself. Hence the necessity, as recognized in our existing treaty relations, of drawing the ties of intimate relationship between us and the Hawaiian Islands so as to make them practically a part of the American system without derogation of their absolute independence. The reciprocity treaty of 1875 has made of Hawaii the sugar-raising field of the Pacific slope and gives to our manufacturers therein the same freedom as in California and Oregon. . . .

The policy of this country with regard to the Pacific is the natural complement to its Atlantic policy. The history of our European relations for fifty years shows the jealous concern with which the United States has guarded its control of the coast from foreign interference, and this without extension of territorial possession beyond the main land. It has always been its aim to preserve the friendly neutrality of the adjacent states and insular possessions. Its attitude toward Cuba is in point. That rich island, the key to the Gulf of Mexico, and the field for our most extended trade in the Western Hemisphere is, though in the hands of Spain, a part of the American commercial system. Our relations, present and prospective, toward Cuba, have never been more ably set forth than in the remarkable note addressed by my predecessor, Mr. Secretary Everett, to the ministers of Great Britain and France in Washington, on the 1st of December, 1852, in rejection of the suggested tripartite alliance to forever determine the neutrality of the Spanish Antilles. In response to the proposal that the United States, Great Britain, and France, should severally and collectively agree to forbid the acquisition of control over Cuba, by any or all of them, Mr. Everett showed that, without forcing or even coveting possession of the island, its condition was essentially an American question; that the renunciation forever by this government of contingent interest therein would be far broader than the like renunciation by Great Britain or France; that if ever ceasing to be Spanish, Cuba must necessarily become American, and not fall under any other European domination, and that the ceaseless movement of segregation of American interests from European control and unification in a broader American sphere of independent life could not and should not be checked by any arbitrary agreement.

Nearly thirty years have demonstrated the wisdom of the attitude then maintained by Mr. Everett and have made indispensable its continuance and its extension to all parts of the American Atlantic system where a disturbance of the existing status might be attempted in the interest of foreign powers. The present attitude of this government toward any European project for the control of an isthmian route is but the logical sequence of the resistance made in 1852 to the attempted pressure of an active foreign influence in the West Indies.

Hawaii, although much farther from the Californian coast than is Cuba from the Floridian peninsula, holds in the western sea much the same position as Cuba in the Atlantic. It is the key to the maritime dominion of the Pacific states, as Cuba is the key to the Gulf trade. The material possession of Hawaii is not desired by the United States any more than was that of Cuba. But under no circumstances can the United States permit any change in the territorial control of either which would cut it adrift from the American system, whereto they both indispensably belong.

In this aspect of the question, it is readily seen with what concern this government must view any tendency toward introducing into Hawaii new social elements, destructive of its necessarily American character. The steady diminution of the native population of the islands, amounting to some ten per cent. between 1872 and 1878, and still continuing, is doubtless a cause of great alarm to the government of the kingdom, and it is no wonder that a solution should be sought with eagerness in any seemingly practicable quarter. The problem, however, is not to be met by a substitution of Mongolian supremacy for native control—as seems at first sight possible through the rapid increase in Chinese immigration to the islands. Neither is a wholesale introduction of the coolie element, professedly Anglo-Indian, likely to afford any more satisfactory outcome to the difficulty. The Hawaiian Islands cannot be joined to the Asiatic system. If they drift from their independent station it must be toward assimilation and identification with the American system, to which they belong by the operation of natural laws, and must belong by the operation of political necessity. . . .

In this line of action the United States does its simple duty both to Hawaii and itself; and it cannot permit such obvious neglect of national interest as would be involved by silent acquiescence in any movement looking to a lessening of those American ties and the substitution of alien and hostile interests. It firmly believes that the position of the Hawaiian Islands as the key to the dominion of the American Pacific demands their neutrality, to which end it will earnestly co-operate with the native government. And if, through any cause, the maintenance of such a position of neutrality should be found by Hawaii to be impracticable, this government would then unhesitatingly meet the altered situation by seeking an avowedly American solution for the grave issues presented. . . .

POLICY REGARDING THE PHILIPPINES*

BY

SENATOR ALBERT J. BEVERIDGE

[1900]

Mr. BEVERIDGE. I ask for the reading of the joint resolution introduced by me on Thursday last.

The PRESIDENT pro tempore. The Chair lays before the Senate the joint resolution introduced by the Senator from Indiana, which was laid on the table subject to his call. The joint resolution will be read.

The Secretary read the joint resolution (S. R. 53) defining the policy of the United States relative to the Philippine Islands, as follows:

> Be it resolved by the Senate and House of Representatives of the United States of America in Congress assembled, That the Philippine Islands are territory belonging to the United States; that it is the intention of the United States to retain them as such and to establish and maintain such governmental control throughout the archipelago as the situation may demand.

Mr. BEVERIDGE. Mr. President, I address the Senate at this time because Senators and Members of the House on both sides have asked that I give to Congress and the country my observations in the Philippines and the Far East, and the conclusions which those observations compel; and because of hurtful resolutions introduced and utterances made in the Senate, every word of which will cost and is costing the lives of American soldiers.

Mr. President, the times call for candor. The Philippines are ours forever, "territory belonging to the United States," as the Constitution calls them. And just beyond the Philippines are China's illimitable markets. We will not retreat from either. We will not repudiate our duty in the archipelago. We will not abandon our opportunity in the Orient. We will not renounce

---

*Adapted from the *Congressional Record*, January 9, 1900. Albert J. Beveridge (1862–1929), American politician and Senator from Indiana, 1899–1911, is the author of famous biographies of Chief Justice John Marshall and Abraham Lincoln.

our part in the mission of our race, trustee, under God, of the civilization of the world. And we will move forward to our work, not howling out regrets like slaves whipped to their burdens, but with gratitude for a task worthy of our strength, and thanksgiving to Almighty God that He has marked us as His chosen people, henceforth to lead in the regeneration of the world.

This island empire is the last land left in all the oceans. If it should prove a mistake to abandon it, the blunder once made would be irretrievable. If it proves a mistake to hold it, the error can be corrected when we will. Every other progressive nation stands ready to relieve us.

But to hold it will be no mistake. Our largest trade henceforth must be with Asia. The Pacific is our ocean. More and more Europe will manufacture the most it needs, secure from its colonies the most it consumes. Where shall we turn for consumers of our surplus? Geography answers the question. China is our natural customer. She is nearer to us than to England, Germany, or Russia, the commercial powers of the present and the future. They have moved nearer to China by securing permanent bases on her borders. The Philippines gives us a base at the door of all the East.

Lines of navigation from our ports to the Orient and Australia; from the Isthmian Canal to Asia; from all Oriental ports to Australia, converge at and separate from the Philippines. They are a self-supporting, dividend-paying fleet, permanently anchored at a spot selected by the strategy of Providence, commanding the Pacific. And the Pacific is the ocean of the commerce of the future. Most future wars will be conflicts for commerce. The power that rules the Pacific, therefore, is the power that rules the world. And, with the Philippines, that power is and will forever be the American Republic.

China's trade is the mightiest commercial fact in our future. Her foreign commerce was $285,738,300 in 1897, of which we, her neighbor, had less than 9 per cent, of which only a little more than half was merchandise sold to China by us. We ought to have 50 per cent, and we will. And China's foreign commerce is

only beginning. Her resources, her possibilities, her wants, all
are undeveloped. She has only 340 miles of railway. I have seen
trains loaded with natives and all the activities of modern life
already appearing along the line. But she needs, and in fifty years
will have, 20,000 miles of railway.

Who can estimate her commerce, then? That statesman commits a crime against American trade—against the American grower
of cotton and wheat and tobacco, the American manufacturer of
machinery and clothing—who fails to put America where she may
command that trade. Germany's Chinese trade is increasing like
magic. She has established ship lines and secured a tangible foothold on China's very soil. Russia's Chinese trade is growing
beyond belief. She is spending the revenues of the Empire to
finish her railroad into Pekin itself, and she is in physical possession of the imperial province of Manchuria. Japan's Chinese
trade is multiplying in volume and value. She is bending her
energy to her merchant marine, and is located along China's very
coast; but Manila is nearer China than Yokohama is. The Philippines command the commercial situation of the entire East. Can
America best trade with China from San Francisco or New York?
From San Francisco, of course. But if San Francisco were closer
to China than New York is to Pittsburg, what then? And Manila
is nearer Hongkong than Habana is to Washington. And yet
American statesmen plan to surrender this commercial throne of
the Orient where Providence and our soldiers' lives have placed us.
When history comes to write the story of that suggested treason to
American supremacy and therefore to the spread of American
civilization, let her in mercy write that those who so proposed
were merely blind and nothing more.

But if they did not command China, India, the Orient, the
whole Pacific for purposes of offense, defense, and trade, the
Philippines are so valuable in themselves that we should hold
them. I have cruised more than 2,000 miles through the archipelago, every moment a surprise at its loveliness and wealth. I
have ridden hundreds of miles on the islands, every foot of the
way a revelation of vegetable and mineral riches.

No land in America surpasses in fertility the plains and valleys of Luzon. Rice and coffee, sugar and cocoanuts, hemp and tobacco, and many products of the temperate as well as the tropic zone grow in various sections of the archipelago. I have seen hundreds of bushels of Indian corn lying in a road fringed with banana trees. The forests of Negros, Mindanao, Mindora, Paluan, and parts of Luzon are invaluable and intact. The wood of the Philippines can supply the furniture of the world for a century to come. At Cebu the best informed man in the island told me that 40 miles of Cebu's mountain chain are practically mountains of coal. Pablo Majia, one of the most reliable men on the islands, confirmed the statement. Some declare that the coal is only lignite; but ship captains who have used it told me that it is better steamer fuel than the best coal of Japan.

I have a nugget of pure gold picked up in its present form on the banks of a Philippine creek. I have gold dust washed out by crude processes of careless natives from the sands of a Philippine stream. Both indicate great deposits at the source from which they come. In one of the islands great deposits of copper exist untouched. The mineral wealth of this empire of the ocean will one day surprise the world. I base this statement partly on personal observation, but chiefly on the testimony of foreign merchants in the Philippines, who have practically investigated the subject, and upon the unanimous opinion of natives and priests. And the mineral wealth is but a small fraction of the agricultural wealth of these islands.

And the wood, hemp, copra, and other products of the Philippines supply what we need and can not ourselves produce. And the markets they will themselves afford will be immense. Spain's export and import trade, with the islands undeveloped, was $11,534,731 annually. Our trade with the islands developed will be $125,000,000 annually, for who believes that we can not do ten times as well as Spain? Consider their imperial dimensions. Luzon is larger and richer than New York, Pennsylvania, Illinois, or Ohio. Mindanao is larger and richer than all New England, exclusive of Maine. Manila, as a port of call and exchange, will, in the time of men now living, far surpass Liverpool. Behold the exhaustless markets they command. It is as if a half dozen of our States were set down between Oceania and the Orient, and those States themselves undeveloped and unspoiled of their primitive wealth and resources.

Nothing is so natural as trade with one's neighbors. The Philippines make us the nearest neighbors of all the East. Nothing is more natural than to trade with those you know. This is the philosophy of all advertising. The Philippines bring us permanently face to face with the most sought-for customers of the world. National prestige, national propinquity, these and commercial activity are the elements of commercial success. The Philippines give the first; the character of the American people supply the last. It is a providential conjunction of all the elements of trade, of duty, and of power. If we are willing to go to war rather than let England have a few feet of frozen Alaska, which affords no market and commands none, what should we not do rather than let England, Germany, Russia, or Japan have all the Philippines? And no man on the spot can fail to see that this would be their fate if we retired.

The climate is the best tropic climate in the world. This is the belief of those who have lived in many tropic countries, with scores of whom I have talked on this point. My own experience with tropical conditions has not been exhaustive; yet, speaking from that experience, I testify that the climate of Iloilo, Sulu, Cebu, and even of Manila, greatly surpasses that of Hongkong. And yet on the bare and burning rock of Hongkong our constructing race has builded one of the noblest cities of all the world, and made the harbor it commands the focus of the commerce of the East. And the glory of that achievement illumines with a rarer splendor than that of Waterloo the flag that floats above it, for from Hongkong's heights civilization is irradiating all the Orient. If this be imperialism, its final end will be the empire of the Son of Man. . . .

It will be hard for Americans who have not studied them to understand the people. They are a barbarous race, modified by three centuries of contact with a decadent race. The Filipino is the South Sea Malay, put through a process of three hundred years of superstition in religion, dishonesty in dealing, disorder in habits of industry, and cruelty, caprice, and corruption in government. It is barely possible that 1,000 men in all the archipelago are capable of self-government in the Anglo-Saxon sense.

My own belief is that there are not 100 men among them who comprehend what Anglo-Saxon self-government even means, and there are over 5,000,000 people to be governed. I know many clever and highly educated men among them, but there are only three commanding intellects and characters—Arellano, Mabini, and Aguinaldo. Arellano, the chief justice of our supreme court, is a profound lawyer and a brave and incorruptible man. Mabini, who, before his capture, was the literary and diplomatic associate of Aguinaldo, is the highest type of subtlety and the most constructive mind that race has yet produced. Aguinaldo is a clever, popular leader, able, brave, resourceful, cunning, ambitious, unscrupulous, and masterful. He is full of decision, initiative, and authority, and had the confidence of the masses. He is a natural dictator. His ideas of government are absolute orders, implicit obedience, or immediate death. He understands the character of his countrymen. He is a Malay Sylla; not a Filipino Washington. . . .

Here, then, Senators, is the situation. Two years ago there was no land in all the world which we could occupy for any purpose. Our commerce was daily turning toward the Orient, and geography and trade developments made necessary our commercial empire over the Pacific. And in that ocean we had no commercial, naval, or military base. Today we have one of the three great ocean possessions of the globe, located at the most commanding commercial, naval, and military points in the eastern seas, within hail of India, shoulder to shoulder with China, richer in its own resources than any equal body of land on the entire globe, and peopled by a race which civilization demands shall be improved. Shall we abandon it? That man little knows the common people of the Republic, little understands the instincts of our race, who thinks we will not hold it fast and hold it forever, administering just government by simplest methods. We may trick up devices to shift our burden and lessen our opportunity; they will avail us nothing but delay. We may tangle conditions by applying academic arrangements of self-government to a crude situation; their failure will drive us to our duty in the end.

The military situation, past, present, and prospective, is no reason for abandonment. Our campaign has been as perfect as possible with the force at hand. We have been delayed, first, by a failure to comprehend the immensity of our acquisition; and, second, by insufficient force; and, third, by our efforts for peace. . . .

Those who complain do so in ignorance of the real situation. We attempted a great task with insufficient means; we became impatient that it was not finished before it could fairly be commenced; and I pray we may not add that other element of disaster, pausing in the work before it is thoroughly and forever done. That is the gravest mistake we could possibly make, and that is the only danger before us. Our Indian wars would have been shortened, the lives of soldiers and settlers saved, and the Indians themselves benefited had we made continuous and decisive war; and any other kind of war is criminal because ineffective. We acted toward the Indians as though we feared them, loved them, hated them—a mingling of foolish sentiment, inaccurate thought, and paralytic purpose. Let us now be instructed by our own experience.

This, too, has been Spain's course in the Philippines. . . . Never since Magellan landed did Spain put enough troops in the islands for complete and final action in war; never did she intelligently, justly, firmly, administer government in peace.

At the outbreak of the last insurrection, in August, 1896, Spain had only 1,500 Spanish soldiers in all the Philippines, and 700 of these were in Manila. In November of that year she had only 10,000 men. The generals in command of these were criticized and assailed in Spain. It is characteristic of Spain that the people at home do not support, but criticize their generals in the field. The Spanish method has always been a mixed policy of peace and war, a contradiction of terms, an impossible combination, rendering war ineffective and peace impossible. . . .

Mr. President, that must not be our plan. This war is like all other wars. It needs to be finished before it is stopped. I am prepared to vote either to make our work thorough or even now to abandon it. A lasting peace can be secured only by overwhelming forces in ceaseless action until universal and absolutely final defeat is inflicted on the enemy. To halt before every armed force, every guerrilla band, opposing us is dispersed or exterminated will prolong hostilities and leave alive the seeds of perpetual insurrection.

Even then we should not treat. To treat at all is to admit that we are wrong. And any quiet so secured will be delusive and fleeting. And a false peace will betray us; a sham truce will curse us. It is not to serve the purposes of the hour, it is not to salve a present situation, that peace should be established. It is for the tranquillity of the archipelago forever. It is for an orderly government for the Filipinos for all the future. It is to give this problem to posterity solved and settled; not vexed and involved. It is to establish the supremacy of the American Republic over the Pacific and throughout the East till the end of time.

It has been charged that our conduct of the war has been cruel. Senators, it has been the reverse. I have been in our hospitals and seen the Filipino wounded as carefully, tenderly cared for as our own. Within our lines they may plow and sow and reap and go about the affairs of peace with absolute liberty. And yet all this kindness was misunderstood, or rather not understood. Senators must remember that we are not dealing with Americans or Europeans. We are dealing with Orientals. We are dealing with Orientals who are Malays. We are dealing with Malays instructed in Spanish methods. They mistake kindness for weakness, forbearance for fear. It could not be otherwise unless you could erase hundreds of years of savagery, other hundreds of years of orientalism, and still other hundreds of years of Spanish character and custom.

Our mistake has not been cruelty; it has been kindness. . . .

The news that 60,000 American soldiers have crossed the Pacific; that, if necessary, the American Congress will make it 100,000 or 200,000 men: that, at any cost, we will establish peace and govern the islands, will do more to end the war than the soldiers themselves. But the report that we even discuss the withdrawal of a single soldier at the present time and that we even debate the possibility of not administering government throughout the archipelago ourselves will be misunderstood and misrepresented and will blow into a flame once more the fires our soldiers' blood has almost quenched.

Mr. President, reluctantly and only from a sense of duty am I forced to say that American opposition to the war has been the chief factor in prolonging it. Had Aguinaldo not understood that in America, even in the American Congress, even here in the Senate, he and his cause were supported; had he not known that it was proclaimed on the stump and in the press of a faction in the United States that every shot his misguided followers fired into the breasts of American soldiers was like the volleys fired by Washington's men against the soldiers of King George, his insurrection would have dissolved before it entirely crystallized.

The utterances of American opponents of the war are read to the ignorant soldiers of Aguinaldo and repeated in exaggerated form among the common people. Attempts have been made by wretches claiming American citizenship to ship arms and ammunition from Asiatic ports to the Filipinos, and these acts of infamy were coupled by the Malays with American assaults on our Government at home. The Filipinos do not understand free speech, and therefore our tolerance of American assaults on the American President and the American Government means to them that our President is in the minority or he would not permit what appears to them such treasonable criticism. It is believed and stated in Luzon, Panay, and Cebu that the Filipinos have only to fight, harass, retreat, break up into small parties, if necessary, as they are doing now, but by any means hold out until the next Presidential election, and our forces will be withdrawn.

All this has aided the enemy more than climate, arms, and battle. Senators, I have heard these reports myself; I have talked with the people; I have seen our mangled boys in the hospital and field; I have stood on the firing line and beheld our dead soldiers, their faces turned to the pitiless southern sky, and in sorrow rather than anger I say to those whose voices in America have cheered those misguided natives on to shoot our soldiers down, that the blood of those dead and wounded boys of ours is on their hands, and the flood of all the years can never wash that stain away. In sorrow rather than anger I say these words, for I earnestly believe that our brothers knew not what they did.

But, Senators, it would be better to abandon this combined garden and Gibraltar of the Pacific, and count our blood and treasure already spent a profitable loss, than to apply any academic arrangement of self-government to these children. They are not capable of self-government. How could they be? They are not of a self-governing race. They are Orientals, Malays, instructed by Spaniards in the latter's worst estate.

They know nothing of practical government except as they have witnessed the weak, corrupt, cruel, and capricious rule of Spain. What magic will anyone employ to dissolve in their minds and characters those impressions of governors and governed which three centuries of misrule has created? What alchemy will change the oriental quality of their blood and set the self-governing currents of the American pouring through their Malay veins? How shall they, in the twinkling of an eye, be exalted to the heights of self-governing peoples which required a thousand years for us to reach, Anglo-Saxon though we are?

Let men beware how they employ the term "self-government." It is a sacred term. It is the watchword at the door of the inner temple of liberty, for liberty does not always mean self-government. Self-government is a method of liberty—the highest, simplest, best—and it is acquired only after centuries of study and struggle and experiment and instruction and all the elements of the progress of man. Self-government is no base and common thing, to be bestowed on the merely audacious. It is the degree which crowns the graduate of liberty, not the name of liberty's infant class, who have not yet mastered the alphabet of freedom. Savage blood, oriental blood, Malay blood, Spanish example—are these the elements of self-government?

We must act on the situation as it exists, not as we would wish it. I have talked with hundreds of these people, getting their views as to the practical workings of self-government. The great majority simply do not understand any participation in any government whatever. The most enlightened among them declare that self-government will succeed because the employers of labor will compel their employees to vote as their employer wills and that this will insure intelligent voting. I was assured that we could depend upon good men always being in office because the officials who constitute the government will nominate their successors, choose those among the people who will do the voting, and determine how and where elections will be held.

The most ardent advocate of self-government that I met was anxious that I should know that such a government would be tranquil because, as he said, if anyone criticised it, the government would shoot the offender. A few of them have a sort of verbal understanding of the democratic theory, but the above are the examples of the ideas of the practical workings of self-government entertained by the aristocracy, the rich planters and traders, and heavy employers of labor, the men who would run the government.

Example for decades will be necessary to instruct them in American ideas and methods of administration. Example, example; always example—this alone will teach them. As a race, their general ability is not excellent. Educators, both men and women, to whom I have talked in Cebu and Luzon, were unanimous in the opinion that in all solid and useful education they are, as a people, dull and stupid. In showy things, like carving and painting or embroidery or music, they have apparent aptitude, but even this is superficial and never thorough. They have facility of speech, too.

The three best educators on the island at different times made to me the same comparison, that the common people in their stupidity are like their caribou bulls. They are not even good agriculturists. Their waste of cane is inexcusable. Their destruction of hemp fiber is childish. They are incurably indolent. They have no continuity or thoroughness of industry. They will quit work without notice and amuse themselves until the money they have earned is spent. They are like children playing at men's work.

No one need fear their competition with our labor. No reward could beguile, no force compel, these children of indolence to leave their trifling lives for the fierce and fervid industry of high-wrought America. The very reverse is the fact. One great problem is the necessary labor to develop these islands—to build the roads, open the mines, clear the wilderness, drain the swamps, dredge the harbors. The natives will not supply it. A lingering prejudice against the Chinese may prevent us from letting them supply it. Ultimately, when the real truth of the climate and human conditions is known, it is barely possible that our labor will go there. Even now young men with the right moral fiber and a little capital can make fortunes there as planters. . . .

Mr. President, self-government and internal development have been the dominant notes of our first century; administration and the development of other lands will be the dominant notes of our second century. And administration is as high and holy a function as self-government, just as the care of a trust estate is as sacred an obligation as the management of our own concerns. Cain was the first to violate the divine law of human society which makes of us our brother's keeper. And administration of good government is the first lesson in self-government, that exalted estate toward which all civilization tends.

Administration of good government is not denial of liberty. For what is liberty? It is not savagery. It is not the exercise of individual will. It is not dictatorship. It involves government, but not necessarily self-government. It means law. First of all, it is a common rule of action, applying equally to all within its limits. Liberty means protection of property and life without price, free speech without intimidation, justice without purchase or delay, government without favor or favorites. What will best give all this to the people of the Philippines—American administration, developing them gradually toward self-government, or self-government by a people before they know what self-government means?

The Declaration of Independence does not forbid us to do our part in the regeneration of the world. If it did, the Declaration would be wrong, just as the Articles of Confederation, drafted by the very same men who signed the Declaration, was found to be wrong. The Declaration has no application to the present situation. It was written by self-governing men for self-governing men.

It was written by men who, for a century and a half, had been experimenting in self-government on this continent, and whose ancestors for hundreds of years before had been gradually developing toward that high and holy estate. The Declaration applies only to people capable of self-government. How dare any man prostitute this expression of the very elect of self-governing peoples to a race of Malay children of barbarism, schooled in Spanish methods and ideas? And you, who say the Declaration applies to all men, how dare you deny its application to the American Indian? And if you deny it to the Indian at home, how dare you grant it to the Malay abroad?

The Declaration does not contemplate that all government must have the consent of the governed. It announces that man's "inalienable rights are life, liberty, and the pursuit of happiness; that to secure these rights governments are established among men deriving their just powers from the consent of the governed; that when any form of government becomes destructive of those rights, it is the right of the people to alter or abolish it." "Life, liberty, and the pursuit of happiness" are the important things; "consent of the governed" is one of the means to those ends.

If "any form of government becomes destructive of those ends, it is the right of the people to alter or abolish it," says the Declaration. "Any form" includes all forms. Thus the Declaration itself recognizes other forms of government than those resting on the consent of the governed. The word "consent" itself recognizes other forms, for "consent" means the understanding of the thing to which the "consent" is given; and there are people in the world who do not understand any form of government. And the sense in which "consent" is used in the Declaration is broader than mere understanding; for "consent" in the Declaration means participation in the government "consented" to. And yet these people who are not capable of "consenting" to any form of government must be governed.

And so the Declaration contemplates all forms of government which secure the fundamental rights of life, liberty, and the pursuit of happiness. Self-government, when that will best secure these ends, as in the case of people capable of self-government; other appropriate forms when people are not capable of self-government. And so the authors of the Declaration themselves governed the Indian without his consent; the inhabitants of Louisiana without their consent; and ever since the sons of the makers of the Declaration have been governing not by theory, but by practice, after the fashion of our governing race, now by one form, now by another, but always for the purpose of securing the great eternal ends of life, liberty, and the pursuit of happiness, not in the savage, but in the civilized meaning of those terms—life according to orderly methods of civilized society; liberty regulated by law; pursuit of happiness limited by the pursuit of happiness by every other man.

If this is not the meaning of the Declaration, our Government itself denies the Declaration every time it receives the representative of any but a republican form of government, such as that of the Sultan, the Czar, or other absolute autocrats, whose governments, according to the opposition's interpretation of the Declaration, are spurious governments, because the people governed have not "consented" to them.

Senators in opposition are estopped from denying our constitutional power to govern the Philippines as circumstances may demand, for such power is admitted in the case of Florida, Louisiana, Alaska. How, then, is it denied in the Philippines? Is there a geographical interpretation to the Constitution? Do degrees of longitude fix constitutional limitations? Does a thousand miles of ocean diminish constitutional power more than a thousand miles of land?

The ocean does not separate us from the field of our duty and endeavor—it joins us, an established highway needing no repair,

and landing us at any point desired. The seas do not separate the
Philippine Islands from us or from each other. The seas are highways through the archipelago, which would cost hundreds of
millions of dollars to construct if they were land instead of water.
Land may separate men from their desire, the ocean never. Russia
has been centuries in crossing Siberian wastes; the Puritans crossed
the Atlantic in brief and flying weeks.

If the Boers must have traveled by land, they would never have
reached the Transvaal; but they sailed on liberty's ocean; they
walked on civilization's untaxed highway, the welcoming sea. Our
ships habitually sailed round the cape and anchored in California's
harbors before a single trail had lined the desert with the whiten-
ing bones of those who made it. No! No! The ocean unites us;
steam unites us; electricity unites us; all the elements of nature
unite us to the region where duty and interest call us. There is in
the ocean no constitutional argument against the march of the
flag, for the oceans, too, are ours. With more extended coast
lines than any nation of history; with a commerce vaster than any
other people ever dreamed of, and that commerce as yet only in its
beginnings; with naval traditions equaling those of England or of
Greece, and the work of our Navy only just begun; with the air of
the ocean in our nostrils and the blood of a sailor ancestry in our
veins; with the shores of all the continents calling us, the Great
Republic before I die will be the acknowledged lord of the world's
high seas. And over them the Republic will hold dominion, by
virtue of the strength God has given it, for the peace of the world
and the betterment of man.

No; the oceans are not limitations of the power which the Constitution expressly gives Congress to govern all territory the nation
may acquire. The Constitution declares that "Congress shall have
power to dispose of and make all needful rules and regulations
respecting the territory belonging to the United States." Not the
Northwest Territory only; not Louisiana or Florida only; not territory on this continent only, but any territory anywhere belonging
to the nation. The founders of the nation were not provincial.
Theirs was the geography of the world. They were soldiers as
well as landsmen, and they knew that where our ships should go

our flag might follow. They had the logic of progress, and they knew that the Republic they were planting must, in obedience to the laws of our expanding race, necessarily develop into the greater Republic which the world beholds today, and into the still mightier Republic which the world will finally acknowledge as the arbiter, under God, of the destinies of mankind. And so our fathers wrote into the Constitution these words of growth, of expansion, of empire, if you will, unlimited by geography or climate or by anything but the vitality and possibilities of the American people: "Congress shall have power to dispose of and make all needful rules and regulations respecting the territory belonging to the United States."

The power to govern all territory the nation may acquire would have been in Congress if the language affirming that power had not been written in the Constitution. For not all powers of the National Government are expressed. Its principal powers are implied. The written Constitution is but the index of the living Constitution. Had this not been true, the Constitution would have failed. For the people in any event would have developed and progressed. And if the Constitution had not had the capacity for growth corresponding with the growth of the nation, the Constitution would and should have been abandoned as the Articles of Confederation were abandoned. For the Constitution is not immortal in itself, is not useful even in itself. The Constitution is immortal and even useful only as it serves the orderly development of the nation. The nation alone is immortal. The nation alone is sacred. The Army is its servant. The Navy is its servant. The President is its servant. The Senate is its servant. Our laws are its methods. Our Constitution is its instrument.

This is the golden rule of constitutional interpretation: The Constitution was made for the people, not the people for the Constitution. . . .

Mr. President, this question is deeper than any question of party politics; deeper than any question of the isolated policy of our country even; deeper even than any question of constitutional power. It is elemental. It is racial. God has not been preparing the English-speaking and Teutonic peoples for a thousand years for nothing but vain and idle self-contemplation and self-admiration. No! He has made us the master organizers of the world to establish system where chaos reigns. He has given us the spirit of progress to overwhelm the forces of reaction throughout the earth. He has made us adepts in government that we may administer government among savage and senile peoples. Were it not for such a force as this the world would relapse into barbarism and night. And of all our race He has marked the American people as His chosen nation to finally lead in the regeneration of the world. This is the divine mission of America, and it holds for us all the profit, all the glory, all the happiness possible to man. We are trustees of the world's progress, guardians of its righteous peace. The judgment of the Master is upon us: "Ye have been faithful over a few things; I will make you ruler over many things."

What shall history say of us? Shall it say that we renounced that holy trust, left the savage to his base condition, the wilderness to the reign of waste, deserted duty, abandoned glory, forgot our sordid profit even, because we feared our strength and read the charter of our powers with the doubter's eye and the quibbler's mind? Shall it say that, called by events to captain and command the proudest, ablest, purest race of history in history's noblest work, we declined that great commission? Our fathers would not have had it so. No! They founded no paralytic government, incapable of the simplest acts of administration. They planted no sluggard people, passive while the world's work calls them. They established no reactionary nation. They unfurled no retreating flag.

That flag has never paused in its onward march. Who dares halt it now—now, when history's largest events are carrying it forward; now, when we are at last one people, strong enough for any task, great enough for any glory destiny can bestow? How comes it that our first century closes with the process of consolidating the American people into a unit just accomplished, and quick upon the stroke of that great hour presses upon us our world opportunity, world duty, and world glory, which none but a people welded into an indivisible nation can achieve or perform?

Blind indeed is he who sees not the hand of God in events so vast, so harmonious, so benign. Reactionary indeed is the mind that perceives not that this vital people is the strongest of the saving forces of the world; that our place, therefore, is at the head of the constructing and redeeming nations of the earth; and that to stand aside while events march on is a surrender of our interests, a betrayal of our duty as blind as it is base. Craven indeed is the heart that fears to perform a work so golden and so noble; that dares not win a glory so immortal.

Do you tell me that it will cost us money? When did Americans ever measure duty by financial standards? Do you tell me of the tremendous toil required to overcome the vast difficulties of our task? What mighty work for the world, for humanity, even for ourselves, has ever been done with ease? Even our bread must we eat by the sweat of our faces. Why are we charged with power such as no people ever knew, if we are not to use it in a work such as no people ever wrought? Who will dispute the divine meaning of the fable of the talents?

Do you remind me of the precious blood that must be shed, the lives that must be given, the broken hearts of loved ones for their slain? And this is indeed a heavier price than all combined. And yet as a nation every historic duty we have done, every achievement we have accomplished, has been by the sacrifice of our noblest sons. Every holy memory that glorifies the flag is of those heroes who have died that its onward march might not be stayed. It is the nation's dearest lives yielded for the flag that makes it dear to us; it is the nation's most precious blood poured out for it that makes it precious to us. That flag is woven of heroism and grief, of the bravery of men and women's tears, of righteousness and battle, of sacrifice and anguish, of triumph and of glory. It is these which make our flag a holy thing. Who would tear from that sacred banner the glorious legends of a single battle where it has waved on land or sea? What son of a soldier of the flag whose father fell beneath it on any field would surrender that proud record for the heraldry of a king? In the cause of civilization, in the service of the Republic anywhere on earth, Americans consider wounds the noblest decorations man can win, and count the giving of their lives a glad and precious duty.

Pray God that spirit never fails. Pray God the time may never come when Mammon and the love of ease shall so debase our blood that we will fear to shed it for the flag and its imperial destiny. Pray God the time may never come when American heroism is but a legend like the story of the Cid, American faith in our mission and our might a dream dissolved, and the glory of our mighty race departed.

And that time will never come. We will renew our youth at the fountain of new and glorious deeds. We will exalt our reverence for the flag by carrying it to a noble future as well as by remembering its ineffable past. Its immortality will not pass, because everywhere and always we will acknowledge and discharge the solemn responsibilities our sacred flag, in its deepest meaning, puts upon us. And so, Senators, with reverent hearts, where dwells the fear of God, the American people move forward to the future of their hope and the doing of His work.

Mr. President and Senators, adopt the resolution offered, that peace may quickly come and that we may begin our saving, regenerating, and uplifting work. Adopt it, and this bloodshed will cease when these deluded children of our islands learn that this is the final word of the representatives of the American people in Congress assembled. Reject it, and the world, history, and the American people will know where to forever fix the awful responsibility for the consequences that will surely follow such failure to do our manifest duty. How dare we delay when our soldiers' blood is flowing? [Applause in the galleries.]

The PRESIDENT pro tempore. Applause is not permitted in the United States Senate. . . .

CIVIL GOVERNMENT FOR THE PHILIPPINE ISLANDS*

BY

SENATOR WILLIAM E. MASON

[1902]

Mr. President: In Herbert Spencer's last book, just published, *Facts and Comments*, speaking of slavery, he says:

"Let me begin with the earliest and simplest, which well serves to symbolize the whole.

"Here is a prisoner, with his hands tied and a cord round his neck (as suggested by figures in Assyrian bas-reliefs), being led home by his savage conqueror, who intends to make him a slave. The one, you say, is captive and the other free? Are you quite sure the other is free? He holds one end of the cord, and unless he means to let his captive escape he must continue to be fastened by keeping hold of the cord in such a way that it can not easily be detached. He must be himself tied to the captive while the captive is tied to him. In other words, his activities are impeded and certain burdens are imposed on him. A wild animal crosses the track, and he cannot pursue. If he wishes to drink of the adjacent stream, he must tie up his captive lest advantage be taken of his defenseless position. Moreover, he has to provide food for both. In various ways, then, he is no longer completely at liberty; and these ways adumbrate in a simple manner the universal truth that the instrumentalities by which the subordination of others is effected themselves subordinate the victor, the master, or the ruler."

Mr. President, I am not here representing the Filipino. While I cannot find words in the short time I have to speak to-day to express the sorrow I feel for that poor unhappy people in the Philippine Islands, I beg to be heard in behalf of the man at the

---

*From a speech delivered in the Senate, June 2, 1902. William E. Mason (1850–1921) was a Senator from Illinois, 1887–1891, 1897–1903, 1917–1921.

other end of the cord, our people who are citizens of the United States, covered and protected by the Constitution which we have sworn solemnly to uphold.

I believe with Herbert Spencer, the philosopher, and with Abraham Lincoln, the patriot, that no man is good enough to govern another without that other man's consent, and therefore no nation is good enough to govern another nation without that other nation's consent. No man can be free who owns a slave, and no nation is free that holds another nation in subjugation. I desire to be free from unkindness, and certainly shall not deal in harsh criticism, not withstanding the almost brutal assaults that have been made upon me for having simply expressed my opinion on these questions according to the best light which God has given me.

I cannot find words to express my feelings when I hear learned Senators, who are familiar with our form of government, talking about "giving" liberty to other people. That we may start right let me read to you in four lines what Daniel Webster thought of one people "giving" liberty to another:

"No matter how easy may be the yoke of a foreign power, no matter how lightly it sits upon the shoulders, if it is not imposed by the voice of his own nation and of his own country, he will not, he cannot, and he means not to be happy under its burden."

I wish to read just two lines from the president of the first Commission, Dr. Schurman, which he spoke day before yesterday:

"The Filipinos will never be content until we allow them to govern themselves."

In the multitude of changes that occur in the march of time, principles never change. That principle was true when Webster pronounced it; when Hungary sought to lift the yoke of Austria. It was true on the day of the Boston tea party. It was true when the little republics of South America, under the guidance of Bolivar, shook off the yoke of Spain. It was true in Cuba, until they were able to set their own flag in the sky. It is true to-day in South Africa; and it is true to-day, God help us, in the far-off island of Luzon.

I have no disposition to find fault, or to debate long and loud upon the facts. Enough of the facts are agreed upon to show that the purchase of the Philippine Islands, and our attempt to govern them, is the saddest and most unhappy mistake our beloved country has made since the day we began to traffic in slaves. How much, under the law of compensation, we must pay in the future for this mistake the all-wise God only knows. The amount we have already paid for this mistake the human mind can neither compute nor comprehend. The money we have spent would make a chain of gold that would encircle the world.

It would construct our Nicaragua Canal over and over again. One year of our expenditure upon the Philippines would redeem every acre of our arid land and make the American desert to blossom as the rose. Our total expenses there would pay the salaries of the President, the Cabinet, and Senators for a thousand years. It would more than double the public buildings of the nation. It would more than pay our annual pension roll. It would provide for our rivers and harbors for a quarter of a century. The human mind can hardly comprehend the hundreds of millions of dollars which we have taken from the people's pockets in this mighty national blunder. I am speaking now not of the slave but of the man, the master, at the other end of the chain.

Who will estimate the cost in other things? Who will count our heroic dead? I remember very well begging and protesting against this war in the Philippines, when one distinguished Senator said that if there was war a regiment of bluecoats would march across the archipelago and make peace.

Ten thousand American boys have gone to their long home, and the end is not yet. Coffin them, beginning here at the Senate Chamber, and lay them out for the world to see. March by the row of coffins until you have seen the faces of thousands of our heroic dead. Look, then, beyond into the desolate homes of mourning and despair; count, weigh, or measure, if you can, the tears of the widow and the orphan. Then, go to St. Elizabeth's Asylum, within a gunshot of the Senate Chamber, and estimate if you can the misery of the hopelessly insane whom we have brought back from the climate of the Philippines, and after looking into the faces of those who are worse than dead, then blame me, if you can and will, for pleading here to-day for Herbert Spencer's man—for the American master at our end of the chain.

* * *

PRESIDENT McKINLEY'S DECISION*

[1899]

How the President came to this decision [to demand cession of all of the Philippine Islands from Spain] was told in a well-authenticated interview at the White House, November 21, 1899. He was receiving a committee representing the General Missionary Committee of the Methodist Episcopal Church, then in session in Washington. . . . After the visitors had presented a resolution of thanks to the President for his courtesy to the convention and listened to an appropriate response, they turned to leave, when the President said, earnestly:—

"Hold a moment longer! Not quite yet, gentlemen! Before you go I would like to say just a word about the Philippine business. I have been criticized a good deal about the Philippines, but don't deserve it. The truth is I didn't want the Philippines, and when they came to us, as a gift from the gods, I did not know what to do with them. When the Spanish War broke out, Dewey was at Hongkong, and I ordered him to go to Manila and to capture or destroy the Spanish fleet, and he had to; because, if defeated, he had no place to refit on that side of the globe, and if the Dons were victorious, they would likely cross the Pacific and ravage our Oregon and California coasts. And so he had to destroy the Spanish fleet, and did it! But that was as far as I thought then.

"When next I realized that the Philippines had dropped into our laps I confess I did not know what to do with them. I sought counsel from all sides—Democrats as well as Republicans—but got little help. I thought first we would take only Manila; then Luzon; then other islands, perhaps, also. I walked the floor of the White House night after night until midnight; and I am not ashamed to tell you, gentlemen, that I went down on my knees and prayed Almighty God for light and guidance more than one night. And one night late it came to me this way—I don't know

* From Charles S. Olcott, *The Life of William McKinley*. Copyright 1916 by Charles S. Olcott. Published by Houghton Mifflin Co. Reprinted by permission.

how it was, but it came: (1) That we could not give them back to Spain—that would be cowardly and dishonorable; (2) that we could not turn them over to France or Germany—our commercial rivals in the Orient—that would be bad business and discreditable; (3) that we could not leave them to themselves—they were unfit for self-government—and they would soon have anarchy and misrule over there worse than Spain's was; and (4) that there was nothing left for us to do but to take them all, and to educate the Filipinos, and uplift and civilize and Christianize them, and by God's grace do the very best we could by them, as our fellow-men for whom Christ also died. And then I went to bed, and went to sleep, and slept soundly, and the next morning I sent for the chief engineer of the War Department (our map-maker), and I told him to put the Philippines on the map of the United States [pointing to a large map on the wall of his office], and there they are, and there they will stay while I am President!"[1]

---

[1]From a report of the interview written by General James F. Rusling, and confirmed by the others who were present.

THE CONQUEST OF THE UNITED STATES BY SPAIN*

BY

WILLIAM GRAHAM SUMNER

[1898]

During the last year the public has been familiarized with descriptions of Spain and of Spanish methods of doing things until the name of Spain has become a symbol for a certain well-defined set of notions and policies. On the other hand, the name of the United States has always been, for all of us, a symbol for a state of things, a set of ideas and traditions, a group of views about social and political affairs. Spain was the first, for a long time the greatest, of the modern imperialistic states. The United States, by its historical origin, its traditions, and its principles, is the chief representative of the revolt and reaction against that kind of a state. I intend to show that, by the line of action now proposed to us, which we call expansion and imperialism, we are throwing away some of the most important elements of the American symbol and are adopting some of the most important elements of the Spanish symbol. We have beaten Spain in a military conflict, but we are submitting to be conquered by her on the field of ideas and policies. Expansionism and imperialism are nothing but the old philosophies of national prosperity which have brought Spain to where she now is. Those philosophies appeal to national vanity and national cupidity. They are seductive, especially upon the first view and the most superficial judgment, and therefore it cannot be denied that they are very strong for popular effect. They are delusions, and they will lead us to ruin unless we are hard-headed enough to resist them. . . .

. . . The original and prime cause of the war was that it was a move of partisan tactics in the strife of parties at Washington. As soon as it seemed resolved upon, a number of interests began to

*From *War and Other Essays*, published by Yale University Press. Reprinted by permission. William Graham Sumner (1840–1910), American sociologist and educator, Professor of Political and Social Science at Yale University, 1872–1909, was the most famous American representative of a thorough *laissez-faire* philosophy.

see their advantage in it and hastened to further it. It was necessary to make appeals to the public which would bring quite other motives to the support of the enterprise and win the consent of classes who would never consent to either financial or political jobbery. Such appeals were found in sensational assertions which we had no means to verify, in phrases of alleged patriotism, in statements about Cuba and the Cubans which we now know to have been entirely untrue.

Where was the statesmanship of all this? If it is not an established rule of statecraft that a statesman should never impose any sacrifices on his people for anything but their own interests, then it is useless to study political philosophy any more, for this is the alphabet of it. It is contrary to honest statesmanship to imperil the political welfare of the state for party interests. It was unstatesmanlike to publish a solemn declaration that we would not seize any territory, and especially to characterize such action in advance as "criminal aggression," for it was morally certain that we should come out of any war with Spain with conquered territory on our hands, and the people who wanted the war, or who consented to it, hoped that we should do so. . . . It is a rule of sound statesmanship not to embark on an adventurous policy. A statesman could not be expected to know in advance that we should come out of the war with the Philippines on our hands, but it belongs to his education to warn him that a policy of adventure and of gratuitous enterprise would be sure to entail embarrassments of some kind. What comes to us in the evolution of our own life and interests, that we must meet; what we go to seek which lies beyond that domain is a waste of our energy and a compromise of our liberty and welfare.

*   *   *

There are some now who think that it is the perfection of statesmanship to say that expansion is a fact and that it is useless to discuss it. We are told that we must not cross any bridges until we come to them; that is, that we must discuss nothing in advance, and that we must not discuss anything which is past because it is irretrievable. No doubt this would be a very acceptable doctrine to the powers that be, for it would mean that they were relieved from responsibility, but it would be a marvelous doctrine to be accepted by a self-governing people. . . . Yet within a year it has become almost a doctrine with us that patriotism requires that we should hold our tongues while our interests, our institutions, our most sacred traditions, and our best established maxims have been trampled underfoot.   There is no doubt that moral courage is the virtue which is more needed than any other in the modern democratic state, and that truckling to popularity is the worst political vice.   The press, the platform, and the pulpit have all fallen under this vice, and there is evidence that the university also, which ought to be the last citadel of truth, is succumbing to it likewise. I have no doubt that the conservative classes of this country will yet look back with great regret to their acquiescence in the events of 1898 and the doctrines and precedents which have been silently established. . . . The perpetuity of self-government depends on the sound political sense of the people, and sound political sense is a matter of habit and practice.   We can give it up and we can take instead pomp and glory.   That is what Spain did.   She had as much self-government as any country in Europe at the beginning of the sixteenth century.   The union of the smaller states into one big one gave an impulse to her national feeling and national development.   The discovery of America put into her hands the control of immense territories.   National pride and ambition were stimulated.   Then came the struggle with France for world-dominion, which resulted in absolute monarchy and bankruptcy for Spain.   She lost self-government and saw her resources spent on interests which were foreign to her, but she could talk about an empire on which the sun never set and boast of her colonies, her gold-mines, her fleets and armies and debts.   She had glory and pride, mixed, of course, with defeat and disaster, such as must be experienced by any nation on that course of policy; and she grew weaker in her industry and commerce and poorer in the status of the population all the time.   She has never been able to recover real self-government yet.   If we Americans believe in self-government, why do we let it slip away from us?   Why do we barter it away for military glory as Spain did?

There is not a civilized nation which does not talk about its civilizing mission just as grandly as we do. The English, who really have more to boast of in this respect than anybody else, talk least about it, but the Phariseeism with which they correct and instruct other people has made them hated all over the globe. The French believe themselves the guardians of the highest and purest culture, and that the eyes of all mankind are fixed on Paris, whence they expect oracles of thought and taste. The Germans regard themselves as charged with a mission, especially to us Americans, to save us from egoism and materialism. The Russians, in their books and newspapers, talk about the civilizing mission of Russia in language that might be translated from some of the finest paragraphs in our imperialistic newspapers. The first principle of Mohammedanism is that we Christians are dogs and infidels, fit only to be enslaved or butchered by Moslems. It is a corollary that wherever Mohammedanism extends it carries, in the belief of its votaries, the highest blessings, and that the whole human race would be enormously elevated if Mohammedanism should supplant Christianity everywhere. To come, last, to Spain, the Spaniards have, for centuries, considered themselves the most zealous and self-sacrificing Christians, especially charged by the Almighty, on this account, to spread true religion and civilization over the globe. They think themselves free and noble, leaders in refinement and the sentiments of personal honor, and they despise us as sordid money-grabbers and heretics. I could bring you passages from peninsular authors of the first rank about the grand rôle of Spain and Portugal in spreading freedom and truth. Now each nation laughs at all the others when it observes these manifestations of national vanity. You may rely upon it that they are all ridiculous by virtue of these pretensions, including ourselves. The point is that each of them repudiates the standards of the others, and the outlying nations, which are to be civilized, hate all the standards of civilized men. We assume that what we like and practice, and what we think better, must come as a welcome blessing to Spanish-Americans and Filipinos. This is grossly and obviously untrue. They hate our ways. They are hostile to our ideas. Our religion, language, institutions, and manners offend them. They like their own ways, and if we appear amongst them as rulers, there will be social discord in all the great departments of social interest. The most important thing which we shall inherit from the Spaniards will be the task of suppressing rebellions. If the United States takes out of the hands of Spain her mission, on the ground that Spain is not executing it well, and if this nation in its turn attempts to be school-mistress to others, it will shrivel up into the same vanity and self-conceit of which Spain now presents an example. To read our current literature one would think that we were already well on the way to it. Now, the great reason why all these enterprises which begin by saying to somebody else, We know what is good for you better than you know yourself and we are going to make you do it, are false and wrong is that they violate liberty; or, to turn the same statement into other words, the reason why liberty, of which we Americans talk so much, is a good thing is that it means leaving people to live out their own lives in their own way, while we do the same. If we believe in liberty, as an American principle, why do we not stand by it? Why are we going to throw it away to enter upon a Spanish policy of dominion and regulation?

*   *   *

The Americans have been committed from the outset to the doctrine that all men are equal. We have elevated it into an absolute doctrine as a part of the theory of our social and political fabric. It has always been a domestic dogma in spite of its absolute form, and as a domestic dogma it has always stood in glaring contradiction to the facts about Indians and Negroes and to our legislation about Chinamen. In its absolute form it must, of course, apply to Kanakas, Malays, Tagals, and Chinese just as much as to Yankees, Germans, and Irish. It is an astonishing event that we have lived to see American arms carry this domestic dogma out where it must be tested in its application to uncivilized and half-civilized peoples. At the first touch of the test we throw the doctrine away and adopt the Spanish doctrine. We are told by all the imperialists that these people are not fit for liberty and self-government; that it is rebellion for them to resist our benefi-

cence; that we must send fleets and armies to kill them if they do
it; that we must devise a government for them and administer it
ourselves; that we may buy them or sell them as we please, and
dispose of their "trade" for our own advantage. What is that
but the policy of Spain to her dependencies? What can we expect
as a consequence of it? Nothing but that it will bring us where
Spain is now.

*   *   *

The doctrine that we are to take away from other nations any
possessions of theirs which we think that we could manage better
than they are managing them, or that we are to take in hand any
countries which we do not think capable of self-government, is
one which will lead us very far. With that doctrine in the background, our politicians will have no trouble to find a war ready
for us the next time that they come around to the point where they
think that it is time for us to have another. We are told that we
must have a big army hereafter. What for; unless we propose to
do again by and by what we have just done? In that case our
neighbors have reason to ask themselves whom we will attack
next. They must begin to arm, too, and by our act the whole
western world is plunged into the distress under which the eastern
world is groaning. Here is another point in regard to which the
conservative elements in the country are making a great mistake to
allow all this militarism and imperialism to go on without protest.
It will be established as a rule that, whenever political ascendency
is threatened, it can be established again by a little war, filling the
minds of the people with glory and diverting their attention from
their own interests. Hard-headed old Benjamin Franklin hit the
point when, referring back to the days of Marlborough, he talked
about the "pest of glory." The thirst for glory is an epidemic
which robs a people of their judgment, seduces their vanity, cheats
them of their interests, and corrupts their consciences.

*   *   *

. . . A great many people talk about the revenue which we are
to get from these possessions. If we attempt to get any revenues

from them we shall repeat the conduct of England towards her
colonies against which they revolted. England claimed that it was
reasonable that the colonies should pay their share of imperial
expenses which were incurred for the benefit of all. I have never
been able to see why that was not a fair demand. As you know,
the colonies spurned it with indignation, on the ground that the
taxation, being at the discretion of a foreign power, *might* be
made unjust. Our historians and publicists have taught us that
the position of the colonists was right and heroic, and the only one
worthy of freemen. The revolt was made on the *principle* of no
taxation, not on the size of the tax. The colonists would not pay
a penny. Since that is so, we cannot get a penny of revenue from
the dependencies, even for their fair share of imperial expenditures, without burning up all our histories, revising all the great
principles of our heroic period, repudiating our great men of that
period, and going over to the Spanish doctrine of taxing dependencies at the discretion of the governing State. Already one of
these dependencies is in arms struggling for liberty against us.
Read the threats of the imperialists against these people, who dare
to rebel against us, and see whether I am misstating or exaggerat-
ing the corruption of imperialism on ourselves. The question is
once more, whether we are prepared to repudiate the principles
which we have been insisting on for one hundred and fifty years,
and to embrace those of which Spain is the oldest and most conspicuous representative, or not.

* * *

Our modern protectionists have always told us that the object
of their policy is to secure the home market. They have pushed
their system to an extravagant excess. The free traders used to
tell them that they were constructing a Chinese wall. They answered that they wished we were separated from other nations by
a gulf of fire. Now it is they who are crying out that they are shut
in by a Chinese wall. When we have shut all the world out, we
find that we have shut ourselves in. The protective system is
applied especially to certain selected lines of production. Of

course these are stimulated out of proportion to the requirements
of the community, and so are exposed to sharp fluctuations of high
profits and over-production. At great expense and loss we have
carried out the policy of the home market, and now we are called
upon at great expense and loss to go out and conquer territory in
order to widen the market. In order to have trade with another
community the first condition is that we must produce what they
want and they must produce what we want. That is the economic
condition. The second condition is that there must be peace and
security and freedom from arbitrary obstacles interposed by government. This is the political condition. If these conditions are
fulfilled, there will be trade, no matter whether the two communities are in one body politic or not. If these conditions are
not fulfilled, there will be no trade, no matter what flag floats.
If we want more trade we can get it any day by a reciprocity treaty
with Canada, and it will be larger and more profitable than that
of all the Spanish possessions. It will cost us nothing to get it.
Yet while we were fighting for Puerto Rico and Manila, and
spending three or four hundred millions to get them, negotiations
with Canada failed through the narrow-mindedness and bigotry
which we brought to the negotiation. Conquest can do nothing
for trade except to remove the political obstacles which the conquered could not, or would not, remove. From this it follows
that the only justification for territorial extension is the extension
of free and enlightened policies in regard to commerce. Even
then extension is an irksome necessity. The question always is,
whether you are taking an asset or a liability. Land grabbing
means properly taking territory and shutting all the rest of the
world out of it, so as to exploit it ourselves. It is not land grabbing to take it and police it and throw it open to all. This is the
policy of the "open door." Our external commercial policy is, in
all its principles, the same as that of Spain. We had no justification, on that ground, in taking anything away from her. If we
now seek to justify ourselves, it must be by going over to the free
policy; but, as I have shown, that forces to a crisis the contradiction
between our domestic and our external policy as to trade. It is
very probable, indeed, that the destruction of our restrictive system

will be the first good result of expansion, but my object here has been to show what a network of difficulties environ us in the attempt to establish a commercial policy for these dependencies. We have certainly to go through years of turmoil and political bitterness, with all the consequent chances of internal dissension, before these difficulties can be overcome.

Another phenomenon which deserves earnest attention from the student of contemporaneous history and of the trend of political institutions is the failure of the masses of our people to perceive *the inevitable effect of imperialism on democracy*. On the twenty-ninth of last November [1898] the Prime Minister of France was quoted in a cable dispatch as follows: "For twenty-eight years we have lived under a contradiction. The army and democracy subsist side by side. The maintenance of the traditions of the army is a menace to liberty, yet they assure the safety of the country and its most sacred duties."

* * *

Everywhere you go on the continent of Europe at this hour you see the conflict between militarism and industrialism. You see the expansion of industrial power pushed forward by the energy, hope, and thrift of men, and you see the development arrested, diverted, crippled, and defeated by measures which are dictated by military considerations. At the same time the press is loaded down with discussions about political economy, political philosophy, and social policy. They are discussing poverty, labor, socialism, charity, reform, and social ideals, and are boasting of enlightenment and progress, at the same time that the things which are done are dictated by none of these considerations, but only by military interests. It is militarism which is eating up all the products of science and art, defeating the energy of the population and wasting its savings. It is militarism which forbids the people to give their attention to the problems of their own welfare and to give their strength to the education and comfort of their children. It is militarism which is combating the grand efforts of science and art to ameliorate the struggle for existence.

The American people believe that they have a free country, and we are treated to grandiloquent speeches about our flag and our reputation for freedom and enlightenment. The common opinion is that we have these things because we have chosen and adopted them, because they are in the Declaration of Independence and the Constitution. We suppose, therefore, that we are sure to keep them and that the follies of other people are things which we can hear about with complacency. People say that this country is like no other; that its prosperity proves its exceptionality, and so on. These are popular errors which in time will meet with harsh correction. The United States is in a protected situation. It is easy to have equality where land is abundant and where the population is small. It is easy to have prosperity where a few men have a great continent to exploit. It is easy to have liberty when you have no dangerous neighbors and when the struggle for existence is easy. There are no severe penalties, under such circumstances, for political mistakes. Democracy is not then a thing to be nursed and defended, as it is in an old country like France. It is rooted and founded in the economic circumstances of the country. The orators and constitution-makers do not make democracy. They are made by it. This protected position, however, is sure to pass away. As the country fills up with population, and the task of getting a living out of the ground becomes more difficult, the struggle for existence will become harder and the competition of life more severe. Then liberty and democracy will cost something, if they are to be maintained.

Now what will hasten the day when our present advantages will wear out and when we shall come down to the conditions of the older and densely populated nations? The answer is: war, debt, taxation, diplomacy, a grand governmental system, pomp, glory, a big army and navy, lavish expenditures, political jobbery—in a word, imperialism. In the old days the democratic masses of this country, who knew little about our modern doctrines of social philosophy, had a sound instinct on these matters, and it is no small ground of political disquietude to see it decline. They resisted every appeal to their vanity in the way of pomp and glory which they knew must be paid for. They dreaded a public debt and a standing army. They were narrow-minded and went too far with these notions, but they were, at least, right, if they wanted to strengthen democracy.

The great foe of democracy now and in the near future is plutocracy. Every year that passes brings out this antagonism more distinctly. It is to be the social war of the twentieth century. In that war militarism, expansion and imperialism will all favor plutocracy.

*   *   *

The point which I have tried to make in this lecture is that expansion and imperialism are at war with the best traditions, principles, and interests of the American people, and that they will plunge us into a network of difficult problems and political perils, which we might have avoided, while they offer us no corresponding advantage in return. . . . The imperialists [say] that Americans can do anything. They say that they do not shrink from responsibilities. They are willing to run into a hole, trusting to luck and cleverness to get out. There are some things that Americans cannot do. Americans cannot make $2 + 2 = 5$. You may answer that that is an arithmetical impossibility and is not in the range of our subject. Very well; . . . so far as yet appears, Americans cannot govern a city of one hundred thousand inhabitants so as to get comfort and convenience in it at a low cost and without jobbery. The fire department of this city is now demoralized by political jobbery—and Spain and all her possessions are not worth as much to you and me as the efficiency of the fire department of New Haven. The Americans in Connecticut cannot abolish the rotten borough system. The English abolished their rotten borough system seventy years ago, in spite of nobles and landlords. We cannot abolish ours in spite of the small towns. Americans cannot reform the pension list. Its abuses are rooted in the methods of democratic self-government, and no one dares to touch them. It is very doubtful indeed if Americans can keep up an army of one hundred thousand men in time of peace. Where can one hundred thousand men be found in this country who are willing to spend their lives as soldiers; or if they are found, what pay will it require to induce them to take this career? Americans cannot disentangle their currency from the confusion into which it was thrown by the Civil War, and they cannot put it on a simple, sure, and sound basis which would give stability to the business of the country. This is a political impossibility. Americans cannot assure the suffrage to Negroes throughout the United States; they have tried it for thirty years and now, contemporaneously with this war with Spain, it has been finally demonstrated that it is a failure. . . . Upon a little serious examination the off-hand disposal of an important question of policy by the declaration that Americans can do anything proves to be only a silly piece of bombast, and upon a little reflection we find that our hands are quite full at home of problems by the solution of which the peace and happiness of the American people could be greatly increased. The laws of nature and of human nature are just as valid for Americans as for anybody else, and if we commit acts we shall have to take consequences, just like other people. Therefore prudence demands that we look ahead to see what we are about to do, and that we gauge the means at our disposal, if we do not want to bring calamity on ourselves and our children. We see that the peculiarities of our system of government set limitations on us. We cannot do things which a great centralized monarchy could do. The very blessings and special advantages which we enjoy, as compared with others, bring disabilities with them. That is the great fundamental cause of what I have tried to show throughout this lecture, that we cannot govern dependencies consistently with our political system, and that, if we try it, the State which our fathers founded will suffer a reaction which will transform it into another empire just after the fashion of all the old ones. That is what imperialism means. That is what it will be; and the democratic republic, which has been, will stand in history, like the colonial organization of earlier days, as a mere transition form.

And yet this scheme of a republic which our fathers formed was a glorious dream which demands more than a word of respect and affection before it passes away. Indeed, it is not fair to call it a dream or even an ideal; it was a possibility which was within our reach if we had been wise enough to grasp and hold it. It was favored by our comparative isolation, or, at least, by our distance from other strong states. The men who came here were able to throw off all the trammels of tradition and established doctrine. They went out into a wilderness, it is true, but they took with them all the art, science, and literature which, up to that time, civilization had produced. They could not, it is true, strip their minds of the ideas which they had inherited, but in time, as they lived on in the new world, they sifted and selected these ideas, retaining what they chose. Of the old-world institutions also they selected and adopted what they chose and threw aside the rest. It was a grand opportunity to be thus able to strip off all the follies and errors which they had inherited, so far as they chose to do so. They had unlimited land with no feudal restrictions to hinder them in the use of it. Their idea was that they would never allow any of the social and political abuses of the old world to grow up here. There should be no manors, no barons, no ranks, no prelates, no idle classes, no paupers, no disinherited ones except the vicious. There were to be no armies except a militia, which would have no functions but those of police. They would have no court and no pomp; no orders, or ribbons, or decorations, or titles. They would have no public debt. They repudiated with scorn the notion that a public debt is a public blessing; if debt was incurred in war it was to be paid in peace and not entailed on posterity. There was to be no grand diplomacy, because they intended to mind their own business and not be involved in any of the intrigues to which European statesmen were accustomed. There was to be no balance of power and no "reason of state" to cost the life and happiness of citizens. The only part of the Monroe doctrine which is valid was their determination that the social and political systems of Europe should not be extended over any part of the American continent, lest people who were weaker than we should lose the opportunity which the new continent gave them to escape from those systems if they wanted to. Our fathers would have an economical government, even if grand people called it a parsimonious one, and taxes should be no greater than were absolutely necessary to pay for such a government. The citizen was to keep all the rest of his earnings and use them as he thought best for the happiness of himself and his family; he was, above all, to be insured peace and quiet while he pursued his honest industry and obeyed the laws. No adventurous policies of conquest or ambition, such as, in the belief of our fathers, kings and nobles had forced, for their own advantage, on European states, would ever be undertaken by a free democratic republic. Therefore the citizen here would never be forced to leave his family or to give his sons to shed blood for glory and to leave widows and orphans in misery for nothing. Justice and law were to reign in the midst of simplicity, and a government which had little to do was to offer little field for ambition. In a society where industry, frugality, and prudence were honored, it was believed that the vices of wealth would never flourish.

We know that these beliefs, hopes, and intentions have been only partially fulfilled. We know that, as time has gone on and we have grown numerous and rich, some of these things have proved impossible ideals, incompatible with a large and flourishing society, but it is by virtue of this conception of a commonwealth that the United States has stood for something unique and grand in the history of mankind and that its people have been happy. It is by virtue of these ideals that we have been "isolated," isolated in a position which the other nations of the earth have observed in silent envy; and yet there are people who are boasting of their patriotism, because they say that we have taken our place now amongst the nations of the earth by virtue of this war. My patriotism is of the kind which is outraged by the notion that the United States never was a great nation until in a petty three months' campaign it knocked to pieces a poor, decrepit, bankrupt old state like Spain. To hold such an opinion as that is to abandon all American standards, to put shame and scorn on all that our ancestors tried to build up here, and to go over to the standards of which Spain is a representative.

III

THE UNITED STATES AND EUROPE

THE FAREWELL ADDRESS

Selections

BY

GEORGE WASHINGTON

[1796]

Observe good faith and justice towards all nations; cultivate peace and harmony with all; religion and morality enjoin this conduct; and can it be that good policy does not equally enjoin it? It will be worthy of a free, enlightened, and, at no distant period, a great nation, to give to mankind the magnanimous and too novel example of a people always guided by an exalted justice and benevolence. Who can doubt that, in the course of time and things, the fruits of such a plan would richly repay any temporary advantages that might be lost by a steady adherence to it? Can it be, that Providence has not connected the permanent felicity of a nation with its virtue? The experiment, at least, is recommended by every sentiment which ennobles human nature. Alas! is it rendered impossible by its vices?

In the execution of such a plan, nothing is more essential than that permanent, inveterate antipathies against particular nations, and passionate attachments for others, should be excluded; and that in place of them, just and amicable feelings towards all should be cultivated. The nation, which indulges towards another an habitual hatred, or an habitual fondness, is in some degree a slave. It is a slave to its animosity or to its affection, either of which is sufficient to lead it astray from its duty and its interest. Antipathy in one nation against another, disposes each more readily to offer insult and injury, to lay hold of slight causes of umbrage, and to be haughty and intractable, when accidental or trifling occasions of dispute occur.

Hence frequent collisions, obstinate, envenomed, and bloody contests. The nation, prompted by ill-will and resentment, sometimes impels to war the government, contrary to the best calculations of policy. The government sometimes participates in the national propensity, and adopts through passion what reason would reject; at other times, it makes the animosity of the nation subservient to projects of hostility instigated by pride, ambition and other sinister and pernicious motives. The peace often, and sometimes, perhaps, the liberty of nations, has been the victim.

So, likewise, a passionate attachment of one nation for another produces a variety of evils. Sympathy for the favorite nation facilitating the illusion of an imaginary common interest in cases where no real common interest exists, and infusing into one the enmities of the other, betrays the former into a participation in the quarrels and wars of the latter, without adequate inducement or justification. It leads also to concessions to the favorite nation of privileges denied to others, which is apt doubly to injure the nation making the concessions; by unnecessarily parting with what ought to have been retained; and by exciting jealousy, ill-will, and a disposition to retaliate, in the parties from whom equal privileges are withheld; and it gives to ambitious, corrupted, or deluded citizens (who devote themselves to the favorite nation) facility to betray, or sacrifice the interests of their own country, without odium, sometimes even with popularity; gilding, with the appearances of a virtuous sense of obligation, a commendable deference for public opinion, or laudable zeal for public good, the base or foolish compliances of ambition, corruption, or infatuation.

As avenues to foreign influence, in innumerable ways, such attachments are particularly alarming to the truly enlightened and independent patriot. How many opportunities do they afford to tamper with domestic factions; to practise the arts of seduction; to mislead public opinion; to influence or awe the public councils! Such an attachment of a small or weak nation, toward a great and powerful one, dooms the former to be the satellite of the latter.

Against the insidious wiles of foreign influence (I conjure you to believe me, fellow-citizens), the jealousy of a free people ought to be constantly awake; since history and experience prove, that foreign influence is one of the most baneful foes of republican government. But that jealousy, to be useful, must be impartial; else it becomes the instrument of the very influence to be avoided, instead of a defence against it. Excessive partiality for one foreign nation, and excessive dislike of another, cause those whom they actuate, to see danger only on one side; and serve to veil and even second the arts of influence on the other. Real patriots, who may resist the intrigues of the favorite, are liable to become suspected and odious; while its tools and dupes usurp the applause and confidence of the people, to surrender their interests.

The great rule of conduct for us, in regard to foreign nations, is, in extending our commercial relations, to have with them as little political connection as possible. So far as we have already formed engagements, let them be fulfilled with perfect good faith. Here let us stop.

Europe has a set of primary interests, which to us have none, or a very remote relation. Hence she must be engaged in frequent controversies, the causes of which are essentially foreign to our concerns. Hence, therefore, it must be unwise in us to implicate ourselves, by artificial ties, in the ordinary vicissitudes of her politics, or the ordinary combinations and collisions of her friendships and enmities.

Our detached and distant situation invites and enables us to pursue a different course. If we remain one people, under an efficient government, the period is not far off when we may defy material injury from external annoyance; when we may take such an attitude as will cause the neutrality we may at any time resolve upon, to be scrupulously respected; when belligerent nations, under the impossibility of making acquisitions upon us, will not lightly hazard the giving us provocation; when we may choose peace or war, as our interest, guided by justice, shall counsel.

Why forego the advantages of so peculiar a situation? Why quit our own to stand upon foreign ground? Why, by interweaving our destiny with that of any part of Europe, entangle our peace and prosperity in the toils of European ambition, rivalship, interest, humor, or caprice?

'Tis our true policy to steer clear of permanent alliances with any portion of the foreign world; so far, I mean, as we are now at liberty to do it; for let me not be understood as capable of patronizing infidelity to existing engagements. I hold the maxim no less applicable to public than to private affairs, that honesty is always the best policy. I repeat it, therefore, let those engagements be observed in their genuine sense. But, in my opinion, it is unnecessary, and would be unwise, to extend them.

Taking care always to keep ourselves, by suitable establishments, in a respectable defensive posture, we may safely trust to temporary alliances for extraordinary emergencies.

Harmony, and a liberal intercourse with all nations, are recommended by policy, humanity, and interest. But even our commercial policy should hold an equal and impartial hand; neither seeking nor granting exclusive favors or preferences; consulting the natural course of things; diffusing and diversifying, by gentle means, the streams of commerce, but forcing nothing; establishing, with powers so disposed, in order to give trade a stable course, to define the rights of our merchants, and to enable the government to support them, conventional rules of intercourse, the best that present circumstances and mutual opinion will permit, but temporary, and liable to be, from time to time, abandoned or varied, as experience and circumstances shall dictate; constantly keeping in view, that it is folly in one nation to look for disinterested favors from another; that it must pay, with a portion of its independence, for whatever it may accept under that character; that, by such acceptance, it may place itself in the condition of having given equivalents for nominal favors, and yet of being reproached with ingratitude for not giving more. There can be no greater error than to expect to calculate upon real favors from nation to nation. It is an illusion, which experience must cure, which a just pride ought to discard.

In offering to you, my countrymen, these counsels of an old and affectionate friend, I dare not hope they will make the strong and lasting impression I could wish; that they will control the usual current of the passions, or prevent our nation from running the course which has hitherto marked the destiny of nations! But, if I may even flatter myself, that they may be productive of some partial benefit, some occasional good; that they may now and then recur to moderate the fury of party spirit; to warn against the mischiefs of foreign intrigues; to guard against the impostures of pretended patriotism; this hope will be a full recompense for the solicitude for your welfare, by which they have been dictated.

How far, in the discharge of my official duties, I have been guided by the principles which have been delineated, the public records and other evidences of my conduct must witness to you and to the world. To myself the assurance of my own conscience is, that I have at least believed myself to be guided by them.

In relation to the still subsisting war in Europe, my proclamation of April 22, 1793, is the index to my plan. Sanctioned by your approving voice, and by that of your representatives in both Houses of Congress, the spirit of that measure has continually governed me, uninfluenced by any attempts to deter or divert me from it.

After deliberate examination, with the aid of the best lights I could obtain, I was well satisfied that our country, under all the circumstances of the case, had a right to take, and was bound in duty and interest to take, a neutral position. Having taken it, I determined, as far as should depend upon me, to maintain it with moderation, perseverance, and firmness.

The considerations which respect the right to hold this conduct, it is not necessary, on this occasion, to detail. I will only observe, that, according to my understanding of the matter, that right, so far from being denied by any of the belligerent powers, has been virtually admitted by all.

The duty of holding a neutral conduct may be inferred, without anything more, from the obligation which justice and humanity impose on every nation, in cases in which it is free to act, to maintain inviolate the relations of peace and amity towards other nations.

The inducements of interest for observing that conduct will best be referred to your own reflection and experience. With me, a predominant motive has been to endeavor to gain time to our country to settle and mature its yet recent institutions, and to progress, without interruption, to that degree of strength and consistency which is necessary to give it, humanly speaking, the command of its own fortunes.

GIDDY MINDS AND FOREIGN QUARRELS*

BY

CHARLES A. BEARD

[1939]

In the fourth act of "Henry IV" the King on his death-bed gives his son and heir the ancient advice dear to the hearts of rulers in dire straits at home:

> I . . . had a purpose now
> To lead out many to the Holy Land,
> Lest rest and lying still might make them look
> Too near unto my state. Therefore, my Harry,
> Be it thy course, to busy giddy minds
> With foreign quarrels; that action, hence borne out,
> May waste the memory of the former days.

* * *

On what . . . should the foreign policy of the United States be based? Here is one answer and it is not excogitated in any professor's study or supplied by political agitators. It is the doctrine formulated by George Washington, supplemented by James Monroe, and followed by the Government of the United States until near the end of the nineteenth century, when the frenzy for foreign adventurism burst upon the country. This doctrine is simple. Europe has a set of "primary interests" which have little or no relation to us, and is constantly vexed by "ambition, rivalship, interest, humor, or caprice." The United States is a continental power separated from Europe by a wide ocean which, despite all changes in warfare; is still a powerful asset of defense. In the ordinary or regular vicissitudes of European politics the United States should not become implicated by any permanent

*Published by Macmillan and Co. Copyright 1939 by Charles A. Beard. Reprinted by permission. Charles A. Beard (1874–1948) is the author of numerous books on American history and foreign policy. He was the foremost American proponent of the economic interpretation of history.

ties. We should promote commerce, but force "nothing." We should steer clear of hates and loves. We should maintain correct and formal relations with all established governments without respect to their forms or their religions, whether Christian, Mohammedan, Shinto, or what have you. Efforts of any European powers to seize more colonies or to oppress independent states in this hemisphere, or to extend their systems of despotism to the New World will be regarded as a matter of concern to the United States as soon as they are immediately threatened and begin to assume tangible shape.

This policy was stated positively in the early days of our Republic. It was clear. It was definite. It gave the powers of the earth something they could understand and count upon in adjusting their policies and conflicts. It was not only stated. It was acted upon with a high degree of consistency until the great frenzy overtook us. It enabled the American people to go ahead under the principles of 1776, conquering a continent and building here a civilization which, with all its faults, has precious merits for us and is, at all events, our own. Under the shelter of this doctrine, human beings were set free to see what they could do on this continent, when emancipated from the privilege-encrusted institutions of Europe and from entanglement in the endless revolutions and wars of that continent.

Grounded in strong common sense, based on deep and bitter experience, Washington's doctrine has remained a tenacious heritage, despite the hectic interludes of the past fifty years. Owing to the growth of our nation, the development of our own industries, the expulsion of Spain from this hemisphere, and the limitations now imposed upon British ambition by European pressures, the United States can pursue this policy more securely and more effectively today than at any time in our history. In an economic sense the United States is far more independent than it was in 1783, when the Republic was launched and, what is more, is better able to defend itself against all comers. Why, as Washington asked, quit our own to stand on foreign ground?

This is a policy founded upon our geographical position and our practical interests. It can be maintained by appropriate military and naval establishments. Beyond its continental zone and adjacent waters, in Latin America, the United States should have a care; but it is sheer folly to go into hysterics and double military and naval expenditures on the rumor that Hitler or Mussolini is about to seize Brazil, or that the Japanese are building gun emplacements in Costa Rica. Beyond this hemisphere, the United States should leave disputes over territory, over the ambitions of warriors, over the intrigues of hierarchies, over forms of government, over passing myths known as ideologies—all to the nations and peoples immediately and directly affected. They have more knowledge and power in the premises than have the people and the Government of the United States.

This foreign policy for the United States is based upon a recognition of the fact that no kind of international drum beating, conferring, and trading can do anything material to set our industries in full motion, raise the country from the deeps of the depression. Foreign trade is important, no doubt, but the main support for our American life is production and distribution in the United States and the way out of the present economic morass lies in the acceleration of this production and distribution at home, by domestic measures. Nothing that the United States can do in foreign negotiations can raise domestic production to the hundred billions a year that we need to put our national life, our democracy, on a foundation of internal security which will relax the present tensions and hatreds.

It is a fact, stubborn and inescapable, that since the year 1900 the annual value of American goods exported has never risen above ten per cent of the total value of exportable or movable goods produced in the United States, except during the abnormal conditions of the war years. The exact percentage was 9.7 in 1914, 9.8 in 1929, and 7.3 in 1931. If experience is any guide we may expect the amount of exportable goods actually exported to be about ten per cent of the total, and the amount consumed at home to be about ninety per cent. High tariff or low tariff, little Navy or big, good neighbor policy or saber-rattling policy, hot air or cold air, this proportion seems to be in the nature of a fixed law, certainly more fixed than most of the so-called laws of political economy.

Since this is so, then why all the furor about attaining full prosperity by "increasing" our foreign trade? Why not apply stimulants to domestic production on which we can act directly? I can conceive of no reason for all this palaver except to divert the attention of the American people from things they can do at home to things they cannot do abroad.

In the rest of the world, outside this hemisphere, our interests are remote and our power to enforce our will is relatively slight. Nothing we can do for Europeans will substantially increase our trade or add to our, or their, well-being. Nothing we can do for Asiatics will materially increase our trade or add to our, or their, well-being. With all countries in Europe and Asia, our relations should be formal and correct. As individuals we may indulge in hate and love, but the Government of the United States embarks on stormy seas when it begins to love one power and hate another officially. Great Britain has never done it. She has paid Prussians to beat Frenchmen and helped Frenchmen to beat Prussians, without official love or hatred, save in wartime, and always in the interest of her security. The charge of perfidy hurled against Britain has been the charge of hypocrites living in glass houses while throwing bricks.

Not until some formidable European power comes into the western Atlantic, breathing the fire of aggression and conquest, need the United States become alarmed about the ups and downs of European conflicts, intrigues, aggressions, and wars. And this peril is slight at worst. To take on worries is to add useless burdens, to breed distempers at home, and to discover, in the course of time, how foolish and vain it all has been. The destiny of Europe and Asia has not been committed, under God, to the keeping of the United States; and only conceit, dreams of grandeur, vain imaginings, lust for power, or a desire to escape from our domestic perils and obligations could possibly make us suppose that Providence has appointed us his chosen people for the pacification of the earth.

And what should those who hold to such a continental policy for the United States say to the powers of Europe? They ought not to say: "Let Europe stew in its own juice; European statesmen are mere cunning intriguers; and we will have nothing to do with Europe." A wiser and juster course would be to say: "We cannot and will not underwrite in advance any power or combination of powers; let them make as best they can the adjustments required by their immediate interests in Europe, Africa, and Asia, about which they know more and over which they have great force; no European power or combination of powers can count upon material aid from the United States while pursuing a course of power politics designed to bolster up its economic interests and its military dominance; in the nature of things American sympathy will be on the side of nations that practice self-government, liberty of opinion and person, and toleration and freedom of thought and inquiry—but the United States has had one war for democracy; the United States will not guarantee the present distribution of imperial domains in Africa and Asia; it will tolerate no attempt to conquer independent states in this hemisphere and make them imperial possessions; in all sincere undertakings to make economic adjustments, reduce armaments, and co-operate in specific cases of international utility and welfare that comport with our national interest, the United States will participate within the framework of its fundamental policy respecting this hemisphere; this much, nations of Europe, and may good fortune attend you." . . .

American people are resolutely taking stock of their past follies. Forty years ago bright young men of tongue and pen told them they had an opportunity and responsibility to go forth and, after the manner of Rome and Britain, conquer, rule, and civilize backward peoples. And the same bright boys told them that all of this would "pay," that it would find outlets for their "surpluses" of manufactures and farm produce. It did not. Twenty-two years ago American people were told that they were to make the world safe for democracy. They nobly responded. Before they got through they heard about the secret treaties by which the Allies divided the loot. They saw the Treaty of Versailles which distributed the spoils and made an impossible "peace." What did they get out of the adventure? Wounds and deaths. The contempt of former associates—until the Americans were needed again in another war for democracy. A repudiation of debts. A huge bill of expenses. A false boom. A terrific crisis.

Those Americans who refuse to plunge blindly into the maelstrom of European and Asiatic politics are not defeatist or neurotic. They are giving evidence of sanity, not cowardice; of adult thinking as distinguished from infantilism. Experience has educated them and made them all the more determined to concentrate their energies on the making of a civilization within the circle of their continental domain. They do not propose to withdraw from the world, but they propose to deal with the world as it is and not as romantic propagandists picture it. They propose to deal with it in American terms, that is, in terms of national interest and security on this continent. Like their ancestors who made a revolution, built the Republic, and made it stick, they intend to preserve and defend the Republic, and under its shelter carry forward the work of employing their talents and resources in enriching American life. They know that this task will call for all the enlightened statesmanship, the constructive energy, and imaginative intelligence that the nation can command. America is not to be Rome or Britain. It is to be America.

DOCUMENTS ON RECENT
AMERICAN FOREIGN POLICY

1. THE TRUMAN DOCTRINE, 1947*

Mr. President, Mr. Speaker, Members of the
Congress of the United States:

The gravity of the situation which confronts the world today necessitates my appearance before a joint session of the Congress.

The foreign policy and the national security of this country are involved.

One aspect of the present situation, which I wish to present to you at this time for your consideration and decision, concerns Greece and Turkey.

The United States has received from the Greek Government an urgent appeal for financial and economic assistance. . . .

When forces of liberation entered Greece they found that the retreating Germans had destroyed virtually all the railways, roads, port facilities, communications, and merchant marine. More than a thousand villages had been burned. Eighty-five percent of the children were tubercular. Livestock, poultry, and draft animals had almost disappeared. Inflation had wiped out practically all savings.

As a result of these tragic conditions, a militant minority, exploiting human want and misery, was able to create political chaos which, until now, has made economic recovery impossible.

Greece is today without funds to finance the importation of those goods which are essential to bare subsistence. . . . Greece must have help to import the goods necessary to restore internal order and security so essential for economic and political recovery.

The Greek Government has also asked for the assistance of experienced American administrators, economists and technicians to insure that the financial and other aid given to Greece shall be

*From President Truman's Message to Congress, "Recommendations on Greece and Turkey," March 12, 1947.

used effectively in creating a stable and self-sustaining economy and in improving its public administration.

The very existence of the Greek state is today threatened by the terrorist activities of several thousand armed men, led by Communists, who defy the government's authority at a number of points, particularly along the northern boundaries. A Commission appointed by the United Nations Security Council is at present investigating disturbed conditions in northern Greece and alleged border violations along the frontier between Greece on the one hand and Albania, Bulgaria, and Yugoslavia on the other.

Meanwhile, the Greek Government is unable to cope with the situation. The Greek army is small and poorly equipped. It needs supplies and equipment if it is to restore the authority of the government throughout Greek territory.

Greece must have assistance if it is to become a self-supporting and self-respecting democracy.

The United States must supply that assistance. We have already extended to Greece certain types of relief and economic aid but these are inadequate.

There is no other country to which democratic Greece can turn.

No other nation is willing and able to provide the necessary support for a democratic Greek government. . . .

We have considered how the United Nations might assist in this crisis. But the situation is an urgent one requiring immediate action, and the United Nations and its related organizations are not in a position to extend help of the kind that is required.

It is important to note that the Greek Government has asked for our aid in utilizing effectively the financial and other assistance we may give to Greece, and in improving its public administration. It is of the utmost importance that we supervise the use of any funds made available to Greece, in such a manner that each dollar spent will count toward making Greece self-supporting, and will help to build an economy in which a healthy democracy can flourish.

No government is perfect. One of the chief virtues of a democracy, however, is that its defects are always visible and under democratic processes can be pointed out and corrected. The government of Greece is not perfect. Nevertheless it represents eighty-five percent of the members of the Greek Parliament who were chosen in an election last year. Foreign observers, including 692 Americans, considered this election to be a fair expression of the views of the Greek people.

The Greek Government has been operating in an atmosphere of chaos and extremism. It has made mistakes. The extension of aid by this country does not mean that the United States condones everything that the Greek Government has done or will do. We have condemned in the past, and we condemn now, extremist measures of the right or the left. We have in the past advised tolerance, and we advise tolerance now.

Greece's neighbor, Turkey, also deserves our attention.

The future of Turkey as an independent and economically sound state is clearly no less important to the freedom-loving peoples of the world than the future of Greece. The circumstances in which Turkey finds itself today are considerably different from those of Greece. Turkey has been spared the disasters that have beset Greece. And during the war, the United States and Great Britain furnished Turkey with material aid.

Nevertheless, Turkey now needs our support.

Since the war Turkey has sought financial assistance from Great Britain and the United States for the purpose of effecting that modernization necessary for the maintenance of its national integrity.

That integrity is essential to the preservation of order in the Middle East.

The British Government has informed us that, owing to its own difficulty, it can no longer extend financial or economic aid to Turkey.

As in the case of Greece, if Turkey is to have the assistance it needs, the United States must supply it. We are the only country able to provide that help.

I am fully aware of the broad implications involved if the

United States extends assistance to Greece and Turkey, and I shall discuss these implications with you at this time.

One of the primary objectives of the foreign policy of the United States is the creation of conditions in which we and other nations will be able to work out a way of life free from coercion. This was a fundamental issue in the war with Germany and Japan. Our victory was won over countries which sought to impose their will, and their way of life, upon other nations.

To ensure the peaceful development of nations, free from coercion, the United States has taken a leading part in establishing the United Nations. The United Nations is designed to make possible lasting freedom and independence for all its members. We shall not realize our objectives, however, unless we are willing to help free peoples to maintain their free institutions and their national integrity against aggressive movements that seek to impose upon them totalitarian regimes. This is no more than a frank recognition that totalitarian regimes imposed on free peoples, by direct or indirect aggression, undermine the foundations of international peace and hence the security of the United States.

The peoples of a number of countries of the world have recently had totalitarian regimes forced upon them against their will. The Government of the United States has made frequent protests against coercion and intimidation, in violation of the Yalta agreement, in Poland, Rumania, and Bulgaria. I must also state that in a number of other countries there have been similar developments.

At the present moment in world history nearly every nation must choose between alternative ways of life. The choice is too often not a free one.

One way of life is based upon the will of the majority, and is distinguished by free institutions, representative government, free elections, guarantees of individual liberty, freedom of speech and religion, and freedom from political oppression.

The second way of life is based upon the will of a minority forcibly imposed upon the majority. It relies upon terror and oppression, a controlled press and radio, fixed elections, and the suppression of personal freedoms.

I believe that it must be the policy of the United States to support free peoples who are resisting attempted subjugation by armed minorities or by outside pressures.

I believe that we must assist free peoples to work out their own destinies in their own way.

I believe that our help should be primarily through economic and financial aid which is essential to economic stability and orderly political processes.

The world is not static, and the *status quo* is not sacred. But we cannot allow changes in the *status quo* in violation of the Charter of the United Nations by such methods as coercion, or by such subterfuges as political infiltration. In helping free and independent nations to maintain their freedom, the United States will be giving effect to the principles of the Charter of the United Nations.

It is necessary only to glance at a map to realize that the survival and integrity of the Greek nation are of grave importance in a much wider situation. If Greece should fall under the control of an armed minority, the effect upon its neighbor, Turkey, would be immediate and serious. Confusion and disorder might well spread throughout the entire Middle East.

Moreover, the disappearance of Greece as an independent state would have a profound effect upon those countries in Europe whose peoples are struggling against great difficulties to maintain their freedoms and their independence while they repair the damages of war. . . .

Should we fail to aid Greece and Turkey in this fateful hour, the effect will be far-reaching to the West as well as to the East.

We must take immediate and resolute action.

I therefore ask the Congress to provide authority for assistance to Greece and Turkey in the amount of $400,000,000 for the period ending June 30, 1948. . . .

In addition to funds, I ask the Congress to authorize the detail of American civilian and military personnel to Greece and Turkey, at the request of those countries, to assist in the tasks of reconstruction, and for the purpose of supervising the use of such financial and material assistance as may be furnished. I recommend that authority also be provided for the instruction and training of selected Greek and Turkish personnel.

Finally, I ask that the Congress provide authority which will permit the speediest and most effective use, in terms of needed commodities, supplies, and equipment, of such funds as may be authorized. . . .

This is a serious course upon which we embark.

I would not recommend it except that the alternative is much more serious.

The United States contributed $341,000,000,000 toward winning World War II. This is an investment in world freedom and world peace.

The assistance that I am recommending for Greece and Turkey amounts to little more than one tenth of one percent of this investment. It is only common sense that we should safeguard this investment and make sure that it was not in vain.

The seeds of totalitarian regimes are nurtured by misery and want. They spread and grow in the evil soil of poverty and strife. They reach their full growth when the hope of a people for a better life has died.

We must keep that hope alive.

The free peoples of the world look to us for support in maintaining their freedoms.

If we falter in our leadership, we may endanger the peace of the world—and we shall surely endanger the welfare of our own nation.

Great responsibilities have been placed upon us by the swift movement of events.

I am confident that the Congress will face these responsibilities squarely.

2. THE MARSHALL PLAN, 1947*

I need not tell you gentlemen that the world situation is very

---

* An address, "European Recovery," by Secretary of State George C. Marshall, made at commencement exercises at Harvard University, June 5, 1947.

serious. That must be apparent to all intelligent people. I think one difficulty is that the problem is one of such enormous complexity that the very mass of facts presented to the public by press and radio make it exceedingly difficult for the man in the street to reach a clear appraisement of the situation. Furthermore, the people of this country are distant from the troubled areas of the earth and it is hard for them to comprehend the plight and consequent reactions of the long-suffering peoples, and the effect of those reactions on their governments in connection with our efforts to promote peace in the world.

In considering the requirements for the rehabilitation of Europe, the physical loss of life, the visible destruction of cities, factories, mines, and railroads was correctly estimated, but it has become obvious during recent months that this visible destruction was probably less serious than the dislocation of the entire fabric of European economy. For the past 10 years conditions have been highly abnormal. The feverish preparation for war and the more feverish maintenance of the war effort engulfed all aspects of national economies. Machinery has fallen into disrepair or is entirely obsolete. Under the arbitrary and destructive Nazi rule, virtually every possible enterprise was geared into the German war machine. Long-standing commercial ties, private institutions, banks, insurance companies, and shipping companies disappeared, through loss of capital, absorption through nationalization, or by simple destruction. In many countries, confidence in the local currency has been severely shaken. The breakdown of the business structure of Europe during the war was complete. Recovery has been seriously retarded by the fact that two years after the close of hostilities a peace settlement with Germany and Austria has not been agreed upon. But even given a more prompt solution of these difficult problems, the rehabilitation of the economic structure of Europe quite evidently will require a much longer time and greater effort than had been foreseen.

There is a phase of this matter which is both interesting and serious. The farmer has always produced the foodstuffs to exchange with the city dweller for the other necessities of life. This division of labor is the basis of modern civilization. At the present time it is threatened with breakdown. The town and city industries are not producing adequate goods to exchange with the food-producing farmer. Raw materials and fuel are in short supply. Machinery is lacking or worn out. The farmer or the peasant cannot find the goods for sale which he desires to purchase. So the sale of his farm produce for money which he cannot use seems to him an unprofitable transaction. He, therefore, has withdrawn many fields from crop cultivation and is using them for grazing. He feeds more grain to stock and finds for himself and his family an ample supply of food, however short he may be on clothing and the other ordinary gadgets of civilization. Meanwhile people in the cities are short of food and fuel. So the governments are forced to use their foreign money and credits to procure these necessities abroad. This process exhausts funds which are urgently needed for reconstruction. Thus a very serious situation is rapidly developing which bodes no good for the world. The modern system of the division of labor upon which the exchange of products is based is in danger of breaking down.

The truth of the matter is that Europe's requirements for the next three or four years of foreign food and other essential products—principally from America—are so much greater than her present ability to pay that she must have substantial additional help or face economic, social, and political deterioration of a very grave character.

The remedy lies in breaking the vicious circle and restoring the confidence of the European people in the economic future of their own countries and of Europe as a whole. The manufacturer and the farmer throughout wide areas must be able and willing to exchange their products for currencies the continuing value of which is not open to question.

Aside from the demoralizing effect on the world at large and the possibilities of disturbances arising as a result of the desperation of the people concerned, the consequences to the economy of the United States should be apparent to all. It is logical that the United States should do whatever it is able to do to assist in the return of normal economic health in the world, without which there can be no political stability and no assured peace. Our policy is directed not against any country or doctrine but against hunger, poverty, desperation, and chaos. Its purpose should be the revival of a working economy in the world so as to permit the emergence of political and social conditions in which free institutions can exist. Such assistance, I am convinced, must not be on a piece-meal basis as various crises develop. Any assistance that this Government may render in the future should provide a cure rather than a mere palliative. Any government that is willing to assist in the task of recovery will find full cooperation, I am sure, on the part of the United States Government. Any government which maneuvers to block the recovery of other countries cannot expect help from us. Furthermore, governments, political parties, or groups which seek to perpetuate human misery in order to profit therefrom politically or otherwise will encounter the opposition of the United States.

It is already evident that, before the United States Government can proceed much further in its efforts to alleviate the situation and help start the European world on its way to recovery, there must be some agreement among the countries of Europe as to the requirements of the situation and the part those countries themselves will take in order to give proper effect to whatever action might be undertaken by this Government. It would be neither fitting nor efficacious for this Government to undertake to draw up unilaterally a program designed to place Europe on its feet economically. This is the business of the Europeans. The initiative, I think, must come from Europe. The role of this country should consist of friendly aid in the drafting of a European program and of later support of such a program so far as it may be practical for us to do so. The program should be a joint one, agreed to by a number, if not all, European nations.

An essential part of any successful action on the part of the United States is an understanding on the part of the people of America of the character of the problem and the remedies to be applied. Political passion and prejudice should have no part. With foresight, and a willingness on the part of our people to face up to the vast responsibility which history has clearly placed upon our country, the difficulties I have outlined can and will be overcome.

3. THE NORTH ATLANTIC TREATY, 1949*

PREAMBLE

The parties to this treaty reaffirm their faith in the purposes and principles of the Charter of the United Nations and their desire to live in peace with all peoples and all governments.

They are determined to safeguard the freedom, common heritage and civilization of their peoples, founded on the principles of democracy, individual liberty and the rule of law.

They seek to promote stability and well-being in the North Atlantic area.

They are resolved to unite their efforts for collective defense and for the preservation of peace and security.

They therefore agree to this North Atlantic Treaty:

ARTICLE 1

The parties undertake, as set forth in the Charter of the United Nations, to settle any international disputes in which they may be involved by peaceful means in such a manner that international peace and security, and justice, are not endangered, and to refrain in their international relations from the threat or use of force in any manner inconsistent with the purpose of the United Nations.

ARTICLE 2

The parties will contribute toward the further development of peaceful and friendly international relations by strengthening their free institutions, by bringing about a better understanding of the principles upon which these institutions are founded, and by promoting conditions of stability and well-being. They will seek to eliminate conflict in their international economic policies and will encourage economic collaboration between any or all of them.

ARTICLE 3

In order more effectively to achieve the objectives of this treaty, the parties, separately and jointly, by means of continuous and

---

*The treaty was signed in Washington on April 4, 1949, by the United States, Canada, Belgium, Denmark, France, Iceland, Italy, Luxembourg, the Netherlands, Norway, Portugal, and the United Kingdom. In February 1952 Greece and Turkey also acceded to the treaty. The German Federal Republic (West Germany) was admitted to NATO on May 9, 1955.

UNITED STATES COLLECTIVE DEFENSE ARRANGEMENTS

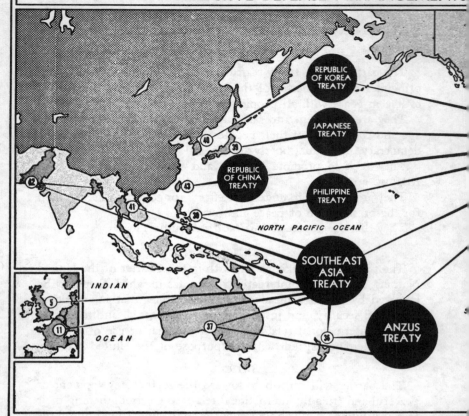

REPUBLIC OF KOREA TREATY

JAPANESE TREATY

REPUBLIC OF CHINA TREATY

PHILIPPINE TREATY

NORTH PACIFIC OCEAN

SOUTHEAST ASIA TREATY

ANZUS TREATY

INDIAN

OCEAN

NORTH ATLANTIC TREATY (15 NATIONS)

A treaty signed April 4, 1949, by which "the parties agree that an armed attack against one or more of them in Europe or North America shall be considered an attack against them all; and . . . each of them . . . will assist the . . . attacked by taking forthwith, individually and in concert with the other Parties, such action as it deems necessary including the use of armed force . . ."

1 UNITED STATES	9 LUXEMBOURG
2 CANADA	10 PORTUGAL
3 ICELAND	11 FRANCE
4 NORWAY	12 ITALY
5 UNITED KINGDOM	13 GREECE
6 NETHERLANDS	14 TURKEY
7 DENMARK	15 FEDERAL REPUBLIC
8 BELGIUM	OF GERMANY

RIO TREATY (21 NATIONS)

A treaty signed September 2, 1947, which provides that an armed attack against any American State "shall be considered as an attack against all the American States and . . . each one . . . undertakes to assist in meeting the attack . . ."

1 UNITED STATES	22 EL SALVADOR	29 PERU
16 MEXICO	23 NICARAGUA	30 BRAZIL
17 CUBA	24 COSTA RICA	31 BOLIVIA
18 HAITI	25 PANAMA	32 PARAGUAY
19 DOMINICAN	26 COLOMBIA	33 CHILE
REPUBLIC	27 VENEZUELA	34 ARGENTINA
20 HONDURAS	28 ECUADOR	35 URUGUAY
21 GUATEMALA		

ANZUS (Australia–New Zealand–United States) TREATY (3 NATIONS)

A treaty signed September 1, 1951, whereby each of the parties "recognizes that an armed attack in the Pacific Area on any of the Parties would be dangerous to its own peace and safety and declares that it would act to meet the common danger in accordance with its constitutional processes."

1 UNITED STATES
36 NEW ZEALAND
37 AUSTRALIA

Reprinted from *The Department of State Bulletin*, March 21, 1955.

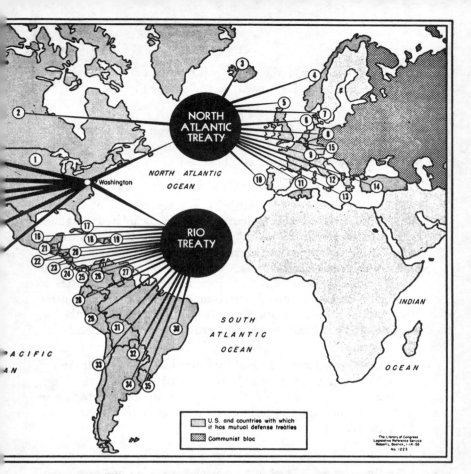

NORTH ATLANTIC TREATY

RIO TREATY

NORTH ATLANTIC OCEAN

SOUTH ATLANTIC OCEAN

INDIAN OCEAN

Washington

□ U.S. and countries with which it has mutual defense treaties

▨ Communist bloc

The Library of Congress
Legislative Reference Service
Robert L. Bostick, 1-14-55
No. 1223

JAPANESE TREATY (BILATERAL)

A treaty signed September 8, 1951, whereby Japan on a provisional basis requests, and the United States agrees, to "maintain certain of its armed forces in and about Japan . . . so as to deter armed attack upon Japan."

**1 UNITED STATES
39 JAPAN**

PHILIPPINE TREATY (BILATERAL)

A treaty signed August 30, 1951, by which the parties recognize "that an armed attack in the Pacific Area on either of the Parties would be dangerous to its own peace and safety" and each party agrees that it will act "to meet the common dangers in accordance with its constitutional processes."

**1 UNITED STATES
38 PHILIPPINES**

REPUBLIC OF KOREA (South Korea) TREATY (BILATERAL)

A treaty signed October 1, 1953, whereby each party "recognizes that an armed attack in the Pacific area on either of the Parties . . . would be dangerous to its own peace and safety" and that each Party "would act to meet the common danger in accordance with its constitutional processes."

**1 UNITED STATES
40 REPUBLIC OF KOREA**

SOUTHEAST ASIA TREATY (8 NATIONS)

A treaty signed September 8, 1954, whereby each Party "recognizes that aggression by means of armed attack in the treaty area against any of the Parties . would endanger its own peace and safety" and each will "in that event act to meet the common danger in accordance with its constitutional processes."

**1 UNITED STATES
5 UNITED KINGDOM
11 FRANCE
36 NEW ZEALAND
37 AUSTRALIA
38 PHILIPPINES
41 THAILAND
42 PAKISTAN**

REPUBLIC OF CHINA (Formosa) TREATY (BILATERAL)

A treaty signed December 2, 1954, whereby each of the parties "recognizes that an armed attack in the West Pacific Area directed against the territories of either of the Parties would be dangerous to its own peace and safety," and that each "would act to meet the common danger in accordance with its constitutional processes." The territory of the Republic of China is defined as "Taiwan (Formosa) and the Pescadores."

**1 UNITED STATES
43 REPUBLIC OF CHINA (FORMOSA)**

effective self-help and mutual aid, will maintain and develop their individual and collective capacity to resist armed attack.

ARTICLE 4

The parties will consult together whenever, in the opinion of any of them, the territorial integrity, political independence or security of any of the parties is threatened.

ARTICLE 5

The parties agree that an armed attack against one or more of them in Europe or North America shall be considered an attack against them all; and consequently they agree that, if such an armed attack occurs, each of them, in exercise of the right of individual or collective self-defense recognized by Article 51 of the Charter of the United Nations, will assist the party or parties so attacked by taking forthwith, individually and in concert with the other parties, such action as it deems necessary, including the use of armed force, to restore and maintain the security of the North Atlantic area.

Any such armed attack and all measures taken as a result thereof shall immediately be reported to the Security Council. Such measures shall be terminated when the Security Council has taken the measures necessary to restore and maintain international peace and security.

ARTICLE 6

For the purpose of Article 5 an armed attack on one or more of the parties is deemed to include attack on the territory of any of the parties in Europe or North America, on the Algerian Departments of France, on the occupation forces of any party in Europe, on the islands under the jurisdiction of any party in the North Atlantic area north of the Tropic of Cancer or on the vessels or aircraft in this area of any of the parties.

ARTICLE 7

This treaty does not affect, and shall not be interpreted as affecting, in any way the rights and obligations under the Charter of the parties which are members of the United Nations, or the

primary responsibility of the Security Council for the maintenance
of international peace and security.

ARTICLE 8

Each party declares that none of the international engagements
now in force between it and any other of the parties or any third
state is in conflict with the provisions of this treaty, and undertakes not to enter into any international engagements in conflict
with this treaty.

ARTICLE 9

The parties hereby establish a Council, on which each of them
shall be represented, to consider matters concerning the implementation of this treaty. The Council shall be so organized as to
be able to meet promptly at any time. The Council shall set up
such subsidiary bodies as may be necessary; in particular it shall
establish immediately a defense committee which shall recommend
measures for the implementation of Articles 3 and 5.

ARTICLE 10

The parties may, by unanimous agreement, invite any other
European state in a position to further the principles of this treaty
and to contribute to the security of the North Atlantic area to
accede to this treaty. Any state so invited may become a party to
the treaty by depositing its instrument of accession with the Government of the United States of America. The Government of
the United States of America will inform each of the parties of
the deposit of each such instrument of accession.

ARTICLE 11

This treaty shall be ratified and its provisions carried out by the
parties in accordance with their respective constitutional processes.
The instruments of ratification shall be deposited as soon as possible with the Government of the United States of America, which
will notify all the other signatories of each deposit. The treaty
shall enter into force between the states which have ratified it as
soon as the ratifications of the majority of the signatories, including the ratifications of Belgium, Canada, France, Luxembourg, the

Netherlands, the United Kingdom and the United States, have been deposited and shall come into effect with respect to other states on the date of the deposit of their ratifications.

ARTICLE 12

After the treaty has been in force for ten years, or at any time thereafter, the parties shall, if any of them so requests, consult together for the purpose of reviewing the treaty, having regard for the factors then affecting peace and security in the North Atlantic area, including the development of universal as well as regional arrangements under the Charter of the United Nations for the maintenance of international peace and security.

ARTICLE 13

After the treaty has been in force for twenty years, any party may cease to be a party one year after its notice of denunciation has been given to the Government of the United States of America, which will inform the Governments of the other parties of the deposit of each notice of denunciation.

ARTICLE 14

This treaty, of which the English and French texts are equally authentic, shall be deposited in the archives of the Government of the United States of America. Duly certified copies thereof will be transmitted by that Government to the Governments of the other signatories.

ISOLATION AND EXPANSION*

BY

WALTER LIPPMANN

[1952]

American history is brief. It is, I know, tiresome to hear this
said again. But we are indeed a young nation. And in remarkable degree, the main ideas with which we approach foreign affairs
are still those of provincial America. They are the ideas which
became habitual during the century and a half before the American nation became a Great Power. The traditional and fundamental themes of American foreign policy are now known as
isolationism. That is a term, however, which must be handled
with the greatest care, or it can do nothing but confuse and
mislead.

It began to be used about 1900 after the Spanish-American
War, but it was not widely used until 1914—until the great debates about American intervention in the two world wars and
about American participation in affairs outside the Western Hemisphere. The word isolation is highly charged with emotion—
with the acute anxiety which twice in this century, so many, on
both sides of the ocean, have suffered, as, facing defeat and disaster, they waited for American intervention, waited until it was
almost too late—waited perhaps until it was too late to make a
good peace. I have shared these anxieties. Yet, speaking as an
old hand in these debates, I should like to point out to you that
the term isolation is misleading as the name of any significant
contemporary American movement in foreign affairs.

During the hard-fought battles over intervention the isolationists were the party of neutrality and of pacifism. They prevailed
in the sense that the American nation refused to enter either world
war until we ourselves were attacked and were, therefore, compelled to go to war. This has caused many abroad and at home to
think of the United States as trying—rather foolishly and in vain

*From *Isolation and Alliances: An American Speaks to the British*, published by Little, Brown and Co. Copyright 1952 by Walter Lippmann.
Reprinted by permission.

151

—to be a kind of big and boisterous Switzerland, a sort of pushing and untidy Sweden—until, at long last, by dint of great argument and exhortation the Americans were aroused, though they are always in danger of relapsing, to do their duty as befits their power in the great world.

According to this legend, the American colonists along the Atlantic seaboard achieved their independence because of the follies of King George III and his Ministers. They found themselves with a vast, an empty and an enormously rich continent at their backs. The legend has it that as they moved into this vacant paradise, they forgot their European heritage. They became wholly immersed in their internal affairs, chiefly in making money. Thanks to the Pax Britannica, they were so secure that they did not need to bother themselves with the affairs of the Old World. In the enjoyment of their too many blessings, which they never seem to weary of boasting about, they became soft and timid—until they were stung into action first by the Kaiser and Admiral von Tirpitz, and then by Hitler and the Japanese.

This is, of course, a false picture and many Europeans are now beginning to appreciate that fact when they discover, often to their dismay, that if it was hard to arouse the sleeping giant, it is also hard to quiet him down again. The term isolationists, and the mythology which has grown up around it, suggest passivity and lethargy. The word isolationist conceals the dynamic and expansionist energy of the American nation. It suggests that the United States did not have a foreign policy until recently. All that is quite untrue. The United States has never been neutral in the European sense. It has always had a very active foreign policy, of which the central purpose has been the determination to expand across the continent from the Atlantic seaboard to the Pacific Ocean.

American foreign policy has been in this sense continuous from the middle of the eighteenth century and throughout the nineteenth century. It has been a policy designed to open up the continental territory, to consolidate that territory firmly within the American union, and to make that territory and the approaches to it invulnerably secure as against all other powers. To accomplish these ends the American people have used diplomacy and war.

The struggle to acquire and consolidate what is now the national territory of the United States lasted until the close of the nineteenth century. It began with the French wars of the eighteenth century. The American colonists participated in these wars, always for American reasons. Officially, so to speak, the struggle for the national territory ended in 1890, when the last of our thirty-seven wars with the Indians was concluded.

Those whom we now call isolationists are the true believers in the foreign policy of the men who conquered and settled the American continental domain. The memory of their struggles against foreign powers, and against the Indians and against the wilderness, has been the living tradition of the Americans who have played leading parts in this century.

Isolationism, then, is not pacifism and withdrawal. It is a deposit of ideas from the experience of conquering, consolidating and securing the national homeland. The traditional American attitude towards European powers, towards alliances with foreign nations, towards war and towards peace, can be understood only when the words of American statesmen—of Washington, Jefferson, Monroe, Wilson, Roosevelt and Truman—are read in the historical context of this struggle for the continent.

American foreign policy has not been so much a reflection of the old colonial cities on the Atlantic seaboard as it has been the instrument of the pioneers and settlers who pushed their way across the Appalachian Mountains into the Mississippi Valley, across the Rocky Mountains and on to the Pacific coast. They did not find that this territory was a vacant paradise. They had to open it up. They had to clear the wilderness. They had by diplomacy and war to work their way past the Great Powers—past Great Britain, France and Spain. They fought the Indians, who in the early days had often been armed against them by the Great Powers. They fought the Mexicans, who were the heirs of Spain in North America.

The famous phrases and injunctions and precepts which are the currency of the American tradition were minted in this struggle.

Consider, for example, Washington's injunction in the Farewell Address, which he published in 1796, when he had decided not to be a candidate for a third term. "The great rule of conduct for us in regard to foreign nations," he said, "is in extending our commercial relations to have with them as little political connection as possible." For, he went on to say, "Europe has a set of primary interests which to us have none or a very remote relation."

When Washington laid down this rule that we must have as little connection as possible with Europe, he had just completed the ratification of Jay's Treaty with the British Government. This treaty was being attacked bitterly on the ground that the United States was being forced to ransom its own property, the northwest posts, by humiliating concessions in commerce, shipping and maritime rights. But Washington and his Cabinet insisted on ratification because the treaty meant that the last frontier post occupied by British soldiers on American soil would be evacuated and the Ohio Valley opened up to settlement. When Washington spoke of political separation from Europe, he was deeply conscious of being surrounded—of being contained—by great unfriendly foreign powers.

Let me say a few words about another of the texts. It is from the address which Thomas Jefferson delivered at his first inauguration in 1801. The famous words are "peace, commerce, and honest friendship with all nations, entangling alliances with none." Shortly after this disavowal of entangling alliances Jefferson performed the diplomatic feat of buying the Louisiana territory from Napoleon Bonaparte. He seized a golden opportunity which was presented to him because France and Great Britain were at war. Jefferson, having no entangling alliance, did in fact negotiate with both powers, and he used his neutral position to make a bargain which brought into the union the Mississippi and Missouri Valleys.

Isolationism, I repeat, is the deposit of this fundamental American foreign policy. The principle of the policy was to keep a free hand in order to expand westward to the continental limits. In any current European usage of the words American isolationism is not neutralist or pacifist. By nature and by mood it is not prudent and it is not retiring. The isolationists of the twentieth century have wished to isolate not merely the American continental domain and the Western Hemisphere. In the last analysis they have wanted to isolate American decisions and actions, to have the final word wherever Americans are involved. They carry with them the thought and feeling which has come down from those who in the eighteenth and nineteenth centuries managed in one way or another, by war and by diplomacy, to expel all the foreign powers who blocked the westward expansion of the American people.

Many other influences have reinforced this basic pattern. Americans have always had a moral conviction that they were conquering a continent not as an empire to be exploited but as Jefferson, or perhaps it was Madison, put it, to be a new domicile of freedom. Americans have never thought of their territorial expansion as imperial conquest. They have always believed that they were opening the territory to all mankind—by which they meant all of the European mankind from which they were themselves descended. It was the European governments which they hoped to see expelled from the New World. The governments, they believed, were political tyrannies. The European social order, moreover, did not recognize that all men are equal. The Americans were mastering a wilderness which was inhabited by savages, and they were opening it up to all men who wished to escape from class, from privilege, from bigotry, and from persecution.

But the new nation formed out of families emigrating from all the countries of Europe was bound to know a certain tension. The ancestral lands in Europe are not altogether foreign. The separation is not complete. In times when feeling runs high, Americans are drawn back to, and then they push themselves away from, the old fatherlands. Whenever the United States has been the ally of one European power and the enemy of another the assimilation of Europeans into the American nationality has been interrupted. This morbid experience is known in America as hyphenization.

The traditional foreign policy—that of regarding the American system as separate from Europe—of keeping Americanism unentangled with loyalties in Europe, is adapted to this inner problem. . . .

Around about the turn of the century the central purpose of the traditional American foreign policy had been achieved. In the eyes of all but a small adventurous and romantic minority our western expansion was completed: in the conquest of the Philippines we had in fact been carried beyond our natural and proper limits.

The Philippines were much too far away to be thought of as destined to become American territory. More than that, a permanent occupation of the Philippines would have violated the basic assumption, the inner moral sanction of the American expansion. Americans had always regarded it as self-evident that any territory they acquired would be organized into states and would be admitted into the Union, and that the inhabitants—who would be predominantly of European stock—would then be assimilated into equal American citizenship.

Americans have never wanted to rule over any territory which could not be admitted as a state into the Union or to govern peoples who could not be assimilated. The Philippines, obviously, could not be admitted into the Union and their people could not be assimilated into the American nation. In American eyes, therefore, they were beyond the natural and the moral limits of American interest and American destiny, and in conquering them from Spain our western expansion had, so to speak, overshot its mark.

The fulfillment of the historic purpose of American policy coincided with the radical change in the world balance of power. The necessary condition under which the United States had been able to expand to the Pacific Ocean and to consolidate its continental territory had been the European equilibrium under the Pax Britannica. The architects of our foreign policy—Washington, Jefferson, the two Adamses, Madison, Monroe—had known quite well that it was the preservation of the balance of power in the Old World which made it possible for the weak nations of the New World to isolate themselves, while they were developing, from interference by the Great Powers of Europe. This had, however, been forgotten by the later generations.

The German challenge of 1914 put in doubt what no American then alive had supposed could ever be put in doubt. It challenged the existing order which was deemed to be natural and not historical. No one in America had anticipated this, and few were prepared to understand it. The nation had always faced towards the west. Now it had to turn around and to recognize that there was a great threat from the rear, where all had so long been so secure.   Instead of continuing to look forward towards the west, where there had always been the American promised lands, the nation had to look backward across the ocean to the countries from which it had come.

Ever since then we have been learning by hard experience that the old order of the world is broken, and that it cannot be restored, and that the making of a new order is a task which our generation may hope to see begun but cannot hope to see completed.

The task of Americans who have had a part in events since 1914 has been to adjust, transform and convert traditional American ideas to the new necessities.   That has been, that is proving to be, a most difficult thing to do.

Within the lives of one generation we have been called upon to remake our fundamental conceptions of the nature of the political world.   By conscious reasoning, by imagination rather than long experience, we are having to transform our deepest habits and our oldest traditions.   I do not think I have misled you in dwelling so much upon the American tradition.   The great revision of the tradition, which history demands of us now, has to be made against the well-nigh instinctive feeling ingrained by the experience of a century and a half, that our expansion, our union as a single nation, and the security which we have enjoyed, were achieved *despite* the powers of Europe—were achieved, to use the contemporary words for these things, not by co-operation but by unilateralism and by insisting upon a free hand.

There lies the explanation of the Wilsonian ideology—the first great American effort to meet the New World situation.   The principles which President Wilson enunciated when we were drawn—so reluctantly and with such deep misgivings—into a war on the continent of Europe were the improvisation of a man who knew he was forced by events to take a course which he, like all the older Americans, thought we had forever renounced.   The Wilsonian doctrine was the adaptation of the American tradition to an unexpected necessity—that of returning to Europe, of fighting on the soil of Europe, and of reuniting politically with European nations.

President Wilson had hoped that he could avoid it, but he was finally driven to accept the necessity of following a policy of inter-

vention in Europe. He was himself, however, an American funda-
mentalist, a sincere and deeply convinced believer in the postulates
of the traditional policy. Only the extreme provocation of the
unlimited submarine war, combined with the dire peril of the
West in 1917, brought him to take the epoch-making decision to
raise an army by conscription and to send it across the Atlantic
Ocean.

The Wilsonian ideology was President Wilson's attempt to
reconcile these new and heretical imperatives with the old, with
his own deeply personal American orthodoxy. The Wilsonian
thesis was, if I may put it in this way, that, since the world was no
longer safe for the American democracy, the American people
were called upon to conduct a crusade to make the world safe for
the American democracy. In order to do this the principles of the
American democracy would have to be made universal throughout
the world. The Wilsonian ideology is American fundamentalism
made into a universal doctrine.

The Wilsonian system of ideas does not recognize that America
is one nation among many other nations with whom it must deal
as rivals, as allies, as partners. The Wilsonian vision is of a world
in which there are no lasting rivalries, where there are no deep
conflicts of interest, where no compromises of principle have to be
made, where there are no separate spheres of influence, and no
alliances. In this world there will be no wars except universal
war against criminal governments who rebel against the universal
order. The Wilsonian ideology is a crusading doctrine, generating
great popular fervor from the feeling that war is an intolerable
criminal interference with the nature of things. The necessity of
going to war is an outrage upon our privacy and upon our rights.

Therefore, all wars are wars to end wars, all wars are crusades
which can be concluded only when all the peoples have submitted
to the only true political religion. There will be peace only when
all the peoples hold and observe the same self-evident principles.

In the Wilsonian ideology an aggression is an armed rebellion
against the universal and eternal principles of the world society.
No war can end rightly, therefore, except by the unconditional
surrender of the aggressor nation and by the overthrow and transformation of its political regime.

The Wilsonian ideology has, it is fair to say, dominated American political thinking and has shaped American policy ever since it was formulated. As late as 1943, for example, Secretary Hull, who was a personal disciple of Wilson, and a lifelong true believer, came home from the Moscow Conference and announced that "as the provisions of the four-nation declaration were carried into effect there will no longer be need for spheres of influence, for alliances, for balance of power, or any other of the special arrangements by which, in the unhappy past, the nations strove to safeguard their security or to promote their interests."

One can hardly exaggerate the compelling, and until very recently, the all-pervading acceptance of this ideology. The explanation of its enormous influence is, as I have been arguing, that in its motives, its modes and its manners, the Wilsonian ideology is a twentieth-century variant of the historic American fundamentalism.

In all the debates, beginning in 1914, and in the debates which are still in progress—for example over the appropriations for foreign aid in the present Congress—the Wilsonian ideology has shaped the arguments of those who have favored intervention, participation in the League of Nations and the United Nations, the Truman Doctrine, the Marshall Plan, the North Atlantic Treaty, the intervention in Korea, the Mutual Security Act.

One can argue, in fact it is often argued at home, that this extraordinary series of measures could never have won popular support unless the highly charged emotions of the Wilsonian ideology had been aroused to support them. The American people and the Congress, it is argued, would have refused and resisted these measures had they not been backed by the proclamation of crusades against the Germans, the Japanese, the Soviets, the Chinese Communists, and Communism in general—had the American people not been fired by promises that these crusades would end in a universal order where all peoples, including the objects of the current crusade, would swear allegiance to the same purposes and would observe the same principles.

There is no denying that this has been the easiest and the quickest way to force through Congress measures which call for the use of American troops and the appropriation of American money for grants abroad. But this method of dealing with our people has, as many are now coming to see, established no political and moral foundation for a settled and steadfast policy. The great Utopian promises have too often turned out to be dust and ashes, and they no longer arouse the fervor and the ardent hopes of 1918 and of 1945.

The measures, it is becoming evident to many, which are promoted by resorting to the ideological incitement, by applying the technique of the crusade, tend to become gravely, and sometimes irreparably, deformed in the very process of getting them enacted. The original ends and intentions of these measures have been almost invariably noble and necessary. But the means employed to carry Congress and the people to accept those ends have often aggravated the troubles which the measures were meant to alleviate.

In my view it is becoming increasingly plain that the Wilsonian ideology is an impossible foundation for the foreign policy of a nation, placed as we are and carrying the burden of our responsibilities. Our people are coming to realize that in this century one crusade has led to another. After the first crusade we were not able to prevent the next war that was coming. We were not prepared for the war when we had to fight it. And twice we have not known how to settle the war when we had won it. Twice in one generation we have gone around this deadly cycle.

Voices are beginning to be heard, asking whether we can break the deadly cycle, and by taking thought and by mastering ourselves resist the destructive impulses of our democracy—which is to be too pacifist in time of peace and too bellicose in time of war. In this deadly cycle of pacifism and bellicosity we, and perhaps the other democracies as well, have wanted disarmament, neutrality, isolation, and if necessary appeasement. Then, as the wars which we did not avert, which we entered reluctantly and unready, rose to their climax of violence and victory, we have felt that our righteous wrath could do with nothing less than unconditional surrender, total victory, the total reform and regeneration of the vanquished—all of them the necessary conditions of the everlasting peace in which we could again disarm ourselves and could again relapse into a private and self-regarding existence.

There is, I need hardly tell you, no ready-made and well-tested philosophy and doctrine of international society which we can confidently and easily turn to. I do not suppose you have such a doctrine and philosophy either, or we should have heard something about it from you. But perhaps together, by genuine frankness in our discourse with one another, we may be able to fashion out of the old wisdom of mankind and a fresh appreciation of the new realities a philosophy which can guide our policy. . . .

DISENTANGLEMENT*

BY

JOSEPH P. KENNEDY

[1951]

Peace is, of course, the broad objective of American foreign policy. The survival of our democratic institutions, our country, even our civilization depends upon how successful we are in attaining that objective. For to fail means war, which in turn destroys lives, institutions and ideals, which no amount of money or energy can ever rebuild. The consequences of war, whether it ends in victory or defeat, is to move us inevitably toward making the state more and more the master of the individual. Inevitably reconstruction ushers in some form of state control, such as the socialistic pattern that now dominates Western Europe, and the very institutions whose preservation may have been the motivation for war are themselves destroyed by war's overpowering demands. Modern war, in short, solves nothing.

But a foreign policy that is short of war, has an overpowering influence on everything else we do. It, and not domestic needs, determines the size of our budgets and the amount of our taxes. Tax reform, even the correction of tax scandals, is a drop in the bucket beside the tremendous drain of the billions demanded by the direction of our present foreign policy. That policy, and not the absence of some scheme of controls, is what is responsible for inflation, for the cheapening of the dollar and ever-higher prices —a process which has only just begun and whose end no one can foresee. That policy determines how much we can and dare expend for social services. It will determine whether we, as a nation, can continue to afford them on our present scale or on any satisfactory basis. Indeed foreign policy permeates all trade, all commerce, all living.

* From "Our Foreign Policy, Its Casualties and Prospects," an address before the Economic Club of Chicago, December 17, 1951. Reprinted by special permission. Joseph P. Kennedy (1888–1969), businessman and diplomat, was United States Ambassador to Great Britain, 1937–1941.

Our foreign policy since 1946 is said to have been dominated by the threat of expansion on the part of Communist Russia. The re-arming of Greece and Turkey, the Marshall Plan, the Korean War, are all ascribed to that cause. Russian tactics have, however, been directed toward weakening the democratic states of the world in order to permit the entry of Communism and its doctrines. If we measure the success of our foreign policy in terms of its checking of that tactic, we appear to be on the edge of failure. For, today, without firing a single shot or sacrificing the life of a single soldier, the Russians have impoverished most of Western Europe, forced upon us peacetime expenditures beyond what could have been their wildest hopes, taken from us the long traditional friendship of a nation of more than 400,000,000 Chinese, and in Korea brought tragedy or death to more than 100,000 American homes. Certainly, we are infinitely worse off today than we were in 1946.

Just a year ago, at Charlottesville, in raising a series of questions with regard to our foreign policy, I touched off what became known as the Great Debate. I said then that we were wasting our resources in the pursuit of a dream which, worthy though it might be, was impossible of accomplishment. I said then that, instead of scattering our dollars and our troops throughout Europe, we would do well to think first of our own destiny and its realization, and second of how within our capabilities we could assist those whose ideals were such that they would wholeheartedly link their survival to ours. I also said then that the chief fortress of resistance must be ourselves, not Europe, not Korea, not even the United Nations, although we might, indeed, from the largesse of our own industrial output help those who made clear that they were willing to help themselves. . . .

The basic difficulty is . . . policy—a policy that purports to reach for security by reliance on the United Nations, and on alliances with nations from Norway to Australia. It is a policy that builds on the theory that our dollars can buy things that are not purchasable—the will to resist, the will to re-arm, the will to fight in another man's cause. From a one-time conception of generous economic aid, our policy is made to appear as an attempt to make Europe a breeding ground of Hessian troops. . . .

Realizing the ineffectiveness of the United Nations as an agency to preserve the peace, we have reached out under the guise of collective security to build smaller and more malleable aggregates of nations. In the Atlantic, we have formed the North Atlantic Treaty Organization. In the Pacific, we have guaranteed the integrity of Australia and New Zealand. In the Middle East, we have proposed the imposition of a Middle East Command on the nations of that explosive area. Perhaps, our next effort will be to ally to ourselves the Eskimos of the North Pole and the Penguins of the Antarctic.

Such alliances have a meaning if they are the source of strength; otherwise, they provide nothing but weakness. Today aggression anywhere within this huge perimeter is potentially an act of war against the United States. Its occurrence automatically authorizes the President, without reference to the Congress of the United States, to use all the armed forces at his disposal, even the atomic bomb, in repelling that far-off aggression. Just as England in 1939, by its guaranty of Polish territorial integrity, made its power to declare war hinge on events over which it had no control, by our guaranty to maintain peace in an area that stretches now from the Dardanelles to the North Cape, we have delegated to others the power to determine our own fate. We were once strong enough to be able to neglect, so far as conscription and mobilization were concerned, wars between the British and the Boers or the Russians and the Japanese. Today, a student riot in Cairo, a pistol shot in Athens, and, as in the case of Korea, we can be committed before there has been time to seek the sober judgment of the Congress of the United States.

This forming of regional alliances purports to pursue the policy of collective security. In theory, through grants to other nations, we seek to achieve parity with the Communist world at points and on borders far removed from our shores. Some thirty billion dollars have already been spent or allocated for that purpose in Europe alone. . . .

The chances of realizing this policy of parity on European soil seem small, but let us assume we do succeed. Suppose that the billions of dollars necessary for such an achievement would have been forthcoming in some ration from us and our allies. What happens next? This is a question to which the men who have proposed this policy must address themselves—given parity with Russia, given the achievement of their goals, what next?

I see only three choices—war, disarmament, or the continuation of parity. The first is horrible to contemplate. It may be that given parity, the chances of war are lessened, but neither you nor I can cite history to prove that. The second choice of disarmament, as recent events indicate, will be unacceptable, particularly since Soviet Russia knows that if she rejects or delays such a choice, she can force us to the third choice—that of the maintenance of parity. Since armaments quickly become obsolescent and need replacement, this will mean the continuation of vast expenditures for the North Atlantic world. It will mean continuing a huge wastage of manpower. Already the demands of conscription are beginning to dry up the sources of our own technical strength. Fewer engineers, fewer chemists, fewer professional men of every category are being trained this year than last, and many fewer will be trained next year and the years that stretch out after that. Taxes will remain extravagantly high and life regimented to the austere needs of a war economy. It is not too difficult to predict that our democratic institutions cannot long survive such a strain. The very economics of such a situation spells disaster and in that disaster Communism or some form of totalitarianism will arise. Russia, on the other hand, can easily continue on her present course. She need do nothing more. Once more, she will have won a stupendous victory without losing a single soldier or firing a single shot.

If this is to be the outcome of our present policy, assuming the successful realization of its goal of parity, it is obviously self-defeating. It will destroy exactly what it hopes to achieve. No wonder Europe reacts toward us with a dull fatalism that sees defeat wherever she turns and sees hope only in the revival of a belief in asserting herself for herself rather than for us. She is tired of our present method, so aptly described as "an approach by reproach." Neither our dollars nor our persistent reprovals to European statesmen for failing to accept our patterns will move them, for they begin to see more clearly, I believe, than we do, the end-result of our actions. . . .

In Asia and in the Middle East, the defection from this American leadership is even more evident. Whether it be Arab or Indian, no patriot of that area wants to become the pawn in a battle between East and West. Anti-Communist as the government of India is, her Prime Minister, watching the Communist states bordering India on the north, hesitates in the light of India's great internal weaknesses to follow us in a policy that inevitably makes tenser situations already tense enough. Were I of his race, I could easily join in his hesitation. In the Middle East, the defection is even worse, for there, anti-Westernism is turning more and more to Russia and her promises. The seriousness of this defection in the Middle East cannot be over-estimated, for it must be remembered that the Moslem World, whose loyalties run to that area, stretches westward to Morocco and eastward to the Philippines.

Obviously, there must be some answer other than that which has been fashioned for us over these last years. For the billions of dollars we have spent, we deserve more fruits than the loss of friendships, ever-increasing hazards, economic insecurity, and a war that we were told once is no war and about which, as it has been so neatly put, even now we cannot seem to make up our minds whether to win it or lose it or just to let it sit there.

The answer, of course, does not lie in the severance of our relationships abroad. Sinews of our strength and nerve tissues of our culture reach out to many lands and many peoples. Certainly we have neither the desire nor the intention to turn our backs on the rest of the world with whose welfare and whose security we have an intimate concern.

But our policy, for the past four years, has achieved for the rest of the world neither its welfare nor its security. Instead, it has endangered both. Nor has it furthered our defense. The threat of Russia lies not in the expanse of her territory but in her military might. We have expanded our territory at the expense of our military might.

I come, therefore, to suggestions that I believe would make our foreign policy meaningful and make for our security as well as for the peace and security of the world. There are at least four of them.

First: we must make certain of the economic, political and military strength of this country. For, if America collapses, the democratic world collapses. No one will create a Marshall Plan for us. Youth must be certain that life offers repayment for ambition and hard work and not see itself destined either for bureaucratic mediocrity or to having its earnings siphoned away by a crushing burden of taxation. Similarly, the savings of our great middle class must be kept intact and not be destroyed by depreciating their value in terms of goods. Both of these are already in danger by spending that has been unproductive and wasteful. This does not mean that we cannot afford or should not spend adequately and even lavishly in our own defense. We can afford that, but we cannot re-arm all the rest of the democratic world and expect also to arm ourselves. That burden would weigh so heavily upon us as to destroy the sense of individual incentive that is central to our democratic institutions and to American life. If we lose ideals because of making it impossible to realize them, we lose the very things we had hoped to save.

Second: we must develop the resources of this hemisphere. We have put billions, by way of lend-lease and Marshall Plan aid, into the development of the resources of other nations in West Africa, in Iran, in Burma, in Malaya. They can too easily be imperilled. . . . Burmese tin and Malayan rubber, are even now in danger. As against these billions, we have put only thousands into the defensible and accessible resources of our neighbors to the South. The oil of Venezuela and the tin of Bolivia lie closer to us than the oil of the Persian Gulf and the tin of Sumatra. It is just plain horse-sense to shorten as much as possible the perimeter of self-sufficiency, rather than to expand it to embrace the world.

Third: we should make a realistic re-appraisal of the needs of Europe or the Middle East or any other region for that matter, and see what we can or should do about them. What we have done has produced neither political or economic stability in Europe—matters essential to the creation of any defensive force in that area.

There is much our European allies can do for themselves which they should do for themselves. If they are unwilling to do what it is within their power to do to restore their productivity, they will be useless allies in a fight. . . .

Certainly all of us wish and desire the friendship of Western Europe, for without that friendship, Europe's industrial productivity means nothing to us. The curious fact is that today, despite our admitted generosity, we have failed to gain that friendship, and we should find out why this is so, before we continue down the same road that we have been travelling. Normally, any man in a fight welcomes assistance. Is it that Europe does not conceive of herself as being in a fight and thus fears the very proffer of our help because it forces her to take sides on an issue of our making rather than hers? If so, there is nothing basic upon which we can build. Or is it that the manner or the nature of the help that we are ready to offer is somehow contrary to her own traditions and aims? If so, we must find a different and more effective means of approach. Or is it that she wants us to shoulder substantially the whole burden of her defense effort? If so, in our interest, we must respectfully decline.

These are questions that must be answered before we can shape for the years to come any realistic and productive program of European aid. We must find an approach that does not seek to superimpose upon Europe patterns of our thinking that may well be contrary to age-old traditions and aims, or patterns that encourage nations not to tackle on their own responsibility problems within their own capabilities to solve. Western Europe's strength has been sapped greatly by war and the loss of portions of her colonial empires. We cannot pretend that this is not so and in an ostrich-like fashion seek to bury those facts by a flood of dollars. To do so is suicidal for Europe; it is equally suicidal for us.

Fourth: we must seek to disentangle ourselves from the far-flung commitments that we have recently made. Today, a border incident in Norway is an act of aggression against the United States. I do not say that such an act should not be a cause of war, but I do say that whether such an act should be treated as a cause for war should be a matter for our determination and not that of some foreign power. And by our determination, I mean the determination of the Congress and not that of the President. In short, I would restore to Congress its constitutional power to make war.

Disentanglement of our commitments requires a similar reversal of our attitude towards the United Nations. We can look to it for a forum to exchange ideas, but not for governance. It cannot govern; it cannot reconcile, as diplomacy has reconciled, conflicting claims. To base, as our present spokesmen say they do, the core of their policy on the United Nations is simply to spread abroad as our policy the vacillation, the indetermination of that organization. America had a clearer voice when she spoke directly to the world rather than through the throat of that assembly.

Peace, I said, is the objective of our foreign policy. But today there is no peace. . . . There are the clouds of dust cast up by atomic explosions in Nevada and in the wastes of Siberia. . . . There are sirens in New York and in Seattle, and millions of men and women devoted not to productive enterprise but to the building of guns and tanks and guided missiles.

It was remarked about a month ago that foreign policy should not be an issue of our coming political campaigns. But if there ever was a need to discuss it, to explore it, and to assay it, that need is now. We must somehow find stars to steer our course by, somehow avoid the thunderheads of war and the equally treacherous fog of an embattled peace. To do so will require the best that is in us. But with the help of God, we may again be able, as young men and old, to live not for today but for a morrow of dreams and freedom and an ever-abounding life.

THE GOAL OF AN ATLANTIC PARTNERSHIP *

BY

JOHN F. KENNEDY

[1962]

It is a high honor for any citizen of the great Republic to speak at this hall of independence on this day of independence. . . .

Today, 186 years later, that Declaration—whose yellowing parchment and fading, almost illegible lines I saw in the past week in the National Archives in Washington—is still a revolutionary document. To read it today is to hear a trumpet call. For that Declaration unleashed not merely a revolution against the British but a revolution in human affairs. Its authors were highly conscious of its worldwide implications, and George Washington declared that liberty and self-government were, in his words, "finally staked on the experiment intrusted to the hands of the American people."

This prophecy has been borne out for 186 years. This doctrine of national independence has shaken the globe, and it remains the most powerful force anywhere in the world today. There are those struggling to eke out a bare existence in a barren land who have never heard of free enterprise but who cherish the idea of independence. There are those who are grappling with overpowering problems of illiteracy and ill health and who are ill equipped to hold free elections, but they are determined to hold fast to their national independence. Even those unwilling or unable to take part in any struggle between East and West are strongly on the side of their own national independence. If there is a single issue in the world today which divides the world, it is independence— the independence of Berlin or Laos or Viet-Nam, the longing for independence behind the Iron Curtain, the peaceful transition to independence in those newly emerging areas whose troubles some hope to exploit.

* Selections from an address by President John F. Kennedy at Independence Hall, Philadelphia, Pennsylvania, July 4, 1962. Reprinted from *The Department of State Bulletin,* July 23, 1962.

The theory of independence—as old as man himself—was not invented in this hall, but it was in this hall that the theory became a practice—that the word went out to all the world that "The God who gave us life, gave us liberty at the same time."

And today this nation—conceived in revolution, nurtured in liberty, matured in independence—has no intention of abdicating its leadership in that worldwide movement for independence to any nation or society committed to systematic human suppression.

As apt and applicable as this historic Declaration of Independence is today, we would do well to honor that other historic document drafted in this hall—the Constitution of the United States—for it stressed not independence but interdependence, not the individual liberty of one but the indivisible liberty of all.

In most of the old colonial world the struggle for independence is coming to an end. Even in areas behind the Curtain, that which Jefferson called "the disease of liberty" still appears to be infectious. With the passing of ancient empires, today less than 2 percent of the world's population lives in territories officially termed "dependent." As this effort for independence, inspired by the spirit of the American Declaration of Independence, now approaches a successful close, a great new effort—for interdependence—is transforming the world about us. And the spirit of that new effort is the same spirit which gave birth to the American Constitution.

That spirit is today most clearly seen across the Atlantic Ocean. The nations of Western Europe, long divided by feuds more bitter than any which existed among the Thirteen Colonies, are joining together, seeking, as our forefathers sought, to find freedom in diversity and unity in strength.

The United States looks on this vast new enterprise with hope and admiration. We do not regard a strong and united Europe as a rival but as a partner. To aid its progress has been the basic objective of our foreign policy for 17 years. We believe that a united Europe will be capable of playing a greater role in the common defense, of responding more generously to the needs of poorer nations, of joining with the United States and others in lowering trade barriers, resolving problems of currency and commodities, and developing coordinated policies in all other economic, diplomatic, and political areas. We see in such a Europe a partner with whom we could deal on a basis of full equality in all the great and burdensome tasks of building and defending a community of free nations.

It would be premature at this time to do more than to indicate the high regard with which we view the formation of this partnership. The first order of business is for our European friends to go forward in forming the more perfect union which will some day make this partnership possible.

A great new edifice is not built overnight. It was 11 years from the Declaration of Independence to the writing of the Constitution. The construction of workable Federal institutions required still another generation. The greatest works of our nation's founders lay not in documents and declarations but in creative, determined action. The building of the new house of Europe has followed this same practical and purposeful course. Building the Atlantic partnership will not be cheaply or easily finished.

But I will say here and now on this day of independence that the United States will be ready for a "Declaration of Interdependence," that we will be prepared to discuss with a United Europe the ways and means of forming a concrete Atlantic partnership, a mutually beneficial partnership between the new union now emerging in Europe and the old American Union founded here 175 years ago.

All this will not be completed in a year, but let the world know it is our goal.

In urging the adoption of the United States Constitution, Alexander Hamilton told his fellow New Yorkers to "think continentally." Today Americans must learn to think intercontinentally.

Acting on our own by ourselves, we cannot establish justice throughout the world. We cannot insure its domestic tranquillity, or provide for its common defense, or promote its general welfare, or secure the blessings of liberty to ourselves and our posterity. But joined with other free nations, we can do all this and more. We can assist the developing nations to throw off the yoke of poverty. We can balance our worldwide trade and payments at the highest possible level of growth. We can mount a deterrent powerful enough to deter any aggression, and ultimately we can help achieve a world of law and free choice, banishing the world of war and coercion.

For the Atlantic partnership of which I speak would not look inward only, preoccupied with its own welfare and advancement. It must look outward to cooperate with all nations in meeting their common concern. It would serve as a nucleus for the eventual union of all free men—those who are now free and those who are avowing that some day they will be free.

On Washington's birthday in 1861, standing right there, President-elect Abraham Lincoln spoke at this hall on his way to the Nation's Capital. And he paid a brief and eloquent tribute to the men who wrote, and fought for, and who died for, the Declaration of Independence. Its essence, he said, was its promise not only of liberty "to the people of this country, but hope to the world . . . (hope) that in due time the weights would be lifted from the shoulders of all men, and that all should have an equal chance."

On this 4th day of July 1962, we who are gathered at this same hall, entrusted with the fate and future of our States and Nation, declare now our vow to do our part to lift the weights from the shoulders of all, to join other men and nations in preserving both peace and freedom, and to regard any threat to the peace or freedom of one as a threat to the peace and freedom of all. "And for the support of this Declaration, with a firm reliance on the Protection of Divine Providence, we mutually pledge to each other our Lives, our Fortunes and our sacred Honor."

DILEMMAS OF THE WESTERN ALLIANCE *

BY

HENRY A. KISSINGER

[1969]

No area of policy illustrates more dramatically the tensions between political multipolarity and military bipolarity than the field of alliance policy. For a decade and a half after the Second World War, the United States identified security with alliances. A global network of relationships grew up based on the proposition that deterrence of aggression required the largest possible grouping of powers.

This system of alliances was always in difficulty outside the Atlantic area because it tried to apply principles drawn from the multipolar world of the eighteenth and nineteenth centuries when several major powers of roughly equal strength existed. Then, indeed, it was impossible for one country to achieve dominance if several others combined to prevent it. But this was not the case in the era of the superpowers of the forties and fifties. Outside Europe, our allies added to our strength only marginally; they were in no position to reinforce each other's capabilities.

Alliances, to be effective, must meet four conditions: (1) a common objective—usually defense against a common danger; (2) a degree of joint policy at least sufficient to define the *casus belli;* (3) some technical means of cooperation in case common action is decided upon; (4) a penalty for noncooperation—that is, the possibility of being refused assistance must exist—otherwise protection will be taken for granted and the mutuality of obligation will break down.

In the system of alliances developed by the United States after the Second World War, these conditions have never been met

* From *American Foreign Policy,* published by W.W. Norton, copyright 1969 by Henry A. Kissinger. Reprinted by permission. Henry A. Kissinger (b. 1923) is currently Assistant to the President for National Security Affairs. He had been Professor of Government at Harvard University. His publications include *The Necessity for Choice* and *The Troubled Partnership.*

outside the North Atlantic Treaty Organization (NATO). In the Southeast Asia Treaty Organization (SEATO) and the Central Treaty Organization (CENTO), to which we belong in all but name, there has been no consensus as to the danger. Pakistan's motive for obtaining U.S. arms was not security against a Communist attack but protection against India. The Arab members of CENTO armed not against the U.S.S.R. but against Israel. Lacking a conception of common interests, the members of these alliances have never been able to develop common policies with respect to issues of war and peace. Had they been able to do so, such policies might well have been stillborn anyway, because the technical means of cooperation have been lacking. Most allies have neither the resources nor the will to render mutual support. A state which finds it difficult to maintain order or coherence of policy at home does not increase its strength by combining with states suffering similar disabilities.

In these circumstances, SEATO and CENTO have grown moribund as instruments of collective action. Because the United States has often seemed more eager to engage in the defense of its SEATO and CENTO allies than they themselves, they have become convinced that noncooperation will have no cost. In fact, they have been able to give the impression that it would be worse for us than for them if they fell to Communism. SEATO and CENTO have become, in effect, unilateral American guarantees. At best, they provide a legal basis for bilateral U.S. aid.

The case is different with NATO. Here we are united with countries of similar traditions and domestic structures. At the start, there was a common conception of the threat. The technical means for cooperation existed. Mechanisms for developing common policies came into being—especially in the military field. Thus in its first decade and a half, NATO was a dynamic and creative institution.

Today, however, NATO is in disarray as well. Actions by the United States—above all, frequent unilateral changes of policy— are partially responsible. But the most important cause is the transformation of the international environment, specifically the decline in the preeminence of the superpowers and the emergence of political multipolarity. Where the alliances outside of Europe have never been vital because they failed to take into account the military bipolarity of the fifties, NATO is in difficulties because it has yet to adjust to the political multipolarity of the late sixties.

When NATO was founded in 1949, Europeans had a dual fear: the danger of an imminent Soviet attack and the prospect of eventual U.S. withdrawal. In the late 1960s, however, the fear of Soviet invasion has declined. Even the attack on Czechoslovakia is likely to restore anxiety about Soviet military aggression only temporarily. At the same time, two decades of American military presence in Europe coupled with American predominance in NATO planning have sharply reduced the fear that America might wash its hands of European concerns.

When NATO was formed, moreover, the principal threat to world peace seemed to lie in a Soviet attack on Europe. In recent years, the view has grown that equally grave risks are likely to arise in trouble spots outside Europe. To most Europeans, these do not appear as immediate threats to their independence or security. The irony here is striking. In the fifties, Europeans were asking for American assistance in Asia and the Middle East with the argument that they were defending the greater interests of freedom. The United States replied that these very interests required American aloofness. Today, the roles are precisely reversed. It is Europe that evades our entreaties to play a global role; that is to say, Europeans do not consider their interests at stake in America's extra-European involvement.

These are symptoms of deeper, structural problems, however. One problem, paradoxically, is the growth of European economic strength and political self-confidence. At the end of the Second World War, Europe was dependent on the United States for economic assistance, political stability, and military protection. As long as Europe needed the shelter of a superpower, American predominance was inevitable. In relations with the United States, European statesmen acted as lobbyists rather than as diplomats. Their influence depended less on the weight of their countries than on the impact of their personalities. A form of consultation evolved whereby Europeans sought to influence American actions by giving us a reputation to uphold or—to put it more crudely—by oscillating between flattery and almost plaintive appeals for reassurance. The

United States, secure in its predominance, in turn concentrated on soothing occasional European outbreaks of insecurity rather than on analyzing their causes.

Tutelage is a comfortable relationship for the senior partner, but it is demoralizing in the long run. It breeds illusions of omniscience on one side and attitudes of impotent irresponsibility on the other. In any event, the United States could not expect to perpetuate the accident of Europe's postwar exhaustion into a permanent pattern of international relations. Europe's economic recovery inevitably led to a return to more traditional political pressures.

These changes in Europe were bound to lead to a difficult transitional period. They could have resulted in a new partnership between the United States and an economically resurgent and politically united Europe, as had been envisaged by many of the early advocates of Atlantic unity. However, the European situation has not resolved itself in that way. Thoughtful Europeans know that Europe must unite in some form if it is to play a major role in the long run. They are aware, too, that Europe does not make even approximately the defense effort of which it is capable. But European unity is stymied, and domestic politics has almost everywhere dominated security policy. The result is a massive frustration which expresses itself in special testiness toward the United States.

These strains have been complicated by the growth of Soviet nuclear power. The changed nature of power in the modern period has affected NATO profoundly. As the risks of nuclear war have become enormous, the credibility of traditional pledges of support has inevitably been reduced. In the past, a country would carry out a commitment because, it could plausibly be argued, the consequences of not doing so were worse than those of coming to the ally's assistance. This is no longer self-evident. In each of the last three annual statements by the Secretary of Defense on the U.S. defense posture, the estimate of *dead* in a general nuclear war ranged from 40 to 120 million. This figure will, if anything, increase. It will become more and more difficult to demonstrate that *anything* is worse than the elimination of over half of a society in a matter of days. The more NATO relies on strategic nuclear war as a counter to all forms of attack, the less credible its pledges will be.

The consciousness of nuclear threat by the two superpowers has undermined allied relationships in yet another way. For understandable reasons, the superpowers have sought to make the nuclear environment more predictable—witness the nuclear test ban treaty and the nonproliferation treaty. But the blind spot in our policy has been the failure to understand that, in the absence of full consultation, our allies see in these talks the possible forerunner of a more comprehensive arrangement affecting their vital interests negotiated without them. Strategic arms talks thus emphasize the need of political understanding in acute form. The pattern of negotiating an agreement first and then giving our allies an opportunity—even a full one—to comment is intolerable in the long run. It puts the onus of failure on them, and it prevents them from doing more than quibble about a framework with which they may disagree. Strains have been reinforced by the uncertain American response to the Soviet invasion of Czechoslovakia— especially the reluctance to give up the prospect of a summit meeting. Atlantic relations, for all their seeming normalcy, thus face a profound crisis.

This state of affairs has been especially difficult for those Americans who deserve most credit for forging existing Atlantic relations. Two decades of hegemony have produced the illusion that present Atlantic arrangements are "natural," that wise policy consists of making the existing framework more tolerable. "Leadership" and "partnership" are invoked, but the content given to these words is usually that which will support the existing pattern. European unity is advocated to enable Europeans to share burdens on a world-wide scale.

Such a view fails to take into account the realities of political multipolarity. The aim of returning to the "great days of the Marshall Plan" is impossible. Nothing would sunder Atlantic relationships so surely as the attempt to reassert the notions of leadership appropriate to the early days of NATO. In the bipolar world of the forties and fifties, order could be equated with military security; integrated command arrangements sufficed as the principal bond of unity. In the sixties, security, while still important, has not been enough. Every crisis from Berlin to Czechoslovakia has seen the call for "strengthening NATO" confined to military dispositions. Within months a malaise has become obvious again because the overriding need for a common political conception has not been recognized. The challenge of the seventies will be to forge unity with political measures.

It is not "natural" that the major decisions about the defense of an area so potentially powerful as Western Europe should be made three thousand miles away. It is not "normal" that Atlantic policies should be geared to American conceptions. In the forties and fifties, practicing unity—through formal resolutions and periodic reassurances—was profoundly important as a symbol of the end of our isolationism. In the decade ahead, we cannot aim at unity as an end in itself; it must emerge from common conceptions and new structures.

"Burden-sharing" will not supply that impetus. Countries do not assume burdens because it is fair, only because it is necessary. While there are strong arguments for Atlantic partnership and European unity, enabling Europe to play a global role is not one of them. A nation assumes responsibilities not only because it has resources but because it has a certain view of its own destiny. Through the greater part of its history—until the Second World War—the United States possessed the resources but not the philosophy for a global role. Today, the poorest Western European country—Portugal—has the widest commitments outside Europe because its historic image of itself has become bound up with its overseas possessions. This condition is unlikely to be met by any other European country—with the possible exception of Great Britain—no matter what its increase in power. Partially as the result of decolonization, Europeans are unlikely to conduct a significant global policy whatever their resources or their degree of unity. Cooperation between the United States and Europe must concentrate on issues within the Atlantic area rather than global partnership.

Even within the Atlantic area, a more equitable distribution of responsibilities has two prerequisites: there must be some consensus in the analysis of the international situation, at least as it affects Europe; there must be a conviction that the United States cannot or will not carry all the burdens alone. Neither condition is met today. The traditional notion of American leadership tends to stifle European incentives for autonomy. Improved consultation —the remedy usually proposed—can only alleviate, not remove, the difficulty.

The problem of consultation is complex, of course. No doubt unilateral American action has compounded the uneasiness produced by American predominance and European weakness. The shift in emphasis of American policy, from the NATO multilateral force to the nonproliferation treaty, and frequent unilateral changes in strategic doctrine, have all tended to produce disquiet and to undermine the domestic position of ministers who had staked their futures on supporting the American viewpoint.

It is far from self-evident, however, that more extensive consultation within the existing framework can be more than a palliative. One problem concerns technical competence. In any large bureaucracy—and an international consultative process has many similarities to domestic administrative procedures—the weight given to advice bears some relation to the competence it reflects. If one partner possesses all the technical competence, the process of consultation is likely to remain barren. The minimum requirement for effective consultation is that each ally have enough knowledge to give meaningful advice.

But there are even more important limits to the process of consultation. The losing party in a domestic dispute has three choices: (a) it can accept the setback with the expectation of winning another battle later on—this is the usual bureaucratic attitude and it is based on the assurance of another hearing; (b) if advice is consistently ignored, it can resign and go into opposition; (c) as the opposition party, it can have the purpose either of inducing the existing government to change its course or of replacing it. If all these avenues are closed, violence or mounting frustration are the consequences.

Only the first option is open to sovereign states bound together by an alliance, since they obviously cannot resign or go into opposition without wrecking the alliance. They cannot affect the process by which their partners' decisionmakers are chosen despite the fact that this may be crucial for their fate. Indeed, as long as the need to maintain the alliance overrides all other concerns, disagreement is likely to be stifled. Advice without responsibility and disagreement without an outlet can turn consultation into a frustrating exercise which compounds rather than alleviates discord.

Consultation is especially difficult when it lacks an integrating over-all framework. The consultation about the nonproliferation treaty concerned specific provisions but not the underlying general philosophy which was of the deepest concern to many of our allies, especially Italy and the Federal Republic of Germany. During periods of détente, each ally makes its own approach to Eastern Europe or the U.S.S.R. without attempting to further a coherent Western enterprise. During periods of crises, there is pressure for American reassurance but not for a clearly defined common philosophy. In these circumstances, consultation runs the risk of being irrelevant. The issues it "solves" are peripheral; the central issues are inadequately articulated. It deals haphazardly in answers to undefined questions.

Such a relationship is not healthy in the long run. Even with the best will, the present structure encourages American unilateralism and European irresponsibility. This is a serious problem for the United States. If the United States remains the trustee of every non-Communist area, it will exhaust its psychological resources. No country can act wisely simultaneously in every part of the globe at every moment of time. A more pluralistic world—especially in relationships with friends—is profoundly in our long-term interest. Political multipolarity, while difficult to get used to, is the precondition for a new period of creativity. Painful as it may be to admit, we could benefit from a counterweight that would discipline our occasional impetuosity and, by supplying historical perspective, modify our penchant for abstract and "final" solutions.

All of this suggests that there is no alternative to European unity either for the United States or for Europe. In its absence, the malaise can only be alleviated, not ended. Ultimately, this is a problem primarily for the Europeans. In the recent past, the United States has often defeated its purposes by committing itself to one particular form of European unity—that of federalism. It has also complicated British membership in the Common Market by making it a direct objective of American policy.

In the next decade the architectonic approach to Atlantic policy will no longer be possible. The American contribution must be more philosophical; it will have to consist more of understanding and quiet, behind-the-scenes encouragement than of the propagation of formal institutional structures. Involved here is the American conception of how nations cooperate. A tradition of legalism and habits of predominance have produced a tendency to multiply formal arrangements.

But growing European autonomy forces us to learn that nations cooperate less because they have a legal obligation to do so than because they have common purposes. Command arrangements cannot substitute for common interests. Coordinated strategy will be empty unless it reflects shared political concepts. The chance of disagreements on peripheral issues may be the price for unity on issues that really matter. The memory of European impotence and American tutelage should not delude us into believing that we understand Europe's problems better than it does itself. Third-force dangers are not avoided by legal formulas, and, more important, they have been overdrawn. It is hard to visualize a "deal" between the Soviet Union and Europe which would jeopardize our interests without jeopardizing European interests first. In any event, a sense of responsibility in Europe will be a much better counter to Soviet efforts to undermine unity than American tutelage.

In short, our relations with Europeans are better founded on developing a community of interests than on the elaboration of formal legal obligations. No precise blueprint for such an arrangement is possible because different fields of activity have different needs. In the military sphere, for example, modern technology will impose a greater degree of integration than is necessary in other areas. Whatever their formal autonomy, it is almost inconceivable that our allies would prefer to go to war without the support of the United States, given the relatively small nuclear forces in prospect for them. Close coordination between Europe and the United States in the military sphere is dictated by self-interest, and Europe has more to gain from it than the United States.

For this very reason, it is in our interest that Europeans should assume much greater responsibility for developing doctrine and force levels in NATO, perhaps by vitalizing such institutions as the West European Union (WEU), perhaps by alternative arrangements. The Supreme Allied Commander should in time be a European.

Military arrangements are not enough, however. Under current conditions, no statesman will risk a cataclysm simply to fulfill a legal obligation. He will do so only if a degree of *political* cooperation has been established which links the fate of each partner with the survival of all the others. This requires an entirely new order of political creativity.

Coordination is especially necessary in East-West relations. The conventional view is that NATO can be as useful an instrument for détente as for defense. This is doubtful—at least in NATO's present form. A military alliance, one of the chief cohesive links of which is its integrated command arrangement, is not the best instrument for flexible diplomacy. Turning NATO into an instrument of détente might reduce its security contribution without achieving a relaxation of tensions. A diplomatic confrontation of NATO and the Warsaw Pact would have all the rigidities of the bipolar military world. It would raise fears in Western Europe of an American-Soviet condominium, and it would tend to legitimize the Soviet hegemonical position in Eastern Europe. Above all, it would fail to take advantage of the flexibility afforded by greater Western European unity and autonomy. As Europe gains structure, its attraction for Eastern Europe is bound to increase. The major initiatives to improve relations between Western and Eastern Europe should originate in Europe with the United States in a reserve position.

Such an approach can work only if there is a real consensus as to objectives. Philosophical agreement can make possible flexibility of method. This will require a form of consultation much more substantial than that which now exists and a far more effective and coherent European contribution.

To be sure, events in Czechoslovakia demonstrate the limits of Eastern European autonomy that the Soviet Union is now prepared to tolerate. But the Soviet Union may not be willing indefinitely to use the Red Army primarily against allies as it has done three times in a decade and a half. In any event, no Western policy can guarantee a more favorable evolution in Central Europe; all it can do is to take advantage of an opportunity if it arises.

Policy outside Europe is likely to be divergent. Given the changed European perspective, an effort to bring about global burden-sharing might only produce stagnation. The allies would be able to agree primarily on doing nothing. Any crisis occurring anywhere would turn automatically and organically world-wide. American acceptance of European autonomy implies also European acceptance of a degree of American autonomy with respect to areas in which, for understandable reasons, European concern has lessened.

There may be opportunities for cooperation in hitherto purely national efforts—for example, our space program. European participation in it could help to remedy the "technological gap."

Finally, under present circumstances, an especially meaningful community of interests can be developed in the social sphere. All modern states face problems of bureaucratization, pollution, environmental control, urban growth. These problems know no national considerations. If the nations of the Atlantic work together on these issues—through either private or governmental channels or both—a new generation habituated to cooperative efforts could develop similar to that spawned in different circumstances by the Marshall Plan.

It is high time that the nations bordering the Atlantic deal—formerly, systematically, and at the highest level—with questions such as these: (a) What are the relative roles of Europe and the United States in East-West contacts? (b) Is a division of functions conceivable in which Western Europe plays the principal role in relation to Eastern Europe while the United States concentrates on relationships with the U.S.S.R.? (c) What forms of political consultation does this require? (d) In what areas of the world is common action possible? Where are divergent courses indicated? How are differences to be handled?

Thus, we face the root questions of a multipolar world. How much unity should we want? How much diversity can we stand? These questions never have a final answer within a pluralistic society. Adjusting the balance between integration and autonomy will be the key challenge of emerging Atlantic relations.

AMERICAN POLICY TOWARD EUROPE *

BY

EDMUND STILLMAN AND WILLIAM PFAFF

[1966]

It seems fair to say that present American policy in Europe has lost sight of its aims. Once these were merely to shield Western Europe from the Soviet attack, help restore European political, social, and economic stability, and so right the imbalance created by the devastation of Europe in World War II. American post-war policy did not look to a unification of Europe, construction of an Atlantic community, or the dozen or so vaguer schemes now put forward as "permanent" rationales for a tightly integrated American-European alliance. Nor had the world· responsibility then so corrupted our vision that the United States expected to exercise a permanent tutelage in Europe or discounted utterly the possibility of independent European action in world affairs.

Europe today is once again secure, prosperous, and apparently stable as well. Sound policy must be based on a realization of these facts. Even the East European states are dramatically changed from their prewar condition of underdevelopment, chronic instability, and incompetent government. They have belatedly, and at heavy cost, begun the modernizing experience which the rest of Europe began in the nineteenth and early twentieth centuries. The feudal heritage has been extirpated. The middle classes have survived the first shock of proletarian revolution (which in Eastern Europe was far less complete than in the Soviet Union) and are in process of coming to terms and intermixing with the communists. Having experienced a nominal "people's democracy" for a generation now, the masses of Eastern Europe, even in any post-communist phase, are unlikely to withdraw from the political process. "Popular"

* From *Power and Impotence: The Failure of America's Foreign Policy,* published by Random House, copyright 1966 by Edmund Stillman and William Pfaff. Reprinted by permission. Edmund Stillman (b. 1924) and William Pfaff (b. 1928) have been affiliated with the Hudson Institute and have collaborated on several books including *The Politics of Hysteria* and *The New Politics*.

politics—mass politics, democratic politics—has not been practiced but it has effectively been preached.

Moreover, Eastern Europe has been industrialized. It is no longer the agrarian appendage to industrial Europe it largely was in the years before Hitler. . . .

Eastern Europe has become part of modern Europe. Together we and the Russians—we consciously and the Russians unconsciously—have created the preconditions, in succession to Hitler's devastations, of a powerful and increasingly independent all-European society. Our shared dilemma today arises from the fact that we both are not quite reconciled to the result; we are half desirous of denying its reality, half willing somehow to perpetuate a domination of new Europe which our own policies and actions have brought into being.

The first principle of American diplomatic policy in Europe, then, should be to acknowledge and deal with Europe's restoration and strength and seek a withdrawal of America and Russia. The Soviets—like us—will eventually have to leave Europe; it is inconceivable that thirty or so years after the cessation of hostilities in World War II, there should be no peace treaty bringing that war to a formal close. But there is a serious question as to the Soviets' ability to get out easily, without provoking political crisis or leaving a dangerous legacy of hostility.

Standing in the way of this objective as much as anything else is the fact that the United States in fact, if not in intention, persists in fostering in Western Europe a helplessness to deal with its political problems in the absence of an American tutelary and guardian power. Our policies in Europe, moreover, are predicated on an almost indefinite prolongation of the division of Europe—on the prolongation of that Cold War which on the other hand our diplomacy with the Soviets seeks to abate. America works for friendship with the Soviets; this is true to a considerable degree. But we have no notion, it sometimes seems, of what such an understanding and friendship would mean for Europe: the old divisions would be healed and America would find itself superfluous so far as the day-to-day security of the Continent is concerned.

American schemes—the multilateral force, or the integration of West Germany into a political community (or further in the future, an "Atlantic" community)—imply a permanent division of Europe, and of Germany within that Europe. There is a curious tension within our policy at this point. Because both America and West Germany profess to believe in the still-continuing threat of Soviet attack in Europe, we are locked in close alliance. But in fact neither Washington nor Bonn any longer believes, in fundamental terms, in the imminence of this threat. The result is that to an increasing degree both Washington and Bonn are hindrances to each other— Bonn to Washington, because the United States wishes to strike an accommodation with the Soviets, which will almost certainly require some considerable sacrifice of German national interest; Washington to Bonn, because West Germany cannot bargain for its occupied eastern zone, to say nothing of its lost territories still farther east, so long as it is tightly integrated into an alliance that is, and a possible future political entity which might be, inimical to Soviet concerns.

The chief result of overestimating the Soviet threat and the utility of West Germany's military contribution to NATO is that we have come to believe that Germany's interest in national reunion is an interest of our own—which it is not. That Germany seeks unification, which is to say a rectification of the losses it suffered in World War II, is comprehensible and legitimate enough. But it is not necessarily in anyone else's interest. The truth is that Europeans as a whole, as well as Russians, and most Americans— official policy notwithstanding—are content with Germany's present division. This is not, as such, an anti-German remark, for the truth is, as Germans know, that Germany has been a deviant in European society in this century, and that its present hard condition is a result of its own national follies. In any case, Germany cannot be reunited without the consent of its neighbors, and this consent cannot conceivably be forthcoming so long as they are afraid of the consequences of a German reunification. Thus, since no one in Washington seriously considers the possibility of, or would want, a settlement in Europe that would be imposed by force on the Soviets, such a settlement of the German, and European, problem can only come about by "normalization" of the European scene.

Such a normalization brings us once again to the question of a peace treaty for Germany. A European settlement means in fact a settlement of World War II. The conflict with the Soviets has obscured this fact, but it will re-emerge as the Cold War continues to wane. Neither we nor the West Germans are quite prepared for this; we have, if anything, permitted West Germany to retain political fantasies of solutions that spring from "rollback" or "victory" in a war we no longer wish to win.

It may also be true that the conditions responsible for Germany's past deviance from Europe's better tradition have now been eliminated. West Germany, certainly, seems firmly lodged in the West European intellectual community—freed of the old German (and largely Prussian–Brandenburgian) lure to the Slavic and Baltic regions, the old ambivalence between Atlantic Europe and an unspecified but unique mission in the East. Conditions suggest that the German future will be different; but the German past has yet to be fully laid to rest.

There must eventually be a peace settlement, and it will come fairly soon. Berlin cannot conceivably be maintained by rights of belligerent occupation half a century after the 1945 armistice. East Germany cannot long be the last colony in a decolonized world.

The objective of a European settlement should be to get Soviet troops behind Soviet borders and to remove the artificial or arbitrary constraints that still influence the conduct of the East European nations—to bring about the long-delayed European "normalization." The price certainly will include an American troop withdrawal, and constraints on Germany. Such an American withdrawal need not be on the worst possible terms, as sometimes seems to be the fear in Washington, and leave Europe helpless to Soviet invasion. Indeed, such a withdrawal need not be total; it could stop short in Britain, say, at least for some years. Nor should the treaty constraints on Germany be excessively harsh; a long time has passed since World War II, a new generation is coming to the fore in Germany, and Germans cannot forever be expected to accept a subordinate role in world affairs. Germany's present division might thus be formalized for a time, on the theory that once Soviet troops were withdrawn, popular pressure within East Germany would bring a rapid amelioration of the regime there. The military and diplomatic freedom of a united Germany might be limited. But it would be best if these limits were for a specified term—a twenty-year prohibition on nuclear weapons, for example—rather than "permanent," for the obvious reason that a limited term is likely to be observed and is enforceable, whereas an unlimited one is impossible to maintain. . . .

In any case, events will move fast in Europe. The NATO treaty is to be reconsidered in 1969, and it is difficult to imagine that it will survive that reconsideration in recognizable form, or that there will not by then be measures of disengagement or settlement. Most Europeans are prepared for a settlement; they have the power to force it against American wishes, and increasingly (not only among Gaullists in France) there is a will to do so. America has it in its power to help shape a useful settlement, or by resistance to provoke a dangerous one. We surely need now to face the prospect of this settlement and consider the price we are willing to pay. The Germans and Soviets must be encouraged to do as much.

A dialogue on normalization will open new possibilities in Europe. They may not all be agreeable possibilities—we have already discussed the European potentialities for violence and political excess. Nor can these possibilities be formulated in too great detail by the United States. The shape of the European future, so long as it does not threaten America's narrowly defined interests, is, after all, Europe's affair, not ours. The American role ought instead be to encourage the sound European politics which has dominated the Continent since the war, and to avoid those conditions wherein Europe's legitimate interests (which include the interest in being freed of American and Russian presence) are frustrated and provoke intemperate responses. America's policy record in Europe in the first decade after the war was brilliant; but our policy today includes elements of complacency and arrogance—not to speak of a shadow of hegemonism—which could wreck our earlier success and provoke the reemergence of European nationalism and political ambition on terms hostile to us and inimical to world stability.

IV

THE UNITED STATES AND LATIN AMERICA

DOCUMENTS ON
LATIN AMERICAN POLICY

1. THE MONROE DOCTRINE, 1823*

At the proposal of the Russian Imperial Government, made through the minister of the Emperor residing here, a full power and instructions have been transmitted to the minister of the United States at St. Petersburg, to arrange, by amicable negotiation, the respective rights and interests of the two nations on the northwest coast of this continent. . . . The Government of the United States has been desirous, by this friendly proceeding, of manifesting the great value which they have invariably attached to the friendship of the Emperor, and their solicitude to cultivate the best understanding with his Government. In the discussions to which this interest has given rise, and in the arrangements by which they may terminate, the occasion has been judged proper for asserting as a principle in which the rights and interests of the United States are involved, that the American continents, by the free and independent condition which they have assumed and maintain, are henceforth not to be considered as subjects for future colonization by any European powers. . . .

It was stated at the commencement of the last session that a great effort was then making in Spain and Portugal to improve the condition of the people of those countries, and that it appeared to be conducted with extraordinary moderation. It need scarcely be remarked that the result has been, so far, very different from what was then anticipated. Of events in that quarter of the globe with which we have so much intercourse, and from which we derive our origin, we have always been anxious and interested spectators. The citizens of the United States cherish sentiments the most friendly in favor of the liberty and happiness of their fellow-men on that side of the Atlantic. In the wars of the European powers in matters relating to themselves we have never taken any part, nor does it comport with our policy to do so. It is only when our rights are invaded or seriously menaced that we

*From President Monroe's Annual Message to Congress, December 2, 1823.

resent injuries or make preparation for our defense. With the movements in this hemisphere we are, of necessity, more immediately connected, and by causes which must be obvious to all enlightened and impartial observers. The political system of the allied powers is essentially different in this respect from that of America. This difference proceeds from that which exists in their respective Governments. And to the defense of our own, which has been achieved by the loss of so much blood and treasure, and matured by the wisdom of their most enlightened citizens, and under which we have enjoyed unexampled felicity, this whole nation is devoted. We owe it, therefore, to candor, and to the amicable relations existing between the United States and those powers, to declare that we should consider any attempt on their part to extend their system to any portion of this hemisphere as dangerous to our peace and safety. With the existing colonies or dependencies of any European power we have not interfered and shall not interfere. But with the governments who have declared their independence and maintained it, and whose independence we have, on great consideration and on just principles, acknowledged, we could not view any interposition for the purpose of oppressing them, or controlling in any other manner their destiny, by any European power, in any other light than as the manifestation of an unfriendly disposition toward the United States. In the war between these new governments and Spain we declared our neutrality at the time of their recognition, and to this we have adhered and shall continue to adhere, provided no change shall occur which, in the judgment of the competent authorities of this Government, shall make a corresponding change on the part of the United States indispensable to their security.

The late events in Spain and Portugal show that Europe is still unsettled. Of this important fact no stronger proof can be adduced than that the allied powers should have thought it proper, on any principle satisfactory to themselves, to have interposed, by force, in the internal concerns of Spain. To what extent such interposition may be carried, on the same principle, is a question in which all independent powers whose governments differ from theirs are interested, even those most remote, and surely none more so than the United States. Our policy in regard to Europe, which was adopted at an early stage of the wars which have so long agitated that quarter of the globe, nevertheless remains the same, which is, not to interfere in the internal concerns of any of its powers; to consider the government *de facto* as the legitimate government for us; to cultivate friendly relations with it, and to preserve those relations by a frank, firm, and manly policy, meeting, in all instances, the just claims of every power, submitting to injuries from none. But in regard to these continents, circumstances are eminently and conspicuously different. It is impossible that the allied powers should extend their political system to any portion of either continent without endangering our peace and happiness; nor can anyone believe that our southern brethren, if left to themselves, would adopt it of their own accord. It is equally impossible, therefore, that we should behold such interposition, in any form, with indifference. If we look to the comparative strength and resources of Spain and those new governments, and their distance from each other, it must be obvious that she can never subdue them. It is still the true policy of the United States to leave the parties to themselves, in the hope that other powers will pursue the same course. . . .

2. SECRETARY OLNEY'S "FIAT," 1895*

That there are circumstances under which a nation may justly interpose in a controversy to which two or more other nations are the direct and immediate parties is an admitted canon of international law. The doctrine is ordinarily expressed in terms of the most general character and is perhaps incapable of more specific statement. It is declared in substance that a nation may avail itself of this right whenever what is done or proposed by any of the parties primarily concerned is a serious and direct menace to its own integrity, tranquillity, or welfare. The propriety of the rule when applied in good faith will not be questioned in any quarter.

---

*From a State Department communication from Richard Olney, Secretary of State, to Thomas F. Bayard, U. S. Ambassador to Great Britain, July 20, 1895, for presentation to the British foreign minister. At the time, Great Britain and Venezuela were involved in a dispute over the Venezuelan boundary. The matter was later submitted to arbitration.

On the other hand, it is an inevitable though unfortunate consequence of the wide scope of the rule that it has only too often been made a cloak for schemes of wanton spoliation and aggrandizement. We are concerned at this time, however, not so much with the general rule as with a form of it which is peculiarly and distinctively American. . . .

. . . The Farewell Address, while it took America out of. the field of European politics, was silent as to the part Europe might be permitted to play in America. . . . The Monroe Administration . . . did not hesitate to accept and apply the logic of the Farewell Address by declaring in effect that American nonintervention in European affairs necessarily implied and meant European nonintervention in American affairs. . . .

The Monroe Administration, however, did not content itself with formulating a correct rule for the regulation of the relations between Europe and America. It aimed at also securing the practical benefits to result from the application of the rule. Hence the message [of December 2, 1823] declared that the American continents were fully occupied and were not the subjects for future colonization by European powers. To this spirit and this purpose, also, are to be attributed the passages of the same message which treat any infringement of the rule against interference in American affairs on the part of the powers of Europe as an act of unfriendliness to the United States. It was realized that it was futile to lay down such a rule unless its observance could be enforced. It was manifest that the United States was the only power in this hemisphere capable of enforcing it. It was therefore courageously declared not merely that Europe ought not to interfere in American affairs, but that any European power doing so would be regarded as antagonizing the interests and inviting the opposition of the United States.

That America is in no part open to colonization, though the proposition was not universally admitted at the time of its first enunciation, has long been universally conceded. We are now concerned, therefore, only with that other practical application of the Monroe doctrine the disregard of which by an European power is to be deemed an act of unfriendliness towards the United States.

The precise scope and limitations of this rule can not be too clearly apprehended. It does not establish any general protectorate by the United States over other American states. It does not relieve any American state from its obligations as fixed by international law nor prevent any European power directly interested from enforcing such obligations or from inflicting merited punishment for the breach of them. It does not contemplate any interference in the internal affairs of any American state or in the relations between it and other American states. It does not justify any attempt on our part to change the established form of government of any American state or to prevent the people of such state from altering that form according to their own will and pleasure. The rule in question has but a single purpose and object. It is that no European power or combination of European powers shall forcibly deprive an American state of the right and power of self-government and of shaping for itself its own political fortunes and destinies.

* * *

If the forcible intrusion of European powers into American politics is to be deprecated—if, as it is to be deprecated, it should be resisted and prevented—such resistance and prevention must come from the United States. They would come from it, of course, were it made the point of attack. But, if they come at all, they must also come from it when any other American state is attacked, since only the United States has the strength adequate to the exigency.

Is it true, then, that the safety and welfare of the United States are so concerned with the maintenance of the independence of every American state as against any European power as to justify and require the interposition of the United States whenever that independence is endangered? The question can be candidly answered in but one way. The States of America, South as well as North, by geographical proximity, by natural sympathy, by similarity of governmental constitutions, are friends and allies, commercially and politically of the United States. To allow the subjugation of any of them by an European power is, of course, to completely reverse that situation and signifies the loss of all the advantages incident to their natural relations to us. But that is not all. The people of the United States have a vital interest in the cause of popular self-government. They have secured the right for themselves and their posterity at the cost of infinite blood and treasure. They have realized and exemplified its beneficent operation by a career unexampled in point of natural greatness or individual felicity. They believe it to be for the healing of all nations, and that civilization must either advance or retrograde accordingly as its supremacy is extended or curtailed. Imbued with these sentiments, the people of the United States might not impossibly be wrought up to an active propaganda in favor of a cause so highly valued both for themselves and for mankind. But the age of the Crusades has passed, and they are content with such assertion and defense of the right of popular self-government as their own security and welfare demand. It is in that view more than in any other that they believe it not to be tolerated that the political control of an American state shall be forcibly assumed by an European power.

The mischiefs apprehended from such a source are none the less real because not immediately imminent in any specific case, and are none the less to be guarded against because the combination of circumstances that will bring them upon us can not be predicted. The civilized states of Christendom deal with each other on substantially the same principles that regulate the conduct of individuals. The greater its enlightenment, the more surely every state perceives that its permanent interests require it to be governed by the immutable principles of right and justice. Each, nevertheless, is only too liable to succumb to the temptations offered by seeming special opportunities for its own aggrandizement, and each would rashly imperil its own safety were it not to remember that for the regard and respect of other states it must be largely dependent upon its own strength and power. To-day the United States is practically sovereign on this continent, and its fiat is law upon the subjects to which it confines its interposition. Why? It is not because of the pure friendship or good will felt for it. It is not simply by reason of its high character as a civilized state, nor because wisdom and justice and equity are the invariable characteristics of the dealings of the United States. It is because, in addition to all other grounds, its infinite resources combined with its isolated position render it master of the situation and practically invulnerable as against any or all other powers. . . .

3. THEODORE ROOSEVELT'S "COROLLARY," 1901-1905*

A. The Monroe Doctrine should be the cardinal feature of the foreign policy of all the nations of the two Americas, as it is of the United States. Just seventy-eight years have passed since President Monroe in his Annual Message announced that "The American continents are henceforth not to be considered as subjects for future colonization by any European power." In other words, the Monroe Doctrine is a declaration that there must be no territorial aggrandizement by any non-American power at the expense of any American power or American soil. It is in no wise intended as hostile to any nation in the Old World. Still less is it intended to give cover to any aggression by one New World power at the expense of any other. It is simply a step, and a long step, toward assuring the universal peace of the world by securing the possibility of permanent peace on this hemisphere.

During the past century other influences have established the permanence and independence of the smaller states of Europe. Through the Monroe Doctrine we hope to be able to safeguard like independence and secure like permanence for the lesser among the New World nations.

This doctrine has nothing to do with the commercial relations of any American power, save that it in truth allows each of them to form such as it desires. In other words, it is really a guaranty of the commercial independence of the Americans. We do not ask under this doctrine for any exclusive commercial dealings with

---

*From (a) President Roosevelt's Annual Message to Congress, December 3, 1901; (b) an address at Chicago, April 2, 1903; (c) the Annual Message to Congress, December 6, 1904; and (d) the Annual Message to Congress, December 5, 1905.

any other American state. We do not guarantee any state against punishment if it misconducts itself, provided that punishment does not take the form of the acquisition of territory by any non-American power.

Our attitude in Cuba is a sufficient guaranty of our own good faith. We have not the slightest desire to secure any territory at the expense of any of our neighbors. We wish to work with them hand in hand, so that all of us may be uplifted together, and we rejoice over the good fortune of any of them, we gladly hail their material prosperity and political stability, and are concerned and alarmed if any of them fall into industrial or political chaos. We do not wish to see any Old World military power grow up on this continent, or to be compelled to become a military power ourselves. The peoples of the Americas can prosper best if left to work out their own salvation in their own way. . . .

Our people intend to abide by the Monroe Doctrine and to insist upon it as the one sure means of securing peace of the Western Hemisphere. The Navy offers us the only means of making our insistence upon the Monroe Doctrine anything but a subject of derision to whatever nation chooses to disregard it. We desire the peace which comes as of right to the just man armed; not the peace granted on terms of ignominy to the craven and the weakling. . . .

B. I believe in the Monroe Doctrine with all my heart and soul; I am convinced that the immense majority of our fellow-countrymen so believe in it; but I would infinitely prefer to see us abandon it than to see us put it forward and bluster about it, and yet fail to build up the efficient fighting strength which in the last resort can alone make it respected by any strong foreign power whose interest it may ever happen to be to violate it.

There is a homely old adage which runs: "Speak softly and carry a big stick; you will go far." If the American nation will speak softly and yet build and keep at a pitch of the highest training a thoroughly efficient navy the Monroe Doctrine will go far.

C. It is not true that the United States feels any land hunger or entertains any projects as regards the other nations of the Western

Hemisphere save such as are for their welfare. All that this country desires is to see the neighboring countries stable, orderly, and prosperous. Any country whose people conduct themselves well can count upon our hearty friendship. If a nation shows that it knows how to act with reasonable efficiency and decency in social and political matters, if it keeps order and pays its obligations, it need fear no interference from the United States. Chronic wrongdoing, or an impotence which results in a general loosening of the ties of civilized society, may in America, as elsewhere, ultimately require intervention by some civilized nation, and in the Western Hemisphere the adherence of the United States to the Monroe Doctrine may force the United States, however reluctantly, in flagrant cases of such wrongdoing or impotence, to the exercise of an international police power. . . . We would interfere with them only in the last resort, and then only if it became evident that their inability or unwillingness to do justice at home and abroad had violated the rights of the United States or had invited foreign aggression to the detriment of the entire body of American nations. It is a mere truism to say that every nation, whether in America or anywhere else, which desires to maintain its freedom, its independence, must ultimately realize that the right of such independence can not be separated from the responsibility of making good use of it.

D. There are certain essential points which must never be forgotten as regards the Monroe Doctrine. In the first place we must as a nation make it evident that we do not intend to treat it in any shape or way as an excuse for aggrandizement on our part at the expense of the republics to the south. We must recognize the fact that in some South American countries there has been much suspicion lest we should interpret the Monroe Doctrine as in some way inimical to their interests, and we must try to convince all the other nations of this continent once and for all that no just and orderly government has anything to fear from us. There are certain republics to the south of us which have already reached such a point of stability, order, and prosperity that they themselves, though as yet hardly consciously, are among the guarantors of this Doctrine. These republics we now meet not only on a basis of entire equality, but in a spirit of frank and respectful friendship, which we hope is mutual. If all of the republics to the south of us will only grow as those to which I allude have already grown, all need for us to be the especial champions of the Doctrine will disappear, for no stable and growing American Republic wishes to see some great non-American military power acquire territory in its neighborhood. All that this country desires is that the other republics on this Continent shall be happy and prosperous; and they can not be happy and prosperous unless they maintain order within their boundaries and behave with a just regard for their obligations toward outsiders. It must be understood that under no circumstances will the United States use the Monroe Doctrine as a cloak for territorial aggression. We desire peace with all the world, but perhaps most of all with the other peoples of the American Continent. There are of course limits to the wrongs which any self-respecting nation can endure. It is always possible that wrong actions toward this Nation, or toward citizens of this Nation, in some State unable to keep order among its own people, unable to secure justice from outsiders, and unwilling to do justice to those outsiders who treat it well, may result in our having to take action to protect our rights; but such action will not be taken with a view to territorial aggression, and it will be taken at all only with extreme reluctance and when it has become evident that every other resource has been exhausted.

Moreover, we must make it evident that we do not intend to permit the Monroe Doctrine to be used by any nation on this Continent as a shield to protect it from the consequences of its own misdeeds against foreign nations. If a republic to the south of us commits a tort against a foreign nation, such as an outrage against a citizen of that nation, then the Monroe Doctrine does not force us to interfere to prevent punishment of the tort, save to see that the punishment does not assume the form of territorial occupation in any shape. The case is more difficult when it refers to a contractual obligation. Our own Government has always refused to enforce such contractual obligations on behalf of its citizens by an appeal to arms. It is much to be wished that all foreign governments would take the same view. But they do not; and in consequence we are liable at any time to be brought face to face with disagreeable alternatives. On the one hand, this country would certainly decline to go to war to prevent a foreign government from collecting a just debt; on the other hand, it is very inadvisable to permit any foreign power to take possession, even temporarily, of the customhouses of an American Republic in order to enforce the payment of its obligations; for such temporary occupation might turn into a permanent occupation. The only escape from these alternatives may at any time be that we must ourselves undertake to bring about some arrangement by which so much as possible of a just obligation shall be paid. It is far better that this country should put through such an arrangement, rather than allow any foreign country to undertake it. To do so insures the defaulting republic from having to pay debts of an improper character under duress, while it also insures honest creditors of the republic from being passed by in the interest of dishonest or grasping creditors. Moreover, for the United States to take such a position offers the only possible way of insuring us against a clash with some foreign power. The position is, therefore, in the interest of peace as well as in the interest of justice. It is of benefit to our people; it is of benefit to foreign peoples; and most of all it is really of benefit to the people of the country concerned.

This brings me to what should be one of the fundamental objects of the Monroe Doctrine. We must ourselves in good faith try to help upward toward peace and order those of our sister republics which need such help. Just as there has been a gradual growth of the ethical element in the relations of one individual to another, so we are, even though slowly, more and more coming to recognize the duty of bearing one another's burdens, not only as among individuals, but also as among nations.

4. CLARK'S MEMORANDUM, 1928*

The Secretary:

Herewith I transmit a Memorandum on the Monroe Doctrine, prepared by your direction, given a little over two months ago. . . .

Obviously the views set out, both herein and in the Memo-

_____

*From a memorandum from J. Reuben Clark, Under Secretary of State, to Frank B. Kellogg, Secretary of State, December 17, 1928.

randum, are not authoritative statements, but merely personal expressions of the writer. . . .

. . . It is of first importance to have in mind that Monroe's declaration in its terms, relates solely to the relationships between European states on the one side, and, on the other side, the American continents, the Western Hemisphere, and the Latin American Governments which on December 2, 1823, had declared and maintained their independence which we had acknowledged.

It is of equal importance to note, on the other hand, that the declaration does not apply to purely inter-American relations.

Nor does the declaration purport to lay down any principles that are to govern the interrelationship of the states of this Western Hemisphere as among themselves.

The Doctrine states a case of United States *vs.* Europe, not of United States *vs.* Latin America.

Such arrangements as the United States has made, for example, with Cuba, Santo Domingo, Haiti, and Nicaragua, are not within the Doctrine as it was announced by Monroe. They may be accounted for as the expression of a national policy which, like the Doctrine itself, originates in the necessities of security or self-preservation—a policy which was outlined in what is known as the "Roosevelt corollary" to the Monroe Doctrine (1905) in connection with the Dominican debt protocol of 1904; but such arrangements are not covered by the terms of the Doctrine itself.

Should it become necessary to apply a sanction for a violation of the Doctrine as declared by Monroe, that sanction would run against the European power offending the policy, and not against the Latin American country which was the object of the European aggression, unless a conspiracy existed between the European and the American states involved.

In the normal case, the Latin American state against which aggression was aimed by a European power, would be the beneficiary of the Doctrine not its victim. This has been the history of its application. The Doctrine makes the United States a guarantor, in effect, of the independence of Latin American states, though without the obligations of a guarantor to those states, for the United States itself determines by its sovereign will when, where, and concerning what aggressions it will invoke the Doctrine, and by what measures, if any, it will apply a sanction. In none of these things has any other state any voice whatever.

Furthermore while the Monroe Doctrine as declared, has no relation in its terms to an aggression by any other state than a European state, yet the principle "self-preservation" which underlies the Doctrine—which principle, as we shall see, is as fully operative without the Doctrine as with it—would apply to any non-American state in whatever quarter of the globe it lay, or even to an American state, if the aggressions of such state against other Latin American states were "dangerous to our peace and safety," or were a "manifestation of an unfriendly disposition towards the United States," or were "endangering our peace and happiness"; that is, if such aggressions challenged our existence.

In other words, there is a broad domain occupied by self-preservation which is incapable of definite boundary as to its extent, or of definition as to the kind of act which lies within it, because new conditions, new advances in the arts and sciences, new instrumentalities of international contact and communication, new political theories and combinations, vary from age to age and can not be certainly foretold. As the law stands, whatever falls within the necessities of self-preservation, under existing or future conditions, lies within the boundaries of the domain of the principle.

By his declaration President Monroe occupied and bounded but a narrow portion of this whole domain—that portion which contained situations immediately threatening. But that can hardly be said to have changed under the rules and principles of international law the fundamental character of the acts defined and bounded. These acts still remained within the domain of self-preservation, for, obviously, if they would constitute a menace to our existence, such menace would not disappear by virtue of their being listed.

In this view, the Monroe Doctrine as such might be wiped out and the United States would lose nothing of its broad, international right; it would still possess, in common with every other member of the family of nations, the internationally recognized right of self-preservation, and this right would fully attach to the matters specified by the Doctrine if and whenever they threatened our existence, just as the right would attach in relation to any other act carrying a like menace.

The Doctrine has been useful, and such indeed was the real motive of its announcement, and it will remain of such use that it should never be abandoned, as a forewarning to European powers as to what this country would regard, in a restricted field, as inimical to its safety. It has been equally useful to the Americas as forecasting our attitude towards certain international problems and relations in which they might be involved.

But, recalling that the Doctrine is based upon the recognized right of self-preservation, it follows (it is submitted) that by the specification of a few matters in the Doctrine, the United States has not surrendered its right to deal, as it may be compelled, and under the rules and principles of international law, with the many others which are unspecified as these may arise, which others might, indeed, have been included in the declaration with as much propriety, legally, as those which were mentioned. By naming either one act or a series of acts which challenges our self-preservation, we do not estop ourselves from naming others as they may arise; otherwise the mention of one such act would foreclose all others. The custom of nations shows that invoking the right as to one menace does not foreclose a power from invoking it as to others.

Moreover, by specifying a few of the world powers which, if they performed the prohibited acts, would bring themselves within the inhibitions of the Doctrine, the United States has not estopped itself from asserting the same principles against other and unnamed powers making the same sort of aggression. That against these other powers, the United States might, in its intervention, speak of the right of self-preservation and not of the Monroe Doctrine, would neither enlarge nor diminish its rights under international law as to the Monroe Doctrine or otherwise.

It is evident from the foregoing that the Monroe Doctrine is not an equivalent for "self-preservation"; and therefore the Monroe Doctrine need not, indeed should not, be invoked in order to cover situations challenging our self-preservation but not within the terms defined by Monroe's declaration. These other situations may be handled, and more wisely so, as matters affecting the national security and self-preservation of the United States as a great power.

* * *

The so-called "Roosevelt corollary" was to the effect, as generally understood, that in case of financial or other difficulties in weak Latin American countries, the United States should attempt an adjustment thereof lest European Governments should intervene, and intervening should occupy territory—an act which would be contrary to the principles of the Monroe Doctrine. . . .

As has already been indicated above, it is not believed that this corollary is justified by the terms of the Monroe Doctrine, however much it may be justified by the application of the doctrine of self-preservation. . . .

Finally, it should not be overlooked that the United States declined the overtures of Great Britain in 1823 to make a joint declaration regarding the principles covered by the Monroe Doctrine, or to enter into a conventional arrangement regarding them. Instead this Government determined to make the declaration of high national policy on its own responsibility and in its own behalf. The Doctrine is thus purely unilateral. The United States determines when and if the principles of the Doctrine are violated, and when and if violation is threatened. We alone determine what measures, if any, shall be taken to vindicate the principles of the Doctrine, and we of necessity determine when the principles have been vindicated. No other power of the world has any relationship to, or voice in, the implementing of the principles which the Doctrine contains. It is our Doctrine, to be by us invoked and sustained, held in abeyance, or abandoned as our high international policy or vital national interests shall seem to us, and to us alone, to demand.

It may, in conclusion, be repeated: The Doctrine does not concern itself with purely inter-American relations; it has nothing to do with the relationship between the United States and other

American nations, except where other American nations shall become involved with European governments in arrangements which threaten the security of the United States, and even in such cases, the Doctrine runs against the European country, not the American nation, and the United States would primarily deal thereunder with the European country and not with the American nation concerned. The Doctrine states a case of the United States *vs.* Europe, and not of the United States *vs.* Latin America. Furthermore, the fact should never be lost to view that in applying this Doctrine during the period of one hundred years since it was announced, our Government has over and over again driven it in as a shield between Europe and the Americas to protect Latin America from the political and territorial thrusts of Europe; and this was done at times when the American nations were weak and struggling for the establishment of stable, permanent governments; when the political morality of Europe sanctioned, indeed encouraged, the acquisition of territory by force; and when many of the great powers of Europe looked with eager, covetous eyes to the rich, undeveloped areas of the American hemisphere. Nor should another equally vital fact be lost sight of, that the United States has only been able to give this protection against designing European powers because of its known willingness and determination, if and whenever necessary, to expend its treasure and to sacrifice American life to maintain the principles of the Doctrine. So far as Latin America is concerned, the Doctrine is now, and always has been, not an instrument of violence and oppression, but an unbought, freely bestowed, and wholly effective guaranty of their freedom, independence, and territorial integrity against the imperialistic designs of Europe.

J. REUBEN CLARK

5. FRANKLIN D. ROOSEVELT'S "GOOD NEIGHBOR" POLICY, 1933*

... In my Inaugural Address I stated that I would "dedicate this Nation to the policy of the good neighbor—the neighbor who resolutely respects himself and, because he does so, respects the

*From an address by President Franklin D. Roosevelt before the Governing Board of the Pan-American Union, Washington, D. C., April 12, 1933.

rights of others—the neighbor who respects his obligations and respects the sanctity of his agreements in and with a world of neighbors." Never before has the significance of the words "good neighbor" been so manifest in international relations. Never have the need and benefit of neighborly cooperation in every form of human activity been so evident as they are today.

Friendship among Nations, as among individuals, calls for constructive efforts to muster the forces of humanity in order that an atmosphere of close understanding and cooperation may be cultivated. It involves mutual obligations and responsibilities, for it is only by sympathetic respect for the rights of others and a scrupulous fulfillment of the corresponding obligations by each member of the community that a true fraternity can be maintained.

The essential qualities of a true Pan Americanism must be the same as those which constitute a good neighbor, namely, mutual understanding, and, through such understanding, a sympathetic appreciation of the other's point of view. It is only in this manner that we can hope to build up a system of which confidence, friendship and good-will are the cornerstones.

In this spirit the people of every Republic on our continent are coming to a deep understanding of the fact that the Monroe Doctrine, of which so much has been written and spoken for more than a century, was and is directed at the maintenance of independence by the peoples of the continent. It was aimed and is aimed against the acquisition in any manner of the control of additional territory in this hemisphere by any non-American power.

Hand in hand with this Pan American doctrine of continental self-defense, the peoples of the American Republics understand more clearly, with the passing years, that the independence of each Republic must recognize the independence of every other Republic. Each one of us must grow by an advancement of civilization and social well-being and not by the acquisition of territory at the expense of any neighbor.

In this spirit of mutual understanding and of cooperation on this continent you and I cannot fail to be disturbed by any armed strife between neighbors. . . .

Your Americanism and mine must be a structure built of confidence, cemented by a sympathy which recognizes only equality and fraternity. It finds its source and being in the hearts of men and dwells in the temple of the intellect.

* * *

6. THE BUENOS AIRES DECLARATION, 1936*

The Governments of the American Republics, having considered:

That they have a common likeness in their democratic form of government and their common ideals of peace and justice, manifested in the several Treaties and Conventions which they have signed for the purpose of constituting a purely American system tending towards the preservation of peace, the proscription of war, the harmonious development of their commerce and of their cultural aspirations in the various fields of political, economic, social, scientific and artistic activities;

That the existence of continental interests obliges them to maintain solidarity of principles as the basis of the life of the relations of each to every other American nation;

That Pan Americanism, as a principle of American International Law, by which is understood a moral union of all of the American Republics in defence of their common interests based upon the most perfect equality and reciprocal respect for their rights of autonomy, independence and free development, requires the proclamation of principles of American International Law; and

That it is necessary to consecrate the principle of American solidarity in all non-continental conflicts, especially since those limited to the American Continent should find a peaceful solution by the means established by the Treaties and Conventions now in force or in the instruments hereafter to be executed,

The Inter-American Conference for the Maintenance of Peace

Declares:

1. That the American Nations, true to their republican institutions, proclaimed their absolute juridical liberty, their unqualified

---

*Declaration of the Inter-American Conference for the Maintenance of Peace: Principles of Inter-American Solidarity and Co-operation, at Buenos Aires, December 21, 1936.

respect for their respective sovereignties and the existence of a common democracy throughout America;

2. That every act susceptible of disturbing the peace of America affects each and every one of them, and justifies the initiation of the procedure of consultation provided for in the Convention for the Maintenance, Preservation and Re-establishment of Peace, signed at this Conference; and

3. That the following principles are accepted by the American community of Nations:

(a) Proscription of territorial conquest and that, in consequence, no acquisition made through violence shall be recognized;

(b) Intervention by one State in the internal or external affairs of another State is condemned;

(c) Forcible collection of pecuniary debts is illegal; and

(d) Any difference or dispute between the American nations, whatever its nature or origin, shall be settled by the methods of conciliation, or unrestricted arbitration, or through operation of international justice.

7. THE RIO TREATY, 1947*

In the name of their Peoples, the Governments represented at the Inter-American Conference for the Maintenance of Continental Peace and Security, desirous of consolidating and strengthening their relations of friendship and good neighborliness, . . .

Have resolved . . . to conclude the following Treaty, in order to assure peace, through adequate means, to provide for effective reciprocal assistance to meet armed attacks against any American State, and in order to deal with threats of aggression against any of them:

ARTICLE 1. The High Contracting Parties formally condemn war and undertake in their international relations not to resort to the threat or the use of force in any manner inconsistent with the provisions of the Charter of the United Nations or of this Treaty.

---

*The Inter-American Treaty of Reciprocal Assistance, signed at the Rio de Janeiro Conference for the Maintenance of Continental Peace and Security, August 15–September 2, 1947.

ARTICLE 2.   As a consequence of the principle set forth in the preceding Article, the High Contracting Parties undertake to submit every controversy which may arise between them to methods of peaceful settlement and to endeavor to settle any such controversy among themselves by means of the procedures in force in the Inter-American System before referring it to the General Assembly or the Security Council of the United Nations.

ARTICLE 3.

1.   The High Contracting Parties agree that an armed attack by any State against an American State shall be considered as an attack against all the American States and, consequently, each one of the said Contracting Parties undertakes to assist in meeting the attack in the exercise of the inherent right of individual or collective self-defense recognized by Article 51 of the Charter of the United Nations.

2.   On the request of the State or States directly attacked and until the decision of the Organ of Consultation of the Inter-American System, each one of the Contracting Parties may determine the immediate measures which it may individually take in fulfillment of the obligation contained in the preceding paragraph and in accordance with the principle of continental solidarity. The Organ of Consultation shall meet without delay for the purpose of examining those measures and agreeing upon the measures of a collective character that should be taken. . . .

4.   Measures of self-defense provided for under this Article may be taken until the Security Council of the United Nations has taken the measures necessary to maintain international peace and security. . . .

ARTICLE 5.   The High Contracting Parties shall immediately send to the Security Council of the United Nations, in conformity with Article 51 and 54 of the Charter of the United Nations, complete information concerning the activities undertaken or in contemplation in the exercise of the right of self-defense or for the purpose of maintaining inter-American peace and security.

ARTICLE 6.   If the inviolability or the integrity of the territory or the sovereignty or political independence of any American State should be affected by an aggression which is not an armed attack

The region included in the Rio Treaty, 1947.

or by an extra-continental or intra-continental conflict, or by any other fact or situation that might endanger the peace of America, the Organ of Consultation shall meet immediately in order to agree on the measures which must be taken in case of aggression to assist the victim of the aggression or, in any case, the measures which should be taken for the common defense and for the maintenance of the peace and security of the Continent.

ARTICLE 7. In the case of a conflict between two or more American States, without prejudice to the right of self-defense in conformity with Article 51 of the Charter of the United Nations, the High Contracting Parties, meeting in consultation, shall call upon the contending States to suspend hostilities and restore matters to the *status quo ante bellum*, and shall take in addition all other necessary measures to re-establish or maintain inter-American peace and security and for the solution of the conflict by peaceful means. The rejection of the pacifying action will be considered in the determination of the aggressor and in the application of the measures which the consultative meeting may agree upon.

ARTICLE 8. For the purposes of this Treaty, the measures on which the Organ of Consultation may agree will comprise one or more of the following: recall of chiefs of diplomatic missions; breaking of diplomatic relations; breaking of consular relations; partial or complete interruption of economic relations or of rail, sea, air, postal, telegraphic, telephonic, and radiotelephonic or radiotelegraphic communications; and use of armed force. . . .

ARTICLE 10. None of the provisions of this Treaty shall be construed as impairing the rights and obligations of the High Contracting Parties under the Charter of the United Nations. . . .

ARTICLE 17. The Organ of Consultation shall take its decisions by a vote of two-thirds of the Signatory States which have ratified the Treaty.

ARTICLE 18. In the case of a situation or dispute between American States, the parties directly interested shall be excluded from the voting. . . .

ARTICLE 20. Decisions which require the application of the measures specified in Article 8 shall be binding upon all the Signatory States which have ratified this Treaty, with the sole exception that no State shall be required to use armed force without its consent. . . .

ARTICLE 26. The principles and fundamental provisions of this Treaty shall be incorporated in the Organic Pact of the Inter-American System.

Done in the City of Rio de Janeiro, in four texts in the English, French, Portuguese and Spanish languages, on the second of September, nineteen hundred forty-seven.

*   *   *

U. S. AGAINST US*

BY

LUIS QUINTANILLA

[1943]

At the time of its enunciation, the Monroe Doctrine was intended to be, essentially, a policy toward Europe; not a policy for the Hemisphere. It was a toothless warning indeed, but one definitely aimed at Europe. As such, there is nothing that we can hold against it. To reject its original intention would be tantamount to accepting the right of Europe to meddle with the nations of our Hemisphere: and that, no Latin American wants.

It is only by virtue of later interpretations—or rather "misinterpretations"—that the momentous Message was gradually fashioned into a Machiavellian policy for *intra*-Hemisphere consumption. From a candid but commendable United States gesture against European interference, the Doctrine was turned into a ruthless axiom, utilized by Washington administrations to suit the interests of what is known as *"Yankee Imperialism."* Because the Doctrine—certainly through no fault of its victims—was perverted to the point of being invoked as a justification for attacks against the sovereignty of the nations which it claimed to protect, it bulks large today as a stumbling block in the way of inter-American relations. "Paramount Interests," "Manifest Destiny," "Big-Stick Policy," "Watchful Waiting," "Dollar Diplomacy," "Paternalism," "Protectionism"—in short, "Yankee Imperialism"—those slogans have become irrevocably connected, in the minds of Latin Americans, with the two words, *"Monroe Doctrine."*

Yes, it may be said that historically there are *two* Monroe Doctrines: the one, promulgated by the President; and the other, the distorted Doctrine of the Corollaries. But the authentic one has been pushed into the background. Today people have not in

*From Luis Quintanilla, A Latin American Speaks. Macmillan Company, 1943. Reprinted by permission. Luis Quintanilla (b. 1900), Mexican diplomat and writer, is now Mexican Ambassador to the Organization of American States.

mind the mild offering of the fifth President of the United States, but the subsequent concoction into which entered all the imperialistic ingredients added by more voracious occupants of the White House, among whom Theodore Roosevelt—twenty-sixth President of the United States of America—stands out conspicuously.

"The Monroe Doctrine, first enunciated by President Monroe in 1823," writes Professor Schuman, "was a warning to the European powers to keep out of the American Hemisphere and, by implications and successive reinterpretations, an assertion of the hegemony of the United States over the American continents." That is precisely the point! The Doctrine has come to mean "an assertion of the hegemony of the United States over the American continents": a policy of bloody military occupation and outright diplomatic intervention.

Practically any Spanish American could put forward an impressive list of perfectly legitimate reasons why he rejects vehemently the Monroe Doctrine. A striking sample of genuine Latin American attitude in this respect, can be found in Gaston Nerval's book, significantly entitled *Autopsy of the Monroe Doctrine*.

"Autopsy" is perhaps wishful thinking. The *original* Doctrine is not dead. The Axis has given it a shot in the arm. To handle the *original* Doctrine as if it were dead would be not "autopsy" but vivisection. It is not dead, yet the weight of its additions places it beyond redemption. The Corollaries have become an intrinsic part of it. We cannot and must not forget them. No historical or diplomatic surgeon could sever the Doctrine from the acts of aggression committed in its name; not even Professor Perkins, family doctor of Monroe's troublesome child, nor official interpreter Reuben Clark and his authoritative Memorandum. After all, a political Doctrine should not be judged by its intent only, but also by its results. Scores of charges can be leveled at the Monroe Doctrine by a Latin American. For the sake of clearness, I will limit the counts of my indictment to five:

1) It is *unilateral*.
2) It proved *inefficient*.
3) It was *perverted*.
4) It is *unpopular*.
5) It has become *outmoded*.

1) There can be no argument concerning the first count. Practically all historians, Anglo-Saxon as well as Latin, agree on that. Even Dr. Perkins writes: "The Monroe Doctrine was not, and was not intended to be, anything else than a unilateral declaration of policy. From that day to this American statesmen have insisted upon its purely American character, upon the right of the United States to interpret it in its own fashion, and on the basis of its own interests." . . . Also Reuben Clark, most unbiased *official* United States interpreter, writes: "The United States determines *when* and *if* the principles of the Doctrine are violated, and when and if violation is threatened. We *alone* determine what measures, if any, shall be taken to vindicate the principles of the Doctrine, and *we* of necessity determine when the principles have been vindicated. No *other* power in the world has *any* relationship to, or voice in, the implementing of the principles which the Doctrine contains. It is *our* Doctrine, to be by *us* invoked and sustained, held in abeyance, or abandoned as *our* high international policy or vital national interest shall seem to *us*, and to *us alone*, to demand." Here again, I have italicized some words to bring out the point. There is nothing the matter with a *unilateral* policy. But its interpreters have no right to make it multilateral. The Monroe Doctrine was never meant to be anything but a one-sided policy. To pretend otherwise, is to commit historical heresy. It is not saving the Monroe Doctrine but rather confessing, by implication, that it has ceased to exist.

The Doctrine was a *monologue*, not a dialogue. It assumed, after the Theodore Roosevelt Corollary, an order of things entirely created and maintained by a self-appointed *guardian*; not one agreed to by equal partners. Why speak of "Americanization" or "continentalization"? Whatever rabbits Monroeist magicians pull out of their hats, that thing called Pan Americanism will never come out of it!

The Doctrine was unilateral not only in its proclamation, definition, and application, but also in its original motive, which was not the safety of the Hemisphere, but the security of the United States. So well known an authority as Professor Charles Edward Chapman, states: "The benevolent feature never was, and is not, the primary purpose of the doctrine. Its fundamental idea has always been *the security of the United States*. In this *all-important* respect, the Monroe Doctrine has not 'changed,' as so often alleged." The security of the United States: again, there is nothing the matter with that. Pan Americanism also includes it—but does not stop there. It cares not only for the security of the United States but for that of all and each of the American Republics. *Good-Neighbor Pan Americanism is a joint enterprise freely undertaken by partners with equal rights and mutual obligations.* And that is precisely what the Monroe Doctrine is not!

2) *The Doctrine proved inefficient.* To be accurate, one should say that it was created impotent. It was the expression of a wish: to remove from the Western Hemisphere the threat of European military or political interference. But there was never mention of specific measures to be taken, should that wish go unheeded. Every North American statesman made it clear that the Doctrine never implied the slightest pledge by the United States actually to fight for the sovereignty of any American Republic. The man who as Secretary of State is credited with the drafting of the Message read by President Monroe to Congress—John Quincy Adams—said in a Message to the Senate December 26, 1825, after he had become President of his country: "An agreement between all the parties represented at the meeting that each will guard *by its own means* against the establishment of any future European colony within its border may be found advisable. This was more than two years since announced by my predecessor." It could not be clearer: *"each by its own means."* From the outset and from the lips of the statesmen who played the principal parts in the elaboration of the Doctrine, the world was advised that it was up to every country by its own means to uphold Monroe's recommendation, with the inference that, should any European nation violate such recommendation, the United States would not consider itself obligated to act; nor, of course, the other American republics. The Monroe Doctrine was too platonic to be effective. Later on, President Adams' Secretary of State, Henry Clay, in his instructions to the United States delegates—who did not reach Panama in time for Bolivar's Congress—made a similar statement: "The President wishes you to propose a joint declaration of the several American states, each, however, acting for and binding only itself, that

within the limits of their respective territories no new European colony will hereafter be allowed to be established." *Each* by its *own* territory, binding only *itself*: that is the only type of Pan Americanism which legitimately could be built on the foundation of the real Monroe Doctrine. That, again, is as different from our modern concept of Pan Americanism as anything we can think of. A policy along those lines is precisely what our Pan Americanism does not want to be! . . . When there is no sanction, any transgressor is willing to take the risk. To consider European infringements as "the manifestation of an unfriendly disposition toward the United States," was not enough. Monroe did not say "act of hostility" but simply "unfriendly disposition." Little wonder that European interventions, of all kinds, took place from 1823 on.

The Doctrine was appealed to in vain by some Latin American countries because of optimistic misinterpretations (improving the essence of the Message, not perverting it). The Doctrine did not bind the United States to any joint resistance against Europe. It never placed upon the United States the heavy burden of protecting the Hemisphere. The Corollaries of the Doctrine tended in that direction, but Monroe and the original Monroeists took pains to make it clear that it made no promise as to the international action of the United States.

It was appealed to in vain by Colombia in 1824; by Venezuela, Peru, and Ecuador, in 1846; by Nicaragua in 1848; again by Nicaragua, plus Honduras and El Salvador in 1849; by Mexico in 1862; by Venezuela, on five occasions (1876, 1880, 1881, 1884, 1887); by the Dominican Republic in 1905; and by Argentina in 1902-1903. Although impressive, this record is far from complete. I quote from Professor Perkins: "We must not imagine, however, that, speaking broadly, the United States, in the period with which we are dealing, pursued a consistent policy looking to the discouragement of a show of force against American republics by the states of the Old World. The recurrent chastisement of the Haitians, for example, never seems to have been regarded with much emotion in Washington. France in 1869, Spain in 1871, Germany in 1872, Great Britain in 1877, France, Spain, and Great Britain in concert in 1883, Russia in 1885, Great Britain again in

1887, resorted to force or the threat of force against the black politicians of Port-au-Prince without a word of protest from the State Department. The British in 1874, the Germans in 1878, the French in 1882, made minatory gestures against the Nicaraguans without arousing any concern in the United States. The Italians had a short-lived brawl with Colombia in 1886 which awakened no mention of the Monroe Doctrine. The French used coercive measures against the Dominican Republic in 1893 without the lifting of a hand at Washington." There were other violations, treated in detail by Nerval in a chapter significantly entitled "Violations Wholesale":

"In 1833, the United States did not prevent, nor even oppose, the seizure of the Argentine Islas Malvinas, or Falkland Islands, by Great Britain." Two years later, "the United States failed to support the government of Central America against the colonization which England was carrying on in Honduras Bay." "In 1838 France, and in 1845 France and England jointly, intervened by armed force in the Rio de la Plata." "New British encroachments on territory of Central America occurred in 1838, when the Bay Islands, of which the most important was Ruatan, were seized by the authorities of British Honduras." "In 1837, a British squadron, in reprisal for alleged indignities heaped upon a British consul, proclaimed the closing of the ports of New Granada (Colombia) and actually blockaded the main port of Cartagena." In 1838 again French naval forces blockaded the Mexican port of Veracruz, "in order to insure the collection of private claims of French citizens from the Mexican government." In 1850 the United States and Great Britain signed the Clayton-Bulwer treaty which "provided for construction of a ship canal from the Atlantic to the Pacific Ocean by way of the San Juan River and the lakes of Managua and Nicaragua." "Thus," writes Nerval, "intervention by a European power in Latin America was not only accepted, but, in this case, invited and solemnly sanctioned by the country which had given the Monroe Doctrine to the world." In the same year "the government of the United States, after confidential conversations in Washington between the Secretary of State and the British and French Ministers, agreed to join France and England in a mediation to bring about the conclusion of the war between the Dominican Republic and Haiti." "In 1861, Spain, following several years of open intermeddling with the domestic affairs of the Dominican Republic, finally proclaimed its annexation to the Spanish Crown." "In 1864, the greatest violation of the Monroe Doctrine, and by far the most famous one, was consummated. This was the overthrow of the republican form of government in Mexico by French troops, and the enthronement of the Archduke Maximilian of Austria as the Emperor of Mexico."

These are the ten major violations of the original Monroe Doctrine. Nerval mentions "secondary" violations: "the invitation by the United States to England and France, in 1862, to aid in insuring the free transit through the Panama Isthmus and in restoring internal order in Colombia; the seizure of the Chincha Islands by Spain as a reprisal against the Peruvian government, in 1864; the bombardment of Valparaiso, major Chilean port, by Spanish naval forces, in 1866, as a coercive measure; the collective intervention of the United States and certain European powers, suggested by the former though never materialized, during the Cuban insurrection of 1868-78; the retrocession of the Island of St. Bartholomew by Sweden to France, in 1877; the refusal of the United States to prevent German military action against Haiti, in the controversy of 1897; etc., etc." . . .

But ineffectiveness implies exclusively a negative criticism. A more serious charge could be made against the Monroe Doctrine when it was fashioned into a positive, aggressive policy.

3) *The Doctrine was perverted.* Originally it meant, "America not for Europe," but the Corollaries made it say, "America for the U.S.A." Cuba, Puerto Rico, Panama, the Dominican Republic, Haiti, Nicaragua—six United States "protectorates" in less than fifteen years. Outright interventions, with Marines landing, occupying territories, setting up governments and running the country: in Cuba from 1898 to 1903, then from 1906 to 1909, again in 1912, and finally from 1917 to 1922; in the Dominican Republic, from 1916 to 1924; in Nicaragua, from 1912 to 1933, practically without interruption; in Haiti, from 1915 to 1934. We can mention these facts because they represent a policy which belongs to the past. We *must* mention them because, since they cannot be forgotten, we expect the United States at least to admit them and

never to minimize their historical significance. Wrongs belong to the past only when you are able to talk about them and still be friends. That is precisely our attitude today: do not keep wrongs bottled up inside. Friendship is a positive, driving force. Frustrated rancor cannot be taken for love. Not to fear is necessary but not sufficient. Friendship is not restraint but forward impulse.

The Monroe Doctrine is guilty—not only because it did not prevent but because it even was invoked to justify manifestations of imperialism. Rather, not the original Message, but its inglorious additions. There are a good many Corollaries. I will mention the most significant ones:

In 1825, Secretary of State Clay declared that the United States could not consent to the occupation of Cuba and Puerto Rico, by "any other power than Spain." The idea was good, as is often the case in the history of Monroe's Problem Doctrine. It is better known today as the "No transfer" principle, reiterated by Van Buren in 1829, Forsyth in 1840, Webster in 1843, and consecrated at the Habana 1940 Conference. Yet the timely warning did not apply to the United States, which, for too many years, made of Cuba a virtual Protectorate. Until 1936, when Franklin D. Roosevelt's Administration renounced the right of intervention granted to its country by the well known Platt Amendment, Cuba was freed from Spain but remained subjugated to the U.S.A.

In 1845, President Polk—of whom Abraham Lincoln said, "He feels the blood of this [Mexican] war, like the blood of Abel crying to heaven against him"—added his Corollary, intended to justify the annexation of Texas. Said he: "We can never consent that European powers shall interfere to prevent such a union [of Texas and the United States] because it might disturb the 'balance of power,' which they [European countries] may desire to maintain upon this continent." So, having promulgated the Doctrine to redress and maintain the balance of power *in Europe,* a North American President claimed that Europe, in turn, had no right to be concerned over changes in the balance of power of the Western Hemisphere. . . .

Under President Cleveland, Secretary of State Bayard said that the United States had "proclaimed herself *the protector of this Western World,* in which she is by far the strongest power."

Then, in 1895, came the arrogant Olney Corollary, added by that Secretary of State who shouted to the world: "Today the United States *is practically sovereign on this continent and its fiat is law* upon the subjects to which it confines its interposition . . . its infinite resources combined with its isolated position render it *master of the situation* and practically invulnerable as against any or all other powers. . . . " It is recorded in history as "Olney's Fiat." The word of the United States was to be a command, not only to European meddlers but to the "subjects" of Latin America's protectorates—and this bombastic attitude was based on the fact that "its infinite resources combined with its isolated position render it *master of the situation* and practically invulnerable as against any or all other powers"! How foolish it all sounds today! Nothing could be more opposed to contemporary Pan Americanism, nothing less acceptable to Latin America. Olney's Fiat was a new expression of United States hegemony. So was the well known Theodore Roosevelt addition: the famous Roosevelt Corollary which dealt the Doctrine its death blow.

On December 6, 1904, "Big Stick" T. R. solemnly declared: "Any country whose people conduct themselves well, can count upon our hearty friendship. If a nation shows that it knows how to act with reasonable efficiency and decency in social and political matters, if it keeps order and pays its obligations, it need fear no interference from the United States. Chronic wrongdoing or an impotence which results in a general loosening of the ties of civilized society, may in America, as elsewhere, ultimately require intervention by some civilized nation, and in the Western Hemisphere the adherence of the United States to the Monroe Doctrine may force the United States, however reluctantly, in flagrant cases of such wrongdoing or impotence, to the exercise of an international power."

No document has proved more harmful to the prestige of the United States in the Western Hemisphere. No White House policy could be more distasteful to Latin Americans—not even, perhaps, outspoken imperialism. Latin Americans are usually inclined to admire strength, force, a nation *muy hombre*. This was imperialism without military glamour: this was imperialism *à la* Tartufe, not even *à la* Napoleon. Moreover, it was a total distortion of the original Message. Monroe's Doctrine was defensive and negative: defensive, in that it was essentially an opposition to eventual aggression from Europe; negative, in that it simply told Europe what it *should not* do—not what the United States *should* do. The Monroe Doctrine of later Corollaries became aggressive and positive: aggressive, because even without actual European attack, it urged United States "protection" of Latin America—and that was outright intervention; positive, because instead of telling Europe what *not* to do, it told the United States what it *should* do in the Western Hemisphere. From a case of America *vs.* Europe, the Corollaries made of the Doctrine a case of United States *vs.* America. President Monroe had merely shaken his head, brandished his finger, and said to Europe, "Now, now, gentlemen, if you meddle with us, we will not love you any more," while Teddy Roosevelt, brandishing a big stick, had shouted, "Listen, you guys, don't muscle in—this territory is ours."

In still another Corollary, enunciated to justify United States intervention, the same Roosevelt said: "It is far better that this country should put through such an arrangement [enforcing fulfill- ment of financial obligations contracted by Latin American states] rather than to allow any foreign country to undertake it." To intervene in order to protect: to intervene, in order to prevent others from so doing. It is the "Invasion for Protection" corollary, so much in the limelight recently, in other parts of the world. . . .

4) Thus, in the light of historical facts—laying aside consid- erations of theoretical value—one can easily understand why the Monroe Doctrine became so *unpopular* not only among Latin Americans but also among an increasing number of people of the United States. Those who do not yet see the point would do well to put themselves, by a stretch of the imagination, in the victims' shoes. Latin Americans—Professor Chapman to the contrary— are just as patriotic and liberty-loving as Anglo-Americans. Unless you begin your analysis on that assumption, you are not qualified to judge the problem of inter-Americanism. Latin Americans, even those who admire the technical superiority of their powerful industrial neighbor, do not recognize the political or moral tutelage of the United States. We have seen that some Latin American countries are ahead of the United States in social legislation. Mex-

ico's agrarian policy, for instance, is certainly more advanced than that of the United States. I could name many other important fields in which Latin America maintains a moral leadership. But one should avoid unnecessary comparisons. It is enough to proclaim that Latin Americans love "life, liberty, and the pursuit of happiness" as ardently as their northern neighbors. So, any reminder directly or indirectly connected with brutal attacks from without, whoever the aggressor, automatically revives legitimate Latin American resentment. . . .

5) Finally, in the light of authentic, genuine Pan Americanism *à la* Bolivar or *à la* F. D. Roosevelt, it is obvious that the Doctrine seems completely *outmoded*. The days in which a single country—however powerful—could claim the exclusive right to behave, on the world stage, as a "rugged individualist," are gone forever. Ask Napoleon, ask the Kaiser, or ask Hitler! Civilized order is a joint enterprise, freely accepted by all partners. Mankind does not allow gangsters, be they individuals or nations. Order was established, first among the members of the family, then among the residents of the community, later among the citizens of a nation. Finally the day is near when a cooperative international order will be established among the nations of the earth. That order, whether local or national, continental or international, can be conceived only as a joint enterprise. America was the first continent in history to struggle for the establishment of such order. There can be no room in this continent for a doctrine which, even at its best and in its original intention, rests essentially on the arbitrary decision of one self-appointed "leader." The hour of selfish nationalism is past. There is no room for anarchy in organized society. Because the welfare of the many must prevail over that of the few, Monroeist Pan Americanism has been gradually but irrevocably displaced by democratic Pan Americanism.

The Monroe Doctrine may not be dead, but there is little use for it today. And there certainly will be less room for it in the world of tomorrow.

THE TWO FACES OF LATIN AMERICA*

BY

GERMÁN ARCINIEGAS

[1952]

There are two Americas: the visible and the invisible. The visible America, the America of presidents and embassies, expresses itself through official organs, through a controlled press. This America takes its seat at the conference table of the Pan American Union and has many votes in the United Nations. And there is the mute, repressed America, which is a vast reservoir of revolution. Both Americas are misleading in appearance.

Under its dictatorial regimes, visible America makes fervent protestations of its democratic faith, signs charters of liberties, manufacturing one line of goods for foreign and another for domestic consumption. This double personality has achieved a dexterity that is almost unbelievable. Even though everywhere and in all periods of history there has been something of this same split between what is said and what is done, the contrast has rarely been so brutal as that afforded today by the Latin American dictatorships. Laureano Gómez who had come to power on a wave of violence once said to a group of North American journalists: "This is a people of savage Communists; they have killed one hundred police officers. Is there a civilized nation anywhere that would tolerate the killing of one hundred police?" To understand this sophism we must analyze two words: "Communism" and "police." For the purposes of their practical dealings with the United States the dictators describe as Communists all those who do not support them. According to General Odría, the people of Peru are communists; according to the military *junta* of Venezuela, the people of Venezuela; according to the dictator of Bogotá, the people of Colombia; according to General Trujillo,

---

*From Germán Arciniegas, *The State of Latin America*. Published by Alfred A. Knopf, 1952. Reprinted by permission. Germán Arciniegas (b. 1900), Columbian author and diplomat, formerly Minister of Education, has been Professor of Spanish-American Literature at Columbia University since 1947.

the people of the Dominican Republic. The word "police" likewise requires definition. A policeman in the United States or London is a human being who helps an old lady across the street, a guardian angel for the children coming out of school, the protecting arm of the law. A policeman under a Latin American despot is a shady character not too far removed from the criminal, a man of dubious past who is handed a uniform and a revolver with orders to crush the opposition and maintain order by terror. The one hundred police officers over whom the North American journalists were asked to weep had been one hundred weapons turned on the peasants, members of a shock force that burned down homes, stole cattle, and attacked the wives and daughters of the peasants in scenes of barbarity that beggar description. When they got a chance the peasants fought back and killed. They were not Communists; the police officers were not police.

This arbitrary use of words has given rise to the greatest confusion. The despots use the word "democracy" to set up governments such as those described in the pages of this book. The common man asks himself if this can be democracy. The same thing holds true of the other words in the political lexicon: army, religion, freedom, Christianity, faith, republic, justice, judge, president, elections, congress, priest, university, peace, public opinion. By turning words inside out, dictators destroy the natural medium of communication among people. When one of the presidents of visible America speaks, his every word must be analyzed against the background of its accepted meaning and the application given to it by him inside his own country.

Although this theme may seem academic, its implications go very deep, because as a result of this deception moral principles are being undermined, good faith is being corrupted, and an atmosphere of cynicism and distrust is growing up. The story of the tower of Babel is not a fairy tale. At this very moment the greatest political campaign in the world is based on one word: peace. With special reference to Russia, her brand of peace is familiar to those Latin Americans who have suffered dictatorships. Paraguay enjoyed peace of this sort under Dr. Francia; this was the peace of Argentina under Rosas, of Venezuela under Juan Vicente Gómez. This peace is the objective of their legitimate successors. We call it a living cemetery. There are peace and order because no one can talk or criticize or object or join his fellows in assembly. It is the kind of peace guarded by the family servant who acts as a spy on the household.

Latin America, like other parts of the world, has fought against the peace of the colony, the peace of slavery, the peace of servility. At times with maximum passion and heroism. In his war against these kinds of peace, man has grown in dignity, intelligence has had a mission to fulfill, people have learned that they are entitled to an existence better than that of the beasts of the field, and a little decency has been brought into the world.

Theoretically it would seem that Latin America is a fertile field for Communism. Yet it is amazing how few addicts this party has made. In fact it may be said that in Latin America Communism is non-existent. France has many more Communists than all of Latin America despite the fact that the people of Latin America, badly fed, badly dressed, badly housed, and badly treated, are in much closer contact than any other with the capitalist world of their next-door neighbor. Why does Communism fail to take hold there? Because in Latin America the thirst for freedom is as great as the thirst for justice. Because there is a sense of national pride. The Mexican wants to be the master of his house, not the lackey of Moscow. What Schuyler said of the Negroes—that they cannot be Communists because they have emerged from slavery and are not buying a return ticket—holds true of the Latin Americans. They are through with being colonials.

By reasons of their historic formation the Latin American masses are well conditioned to absorb and spread ideas of representative government, the spirit of liberty, the doctrines of social justice. This is a world in which, from the beginning, different races have had to live together and have fused, where no old aristocracy exists, where privilege is not entrenched. But this potentiality which exists in the Latin American republics that enjoy free government must be assured to the others.

Like visible America, invisible America lies. The humble folk know that they cannot say what they think, and the upper classes have learned this too. On one occasion, at the beginning of Perón's

dictatorship, a group of ladies of the best families gathered in the
street and began to sing the Argentine national anthem:

> Hark, mortals, the sacred cry:
> Liberty, liberty, liberty!

The ladies spent the night in jail. In Barranquilla, Colombia, the
director of one of the factories in that prosperous industrial city
shouted in the lobby of the Hotel del Prado—the best in the city—
"Long live the Liberal Party." A bullet from a policeman's revolver dropped him dead. If this can happen to persons who, by
reason of their social position and wealth, generally receive prefer-
ential treatment from the authorities, what can the peasant expect?
This book has touched only lightly on instances of the brutality
that is of constant occurrence. The full account of the violence,
the tortures, the concentration camps has not been told outside the
frontiers. But if in one of the most cultured countries of Europe
Nazism could unleash the dark forces it did, why wonder that
similar things have taken place in backward lands? In invisible
America, where a vast mass of the population lives with the cold
breath of terror on its neck, the least word may bring reprisals.
The part of prudence is to keep quiet, to wear a mask. Where
machine guns have the floor a deep silence reigns. Life goes on
under the cover of conventional phrases, lip-service, extorted votes.
A Peruvian poet has described the attitude of the Indian in
a famous poem in which each stanza ends with: "¿Quien sabe,
señor?"

Nobody knows exactly what these 150,000,000 silent men and
women think, feel, dream, or await in the depths of their being.

The attitude of the Indian is not the result of racial shortcoming;
it has been developed by the life he has been forced to live. The
same dissimulation is now found among white "Sons of the American Revolution," newly arrived immigrants—even in the third
party, made up of business men, that is to be found in all the Latin
American countries. Latin America's natural rate of growth is
very rapid. The industrial world in the process of development
there is creating great wealth. This is apparent in the cities, where
the skyscrapers, shops, hotels, theaters, and apartment houses are
among the best to be found anywhere in the world. Yet all this
could be multiplied if only there were security, if the storm clouds

could be rolled away from invisible America. Native capital flees from Latin America. Only in Montevideo and Mexico City have large fortunes found refuge. If the amount of Latin American funds on deposit today in the banks of New York and Switzerland were accurately known, one would conclude that Latin America possesses all the capital it needs. Even capital is invisible in America.

Europe had a brief span of security which reached its apex before the First World War. People there still preserve the habits of a safe world. Insecurity is Latin America's political tradition, and underlies the history of its economic crises. There was a day when its wealth was rubber; when rubber began to be produced in great quantity by the Far East, this wealth vanished. The same thing has happened for this or an analogous reason with quinine, cacao, nitrates, coffee, sugar, diamonds, Panama hats. At this very moment the vast development of colonial Africa holds a tremendous threat for Latin America. Carlos Dávila, who has studied these matters, says:

"Before World War II the United States was buying 94 per cent of its tropical imports, mostly strategic materials, from an undependable Orient ten thousand miles away, instead of from its neighbors in near-by Latin America, and was paying for this unsound course in mounting scarcities. In 1939 the United States' imports of essential and strategic commodities amounted to $400 million. Of this, six million, or 1½%, came from Latin America. When World War II broke out, it was freely stated this would 'never happen again.' But as events are shaping up now, it may very well happen again."

What is the approach to Latin America? With two Americas, visible and invisible, each having a double personality, it is a region of complexities shot through with reserves, suspicion, resentment, wariness, and fears. There is one word that arouses an immeasurable reaction on the part of those who have emerged from a colonial world and have heard about a semi-colonial one: "intervention." Intervention, too, has a double personality. It may take the form of landing marines, a diplomatic offensive, threats. It may also take the form of omission. For years Perón's best campaign slogan has been "Braden or Perón." Braden's speeches were looked upon in Argentina as American intervention. This intervention was violently denounced by Perón, who, however, was more than willing to accept another more effective intervention: a $125,000,000 loan and the honeyed words of Mr. Braden's successor.

Everything in Latin American politics depends on the approach. On analysis things turn out to be simpler than they look. The thing to do is to decide between two opposed methods and then adjust each action and the evaluation of each incident to the method decided upon. Either one accepts the position that the invisible America is a real factor that will sooner or later swing into action or one takes the position that it is negligible and that its people are a kind of still life that can be handled as seems most convenient. One of the dictators said not long ago at an intimate gathering: "What we have proved is that the people does not exist; nobody can frighten us any more with a ghost that has been laid." This is one opinion. If this is adopted, it should be carried to its ultimate conclusions. The dictatorships should be given arms, the police state strengthened, and the way paved for a silent, zombie continent where good business can be carried on and a new age of wizards established.

If, on the other hand, it is assumed that the love of liberty is still alive in the heart of Latin America, and that along with its material resources there is a human reserve that can produce more and better on a basis of dignity and justice, or that may kick over the traces any day, the approach to the problem must become radically different. In the light of this a Pan American Union of Public Opinion becomes a possibility. It will be conceded that the coming generations, the young people trained in the universities, are equipped to carry on a tradition of learning, scientific studies, and art, fields in which contributions of universal value already have been made. When Bernardo Houssay receives the Nobel Prize for his work as head of the Institute of Physiology of Buenos Aires, when the Nobel Prize for Literature is awarded to Gabriela Mistral for her poetry, when the work of the Mexican painters is accepted as one of the important artistic achievements of our century, there can be no quibbling about Latin America's cultural status.

During the first half of this century no other section of the world showed so high an index of material progress as Latin America. If this rate was formerly surpassed by that of the United States, the two are now on a level. In the briefest space of time— during the years from 1920 to 1950—six of the most beautiful cities in the world have grown up in Latin America. And, looking backwards, several of the most impressive civilizations history records once flourished in this same area. Is all this to end in a cemetery of living dead?

Using a little common sense, and with an eye to the future, it would seem far better to regard the Latin Americans as one of mankind's reserves that should be put to active use. Inside Latin America this is not accepted by those who favor a political system of servility. Nor is it accepted by those outside Latin America who share that idea. And yet, what today look like insurmountable difficulties may tomorrow be but the memory of a hideous nightmare. In America, where a handful of dictators struts and frets, there are great zones of light. And throughout the hemisphere, in the background, stands the people. The day they can make themselves heard they may be a consuming fire or a flood of light. In any case, they hold the light of that *mañana* which is omnipresent and enigmatic in the language of the Latin Americans.

THE ALLIANCE FOR PROGRESS *

BY

JOHN F. KENNEDY

[1961]

. . . One hundred and thirty-nine years ago this week the
United States, stirred by the heroic struggles of its fellow Americans, urged the independence and recognition of the new Latin
American Republics. It was then, at the dawn of freedom throughout this hemisphere, that Bolívar spoke of his desire to see the
Americas fashioned into the greatest region in the world, "greatest," he said, "not so much by virtue of her area and her wealth,
as by her freedom and her glory."

Never, in the long history of our hemisphere, has this dream
been nearer to fulfillment, and never has it been in greater danger.

The genius of our scientists has given us the tools to bring
abundance to our land, strength to our industry, and knowledge to
our people. For the first time we have the capacity to strike off the
remaining bonds of poverty and ignorance—to free our people for
the spiritual and intellectual fulfillment which has always been
the goal of our civilization.

Yet at this very moment of maximum opportunity, we confront
the same forces which have imperiled America throughout its
history—the alien forces which once again seek to impose the despotisms of the Old World on the people of the New. . . .

We meet together as firm and ancient friends, united by history
and experience and by our determination to advance the values of
American civilization. For this new world of ours is not merely
an accident of geography. Our continents are bound together by a
common history—the endless exploration of new frontiers. Our
nations are the product of a common struggle—the revolt from
colonial rule. And our people share a common heritage—the quest
for the dignity and the freedom of man.

The revolutions which gave us birth ignited, in the words of

---

* From an address by President John F. Kennedy to a White House reception
for Latin American diplomats, March 13, 1961. Reprinted from *The Department
of State Bulletin*, April 3, 1961.

Thomas Paine, "a spark never to be extinguished." And across vast, turbulent continents these American ideals still stir man's struggle for national independence and individual freedom. But as we welcome the spread of the American Revolution to other lands, we must also remember that our own struggle—the revolution which began in Philadelphia in 1776 and in Caracas in 1811—is not yet finished. Our hemisphere's mission is not yet completed. *For our unfulfilled task is to demonstrate to the entire world that man's unsatisfied aspiration for economic progress and social justice can best be achieved by free men working within a framework of democratic institutions.* If we can do this in our own hemisphere, and for our own people, we may yet realize the prophecy of the great Mexican patriot, Benito Juarez, that "democracy is the destiny of future humanity."

As a citizen of the United States let me be the first to admit that we North Americans have not always grasped the significance of this common mission, just as it is also true that many in your own countries have not fully understood the urgency of the need to lift people from poverty and ignorance and despair. But we must turn from these mistakes—from the failures and the misunderstandings of the past—to a future full of peril but bright with hope.

Throughout Latin America—a continent rich in resources and in the spiritual and cultural achievements of its people—millions of men and women suffer the daily degradations of hunger and poverty. They lack decent shelter or protection from disease. Their children are deprived of the education or the jobs which are the gateway to a better life. And each day the problems grow more urgent. Population growth is outpacing economic growth, low living standards are even further endangered, and discontent—the discontent of a people who know that abundance and the tools of progress are at last within their reach—that discontent is growing. In the words of José Figueres, "once dormant peoples are struggling upward toward the sun, toward a better life."

If we are to meet a problem so staggering in its dimensions, our approach must itself be equally bold, an approach consistent with the majestic concept of Operation Pan America. Therefore I have called on all the people of the hemisphere to join in a new Alliance for Progress—*Alianza para Progreso*—a vast cooperative effort, unparalleled in magnitude and nobility of purpose, to satisfy the basic needs of the American people for homes, work and land, health and schools—*techo, trabajo y tierra, salud y escuela.*

I propose that the American Republics begin on a vast new 10-year plan for the Americas, a plan to transform the 1960's into an historic decade of democratic progress. These 10 years will be the years of maximum progress, maximum effort—the years when the greatest obstacles must be overcome, the years when the need for assistance will be the greatest.

And if we are successful, if our effort is bold enough and determined enough, then the close of this decade will mark the beginning of a new era in the American experience. The living standards of every American family will be on the rise, basic education will be available to all, hunger will be a forgotten experience, the need for massive outside help will have passed, most nations will have entered a period of self-sustaining growth, and, although there will be still much to do, every American Republic will be the master of its own revolution and its own hope and progress.

Let me stress that only the most determined efforts of the American nations themselves can bring success to this effort. They, and they alone, can mobilize their resources, enlist the energies of their people, and modify their social patterns so that all, and not just a privileged few, share in the fruits of growth. If this effort is made, then outside assistance will give a vital impetus to progress; without it, no amount of help will advance the welfare of the people.

Thus if the countries of Latin America are ready to do their part —and I am sure they are—then I believe the United States, for its part, should help provide resources of a scope and magnitude sufficient to make this bold development plan a success, just as we helped to provide, against nearly equal odds, the resources adequate to help rebuild the economies of Western Europe. For only an effort of towering dimensions can insure fulfillment of our plan for a decade of progress.

I will shortly request a ministerial meeting of the Inter-American Economic and Social Council, a meeting at which we can begin the massive planning effort which will be at the heart of the Alliance for Progress.

For if our alliance is to succeed, each Latin nation must formulate long-range plans for its own development—plans which establish targets and priorities, insure monetary stability, establish the machinery for vital social change, stimulate private activity and initiative, and provide for a maximum national effort. These plans will be the foundation of our development effort and the basis for the allocation of outside resources. . . .

We must support all economic integration which is a genuine step toward larger markets and greater competitive opportunity. The fragmentation of Latin American economies is a serious barrier to industrial growth. . . .

The United States is ready to cooperate in serious, case-by-case examinations of commodity market problems. . . .

We will immediately step up our food-for-peace emergency program. . . .

All the people of the hemisphere must be allowed to share in the expanding wonders of science. . . .

We must rapidly expand the training of those needed to man the economies of rapidly developing countries. . . .

We reaffirm our pledge to come to the defense of any American nation whose independence is endangered. . . .

We invite our friends in Latin America to contribute to the enrichment of life and culture in the United States. We need teachers of your literature and history and tradition, opportunities for our young people to study in your universities. . . .

With steps such as these we propose to complete the revolution of the Americas, to build a hemisphere where all men can hope for a suitable standard of living and all can live out their lives in dignity and in freedom.

To achieve this goal political freedom must accompany material progress. Our Alliance for Progress is an alliance of free governments—and it must work to eliminate tyranny from a hemisphere in which it has no rightful place. Therefore let us express our special friendship to the people of Cuba and the Dominican Republic —and the hope they will soon rejoin the society of free men, uniting with us in our common effort.

This political freedom must be accompanied by social change. For unless necessary social reforms, including land and tax reform, are freely made, unless we broaden the opportunity of all of our people, unless the great mass of Americans share in increasing prosperity, then our alliance, our revolution, our dream, and our freedom will fail. But we call for social change by free men—change in the spirit of Washington and Jefferson, of Bolívar and San Martín and Martí—not change which seeks to impose on men tyrannies which we cast out a century and a half ago. Our motto is what it has always been—progress yes, tyranny no—*progreso sí, tiranía no!*

But our greatest challenge comes from within—the task of creating an American civilization where spiritual and cultural values are strengthened by an ever-broadening base of material advance, where, within the rich diversity of its own traditions, each nation is free to follow its own path toward progress.

The completion of our task will, of course, require the efforts of all the governments of our hemisphere. But the efforts of governments alone will never be enough. In the end the people must choose and the people must help themselves.

And so I say to the men and women of the Americas—to the *campesino* in the fields, to the *obrero* in the cities, to the *estudiante* in the schools—prepare your mind and heart for the task ahead, call forth your strength, and let each devote his energies to the betterment of all so that your children and our children in this hemisphere can find an ever richer and a freer life.

Let us once again transform the American Continent into a vast crucible of revolutionary ideas and efforts, a tribute to the power of the creative energies of free men and women, an example to all the world that liberty and progress walk hand in hand. Let us once again awaken our American revolution until it guides the struggles of people everywhere—not with an imperialism of force or fear but the rule of courage and freedom and hope for the future of man.

REVOLUTION IN
LATIN AMERICA *

BY

J. WILLIAM FULBRIGHT

[1966]

Nowhere has the ambivalence in the American attitude toward revolution been more apparent and more troublesome than in the relations of the United States with Latin America. In Latin America as in Asia the United States, a profoundly unrevolutionary nation, is required to make choices between accepting revolution and trying to suppress it.

Caught between genuine sympathy for social reform on the one hand and an intense fear of revolution on the Cuban model on the other, we have thus far been unwilling, or unable, to follow a consistent course. On the one hand, we have made ourselves the friend of certain progressive democratic governments and have joined with Latin America in the Alliance for Progress, the purpose of which is social revolution by peaceful means. On the other hand, we have allowed our fear of communism to drive us into supporting a number of governments whose policies, to put it charitably, are inconsistent with the aims of the Alliance, and on three occasions—Guatemala in 1954, Cuba in 1961, and the Dominican Republic in 1965—we resorted to force, illegally, unwisely, and inasmuch as each of these interventions almost certainly strengthened the appeal of communism to the younger generation of educated Latin Americans, unsuccessfully as well.

The United States thus pursues two largely incompatible policies in Latin America—discriminating support for social reform and an undiscriminating anti-communism that often makes us the friend of military dictatorships and reactionary oligarchies. Anti-communism is increasingly being given precedence over support for re-

---

* From *The Arrogance of Power*, published by Random House, copyright 1966 by J. William Fulbright. Reprinted by permission. J. William Fulbright (b. 1905), Democrat, is United States Senator from Arkansas (1945–   ) and Chairman of the Committee on Foreign Relations.

form. American policy-makers clearly prefer reformist democratic governments to economic oligarchies and military juntas as long as the former are aggressively anti-communist; but the slightest suspicion of communist support seems to be enough to discredit a reform movement in North American eyes and to drive United States policy-makers into the stifling embrace of the generals and the oligarchs.

Guided by a reflex bred into them by Fidel Castro, American policy-makers have developed a tendency to identify revolution with communism, assuming, because they have something to do with each other, as indeed they do, that they are one and the same thing, as indeed they are not. The pervading suspicion of social revolutionary movements on the part of United States policy-makers is unfortunate indeed because there is the strong possibility of more explosions in Latin America and, insofar as the United States makes itself the enemy of revolutionary movements, communism is enabled to make itself their friend. The anti-revolutionary bias in United States policy, which is rooted in the fear of communism on the Cuban model, can only have the effect of strengthening communism.

The Alliance for Progress encouraged the hope in Latin America that the United States would not only tolerate but actively support domestic social revolution. The Dominican intervention at least temporarily destroyed that hope.

The election on June 1, 1966, of Joachin Balaguer as President of the Dominican Republic, in an election regarded by most observers as having been fair and free, has been widely interpreted as a vindication of the American military intervention of April 1965, as proof that the intervention was necessary, justified, and wise. Those of us who criticized the American intervention must concede that a degree of order and stability in the Dominican Republic was restored more quickly than seemed likely in the spring and summer of 1965 and that credit for this properly belongs to United States diplomacy, to the Organization of American States, and to the Inter-American Force which remained in the Dominican Republic until the summer of 1966, as well as to the provisional government which held office from September 1965 to July 1966 and to the elected government which succeeded it.

That, however, is all that must or can be conceded. The facts remain that the United States engaged in a unilateral military intervention in violation of inter-American law, the "good neighbor" policy of thirty years' standing, and the spirit of the Charter of Punta del Este; that the Organization of American States was gravely weakened as the result of its use—with its own consent—as an instrument of the policy of the United States; that the power of the reactionary military oligarchy in the Dominican Republic remains substantially unimpaired; that the intervention alienated from the United States the confidence and good opinion of reformers and young people throughout Latin America, the very people, that is, whose efforts are essential to the success of peaceful revolution through the Alliance for Progress; and that confidence in the word and in the intentions of the United States Government has been severely shaken, not only in Latin America but in Europe and Asia and even in our own country.

Recovery from a disaster does not turn the disaster into a triumph. To regard the restoration of constitutional government in the Dominican Republic as a vindication of the intervention is like regarding the reconstruction of a burned-out house as a vindication of the fire. The effects of the Dominican intervention abroad have been described by a good friend of the United States, the former President of Colombia, Alberto Lleras Camargo, who was touring Europe at the time and who later wrote ". . . The general feeling was that a new and openly imperialistic policy in the style of Theodore Roosevelt had been adopted by the White House and that, if there was intervention with Marines in the Hemisphere, against unequivocal standards of law, one can only expect—in Asia, in Africa, and in wherever—new acts of force and, perhaps, the escalation of the cold war to the hot in a very short time. . . ."

The central fact about the intervention of the United States in the Dominican Republic was that we had closed our minds to the causes and to the essential legitimacy of revolution in a country in which democratic procedures had failed. The involvement of an undetermined number of communists in the Dominican Revolution was judged to discredit the entire reformist movement, like poison in a well, and rather than use our considerable resources to compete with the communists for influence with the democratic forces who actively solicited our support, we intervened militarily on the side of a corrupt and reactionary military oligarchy. We thus lent credence to the idea that the United States is the enemy of social revolution, and therefore the enemy of social justice, in Latin America.

The evidence is incontrovertible that American forces landed in Santo Domingo on April 28, 1965, not, as was and is officially contended, for the primary purpose of saving American lives but for the primary if not the sole purpose of defeating the revolution, which, on the basis of fragmentary evidence and exaggerated estimates of communist influence, was judged to be either communist-dominated or certain to become so. . . . .

The United States intervened in the Dominican Republic for the purpose of preventing the victory of a revolutionary force which was judged to be communist-dominated. On the basis of Ambassador Bennett's messages to Washington, there is no doubt that the fear of communism rather than danger to American lives was his primary or sole reason for recommending military intervention. In fact, no American lives were lost in Santo Domingo until the Marines began exchanging fire with the rebels after April 28; reports of widespread shooting that endangered American lives turned out to be greatly exaggerated.

The question of the degree of communist influence is therefore crucial but it cannot be answered with certainty. The weight of the evidence is that communists did not participate in planning the revolution—indeed, there is some indication that it took them by surprise—but that they very rapidly began to try to take advantage of it and to seize control of it. The evidence does not establish that the communists at any time actually had control of the revolution. There is little doubt that they had influence within the revolutionary movement, but the degree of that influence remains a matter of speculation.

The United States government, however, assumed almost from the beginning that the revolution was communist-dominated, or would certainly become so, and that nothing short of forcible opposition could prevent a communist takeover. In their panic lest the Dominican Republic become "another Cuba," some of our officials seem to have forgotten that virtually all reform movements attract

some communist support, that there is an important difference between communist support and communist control of a political
movement, that it is quite possible to *compete* with the communists
for influence in a reform movement rather than abandon it to them,
and, most important of all, that economic development and social
justice are themselves the primary and most reliable security against
communist subversion. The point I am making is not—most emphatically not—that there was no communist participation in the
Dominican crisis, but simply that the Administration acted on the
premise that the revolution was *controlled* by communists—a premise which it failed to establish at the time and has not established
since.

Intervention on the basis of communist participation as distinguished from control of the Dominican Revolution was a mistake
of panic and timidity which also reflects a grievous misreading of
the temper of contemporary Latin American politics. Communists
are present in all Latin American countries, and they are going to
inject themselves into almost any Latin American revolution and
try to seize control of it. If any group or any movement with which
the communists associate themselves is going to be automatically
condemned in the eyes of the United States, then we have indeed
given up all hope of influencing even to a marginal degree the
revolutionary movements and the demands for social change which
are sweeping Latin America. Worse, if that is our view, then we
have made ourselves the prisoners of the Latin American oligarchs
who are engaged in a vain attempt to preserve the status quo—reactionaries who habitually use the term "communist" very loosely,
in part out of emotional predilection and in part in a calculated
effort to scare the United States into supporting their selfish and
discredited aims.

The movement of the future in Latin America is social revolution. The question is whether it is to be communist or democratic
revolution and the choice which the Latin Americans make will
depend in part on how the United States uses its great influence. It
should be very clear that the choice is not between social revolution
and conservative oligarchy but whether, by supporting reform, we
bolster the popular non-communist left, or, by supporting unpopular oligarchies, we drive the rising generation of educated and pa-

triotic young Latin Americans to an embittered and hostile form of communism like that of Fidel Castro in Cuba.

We simply cannot have it both ways; we must choose between the objectives of the Alliance for Progress and a foredoomed effort to sustain the status quo in Latin America. The choice which we are to make is the principal unanswered question arising out of the unhappy events in the Dominican Republic and, indeed, the principal unanswered question for the future of our relations with Latin America.

OUR DOMINICAN INTERVENTION *

BY

WALTER LIPPMANN

[1965]

The crucial point in the Dominican affair is that the decision to rescue Americans and other foreigners became almost immediately a decision also to stop the rebellion. The disorders began, said the President on Sunday evening "as a popular democratic revolution committed to democracy and social justice." The purpose of the revolution was to restore the duly elected President, Juan Bosch, who had been deposed in 1963 by reactionary military forces 7 months after taking office. "But, the revolutionary movement took a tragic turn."

A number of Communists trained in Cuba "took increasing control, . . . many of the original leaders of the rebellion, the followers of President Bosch, took refuge in foreign embassies because they had been superseded by other evil forces, and the secretary general of the rebel government, Martinez Francisco, appealed for a cease-fire. But he was ignored. The revolution was now in other and dangerous hands."

In the state of the emergency, there was no time for a thorough investigation of all the facts. President Johnson took his decision to halt the rebellion on what, it seems to me, was the right ground.

It was that, if the Communists in the revolutionary forces took over the government, the result would be for all practical purposes irreversible. There would never be another election while they were in power in Santo Domingo. On the other hand, while the Bosch restoration has been halted, the way is still open to the return of the party which won the 1965 elections. By acting promptly and decisively the President has kept the way open as otherwise it might well have been closed forever.

It is quite plain from the President's speech that the United States does not want to see a restoration of the old reactionary regime and that it does want the kind of popular democratic revo-

---

* From *The Washington Post*, May 4, 1965. Reprinted by permission.

lution, committed to "democracy and social justice" which President Bosch represents.

It is a question whether a country like the Dominican Republic can find stability somewhere in the center between the extreme left and the extreme right. Cuba did not find this stability. There was nothing, it turned out, between Batista and Castro. Is there in the Dominican Republic something between the corrupt and cruel dictatorship of Trujillo and a Communist dictatorship, like Castro's. which would be far to the left of President Bosch?

If President Johnson, working with the OAS, can help the Dominicans find that something in between, can restore President Bosch and shore him up while he carries through the drastic reforms which are necessary in order to extirpate the evils of Trujillo, evils that breed communism, it will be a bright day for the American Republics.

We must not think it is impossible to do this. Mexico has found the middle way. There are new currents flowing in this hemisphere, most notably in Chile and Brazil. They flow toward the center, from the left in Chile and from the right in Brazil.

Our intervention in the Caribbean island will, of course, be looked upon all over the world in the context of our intervention in southeast Asia. We need to consider it ourselves in this context.

We must start from the basic fact that what we have done is literally forbidden by article 15 of the Charter of the OAS—"No State or group of States has the right to intervene, directly or indirectly, for any reason whatever, in the internal or external affairs of any other State."

How then can we defend and justify ourselves? Shall we do it on the ground that the United States is the global policeman, or the global fire department, appointed to stop communism everywhere? After such a plea the best we could hope for even from our best friends is that they will smile indulgently at our innocent self-righteousness. The addicts of the global and crusading theory should ask themselves how many more Vietnams and Dominican Republics they are prepared and able to police.

The other ground, which is the one I take, is the old-fashioned and classical diplomatic ground that the Dominican Republic lies squarely within the sphere of influence of the United States, and that it is normal, not abnormal, for a great power to insist that within its sphere of influence, no other great power shall exercise hostile military and political force.

Since we emerged from isolation in the beginning of this century, American foreign policy has been bedeviled by the utopian fallacy that because this is one world, special spheres of influence are an inherent evil and obsolete. Wilson proclaimed this globalism. Franklin Roosevelt, under the prodding of Cordell Hull, adhered to it against Churchill's better judgment. And Johnson continues to invoke it without, I think, a sufficient study of it.

As a matter of fact, experience must soon verify the truth that spheres of influence are fundamental in the very nature of international society. They are as much a fact of life as are birth and death. Great powers will resist the invasion of their spheres of influence. The Soviet Union did that in Hungary, France did it recently in Gabon, the British have always done it when the Low Countries were attacked, the United States has done it in the Dominican Republic. And, if and when we want to know and face the truth, how much of what China is doing is something very similar?

Recognition of spheres of influence is a true alternative to globalism. It is the alternative to Communist globalism which proclaims a universal revolution. It is the alternative to anti-Communist globalism which promises to fight anti-Communist wars everywhere. The acceptance of spheres of influence has been the diplomatic foundation of the détente in Europe between the Soviet Union and the West. Eventually, it will provide the formula of coexistence between Red China and the United States.

THE NEED FOR
RADICAL CHANGE *

BY

GEORGE C. LODGE

[1969]

We are confronting in Latin America what is in essence an ideological crisis—a question of purpose. Given our national predilections this is the kind of problem we find most difficult to deal with. The temptation is to retreat, retrench and look inward. This is an impossibility: our wealth is too great not to share, our enterprise too successful and too useful not to expand, our interests— and the peace of the world—too vulnerable not to protect.

The central issue is revolution—radical, structural change in the political, economic and social systems of Latin America—and the relationship to it of the United States. Comforting and noncontroversial as it may be to speak in familiar technical terms of "development," particularly "economic development," we must accept the fact that real development is change; and that change necessarily raises questions of speed, direction and control which are in the largest sense inherently political and deeply controversial. In the Latin American environment particularly, the introduction of seemingly innocuous economic or technological change often in fact requires profound, permanent and radical alteration of existing systems.

Let us take food production, which has been hobbling along beneath the burden of rising population. We have generally supposed improving agricultural output to be a matter of better seed, more fertilizer, irrigation and the like. We have proceeded on the vague assumption that Latin American peasants resemble in some half-formed way the homesteaders of our own West—confident,

---

* From *Foreign Affairs,* July 1969, copyright by the Council on Foreign Relations. Reprinted by permission. George C. Lodge (b. 1927) is an Associate Professor of Business Administration at the Harvard Business School. He was Assistant Secretary of Labor for International Affairs (1958–1962) and is the author of *Engines of Change, United States Interests and Revolution in Latin America.*

Protestant entrepreneurs eagerly waiting for the means to a better life. We have treated Latin American states as though they were in fact representative of their people, able and willing to introduce the manifold changes which we encourage—and pay—them to promise, and prepared to mobilize efficiently a vast spread of governmental services to their rural areas. While some governments receiving assistance may have such capacity and determination, most do not. The Latin American peasant, generally speaking, is snared in an historical web of pressures and powers which allows him little control over his environment and deprives him of confidence and motivation. He feels little or no identification with his government or with what is called his nation; his sole concern is survival and the agonies that it involves. Disorganized, isolated and detached, he, like the Black American, has been denied power in his own country. While this condition has afflicted roughly only 20 percent of North Americans, it circumscribes the existence of perhaps 80 percent of Latin Americans. A change in the production of food, or any other sort of meaningful change, requires a fundamental realignment of the structures and the power which contain this condition. More than technology, it is a problem of land tenure, of markets, of credit, of motivation, of organization and of commitment. It is in the largest sense a political problem. The bonds that tie the peasants to their traditional marginal existence are not to be undone by governments dependent upon the existing power structure. That would constitute an unreal form of self-subversion. The job must be done by a variety of self-sustaining, largely nongovernmental, engines of change.

Here and there these engines are at work; campesino federations in Venezuela and the Dominican Republic; organizations of the radical Church, like those in Brazil, Chile and Panama; some trade unions; and various enterprises, such as the large commercial farms of Mexico, and certain integrated food production, processing and distribution activities of some U.S.-based multinational corporations.

They are contributing to the development of true communities in Latin America, helping them to form and organize in such a way that they can govern themselves, determine their values and goals and build the institutions and organizations necessary for a vigorous, responsive and lasting political system. These engines of change are providing a new confidence that power in the environment is not permanently fixed, that movement is possible; a new sense of purpose and legitimacy. And this matter of purpose is at the heart of Latin America's difficulties. . . .

Student organizations and nationalist guerrilla movements are also endeavoring to operate as engines of change, but so far with limited success. And, surprisingly perhaps, communism in Latin America has been dramatically unsuccessful in causing change. Its European-based Marxist ideology has consistently shown itself to be irrelevant to the Latin American reality. Its fealty to Moscow has made it an unacceptable form of neocolonialism, an affront to nationalism; and in the clinch, Moscow has been unable to protect its Latin American offspring. Although the Soviet Union is stuck with the economic burden of Castro, it is plain that it does not support his brand of revolutionary warfare, and indeed, given Castro's open defiance of the party line as laid down by the Kremlin, it is questionable whether it is accurate or useful to call him and his followers elsewhere in Latin America communists. They are more precisely described as revolutionary nationalists who may or may not receive assistance from Moscow. The Soviet Union's principal efforts in Latin America are devoted to increasing its general influence by promoting trade and commerce and securing friendly governments by exerting pressure within the existing political structures—most notably today in Chile, Peru and Uruguay.

The changing nature of the cold war and the demise of the communist apparatus as an important threat in Latin America have removed the most readily understood and for some the most compelling purpose of our foreign policy and program in Latin America. While we have always denied that foreign aid was necessarily tied to protection against communists, there has been some question whether anyone really believed it. Anti-communism has served a useful purpose for us; it has allowed us to defer clarifying our own ideology, our vision of what we mean by a good community. It has permitted us to live with a fundamental contradiction between stability and change. We could insist upon changes of all sorts, as in the Alliance for Progress, but at the same time we could sustain institutions which thwarted change, arguing the necessity of stability. We have spoken regularly of freedom, democracy and self-determination, the inference being that both change and stability were preconditions for the fulfillment of these political ideals. Because of communism, however, we were able to avoid facing the hard reality that in much of Latin America democracy is a euphemism and will remain so until the advent of the widespread political organization upon which democracy must rest. And because of communism we were able to skirt the issue of who was "determining" what for whom. Thus, because of communism we have been conducting a policy which has combined an offering of lip service to radical structural change with support for the status quo.

This is not to say that the Agency for International Development and the Alliance for Progress have not done good things. They have built roads, schoolhouses, hospitals and dams; they have financed housing, training and the introduction of new industry and technology; they have promoted exports, economic diversification and the passage of a sizable amount of reform legislation (much of it unimplemented). All this has been done, however, for the most part through local government and in collaboration with members of the existing power structure. While our assistance may have caused a marginal improvement in the standard of life for some, it has also, equally importantly, provided a source of patronage and political strength for the status quo.

And all too often a road, a bridge or a hydroelectric station has been considered to be in and of itself a good thing. All too often the question of whether the road or the bridge is located properly to promote the organization of the population for its inclusion into the nation, or whether the hydroelectric station and its output are so arranged as to bring power and light more cheaply to more people, receives little consideration. Our aid has in reality changed Latin America very little. . . .

Stripped of the protective rationale of anti-communism, we must now face the unveiled question of where we stand on revolution or radical change in Latin America. To answer this question we must identify our interests precisely. Our priorities would seem to be in the following order:

The chief concern of the Government of the United States must be the survival of the American people. Survival is threatened by the existence anywhere of chaos and disorganization. These produce socio-political vacuums which the bully and the predator are tempted to fill aggressively. In this day and age such aggression can bring the threat of total war.

The second concern of the U.S. Government must be the protection of the rights and interests of U.S. citizens in Latin America.

It follows from these primary and secondary objectives that the control of violent conflict is a vital interest of the United States. The control of conflict requires the presence in any community—national or international—of an effective police capable of apprehending and confining the bandit and the criminal. But in Latin America, banditry and criminality are neither the root nor the principal potential cause of violence; and care must be taken not to confuse such lawlessness with revolution, the right to which is deep in our own political and moral heritage. Our reason for being as a nation is linked to the pledge that *all* men have certain rights to life, liberty and the pursuit of happiness; that governments are instituted "to secure these rights"; and that "whenever any form of government becomes destructive of these ends, it is the Right of the People to alter or abolish it, and to institute new Government. . . ."

The cause of conflict in Latin America comes in large measure from the desire of increasing numbers to achieve these rights. In the context of the Latin American environment this achievement requires change which is sufficiently radical to deserve the name of revolution. It thus becomes the interest of the United States to promote that revolution; and it is a subsidiary interest to promote the revolution in such a way that the violent conflict which often accompanies radical change is minimized.

It should be emphasized that this objective is also in accord with our moral stance, corresponding to what we proclaim as the definition of the good community. And in as much as the revolution is inevitable it is axiomatic that our political interest lies in closer coöperation with it. We cannot win a war with the inevitable even though today we are dangerously close to trying.

The revolution in Latin America requires the mobilization of those political institutions which I have already referred to as engines of change, and which are essential for self-determination.

Our policy thus should become solidly oriented toward sustaining these institutions rather than those of the status quo. This will undoubtedly arouse controversy between us and those who hold power in Latin America. They will tend to regard it as a policy of subversion, which in a sense it is. They will speak of intervention in the internal political affairs of sovereign states, which it is. They should be reminded, however, that our present policy also constitutes intervention, only on their behalf. It is time to recognize that almost any foreign assistance in Latin America is bound to be interventionary in one way or another.

It is easy, however, to overestimate the controversy and to ignore means by which it can be minimized. The fact is that many government leaders in Latin America are themselves keenly aware of the need for radical change. But they are hobbled in their efforts to introduce it by recalcitrant oligarchs and conservative bureaucracies, both of which tend to be bolstered by our aid program; they are also impeded by insufficient organization for change outside of government. Many of these leaders would, therefore, secretly, if not publicly, welcome such a shift in U.S. policy.

Our alternative to adopting this policy would seem to be to continue our equivocation in the matter of change. This in turn will tend to force those urging change, from the radical Church to the revolutionary nationalists, into seeking assistance from other world powers, including the Soviet Union. In spite of the weakness of its hemispheric apparatus and its recent peaceful policies in Latin America, the U.S.S.R. still, of course, has the power to intervene if it feels it necessary to its world position.

The implementation of such a policy calls for substantial changes in the organization of our foreign assistance. What follows is an outline of such a reorganization, not intended as a full-fledged or final proposal but as an indicator of the direction in which U.S. policy must move.

II

Although the total thrust of a new foreign assistance policy should be directed at the purposes set by the Alliance for Progress, this policy is best achieved by dividing programs into two general categories—those which work within existing structures and those which are designed to introduce basic, structural change. For this purpose AID, both in Washington and Latin America, should be replaced by two principal alternative assistance channels and perhaps several subsidiary ones. (A similar reorganization of U.S. assistance elsewhere in the world should undoubtedly follow.)

The first channel, which we shall call the New Alliance for Progress, should be a multilateral structure receiving perhaps 70 percent of U.S. assistance for Latin America. The second, which will be called the American Foundation, would distribute about 25 percent. The remainder might be distributed through other routes, such as the overseas investment corporation which has been proposed for encouraging private investment in less developed countries.

The New Alliance would include programs designed to sustain, nourish and improve existing national growth structures. Essentially supplemental in nature, such programs would presuppose the existence of effective local structures capable of directing economic inputs into a coherent, purposeful development scheme. They would be designed, therefore, to assist national governments and those public and private institutions and enterprises which are generally connected with or endorsed by government. These programs, for example, would concern: health, education and public works; routine industrial development; military, police and civil administration training and assistance; trade and tariffs and export development.

Such programs are in essence nonrevolutionary. Although they may well contribute to the gradual evolution of existing structures, they are primarily aimed at improving the conditions of life within them. While they are necessary and consistent with our interests, they may often obstruct change because they are still tied to national governments and therefore tend to support the status quo. For this reason they should be channeled through multilateral agencies, relieving the United States of sole responsibility for their effect. The blame should be shared regionally.

Latin American leadership would be better suited than the U.S. Government to harass and chide Latin American governments to make the most efficient use of large quantities of assistance; it would also be more sensitive to questions of priority, timing, concentration and focus. . . .

Programs under the New Alliance for Progress would be financed by contributions from Latin American governments, the United States Government, and European government members of the Organization for Economic Coöperation and Development. The task of insuring that these funds were being used honestly and efficiently would fall upon the international institutions themselves, which experience has shown can be hard and tough in this regard—often more so than U.S. officials can or want to be. This proposal envisages an expansion of the existing programs which for the most part have worked well, and an extension and strengthening of Latin American control over these programs. The Alliance for Progress would continue as a true "alliance"; and opportunities for regional growth and integrated development independent of U.S. pressures and influence would be increased. Because of its regional character, the New Alliance would be more appealing to Europe and Japan, perhaps even enticing assistance from the Soviet Union. Training and technical assistance could be brought from many countries other than the United States. Israel in particular has much to offer. It is difficult today for AID to arrange for Israeli assistance to Latin America for a variety of reasons, not the least of which is the Arabs. Then, too, regional control of military and police assistance and training would be a particularly salutary innovation, removing the United States at least one step from this sticky area and providing us with political distance and manœuvring room which we do not now have.

But perhaps the most important effect of the New Alliance would be the added impetus which it would give to national and regional planning and thus to the integration of Latin America—at first commercially and economically and then politically. We have seen how damaging the close proximity of the United States and its officialdom can be to Latin American initiative. We cannot help ourselves; it is in the nature of things; we are large and powerful and our breath is heavy. The closer we are to the processes by which Latin Americans plan, establish priorities, identify their interests and determine actions, the more these processes will be distorted, dampened and defeated. We have long spoken about the necessity of "giving the Latin Americans the tools and letting them do the job for themselves," but we have found it difficult to act accordingly. Our AID programs have become an increasingly self-defeating exercise with almost the opposite effect. We are fond of using the word "self-help," but it is generally more a sham than a reality.

The regional organization of foreign assistance would also facilitate foreign investment. . . .

The purposes of the New Alliance would be very much like those of its predecessor. While we can hope that it will find new and better ways to achieve them, we cannot expect the Alliance, by itself, to speed up the revolutionary process to the extent that U.S. and Latin American interests dictate.

III

U.S. objectives, therefore, require a second and quite distinct system of assistance programs to find and fuel the engines of change which work directly to revolutionize Latin American social and political structures. As the New Alliance would sustain local growth structures, the second category of programs would help to design and construct such structures where they do not exist and assist in the formation of new local organizations to exert pressure for radical change in existing structures.

It may appear that the two program categories are contradictory. In a sense they are and must be. Our purpose, however, is to make the contradiction more precise and manageable. The contradiction between change and stability exists today; we can be sure it will exist tomorrow. The vital interests of both the United States and Latin America lie in designing better ways of handling it.

Second-category programs would be essentially non-governmental. They would seek to strengthen those organizations and institutions which can bring pressure to bear upon government and establish useful links with it. But they would be definitely distinct from government and in fact might often be hostile to the régime in power, or to parts of that régime. They are the critical levers required to set the process of change in motion and keep it moving.

These programs must by their nature be local—aimed at a particular community, organization, group or institution. The workings of our engines of change are fundamentally rooted in a particular place and a particular group of leaders and followers. Confidence and participation in representative government develop at the local level. As continuing pressure comes to be exerted on the decision-making processes of the national government, the motivation and capacity for rural action on the part of government administrative officials grow. The campesino's trust in, and ability to use, his government increase in turn.

For some time Category Two programs would obviously be controversial; they would have to be handled with great care and delicacy, moving experimentally from small to larger undertakings. Even so, this new idea will be attacked; it would never survive the onslaught of the status quo if it were part of a large international bureaucracy.

Congress should, therefore, establish and fund an American Foundation for the purpose of launching Category Two programs, using a diversity of nongovernmental groups, institutes, centers and organizations, representing a broad spectrum of U.S. interests and talents, each with special capability to work with and assist a Latin American purpose-making institution. I am here suggesting that we make the most of the pluralism of American society, accentuating its great and varied strength and employing it to connect U.S. groups naturally to Latin American counterparts. . . . The reasons for the Foundation are fundamental: revoluntionary change is underway; it is inevitable; it is in many ways essential and morally justified; the interests of world peace and of the United States require that this change be assisted: while it may require some conflict, the objective should be clearly to minimize violence. The objectives of the Foundation would be to make the revolution peaceful; to make it effective; to make it consistent with the best interests of the United States and Latin America. The commitment of the Trustees to these purposes would be an important factor in their selection. Before critics cry "sham" let it be emphasized that the Foundation would be frankly an instrument of the United States to foster nongovernmental U.S. organizations to find and fuel engines of change in Latin America. But while a creation of the U.S. Government, it would be distinct from it. Indeed, much of its validity would derive from its independence of government control.

Acting in accordance with the principles of the Charter of Punta del Este and subsequent Alliance doctrine, the Foundation would, through grant and agreement, fund the activities of those U.S. institutions best suited to establish constructive relationships with change and purpose-making institutions in Latin America—such as organizations of the radical Church, peasant unions, trade unions, universities and change-oriented varieties of local and multinational enterprises. AID cannot reach many of these at all today; and its governmental connection prevents it from reaching others effectively and efficiently.

Perhaps most important would be the role of the Foundation in making possible direct ties between U.S. and Latin American universities, uncluttered by governmental considerations on either side. . . .

Latin America needs above all else the study and the insight necessary to formulate its own independent purposes and goals. This study requires the discipline and detachment which only a great university can provide. It is perhaps presumptuous to suppose that the United States can play a significant role in such an important and precarious venture. But I believe that our Foundation, working with the best of North America's universities, could be of great use, if only perhaps in one pursuit: the support of greatly expanded research by Latin American scholars, with young U.S. counterparts and assistants, into the real nature and problems of their respective communities. . . .

But what happens, you may ask, when a Foundation-supported group is drawn into conflict with the status quo in Latin America? How do you deal with the implication of subversion in this situation? After all, we are bypassing government to introduce change to which government may be resistant.

Here is where the great advantage of separation from the U.S. governmental apparatus—the embassy and AID—becomes clear. Under our proposed scheme of things, although the Ambassador would be informed about Foundation-supported activities in his country of assignment, he would have no official responsibility for them. . . .

The fundamental idea here is that we stop running our foreign assistance activities as though we were a statist monolith like the Soviet Union. Our greatest strength lies in our plurality of interests, points of view and competences. And by working through a number of independent groups we will also be better able to avoid the kind of cultural imperialism which tends to be a by-product of monolithic government-centered undertakings. Much of our current effort kindles this fear, which is entirely consistent with the apprehension of many U.S. critics about our own activities abroad. . . .

Only by some such new approach can we hope to arouse the national enthusiasm required to raise the levels of U.S. foreign assistance to where they should be—at least 1 percent of the gross national product and in time hopefully more.

V

THE UNITED STATES AND THE
FAR EAST

THE MYSTERY OF OUR
CHINA POLICY*

BY

WALTER LIPPMANN

[1944]

We shall fix our attention on those critical facts and events
which made the conflict with Japan . . . irreconcilable. I must
emphasize the word *irreconcilable* because every country has disputes. But only those disputes are irreconcilable where the interest
at stake is so vital to both countries that they would rather fight
than give way.

We may begin by asking how we have come to be at war with
Japan. It is true that Japan attacked Pearl Harbor on December
7, 1941, and that then we had no choice. But we cannot leave it
at that. For the Japanese would not have attacked Pearl Harbor
if we had accepted the terms they offered us. They did not attack
Pearl Harbor for the sake of sinking our Pacific fleet. They tried
to sink our Pacific fleet because we were opposing them on matters that they were determined to carry through.

There is no mystery about what these were. Japan was committed to the conquest of China. Japan was also planning and
preparing the conquest of the East Indies, the Philippines, Malaya,
and Indo-China. She was certainly contemplating an attack on the
Soviet Union. But the irrevocable commitment was to conquer
China: the rest, though there is no doubt that it was intended,
was not an absolute and immediate commitment. The Japanese
were willing to negotiate, to compromise, and at least to postpone,
their demands outside of China. There was the irreconcilable
issue. When the United States refused finally to assent to the

---

* From *U. S. War Aims*, copyright 1944 by Walter Lippmann. Reprinted
by permission of Little, Brown and Co., Atlantic Monthly Press. Walter
Lippmann (b. 1889), is an American columnist and author of many books on
political subjects. His most recent book is *The Public Philosophy*.

conquest of China, and to desist from opposing Japan in China, Japan went to war.

The Emperor's rescript declaring war against the United States and Britain[1] stated that war

> has been truly unavoidable [*because* the Chinese] regime which has survived at Chungking, relying upon American and British protection, still continues its fratricidal opposition

to the Nanking regime which accepts Japanese rule in occupied China. The Emperor went on to say that the United States and Britain,

> inducing other countries to follow suit, increased military preparations on all sides of our empire to challenge us. They have obstructed by every means our peaceful commerce, and finally have resorted to the direct severance of economic relations, menacing gravely the existence of our empire.

The statements are true. We did support the Chinese regime at Chungking. We encouraged it and helped it wage war against the Japanese invaders and their Chinese puppet government. We did induce Britain and the Netherlands to join us in preparing for war with Japan. We did sever economic relations, and our purpose was to impair the military power of the Japanese Empire.

On November 26, 1941, eleven days before Pearl Harbor, Secretary Hull gave the Japanese Ambassador the outline of an agreement to preserve the peace: it stipulated that

> the Government of Japan will withdraw all military, naval, air and police forces from China and from Indo-China.

Mr. Hull's memorandum was the American reply to the Japanese proposal (November 20) which contained no offer to evacuate China, and in fact demanded that the United States "refrain" from intervening in the relations between Japan and China. This

---

[1] Japan declared war on December 7, 1941, at 4 P.M. E.S.T.; the attack on Pearl Harbor began at 1:20 P.M. E.S.T. The text is from the London *Times* translation.

was the irreconcilable issue. On the American demand that Japan evacuate China and the Japanese demand that the United States abandon China, the final negotiations broke down.[2] Mr. Kurusu told Mr. Hull that our position would be interpreted in Tokyo "as tantamount to meaning the end." Three days later Mr. Hull told the British Ambassador that

> the diplomatic part of our relations with Japan was virtually over and that the matter will now go to the officials of the Army and Navy.

A week later the Japanese attacked Pearl Harbor.

The question, then, is why and how the United States, rather than assent to the conquest of China, chose to accept the Japanese challenge. The record shows that the American nation reached this momentous decision gradually, reluctantly, but with increasing unanimity and finality, over a period of about forty years. The remarkable thing about the record of these forty years is the constancy with which the United States government has stood for the integrity of Chinese territory.

The first President to take this position was McKinley: in 1900 his Secretary of State, John Hay, declared that

> the policy of the government of the United States is to seek a solution which may bring about permanent peace and safety to China, preserve Chinese territorial and administrative entity, protect all rights guaranteed to friendly powers by treaty and

---

[2]"Hope of concluding any arrangement, however, became slender indeed in the light of clear indication given by the Japanese authorities that they had no intention of desisting from the menace which they were creating to the United States, to the British Empire, to the Netherlands East Indies, to Thailand, and to China, by the substantial increasing of their armed forces in Indochina and in adjacent waters. In view of that growing menace, of the continuation of the hostilities in China, of the mobilization of Japanese forces in Manchuria, and of the fact that the Japanese proposal of November 20 offered, as outlined above, no basis for a practical and reassuring settlement, it was obvious that the chance of meeting the crisis by measures of diplomacy had practically vanished." (*Foreign Relations of the United States. Japan: 1931–1941.* Vol. II, pp. 370–371.)

international law, and safeguard for the world the principle of equal and impartial trade with all parts of the Chinese Empire.

The American decision to become the champion of China was, second only to Monroe's commitment to defend the Latin-American republics, the most momentous event in our foreign relations.

How did Hay happen to make this commitment in the summer of 1900? The first clue to the answer is to be found in his action in the autumn of 1899 when he sent diplomatic notes to the six powers interested in China asking for the maintenance of what was called the Open Door for commercial interests in respect to equal tariffs, railroad rates, and port dues in their Chinese spheres of interest.* Although, after receiving their replies, Hay an-

---

* EDITOR'S NOTE: Following is the text of Secretary of State Hay's "Open Door" note to the U. S. Ambassador in Great Britain. Similar instructions were sent to American diplomatic representatives in Paris, Berlin, St. Petersburg, Rome, and Tokyo.

Washington, September 6, 1899

SIR: The Government of Her Britannic Majesty has declared that its policy and its very traditions precluded it from using any privileges which might be granted it in China as a weapon for excluding commercial rivals, and that freedom of trade for Great Britain in that Empire meant freedom of trade for all the world alike. While conceding by formal agreements, first with Germany and then with Russia, the possession of "spheres of influence or interest" in China in which they are to enjoy special rights and privileges, more especially in respect of railroads and mining enterprises, Her Britannic Majesty's Government has therefore sought to maintain at the same time what is called the "open-door" policy, to insure to the commerce of the world in China equality of treatment within said "spheres" for commerce and navigation. This latter policy is alike urgently demanded by the British mercantile communities and by those of the United States, as it is justly held by them to be the only one which will improve existing conditions, enable them to maintain their positions in the markets of China, and extend their operations in the future. While the Government of the United States will in no way commit itself to a recognition of exclusive rights of any power within or control over any portion of the Chinese Empire under such agreements as have within the last year been made, it can not conceal its apprehension that under existing conditions there is a possibility, even a probability, of complications arising between the treaty powers which may imperil the rights insured to the United States under our treaties with China.

This Government is animated by a sincere desire that the interests of our citizens may not be prejudiced through exclusive treatment by any of the controlling powers within their so-called "spheres of interest" in China, and hopes also to retain there an open market for the commerce of the world, remove dangerous sources of international irritation, and hasten thereby united or concerted action of the powers at Pekin in favor of the administrative reforms so urgently needed for strengthening the Imperial Government and maintaining the integrity of China in which the whole western world is alike concerned. It believes that such a result may be greatly assisted by a declaration by the various powers claiming "spheres of interest" in China of their intentions as regards treatment of foreign trade therein. The present moment seems a particularly opportune one for informing Her Britannic Majesty's Government of the desire of the United States to see it make a formal declaration and to lend its support in obtaining similar declarations from the various powers claiming "spheres of influence" in China, to the effect that each in its respective spheres of interest or influence

First. Will in no wise interfere with any treaty port or any vested interest within any so-called "sphere of interest" or leased territory it may have in China.

Second. That the Chinese treaty tariff of the time being shall apply to all merchandise landed or shipped into all such ports as are within said "sphere of interest" (unless they be "free ports"), no matter to what nationality it may belong, and that duties so leviable shall be collected by the Chinese Government.

Third. That it will levy no higher harbor duties on vessels of another nationality frequenting any port in such "sphere" than shall be levied on vessels of its own nationality, and no higher railroad charges over lines built, controlled, or operated within its "sphere" on merchandise belonging to citizens or subjects of other nationalities transported through such "sphere" than shall be levied on similar merchandise belonging to its own nationals transported over equal distances.

The recent ukase of His Majesty the Emperor of Russia, declaring the port of Ta-lien-wan open to the merchant ships of all nations during the whole of the lease under which it is to be held by Russia, removing as it does all uncertainty as to the liberal and conciliatory policy of that power, together with the assurances given this Government by Russia, justifies the expectation that His Majesty will cooperate in such an understanding as is here proposed, and our ambassador at the court of St. Petersburg has been instructed accordingly to submit the propositions above detailed to His Imperial Majesty, and ask their early consideration. Copy of my instruction to Mr. Tower is herewith inclosed for your confidential information.

The action of Germany in declaring the port of Kiaochow a "free port," and the aid the Imperial Government has given China in the establishment there of a Chinese custom-house, coupled with the oral assurance conveyed the United States by Germany that our interests within its "sphere" would in no wise be affected by its occupation of this portion of the province of Shang-tung, tend to show that little opposition may be anticipated from that power to the desired declaration.

The interests of Japan, the next most interested power in the trade of China, will be so clearly served by the proposed arrangement, and the declaration of its statesmen within the last year are so entirely in line with the views here expressed, that its hearty cooperation is confidently counted on. . . .

I have the honor to be [etc.]   JOHN HAY.

nounced that the powers had come to a "final and definitive" agreement, and his achievement was hailed by his predecessor, William R. Day, as "a diplomatic triumph of the first importance," the replies had actually been in some instances conditional and evasive.

He was unable to do more at that time because of the crushing defeat of China by Japan in 1894-1895, which had wrecked the so-called Middle Kingdom. There was a vacuum opened up by the collapse of the Chinese government authority; the European powers and Japan were moving rapidly into it, and were establishing spheres of interest which meant the partition of China into a collection of colonies.[3]   In a China which had been dismembered and reduced to colonial status, there could obviously be no Open Door for commerce.

But neither could there be peace, or law and order, or indeed satisfactory intercourse in a colonial China. The Chinese are too mature to tolerate it. The partition of China turned the Boxer Rebellion into an uprising against all foreigners, which became acute in May 1900. The legations of Great Britain, France, Germany, Russia, Japan, and the United States were besieged on June 20, and the siege was raised by an international relief expedition on August 14. The dates are significant. It was in July, during this siege, that Secretary Hay for the first time committed the United States to being the champion of Chinese unity and independence.

It seems clear that Hay's decision to oppose the dismemberment of China was based on a realization that, on the one hand, the Chinese would fight against partition and that, on the other, the United States would never achieve the Open Door if China was partitioned. That is how the American interest in China first became identified with the maintenance of Chinese independence.

We must fix clearly in our minds this fundamental fact—that

[3]On March 6, 1898, Germany took Kiaochow on the Shantung peninsula; on March 27, Russia took Port Arthur; on April 10, France took Kwangchow, and on June 9, Great Britain extended her holdings in Hong Kong and on July 1, took Weihaiwei. Admiral Dewey, we may note, fought the battle of Manila Bay on May 1—while these events were happening.

what the Chinese did for themselves and what the United States has desired in China have in the past been reciprocal. We cannot understand why we are fighting in the Pacific, and therefore what we are fighting for, unless we remember how related, the one with the other, have been Chinese independence and American rights.

Why Americans should care so much about Asia as to fight a great war about it is a question that we shall have to examine thoroughly.

* * *

. . . How and why did the United States come to be so deeply concerned about the fate of an Oriental people from whom they are separated by the immense distances of the Pacific Ocean?

American interest in China originated in what President Fillmore called

> the consideration . . . of the great trade which must at no distant day be carried on between the Western Coast of North America and Eastern Asia. . . . I need not say that the importance of these considerations has been greatly influenced by the sudden and vast development which the interests of the United States have attained in California and Oregon. . . .

These words were addressed to Congress in 1849 in order to explain why the President had denied the French claims and had recognized the independence of Hawaii, then known as the Sandwich Islands. The islands were regarded as a necessary commercial outpost for American trade. By 1840 Honolulu had already become a repair port for American whalers and the center of a three-cornered trade with China.

The early exports to China were chiefly silver dollars and ginseng; the imports were silk and tea. After 1790, or thereabouts, the Yankee merchants traded clothing, hardware, and other manufactures for sea-otter peltries in the Pacific Northwest, and then sold the peltries in Canton for silk, tea, enameled ware, and a yellow cotton cloth called nankeen. In 1818-1819 the value of the combined exports and imports was about $19,000,000: the risks were great and the profits of this China trade were high.

This old China trade came to an end in the 1850's, and for about half a century, until the 1890's, there was little American interest in that or any other foreign trade. This was, of course, the period of the Civil War, the Reconstruction, the settlement of the Western country, and the industrialization of America. But, as Peffer points out, when the transcontinental railroads had been built and the bonanzas had been staked out, the free land was gone and manufacturers were looking for markets. Then the American interest in "the great trade" with East Asia revived.

On July 7, 1898, during the war with Spain, Hawaii was annexed, and on December 10, 1898, the treaty in which Spain ceded the Philippine Islands was signed. It is clear that the paramount consideration in taking the Philippines was the belief that Manila would be an entrepôt for the China trade. Strategic considerations of military power in the Pacific appear to have played no part in the mind of President McKinley and his advisers; this is evident from the fact that they were not sure whether they wanted *all* of the Philippine Islands. Not even Admiral Mahan, the great exponent of sea power, objected when Spain sold the Caroline Islands to Germany.

Yet the China trade was never very large. At no time has it amounted to as much as 4 per cent of our whole foreign commerce. Until 1860 the trade with Cuba was almost twice as valuable as the China trade. From 1861 to 1938 the China trade was about 3 per cent of our total trade; our trade with Japan was about 5 per cent of the whole; that with the British Empire, including Canada, was over 40 per cent.

Although our interest in China grew to be a vital interest, it was not because of the profits of the China trade.

Yet from the earliest days we have contended for an Open Door, so that American traders would have the same commercial rights as those of any other nation. Dennett shows that the policy of the Open Door is as old as our relations with Asia, that it was not limited to China, but was upheld also for Japan and Korea, and on the coast of Africa as early as 1832.

The ardor with which Americans have espoused this principle is the heart of the mystery. The importance to the American people of the whole Oriental trade was, as we have seen, small. The merchants and the investors directly concerned in it could have done fully as well for themselves, probably much better, by entering into combinations with other nations for the colonial exploitation of China. During the past generation, certainly, Japan would have been only too pleased to take the United States into a business partnership, provided we assented to her political domination of China. Had profits been the determining motive, Americans could have had them without the risks of war.

Yet, with deviations from the main line of our principles, which were soon corrected, Americans preached the Open Door incessantly to other nations, and whenever the Chinese asserted their own independence, we gave them moral and material support. It is evident that the Open Door meant something more to Americans than a commercial policy, and that the missionary zeal with which we have propagated it touches chords of memory and of faith, and is somehow the expression of the American political religion.

The explanation is not far to seek. The American nation was born in a rebellion by the colonists against the mercantilist empire of Great Britain. The Open Door is simply a short name to describe American opposition to the trade monopolies and privileges of the mercantilist system. In the struggle for independence the American people acquired an indelible antipathy to monopolies and privileges established by imperial rule. Thus Americans react by long tradition, which is now well-nigh instinctive, against colonial imperialism. When they have themselves acquired colonies, as in the Philippines, they could not rest until they had promised the colonies independence; they were glad to provide the means by which the colonies could achieve independence; and the great majority were pleased when Congress, yielding to the pressure of the sugar lobby and the like, fixed a definite date for Philippine independence.

The American antipathy to imperialism is not a humanitarian sentiment acquired in some casual way. It is organic in the American character, and is transmitted on American soil to all whose minds are molded by the American tradition. It is a deep and pervasive habit of thought because it comes directly from the original conflict in which the colonists became Americans. That explains the missionary zeal with which Americans have championed what is apparently a merely commercial policy. English mercantilism, says Miller, "required the colonies to send many of their most important raw products to Britain and to purchase almost all their manufactured goods in the same market."[4] . . . Towards the end of the colonial period "the British government sought to tighten the screws of commercial monopoly . . . and even the staunchest defenders of colonial liberty in England, including William Pitt, insisted upon keeping the colonies in economic leading strings." The revolt against this system, and against the police measures used to enforce it, shaped the American conception of liberty and the rights of man.

Yet even after the outbreak of hostilities in 1775, the immediate object of the colonists was not independence; it was the recapture and the propagation of English liberty. They declared their independence more than a year *after* they were at war and not until they were convinced that only through independence could they achieve liberty.

Many of the patriots had a "veneration for the British Empire" which was "based upon the belief that it stood for liberty and the rights of man." Benjamin Franklin, who embodied the highest common sense of the patriot leaders, believed until the eve of independence that the best hope of human liberty lay in the extension of the English constitution. He advised Englishmen to recognize gracefully the potentiality of American growth, to make no laws which would hinder American trade and manufacture. He told them that their laws would be swept aside. He pleaded with them to think in terms of an Atlantic World, peopled by Englishmen, who, whether born in England or America, possessed equal rights and privileges.

But in 1775, writes Miller, "instead of founding the empire upon liberty and human rights," as enjoyed by Englishmen in England, "British imperialists thought almost exclusively in terms of revenue and enforcement of the Laws of Trade, and by their

---

[4] John C. Miller, *Origins of the American Revolution.* Atlantic-Little, Brown, Boston, 1943, p. 7.

efforts to tax the colonies raised the question 'whether the rising empire of America shall be an empire of slaves or freemen.' " As a result, the colonists lost all their enthusiasm for extending the British Empire over the world. They turned to the idea of creating in this hemisphere a new world. "Here a new civilization was to be established while Europe sank into slavery. Only through independence, it was contended, could America attain its destiny and become . . . what Great Britain refused to be: 'the Glory of the World and the Terror of the Wicked Oppressors among the Nations' (*Boston Gazette*, August 24, 1772)."

The success of the Revolution meant, of course, that the monopolies and privileges of the British mercantilist system were abolished on American soil. The merchants and manufacturers who carried on American business practised what it is now the fashion to call "free enterprise." When they sought for themselves, as indeed being human they often did, governmental favors, or when they formed monopolistic combinations, they quickly encountered the indigenous American radicalism which has always had as its watchword "Equal rights for all, special privileges to none." There never was established on American soil a ruling class which had recognized legal privileges. Consequently, though wealth has exercised much power, no hereditary governing class could be founded. The one notable exception was the great plantation owners of the South and their "peculiar institution" of chattel slavery.

Now without a hereditary governing class it has always been impossible for long to govern an empire: imperial rule over alien peoples abroad is vigorous and long-continuing only when there are great families which possess at home the traditions and prerogatives of governing others.

Having no ruling class which could administer an empire, the Americans have in the end always been anti-imperialists abroad: that is, they have disliked to see peoples ruled by alien powers. "Sometimes," said Jefferson, "it is said that man cannot be trusted with the government of himself. Can he, then, be trusted with the government of others? Or have we found angels in the forms of kings to govern him? Let History answer this question."

This is the spirit which has made Americans the missionaries of the Open Door. As Dennett says, "they desired to see the Asiatic states sustained and made strong to withstand by their own might the encroachments of European powers." The Open Door is, at bottom, a short name for the American way of life, projected abroad; the support of China by Americans, and their sympathy with all other colonial peoples seeking independence, reflect the fact that Americans, being incapable by the nature of their own society of sustained imperialism, are the opponents of imperialism wherever they encounter it.

For intuitively Americans have always felt, however little they measured the risks and were prepared for the costs, that they could not prosper and live securely in contact with states where governments worked on principles radically different from their own. They have believed profoundly that their own principles of liberty were founded upon the laws of nature and of nature's God, and that at last they would prevail everywhere. I believe that the history of our relations with Eastern Asia has proved that these convictions are the mainspring of the foreign relations of the United States.

The contrary view, that it is no concern of the Americans what happens in any other country, is not the normal American way of thinking. The Monroe Doctrine, which antedates our China policy by more than three quarters of a century, is founded on the open avowal that the principles of national freedom may not be attacked in this hemisphere by the great powers of the earth. Nothing could be further than this from the idea that what goes on outside our borders does not concern us. The argument that nothing abroad really matters vitally has frequently been advanced in controversies, but almost always as a reason for not taking some particular step on which men's judgments differed—as, for example, during Washington's administration over intervention on behalf of revolutionary France, in Lincoln's over support of the Polish insurrection, in Wilson's and Franklin Roosevelt's over intervention in Europe.

There have never been many isolationists who were so consistently noninterventionist that they did not at least vent their feelings by uttering ardent views about the internal affairs of other countries: about British rule in Ireland or India, Turkish rule in Armenia, Spanish rule in Cuba; about czarist and bolshevist rule in Russia, the Kaiser's and Hitler's in Germany. In fact, no other nation in modern times has ever preached so much about, or has passed so many judgments upon, the affairs of so many other peoples.

This persistent evangel of Americanism in the outer world must reflect something more than meddlesome self-righteousness. It does. It reflects the fact that no nation, and certainly not this nation, can endure in a politically alien and morally hostile environment; and the profound and abiding truth that a people which does not advance its faith has already begun to abandon it.

THE OPEN DOOR CLOSED TIGHT*

BY

WILLIAM L. NEUMANN

[1953]

I

The war between the United States and Japan was neither, as official and semi-official histories paint it, a struggle between good and evil nor a contest between a peace-loving nation and an arrogant proponent of aggression and chaos. These are the conventional labels used by nations to describe their enemies. Every victorious power attempts to certify similar interpretations of recent wars as eternal truths. While such moralistic simplifications have their value as nationalist propaganda, they have no place in an honest attempt at an unbiased study of international issues. Righteousness has never been the exclusive preserve of any one nation, nor has virtue been completely wanting among even the most chauvinistic peoples. If the Pacific conflict is to be the subject of moralizing, it might better be described as a tragedy of errors and as the unwanted offspring of false assumptions and follies on both sides of the Pacific.

The errors and fallacies of Japanese policy have often been set forth for Americans with a rich collection of assorted invectives. Stripped of all gratuitous adjectives and adverbs, Japan's course is clear and the errors of Japanese assumptions then become patent. An island nation with a growing population, stimulated by Western penetration, found its resources inadequate to achieve its aspirations for a higher standard of living. Following the Western pattern, Japan looked abroad for land, markets, and raw materials. Japan also developed aspirations for the status of a major power, again stimulated by Western influences, particularly by the humiliating experiences of the early post-Perry decades. It was in these

---

*From "How American Policy Toward Japan Contributed to War in the Pacific," in Harry E. Barnes (editor), Perpetual War for Perpetual Peace. Copyright 1953 by The Caxton Printers, Ltd. Reprinted by permission. William L. Neumann (b. 1915), Professor of History, Goucher College, has written widely on American diplomacy in the Far East.

formative years that Japan learned how helpless a small power could be in the face of energetic Western imperialism, backed by hostile naval squadrons. These two aspirations combined to create an expansionist movement in Japan which looked primarily to Asia for its fulfillment. When economic penetration of Asia was checked by political obstacles in the form of intransigent Chinese war lords, Japan turned to the ultimate weapon of imperialism, military force.

Japanese expansionism also brought to the fore a chauvinistic group of military leaders who developed a racialist concept of Japan's manifest destiny. They believed that Asia was at last to find peace and economic progress under Japanese leadership in the form of the Greater East Asia Co-prosperity sphere. No alien nation, neither Russia nor the United States, was to be permitted to stand in the way of this goal. To this end Japan fought a border war in Manchuria against the Soviet Union from 1937 to 1939. When the United States, from 1931 onward, stood firmly behind the Chinese Nationalist government, Japan's best customer became Japan's enemy. When other methods seemed unavailing, Japan prepared for a trans-Pacific war to remove the American barrier to an area which Japan believed was vital for national security and prosperity. But the willingness of the people of the United States, once attacked, to fight a long and costly war over a cause remote from their shores was not foreseen by Japan's leaders. This was the fatal error of Japanese policy. This was the false assumption which was to bring that nation to defeat and to destroy the accomplishments of two generations of vigorous diplomacy.

Americans have given little attention to the errors of their own Far Eastern policies. Self-examination is not a characteristic of the victor, even when the fruits of victory prove bitter. Most studies of the coming of the Pacific war by Americans still accept the official assumptions as valid. The United States is seen as a force exerted in behalf of peace and stability in Asia. American attempts to maintain the *status quo* and uphold the integrity of China are judged wise even though they failed. More important, the basic premise of American policy from 1931 onward—that the United States had a vital national interest in blocking the expansion of Japan in Asia—is seldom questioned. Yet on this premise any justification of the diplomacy of Secretary of State Henry Stimson or of the foreign policy of the Franklin D. Roosevelt administration must make its case. . . .

It is possible to outline the misconceptions of American policy makers and to see in what respects they were blinded to basic facts and key relationships in Far Eastern international policies. No consideration was given to the historic ambitions of Russia in Asia nor to the expansionist element in Stalinist Communism. As a result there was a complete disregard for the role which a strong Japan played in the Far Eastern balance of power. Gross errors were also made in calculating that Japan could be coerced by economic pressure and naval force to follow American bidding in its relations with China. The political and economic importance of China for Japan was not grasped, despite the fact that Japanese leaders spoke of it as a national interest to be defended regardless of costs. This blindness to the importance of China for Japan contrasts with the gross overrating of the importance of a Japan-free China for the United States. It was assumed by some key figures in the Roosevelt administration that this objective was worth the blood and toil which a costly trans-Pacific conflict would entail. Behind this premise was another, equally invalid. This was the assumption that the power relationships of Asia of the 1920's could be maintained—or, after 1931, restored—despite the rising power of Japan and the Soviet Union and the internal political disintegration of the Chinese Nationalist government. The instrument of maintenance or restoration was not to be forces within Asia itself but the pronouncements and threats of American power with its center thousands of miles from Asia's shores. Faith in the growth of American naval power under the Roosevelt administration disregarded the strength by which the Japanese navy sought to counter American building.

The history of American policy in the Far East from 1931 onward is largely a story of these blunders and fallacies in the interpretation and implementation of American interests. It was Henry L. Stimson, twice Secretary of War, who, as President Hoover's Secretary of State, first set the course of American opposition to Japanese expansion. When Japan established in Manchuria a puppet government to protect its economic interests in that area, Stimson announced to the world that the United States would not accept the legality of the new government established by force. Japan was charged with a violation of the Kellogg-Briand Pact of 1928 as a result of its undeclared war with China. In taking this step Stimson set the direction of American diplomacy for the next decade. The influence and, finally, the force of the United States was to be employed in the hopeless task of maintaining the disintegrating *status quo* of Asia. . . . *

Arguments were presented in behalf of American intervention in the Sino-Japanese conflict which went beyond the traditional political and economic concepts of national interest. World peace, in which the United States was said to have a vital stake, was also to be preserved by the Stimson-Roosevelt Far Eastern policy, according to its supporters. Stimson believed that American sponsorship of the Kellogg-Briand antiwar pact called for active steps to maintain peace by opposing Japanese expansionism. Secretary Hull thought along similar lines. In January, 1938, the Secretary was asked for statistics by the Senate on American economic interests in China. The Secretary replied that there was in China "a broader and much more fundamental interest—which is that orderly processes in international relationships must be maintained." Spokesmen for the Roosevelt administration frequently made similar claims for their policy's peace-spreading characteristics.

Two assumptions were made in these arguments. The first was that peace between two Asiatic powers was a matter of direct con-

---

* EDITOR'S NOTE: The Stimson (Non-Recognition) Doctrine was announced in the following note sent by the United States to China and Japan on January 7, 1932:

In view of the present situation and of its own rights and obligations therein, the American Government deems it to be its duty to notify both the Government of the Chinese Republic and the Imperial Japanese Government that it cannot admit the legality of any situation *de facto* nor does it intend to recognize any treaty or agreement entered into between these governments, or agents thereof, which may impair the treaty rights of the United States or its citizens in China, including those which relate to the sovereignty, the independence or the territorial and administrative integrity of the Republic of China, or to the international policy relative to China, commonly known as the Open Door Policy; and that it does not intend to recognize any situation, treaty, or agreement which may be brought about by means contrary to the covenants and obligations of the Pact of Paris of August 27, 1928, to which treaty both China and Japan, as well as the United States, are parties.

cern for the United States and an important enough national interest to justify the risk of spreading the war. The second
assumption was again the optimistic one that a third power, far
from the seat of conflict, could adjust the differences of the warring
powers by supporting the weaker against the stronger. For over a
century the American policy of neutrality had been based on the
assumption that peace was divisible and that it was to the interest
of this country to avoid wars in which national security and
national prosperity were not endangered. That policy, dating
back to the precepts of George Washington and Thomas Jefferson,
was now discarded on the assumption that neutrality was no longer
a workable policy and that the use of American political, economic,
and military strength could effectively check wars on other continents by exerting pressure on one of the contestants. The validity
of these assumptions can most objectively be tested by their
results. . . .

II

When the Hoover administration was replaced in March, 1933,
the direction which Stimson had tried to give to American policy
in the Far East was . . . greatly expanded. Not only was there to
be political and economic pressure on Japan but the United States
Navy was to be greatly increased in strength and the building
program pointed directly at Japan. . . .

Within a year in office President Roosevelt was to launch the
largest naval building program in the history of the United States.
Two months before he took office the President-elect announced
that he would give his support to the Stimson doctrine of non-
recognition of the Japanese puppet state of Manchukuo. When
this announcement was made the New York *Daily News* editorial-
ized: ". . . he had better begin building up the Navy the moment
he becomes President. You cannot make a war-provoking policy
stick unless you have war-like weapons and plenty of them. . . ."
The logic of the editorial writer's assumption seems to have been
fully accepted by Roosevelt in his first years in office. . . .

On June 16 Roosevelt issued an executive order allotting
$238,000,000 of the National Recovery Administration's funds to
increasing the size of the Navy. The President's critics were quick

to question the value of spending these funds in shipyards when there were areas of more pressing needs. But such complaints from the supporters of the President's economic program went unanswered. Before the first year of his administration was over, liberal critics were suggesting that the New Deal was "drifting into militarism."

Although the new ships to be built with N.R.A. funds would not bring American strength beyond the 1930 treaty limits, Tokyo and many European capitals viewed the American program as again starting the world on a naval race. Naval building had been declining in all countries as national budgets were cut under the stress of the world depression. Japanese appropriations for new naval construction declined from $40,900,00 in 1930-31 to $33,500,000 in 1931-32, and were further cut to $26,900,000 in 1932-33. The Roosevelt administration, by beginning the largest single program of naval construction undertaken by any nation since the end of World War I, was taking the initiative in reversing the trend.

In January, 1934, the Roosevelt administration presented new evidence that assumptions about the use of naval power in dealing with Japan played an important part in its thinking. Congressman Vinson at that time introduced a bill authorizing a building program over the next five years to bring the Navy up to the maximum tonnage permitted by the Washington and London treaties in all categories. As finally passed, the Vinson-Trammell Act authorized the construction of over a hundred new vessels at an estimated annual cost of $76,000,000. No battleships were contemplated; the 1935 program began with an aircraft carrier, two light cruisers, fourteen destroyers, and six submarines.

When he signed this bill, Roosevelt assured Americans that it was not a law "for the construction of a single additional United States warship." Its purpose, he said, was only to give general congressional approval to a future program. His administration still favored the limitation of naval armaments, Roosevelt argued, despite appearances to the contrary.

As seen from Japan, the American building program of 1933-34 had radically different implications than those offered by its sponsors. Admiral Osumi, Minister of the Navy, declared that the American program left Japan no alternative but to build more ships if national security was to be maintained. The new American ships thus provided the basis for a campaign by the naval expansionists of Japan. Despite pressure for cuts in the national budget, the Japanese naval estimates were the only ones to survive the Diet's economy slashes virtually intact. Some Japanese also assumed that the American effort at naval intimidation meant eventual war. Admiral Suetsugo, Commander-in-Chief of the Combined Fleet, told Japanese reporters early in 1934 that his country must now be ready for an attack from a large air force carried across the Pacific by the American fleet. . . .

In 1935, Roosevelt sent to Congress a budget message calling for the largest military appropriations in the peacetime history of the United States—$485,000,000 for the Navy alone—a rise of $180,000,000 over the previous year. Counting the sums spent by P.W.A. on shipbuilding in 1934, this was an increase of almost 40 per cent for the fiscal year of 1936 over that of 1934. Such expenditures, liberal critics pointed out, could only be aimed at Japan and would stir the people of that nation to arm with corresponding speed. . . .

In the spring of 1936 Congress was asked to give the Navy Department $530,000,000 for the next fiscal year. Although this figure was cut a few millions in committee, the final bill still set a new high for peacetime naval spending. The Naval Appropriation Act provided for the construction of twelve destroyers, six submarines and some three hundred naval planes. Two battleships were also authorized, if either Britain or Japan began the construction of capital ships.

If, at any point in history, the die is finally cast after years of preparation, that point had been reached in Japanese-American relations in the years 1936 and 1937. In Japan the political and economic developments assured a continuation of the policy of expansion. In the United States the Roosevelt administration committed itself to programs which meant eventually going to war to stop Japanese expansion. It was, thereafter, only a question of time until the two policies converged and exploded into war.

The continuation of the external political and economic pressures upon Japan during the first half of the 1930's, coupled with the world-wide increase of militarism, gave more strength to the Japanese army's hold on the government. In February, 1936, a coup was attempted by military extremists. Important government buildings were seized and held for several days before the revolting troops and their leaders surrendered at the command of the Emperor. As a result, one extremist group in the army, the Kodoha, was eliminated. But this left in power the Control Faction, a rival group which was also chauvinistic but avoided extra-legal means in its striving for power.

Military domination of the government was now almost complete. In May, 1936, an imperial ordinance required that all officers filling either the Ministry of War or Navy be on active status. The army and navy could thus make or break cabinets as they pleased, and the political parties were helpless in attempting to form a cabinet which did not have military approval. When members of the Seiyuki party early in 1937, attacked the dictatorial program of the army and the signing of the German-Japanese Anti-Comintern Pact, the army forced the resignation of the War Minister and the collapse of the Hirota cabinet. Even though the electorate, in May, 1937, repudiated the next cabinet headed by General Hayashi, there was little hope for effective action by the *status quo* forces which favored *rapprochement* with Britain and the United States.

It was on the basis of these facts that a review of American policy toward Japan was called for in 1936-37. The issue of peace or war for the American people now hung on the question of whether or not it was of vital national interest that future Japanese expansion in Asia be blocked. It was clear, even that early, that there was only the remotest of possibilities that this expansion could be checked by methods short of war. The dreams and proposals of amateur strategists for forcing Japan to her knees by economic means merited little consideration by serious students of Japanese character and foreign policy.

In naval as well as in diplomatic policy, two courses were open to the United States. One was the continuation of the American building program on the Roosevelt-approved Mahan hypothesis that the cure for the curse of navalism would be found in more navalism. Accepting this assumption, to win victory at a minimum cost, the United States had to build a tremendous offensive Navy, one which could carry the conflict across the Pacific, cutting off Japan's trade routes and threatening the home islands. As Charles Beard phrased it, the Navy had to be either for "defense or portent." If the latter, the Pacific Fleet had to be strong enough to sweep the Pacific if Japan reacted to a threat of force as proud nations had hitherto responded to this type of diplomacy.

The other course promised peace in the Pacific but peace for a price. It involved recognition of the fact that Japan was in at least portions of China to stay for the foreseeable future. It involved acceptance of the word "parity" in naval relations, but with the knowledge that this did not of necessity mean a change in the actual power relationship. On these terms, friendship with Japan was assured, the security of the Philippines was unlikely to be questioned, and America's profitable economic relations with Japan could continue undisturbed.

Congress, as well as the American people as a whole in 1936-37, assumed that American interests in China were far too small to justify war or even a risk of war with Japan. The apathy and lack of warlike spirit in response to the sinking of the U. S. gunboat *Panay* by Japanese planes in December, 1937, testified to the disinterest in Asia. If the issues of war or peace had been stated clearly, the overwhelming popular as well as congressional vote would have favored nonintervention in Asia.

It was different, however, when it came to appropriating funds for a navy which might eventually fight an unwanted war. At this level Congress and the voter only briefly and infrequently glimpsed the relationship between naval expansion and the administration's diplomatic aspirations in the Far East. As a result the Mahanist hypothesis was accepted without serious challenge and continued large-scale naval building met with little resistance. . . .

III

After 1938 the increase of Hitler's power in Europe and the fall of Austria and Czechoslovakia made it easier to overcome congressional opposition to naval building and to administration pleas for a two-ocean navy. For the fiscal year of 1939, total arms expenditures mounted to more than twice those of 1935. The Navy also drew on the Treasury for over $670,000,000 in 1939, almost $900,000,000 in 1940, and for over $2,000,000,000 in the fiscal year ending in June, 1941. Authorizations later that year, moved by the fall of France, almost doubled the Navy's building goals.

As the Navy grew larger, there was increasing confidence that American naval power could easily threaten Japan into submission or, if necessary, crush the Japanese forces with a minimum of losses for the United States. There was no expectation that the war would be a long one or a hard one. The American racialist stereotype of the Oriental, assuming basic inferiority on the part of the yellow races, did not permit any consideration of the possibility that the Japanese might be a formidable opponent. The surprise victory of the Japanese over the Russians in 1904-5 was forgotten, even though it had once raised the stature of Japan in American eyes. . . .

In October, 1939, a substantial number of ships—eight heavy cruisers, one aircraft carrier, and eighteen destroyers—were detached from the West Coast and stationed at Pearl Harbor. In April, 1940, the fleet was moved in its entirety to Hawaii for the conduct of the annual maneuvers. Although the fleet's plans called for a return to the West Coast in early May, orders were given to postpone the return for two weeks. Before that period expired, the fleet was assigned to Pearl Harbor for an indefinite period. For two decades, since its assignment to the Pacific in 1920, the fleet had been based on the West Coast. This move, shifting the center of American naval power some 2,500 miles closer to Japan, was a highly significant event in the history of the power relations of the two countries. . . .

The major decision, the retention of the entire fleet at Pearl Harbor, was apparently made by the President himself. When the fleet commander asked the meaning of this move, he was told by the Chief of Naval Operations that it was to have a "deterrent effect" on Japanese moves into the East Indies. Admiral Richardson doubted, however, whether the intended effect could be obtained. Japanese espionage in Hawaii, he was certain, was effective enough to inform Tokyo that the American fleet had assembled with only an 85 per cent complement and without the train of auxiliary ships needed for offensive action west of Hawaii. When the admiral presented this argument to the President in person, he found that Roosevelt was certain that the contrary was true and was determined not to permit a withdrawal to the West Coast bases. Admiral Stark agreed with Richardson on the inadvisability of keeping the fleet at Pearl Harbor.

Several Japanese newspapers pointed out that the decision to move the fleet base was an effort to stop rumored Japanese moves toward the Dutch East Indies. But they also suggested that it would be difficult for the fleet to remain at Pearl Harbor because of limited facilities. The information now available on the formulation of Japanese foreign policy, in 1940, gives no support for the President's belief in the effects of his strategy. Roosevelt admitted some uncertainty about his policy, but held out against the opinion of his two top naval commanders and told Stark that he would "sit tight" on his decision.

As an amateur naval strategist, Roosevelt . . . vastly underrated the ability and strength of the Japanese navy and expressed overly-optimistic views about the capabilities of the American fleet. In October, 1939, discussing the possibility of Japan's moving into the Dutch East Indies, he said that "we could easily intercept her fleet"—an operation which American forces would have had to conduct some five thousand miles from their nearest major base. . . .

This myth of overwhelming fighting superiority lulled many Americans into the passive acceptance of the coming conflict. Although it was obvious to many that the Roosevelt administration was taking a position which would force a military showdown, opposition voices were softened or stilled by a belief in a quick and inexpensive victory. The traditional assumptions of white or Anglo-Saxon superiority made it easy for the public as well as for government leaders to believe that an Oriental nation could not equal or outdo the West in adapting itself to the techniques and machines of modern warfare. It was this belief that also contributed to the unpreparedness of Hawaii and the Philippines.

IV

The underrating of Japanese strength and morale also dominated the last phase of American peacetime relations with Japan. Like the naval program, the Roosevelt administration's economic program was based on the assumption that threats and pressure would achieve American ends in dealing with Japan.

The first call for the use of economic pressure against Japan followed the issuance of the Stimson doctrine in 1932. Proponents of sanctions advocated striking two blows at the Japanese, one by an embargo on arms and munitions and the other by a boycott of Japanese goods sold in the United States. . . .

When Japan struck at China again in 1937, the movement for economic measures was revived with great strength. Former Secretary of State Henry Stimson, now a private citizen, took the lead with a letter to the *New York Times* in October, 1937. Stimson called upon the United States to end the sale of arms to Japan and claimed that in this manner the conflict could be brought to a halt. . . .

The application of the so-called "moral embargo" by the Department of State in 1938 was the first official achievement of the supporters of economic sanctions. The decision, in 1939, to terminate the 1911 commercial treaty with Japan was an even greater victory. Within the Roosevelt cabinet the movement for embargoes grew in strength. Secretary Morgenthau was the strongest advocate of ending American trade with Japan, and he gained a strong supporter in Henry Stimson when the latter entered the cabinet in the summer of 1940. Six months earlier, Stimson had written another letter to the *New York Times,* again appealing for an end to the sale of war materials as the first step to a firmer policy. He assured his fellow Americans that Japan did not want war with the United States and that an embargo was the road to peace.

This simple program for winning a bloodless victory over Japan, with its "having one's cake and eating it" solution, began to win wider public support. Public-opinion polls were able to produce larger and larger percentages in favor of embargoes on trade with Japan. The administration kept pace with this movement of opinion and, by its licensing program, made successive inroads on the sale of strategic materials to Japan. By the end of 1940 the only item vital to Japan's effort being shipped by the United States was oil. The sanctionist groups therefore concentrated their efforts in 1941 on ending the trade in oil and in nonessential commodities. . . .

The Navy, and Admiral Stark in particular, argued strongly against cutting off Japanese oil purchases. Little hope was placed by the Navy in this method of forcing a reversal in Japanese policy. The shortage of domestic oil supplies was expected to force Japan into war for the Dutch East Indies oil and into war with the United States as well. The Navy, heavily burdened by its operations in the Atlantic in the convoying of arms to Britain, did not consider itself ready for war in the Pacific. Secretary Hull was also for months reluctant to give the approval of the State Department to this drastic move.

Secretary Morgenthau, warmly supported by Stimson, continued his fight against the moderates in the Roosevelt cabinet and called for the ending of Japanese trade by the freezing of Japanese assets. . . .

President Roosevelt was finally moved to carry out the Morgenthau-Stimson program. On July 26, 1941, following the movement of Japanese troops into Indochina, he issued an order freezing Japanese assets and cutting off all Japanese trade. Britain and the Netherlands followed suit. Pressing the point home, American oil was then sent to the Soviet Union via Vladivostok by American tankers which passed not far from the shores of oil-hungry Japan.

Japan now had no alternative but to bow to American demands or fight for the resources by which her economic and military strength was to be maintained. Short of a miraculous revolution, overthrowing army leadership, no change of course could be expected from the Japanese government. The war with Japan, which Admiral Ingersoll said the navy had confidently expected for the last twenty years, was now at hand. The only question which remained to be answered was where and at what hour the attack would come. Pearl Harbor, the Philippines, and Guam were obvious Japanese objectives. But the vigor which had been applied to pressuring Japan in the previous months was not now applied in preparing to meet the results of that policy.

V

The Far Eastern policy of the Roosevelt administration was born of an exaggerated conception of American political and economic interests in China. It was based on dream stuff rather than on the facts of Far Eastern history and statistics of American trade. It was based on the oft-disproved assumption that one major power can intimidate another by rapidly increasing its striking power without an arms race as the chief result. Yet this was the assumption stated most bluntly by Norman H. Davis, perennial American delegate to the naval disarmament conferences and one of Franklin Roosevelt's closest advisers in the realm of foreign affairs. In a memorandum which he prepared for the President in July, 1937, after the out-break of war in China, Davis advocated the construction of two or three additional battleships "for the sake of peace and ultimate disarmament." By these means American intervention in the Sino-Japanese conflict was to restore the pre-1937 or even the pre-1931 *status quo* of the Far East. When war appeared finally as an almost inescapable certainty, there was still faith in the validity of American policy since out of war were to come order and progress for China and more abundant economic opportunities for the United States.

These assumptions dominated the thinking of President Roosevelt and key figures in his cabinet. When challenged by political opponents and others who were concerned with the maintenance of peace in the Pacific, the assumptions were dogmatically reaffirmed. On the basis of materials now available, there is no evidence that these assumptions were seriously re-examined at any time from 1933 down to Pearl Harbor. The warnings of Ambassador Grew and other students of the Far East, who managed to free themselves from the official frame of reference and the prevalent stereotypes, went unheeded. In 1935, for example, a former chief of the State Department's Division of Far Eastern Affairs warned his superiors that the defeat of Japan ". . . would merely create a new set of stresses, and substitute for Japan the U.S.S.R.— as the successor of Imperial Russia—as a contestant (and at least an equally unscrupulous and dangerous one) for the mastery of the East. Nobody except perhaps Russia would gain from our victory in such a war. . . ."

This profound prophecy was ignored. The President and his policy makers went ahead with a program of resistance to Japan which was logical and consistent, if their assumptions were accepted, but could end only in war.

Any study of the wisdom of American Far Eastern policy must note the unpleasant facts of its results. The end of all foreign policies is the protection and advancement of national interests. If American policy was sound, the results should testify to that soundness. But its results have only been negative. Into the vacuum created by the destruction of Japanese power moved the power of the Soviet Union. In place of Japan, the Soviet Union became the dominant force in the Far East and a China under Soviet influence has yielded far less for American interests than did China under Japan. A war with the "Open Door" as one of its objectives ended with the door closed more tightly than ever. Not only were American interests in China destroyed but in the war the more valuable trade with Japan was eliminated and Japan turned into a subject nation, dependent far into the foreseeable future on an American subsidy for its economic existence. Lastly, instead of bringing peace and order to Asia, World War II let loose in that vast area—as World War I did in Europe—all the passions of long-suppressed nationalism to create tumult and strife for decades to come.

"Wars begin in the minds of men," the framers of the UNESCO constitution concluded. So America's war with Japan began as much in the minds of Stimson, Roosevelt, and other architects of American policy, in the decade before Pearl Harbor, as in the minds of the leaders of Japan. It is unfair to ask that American leaders be endowed with super-human powers of prediction and the ability to foresee all the results of their acts. But it is the responsibility of statesmen and diplomats to avoid war and war-making policies unless there is a high degree of probability that unquestionably vital national interests can be protected only by war. A war policy must then be justified by the sanest of estimates of the outcome, evaluating the experience of the past and weighing the costs in blood and sweat against the benefits to present and future generations. By the standards of results—

mankind's score sheet—the policies of Roosevelt and Stimson failed in their estimates of national interest and of the methods of achieving that interest. Their policy paid for in American lives and resources, netted nought but ruin for Japan and assisted in the birth of an Asia more determined than ever to eject the Western interloper.

UNITED STATES RELATIONS WITH CHINA*

BY

DEAN ACHESON

[1949]

THE PRESIDENT: In accordance with your wish, I have had compiled a record of our relations with China, special emphasis being placed on the last five years. . . .

The record should be read in the light of conditions prevailing when the events occurred. It must not be forgotten, for example, that throughout World War II we were allied with Russia in the struggle to defeat Germany and Italy, and that a prime object of our policy was to bring Russia into the struggle against Japan in time to be of real value in the prosecution of the war. In this period, military considerations were understandably predominant over all others. Our most urgent purpose in the Far East was to defeat the common enemy and save the lives of our own men and those of our comrades-in-arms, the Chinese included. We should have failed in our manifest duty had we pursued any other course.

In the years since V-J Day, as in the years before Pearl Harbor, military considerations have been secondary to an earnest desire on our part to assist the Chinese people to achieve peace, prosperity and internal stability. The decisions and actions of our Government to promote these aims necessarily were taken on the basis of information available at the time. Throughout this tragic period, it has been fully realized that the material aid, the military and technical assistance, and the good will of the United States, however abundant, could not of themselves put China on her feet. In the last analysis, that can be done only by China herself.

Two factors have played a major role in shaping the destiny of modern China.

The population of China during the eighteenth and nineteenth

* From the Letter of Transmittal to the President accompanying the State Department's "White Book," *United States Relations with China*, Department of State Publication 3573, August 1949. Dean Acheson (b. 1893), Secretary of State from 1949 to 1952, now practices law in Washington, D. C.

centuries doubled, thereby creating an unbearable pressure upon the land. The first problem which every Chinese Government has had to face is that of feeding this population. So far none has succeeded. The Kuomintang attempted to solve it by putting many land-reform laws on the statute books. Some of these laws have failed, others have been ignored. In no small measure, the predicament in which the National Government finds itself today is due to its failure to provide China with enough to eat. A large part of the Chinese Communists' propaganda consists of promises that they will solve the land problem.

The second major factor which has shaped the pattern of contemporary China is the impact of the West and of Western ideas. . . . These outsiders brought with them aggressiveness, the unparalleled development of Western technology, and a high order of culture which had not accompanied previous foreign incursions into China. Partly because of these qualities and partly because of the decay of Manchu rule, the Westerners, instead of being absorbed by the Chinese, introduced new ideas which played an important part in stimulating ferment and unrest.

By the beginning of the twentieth century, the combined force of overpopulation and new ideas set in motion that chain of events which can be called the Chinese revolution. It is one of the most imposing revolutions in recorded history and its outcome and consequences are yet to be foreseen. Out of this revolutionary whirlpool emerged the Kuomintang, first under the leadership of Dr. Sun Yat-sen, and later Generalissimo Chiang Kai-shek, to assume the direction of the revolution. The leadership of the Kuomintang was not challenged until 1927 by the Chinese Communist party which had been organized in the early twenties under the ideological impetus of the Russian revolution. . . . To a large extent the history of the period between 1927 and 1937 can be written in terms of the struggle for power between the Kuomintang and the Chinese Communists, with the latter apparently fighting a losing battle. During this period the Kuomintang made considerable progress in its efforts to unify the country and to build up the nation's financial and economic strength. Somewhere during this decade, however, the Kuomintang began to lose the dynamism and revolutionary fervor which had created it, while in the Chinese Communists the fervor became fanaticism.

Perhaps largely because of the progress being made in China, the Japanese chose 1937 as the departure point for the conquest of China proper, and the goal of the Chinese people became the expulsion of a brutal and hated invader. . . .

In contrast also to the unity of the people of China in the war against Japan were the divided interests of the leaders of the Kuomintang and of the Chinese Communists. It became apparent in the early forties that the leaders of the Government, just as much as the Communist leaders, were still as preoccupied with the internal struggle for power as they were with waging war against Japan. Once the United States became a participant in the war, the Kuomintang was apparently convinced of the ultimate defeat of Japan and saw an opportunity to improve its position for a show-down struggle with the Communists. The Communists, for their part, seemed to see in the chaos of China an opportunity to obtain that which had been denied them before the Japanese war, namely, full power in China. . . .

The reports of United States military and diplomatic officers reveal a growing conviction through 1943 and 1944 that the Government and the Kuomintang had apparently lost the crusading spirit that won them the people's loyalty during the early years of the war. In the opinion of many observers they had sunk into corruption, into a scramble for place and power, and into reliance on the United States to win the war for them and to preserve their own domestic supremacy. The Government of China, of course, had always been a one-party rather than a democratic government in the Western sense. The stresses and strains of war were now rapidly weakening such liberal elements as it did possess and strengthening the grip of the reactionaries who were indistinguishable from the war lords of the past. The mass of the Chinese people were coming more and more to lose confidence in the Government.

It was evident to us that only a rejuvenated and progressive Chinese Government which could recapture the enthusiastic loyalty of the people could and would wage an effective war against Japan. American officials repeatedly brought their concern with this situation to the attention of the Generalissimo and he repeatedly assured them that it would be corrected. He made, however, little or no effective effort to correct it and tended to shut himself off from Chinese officials who gave unpalatable advice. In addition to a concern over the effect which this atrophy of the central Chinese administration must have upon the conduct of the war, some American observers . . . were concerned over the effect which this deterioration of the Kuomintang must have on its eventual struggle, whether political or military, with the Chinese Communists. These observers were already fearful in 1943 and 1944 that the National Government might be so isolating itself from the people that in the postwar competition for power it would prove itself impotent to maintain its authority. Nevertheless, we continued for obvious reasons to direct all our aid to the National Government. . . .

When peace came the United States was confronted with three possible alternatives in China: (1) it could have pulled out lock, stock and barrel; (2) it could have intervened militarily on a major scale to assist the Nationalists to destroy the Communists; (3) it could, while assisting the Nationalists to assert their authority over as much of China as possible, endeavor to avoid a civil war by working for a compromise between the two sides.

The first alternative would, and I believe American public opinion at the time so felt, have represented an abandonment of our international responsibilities and of our traditional policy of friendship for China before we had made a determined effort to be of assistance. The second alternative policy, while it may look attractive theoretically and in retrospect, was wholly impracticable. The Nationalists had been unable to destroy the Communists during the 10 years before the war. Now after the war the Nationalists were, as indicated above, weakened, demoralized, and unpopular. They had quickly dissipated their popular support and prestige in the areas liberated from the Japanese by the conduct of their civil and military officials. The Communists on the other hand were much stronger than they had ever been and were in control of most of North China. Because of the ineffectiveness of the Nationalist forces which was later to be tragically demonstrated, the Communists probably could have been dislodged only by American arms. It is obvious that the American people would not have sanctioned such a colossal commitment of our armies in 1945 or later. We therefore came to the third alternative policy whereunder we faced the facts of the situation and attempted to assist in working out a *modus vivendi* which would avert civil war but nevertheless preserve and even increase the influence of the National Government.

It was the Chinese National Government itself which had taken steps to arrive at a working agreement with the Communists. As early as September 1943 in addressing the Kuomintang Central Executive Committee, the Generalissimo said, "we should clearly recognize that the Communist problem is a purely political problem and should be solved by political means." He repeated this view on several occasions. Comprehensive negotiations between representatives of the Government and of the Communists, dealing with both military cooperation and civil administration, were opened in Sian in May 1944. These negotiations, in which Ambassador Hurley later assisted at the invitation of both parties between August 1944 and September 1945, continued intermittently during a year and a half without producing conclusive results and culminated in a comprehensive series of agreements on basic points on October 11, 1945, after Ambassador Hurley's departure from China and before General Marshall's arrival. Meanwhile, however, clashes between the armed forces of the two groups were increasing and were jeopardizing the fulfillment of the agreements. The danger of wide-spread civil war, unless the negotiations could promptly be brought to a successful conclusion, was critical. It was under these circumstances that General Marshall left on his mission to China at the end of 1945. . . .

Our policy at that time was inspired by the two objectives of bringing peace to China under conditions which would permit stable government and progress along democratic lines, and of assisting the National Government to establish its authority over as wide areas of China as possible. As the event proved, the first objective was unrealizable because neither side desired it to succeed: the Communists because they refused to accept conditions which would weaken their freedom to proceed with what remained consistently their aim, the communization of all China; the Nationalists because they cherished the illusion, in spite of repeated advice to the contrary from our military representatives, that they could destroy the Communists by force of arms.

The second objective of assisting the National Government, however, we pursued vigorously from 1945 to 1949. The National Government was the recognized government of a friendly power. Our friendship, and our right under international law alike, called for aid to the Government instead of to the Communists who were seeking to subvert and overthrow it. . . . The National Government had in 1945, and maintained until the early fall of 1948, a marked superiority in manpower and armament over their rivals. Indeed during that period, thanks very largely to our aid in transporting, arming and supplying their forces, they extended their control over a large part of North China and Manchuria. By the time General Marshall left China at the beginning of 1947, the Nationalists were apparently at the very peak of their military successes and territorial expansion. The following year and a half revealed, however, that their seeming strength was illusory and that their victories were built on sand.

The crisis had developed around Manchuria, traditional focus of Russian and Japanese imperialism. On numerous occasions, Marshal Stalin had stated categorically that he expected the National Government to take over the occupation of Manchuria. In the truce agreement of January 10, 1946, the Chinese Communists agreed to the movement of Government troops into Manchuria for the purpose of restoring Chinese sovereignty over this area. In conformity with this understanding the United States transported sizable government armies to the ports of entry into Manchuria. Earlier the Soviet Army had expressed a desire to evacuate Manchuria in December 1945, but had remained an additional two or three months at the request of the Chinese Government. When the Russian troops did begin their evacuation, the National Government found itself with extended lines of communication, limited rolling stock and insufficient forces to take over the areas being evacuated in time to prevent the entry of Chinese Communist forces, who were already in occupation of the countryside. As the Communists entered, they obtained the large stocks of matériel from the Japanese Kwantung Army which the Russians had conveniently "abandoned." To meet this situation the National Government embarked on a series of military campaigns which expanded the line of its holdings to the Sungari River. Toward the end of these campaigns it also commenced hostilities within North China and succeeded in constricting the areas held by the Communists.

In the spring of 1946 General Marshall attempted to restore peace. This effort lasted for months and during its course a seemingly endless series of proposals and counterproposals were made which had little effect upon the course of military activities and produced no political settlement. During these negotiations General Marshall displayed limitless patience and tact and a willingness to try and then try again in order to reach agreement. Increasingly he became convinced, however, that twenty years of intermittent civil war between the two factions, during which the leading figures had remained the same, had created such deep personal bitterness and such irreconcilable differences that no agreement was possible. The suspicions and the lack of confidence were beyond remedy. He became convinced that both parties were merely sparring for time, jockeying for military position and catering temporarily to what they believed to be American desires. General Marshall concluded that there was no hope of accomplishing the objectives of his mission. . . .

In his farewell statement, General Marshall announced the termination of his efforts to assist the Chinese in restoring internal peace. He described the deep-seated mutual suspicion between the Kuomintang and the Chinese Communist Party as the greatest obstacle to a settlement. He made it clear that the salvation of China lay in the hands of the Chinese themselves. . . . He appealed for the assumption of leadership by liberals in and out of the Government as the road to unity and peace. With these final words he returned to Washington to assume, in January 1947, his new post as Secretary of State.

As the signs of impending disaster multiplied, the President in July 1947, acting on the recommendation of the Secretary of State, instructed Lt. Gen. Albert C. Wedemeyer to survey the Chinese scene and make recommendations. In his report, submitted on September 19, 1947, the General recommended that the United

States continue and expand its policy of giving aid to Nationalist
China, subject to these stipulations:

1. That China inform the United Nations of her request for aid.
2. That China request the United Nations to bring about a truce
in Manchuria and request that Manchuria be placed under a Five-
Power guardianship or a trusteeship.
3. That China utilize her own resources, reform her finances,
her Government and her armies, and accept American advisers in
the military and economic fields.

General Wedemeyer's report, which fully recognized the danger
of Communist domination of all China and was sympathetic to
the problems of the National Government, nevertheless listed a
large number of reforms which he considered essential if that Government were to rehabilitate itself.

It was decided that the publication at that time of a suggestion
for the alienation of a part of China from the control of the
National Government, and for placing that part under an international administration to include Soviet Russia, would not be
helpful. . . .

The reasons for the failures of the Chinese National Government appear in some detail in the attached record. They do not
stem from any inadequacy of American aid. Our military observers on the spot have reported that the Nationalist armies did
not lose a single battle during the crucial year of 1948 through
lack of arms or ammunition. The fact was that the decay which
our observers had detected in Chungking early in the war had
fatally sapped the powers of resistance of the Kuomintang. Its
leaders had proved incapable of meeting the crisis confronting
them, its troops had lost the will to fight, and its Government had
lost popular support. The Communists, on the other hand, through
a ruthless discipline and fanatical zeal, attempted to sell themselves as guardians and liberators of the people. The Nationalist
armies did not have to be defeated; they disintegrated. History
has proved again and again that a regime without faith in itself
and an army without morale cannot survive the test of battle.

The record obviously can not set forth in equal detail the inner
history and development of the Chinese Communist Party during
these years. The principal reason is that, while we had regular

diplomatic relations with the National Government and had the benefit of voluminous reports from our representatives in their territories, our direct contact with the Communists was limited in the main to the mediation efforts of General Hurley and General Marshall.

Fully recognizing that the heads of the Chinese Communist Party were ideologically affiliated with Moscow, our Government nevertheless took the view, in the light of the existing balance of forces in China, that peace could be established only if certain conditions were met. The Kuomintang would have to set its own house in order and both sides would have to make concessions so that the Government of China might become, in fact as well as in name, the Government of all China and so that all parties might function within the constitutional system of the Government. Both internal peace and constitutional development required that the progress should be rapid from one party government with a large opposition party in armed rebellion, to the participation of all parties, including the moderate non-communist elements, in a truly national system of government.

None of these conditions has been realized. The distrust of the leaders of both the Nationalist and Communist Parties for each other proved too deep-seated to permit final agreement, notwithstanding temporary truces and apparently promising negotiations. The Nationalists, furthermore, embarked in 1946 on an over-ambitious military campaign in the face of warnings by General Marshall that it not only would fail but would plunge China into economic chaos and eventually destroy the National Government. General Marshall pointed out that though Nationalist armies could, for a period, capture Communist-held cities, they could not destroy the Communist armies. Thus every Nationalist advance would expose their communications to attack by Communist guerrillas and compel them to retreat or to surrender their armies together with the munitions which the United States has furnished them. No estimate of a military situation has ever been more completely confirmed by the resulting facts.

The historic policy of the United States of friendship and aid toward the people of China was, however, maintained in both peace and war. Since V-J Day, the United States Government has authorized aid to Nationalist China in the form of grants and credits totaling approximately 2 billion dollars, an amount equivalent in value to more than 50 percent of the monetary expenditures of the Chinese Government and of proportionately greater magnitude in relation to the budget of that Government than the United States has provided to any nation of Western Europe since the end of the war. In addition to these grants and credits, the United States Government has sold the Chinese Government large quantities of military and civilian war surplus property with a total procurement cost of over 1 billion dollars, for which the agreed realization to the United States was 232 million dollars. A large proportion of the military supplies furnished the Chinese armies by the United States since V-J Day has, however, fallen into the hands of the Chinese Communists through the military ineptitude of the Nationalist leaders, their defections and surrenders, and the absence among their forces of the will to fight.

It has been urged that relatively small amounts of additional aid —military and economic—to the National Government would have enabled it to destroy communism in China. The most trustworthy military, economic, and political information available to our Government does not bear out this view.

A realistic appraisal of conditions in China, past and present, leads to the conclusion that the only alternative open to the United States was full-scale intervention in behalf of a Government which had lost the confidence of its own troops and its own people. Such intervention would have required the expenditure of even greater sums than have been fruitlessly spent thus far, the command of Nationalist armies by American officers, and the probable participation of American armed forces—land, sea, and air—in the resulting war. Intervention of such a scope and magnitude would have been resented by the mass of the Chinese people, would have diametrically reversed our historic policy, and would have been condemned by the American people.

It must be admitted frankly that the American policy of assisting the Chinese people in resisting domination by any foreign power or powers is now confronted with the gravest difficulties. The heart of China is in Communist hands. The Communist leaders have foresworn their Chinese heritage and have publicly announced their subservience to a foreign power, Russia, which during the last 50 years, under czars and communists alike, has been most assiduous in its efforts to extend its control in the Far East. In the recent past, attempts at foreign domination have appeared quite clearly to the Chinese people as external aggression and as such have been bitterly and in the long run successfully resisted. Our aid and encouragement have helped them to resist. In this case, however, the foreign domination has been masked behind the façade of a vast crusading movement which apparently has seemed to many Chinese to be wholly indigenous and national. Under these circumstances, our aid has been unavailing.

The unfortunate but inescapable fact is that the ominous result of the civil war in China was beyond the control of the government of the United States. Nothing that this country did or could have done within the reasonable limits of its capabilities could have changed that result; nothing that was left undone by this country has contributed to it. It was the product of internal Chinese forces, forces which this country tried to influence but could not. A decision was arrived at within China, if only a decision by default.

And now it is abundantly clear that we must face the situation as it exists in fact. We will not help the Chinese or ourselves by basing our policy on wishful thinking. We continue to believe that, however tragic may be the immediate future of China and however ruthlessly a major portion of this great people may be exploited by a party in the interest of a foreign imperialism, ultimately the profound civilization and the democratic individualism of China will reassert themselves and she will throw off the foreign yoke. I consider that we should encourage all developments in China which now and in the future work toward this end.

In the immediate future, however, the implementation of our historic policy of friendship for China must be profoundly affected by current developments. It will necessarily be influenced by the degree to which the Chinese people come to recognize that the Communist regime serves not their interests but those of Soviet Russia and the manner in which, having become aware of the facts, they react to this foreign domination. One point, however, is clear. Should the Communist regime lend itself to the aims of Soviet Russian imperialism and attempt to engage in aggression against China's neighbors, we and the other members of the United Nations would be confronted by a situation violative of the principles of the United Nations Charter, and threatening international peace and security.

Meanwhile our policy will continue to be based upon our own respect for the Charter, our friendship for China, and our traditional support for the Open Door and for China's independence and administrative and territorial integrity.

Respectfully yours,

Dean Acheson

THE GOALS OF
COMMUNIST CHINA *

BY

ROBERT A. SCALAPINO

[1966]

The question is often asked, "Can we anticipate major changes
in China in the near future?" If by major changes, one means an
overthrow of the Communist Party, the chances seem to me remote,
barring global war or some other major and unforeseeable
crisis. . . .

Thus, in all probability, the most meaningful question is that so
frequently posed recently, "Will a younger generation of party
leaders diverge considerably from the group of old Bolsheviks currently holding absolute power, so that the resulting changes, while
taking place within the party, will nonetheless be profound and, in
general, in the direction of realism and moderation?"

This is a crucial question, and one that cannot be answered with
any complete certainty. My own belief is that such changes will
occur, but that the critical element of timing will depend heavily
upon both the internal and the external environment. Even under
the best of circumstances, I am inclined to feel that the struggle
for a more pragmatic, realistic, and moderate political elite in
China will be long and arduous, extending considerably beyond
one generation. But the rate and nature of change will certainly be
affected by the degree to which a wide range of subtle external
pressures and alternatives can be developed.

In certain terms, we are conducting a holding operation in Asia,
and one of the variables with which we must contend is the race
in China itself between the acquisition of power and the acquisition of responsibility. Our policies and those of other foreign

---

* Statement before the United States Senate, Committee on Foreign Relations.
Hearings, U.S. Policy with Respect to Mainland China, 1966. Robert A. Scalapino
(b. 1919) is Professor of Political Science at the University of California,
Berkeley, and editor of Asian Survey. His major publications include *The
Japanese Communist Movement, 1920–66* and *The Communist Revolution in
Asia* (ed.).

states, while not representing the sole determinants of this race, are vitally important elements.

One final point regarding change in China might be added. No political regime can be totally rigid and survive. Clearly, current Chinese leaders have been forced to make substantial adjustments to various programs that have failed, at home and abroad. That will continue. Indeed, just as the Maoists had to retrench in the aftermath of the failure of the Great Leap Forward at home, so now they are engaged in a reassessment of the Great Leap Forward abroad which has also failed on a major scale. . . .

Thus, tactical adjustments and modifications will be made because there is literally no alternative. One must distinguish, however, between belated responses to inescapable realities and the frame of mind which is bound to a minimum of dogma, the mind fundamentally responsive to a wide range of alternatives. China is still ruled by hard-core ideologues who hold to the thesis that being "red" is more important than being "expert," and who have now been driven to the deification of Maoism as the repository of all significant truth. . . .

Perhaps a basic fragility is revealed in a regime that is forced increasingly to rely upon the omnipotence of one man and descend into such irrational depths in the process. But the current scene in China has universal implications. In most emerging societies, a broad and supremely important conflict ensues at some point between elements we may roughly call ideologues and pragmatists. First-generation revolutionaries are generally strongly ideological, highly politicized, possessed of certain "charismatic" qualities, and lacking in most advanced technical skills. Their primary task is nation building, often via mass mobilization. At some point, however, they must give way to an elite who are more pragmatic than ideological, more bureaucratic than charismatic, and more concerned with the technical and administrative skills essential to progress in economic and social terms. The implications of this process for American foreign policy, I would suggest, are far reaching.

The era of the ideologues is likely to be at once dynamic and disappointing—disappointing in the sense that many of the broad goals projected will not be realized. Consequently, mounting pressures upon the elite in power will ensue. The temptation on their part to engage in irrational, distractive behavior will increase. But there will also be ultimate pressures for realistic policies that can achieve results.

It is certainly incumbent upon the United States in these circumstances to take a positive position in affirmation of the broad goals constantly voiced in this era: nationalism; the acceptance of, and involvement in, the world community; democracy; social justice and economic development. It is equally important that we devise policies that in concrete terms will discourage extremism and encourage moderation, primarily by making clear the risks of the former, and setting forth the opportunities of the latter. And these opportunities must involve precisely the types of interaction and assistance that would abet the movement from ideological rigidity toward pragmatic experimentalism.

*　　*　　*

There are two other general questions relating to China upon which I should like to comment prior to discussing the specifics of our China policy. There has been some debate over the nature of Chinese Communist power and intentions. Some emphasize the thesis that China is essentially a weak nation, one thoroughly frightened by the massive power and encirclement policies of the United States, and most likely to respond to us only in a defensive sense—hence constituting no basic threat to us, our allies, or the neutrals. Others argue that we should treat China as a major power and one that clearly has aggressive, expansionist aspirations threatening the whole of the non-Communist world.

In my opinion, the truth is approached as one combines these two views, treating them as more complementary than in conflict. China is weak in a variety of ways. Her economic recovery from the disasters of a few years ago is scarcely complete, and despite remarkable feats in certain areas of production and distribution, overall increases—particularly in agrarian production—appear to be modest, especially when measured against population growth. Moreover, the changing of the political guard is at hand and even if the resulting changes may not be dramatic, some internal tension must be present in the Chinese Communist Party at this point, heightened by the significant setbacks in foreign policy. Finally, China is scarcely a military match for the United States, and she undoubtedly fears American power.

American power confronts China on the east and south. Soviet power lies on the west and north. Without question, the existence of this power contributes to a psychology that is at once fearful and blatantly defiant. It would be extremely unwise, however, to deduce from this that such power being removed, Chinese foreign policy would subsequently be characterized by passivity or moderation. Were it not for American and Soviet power in Asia, the Chinese Communists would almost certainly have advanced much further toward their basic goals there, although I do not for a moment regard American and Soviet interests and objectives in the area as identical.

What are the Chinese goals? Three have been oft proclaimed: To remove all Western influence from Asia; to encourage by a variety of means an ideologically politically uniform Asia cast in the image of "the new China"; and to enlist this "progressive" Asia in the global struggle against both the "revisionists" and the "imperialists." The words are those of the Chinese.

These are scarcely the goals of an elite that is primarily oriented toward defense, and posing its objectives in very limited terms. It is quite true, however, that these goals—and some of the actions that have accompanied them—have triggered a reaction, not alone from us but from many others as well. Thus today, China must calculate defensively because the United States, and in some degree the Soviet Union, will not permit her to calculate offensively on any significant scale.

Her defensive calculations undoubtedly include a determination in each specific instance as to what she can and cannot tolerate from the standpoint of her own national interests, and what risks, correspondingly, she is prepared to run. . . .

The fact, however, that China is forced to react defensively and partly from fear at this point should not obscure the very strong commitment which the current generation of Chinese leaders have had to global influence. From the moment they emerged into full control, these leaders committed themselves and their society to the cultivation of power in all of its forms: military, political, psychological, and economic. . . .

Since the Communist era began in China, no Asian state has been capable of matching Chinese power unaided, and it is wise to remember that there is not a pacifist bone in a Maoist body. The Chinese Communists, moreover, have consummated alliances large and small, undertaken aid and technical assistance programs far beyond their economic capacities, and engaged in a range of political activities throughout the world that caused most nations, friend and foe, to label China "major power designate." That is a significant accomplishment, incidentally, because such a status grants certain rights without conveying the requisite responsibilities.

When all of these activities are surveyed, I do not understand how anyone can regard Chinese actions or goals of the past decade as defensive, either in character or intent. . . .

What have been the major source-springs of Chinese foreign policy under the Communists? Three forces seem to me of central importance: Tradition, nationalism, and MLM—Marx-Lenin-Maoism. In certain respects, the current Chinese leaders still think of their problem as how to handle the barbarians. They still divide the world into those who accept Chinese culture (now to be read "ideology") and those who live outside the pale. The former are the "civilized" or the "progressive" people, to use their terms; the latter are barbarians, be they "revisionists," "imperialists," or "neutrals." The barbarian must be handled by a combination of persuasion and coercion. . . . Some of China's difficulties today are unquestionably due to a continuance among her present generation of mandarin rulers of an "imperial complex," an engrained sense of cultural superiority and the attitude of condescension toward other peoples that invariably accompanies this.

The nationalist quotient in Chinese foreign policy is, of course, extremely high. In many respects, China is behaving in much the same fashion as have other major societies en route to power. First, she has sought to define and defend her boundaries as she interprets these; secondly, she has sought to create a buffer state system around her; and finally, she has sought hegemony in the world in which she lives: the Asian world, the non-Western World, and the Communist World.

In pursuit of these objectives, the Chinese Communists have been no more able to follow a totally consistent foreign policy than the leaders of other major states. The main thrust of Chinese Communist foreign policy, as suggested earlier, has been characterized by revolutionary fervor, global commitment, and relatively inflexible division of the world into comrades and enemies. The line has been hard, advanced by practicing ideologues fiercely impatient with the existing order and anxious to challenge it in radical fashion. And yet, for tactical reasons and out of necessity, these leaders have adopted a great variety of approaches. . . . Indeed, one is forced to conclude that the one element of major consistency is that which runs through the policies of all nations: the consistent expression of what appears to the political elite as in their national interests. And it is precisely this fact that offers hope of some flexibility, even among hard-core ideologues.

At its roots, the Sino-Soviet dispute itself is closely connected with the phenomena of nationalism. We now know that nationalism has not only survived Communism, but in many respects triumphed over it. The Sino-Soviet cleavage illustrates the fact that two nations supposedly sharing a common ideology but differing substantially in cultural traditions, timing of revolution, stage of development, generation of leadership and degree of power are almost certain to have different views of the world and of their own needs. Hence, they will have different concepts of national interest which, in the case of Marxists, will be translated into different interpretations of what is truth; namely, what is orthodox Marxism-Leninism. . . .

The Sino-Soviet dispute centers upon the issue of how to treat the United States, although there are other significant issues as well. The Soviet Union basically believes in nation-to-nation competition with the United States, counting upon the ultimate superiority of Soviet productivity and power. Thus it argues that the appropriate method of confrontation is peaceful coexistence, meaning all-out economic, political and social competition but the avoidance of nuclear war. There is, to be sure, an element of ambiguity in the Soviet position surrounding its defense of national wars of liberation, which may be variously defined and supported. Nevertheless, its standard criticisms of the Peking line is that the Chinese leaders have rejected peaceful coexistence, and pursue a left-adventurist policy that risks global war.

China, on the other hand, not being able to conceive of the possibility of nation-to-nation competition with the United States in the near future, and having no basic responsibility for the maintenance of peace or the prosecution of a nuclear war, argues the classical Bolshevik thesis that America must be challenged by the technique of unfolding the world revolution. The Chinese theme is that primary emphasis must be placed upon mobilizing the non-Western World for a rapid, continuous assault upon the "capitalist West, led by the United States." Thus, the Russians are rebuked for their refusal to take massive risks on behalf of global revolution, and they are now charged by Peking with active collaboration with Washington for purposes of world domination. At the moment, China asserts that Vietnam is the supreme test of the validity of her position and her principles. The United States is a paper tiger which, if challenged resolutely and in accordance with Maoist principles, will collapse as a result of internal and external pressures. Maoism will be vindicated on the battlefields of Vietnam—and in the streets of the United States—against the combination of American imperialism and Soviet sabotage. That is the Chinese position.

As the nationalist component in Chinese foreign policy is surveyed, I would suggest that the following conclusions pertinent to policy might be advanced. One critical problem is that of striking a balance between providing Chinese nationalism with legitimate outlets and guarding against those aggressive potentials that lie embedded in any nationalist movement, and particularly one possessed of active messianic goals like that of China. There are some who argue that Chinese domination of Asia is appropriate, or in any case, inevitable. Their thesis is that Asia is the legitimate sphere of influence for China, just as the Western Hemisphere is for us. . . . The simple spheres of influence concept is misleading in terms of fact, unrealistic in terms of current political trends, and untenable in terms of basic morality.

There can be no question that the United States, of all modern nations, has had the greatest unchallenged preponderance of power historically in its own region. Yet even the United States has lived for various periods of time with hostile states in this hemisphere, and with states having intimate ties with foreign powers—from the time of British Canada to the time of Moscow-oriented Cuba. Certainly, the Russians have never had any total dominance of their near neighbors—witness the existence of Finland, Turkey, Greece, and Iran, among others. My own belief, indeed, is that the existence of some elements of competition and neutrality in the vicinity of a major power is healthy. A major state totally secure in its own region may not only be oblivious to the problems of its neighbors, but may also be unduly free to undertake expansionist activities afield. Thus, I do not believe that Chinese dominance of Asia is either inevitable or desirable—and neither, I suspect, do the peoples of India, Japan, Indonesia, and the Soviet Union, among others.

This is not to say, however, that China should be denied—or can be denied—all elements to security. Already, China has a certain buffer state system: North Korea shields the Manchurian complex, at least from the East; North Vietnam stands in front of the Kwantung area; China now controls Tibet; and many of the border states of south and southeast Asia—notably Afghanistan, Pakistan, Nepal, Burma, and Cambodia can either be accounted neutral or friendly. Over time and under conditions where a general balance of power in Asia had been achieved, it might be possible to extend that belt of neutrality to other states. Indeed, nothing should be ruled outside the range of future possibility, including large-scale disarmament and a reliance upon collective security agreements by the major Asian states. Progress on any of these fronts, however, now depends primarily upon China: her willingness to renounce force as a means of effecting international change; her preparedness to enter into negotiations on a wide range of issues; her capacity to accept compromise as an essential ingredient in international agreement; and her ability to abandon the thesis that the destruction of the United States as it is presently constituted takes priority over all other foreign policy objectives.

The final source-spring of Chinese Communist foreign policy, I have labeled MLM. The Maoists think of themselves as orthodox

Marxist-Leninists, indeed, as the only legitimate leaders of the world Marxist movement. At the same time, however, they pride themselves upon having "applied Marxism-Leninism creativity" to the conditions of China. Perhaps it is accurate to define the Maoist element in Chinese Marxism as the practical development of a five-stage revolutionary progression which places heavy reliance initially upon intellectual leadership and a peasant-based radical movement that has its roots in the countryside.

The Maoist revolutionary formula begins with the creation of a Communist Party which must never lose control of the revolutionary movement. That party proceeds to guide the creation of a united front, using nationalist and socio-economic appeals, but relying heavily upon organization, and using freely the instruments of coercion as well as those of persuasion. When the front has been prepared, the movement into guerrilla warfare is the next stage, and then the advance to positional warfare. When military victory has been attained, the so-called People's Democratic Republic is established under the complete control of the Communist Party.

Long before Lin Piao's speech of last summer, it was clear that the Chinese Communists regarded this revolutionary formula broadly applicable to the world scene—from the Congo to Vietnam. In very high degree, indeed, the old Bolsheviks of China, so strongly isolated from world reality, have seen the world mirrored in their own ideological-revolutionary image and history. The need for a true Communist Party means that one must fight such false Marxists-Leninists as the Russians. The united front with its emphasis upon a union of peasants, workers, intellectuals, and national bourgeois under the leadership of the vanguard party spells out the Chinese determination to unite the world peasantry (the Afro-Asian societies) and certain susceptible bourgeois elements (clearly France was once in mind) under Peking's banners.

Thus, MLM makes Chinese Communist foreign policy something more than merely another expression of nationalism in action. It defines both the scope and the techniques of policy in a unique way. China is interested in Albania as well as Korea; in Mali as well as in Vietnam. The definition of national interest, the conceptualization of problem, the vocabulary of dispute are all colored by MLM. It would be as dangerous to underestimate the

Marxist quotient in Chinese foreign policy at this point as to accord it total influence. . . .

Naturally, I am gratified to note that in recent months and weeks, there have been increasing signs that our Government is seeking a more broadly gauged policy. Some of the steps which I advocated in 1959 are now being initiated or at least actively contemplated. These include a willingness to allow American scholars, scientists, journalists, and certain other citizens to travel to China; positive steps to seek the involvement of China in international negotiations on such problems as disarmament, nuclear weapon control, and similar issues of world importance; and the establishment of terms under which mainland China might come in to the United Nations.

Because these steps, and others which should follow will be strongly debated, I should like to reiterate the reasons why I believe such actions, on balance, are highly desirable. A policy of containment by isolation robbed the United States of initiative or leverage, and tended to posit our rigidity against that of Peking. This in turn served to separate us from our allies and the neutrals, making collective thinking and action with respect to China vastly more difficult. It also rendered far less effective the type of multiple external pressures that are essential if the element of extremism in Chinese foreign policy is to be effectively curbed or countered.

Our past policy has been insufficient in certain other respects. To foster isolation is to foster fanaticism. Isolation, indeed, is one of the major weapons of a police state, and there is no reason as to why we should be a party to its support. . . . To be table to engage in selective diplomacy and to bear negligible responsibilities in the world community represent significant tactical advantages which we should not bestow lightly. Such a situation also encourages a purist, uncompromising, and irrational attitude, an air of complete unrealism.

A policy of containment by isolation, in short, not only provides an inadequate approach from the standpoint of international political realities, but it is also highly unsatisfactory from the standpoint of its impact upon the Chinese nation itself. In immediate terms, therefore, we must move from such a policy toward one that heightens the element of choice for the Chinese political elite by providing additional incentives for moderation and firm, explicit deterrents to extremism. We must find a way of making peaceful coexistence the only conceivable path for the next generation of Chinese leaders and we must do this without abandoning any of the basic rights or requirements of the non-Communist World.

I do not claim that this will be easy or that it can be done quickly. The thrust of my earlier analysis was that we face a China both militantly nationalist and strongly ideological at present, a China whose leaders have committed a series of excesses from which they must now beat some retreat, but who still appear to be intent upon cultivating power in all of its aspects and quite prepared to use violence to effect revolutionary change throughout the world. At this point, presumably, the Chinese leaders are sufficiently realistic to want to avoid war with the United States, and even with less powerful forces. The time may not be too long, however, before China's military capacities come closer to matching her political visions. We must prepare for that eventuality now. . . .

The only realistic approach in my opinion, is the complex one of creating an elaborate structure of opportunities and deterrents, and in this task we must have the cooperation of other nations, particularly those of non-Communist Asia. Our first steps seem clear enough. Progressively, we must make it clear by concrete actions that if China is isolated, the initiative lies with her, that we are prepared to enter into cultural relations with her, engage in trade on the same basis as with other Communist nations, and negotiate with her on all matters of international importance. At the same time, we should accept in principle the desirability of universal membership in the United Nations, a principle which among other things would make natural the acceptance of both China and Taiwan as de facto states deserving international representation. Bilateral recognition between the United States and China is not, in my opinion, a first priority item under present circumstances. Once again, however, I believe that we should move toward the establishment of a general principle, namely the complete divorcement of recognition from the question of moral or political approval.

Having supported the above actions, let me make it emphatically clear that I am under no illusions about the initial Chinese response. Peking will not help us develop a new China policy because basically she likes our old one, and does not want us to change. As has already been implied, she believes that our present policy isolates us more than her; makes the United States available as a perfect scapegoat both before her own people and before others; and prevents or at least mitigates the types of pressures developing upon her from the outside that might otherwise be created.

Thus, we can assume that the torrent of abuse against us will continue to flow out of China, and that initial responses to our overtures will be almost completely negative. As in so many other situations today, this will test our patience and our sophistication. We must neither be driven back into rigidity nor panicked into making unwarranted concessions. . . .

Thus far, however, I have advanced and defended only one side of the policy proposed earlier. But it is my firm belief that moderation will be encouraged only if the risks of extremism are made both credible and clear. When the history of this era is written, it may be that the two Asian wars in which we have been engaged since 1950 were both the products of Communist miscalculation for which we must assume some share of responsibility. . . .

Let us not make this type of mistake again. Let us make clear our definition of aggression and neoaggression, and make clear also our commitments and resolves so that miscalculations can be reduced to an absolute minimum.

At this point, for example, we should make it absolutely clear that any attempt to change the status of Taiwan or South Korea by means of the use of externally directed or assisted force will be resolutely countered by the application of American force. We should also continue to make it unmistakably clear that we do not intend to allow these tactics to succeed in South Vietnam. In my opinion, nothing would be more calculated to pump life into the extremist movement within China and within the Communist world than a Maoist victory in Vietnam—and nothing would lead us more quickly into the awful choice between precipitous retreat everywhere and World War III. The Chinese have repeatedly emphasized the fact that Vietnam is a supreme test of Maoist principles in statements to their own people, to other Asians, and to fellow Communists. We can be certain that the path toward moderation and peace will be infinitely longer and more painful if extremism pays in this crucial test.

If we are to be successful in gradually developing a new approach to China, we must also look closely at our total Asian policy, because obviously there must be a close interrelation between our approach to China and our approach to Asia as a whole. . . .

First, if we look at the present political situation in its broadest dimensions, two powers largely external to Asia—the United States and the Soviet Union—are each in somewhat different ways playing a critical role in balancing the thrust of China, primarily because no Asian nation—or combination of nations—is currently prepared to play that role. It is recognized on all sides, however, that ultimately a balance of power must be developed within Asia, if diversity and peace are to be rendered possible, and our most basic planning and support must be directed toward this end.

Second, a major world power like the United States is destined by virtue of its strength and resources to be somewhat apart from other nations. In this era, we are required to bear heavier responsibilities, be subjected to heavier criticism, and on occasion to make grave decisions, the execution of which falls primarily upon us, or upon us alone. In many cases, moreover, the decision not to act is at least as fateful as the decision to act. Thus, we cannot escape from a powerful element of unilateralism, and I see no point in naively or romantically railing against this fact. We are going to do certain things alone, or almost alone, if they are done at all. At the same time, it is incumbent upon us—now more than ever before—to develop programs and also an attitude of mind soliciting international opinions and support, especially from nations like Japan and India, nations that should be taking more responsibility in world affairs and in the affairs of Asia than is currently the case.

Third, until we find better methods of enabling freedom and socio-economic development to go together, we will be under substantial handicaps in the struggle to preserve open societies. I am personally convinced that we have the brains and much of the data needed to make significant progress on this problem, and in the course of making that progress, providing answers to a host of crucial questions that relate to certain basic aspects of American foreign policy. . . . Obviously, we should not be and we are not involved equally in every nation of the world—or even in every region. But under what conditions—assuming that the initiative is largely ours—should we be involved, and how? . . .

I should like to conclude with two final observations that relate to our status in the modern world and our responsibilities. Perhaps we have underestimated the psychological and intellectual problems of moving from a position of regional influence to one of global power. Our intellectual center of gravity, for example, and also the center of our decisionmaking process continues to evidence strong Europocentric tendencies. . . .

Finally, I cannot avoid the observation that perhaps our gravest problem today is the fact that our culture conflicts in certain significant respects with the requirements of our status and power. . . . Whereas power in the mid-19th century was held by small states which had come to the industrial revolution early and had accumulated their resources externally, power in the mid-20th century is held by continental-mass societies whose resources lie largely within themselves, and each of whom has had a long history of relative self-sufficiency, a reasonably high quotient of ethnocentrism, and a strong commitment to isolation not easily removed. . . .

Beyond that, ours is a culture that has placed an enormous premium upon speed and efficiency. I suspect that the critical test of American success or failure in world leadership in the years that lie immediately ahead will hinge upon whether we can modify those cherished qualities in accordance with the dictates of the world in which we live. This requires patience and, more than patience, an appreciation of the signal importance of being able to move from 10 to 11, or 8 to 7, in the broad range of policy alternatives, rather than being forced to operate only on the basis of 0 to 100. I regard this as the single most important test of American maturity. If we continue to live by the all or nothing philosophy— either "all in" or "all out"—we cannot possibly sustain our values of our interests. This is to use a neolithic approach to the problems of a nuclear age. . . .

A NEW CHINA POLICY FOR THE UNITED STATES *

BY

HANS J. MORGENTHAU

[1966]

I. THE INTERESTS AND POLICIES OF CHINA

China poses for the United States three fundamental issues, which can be separated for purposes of analysis but in practice blend into each other. First, China is the most powerful nation of the mainland of Asia and potentially the most powerful nation in the world. Second, China has been for at least a millennium a great power of a peculiar kind in that her outlook upon, and relations with, the outside world have been different from those of other great powers. Third, China is today the fountainhead of the most virulent kind of communism, proclaiming the inevitability of armed conflict and instigating and supporting Communist subversion throughout the world.

1. China as a Great Power

As a great Asian power, China seeks to restore the position she occupied before she was reduced to a semicolonial status about a century ago. That goal has been proclaimed by the Chinese leaders, and the policies actually pursued by them with regard to the off-shore islands and Taiwan, Korea, Vietnam, Burma, Cambodia, Tibet, and India conform to a consistent pattern: restoration of the territorial boundaries and of the influence the Chinese Empire possessed before its modern decline. These boundaries are likely to comprise Taiwan and the offshore islands, Outer Mongolia, and the Asian territories claimed by China and annexed by the Soviet Union during the 19th century. Physically, considering the distri-

---

* Statement before the United States Senate, Committee on Foreign Relations. *Hearings, U.S. Policy with Respect to Mainland China*, 1966. Hans J. Morgenthau (b. 1904) is Director of the Center for Study of American Foreign and Military Policy and Professor of Political Science at the University of Chicago. His most recent book is *A New Foreign Policy for the United States*.

bution of power on the Asian mainland, China could go much further, she could go virtually as far as she wanted to. But she has never done so in the past, and she is not likely to do so in the future. The reasons are to be found in the peculiar Chinese outlook upon the world. . . .

Instead of conquering neighboring states, which she could have conquered without undue risk, China has been traditionally satisfied with the establishment at her southern and southwestern borders of friendly governments, whose political identity was left intact and whose friendliness was assured and symbolized through tributary relationships of different kinds and degrees.

These subtle and indirect relationships are the result of the traditional Chinese conception of China as the center of the political universe, the only sovereign power worthy of the name, to which all other nations owe tribute. This extreme ethnocentrism goes hand in hand with contempt for, and ignorance of, the outside world, which from the Chinese point of view really does not need to be understood and to be dealt with on terms of equality with China. . . .

2. China as a Communist Power

The quandary which the United States faces in its relations with China is created by the addition to these traditional elements of Chinese foreign policy of a new and unprecedented one: the sponsorship of a militant world communism. That quandary is similar to the one the United States dealt with successfully in the immediate aftermath of the Second World War when we had to distinguish between the great power and world Communist aspirations of the Soviet Union. The Soviet Union modified and mitigated its world revolutionary fervor when it began to realize, starting in the twenties, that the risks it ran for its own survival on behalf of world revolution were out of all proportion to the chances to achieve that revolution. It is likely that China will undergo a similar process of adapting world revolutionary aims to political and military realities. The chances for such a development must exist, provided China has a rational government, and they are enhanced by Mao Tse-tung's intellectual characteristics and the nature of his past policies, both at home and abroad.

Mao Tse-tung's approach to the political and military problems at hand is characterized by two main interrelated qualities, as revealed in his writings and actions: a radically independent interpretation of Marxism-Leninism and a highly undogmatic pragmatism. . . . These same qualities mark the foreign policies Mao Tse-tung has pursued in Asia. Their caution and limitation to the traditional national objectives of China stand in stark contrast to the militant rhetoric of the Chinese leaders, in which an ethnocentric disregard for the realities and contempt for the interests of the outside world manifest themselves.

Marshal Lin Piao's famous manifesto of September 2, 1965, provides a particularly impressive but by no means unique example of this ethnocentrism, which is intellectually absurd and politically impractical. The Marshal tries to apply the lessons of the Communist revolution in China to the world scene. As the Communists conquered the countryside, isolating, surrounding, and finally conquering the cities, so, the Marshal suggests, the Communists will conquer the rural areas of the world, and isolates and finally conquer the cities of the world, by which he means the capitalistic nations of the West. To take these geopolitical metaphors as a program for political and military action is to completely misunderstand their ethnocentric source. Marshal Lin Piao's manifesto is not the Chinese equivalent of "Mein Kampf," for the simple reason that even a Chinese Hitler would be incapable of putting it into practice. . . .

3. The Future Policies of China

It can thus be expected that both the present and the coming generation of Chinese leaders will continue to learn from experience and to adapt their policies to the real world. It is also quite possible that the coming generation will be less given to militant Marxist-Leninist rhetoric and to the instigation and support of subversion throughout the world. But it would be futile to expect that the new generation will be more accommodating than is the old one when it comes to the restoration of China's traditional domain in Asia. In this respect, Mao Tse-tung and Chiang Kai-shek see eye to eye, and so must Mao Tse-tung and his successor, whoever he may be. To mention only the most crucial issue where the traditional Chinese national interest is at stake: both Mao Tse-tung and Chiang Kai-shek consider Taiwan to be an integral part of China, they only disagree as to who shall rule China. Regardless of its ideological commitment, no patriotic government of China can be expected to give up the claim to Taiwan, and any Chinese government which believes to have the power will try to recover it. The issue of Taiwan has indeed proven the main stumbling block in the Warsaw negotiations between the United States and China, and it is bound to do so in the future. That it has proven to be no more is due to China's temporary military weakness. Once China has realized its military potential, the issue of Taiwan, if it has not been settled in the meantime, will be the most likely casus belli between the United States and China.

II. THE INTERESTS AND POLICIES OF THE UNITED STATES

What are the interests of the United States with regard to China, and what are the policies most likely to serve those interests? The United States has two such interests: maintenance or, if need be, the restoration of a viable balance of power in Asia and the maintenance of a world balance of power. We have tried to serve these interests for more than 15 years through two policies: the isolation and the peripheral military containment of China.

1. The Policy of Isolating China

The policy of isolating China seeks the downfall of its Communist government. It is intimately connected with the recognition of the Chiang Kai-shek government as the legitimate government of China and with the expectation of its return to the mainland. By maintaining close relations with the Chiang Kai-shek government and none with the Communist government, a policy in which we expected our allies to participate, we tried to destroy the legitimacy of the Communist government. By interdicting all personal and commercial relations with mainland China we expected to make it impossible for the Communist government to govern. This policy has obviously failed. Chiang Kai-shek will not return to the mainland and his government survives only by virtue of the presence of the 7th Fleet in the Straits of Taiwan. The Communist govern-

ment of China enjoys diplomatic, cultural, and commercial relations with many nations, among which there are many allies of the
United States, and it is the United States rather than Communist
China which has been isolated in consequence of its policy of isolation. . . .

Thus from the point of view of China, our policy of isolation is
no longer an important issue. Therefore, no favorable response can
be expected from China if the United States should give up this
policy. The real issue is not isolation but containment. This is the
crucial point at which the traditional national interests of China
and the policy of the United States clash. The slogan "containment
without isolation" obscures that crucial issue. . . .

Similar considerations apply to the proposal to end the isolation
of China by engaging in trade with her. The existence and the volume of trade between the United States and China are irrelevant to
the basic issues that divide the two nations. Furthermore, China
looks at foreign trade not as a series of transactions undertaken for
commercial gain, but as an instrument of national policy. To engage in indiscriminate trade with China, apart from an overall
political settlement, is self-defeating, for such trade strengthens
China politically and militarily without giving an equivalent political or military advantage to the other partner.

Finally, the seating of the Communist government as the representative of China in the United Nations is not likely to be successful if it is conceived merely as the liquidation of the policy of
isolation and not also and primarily as a settlement of the issue of
Taiwan. It is virtually inconceivable that a representative of the
Communist government should set foot in the United Nations while
a representative of the Chiang Kai-shek government is present; for
the idea of "two Chinas" is as repellent to Mao Tse-tung as it is to
Chiang Kai-shek. If the General Assembly should vote this fall
that the representative of the Communist government replace the
representative of the Chiang Kai-shek government, the latter would
no longer be represented in the General Assembly but would still
occupy the seat of China as a permanent member of the Security
Council. It is here that the issue would be joined.

If the Security Council should decide to emulate the General
Assembly and install the representative of the Communist govern-

ment in the permanent seat of China—a decision the United States could nullify by vetoing it—the Chiang Kai-shek government would be deprived of any representation in the United Nations. In consequence, its claim to be the legitimate government of China would be destroyed, and its claim to be the legitimate government of Taiwan would be considerably impaired. Thus our policy of containing Communist China, which we could continue behind the military shield of the 7th Fleet, would be politically undermined. For by weakening Chiang Kai-shek's claim, Communist China would have taken the first step toward achieving the recognition of its own. Thus it becomes obvious again that the real issue is not isolation but containment.

2. *The Policy of Peripheral Military Containment*

We thought that the policy of military containment which worked so well against the Soviet Union in Europe would work equally well elsewhere, and so we applied it to the Middle East through the Baghdad Pact and to Asia through SEATO, and have followed it in our policies vis-à-vis China. Yet what succeeded in Europe was bound to fail elsewhere. The reasons for that failure are twofold.

First, the threat that faced the nations of Western Europe in the aftermath of the Second World War was primarily military. It was the threat of the Red army marching westward. Behind the line of military demarcation of 1945 which the policy of containment declared to the westernmost limits of the Soviet empire, there was an ancient civilization, only temporarily weak and able to maintain itself against the threat of Communist subversion.

The situation is different in the Middle East and Asia. The threat there is not primarily military but political in nature. Weak governments and societies provide opportunities for Communist subversion. Military containment is irrelevant to that threat and may even be counterproductive. Thus the Baghdad Pact did not protect Egypt from Soviet influence and SEATO has had no bearing on Chinese influence in Indonesia and Pakistan, to speak of Asia only.

Second, and more important, China is, even in her present underdeveloped state, the dominant power in Asia. She is this by virtue of the equality and quantity of her population, her geographic position, her civilization, her past power remembered and her future power anticipated. Anybody who has traveled in Asia with his eyes and ears open must have been impressed by the enormous impact which the resurgence of China has made upon all manner of men, regardless of class and political conviction, from Japan to Pakistan.

The issue China poses is political and cultural predominance. The United States can no more contain Chinese influence in Asia by arming Thailand and fighting in South Vietnam than China could contain American influence in the Western Hemisphere by arming, say, Nicaragua and fighting in Lower California. If we are convinced that we cannot live with a China predominant on the mainland of Asia, then we must strike at the heart of Chinese power—that is, rather than try to contain the power of China by power itself. Thus there is logic on the side of that small group of Americans who are convinced that war between the United States and China is inevitable and that the earlier it comes, the better will be the chances for the United States to win it.

Yet, while logic is on their side, practical judgment is against them. For while China is obviously no match for the United States in overall power, China is largely immune to the specific types of power in which the superiority of the United States consists—that is, nuclear, air, and naval power. Certainly, the United States has the power to destroy the nuclear installations and the major industrial and population centers of China, but this destruction would not defeat China; it would only set her development back. To be defeated, China has to be conquered.

Physical conquest would require the deployment of millions of American soldiers on the mainland of Asia. No American military leader has ever advocated a course of action so fraught with incalculable risks, so uncertain of outcome, requiring sacrifices so out of proportion to the interests at stake and the benefits to be expected. . . .

If we do not want to set ourselves goals which cannot be attained with the means we are willing to employ, we must learn to accommodate ourselves to the political and cultural predominance of China on the Asian mainland. It is instructive to note that those Asian nations which have done so—such as Burma and Cambodia —live peacefully in the shadow of the Chinese giant. On the other hand, those Asian nations which have allowed themselves to be transformed into outposts of American military power—such as Laos in the late fifties, South Vietnam and Thailand—have become the actual or prospective victims of Communist aggression and subversion. Thus it appears that peripheral military containment is counterproductive. Challenged at its periphery by American military power at its weakest—that is, by the proxy of client-states —China or its proxies are able to respond with locally superior military and political power.

Thus, even if the Chinese threat were primarily of a military nature, peripheral military containment would be ineffective in the long run in view of China's local military superiority. By believing otherwise, we have fallen heir to a misconception of our containment of the Soviet Union and of the reasons for its success. The Soviet Union has not been contained by the Armed Forces we have been able to put in the field locally in Europe. It has been contained by the near certainty that an attack upon these forces would be countered by the nuclear retaliation of the United States. If we are to assume that the Chinese armies stand, or one day will stand, poised to sweep over Asia, they will not be contained by the Armed Forces we or our allies can put into the field on the mainland of Asia. They will only be deterred by the near certainty that China as an organized society will be destroyed in the process of nuclear retaliation.

China is today protected from the full measure of our nuclear retaliation by her own technological backwardness; for she does not possesss the number of industrial and population centers whose nuclear destruction would spell her defeat. It is for this reason that China is today more daring in words, and might well become more daring in action if her vital interests were sufficiently threatened, than would be justified in view of the overall distribution of power between the United States and China. However, in the measure that China develops her nuclear capability, she also becomes vulnerable to nuclear retaliation; for once China has developed into a modern nation with a high technological capability, she will also have developed a large number of vital industrial and population centers and will then have become as vulnerable to nuclear attack as are the United States and the Soviet Union today. Assuming a modicum of rationality in the government which will then govern

China, fear of nuclear retaliation must be assumed to have the same restraining influence upon Chinese policies as it has had upon the policies of the United States and the Soviet Union since the beginning of the nuclear age. . . .

3. *The Worldwide Containment of China*

The peripheral military containment of China is, however, being justified not only in local terms but also, and to an ever greater extent, in worldwide terms. We are told that by containing China in South Vietnam we are containing here everywhere, and that by frustrating a "war of national liberation" in southeast Asia, we frustrate all "wars of national liberation." This argument has the virtue of simplicity, but it is supported by no historic evidence. . . .

The so-called domino theory is indeed an echo of the Marxist dogma of historic inevitability which asserts that communism will inevitably spread from country to country until in the end it engulfs the world. Nothing of the kind has actually happened. After the Second World War, the nations of Eastern Europe went Communist, but Finland to this day has not. After the collapse of French rule in Indochina in 1954, North Vietnam went Communist, but nobody else did. By 1960, half of Laos had gone Communist, but nobody else followed suit. For almost two decades, the fortunes of communism in Indonesia have fluctuated according to local conditions, not according to what happened or did not happen elsewhere. Can anyone seriously maintain that the fortunes of the guerrilla wars in Guatemala, Colombia, or Venezuela will depend upon what happens or does not happen in South Vietnam? It stands to reason that the triumph or defeat of communism in any particular country is not simply a byproduct of what happens or does not happen in other countries. What will happen in Vietnam can at the very best be no more than one factor among many, and most certainly not the decisive one, that will influence developments in other countries.

III. A NEW CHINA POLICY FOR THE UNITED STATES

What follows from this analysis for the policies of the United States vis-à-vis China? In view of the vital interests of the United

States in the Asian and world balance of power, five basic principles ought to guide the policies of the United States with regard to China:

First, the policy of peripheral military containment ought to be gradually liquidated. This policy is not only irrelevant to the interests of the United States but actually runs counter to them.

Second, both the policy of isolating China and the policy of ending that isolation are essentially irrelevant to the issue at hand. One may aggravate, and the other ameliorate, the international climate; but they have no relevance, one way or the other, to the basic issue of containment.

Third, since the expansion of Chinese power and influence, threatening the Asian and world balance of power, proceeds by political rather than military means, it must be contained by political means. To that purpose, it is necessary to strengthen politically, socially, and economically, the nations of Asia which are within China's reach, without exacting in return political and military alinements directed against China. We ought to pursue a similar policy with regard to the uncommitted nations in which China in the recent past has attempted to gain a foothold.

Fourth, we ought to be clear in our minds that if we should continue the present policy of the peripheral military containment of China, we will find ourselves in all likelihood sooner or later at war with China. If we want to avoid such a war, we must change our policy. If we do not want to change our policy, we must be ready to go to war. That is to say, either we bring the means we are willing to employ into line with our objectives, or we cut down our objectives to the measure of the means we are willing to employ.

Fifth, the ultimate instrument for containing China is the same that has contained the Soviet Union: the retaliatory nuclear capability of the United States. It must be brough home to China, as it was brought home to the Soviet Union, that in the unlikely event that she should embark upon a policy of Asian or world conquest, she is bound to be at war with the United States.

SHOULD THE U.S. WITHDRAW
FROM ASIA?*

BY

OWEN HARRIES

[1968]

Among the more prominent critics of U.S. Viet Nam policy there is substantial agreement that American military power should not be committed again to the Southeast Asian mainland. Some are more explicit than others on this, and some accept that the process of extrication from Viet Nam may require the continuing presence of American troops during a transition period. But there is pretty general agreement that ideally and ultimately the United States should withdraw from the mainland.

This conclusion is supported by a number of arguments. The most far-reaching of these—and, if it is accepted, the most compelling—is that neither in terms of American interests nor the world balance of power is the region important enough to justify such an American commitment. . . .

As far as I can discover, the comparative unimportance of Southeast Asia has been simply asserted rather than demonstrated in any detail. This is surprising, for there is a prima facie case for considering the region to be of great strategic and political importance. Over the last two decades, not only the United States but China, Great Britain and France have certainly behaved as if they had very important interests in the region and have entered into major commitments in relation to it. Russia, too, has behaved as if great issues were at stake there. In so far as the British and French interests in the area have declined, they have done so because of a reluctant recognition by those countries of their inability to sustain commitments there, not because of an acceptance of the view that the region is unimportant. Three important secondary powers—India, Japan and Indonesia—whose fates are certainly a matter of

---

* From *Foreign Affairs*, October 1968, copyright by the Council on Foreign Relations. Reprinted by permission. Owen Harries is Senior Lecturer in the School of Political Science, University of New South Wales.

great concern to the major powers are adjacent to the region, and their futures can hardly be unaffected by developments in it. Two of the major international crises of this decade have centered on the region. . . .

Apart from the assertion that the Southeast Asian mainland is not worth a major American military commitment, a number of arguments have been advanced to show that such a commitment, if entered into, must fail. Although these support the same conclusion, not all of them sit well together. Walter Lippmann, for example, has been concerned with stressing the military disadvantages facing an American presence on the mainland and to bring this out has emphasized the importance of the military strength of communist forces. . . .

Others, Hans Morgenthau for example, concerned with establishing not the disadvantages but the inappropriateness of a military response, have played down what Lippmann emphasizes. . . .

This line of argument has been developed further: not only is a military presence inappropriate but it is counterproductive. It attracts the communist aggression and subversion it is meant to counter, and it weakens and compromises the forces of local nationalism it is meant to sustain.

The division between the approach which emphasizes the military aspect of the Chinese Communist threat and that which depreciates it runs deep through the ranks of the critics. It is reflected in the two diametrically opposed conclusions which have been advanced among them in the course of debate: that Southeast Asia must, inevitably, fall under Chinese domination (and that it is therefore futile to try to prevent this from happening); and that the "Chinese threat" is a myth propagated by anticommunists and devoid of substance (and that it is therefore unnecessary to take measures to counter it). In so far as either view is valid, it detracts from the force of the other. . . .

Three further observations may be made about the line of argument that a military presence is ineffectual, irrelevant or counterproductive. First, this view seems to be based very largely on the Viet Nam experience and to generalize from that experience. Yet in denouncing the rigidly deterministic version of the domino theory many of those who generalize in this way have been adamant in stressing the uniqueness of each Asian country and the importance of local conditions. They have insisted that what is true of one country need not be true of another. If this is accepted, it is difficult to see why it should not apply in assessing the effects and effectiveness of an American military presence in the various countries as well as in assessing the chances of successful insurrection. Secondly, these views seem to ignore important relevant evidence, in particular that provided by the long-standing British military presence in Malaya and later Malaysia. In retrospect this does not appear to have been ineffectual, irrelevant or counterproductive. . . . Thirdly, some formulations of these views seem to polarize the issues unnecessarily and misleadingly, presenting the issues as if a clear choice must be made between a military response and a nonmilitary one. One can accept the view that the struggle is primarily a political one without concluding that a military presence therefore has no bearing upon the threat. . . .

II

The arguments and beliefs so far outlined seem to constitute the case for ending the American commitment to the mainland. How persuasive or unpersuasive one finds them is likely to depend not only on their own force but also on one's assessment of the consequences of withdrawal. What have the critics to say about these? It is possible to discern, at least for purposes of analysis, three distinct viewpoints. There are those, like Lippmann, who accept that withdrawal will mean the domination of the mainland by China, or possibly by China and North Viet Nam. How this conclusion will affect one's attitude to withdrawal is likely to depend on how persuasive one finds the arguments that the fate of the region is of no great importance in terms of international politics, and that in any case Chinese influence must prevail in the long run as a kind of geopolitical necessity. The first of these has already been examined. As to the second, it is open to the same decisive objection as the rigid, deterministic version of the domino theory: it asserts the inevitability of one particular outcome in a situation where there are too many variables to justify doing so.

The more optimistic, who maintain that the independent states of Southeast Asia could survive an American withdrawal, may be divided into those who lay stress on maintaining an international balance of power and those who stress other factors. There are two versions of the balance-of-power thesis. In the first it is maintained that the offshore presence of the United States either in the form of the Seventh Fleet or of an island base or of some combination of the two could maintain a balance. In the second it is maintained that a purely Asian balance of power is possible.

As for the first of these, the American experience in Viet Nam surely speaks decisively against it. If the use of American air power on a massive scale, with the advantage of land as well as sea bases and in conjunction with land forces, was not decisive there, it is difficult to see how it could be so elsewhere when it would not enjoy similar advantages. One cannot simultaneously insist on the ineffectiveness of the bombing of North Viet Nam over the last few years and argue that offshore air power could maintain a balance in the future. Unless, that is, the use of nuclear weapons is envisaged. If one believes that the United States is unlikely to use such weapons in a Southeast Asian conflict, this argument is not convincing; it is similarly unpersuasive if one believes it should not use them.

The case in favor of a purely Asian balance of power has been stated most fully by Alastair Buchan.[1] Buchan explains that what he has in mind is not an integrated military alliance of non-communist states but a diplomatic coalition built around India, Australia and Japan. Its object would not be to deter a full-scale "Hitlerian onslaught" by China against her neighbors (which he thinks unlikely) but to prevent the isolating of individual states and the exploitation of internal strife and of quarrels between states. He points to the advantage of "de-coupling" centers of tension so that a crisis in one of them does not lead immediately to a great-power confrontation. He believes also that China would be more inclined to come to terms with the rest of Asia if such a coalition came into existence and the United States was no longer involved.

---

[1] Alastair Buchan, "An Asian Balance of Power?" *The Australian Journal of Politics and History,* August 1966. See also *Encounter,* December 1966.

Buchan recognizes some of the difficulties facing the implementation of such a concept: the suspicion of Japan among other Asian states, the unpopularity of India, the shortage of investment capital in India and of manpower in Australia. He recognizes the problem posed by the existence of Chinese nuclear weapons and concludes that either Asian countries will have to acquire nuclear weapons or they will want to involve the United States more closely. He prefers the dangers of proliferation to those of an American umbrella.

Two questions pose themselves in relation to the concept of a purely Asian balance of power: Could the necessary coalition be constituted and, if it could, would it do what is claimed for it (*i.e.* stabilize the situation in Southeast Asia)? On the first, an honest appraisal of conditions in Southeast Asia can surely lead only to considerable skepticism. The concept of a balance of power presupposes the existence of stable and effective units which can be organized into alliances and coalitions. The states of this region are characterized neither by stability nor effectiveness. Furthermore, as one commentator has pointed out, in assessing the chances of such a coalition coming into existence, "non-material factors like political will" are of overriding importance.[2] The will for decisive action, action requiring steadfastness of purpose over a long period and the willingness to forego short-term advantage, seems conspicuously absent in the proposed members of the coalition. Neither India nor Japan has shown the slightest inclination to play the role allotted to it, and the current Australian attitude seems to be that it will act in conjunction with the United States or Britain, but not on its own. A serious attempt to create a united will would be likely to involve the United States even more intimately in the affairs of the region than it is at present, and for a considerable period.

If a coalition were created, one's judgment as to whether it would be a stabilizing factor is likely to depend very much on one's assessment of the consequences, both outside and inside the region, of its members' acquiring the nuclear weapons which

[2] Coral Bell, "The Asian Balance of Power: A Comparison with European Precedents," *Adelphi Papers No. 34* (Institute for Strategic Studies). The whole of this paragraph is indebted to this excellent paper.

Buchan realistically concedes would be necessary in order to create an effective balance to China. To the extent that the prospects of nuclear proliferation appall, the coalition will be unattractive.

We have been examining views which stress the importance of maintaining or constructing a balance of power as a necessary condition for the continuing independence of the non-communist states of Southeast Asia. Some put the emphasis on the other factors; for example, internal stability and order. Those who do so see the threat almost exclusively in terms of subversion and guerrilla uprisings. Dismissing the domino theory as an "artificial nightmare," Lowenthal, for instance, stresses that successful indirect aggression depends on the political weakness of the attacked régime, not merely or principally on the will of the aggressor.[3] Many others have made the same point. Accepting it as true, it is difficult to see what comfort can be drawn from it.

Political weakness is endemic throughout the region. Unstable central governments with only very limited capacities to mobilize support, neglected outer provinces, sharp discontinuities between city and countryside, dissatisfied minorities, institutions with shallow roots, military establishments with a keen interest in politics— these are standard features of most of the countries concerned. Indeed, awareness of these political conditions is a major reason for pessimism. . . .

Moreover, it is true and relevant, as the case of Viet Nam shows, that political and social conditions are not simply given factors. To a degree, subversive movements can in time create the conditions that favor them—by the assassination of key figures in the rural administration, by disrupting communications between the center and the provinces, by levying taxes and forced recruiting, and by sustained propaganda.

III

Many of the critics put their faith in the emergence of "Titoist" régimes which would resist any encroachments by China. In view of the importance of the policy decisions being advocated, one would expect such a faith to be sustained by a much more search-

---

[3] R. Lowenthal, "America's Asian Commitment," *Encounter*, October 1965.

ing discussion of the conditions required for the emergence of Titoist régimes than has been evident. As the history of Eastern Europe makes clear, the mere existence of strong nationalist sentiment is not enough. Such a spirit was never absent through the forties and fifties, even within the various communist parties. In fact it was probably stronger there than in the parties of Southeast Asia, several of which—particularly those of Singapore, Malaysia and Thailand—have a very strong Chinese component which one would expect to draw them toward Peking rather than away from it.

One condition which one might assume was conducive, if not essential, to the emergence of a Titoist régime is the presence of two major and competing powers between which the potential Titoist can manœuvre with some freedom. If this is so, then the chances of Titoism may be much better if the United States maintains an effective presence, which means a military presence. It would be ironical if the possibility of Titoism were used to justify a course of action which would itself seriously diminish that possibility.

One further point about Titoism is worth making. In the context of international politics the term implies two characteristics: independence and non-aggression. While these two have gone together in the case of Jugoslavia, there is no reason to assume that they must always go together, that an independent communist state in Southeast Asia will, by definition, be non-aggressive and non-threatening. . . .

It is clear that certain assumptions about the nature of China's foreign policy play a key role in one's view of the post-Viet Nam situation in Southeast Asia. There seems to be substantial agreement among critics of U.S. policy that China's ideological stance does not have much operational significance; that, in the words of one of them, "the basic direction of her policies is determined primarily by her traditional national interests, and that communism only adds a new dynamic dimension to the means by which the policies are to be achieved." [4] That is, ideology is conceived

[4] H. J. Morgenthau, "Vietnam and the United States." Washington: Public Affairs Press, 1965, p. 55.

more as an instrument than a determinant of policy. This view is also likely to lead to the conclusion that China is a regional power with limited ambitions, rather than the world power she claims to be. . . .

As far as the importance of ideology is concerned, it is notoriously difficult to establish criteria which would indicate conclusively what role it does play. One interesting piece of evidence supporting the view that its role is an important one may have been provided inadvertently by Professor C. P. Fitzgerald. . . .

According to Fitzgerald, one of the central principles of traditional policy was contained in "the axiom that it is unwise and very dangerous to quarrel at the same time with the Power which dominates the northern borderlands and the Power which rules the Pacific Ocean." [5] It was an important part of his thesis that this was accepted by the present régime. . . .

Unfortunately for this thesis, at about the time the article was published, the Communist Government of China, already bitterly in conflict with the United States, was deliberately pushing its differences with the Soviet Union to the point of an open and probably irrevocable breach. That is, if Fitzgerald was right about traditional Chinese foreign policy, it was acting in a way which was inexplicable and indefensible in terms of traditional policy and interests, but which *was* understandable if China was regarded as a communist state for whose decision-makers ideological factors were extremely important.

Important does not mean all-important or consistently crucial. The relationship between ideology and policy is not fixed, and surely the degree of caution or boldness, which may seem "innate," will change with circumstance. How boldly or cautiously a régime behaves is likely to depend on how it calculates the rewards and dangers of boldness.

If this is true, it seems unwise to base one's expectations of how China will behave in a Southeast Asia from which the United States is absent on how she has behaved when the American presence was very real. If the Chinese régime has avoided frontal

---

[5] C. P. Fitzgerald, "The Chinese View of Foreign Relations," *The World Today*, January 1963, pp. 9, 12.

attacks, contenting itself with stimulating and aiding local guerrilla movements, may this not be due to a healthy awareness of the danger of acting otherwise rather than to innate propensities or the persistence of traditional styles of behavior? The argument that the indirectness of China's strategy is dictated by ideology has some force, but it is not an argument available to those who deny the importance of ideology.

While some are sanguine because they are convinced that China has little desire to expand southward, others base their optimism on the alleged military incapacity of the Chinese. It is ironic that as Chinese military power has increased the respect paid to it by Western commentators has tended to diminish. Ten years ago it was usual to exaggerate its significance; now it might well be that it is taken too lightly. Much of the argument seems to depend on the logistic difficulties which would face a Chinese move south. If, however, one remembers the success of the Japanese in moving through the region in World War II, of the North Vietnamese in the present war, and of the Chinese themselves in the incredibly difficult terrain of Tibet and on the Sino-Indian border, these difficulties may appear less decisive—especially in circumstances in which the military opposition would be for the most part negligible.

This article has concentrated on a critical examination of the views of those who advocate ending the American commitment on the Southeast Asian mainland. It has not attempted to put forward the positive case for continuing the commitment. Even without bringing this into the reckoning, however, the case for complete withdrawal does not appear strong. . . . Between another "Viet Nam commitment" and total withdrawal there are many possibilities. The time has come to focus attention on these.

VI

THE UNITED STATES AND SOVIET RUSSIA

THE SOURCES OF SOVIET CONDUCT*

BY

X

[1947]

The political personality of Soviet power as we know it today is the product of ideology and circumstances: ideology inherited by the present Soviet leaders from the movement in which they had their political origin, and circumstances of the power which they now have exercised for nearly three decades in Russia. There can be few tasks of psychological analysis more difficult than to try to trace the interaction of these two forces and the relative rôle of each in the determination of official Soviet conduct. Yet the attempt must be made if that conduct is to be understood and effectively countered.

It is difficult to summarize the set of ideological concepts with which the Soviet leaders came into power. Marxian ideology, in its Russian-Communist projection, has always been in process of subtle evolution. The materials on which it bases itself are extensive and complex. But the outstanding features of Communist thought as it existed in 1916 may perhaps be summarized as follows: (a) that the central factor in the life of man, the factor which determines the character of public life and the "physiognomy of society," is the system by which material goods are produced and exchanged; (b) that the capitalist system of production is a nefarious one which inevitably leads to the exploitation of the working class by the capital-owning class and is incapable of developing adequately the economic resources of society or of distributing fairly the material goods produced by human labor; (c) that capitalism contains the seeds of its own destruction and must, in view of the inability of the capital-owning class to adjust itself to economic change, result eventually and inescapably in a

---

*From *Foreign Affairs*, July 1947. Reprinted by permission of *Foreign Affairs*. Copyright by Council on Foreign Relations, New York. The author was later identified as George F. Kennan (b. 1904), a U. S. foreign service officer from 1927 to 1952. Since serving as Ambassador to the Soviet Union in 1952, Mr. Kennan has been a member of the Institute for Advanced Study, Princeton.

revolutionary transfer of power to the working class; and (d) that imperialism, the final phase of capitalism, leads directly to war and revolution.

The rest may be outlined in Lenin's own words: "Unevenness of economic and political development is the inflexible law of capitalism. It follows from this that the victory of Socialism may come originally in a few capitalist countries or even in a single capitalist country. The victorious proletariat of that country, having expropriated the capitalists and having organized Socialist production at home, would rise against the remaining capitalist world, drawing to itself in the process the oppressed classes of other countries."[1] It must be noted that there was no assumption that capitalism would perish without proletarian revolution. A final push was needed from a revolutionary proletariat movement in order to tip over the tottering structure. But is was regarded as inevitable that sooner or later that push be given.

For 50 years prior to the outbreak of the Revolution, this pattern of thought had exercised great fascination for the members of the Russian revolutionary movement. Frustrated, discontented, hopeless of finding self-expression—or too impatient to seek it— in the confining limits of the Tsarist political system, yet lacking wide popular support for their choice of bloody revolution as a means of social betterment, these revolutionists found in Marxist theory a highly convenient rationalization for their own instinctive desires. It afforded pseudo-scientific justification for their impatience, for their categoric denial of all value in the Tsarist system, for their yearning for power and revenge and for their inclination to cut corners in the pursuit of it. It is therefore no wonder that they had come to believe implicitly in the truth and soundness of the Marxian-Leninist teachings, so congenial to their own impulses and emotions. Their sincerity need not be impugned. This is a phenomenon as old as human nature itself. It has has never been more aptly described than by Edward Gibbon, who wrote in "The Decline and Fall of the Roman Empire": "From enthusiasm to imposture the step is perilous and slippery;

---

[1] "Concerning the Slogans of the United States of Europe," August 1915. Official Soviet edition of Lenin's works.

the demon of Socrates affords a memorable instance how a wise man may deceive himself, how a good man may deceive others, how the conscience may slumber in a mixed and middle state between self-illusion and voluntary fraud." And it was with this set of conceptions that the members of the Bolshevik Party entered into power.

Now it must be noted that through all the years of preparation for revolution, the attention of these men, as indeed of Marx himself, had been centered less on the future form which Socialism[2] would take than on the necessary overthrow of rival power which, in their view, had to precede the introduction of Socialism. Their views, therefore, on the positive program to be put into effect, once power was attained, were for the most part nebulous, visionary and impractical. Beyond the nationalizing of industry and the expropriation of large private capital holdings there was no agreed program. The treatment of the peasantry, which according to the Marxist formulation was not of the proletariat, had always been a vague spot in the pattern of Communist thought; and it remained an object of controversy and vacillation for the first ten years of Communist power.

The circumstances of the immediate post-revolution period— the existence in Russia of civil war and foreign intervention, together with the obvious fact that the Communists represented only a tiny minority of the Russian people—made the establishment of a dictatorial power a necessity. The experiment with "war Communism" and the abrupt attempt to eliminate private production and trade had unfortunate economic consequences and caused further bitterness against the new revolutionary régime. While the temporary relaxation of the effort to communize Russia, represented by the New Economic Policy, alleviated some of this economic distress and thereby served its purpose, it also made it evident that the "capitalistic sector of society" was still prepared to profit at once from any relaxation of governmental pressure, and would, if permitted to continue to exist, always constitute a

---

[2]Here and elsewhere in this paper "Socialism" refers to Marxist or Leninist Communism, not to liberal Socialism of the Second International variety.

powerful opposing element to the Soviet régime and a serious rival for influence in the country. Somewhat the same situation prevailed with respect to the individual peasant who, in his own small way, was also a private producer.

Lenin, had he lived, might have proved a great enough man to reconcile these conflicting forces to the ultimate benefit of Russian society,.though this is questionable. But be that as it may, Stalin, and those whom he led in the struggle for succession to Lenin's position of leadership, were not the men to tolerate rival political forces in the sphere of power which they coveted. Their sense of insecurity was too great. Their particular brand of fanaticism, unmodified by any of the Anglo-Saxon traditions of compromise, was too fierce and too jealous to envisage any permanent sharing of power. From the Russian-Asiatic world out of which they had emerged they carried with them a skepticism as to the possibilities of permanent and peaceful coexistence of rival forces. Easily persuaded of their own doctrinaire "rightness," they insisted on the submission or destruction of all competing power. Outside of the Communist Party, Russian society was to have no rigidity. There were to be no forms of collective human activity or association which would not be dominated by the Party. No other force in Russian society was to be permitted to achieve vitality or integrity. Only the Party was to have structure. All else was to be an amorphous mass.

And within the Party the same principle was to apply. The mass of Party members might go through the motions of election, deliberation, decision and action; but in these motions they were to be animated not by their own individual wills but by the awesome breath of the Party leadership and the overbrooding presence of "the word."

Let it be stressed again that subjectively these men probably did not seek absolutism for its own sake. They doubtless believed—and found it easy to believe—that they alone knew what was good for society and that they would accomplish that good once their power was secure and unchallengeable. But in seeking that security of their own rule they were prepared to recognize no restrictions, either of God or man, on the character of their methods. And until such time as that security might be achieved, they placed far down on their scale of operational priorities the comforts and happiness of the peoples entrusted to their care.

Now the outstanding circumstance concerning the Soviet régime is that down to the present day this process of political consolidation has never been completed and the men in the Kremlin have continued to be predominantly absorbed with the struggle to secure and make absolute the power which they seized in November 1917. They have endeavored to secure it primarily against forces at home, within Soviet society itself. But they have also endeavored to secure it against the outside world. For ideology, as we have seen, taught them that the outside world was hostile and that it was their duty eventually to overthrow the political forces beyond their borders. The powerful hands of Russian history and tradition reached up to sustain them in this feeling. Finally, their own aggressive intransigence with respect to the outside world began to find its own reaction; and they were soon forced, to use another Gibbonesque phrase, "to chastise the contumacy" which they themselves had provoked. It is an undeniable privilege of every man to prove himself right in the thesis that the world is his enemy; for if he reiterates it frequently enough and makes it the background of his conduct he is bound eventually to be right.

Now it lies in the nature of the mental world of the Soviet leaders, as well as in the character of their ideology, that no opposition to them can be officially recognized as having any merit or justification whatsoever. Such opposition can flow, in theory, only from the hostile and incorrigible forces of dying capitalism. As long as remnants of capitalism were officially recognized as existing in Russia, it was possible to place on them, as an internal element, part of the blame for the maintenance of a dictatorial form of society. But as these remnants were liquidated, little by little, this justification fell away; and when it was indicated officially that they had been finally destroyed, it disappeared altogether. And this fact created one of the most basic of the compulsions which came to act upon the Soviet régime: since capitalism no longer existed in Russia and since it could not be admitted that there could be serious or widespread opposition to the Kremlin springing spontaneously from the liberated masses under its authority, it became necessary to justify the retention of the dictatorship by stressing the menace of capitalism abroad.

This began at an early date. In 1924 Stalin specifically defended the retention of the "organs of suppression," meaning, among others, the army and the secret police, on the ground that "as long as there is a capitalistic encirclement there will be danger of intervention with all the consequences that flow from that danger." In accordance with that theory, and from that time on, all internal opposition forces in Russia have consistently been portrayed as the agents of foreign forces of reaction antagonistic to Soviet power.

By the same token, tremendous emphasis has been placed on the original Communist thesis of a basic antagonism between the capitalist and Socialist worlds. It is clear, from many indications, that this emphasis is not founded in reality. The real facts concerning it have been confused by the existence abroad of genuine resentment provoked by Soviet philosophy and tactics and occasionally by the existence of great centers of military power, notably the Nazi régime in Germany and the Japanese Government of the late 1930's, which did indeed have aggressive designs against the Soviet Union. But there is ample evidence that the stress laid in Moscow on the menace confronting Soviet society from the world outside its borders is founded not in the realities of foreign antagonism but in the necessity of explaining away the maintenance of dictatorial authority at home.

Now the maintenance of this pattern of Soviet power, namely, the pursuit of unlimited authority domestically, accompanied by the cultivation of the semi-myth of implacable foreign hostility, has gone far to shape the actual machinery of Soviet power as we know it today. Internal organs of administration which did not serve this purpose withered on the vine. Organs which did serve this purpose became vastly swollen. The security of Soviet power came to rest on the iron discipline of the Party, on the severity and ubiquity of the secret police, and on the uncompromising economic monopolism of the state. The "organs of suppression," in which the Soviet leaders had sought security from rival forces, became in large measure the masters of those whom they were designed to serve. Today the major part of the structure of Soviet power is committed to the perfection of the dictatorship and to the maintenance of the concept of Russia as in a state of siege, with the enemy lowering beyond the walls. And the millions of human beings who form that part of the structure of power must defend at all costs this concept of Russia's position, for without it they are themselves superfluous.

As things stand today, the rulers can no longer dream of parting with these organs of suppression. The quest for absolute power, pursued now for nearly three decades with a ruthlessness unparalleled (in scope at least) in modern times, has again produced internally, as it did externally, its own reaction. The excesses of the police apparatus have fanned the potential opposition to the régime into something far greater and more dangerous than it could have been before those excesses began.

But least of all can the rulers dispense with the fiction by which the maintenance of dictatorial power has been defended. For this fiction has been canonized in Soviet philosophy by the excesses already committed in its name; and it is now anchored in the Soviet structure of thought by bonds far greater than those of mere ideology.

So much for the historical background. What does it spell in terms of the political personality of Soviet power as we know it today?

Of the original ideology, nothing has been officially junked. Belief is maintained in the basic badness of capitalism, in the inevitability of its destruction, in the obligation of the proletariat to assist in that destruction and to take power into its own hands. But stress has come to be laid primarily on those concepts which relate most specifically to the Soviet régime itself: to its position as the sole truly Socialist régime in a dark and misguided world, and to the relationships of power within it.

The first of these concepts is that of the innate antagonism between capitalism and Socialism. We have seen how deeply that concept has become imbedded in foundations of Soviet power. It has profound implications for Russia's conduct as a member of international society. It means that there can never be on Moscow's side any sincere assumption of a community of aims between the Soviet Union and powers which are regarded as capitalist. It must invariably be assumed in Moscow that the aims of the capitalist world are antagonistic to the Soviet régime, and therefore to the interests of the peoples it controls. If the Soviet Government occasionally sets its signature to documents which would indicate the contrary, this is to be regarded as a tactical manœuvre permissible in dealing with the enemy (who is without honor) and should be taken in the spirit of *caveat emptor*. Basically, the antagonism remains. It is postulated. And from it flow many of the phenomena which we find disturbing in the Kremlin's conduct of foreign policy: the secretiveness, the lack of frankness, the duplicity, the wary suspiciousness, and the basic unfriendliness of purpose. These phenomena are there to stay, for the foreseeable future. There can be variations of degree and of emphasis. When there is something the Russians want from us, one or the other of these features of their policy may be thrust temporarily into the background; and when that happens there will always be Americans who will leap forward with gleeful announcements that "the Russians have changed," and some who will even try to take credit for having brought about such "changes." But we should not be misled by tactical manœuvres. These characteristics of Soviet policy, like the postulate from which they flow, are basic to the internal nature of Soviet power, and will be with us, whether in the foreground or the background, until the internal nature of Soviet power is changed.

This means that we are going to continue for a long time to find the Russians difficult to deal with. It does not mean that they should be considered as embarked upon a do-or-die program to overthrow our society by a given date. The theory of the inevitability of the eventual fall of capitalism has the fortunate connotation that there is no hurry about it. The forces of progress can take their time in preparing the final *coup de grace*. Meanwhile, what is vital is that the "Socialist fatherland"—that oasis of power which has been already won for Socialism in the person of the Soviet Union—should be cherished and defended by all good Communists at home and abroad, its fortunes promoted, its enemies badgered and confounded. The promotion of premature, "adventuristic" revolutionary projects abroad which might embarrass Soviet power in any way would be an inexcusable, even a counter-revolutionary act. The cause of Socialism is the support and promotion of Soviet power, as defined in Moscow.

This brings us to the second of the concepts important to contemporary Soviet outlook. That is the infallibility of the Kremlin. The Soviet concept of power, which permits no focal points of organization outside the Party itself, requires that the Party leadership remain in theory the sole repository of truth. For if truth were to be found elsewhere, there would be justification for its expression in organized activity. But it is precisely that which the Kremlin cannot and will not permit.

The leadership of the Communist Party is therefore always right, and has been always right ever since in 1929 Stalin formalized his personal power by announcing that decisions of the Politburo were being taken unanimously.

On the principle of infallibility there rests the iron discipline of the Communist Party. In fact, the two concepts are mutually self-supporting. Perfect discipline requires recognition of infallibility. Infallibility requires the observance of discipline. And the two together go far to determine the behaviorism of the entire Soviet apparatus of power. But their effect cannot be understood unless a third factor be taken into account: namely, the fact that the leadership is at liberty to put forward for tactical purposes any particular thesis which it finds useful to the cause at any particular moment and to require the faithful and unquestioning acceptance of that thesis by the members of the movement as a whole. This means that truth is not a constant but is actually created, for all intents and purposes, by the Soviet leaders themselves. It may vary from week to week, from month to month. It is nothing absolute and immutable—nothing which flows from objective reality. It is only the most recent manifestation of the wisdom of those in whom the ultimate wisdom is supposed to reside, because they represent the logic of history. The accumulative effect of these factors is to give to the whole subordinate apparatus of Soviet power an unshakeable stubbornness and steadfastness in its orientation. This orientation can be changed at will by the Kremlin but by no other power. Once a given party line has been laid down on a given issue of current policy, the whole Soviet governmental machine, including the mechanism of diplomacy, moves inexorably along the prescribed path, like a persistent toy automobile wound up and headed in a given direction, stopping only when it meets with some unanswerable force. The individuals who are the components of this machine are unamenable to argument or reason which comes to them from outside sources. Their whole training has taught them to mistrust and discount the glib persuasiveness of the outside world. Like the white dog before the phonograph, they hear only the "master's voice." And if they are to be called off from the purposes last dictated to them, it is the master who must call them off. Thus the foreign representative cannot hope that his words will make any impression on them. The most that he can hope is that they will be transmitted to those at the top, who are capable of changing the party line. But even those are not likely to be swayed by any normal logic in the words of the bourgeois representative. Since there can be no appeal to common purposes, there can be no appeal to common mental approaches. For this reason, facts speak louder than words to the ears of the Kremlin; and words carry the greatest weight when they have the ring of reflecting, or being backed up by, facts of unchallengeable validity.

But we have seen that the Kremlin is under no ideological compulsion to accomplish its purposes in a hurry. Like the Church, it is dealing in ideological concepts which are of long-term validity, and it can afford to be patient. It has no right to risk the existing achievements of the revolution for the sake of vain baubles of the future. The very teachings of Lenin himself require great caution and flexibility in the pursuit of Communist purposes. Again, these precepts are fortified by the lessons of Russian history: of centuries of obscure battles between nomadic forces over the stretches of a vast unfortified plain. Here caution, circumspection, flexibility and deception are the valuable qualities; and their value finds natural appreciation in the Russian or the oriental mind. Thus the Kremlin has no compunction about retreating in the face of superior force. And being under the compulsion of no timetable, it does not get panicky under the necessity for such retreat. Its political action is a fluid stream which moves constantly, wherever it is permitted to move, toward a given goal. Its main concern is to make sure that it has filled every nook and cranny available to it in the basin of world power. But if it finds unassailable barriers in its path, it accepts these philosophically and accommodates itself to them. The main thing is that there should always be pressure, unceasing constant pressure, toward the desired goal. There is no trace of any feeling in Soviet psychology that that goal must be reached at any given time.

These considerations make Soviet diplomacy at once easier and more difficult to deal with than the diplomacy of individual aggressive leaders like Napoleon and Hitler. On the one hand it is more sensitive to contrary force, more ready to yield on individual sectors of the diplomatic front when that force is felt to be too strong, and thus more rational in the logic and rhetoric of power. On the other hand it cannot be easily defeated or discouraged by a single victory on the part of its opponents. And the patient persistence by which it is animated means that it can be effectively countered not by sporadic acts which represent the momentary whims of democratic opinion but only by intelligent long-range policies on the part of Russia's adversaries—policies no less steady in their purpose, and no less variegated and resourceful in their application, than those of the Soviet Union itself.

In these circumstances it is clear that the main element of any United States policy toward the Soviet Union must be that of a long-term, patient but firm and vigilant containment of Russian expansive tendencies. It is important to note, however, that such a policy has nothing to do with outward histrionics: with threats or blustering or superfluous gestures of outward "toughness." While the Kremlin is basically flexible in its reaction to political realities, it is by no means unamenable to considerations of pres· tige. Like almost any other government, it can be placed by tactless and threatening gestures in a position where it cannot afford to yield even though this might be dictated by its sense of realism. The Russian leaders are keen judges of human psychology, and as such they are highly conscious that loss of temper and of self-control is never a source of strength in political affairs. They are quick to exploit such evidences of weakness. For these reasons, it is a *sine qua non* of successful dealing with Russia that the foreign government in question should remain at all times cool and collected. and that its demands on Russian policy should be put forward in such a manner as to leave the way open for a compliance not too detrimental to Russian prestige.

In the light of the above, it will be clearly seen that the Soviet pressure against the free institutions of the western world is something that can be contained by the adroit and vigilant application of counter-force at a series of constantly shifting geographical and political points, corresponding to the shifts and manœuvres of Soviet policy, but which cannot be charmed or talked out of existence. The Russians look forward to a duel of infinite duration, and they see that already they have scored great successes. It must be borne in mind that there was a time when the Communist Party represented far more of a minority in the sphere of Russian national life than Soviet power today represents in the world community.

But if ideology convinces the rulers of Russia that truth is on their side and that they can therefore afford to wait, those of us on whom that ideology has no claim are free to examine objectively the validity of that premise. The Soviet thesis not only implies complete lack of control by the west over its own economic destiny, it likewise assumes Russian unity, discipline and patience over an infinite period. Let us bring this apocalyptic vision down to earth, and suppose that the western world finds the strength and resourcefulness to contain Soviet power over a period of ten to fifteen years. What does that spell for Russia itself?

The Soviet leaders, taking advantage of the contributions of modern technique to the arts of despotism, have solved the question of obedience within the confines of their power. Few challenge their authority; and even those who do are unable to make that challenge valid as against the organs of suppression of the state.

The Kremlin has also proved able to accomplish its purpose of building up in Russia, regardless of the interests of the inhabitants, an industrial foundation of heavy metallurgy, which is, to be sure, not yet complete but which is nevertheless continuing to grow and is approaching those of the other major industrial countries. All of this, however, both the maintenance of internal political security and the building of heavy industry, has been carried out at a terrible cost in human life and in human hopes and energies. It has necessitated the use of forced labor on a scale unprecedented in modern times under conditions of peace. It has involved the neglect or abuse of other phases of Soviet economic life, particularly agriculture, consumers' goods production, housing and transportation.

To all that, the war has added its tremendous toll of destruction, death and human exhaustion. In consequence of this, we have in Russia today a population which is physically and spiritually tired. The mass of the people are disillusioned, skeptical and no longer as accessible as they once were to the magical attraction which Soviet power still radiates to its followers abroad. The avidity with which people seized upon the slight respite accorded to the Church for tactical reasons during the war was eloquent testimony to the fact that their capacity for faith and devotion found little expression in the purposes of the régime.

In these circumstances, there are limits to the physical and nervous strength of people themselves. These limits are absolute ones, and are binding even for the cruelest dictatorship, because beyond them people cannot be driven. The forced labor camps and the other agencies of constraint provide temporary means of compelling people to work longer hours than their own volition or mere economic pressure would dictate; but if people survive them at all they become old before their time and must be considered as human casualties to the demands of dictatorship. In either case their best powers are no longer available to society and can no longer be enlisted in the service of the state.

Here only the younger generation can help. The younger generation, despite all vicissitudes and sufferings, is numerous and vigorous; and the Russians are a talented people. But it still remains to be seen what will be the effects on mature performance of the abnormal emotional strains of childhood which Soviet dictatorship created and which were enormously increased by the war. Such things as normal security and placidity of home environment have practically ceased to exist in the Soviet Union outside of the most remote farms and villages. And observers are not yet sure whether that is not going to leave its mark on the over-all capacity of the generation now coming into maturity.

In addition to this, we have the fact that Soviet economic development, while it can list certain formidable achievements, has been precariously spotty and uneven. Russian Communists who speak of the "uneven development of capitalism" should blush at the contemplation of their own national economy. Here certain branches of economic life, such as the metallurgical and machine industries, have been pushed out of all proportion to other sectors of economy. Here is a nation striving to become in a short period one of the great industrial nations of the world while it still has no highway network worthy of the name and only a relatively primitive network of railways. Much has been done to increase efficiency of labor and to teach primitive peasants something about the operation of machines. But maintenance is still a crying deficiency of all Soviet economy. Construction is hasty and poor in quality. Depreciation must be enormous. And in vast sectors of economic life it has not yet been possible to instill into labor anything like that general culture of production and technical self-respect which characterizes the skilled worker of the west.

It is difficult to see how these deficiencies can be corrected at an early date by a tired and dispirited population working largely under the shadow of fear and compulsion. And as long as they are not overcome, Russia will remain economically a vulnerable, and in a certain sense an impotent, nation, capable of exporting its enthusiasms and of radiating the strange charm of its primitive political vitality but unable to back up those articles of export by the real evidences of material power and prosperity.

Meanwhile, a great uncertainty hangs over the political life of the Soviet Union. That is the uncertainty involved in the transfer of power from one individual or group of individuals to others.

This is, of course, outstandingly the problem of the personal position of Stalin. We must remember that his succession to Lenin's pinnacle of preëminence in the Communist movement was the only such transfer of individual authority which the Soviet Union has experienced. That transfer took 12 years to consolidate. It cost the lives of millions of people and shook the state to its foundations. The attendant tremors were felt all through the international revolutionary movement, to the disadvantage of the Kremlin itself.

It is always possible that another transfer of preëminent power may take place quietly and inconspicuously, with no repercussions anywhere. But again, it is possible that the questions involved may unleash, to use some of Lenin's words, one of those "incredibly swift transitions" from "delicate deceit" to "wild violence" which characterize Russian history, and may shake Soviet power to its foundations.

But this is not only a question of Stalin himself. There has been, since 1938, a dangerous congealment of political life in the higher circles of Soviet power. The All-Union Party Congress, in theory the supreme body of the Party, is supposed to meet not less often than once in three years. It will soon be eight full years since its last meeting. During this period membership in the Party has numerically doubled. Party mortality during the war was enormous; and today well over half of the Party members are persons who have entered since the last Party congress was held. Meanwhile, the same small group of men has carried on at the top through an amazing series of national vicissitudes. Surely there is some reason why the experiences of the war brought basic political changes to every one of the great governments of the west. Surely the causes of that phenomenon are basic enough to be present somewhere in the obscurity of Soviet political life, as well. And yet no recognition has been given to these causes in Russia.

It must be surmised from this that even within so highly disciplined an organization as the Communist Party there must be a growing divergence in age, outlook and interest between the great mass of Party members, only so recently recruited into the movement, and the little self-perpetuating clique of men at the top, whom most of these Party members have never met, with whom they have never conversed, and with whom they can have no political intimacy.

Who can say whether, in these circumstances, the eventual rejuvenation of the higher spheres of authority (which can only be a matter of time) can take place smoothly and peacefully, or whether rivals in the quest for higher power will not eventually reach down into these politically immature and inexperienced masses in order to find support for their respective claims? If this were ever to happen, strange consequences could flow for the Communist Party: for the membership at large has been exercised only in the practices of iron discipline and obedience and not in the arts of compromise and accommodation. And if disunity were ever to seize and paralyze the Party, the chaos and weakness of Russian society would be revealed in forms beyond description. For we have seen that Soviet power is only a crust concealing an amorphous mass of human beings among whom no independent organizational structure is tolerated. In Russia there is not even such a thing as local government. The present generation of Russians have never known spontaneity of collective action. If, consequently, anything were ever to occur to disrupt the unity and efficacy of the Party as a political instrument, Soviet Russia might be changed overnight from one of the strongest to one of the weakest and most pitiable of national societies.

Thus the future of Soviet power may not be by any means as secure as Russian capacity for self-delusion would make it appear to the men in the Kremlin. That they can keep power themselves, they have demonstrated. That they can quietly and easily turn it over to others remains to be proved. Meanwhile, the hardships of their rule and the vicissitudes of international life have taken a heavy toll of the strength and hopes of the great people on whom their power rests. It is curious to note that the ideological power of Soviet authority is strongest today in areas beyond the frontiers of Russia, beyond the reach of its police power. This phenomenon brings to mind a comparison used by Thomas Mann in his great novel "Buddenbrooks." Observing that human institutions often show the greatest outward brilliance at a moment when inner decay is in reality farthest advanced, he compared the Buddenbrook family, in the days of its greatest glamour, to one of those stars whose light shines most brightly on this world when in reality it has long since ceased to exist. And who can say with assurance that the strong light still cast by the Kremlin on the dissatisfied peoples of the western world is not the powerful afterglow of a constellation which is in actuality on the wane? This cannot be proved. And it cannot be disproved. But the possibility remains (and in the opinion of this writer it is a strong one) that Soviet power, like the capitalist world of its conception, bears within it the seeds of its own decay, and that the sprouting of these seeds is well advanced.

It is clear that the United States cannot expect in the foreseeable future to enjoy political intimacy with the Soviet regime. It must continue to regard the Soviet Union as a rival, not a partner, in the political arena. It must continue to expect that Soviet policies will reflect no abstract love of peace and stability, no real faith in the possibility of a permanent happy coexistence of the Socialist and capitalist worlds, but rather a cautious, persistent pressure toward the disruption and weakening of all rival influence and rival power.

Balanced against this are the facts that Russia, as opposed to the western world in general, is still by far the weaker party, that Soviet policy is highly flexible, and that Soviet society may well contain deficiencies which will eventually weaken its own total potential. This would of itself warrant the United States entering with reasonable confidence upon a policy of firm containment, designed to confront the Russians with unalterable counter-force at every point where they show signs of encroaching upon the interests of a peaceful and stable world.

But in actuality the possibilities for American policy are by no means limited to holding the line and hoping for the best. It is entirely possible for the United States to influence by its actions the internal developments, both within Russia and throughout the international Communist movement, by which Russian policy is largely determined. This is not only a question of the modest measure of informational activity which this government can conduct in the Soviet Union and elsewhere, although that, too, is important. It is rather a question of the degree to which the United States can create among the peoples of the world generally the impression of a country which knows what it wants, which is coping successfully with the problems of its internal life and with the responsibilities of a World Power, and which has a spiritual vitality capable of holding its own among the major ideological currents of the time. To the extent that such an impression can be created and maintained, the aims of Russian Communism must appear sterile and quixotic, the hopes and enthusiasm of Moscow's supporters must wane, and added strain must be imposed on the Kremlin's foreign policies. For the palsied decrepitude of the capitalist world is the keystone of Communist philosophy. Even the failure of the United States to experience the early economic depression which the ravens of the Red Square have been predicting with such complacent confidence since hostilities ceased would have deep and important repercussions throughout the Communist world.

By the same token, exhibitions of indecision, disunity and internal disintegration within this country have an exhilarating effect on the whole Communist movement. At each evidence of these tendencies, a thrill of hope and excitement goes through the Communist world; a new jauntiness can be noted in the Moscow tread; new groups of foreign supporters climb on to what they can only view as the band wagon of international politics; and Russian pressure increases all along the line in international affairs.

It would be an exaggeration to say that American behavior unassisted and alone could exercise a power of life and death over the Communist movement and bring about the early fall of Soviet power in Russia. But the United States has it in its power to increase enormously the strains under which Soviet policy must operate, to force upon the Kremlin a far greater degree of moderation and circumspection than it has had to observe in recent years, and in this way to promote tendencies which must eventually find their outlet in either the break-up or the gradual mellowing of Soviet power. For no mystical, Messianic movement—and particularly not that of the Kremlin—can face frustration indefinitely without eventually adjusting itself in one way or another to the logic of that state of affairs.

Thus the decision will really fall in large measure in this country itself. The issue of Soviet-American relations is in essence a test of the over-all worth of the United States as a nation among nations. To avoid destruction the United States need only measure up to its own best traditions and prove itself worthy of preservation as a great nation.

Surely, there was never a fairer test of national quality than this. In the light of these circumstances, the thoughtful observer of Russian-American relations will find no cause for complaint in the Kremlin's challenge to American society. He will rather experience a certain gratitude to a Providence which, by providing the American people with this implacable challenge, has made their entire security as a nation dependent on their pulling themselves together and accepting the responsibilities of moral and political leadership that history plainly intended them to bear.

THE POLICY OF LIBERATION*

BY

JAMES BURNHAM

[1952]

For the United States, foreign policy means policy toward world communism and the Soviet Union. The range of choice is restricted to three possibilities: appeasement, containment, liberation. Other and more elaborate names may be used, but when we strip off the wrapping, we shall find one of just these three.

Besides these three, what policy could there even conceivably be? They empty the barrel. Your purpose can be to stand off the Soviet Empire by firmly bottling it up within its present boundaries (whatever these happen to be at the given moment). That is: *containment*. You can accept communism as a legitimate child of human civilization, and therefore wish to bring the Soviet Empire within the family of nations. Because the Soviet imperial state is a totalitarian power which seeks world domination, this is equivalent to accepting the extension of Soviet control. In a word: *appeasement*. You can aim to get rid of Soviet rule, or at least reduce it to a scale which would no longer threaten all mankind. That is: *liberation*. You must either hold Soviet power where it is or let it advance or thrust it back. . . .

What exactly is meant by a policy of liberation? . . .

There is nothing mysterious about the policy of liberation. Its goal is freedom for the peoples and nations now enslaved by the Russian-centered Soviet state system—freedom for all the peoples and nations now under communist domination, including the Russian people. For the United States to adopt the policy of liberation will mean in the first instance simply that a responsible decision by the government commits the country to that goal. . . . There is no need at the beginning for an official statement of just

*From *Containment or Liberation?* published by The John Day Company. Copyright 1952, 1953, by James Burnham. Reprinted by permission. James Burnham (b. 1905), former Professor of Philosophy, New York University, is the author of *The Managerial Revolution* and other works.

how the goal will be reached, nor would it be proper at any time for Americans to try to prescribe in detail the political and social arrangements that will replace the Soviet state system.

Among those who accept the goal of liberation there will inevitably be disputes over means and methods. However sharp, these will be less deep and more productive than the dispute over general policy, the intensity of which has been increasing since the latter part of 1949—the date when the Soviet atomic explosion and the communist conquest of the Chinese mainland proved objectively that containment had collapsed.

The policy of liberation will affect all fields of national endeavor—diplomatic, economic, psychological, military. Liberation cannot be a Sunday doctrine, but must inform and guide day by day, routine behavior, as well as the great and special actions. So it has been with containment.

The containment principle is to try to hold the line, but never to aim beyond it. Therefore, under containment, the Korean armistice boundary had to be the 38th parallel; Chinese Nationalist units from Formosa cannot be permitted to operate on the mainland; the American spokesmen in the United Nations must repudiate the terms of a law passed by Congress to arm exile military units; the anti-communist majority of the Albanian populace cannot be rallied to take the rather short jump out of the Soviet Empire; . . . American spokesmen everywhere have got to "avoid provocation," yield the initiative, and stay strictly on the defensive. This is the way it has been and had to be, under the policy of containment. Conversely, this is in each case the opposite of the way it will necessarily be if the policy of liberation is translated into action.

Following the commitment of the United States to the objective, the next act under a policy of liberation will be the communication of the decision to the inhabitants of the Soviet Empire, and to the world at large. The Soviet subjects, and the leaders also, know that the survival of the Soviet system depends in the last analysis on the United States. If the United States acquiesces in the system's permanence, if the policy of containment (which is equivalent to acquiescence) continues or is succeeded by appeasement, then the problem is settled. The remaining opposition will wither, and talk of anti-communist Resistance will become mere provocation. A genuine Resistance can develop only out of the conviction that the present state of affairs is temporary, that the system will not endure. This conviction must be shared by the masses. . . . The policy of liberation addresses itself to entire nations and peoples: its goal is freedom, not subversion.

Words alone ("propaganda") will not be enough to convince the masses of the American commitment to liberation. This must be daily demonstrated in action. The content of the demonstration will be threefold: all-sided political warfare; auxiliary military and paramilitary actions where called for; adequate preparation for whatever military action may be required in the future. The United States is of course already busy along these three lines. The shift in policy will step up the scale and tempo, particularly of political warfare, and focus all activities both political and military on the objective of liberation.

Because I am here concerned with the basic issue of policy, I do not want to clutter up the analysis with technical problems of application. I should like merely to use a few examples to show how the perspective of liberation would be concretely expressed in political warfare actions.

The outlook of liberation implies that the peoples and nations now subject to Soviet imperial domination are allies of the United States, and not either enemies or mere agents. The adoption of the policy of liberation would demand, therefore, that so far as possible the United States treat them as allies. This means that the United States would consider authentic representatives of these nations as the spokesmen for friendly state powers. From the point of view of liberation the present communist governments are not authentic, but are illegitimate usurpers. It follows that wherever there is any plausible basis for doing so, some sort of recognition should be extended to "free" (now necessarily exile) governments or to representative national committees.

The United States, even under the policy of containment, has continued to recognize the free governments of the Baltic nations, and to refuse to give legal acceptance to the incorporation of their territories within the Soviet Empire. The perspective of liberation suggests that this recognition should be taken more seriously, and that in terms of diplomacy and material aid the officials of the free Baltic governments should be treated in the same way as those of other allied powers.

It would be entirely proper, and legally justified, to withdraw recognition from the puppet Warsaw government of Poland in favor of the Free Polish ("London") government, which has been continuously recognized by a number of countries, including Spain, Lebanon, Portugal, and several South American nations. It goes without saying that under the policy of liberation any idea of recognizing the Chinese communist government would be dropped.

The exact form of relations with the exile representatives of other captive countries would have to be worked out in terms of the specific situation in each case. It is desirable to preserve a maximum of flexibility, and to realize that the function of exile groups is always transitional. In the end, the political outcome rests on those who remain, not on the exiles. . . .

The essential element of the policy of liberation is *the commitment to a goal*. It will be wise to join clarity and firmness concerning the goal with much flexibility toward the methods used in its pursuit. History is cunning. We cannot be sure by just what steps or at what pace the communist yoke can be lifted. Must the complete overthrow of each of the existing governments within the Soviet sphere invariably take place, or can there be new "Titoist" shifts in which an existing government, if only as a transition move, itself breaks away from Moscow's control? Can the change come more or less peacefully, or must there always be mass violence? Is it conceivable that the Soviet Empire can break up, or begin to break up, without general war? Could a palace revolution some time after the death of Stalin lead to a significant modification of the Soviet system?

We should be modest in attempting to answer such questions ahead of time, and willing to change our answers at the call of new evidence. What we can decide in advance is that we will by our own actions work to strengthen those developments in every field that contribute to the goal of liberation, to the weakening of communism and the dissolution of the Soviet state system.

. . . Can the goal be reached, or at least sufficiently approximated, without shooting and without general nuclear war?

Although only a fool or a liar would guarantee a complete reply, some partial truths may be stated. First, there will certainly be shooting, as there already and continuously has been. Those who talk about not "provoking" the Soviets are inclined to forget that in Greece, Iran, Malaya, the Philippines, Burma, India, Berlin, Indochina—and Korea—there have been hundreds of thousands of casualties in the anti-Soviet ranks. These increase to millions if we add, as we should, the victims of the purges and liquidations inside the Soviet Empire.

Whatever the policy, there will continue to be auxiliary military actions of various sorts. Some will be comparable to one or another of those which have already occurred. There may be new kinds: if, for example, the Albanians, aided by exiles and material help from abroad, decided to break away from the Soviet orbit; if Chinese Nationalist units from Formosa should be permitted to reenter the mainland; if a Titoist Polish government asked recognition and protection; or—at a later but not impossible stage—if the people of Czechoslovakia, East Germany or Bulgaria rose against their communist masters, and called on the nations of the West to prohibit intervention by the Soviet Red Army.

Second, we can conclude from an understanding of the nature of communism and from a review of Soviet history that the Soviet Union is never in fact provoked. If Moscow wants general war, then general war will begin. Not strength but weakness in the attitude of the enemy is the only factor that might speed its beginning. Moscow has not been ready for general war, and as I write (in the latter part of 1952) there is no indication that she will be in the near future. Those strong actions that have been taken since 1947 have not brought on general war, though some of them, as in Greece, Korea and Turkey, have been in themselves undeniably provocative.

Third, the policy of liberation would prove a stronger deterrent to general war than the policy of containment can possibly be. The policy of liberation, insofar as it has any success at all, strikes behind the Soviet front, and throws forces across the Soviet lines of communication. At the same time it arouses what are from the Soviet point of view the most disruptive internal elements. Strategically considered, it is hard to see what could give the Kremlin greater pause.

Fourth, we must understand that in the long run general war, though not inevitable, remains a probability, policy or no policy. Too much is at stake—indeed, the world is at stake—to assume that either side will accept defeat without a total effort to forestall it. The United States, together with whatever allies will join, must therefore prepare for general war. This necessity has no specific relation to the policy of liberation. Under the policy of containment the United States has been preparing for general war, and would have to do so under any conceivable policy except outright capitulation.

Policies either of containment or appeasement share a key defect. No matter what can be said for them during a period of peace or near-peace, they must be dropped on the outbreak of general war. About this there can presumably be no argument. Once general war starts, appeasement no longer has any meaning, and containment would be a direct prescription for defeat. Consequently, the basic policy structure must be overturned. This cannot be done quickly or without loss. Not only nationally but internationally, the pre-war policy will have built up established ways of thinking, acting and feeling, together with a particular estimate of the world situation, the nature of the opponent and what ought to be done. Then, with the beginning of general war, everyone will be expected to reverse himself abruptly, and to substitute a wholly new pattern of opinion and action.

No such discontinuity need interrupt the development of the policy of liberation. Exactly the same basic policy holds for conditions of peace, limited (cold) war, and general war. The outbreak of general war would in no way affect the substance of the policy, but only its tempo and the detailed mode of its application. This means that everything positive done under the policy of liberation counts, and does not have to be jettisoned at a change in the international weather. We are for the freedom of the peoples and nations of the Soviet Empire yesterday, today and tomorrow. In action, we promote the goal of their liberation by the means that are appropriate to the given stage. In peace and semi-peace we deny the permanence of the Soviet tyranny. In full scale war, our blows aim not at the conquest of territory but at the freeing of men and of nations.

It would be criminal if the policy of liberation were so directed as to arouse premature, narrow uprisings that would lead only to bloody repression and the loss of the most active Resistance leaders. At the same time we must ask ourselves: what if, in a captive nation, in a non-Russian Soviet nation or even in Russia itself, a broad mass uprising against the regime began? Or, what if one of the communist governments, supported by the majority of the people, declared against Moscow? And, in either case, what if help were then asked from the free world? Whatever the official policy, will the United States and its allies stand aside while the Red Army and the special troops of the MGB slaughter enough millions to wipe out the challenge not only from those who have come into the open but from any who might dream of freedom in the future? Would not passivity under such circumstances be a final proof of the inevitability of communist world victory?

To intervene even under those circumstances would not necessarily mean general war. Intervention in Greece and Korea have not brought general war, nor is there any indication that operations tomorrow on the Chinese mainland would do so. There are many forms of intervention, and many replies—including, of course, retreat. From Moscow's point of view, a mass revolt in part of her Empire, capable of spreading like fire in the dry season, is hardly a happy moment for starting general war. Indeed, it is not certain that Moscow would ever start general and unlimited war. She would do so only if she felt sure of victory. The fact that she has held back up to now proves that she has feared to lose rather than to gain by general war, and that she has felt more confident about the results of other modes of struggle. If successful anti-Soviet political warfare weakened the Soviet Union, then Moscow would be still less likely to dare the gamble on general war.

Finally, we may note that the policy of liberation throws the Soviet Empire on the defensive, and captures the initiative for the free world. The policy of liberation is by its essence offensive, just as containment and appeasement are essentially and unavoidably defensive. This contrast applies in every field, military, economic, political. In the present struggle for the world as in all conflict, the general law applies: only the offensive can win. When we call a policy "offensive," what we are really saying is simply that it aims to win.

* * *

THREE OBJECTIONS to the policy of liberation deserve special notice. It can be argued that the allies of the United States would be unhappy about it; that it would involve the United States in a fanatic and utopian "crusade"; and that the liberation of the Soviet Empire, however desirable, is none of America's proper business, which is restricted to the defense of its own security.

1

It is a fact that many persons within the non-communist nations are uneasy about a shift to the perspective of liberation. . . . Containment, if successful, would mean a stalemate between Moscow and Washington. To the non-communist nations other than the United States, a stalemate seems to promise protection from all-out world war and at the same time, because of the balancing off of the two major powers, an easier chance for independent maneuvers.

There is another reason why the non-communist nations cling to the stalemate, incline toward neutralism and drag their foot in the job of building anti-Soviet power. They do not yet believe in the seriousness of American purpose. What is the United States up to? what is its objective? To these questions clear answers have not been given. Is the United States determined to weaken and if necessary eliminate the Soviet system? or does it really want some sort of accommodation with the Kremlin? and if the latter, at whose expense? Does the United States really plan to defend Western Europe? Southeast Asia? the Middle East? and if so, how?

Unless these questions are answered convincingly, in American behavior as well as by words, there is no motive for strenuous anti-Soviet action. Outside or inside the Soviet Empire, there will be no firm resistance without a reasonable chance of winning. If Washington hasn't made up its mind, why stick one's neck out? . . .

2

It is the intellectual fashion to be scornful of "crusades."

Crusades, it is said, are as dangerous as they are futile. They arouse a fanatic spirit that hardens on both sides, and leads to insistence on the unconditional surrender of the enemy. The conflict becomes "a holy war." The crusaders' passions rule out any chance for negotiation and reasonable compromise. To adopt the policy of liberation, critics warn, would be to set out on a crusade. . . .

To object to conceiving the struggle against communism as a crusade implies the belief that the opposition between the communist way and ours is not fundamental. If it is not, then the idea of a crusade is light-minded, immoral and in truth fanatic. We ought then to keep the conflict as cool and rational as can be, and to be ready at all times for negotiation, compromise and settlement.

The heart of this matter has always been clear to the communist leaders, who have known themselves to be separated from what they call "the bourgeois world" by an absolute chasm. . . . The communist enterprise proposes to replace society, God and man by a wholly new system of society, a new kind of man with a new "nature," and the new gods of material and historical Necessity. The communists realize that with their proposal there cannot be compromise or negotiation. What is there to compromise? You do not compromise with birth, or death. There are some questions which must be answered just Yes or No.

The communist stand forces us to decide, painful as is the process to liberal sensibilities, whether we really believe that our way is better than theirs. Are we ready to declare that Western civilization is superior—objectively superior—to Soviet totalitarianism? Do we as Americans proclaim that political freedom and representative government are better than political tyranny and the sovereignty of the secret police, better for all men, Poles and Chinese and Russians as well as French and English and Americans? Our ancestors did not doubt the universality of their political ideal, nor did they hesitate to speak and act according to its light. The Declaration of Independence did not confine its truths to the three mile limit. If we do not think that our way is better than the Kremlin's, then what are we disputing? Let us apply for acceptance as another of the Federated Socialist Soviet Republics. We can be sure of the warmth of our welcome.

3

The third objection is related to the second. It is argued that liberation, though in itself good and to be wished for, is none of our business. Suffering, despotism and famine have always been rather widely distributed in the world. We are saddened that this is so, and we rejoice when these plagues are anywhere lightened or removed. But we cannot be every man's keeper. Our task is to strengthen the liberty and well-being of our own land and people. So far as international conflict goes, our problem is our national defense. If we assign ourselves the job of global savior, we shall not only make a mess on the world scale, but will endanger the humbler domestic goals.

Let us agree that national security and defense are the proper objective of a government's general strategy, and that any action in the field of foreign affairs which injures national security is wrong. Let us further grant that no action is justified unless it contributes positively to national defense. The case for a policy of liberation will remain as strong as ever. . . .

This peril can be summed up in a single sentence. If the communists succeed in consolidating what they have *already* conquered, then their complete world victory is certain. The threat does not come only from what the communists may do, but from what they have done. We do not have to bring in speculation about Soviet "intentions." The simple terrible fact is that if things go on as they now are, if for the time being they merely stabilize, then we have already lost. That is why the policy of containment, even if 100% successful, is a formula for Soviet victory. . . .

We are lost if our opponent so much as holds his own. There remains only a limited time during which it will continue to be possible to move against him. Americans will not even be granted much longer the desperate comfort that as a last resort there are always the bombs to turn to. If the political offensive is long delayed, it will be too late for bombs.

THE INTERNATIONAL POSITION
OF THE SOVIET UNION*

BY

NIKITA S. KHRUSHCHEV

[1956]

The emergence of socialism from within the bounds of a single country and its transformation into a world system is the main feature of our era. Capitalism has proved powerless to prevent this process of world-historic significance. The simultaneous existence of two opposite world economic systems, the capitalist and the socialist, developing according to different laws and in opposite directions, has become an indisputable fact.

Socialist economy is developing towards the ever-increasing satisfaction of the material and cultural requirements of àll members of society, the continuous expansion and improvement of production on the basis of higher techniques, and closer co-operation and mutual assistance between the socialist countries.

The trend of capitalist economy is that of the ever-increasing enrichment of the monopolies, the further intensification of exploitation and cuts in the living standards of millions of working people, particularly in the colonial and dependent countries, of increased militarization of the economy, the exacerbation of the competitive struggle among the capitalist countries, and the maturing of new economic crises and upheavals. . . .

Comrades, between the Nineteenth and Twentieth Congresses of the Communist Party of the Soviet Union, very important changes have taken place in international relations.

Soon after the Second World War ended, the influence of reactionary and militarist groups began to be increasingly evident in the policy of the United States of America, Britain and France. Their desire to enforce their will on other countries by economic

* Selections from the *Report of the Central Committee of the Communist Party of the Soviet Union to the 20th Party Congress,* February 14, 1956. Published by Foreign Languages Publishing House, Moscow. N. S. Khrushchev (b. 1894) was formerly Secretary-General of the Central Committee of the Communist Party of the Soviet Union (1953-64) and Chairman of the Council of Ministers (1958-64).

and political pressure, threats and military provocation prevailed. This became known as the "positions of strength" policy. It reflects the aspiration of the most aggressive sections of present-day imperialism to win world supremacy, to suppress the working class and the democratic and national-liberation movements; it reflects their plans for military adventures against the socialist camp.

The international atmosphere was poisoned by war hysteria. The arms race began to assume more and more monstrous dimensions. Many big U.S. military bases designed for use against the U.S.S.R. and the People's Democracies were built in countries thousands of miles from the borders of the United States. "Cold war" was begun against the socialist camp. International distrust was artificially kindled, and nations set against one another. A bloody war was launched in Korea; the war in Indo-China dragged on for years.

The inspirers of the "cold war" began to establish military blocs, and many countries found themselves, against the will of their peoples, involved in restricted aggressive alignments—the North Atlantic bloc, Western European Union, SEATO (military bloc for South-East Asia) and the Baghdad pact.

The organizers of military blocs allege that they have united for defence, for protection against the "communist threat." But that is sheer hypocrisy. We know from history that when planning a redivision of the world, the imperialist powers have always lined up military blocs. Today the "anti-communism" slogan is again being used as a smokescreen to cover up the claims of one power for world domination. The new thing here is that the United States wants, by means of all kinds of blocs and pacts, to secure a dominant position in the capitalist world for itself, and to reduce all its partners in the blocs to the status of obedient executors of its will.

The inspirers of the "positions of strength" policy assert that this policy makes another war impossible, because it ensures a "balance of power" in the world arena. This view is widespread among Western statesmen and it is therefore all the more important to thoroughly expose its real meaning.

Can peace be promoted by an arms race? It would seem that it is simply absurd to pose such a question. Yet the adherents of the "positions of strength" policy offer the arms race as their main recipe for the preservation of peace! It is perfectly obvious that when nations compete to increase their military might, the danger of war becomes greater, not lesser.

The arms race, the "positions of strength" policy, the lining up of aggressive blocs and the "cold war"—all this could not but aggravate the international situation, and it did. This has been one trend of world events during the period under review.

But other processes have also taken place in the international arena during these years, processes showing that in the world today monopolist circles are by no means controlling everything.

The steady consolidation of the forces of socialism, democracy and peace, and of the forces of the national-liberation movement is of decisive significance. The international position of the Soviet Union, the People's Republic of China, and the other socialist countries has been further strengthened during this period, and their prestige and international ties have grown immeasurably. The international camp of socialism is exerting ever-growing influence on the course of international events. *(Applause.)*

The forces of peace have been considerably augmented by the emergence in the world arena of a group of peace-loving European and Asian states which have proclaimed non-participation in blocs as a principle of their foreign policy. The leading political circles of these states rightly hold that to participate in restricted military imperialist alignments would merely increase the danger of their countries being involved in military gambles by the aggressive forces and draw them into the maelstrom of the arms drive.

As a result, a vast Zone of Peace including peace-loving states, both socialist and non-socialist, of Europe and Asia, has emerged in the world. This zone includes vast areas inhabited by nearly 1,500 million people, that is, the majority of the population of our planet. . . .

The October Socialist Revolution struck a most powerful blow at the imperialist colonial system. Under the influence of the Great October Revolution the national-liberation struggle of the colonial peoples developed with particular force, it continued throughout the subsequent years and has led to a deep-going crisis of the entire imperialist colonial system.

The defeat of fascist Germany and imperialist Japan in the Second World War was an important factor stimulating the liberation struggles in the colonies and dependent countries. The democratic forces' victory over fascism instilled faith in the possibility of liberation in the hearts of the oppressed peoples.

The victorious revolution in China struck the next staggering blow at the colonial system; it marked a grave defeat for imperialism.

India, the country with the world's second biggest population, has won political independence. Independence has been gained by Burma, Indonesia, Egypt, Syria, the Lebanon, the Sudan, and a number of other former colonial countries. More than 1,200 million people, or nearly half of the world's population, have freed themselves from colonial or semi-colonial dependence during the last ten years. *(Prolonged applause.)*

The disintegration of the imperialist colonial system now taking place is a post-war development of history-making significance. Peoples who for centuries were kept away by the colonialists from the high road of progress followed by human society are now going through a great process of regeneration. People's China and the independent Indian Republic have joined the ranks of the Great Powers. We are witnessing a political and economic upsurge of the peoples of South-East Asia and the Arab East. The awakening of the peoples of Africa has begun. The national-liberation movement has gained in strength in Brazil, Chile and other Latin-American countries. The outcome of the wars in Korea, Indo-China and Indonesia has demonstrated that the imperialists are unable, even with the help of armed intervention, to crush the peoples who are resolutely fighting for a life of freedom and independence. The complete abolition of the infamous system of colonialism has now been put on the agenda as one of the most acute and pressing problems. *(Applause.)*

The new period in world history which Lenin predicted has arrived, and the peoples of the East are playing an active part in deciding the destinies of the whole world, are becoming a new mighty factor in international relations. In contrast to the pre-war period, most Asian countries now act in the world arena as sovereign states or states which are resolutely upholding their right to an independent foreign policy. International relations have spread beyond the bounds of relations between the countries inhabited chiefly by peoples of the white race and are beginning to acquire the character of genuinely world-wide relations.

The winning of political freedom by the peoples of the former colonies and semi-colonies is the first and most important prerequisite of their full independence, that is, of the achievement of economic independence. The liberated Asian countries are pursuing a policy of building up their own industry, training their own technicians, raising the living standards of the people, and regenerating and developing their age-old national culture. History-making prospects for a better future are opening up before the countries which have embarked upon the path of independent development.

These countries, although they do not belong to the socialist world system, can draw on its achievements to build up an independent national economy and to raise the living standards of their peoples. Today they need not go begging for up-to-date equipment to their former oppressors. They can get it in the socialist countries, without assuming any political or military commitments.

The very fact that the Soviet Union and the other countries of the socialist camp exist, their readiness to help the underdeveloped countries in advancing their industries on terms of equality and mutual benefit are a major stumbling-block to colonial policy. The imperialists can no longer regard the underdeveloped countries solely as potential sources for making maximum profits. They are compelled to make concessions to them.

Not all the countries, however, have thrown off the colonial yoke. A big part of the African continent, some countries of Asia, Central and South America continue to remain in colonial or semi-colonial dependence. They are still retained as agrarian raw-material appendages of the imperialist countries. The living standard of the population in the dependent countries remains exceedingly low.

The contradictions and rivalry between the colonial powers for spheres of influence, sources of raw materials, and markets are growing. The United States is out to grab the colonial possessions of the European powers. South Viet-Nam is passing from France to the United States. The American monopolies are waging an offensive against the French, Belgian and Portugese possessions in Africa. Once Iran's oil riches were fully controlled by the British, but now the British have been compelled to share them with the Americans; moreover, the American monopolists are fighting to oust the British entirely. American influence in Pakistan and Iraq is increasing under the guise of "free enterprise."

The American monopolies, utilizing their dominant position in the Central and South-American countries, have moulded the economies of many of them in a distorted, one-sided way, extremely disadvantageous for the population. They are hampering their industrial development and shackling them with the heavy chains of economic dependence.

To preserve, and in some places also to re-establish their former domination, the colonial powers are resorting to the suppression of the colonial peoples by the force of arms, a method which has been condemned by history. They also have recourse to new forms of colonial enslavement under the guise of so-called "aid" to under-developed countries, which brings colossal profits to the colonialists. Let us take the United States as an example. The United States renders such "aid" above all in the form of deliveries of American weapons to the underdeveloped countries. This enables the American monopolies to load up their industry with arms orders. Then the products of the arms industry, worth billions of dollars and paid for through the budget by the American taxpayers, are sent to the underdeveloped countries. States receiving such "aid" in the form of weapons, inevitably fall into dependence; they increase their armies, which leads to higher taxes and a decline in living standards.

The monopolists are interested in continuing the "positions of strength" policy; the ending of the "cold war" is to their disadvantage. Why? Because the fanning of war hysteria is used to justify imperialist expansion, to intimidate the masses and dope their minds in order to justify the higher taxes which then go to pay for war orders and flow into the safes of the millionaires. Thus, the "cold war" is a means for maintaining the war industry at a high level and for extracting colossal profits.

Naturally, "aid" to underdeveloped countries is granted on

definite political terms, terms providing for their integration into aggressive military blocs, the conclusion of joint military pacts, and support for American foreign policy aimed at world domination, or "world leadership," as the American imperialists themselves call it. . . .

* * *

The peaceful co-existence of the two systems. The Leninist principle of peaceful co-existence of states with different social systems has always been and remains the general line of our country's foreign policy.

It has been alleged that the Soviet Union advances the principle of peaceful co-existence merely out of tactical considerations, considerations of expediency. Yet it is common knowledge that we have always, from the very first years of Soviet power, stood with equal firmness for peaceful co-existence. Hence, it is not a tactical move, but a fundamental principle of Soviet foreign policy.

This means that if there is indeed a threat to the peaceful co-existence of countries with differing social and political systems, it by no means comes from the Soviet Union or the rest of the socialist camp. Is there a single reason why a socialist state should want to unleash aggressive war? Do we have classes and groups that are interested in war as a means of enrichment? We do not. We abolished them long ago. Or, perhaps, we do not have enough territory or natural wealth, perhaps we lack sources of raw materials or markets for our goods? No, we have sufficient of all those and to spare. Why then should we want war? We do not want it, as a matter of principle we renounce any policy that might lead to millions of people being plunged into war for the sake of the selfish interests of a handful of multi-millionaires. Do those who shout about the "aggressive intentions" of the U.S.S.R. know all this? Of course they do. Why then do they keep up the old monotonous refrain about some imaginary "communist aggression"? Only to stir up mud, to conceal their plans for world domination, a "crusade" against peace, democracy, and socialism.

To this day the enemies of peace allege that the Soviet Union is out to overthrow capitalism in other countries by "exporting" revolution. It goes without saying that among us Communists there are no supporters of capitalism. But this does not mean that we have interefered or plan to interfere in the internal affairs of countries where capitalism still exists. Romain Rolland was right when he said that "freedom is not brought in from abroad in baggage trains like Bourbons." *(Animation.)* It is ridiculous to think that revolutions are made to order. We often hear representatives of bourgeois countries reasoning thus: "The Soviet leaders claim that they are for peaceful co-existence between the two systems. At the same time they declare that they are fighting for communism, and say that communism is bound to win in all countries. Now if the Soviet Union is fighting for communism, how can there be any peaceful co-existence with it?" This view is the result of bourgeois propaganda. The ideologists of the bourgeoisie distort the facts and deliberately confuse questions of ideological struggle with questions of relations between states in order to make the Communists of the Soviet Union look like advocates of aggression.

When we say that the socialist system will win in the competition between the two systems—the capitalist and the socialist—this by no means signifies that its victory will be achieved through armed interference by the socialist countries in the internal affairs of the capitalist countries. Our certainty of the victory of communism is based on the fact that the socialist mode of production possesses decisive advantages over the capitalist mode of production. Precisely because of this, the ideas of Marxism-Leninism are more and more capturing the minds of the broad masses of the working people in the capitalist countries, just as they have captured the minds of millions of men and women in our country and the People's Democracies. *(Prolonged applause.)* We believe that all working men in the world, once they have become convinced of the advantages communism brings, will sooner or later take the road of struggle for the construction of socialist society. *(Prolonged applause.)* Building communism in our country, we are resolutely against war. We have always held and continue to hold that the establishment of a new social system in one or another country is the internal affair of the peoples of the countries concerned. This is our attitude, based on the great Marxist-Leninist teaching. . . .

POWER TODAY*

Its Location, Nature, and Growth

BY

DEAN ACHESON

[1958]

Before the present century was two decades old, the system which had provided an international order since Waterloo was mortally stricken. Twenty years later, it had disappeared altogether.

It is true that in the rosy light of retrospect the period after the Congress of Vienna has seemed more peaceful and idyllic than it was. To the men of the time, says a more realistic writer, the period "was one of appalling turmoil. It was an armed peace. Austria's budget, for instance, was so overburdened by expenditure on armaments that it only once avoided a deficit between 1812 and 1848. France was not pacified: on the contrary resentment against the settlement dominated French political life for a generation. The discontent in the victorious countries was almost as great, except where held down—as in Austria—by police tyranny."[1]

All this is true. Nonetheless, the "Concert of Europe" describes a method and a reality. The empires of Europe, controlling hundreds of millions of people in Europe, Asia, and Africa, and decisively affecting the conduct of hundreds of millions more, did keep international conflict limited in scope and minimal in destruction. They did provide an economic system, accepted without protest, and they did establish political coherence unequaled in extent since the Roman Empire. One essential element in all of this was Great Britain's skillful employment of its power to give stability through shifts of its weight from one side to another, much as a gyroscope gives balance to a moving craft. Another essential element was the managerial and material contribution to

---

*From *Power and Diplomacy*, published by Harvard University Press, copyright 1958 by The Fletcher School of Law and Diplomacy, Tufts University. Reprinted by permission.

[1] *Times Literary Supplement* (London), April 26, 1957.

economic development, first, by the British and, later, by Western
European industry and finance.

The First World War ended thé Austro-Hungarian, German,
and Ottoman Empires and the Czarist regime in Russia, unloosed
nationalism in Eastern Europe, and gravely weakened the French
and British Empires. The Second World War eliminated the
empires of Japan and Italy, and the military power of Germany.
France, defeated and occupied, lost her position in the Near East
and Far East, and only with increasing difficulty maintains herself
in Africa, at the expense of power in Europe. Great Britain,
economically exhausted and, save for the African colonies, politically and militarily reduced to her island resources, has by her
recent budget decision made clear that the security of the United
Kingdom lies in association with other states. . . .

The curtain had been rung down upon an era; the stage set for
the unfolding of another, which Alexis de Tocqueville, with amazing vision, forecast almost a century and a quarter ago, in his
Democracy in America:

"There are at the present time two great nations in the world,
which started from different points, but seem to tend towards the
same end. I allude to the Russians and the Americans. Both of
them have grown up unnoticed; and while the attention of mankind was directed elsewhere, they have suddenly placed themselves
in the front rank among the nations, and the world learned their
existence and their greatness at almost the same time.

"All other nations seem to have nearly reached their natural
limits, and they have only to maintain their power; but these are
still in the act of growth. All the others have stopped, or continue
to advance with extreme difficulty; these alone are proceeding with
ease and celerity along a path to which no limit can be perceived.
The American struggles against the obstacles that nature opposes
to him; the adversaries of the Russian are men. The former com-
bats the wilderness and savage life; the latter, civilization with all
its arms. The conquests of the American are therefore gained by
the plowshare; those of the Russian by the sword. The Anglo-
American relies upon personal interest to accomplish his ends and
gives free scope to the unguided strength and common sense of the
people; the Russian centers all the authority of society in a single

arm. The principal instrument of the former is freedom; of the latter, servitude. Their starting-point is different and their courses are not the same; yet each of them seems marked out by the will of Heaven to sway the destinies of half the globe."[2]

Today even the component elements of the world order which had swayed the destinies of the entire globe have been destroyed; beginnings have been made on two alignments to succeed it.

In one of these alignments, Britain, which once had the training and capability to manage a world system, no longer has the capability. The United States, which has the material capability, lacks the experience and the discipline needed for responsible management. This is said in no spirit of belittling those far-reaching, bold, and imaginative steps which this government and people have taken to stop the disintegration of international society and to build anew. Americans, like all sensible people who have had the good fortune to be spared the desire for expansion abroad and the experience of national catastrophe from foreign attack, are primarily interested in their own absorbing and immensely profitable affairs, and only secondarily interested in the doings and business of distant peoples. To understand the bearing and urgency of these takes time and experience.

The disappearance of a world system and of the power which sustained it, together with the growth of Soviet power and ambitions, means that the nations which wish to preserve independent national identity can do so only if the material strength and the political and economic leadership of the United States are enlisted in the effort. However much all of us may dislike this thought, the requisite power does not reside anywhere else.

Europe, however, remains of great importance. Its population is still the largest aggregation of skilled workers in the world, its resources are many and varied. Its industry is second only to our own, though closely pressed in many fields by the Russians. Its traditions of civilization go back through two and a half millennia. If Europe should, by evil chance, become subject to Soviet domination, the problems of the remainder of the non-communist world

---

[2] Alexis de Tocqueville, *Democracy in America* (Alfred A. Knopf, New York, 1945), I, 434.

would become unmanageable.[3] The agreement and support of Western European nations are necessary for any successful foreign policy and defense arrangement on our part. One must not discount the importance of Europe. But the fact remains that Europe without American strength and leadership can neither preserve its own independence nor foster an international system in which anyone's independence will survive.

GROWTH OF RUSSIAN POWER

In the other alignment, Russian power, which has for two centuries been great, appears to be towering now. In part this is so because it stands out like a great tree in a forest where all around it have been felled; in part, because it has fed on the surrounding decay, and grown. In the past Russian strength lay in its vast area and its large and disciplined manpower. The Soviet regime has added to these assets industrial productive power, which is today the indispensable basis of military power, economic penetration, and political attraction. The Soviet regime gives first importance to its own perpetuation. A strong second effort goes to keeping confusion and unrest as widespread as possible outside

---

3 " . . . Were the United States to stand alone against a Communist world which contained all Europe and the Soviet Union, its 1953 production of 102 million metric tons of crude steel would be outweighed by the Communist 113 million metric tons. Our theoretical capacity (112.7 million metric tons at January 1, 1954) would, however, be equal to that production total. By 1960, ignoring the changes in policy and effort that would obviously take place, our anticipated production of 117 million metric tons would be faced by a combined production of 161.5 million metric tons. That is to say, our production now would equal 90 percent of the combined output of our opponents and in 1960 only 72 percent."—*Trends in Economic Growth, A Comparison of the Western Powers and the Soviet Bloc*, prepared for the Joint Committee on the Economic Report by the Legislative Reference Service of the Library of Congress, 83 Cong., 2 Sess., January 3, 1955 (Government Printing Office, Washington, 1955), p. 140.

The impact of this is even greater if it is true, as the subsequent JEC Report believes it is, that "The bulk of it [steel]—perhaps as much steel as in the United States—is available for production of military goods or for items conducive to further economic growth. The same kind of comparisons might be made for petroleum." *Soviet Economic Growth: A Comparison with the United States*, prepared for the Subcommittee on Foreign Economic Policy of the Joint Economic Committee by the Legislative Reference Service of the Library of Congress, 85 Cong., 1 Sess., July 5, 1957 (Government Printing Office, Washington, 1957), pp. 11–12.

the communist area, and to frustrating all attempts to build an international system other than a communist one.   All this paves the way for the inevitable—so the regime believes—collapse of capitalistic governments and systems, and for the hegemony of the Soviet Union in a communist world.   The regime's efforts gain immense vigor, subtlety, and—for the West—deep deceptiveness from the fact that the Soviet is a revolutionary society, repudiating the most fundamental postulates of the established order, and is in the grip of an ideology which imbues it with unquestioning confidence in its superiority and its destined progression to triumph and dominion.

No matter how plainly the Russians talk and act, we simply refuse to believe what they say and to understand the meaning of what they do.   President Eisenhower and Secretary Dulles keep insisting that the test must be deeds, not words.   Floods of deeds follow, amply explained by torrents of words.   Yet our leaders and, indeed, our people cannot believe what they see and hear.

As I write, President Eisenhower tells us that relations between the United States and the Soviet Union might be improved by a visit from Marshal Zhukov.   The President recalls that he and the Marshal "had a most satisfactory acquaintanceship and friend-ship," and remembers having had "a very tough time trying to defend our position" against the Marshal's contention "that their system appealed to the idealistic, and we completely to the material-istic."[4]   The President seems to forget that the same satisfactory friend and persuasive debater insisted upon and carried out the bloody liquidation of the Hungarian revolt.   The friendliness which underlies American life makes it impossible to believe that congeniality can accompany the most profound hostility to our-selves and all we believe.   As Justice Holmes correctly observed, candor is the best form of deception.

"People," Mr. Khrushchev told the East German communist leaders in September of 1955—"People say our smiles are not honest.   That is not true.   Our smile is real and not artificial.   But if anyone believes that our smile means that we have given up the teachings of Marx, Engels and Lenin, they are badly mistaken. Those who are waiting for that to happen can go on waiting until

---

[4] *New York Times*, July 18, 1957.

Easter and Whit Monday fall on the same day. . . . We are honest people and always tell our opponents the truth. We are supporters of peaceful coexistence but also of education for communism. We are supporters of peaceful coexistence only because there happen to be two systems. We do not need a war to ensure the victory of socialism. Peaceful competition itself is enough . . . one cannot stop the course of history."

The object of competition, Khrushchev points out, is the triumph of the Soviet system. He does not *"need"* a war to ensure this victory; but he would quite clearly not reject force if the risks were low, or if, as in Hungary, he felt that the deepest interests of the regime were at stake. Despite all this, we go on seeing in each new move of the Kremlin to divide and weaken us signs that the Russians may at last be "sincere." The very word shows our lack of understanding. The Russians are and have been wholly sincere in what they believe and are pursuing. But their moves and proposals in dealing with other states are coldly and carefully calculated to advance their own purposes, not any common purpose with the West. In this context "sincerity" is a silly and, indeed, a very dangerous word.

TOWARD A RELAXATION
OF TENSIONS *

BY

J. WILLIAM FULBRIGHT

[1964]

There is no longer any validity in the Clausewitz doctrine of war as "a carrying out of policy with other means." Nuclear weapons have rendered it totally obsolete because the instrument of policy is now totally disproportionate to the end in view. Nuclear weapons have deprived force of its utility as an instrument of national policy, leaving the nuclear powers with vastly greater but far less useful power than they had before. So long as there is reason—not virtue, but simply reason—in the foreign policy of the great nations, nuclear weapons are not so much an instrument as an inhibition on policy.

By all available evidence, the Russians are no less aware of this than we. The memory of their 20 million dead in World War II is still fresh in the minds of most Russians. In a speech on July 19, 1963, Chairman Khrushchev castigated the Chinese Communists as "those who want to start a war against everybody . . . Do these men know," he asked, "that if all the nuclear warheads were touched off, the world would be in such a state that the survivors would envy the dead?" . . .

In the pursuit of its ambitions, whether by militant or peaceful means, the Soviet Union, like any other nation, is subject to the unending pressures for change imposed by time and circumstance. "Man," it has been said, "the supreme pragmatist, is a revisionist by nature." Those who attribute to the Soviet leaders a permanent and unalterable determination to destroy the free societies of the West are crediting the Soviet Union with a strength and constancy of will that, so far as I know, has never been achieved by any nation.

---

* From *Old Myths and New Realities,* published by Random House, copyright 1964 by J. William Fulbright. Reprinted by permission.

There is, in fact, every reason to anticipate change, both within the Communist nations and in the relations between the Communist and the free nations. If there is any "law" of history, it is the inevitability and continuity of change. It is sometimes for the better, but often for the worse, and we cannot assume that the future evolution of the Communist world will be toward moderate and peaceful policies. But neither are we helpless and passive spectators to the course which the Communist nations follow. We have the means and resources to influence events in the Soviet Union and in other bloc countries. Our ability to put those means to effective use depends in no small measure on our willingness to go beyond a rigidly ideological view of communism and to deal with the Communist countries as the national entities which they are, each with special national interests and aspirations.

If we look at the Communist bloc objectively, and not through the distorting prism of ideological hostility, we can see that important and encouraging changes have already taken place. We perceive that Soviet society and the Soviet economy are becoming highly complex, too complex to be completely and efficiently controlled by a highly centralized dictatorship. We perceive that under the pressures of growing complexity a degree of economic decentralization has taken place, that the police terror of the Stalin era has been abated, that the Central Committee of the Communist Party may even be developing under Khrushchev into a kind of rudimentary parliamentary body. And most important of all . . . the unity of the Communist bloc has been disrupted, and we find ourselves confronted with a growing diversity of national outlooks and policies, ranging from the harsh orthodoxy of Communist China to the pragmatism of the Soviet Union, the nationalism of Poland and Hungary, and the astonishing diplomatic independence of Rumania.

There are those who maintain that the only valid test of altered Soviet policies must be the explicit repudiation of those tenets of Marxist ideology that call for world revolution and the universal victory of communism. To ask for overt renunciation of a cherished doctrine is to expect too much of human nature. Men do not repudiate the doctrines and dogmas to which they have sworn their loyalty. Instead they rationalize, revise, and reinterpret them to meet new needs and new circumstances, all the while protesting that their heresy is the purest orthodoxy.

Something of this nature is now occurring in the Soviet Union. Khrushchev has not repudiated Marx and Lenin; on the contrary, he vows his fealty to their doctrines at every opportunity. But his "orthodoxy" has not deterred him from some striking interpretations of the scriptures. Contrast, for example, the Marxist-Leninist emphasis on discipline and self-sacrifice and revolution with Khrushchev's famous words in Budapest in April, 1964: "The important thing is that we should have more to eat—good goulash—schools, housing, and ballet. How much more do these things give to the enlargement of man's life? It is worth fighting and working for these things." Or contrast the Marxist-Leninist principle of relentless struggle for the universal victory of communism with Khrushchev's answer to his own rhetorical question as to whether the Soviet Union should help the French working class to take over power. "Who asked us to mix in their affairs?" was his reply. "What do we know about them?"

The attribution of an unalterable will and constancy to Soviet policy has been a serious handicap to our own policy. It has restricted our ability to gain insights into the realities of Soviet society and Soviet foreign policy. It has denied us valuable opportunities to take advantage of changing conditions in the Communist world and to encourage changes which would reduce the Communist threat to the free world. We have overestimated the ability of the Soviets to pursue malevolent aims, without regard to time or circumstances, and, in so doing, we have underestimated our own ability to influence Soviet behavior.

A stigma of heresy has been attached to suggestions by American policy-makers that Soviet policy can change or that it is sometimes altered in response to our own. But it is a fact that in the wake of the failure of the aggressive policies of the Stalin period, the Soviet leaders have gradually shifted to a policy of peaceful, or competitive, coexistence with the West. This policy confronts us with certain dangers but also with important opportunities if we are wise enough to take advantage of them.

The abrupt change in the Soviet position which made possible the signing of the nuclear test ban treaty in 1963 appears to have been motivated by the general failure of competitive coexistence as practiced in the last few years and by a number of specific problems, both foreign and domestic. The most conspicuous of these is the public eruption of the dispute with Communist China. In addition, the Soviet leaders have been troubled by economic difficulties at home, particularly in agriculture, by the increasingly insistent demands of the Russian people for more and better food, clothing, and housing, and by difficulties between the regime and Soviet intellectuals and artists; by increasing centrifugal tendencies in Eastern Europe, aggravated by the dismaying contrast with an increasingly prosperous and powerful Western Europe; and by the negligible rewards of Soviet diplomacy and economic aid in Asia and Africa.

The most crucial failure of Soviet policy has been in its dealings with the West. Contrary to Soviet expectations of a few years ago, it has proven impossible to extract concessions from the West on Berlin and Central Europe by nuclear diplomacy. Thwarted in Europe, Khrushchev embarked in the fall of 1962 on the extremely dangerous adventure of placing missiles in Cuba, hoping, it would seem, to force a solution in Berlin and an unfreezing of Central Europe. The debacle in Cuba led the Soviet leaders to a major reappraisal of their policies.

That reappraisal has apparently resulted in a decision to seek a relaxation of tensions with the West. The nuclear test ban treaty and subsequent limited agreements with the West were clearly calculated to serve that purpose. In addition, the tone of Soviet diplomacy has changed; in matters ranging from Cuba to Vietnam, vituperation has been muted and the Russians have passed up a number of opportunities to quarrel with the United States.

From the Soviet point of view, a limited *détente* with the West appears to offer certain clear advantages. Three reasons for seeking improved relations with the West seem of major importance. First and foremost is the genuine fear of nuclear war which the Soviets share with the West, all the more since the United States demonstrated in the Cuban crisis that it was prepared to use nuclear weapons to defend its vital interests. Secondly, in the mounting conflict with the Chinese, the Soviet Union can claim a success for its policies of "peaceful coexistence" and, more important, can use the world-wide popularity of the test ban and other arms-control measures to strengthen its position both in the Communist bloc and in the non-Communist underdeveloped countries, thereby further isolating the Chinese. Thirdly, Khrushchev appears to be interested in measures which will permit a leveling off, and perhaps a reduction, of weapons expenditures in order to be able to divert scarce resources for meeting some of the demands of the Russian people for a better life. . . .

If the relaxation of tensions is conceived by the Soviets as an interlude in which to consolidate their position, strengthen their power base, and then renew their aggressive policies against the West, is it wise for us to grant them this interlude? It is indeed wise, for two main reasons: first, because it will provide the West with an identical opportunity to strengthen the power base of the free world; and secondly, because it will generate conditions in which the Soviet and Communist bloc peoples will be emboldened to step up their demands for peace and a better life, conditions which the Soviet leadership will find it exceedingly difficult to alter. . . .

The other great advantage to the West of a period of relaxed tensions is that it may release long-suppressed pressures for peace and the satisfaction of civilian needs within the Soviet bloc. Public opinion, even in a dictatorship like the Soviet Union, is an enormously powerful force which no government can safely defy for too long or in too many ways. Russian public opinion is overwhelmingly opposed to war and overwhelmingly in favor of higher wages, of better food, clothing, and housing, and of all the good things of life in a modern industrial society. The Russian *people* may well turn out to be a powerful ally of the free nations, who also want peace and prosperity. It is quite possible that a thaw in Soviet-American relations, even though conceived by the Soviet leadership as a temporary pause, could lead gradually to an entirely new relationship. Motives have a way of becoming lost as the actions to which they give rise generate new attitudes and new and unforeseen motives. Pressed by the demands of an increasingly assertive public opinion, the Soviet leaders may find new reasons to continue a policy of peace and accommodation with the West. Step by step their revolutionary zeal may diminish, as they find that a peaceful and affluent national existence is not really so tragic a fate as they had imagined.

No one knows whether Soviet society will actually evolve along these lines, but the trend of Soviet history suggests that it is by no means impossible. . . .

It is possible, I believe, for the West to encourage a hopeful direction in Soviet policy. We can seek to strengthen Russian public opinion as a brake against dangerous policies by conveying accurate information about Western life and Western aims, and about the heavy price that both sides are paying for the cold war. We can make it clear to the Russians that they have nothing to fear from the West so long as they respect the rights and independence of other nations. We can suggest to them at every possible opportunity, both by persuasion and by example, that there is no greater human vanity than the assumption that one's own values have universal validity, and no enterprise more certain of failure than the attempt to impose the preferences of a single society on an unwilling world. And finally, we can encourage them to recognize, as we must never fail to recognize ourselves, that adventures born of passion are soon severed from their lofty aims, turning idealism into barbarism and men into demons. . . .

*   *   *

The purpose of a realistic foreign policy is not to end the cold war but to modify it, not to resolve the conflict between communism and freedom—a goal which is almost certainly beyond the reach of the present generation—but to remove some of the terror and passion from it. The progress thus far achieved and now in prospect has been small in substance, in the sense that it has brought us scarcely closer to a solution of such great problems as the arms race and the division of Germany. But in another sense—the extremely important psychological sense—it may be that we are doing better than we know. The ultimate criterion of the importance of any issue is its implications for war and peace. The division of Germany is a most important issue in itself, but its global and historical significance, like that of the arms race, is that it has a critical bearing on whether we shall have war or peace. If, by a series of agreements on issues which in substance are much less important than the division of Germany and the arms race—such agreements as the test ban treaty, reductions in the output of fissionable materials, or the opening of consulates and airline connections—we succeed in creating a *state of mind* in which neither side considers war as a likely eventuality or as a real option for itself except under radically changed conditions, then in fact we will have progressed toward precisely the same objective which a German settlement or a general disarmament agreement would help to achieve—a world substantially free of the threat of nuclear incineration.

The point which I am trying, imperfectly, to make is that in our quest for world peace the *alteration of attitudes* is no less important, perhaps more important, than the resolution of issues. It is in the minds of men, after all, that wars are spawned; to act upon the human mind, regardless of the issue or occasion for doing so, is to act upon the source of conflict and the potential source of redemption and reconciliation. It would seem, therefore, that there may be important new things to be learned about international relations through the scholarship of psychologists and pyschiatrists.

When all is said and done, when the abstractions and subtleties of political science have been exhausted, there remain the most basic unanswered questions about war and peace and why we contest the issues we contest and why we even care about them. As Aldous Huxley has written: "There may be arguments about the best way of raising wheat in a cold climate or of re-afforesting a denuded mountain. But such arguments never lead to organized slaughter. Organized slaughter is the result of arguments about such questions as the following: Which is the best nation? The best religion? The best political theory? The best form of government? Why are other people so stupid and wicked? Why can't they see how good and intelligent we are? Why do they resist our beneficent efforts to bring them under our control and make them like ourselves?" [1] . . .

* * *

---

[1] Aldous Huxley, "The Politics of Ecology" (pamphlet, published by The Center for the Study of Democratic Institutions, Santa Barbara, California, 1963), p. 6.

The root question, for which I must confess I have no answer, is how and why it is that so much of the energy and intelligence that men could use to make life better for themselves is used instead to make life difficult and painful for other men. When the subtleties of strategy and power and diplomatic method have all been explained, we are still left with the seemingly unanswerable question of how and why it is that we *care* about such things, which are so remote from the personal satisfactions that bring pleasure and grace and fulfillment into our lives.

The paradoxes of human nature are eternal and perhaps unanswerable, but I do think we know enough about elemental human needs to be able to apply certain psychological principles in our efforts to alleviate the tensions of the cold war.

In this connection, I would suggest that a great deal—more than one would suspect—depends upon the *manner* in which we seek to negotiate reasonable agreements with the Russians. We must remember that we are not dealing with automatons whose sole function in life is to embody an ideology and a party line, but with human beings—people who, like ourselves, have special areas of pride, prejudice, and sensitivity. . . .

If . . . you start out with a compliment about the successes of Soviet society—and there have been a few—or with a candid reference to the shortcomings of our own society—and there have also been a few of these—then it often happens that the response is surprisingly expansive and conciliatory. . . .

The compliments in themselves are of little importance. But the candor and the cordiality are of great importance. As any good businessman knows, they set a tone and an atmosphere in which emotion gives way to reason and it becomes possible to do business, to move on from cordial generalities to specific negotiations. They generate that minimum of mutual confidence which is absolutely essential for reaching concrete agreements. Under existing circumstances, no one can expect such agreements to be more than modest accommodations which are clearly in the mutual interest; but they are at least a start toward more significant arrangements, and as I have already suggested, the critical question of war and peace may have less to do with the specifications of agreements than with the attitudes they engender and the attitudes they dispel.

"Frightened, hostile individuals tend to behave in ways which aggravate their difficulties instead of resolving them," says the distinguished psychiatrist Dr. Jerome D. Frank, "and frightened, hostile nations seems to behave similarly." [2] A nation, like an individual, Dr. Frank suggests, is likely to respond to a feared rival by breaking off communications, by provocative behavior, or by taking measures which promise immediate relief, regardless of their ultimate consequences.

Among the psychiatrically constructive techniques which might be used to cope with the destructive emotions of the cold war, Dr. Frank suggests the following: that we give Russian views our respectful attention as one way of making the Russians more receptive to ours; that we enormously increase communications between the Communist and the free worlds through cultural, scientific, agricultural, and student exchange programs; that we engage in co-operative activities that will enable both sides to achieve desired goals neither can as readily achieve alone. . . .

Through such means we may strive to break through the ideological passions and national animosities that fill men's minds with destructive zeal and blind them to what Aldous Huxley called the simple human preference for life and peace. Through such means we may strive to build strong foundations for our national security and, indeed, for the security of all peoples.

. . . It is not enough to seek security through armaments or even through ingenious schemes of disarmament; nor is it enough to seek security through schemes for the transfer of territories or for the deployment and redeployment of forces. Security is a state of mind rather than a set of devices and arrangements. The latter are important because they contribute, but only to the extent that they contribute, to generating a *psychological process* in which peoples and statesmen come increasingly to think of war as undesirable and unfeasible.

It is this *process* that has critical importance for our security. . . . As long as we are by one means or another cultivating a worldwide state of mind in which peace is favored over war, we are doing the most effective possible thing to strengthen the foundations of our security. . . .

---

[2] Letter from Dr. Frank to the author, September 13, 1960.

The cold war and all the other national rivalries of our time are not likely to evaporate in our lifetimes. The major question of our time is not how to end these conflicts but whether we can find some way to conduct them without resorting to weapons that will resolve them once and for all by wiping out the contestants. A generation ago we were speaking of "making the world safe for democracy." Having failed of this in two World Wars, we must now seek ways of making the world reasonably safe for the continuing contest between those who favor democracy and those who oppose it. It is a modest aspiration, but it is a sane and realistic one for a generation which, having failed of grander things, must now look to its own survival.

Extreme nationalism and dogmatic ideology are luxuries that the human race can no longer afford. It must turn its energies now to the politics of survival. If we do so, we may find in time that we can do better than just survive. We may find that the simple human preference for life and peace has an inspirational force of its own, less intoxicating perhaps than the sacred abstractions of nation and ideology, but far more relevant to the requirements of human life and human happiness.

There are, to be sure, risks in such an approach. There is an element of trust in it, and we can be betrayed. But human life is fraught with risks, and the behavior of the sane man is not the avoidance of all possible danger but the weighing of greater against lesser risks and of risks against opportunities.

We have an opportunity at present to try to build stronger foundations for our national security than armaments alone can ever provide. That opportunity lies in a policy of encouraging the development of a habit of peaceful and civilized contacts between ourselves and the Communist bloc. I believe that this opportunity must be pursued, with reason and restraint, with due regard for the pitfalls involved and for the possibility that our efforts may fail, but with no less regard for the promise of a safer and more civilized world. In the course of this pursuit, both we and our adversaries may find it possible one day to break through the barriers of nationalism and ideology and to approach each other in something of the spirit of Pope John's words to Khrushchev's son-in-law: "They tell me you are an atheist. But you will not refuse an old man's blessing for your children."

LESSONS OF CZECHOSLOVAKIA *

BY

ANATOLE SHUB

[1969]

For the third time in a generation—1938, 1948, 1968—Czechoslovakia has transformed the political atmosphere of the civilized world. The eight-month "Prague spring," the Soviet invasion of August 20 and its grim consequences have stirred strong emotions throughout Europe and beyond. Not since the Hitler-Stalin Pact, perhaps, has the outrage at Kremlin policy been so general, embracing Richard Nixon and Herbert Marcuse, Chou En-lai and Josip Broz-Tito, Bertrand Russell and Yevgeni Yevtushenko, Luigi Longo and Paul VI.

However, the Soviet régime has in fact suffered many such "moral defeats," from its dispersal of the All-Russian Constituent Assembly in 1918 to its intervention in Hungary in 1956. It has, then and now, shown less concern for "bourgeois morals" and for "formalistic juridical" concepts of international law than for power. Lenin crystalized its fundamental outlook in the famous question *Kto kovo?* (Who rules whom?) Stalin asked, "How many divisions has the Pope?" Brezhnev declared on the fiftieth anniversary of Bolshevik rule that Marxism-Leninism was the science of "how to win"—and the Soviet press after the invasion of Czechoslovakia did not hesitate to quote Bismarck: "Whoever rules Bohemia holds the key to Europe."

It is clearly tempting now for the West to consign the Czechoslovak experience to the archives of historical tragedies and lost causes. Yet the West would do so at its own peril. For Soviet conduct in the Czechoslovak crisis has challenged several of the most important assumptions on which Western policy has been tacitly based. These assumptions concern the evolution of communist rule

* From *Foreign Affairs,* January 1969, copyright by the Council on Foreign Relations. Reprinted by permission. Anatole Shub (b. 1928) was the Moscow correspondent of the *Washington Post* from April 1967 until he was expelled by the Soviet authorities in May 1969. He is the author of *The New Russian Tragedy.*

in Russia and its dependencies; such concepts as the status quo and spheres of influence; and the orientation of American policy toward the conflict between Russia and China. These assumptions have never been fully shared by the handful of seasoned experts with thorough personal knowledge of the Soviet Union; but they have nevertheless permeated popular Western opinion and thus, to a large extent, determined the policies of Western governments.

II

Surely the most striking aspect of the Soviet invasion of Czechoslovakia was the way it surprised even the closest observers. To be sure, many had perceived the danger of military intervention earlier in the summer—and particularly during the three tense weeks between the so-called Warsaw Letter (or ultimatum) of the Soviet leaders and their friends, and the climactic conferences at Cierna-nad-Tisou and Bratislava. Following these conferences, however, the entire world, including the Czechoslovak leaders themselves, believed that the crisis had been resolved by compromise agreement. This belief, consonant with the traditional rhythms of political crises over the centuries, proved completely false.

As Professor Leo Mates of Belgrade has observed, Czechoslovakia provided a case, virtually unique in modern history, where enormous military forces were unleashed *after* the climax in tension had passed, with scarcely any new preparation of world or Soviet domestic opinion for such drastic action. Professor Mates has stated the broad implications as follows: "If it is possible for unprovoked military intervention to follow negotiations and agreement, then the danger to peace is transferred to the domain of the unpredictable, which can but leave deep traces on the general behavior of states in international relations." For belief in the rationality, and therefore predictability, of Soviet as well as American conduct has been one of the pillars of international relations in the thermonuclear age.

Belief in Soviet predictability has been called into question not merely by the suddenness of the August 20 invasion but by the peculiar manner in which the decision to intervene appears to have been taken. There was the failure, both immediately before and for months after the invasion, to summon a plenary meeting of the Soviet Communist Party Central Committee. There was the prolonged silence of the nominally highest leaders of the party and state, none of whom seemed to wish to identify himself publicly with the actions taken. There were the persistent reports that the senior Politburo members respectively charged with supervising Soviet relations with foreign governments and foreign communist parties—Alexei Kosygin and Mikhail Suslov—were among those who had opposed the invasion. There was the insistence, all spring and summer, by the Czechs and Slovaks that their most implacable foes had been the supposedly "second line" Politburo members, the Ukrainian leader Pyotr Shelest and party secretary Andrei Kirilenko. And, of course, there was the startling Soviet turnabout toward Alexandre Dubček—embraced publicly by Brezhnev in Bratislava on August 3, arrested on August 21, anathemized by *Pravda* next day as a "right-wing opportunist" who had "betrayed socialism," brought secretly to Russia under armed guard, and then released on August 26 as a signatory of the Moscow "agreement."

These and other curious circumstances provoke two disturbing observations. First, the mysteries of Soviet decision-making appear even more inscrutable than during the Stalin era. For Stalin was an absolute ruler, and a careful reading of his personality and doctrines offered an accurate guide to perceptive statesmen of the calibre of Churchill and de Gaulle. There is no such personality today, and Soviet doctrines (including the most recent attempts to preach a "collective sovereignty") are more than ever impromptu, inconsistent rationalizations of actions hastily decided in the stress of internal and international struggle.

Second, collective leadership in the Kremlin is not, as some had thought, "intrinsically" and under all circumstances a force for conservatism and caution in Soviet policies, and therefore an element of stability in the world. In the crisis over Czechoslovakia, such leadership, anonymous as well as secret, proved to be a factor of instability, capable of generating rash, abrupt and objectively inexplicable turns. Indeed, for the foreign analyst seeking to discern Soviet intentions as well as capabilities, the current system of Soviet government—which one East European observer has labeled a system of "collective irresponsibility"—may well be the most dangerous possible. For it offers neither the relative clarity and continuity of traditional autocracy (Tsarist or Stalinist) nor the safeguards provided by an open society with autonomous, counter-vailing institutions and a free press. It need hardly be added that a system capable of such surprises as the invasion of August 20 is inherently capable of other surprises no less unpleasant. Not the least unfortunate consequence of the Soviet action will be to revive the "Pearl Harbor complex" among large sections of American public opinion.

Yet, even without the element of surprise, even had the Soviet armies marched a month earlier (that is, just after the Warsaw ultimatum), there would be ample grounds for rethinking more basic Western ideas on Soviet development. The most important such assumption has been the traditional liberal faith in the in-evitability of progressive evolution of Soviet Russia after the death of Stalin.

To some degree, this faith was based on a misreading, or faulty memory, of George F. Kennan's measured hopes (expressed in this journal in 1947 and 1951) for an eventual "mellowing of Soviet power" and "erosion from despotism." Ambassador Ken-nan carefully grounded these hopes on the condition that the West found "the strength and resourcefulness to contain Soviet power over a period of ten to fifteen years." The policy of con-tainment, as viewed by its author, involved not merely or even mainly an American arms race with the Soviet Union, but an unstinting political effort "to release and make effective all those forces in the world which, together with our own, can serve to convince the masters of the Kremlin that their grand design is a futile and unachievable one, persistence in which promises no solution of their own predicaments and dilemmas."

From the felicitous nouns "mellowing" and "erosion" rather than from Kennan's actual analysis, and under the impact of the Soviet Twentieth Party Congress and the peculiar charm of Nikita Khrushchev, it was, unfortunately, but a short step to illusions and pseudo-Marxist theories predicting that Soviet power would soon "mellow" and "erode" of itself. From 1956 onward, it was increasingly imagined that this withering of the Bolshevik essence would take place merely under the impact of the arms race, or of limited measures of arms control—without the West's playing its side of the political court, and with rhetorical expressions of willingness to negotiate in place of concrete, serious proposals for the future of the area in which the cold war originated: Central and Eastern Europe. It was largely believed that, however the United States might become absorbed in Southeast Asian jungles, Russia was progressing irreversibly toward rationality, restraint and traditional norms in its foreign policies, as well as toward more humane and responsive government of its own subjects.

To be sure, there were Hungary and Cuba, two Berlin crises and the ugliness of the Pasternak affair; yet these were viewed as unfortunate throwbacks to a Stalinist past which could never be revived. For each step backward (it was argued), there had been —or would be sooner or later—two steps forward. For the Soviet Union had advanced from famine and scarcity to relative economic abundance; the old Stalinist ideology had lost credibility and relevance; and the new generation of scientists, managers and technocrats was gradually compelling changes in the Soviet economic system which in turn would force modification of the political dictatorship.

Such beliefs captured popular imagination not merely because they suited universal hopes but because they contained more than a grain of truth. The Soviet ideology is, indeed, virtually indistinguishable from a crude, xenophobic Russian nationalism, and (as both cause and effect) the world communist movement is in a state of fairly rapid decomposition. The younger generation in Russia is largely free of both the misguided fervor and particular neuroses of its elders, who made and survived Stalin's bloody experiments. The Soviet intelligentsia, as its attitude toward Czechoslovakia showed, is as alienated from official policies as the Russian intelligentsia of a century ago. Straining for supremacy in armaments and space, Russia is losing the peaceful economic competition with the West which Khrushchev proclaimed; and, the longer her rulers resist profound social and political reforms, the more difficult and painful such reforms may have to be.

Nevertheless, despite changes, actual Kremlin policies over the last fifteen years have by no means conformed to a simple pattern of "two steps forward, one step back." A close reëxamination of the period since Stalin's death discloses three distinct phases: the great steps forward, crowned and symbolized by the Twentieth Congress, which took place almost immediately, in the disarray of the struggle over the succession; the seven years from the first Sputnik in October 1957 to the fall of Khrushchev, which witnessed sharply contradictory trends, now liberal and realistic, now dogmatic and adventurous, both at home and abroad; the Brezhnev period, which apart from modest corrections of some of Khrushchev's "hare-brained schemes" in economic management, has been marked by steady regression to Stalinist principles and methods in nearly all fields. If the publication in 1962 of Alexander Solzhenitsyn's *One Day in the Life of Ivan Denisovich* was rightly regarded as a sign of hope, the systematic persecution of that gifted writer since 1965 must be viewed with alarm. If the nuclear physicist Andrei Sakharov's underground blueprint for peaceful coexistence disclosed serious political dissent among the Soviet scientific élite, then it should be recalled that, after Sakharov hailed the Czechoslovak experiment, the Politburo and Red Army crushed it.

To be sure, a full-fledged return to the mass terror and paranoia of the Stalin years still appears improbable. Yet the current régime in the Kremlin is as clearly a deliberate "restoration" of the "old days" as the reign of Alexander III embodied a conscious effort to reimpose the autocratic order of Nicholas I.

There are all too many explanations for the current regression. The Soviet Union is a great power stubbornly embattled on two fronts, Western and Chinese; its rulers fear that any domestic disarray would be exploited by their rivals abroad. The Soviet state is also a multinational empire, in which harsh centralism appears the simplest response to nationalist stirrings on the periphery. The ruling generation of Soviet politicians is one of particular mediocrity, for it consists of precisely those members of the party, state and police apparatus capable of surviving or rising during Stalin's blood purges. The older generations of the intelligentsia were even more thoroughly decimated, terrorized or corrupted, so that their juniors lack leaders. In fact, two world wars, the civil war, two emigrations, successive purges and leveling economic policies have "decapitated" Russian society as no other in modern history, destroying or atomizing the very groups and classes which elsewhere (including nineteenth-century Russia) set moral and cultural standards and were the bearers of liberal ideas.

Among the great Soviet masses, there has been a paralysis or atrophy of what might be called the political sense—the ability of an individual to relate the grim, inchoate details of social life to a larger, coherent political framework and to draw independent conclusions in theory and practice. This political sense, as well as the capacity for civil courage, has been deadened by decades of demeaning propaganda, censorship, police control, exaltation of brutality and thorough isolation from the living world outside. It is the kind of atrophy familiar to students of postwar Germany, where the "middle generation" was (with very few exceptions) hopelessly disoriented by only twelve years of Hitler, Goebbels and Himmler.

The disorientation in Russia is even more grave after half a century; and it is a kind of miracle that young men like Pavel Litvinov and Yuri Galanskov have nevertheless arisen to reënact the lonely protests and martyrdom of the first radical "circles" in Tsarist Russia a century age. Yet such young men are relatively few, and those who sympathize with them are inhibited not merely by the sanctions of the Party and the KGB but by the indifference of the Soviet masses to purely political issues so long as the régime can continue the slow but steady raising of material standards.

All of this suggests that the prospects for positive evolution in Russia should be regarded with greater patience and caution; that neither technology, "prosperity" nor young people automatically produce significant political change in the short run; that the very existence of profound contradictions and rising libertarian aspirations in Russia may well (as they did a century ago) lead its rulers to repression rather than reform; and that a reassertion of police power, some form of military rule, or a new "strongman" must be considered as being at least as possible over the next decade as the "erosion from despotism" or the "violent upthrust of liberty" which Ambassador Kennan discussed at the dawn of the cold war. These may yet come to pass; but after the Czechoslovak experience, it would seem prudent to err on the side of pessimism.

The invasion of Czechoslovakia has also undermined a popular belief that liberalization in Eastern Europe could precede and compel change in the Soviet Union itself. This belief, based partly on the survival of certain East European traditions, partly on the indisputable appeal of Titoism, nevertheless ran counter to the facts of 1955–56, when it was Khrushchev, with his rehabilitation of Tito, spirit of Geneva and de-Stalinization at the Twentieth Congress, who set off the dramatic events in Hungary and Poland. The Czechoslovak experience shows even more clearly that the influence of Eastern Europe on the Kremlin is either limited or perverse. While the East German rebels of 1953 and the Hungarians of 1956 stood virtually alone, the Prague reformers in 1968 enjoyed the support of an "arithmetical majority" in Eastern Europe. They were openly supported by the communist governments of Rumania and Jugoslavia, covertly supported by Hungary, and enjoyed (for what that was worth) the indifference of Bulgaria and benevolent neutrality of Albania. None of this made any difference.

Indeed, a kind of Gresham's Law operated in the Eastern camp, with the dogmatists of occupied East Germany and Poland able to arouse the decisive support in Moscow of the forces of Soviet hegemonism and neo-Stalinism. Neither the legal, bloodless character of the Czechoslovak revolution nor the Prague Communists' repeated assurances of loyalty to the Warsaw Pact affected the outcome. It is realistic to assume, therefore, that no great change is possible in Eastern Europe without corresponding change in Russia itself—so long, that is, as the West (as in 1953, 1956 and 1968) refrains from trying to influence directly Soviet behavior in Eastern Europe.

III

There is no more thorny thicket in which to wander, in discussions of the cold war, than the complex of unexamined assumptions and ground rules conveyed by the phrases "status quo" and "spheres of influence." There is no need here to dwell on the particular controversies aroused by past misunderstandings (such as what did or did not happen at Yalta) or long-standing contradictions (such as the Allied refusal to recognize the Oder-Neisse frontier). It is sufficient to state broadly what has been the dominant Western view, namely:

(1) That the aim of Western policy, in Europe and elsewhere, is the preservation and perfection of the existing order until such time as the Kremlin may be prepared to discuss more just arrangements.

(2) That in Europe this status quo involves a clear line of East-West demarcation (originally drawn from Stettin to Trieste, now partitioning Berlin as well as Germany and rather fuzzy in Southeastern Europe).

(3) That, rightly or wrongly, the communist-ruled nations of Eastern Europe form a Soviet game preserve, or sphere of influence, on which the West can impinge only marginally through conventional diplomatic, commercial and cultural exchange.

These assumptions largely determined the Western stance toward Czechoslovakia in 1968. They were shown there to be highly dubious, if not self-defeating. In the summer of 1968, what in fact *was* the status quo in Czechoslovakia? Was it the free, open society created by the communist reformation between January and April? Was it the Czechoslovakia of Novotny's last five years —clearly in the throes of decisive metamorphosis? Was it the era of pure Stalinism, which led the country to economic ruin and its communists to total disillusion by the early 1960s? Or was the status quo in Czechoslovakia that which had been defined in the Yalta period—namely, the Benes-Gottwald coalition régime of 1944–47, which represented the model for the most extreme aspirations of the non-party "counterrevolutionaries" of 1968? Only if Stalinism is considered the eternal norm can the Soviet intervention properly be called a defense of the status quo.

In fact, the crisis enabled the Soviet Union to make at least one very important change in the state of affairs which had existed since the end of the war. Between 1945 and 1968, Czechoslovakia had been free of Soviet occupation troops. As a result of the undeterred invasion of August 20, however, the Western powers will now be confronted indefinitely with a minimum of six Soviet divisions in Czechoslovakia, possessing the most modern Russian equipment. These forces may not greatly alter the overall strategic balance between the United States and Russia. However, like the steady attrition of Allied rights in Greater Berlin since 1945, the Soviet occupation of Czechoslovakia has considerably reduced the Allies' capacity for diplomatic manœuvre along the most critical sector of the East-West line.

The inadequacy of "status quo" thinking is even more evident in considering the current object of Kremlin pressures, Rumania. Which status quo should Soviet power be permitted to restore therein place of the increasingly independent Rumania of 1964–68? The loyal but unoccupied Rumania of 1958–63? Or the Rumania occupied and controlled by Soviet armed forces before 1957? All may hope that Soviet pressures remain nonmilitary. Yet it should be recognized that the reëntry of Soviet troops into Rumania, a decade or more after their withdrawal, would surely create a new and serious threat to independent Jugoslavia—and (given Bulgaria's traditional posture) probably to Greece and Turkey as well.

It is doubtless be argued that, whatever the wishes of its rulers or people, historically Rumania has, like Czechoslovakia, become part of the acknowledged Soviet sphere of influence. This sphere was most candidly defined by Stalin when he told Djilas in 1944 that each side imposed its system as far as its armies could march. It was formalized by Khrushchev's organization of the Warsaw Pact in 1955. Its immutability has been tacitly accepted by the West in the belief that organization of Europe into two neat military blocs provides greater security than any attempt to risk the free play of political change.

Several objections must be made to this view. First, the frozen bloc system leaves at least four nations—Finland, Albania, Austria and Jugoslavia—in an anomalous position. The West has no obligations whatever to Finland or Albania; and to Austria, only the obligation to consult among the Big Four. Jugoslavia's position is ambiguous. There is no formal Western commitment to its independence; yet the establishment of Soviet military power on the Adriatic could hardly be tolerated. There are grounds here for tragic miscalculation.

Second, permanent acceptance of Soviet control over the Warsaw Pact nations not merely forecloses significant internal change within them but condemns all Europe to the dangers and frustrations arising from the unnatural division of that continent. There have been three major crises over Berlin in the past two decades, and there is little reason to suppose that the Kremlin and its East German agents will not try again. Soviet policy toward West Germany itself has been disquieting. Although Khrushchev sought in 1955 and again in 1964 to open a dialogue with Bonn, his successors have reverted to Stalin's tragic "the worse, the better" strategy of the 1930s. Moscow has done all in its power to keep West Germany in a state of frustration and tension indefinitely, with the obvious hope of stimulating the sort of right-wing nationalist reaction which would either isolate Bonn morally from its allies, or lead to the fulfillment of the eternal dream of anti-Western reactionaries in both Germany and Russia—another Tauroggen, Rapallo or Hitler-Stalin Pact in which the price for some relief of legitimate German national aspirations would be the expulsion of Western influence beyond the Rhine.

Yet, even should these Stalinist tactics toward Germany fail, acceptance of the division of Europe into two hostile armed camps, with no reasonable hope for an abatement of the cold war, involves the condemnation of yet new generations (in the United States as well as Europe) to a future without horizons—to the lifelong strain of the ever costlier, deadlier armaments race. Quite apart from the danger of nuclear and rocket accidents, such prolongation of cold-war frustrations can breed all too easily among the young a spirit of nihilism which might well foster irresponsible illusions or dangerous adventures. Memory is short; and already to "new left" and anarchist students in 1968, the cold war was some kind of myth conjured up by the Western "Establishment" rather than the tragic result of the Soviet armed presence in the heart of Europe.

Finally, Western acquiescence in permanent Soviet rule east of the Elbe may well be, over the long run, a prescription for ultimate suicide on a global scale. For Western respect for the Soviet sphere of influence has been a purely one-sided undertaking. The Kremlin has not hesitated, whenever opportunities arose, to move into areas formerly part of the Western sphere. Despite the Monroe Doctrine, the Kremlin took advantage of the Cuban Revolution to win a new ally and create a center of Latin American mischief ninety miles from the U.S. coast. Similarly, in the wake of three Israeli-Arab wars, the Soviet Union has gained a political influence in the Middle East and a naval presence in the Mediterranean previously denied to both the Tsars and Stalin. Nor did Khrushchev's successors hesitate to pour an estimated billion dollars annually into Vietnamese communist military operations which, by enmeshing the United States in a hopeless quagmire, produced deep fissures in American society itself.

Similar opportunities will doubtless occur in the future, if only in the undeveloped world, where the population explosion, tribalism, falling raw material prices and the inadequacy of received tradition are an invitation to demagogy and adventurism. Yet even in the West, the stability, prosperity and alliance of the last two decades have not been divinely decreed as eternal. It does not take great imagination to foresee all sorts of possible crises in the future—American absorption in domestic racial conflict, a breakdown in the world monetary system, new civil conflict in Spain, war over Cyprus, political instability in France or Italy. Can anyone doubt that the Kremlin would seek to exploit any such opportunities—as well as the certain emergence of new Castros, Lumumbas and Sukarnos—to the maximum disadvantage of the West?

Peace rests ultimately on a balance of power which is political as well as military. The political balance is a subtle tissue composed of diverse elements including hope and will; and it can collapse as rapidly as the Versailles system did between 1934 and 1938. The longer the Kremlin is free to scavenge among the unresolved conflicts of the West and the Third World, while its occupation of half of Europe is permanently guaranteed, the greater the danger that sooner or later the precarious political balance will be upset. Even the best football team cannot indefinitely survive a game in which its adversaries are entitled to recover all its fumbles as well as all their own, and in which movement is permanently restricted to one end of the field.

In such a perspective, and especially when the United States has begun to weary of "playing the world's policeman," the time has surely come to reappraise the West's thoughtless and inconsistent passivity toward the future development of Central and Eastern Europe; and to elaborate, with the aid of the genuine democratic forces in Germany as well as the independent neutral states of Europe, a constructive and realistic approach to the problem of a German peace treaty. The details of concrete proposals are clearly beyond the scope of this article, but they would inevitably involve modification of the existing bloc system as well as some measure of disengagement of American and Soviet forces from Central Europe. Although in the present mood of Kremlin intransigence no such proposals would soon be accepted, they are necessary to clarify European realities—to isolate irrational, chauvinistic elements in Germany and Poland as well as in Russia, and to provide future Soviet leaders with an honorable alternative to the present Germanophobia and military rule of Eastern Europe.

At the same time, it would be tragic if the West did not now realize the necessity of framing a qualitatively different response for the next "Czechoslovakia" or "Hungary," with regard both to the Rumanian case already at hand and to future eventualities. It is neither necessary nor desirable to return to the "dirty tricks" approach symbolized by the Albanian "insurrection" entrusted by Western statesmen to Kim Philby; nor to the misleading "liberation" propaganda conducted by some Western radio stations in the 1950s; nor indeed to any form of interference, overt or covert, in the internal affairs of East European nations.

However, if and when in future the legitimate authorities of any of the East European nations make clear their desire for greater independence, the West should be prepared, swiftly and decisively, to deter Kremlin reprisals by extending to such nations the same assistance and protection which it offered to Jugoslavia in 1948. What is required is neither military bases, pacts nor conspiracies, neither restoration of the old order nor utopian promises—but prompt, vigorous defense of the right to independence and nonalignment of communist as well as other sovereign states.

VII

THE UNITED STATES AND
INTERNATIONAL ORGANIZATION

THE CONDITIONS OF PERMANENT PEACE*

BY

WOODROW WILSON

[1917]

I have sought this opportunity to address you because I thought that I owed it to you, as the council associated with me in the final determination of our international obligations, to disclose to you without reserve the thought and purpose that have been taking form in my mind in regard to the duty of our Government in the days to come when it will be necessary to lay afresh and upon a new plan the foundations of peace among nations.

It is inconceivable that the people of the United States should play no part in that great enterprise. To take part in such a service will be the opportunity for which they have sought to prepare themselves by the very principles and purposes of their polity and the approved practices of their Government ever since the days when they set up a new nation in the high and honorable hope that it might in all that it was and did show mankind the way to liberty. They cannot in honor withhold the service to which they are now about to be challenged. They do not wish to withhold it. But they owe it to themselves and to the other nations of the world to state the conditions under which they will feel free to render it.

That service is nothing less than this, to add their authority and their power to the authority and force of other nations to guarantee peace and justice throughout the world. Such a settlement cannot now be long postponed. It is right that before it comes this Government should frankly formulate the conditions upon which it would feel justified in asking our people to approve its formal and

---

*An address by the President delivered to the Senate, Jan. 22, 1917. From *Messages and Papers of the Presidents*, Vol. XVII. Published by Bureau of National Literature, Inc.

solemn adherence to a League for Peace. I am here to attempt to state those conditions.

The present war must first be ended; but we owe it to candor and to a just regard for the opinion of mankind to say that, so far as our participation in guarantees of future peace is concerned, it makes a great deal of difference in what way and upon what terms it is ended. The treaties and agreements which bring it to an end must embody terms which will create a peace that is worth guaranteeing and preserving, a peace that will win the approval of mankind, not merely a peace that will serve the several interests and immediate aims of the nations engaged. We shall have no voice in determining what those terms shall be, but we shall, I feel sure, have a voice in determining whether they shall be made lasting or not by the guarantees of a universal covenant; and our judgment upon what is fundamental and essential as a condition precedent to permanency should be spoken now, not afterwards when it may be too late.

No covenant or co-operative peace that does not include the peoples of the New World can suffice to keep the future safe against war; and yet there is only one sort of peace that the peoples of America could join in guaranteeing. The elements of that peace must be elements that engage the confidence and satisfy the principles of the American governments, elements consistent with their political faith and with the practical convictions which the peoples of America have once for all embraced and undertaken to defend.

I do not mean to say that any American government would throw any obstacle in the way of any terms of peace the governments now at war might agree upon, or seek to upset them when made, whatever they might be. I only take it for granted that mere terms of peace between the belligerents will not satisfy even the belligerents themselves. Mere agreements may not make peace secure. It will be absolutely necessary that a force be created as a guarantor of the permanency of the settlement so much greater than the force of any nation now engaged or any alliance hitherto formed or projected that no nation, no probable combination of nations could face or withstand it. If the peace presently to be made is to endure, it must be a peace made secure by the organized major force of mankind.

The terms of the immediate peace agreed upon will determine whether it is a peace for which such a guarantee can be secured. The question upon which the whole future peace and policy of the world depends is this: Is the present war a struggle for a just and secure peace, or only for a new balance of power? If it be only a struggle for a new balance of power, who will guarantee, who can guarantee, the stable equilibrium of the new arrangement? Only a tranquil Europe can be a stable Europe. There must be, not a balance of power, but a community of power; not organized rivalries, but an organized common peace.

Fortunately we have received very explicit assurances on this point. The statesmen of both of the groups of nations now arrayed against one another have said, in terms that could not be misinterpreted, that it was no part of the purpose they had in mind to crush their antagonists. But the implications of these assurances may not be equally clear to all—may not be the same on both sides of the water. I think it will be serviceable if I attempt to set forth what we understand them to be.

They imply, first of all, that it must be a peace without victory. It is not pleasant to say this. I beg that I may be permitted to put my own interpretation upon it and that it may be understood that no other interpretation was in my thought. I am seeking only to face realities and to face them without soft concealments. Victory would mean peace forced upon the loser, a victor's terms imposed upon the vanquished. It would be accepted in humiliation, under duress, at an intolerable sacrifice, and would leave a sting, a resentment, a bitter memory upon which terms of peace would rest, not permanently, but only as upon quicksand. Only a peace between equals can last. Only a peace the very principle of which is equality and a common participation in a common benefit. The right state of mind, the right feeling between nations, is as necessary for a lasting peace as is the just settlement of vexed questions of territory or of racial and national allegiance.

The equality of nations upon which peace must be founded if it is to last must be an equality of rights; the guarantees exchanged must neither recognize nor imply a difference between big nations and small, between those that are powerful and those that are weak. Right must be based upon the common strength, not upon the individual strength, of the nations upon whose concert peace will depend. Equality of territory or of resources there of course cannot be; nor any other sort of equality not gained in the ordinary peaceful and legitimate development of the peoples themselves. But no one asks or expects anything more than an equality of rights. Mankind is looking now for freedom of life, not for equipoises of power.

And there is a deeper thing involved than even equality of right among organized nations. No peace can last, or ought to last, which does not recognize and accept the principle that governments derive all their just powers from the consent of the governed, and that no right anywhere exists to hand peoples about from sovereignty to sovereignty as if they were property. I take it for granted, for instance, if I may venture upon a single example, that statesmen everywhere are agreed that there should be a united, independent, and autonomous Poland, and that henceforth inviolable security of life, of worship, and of industrial and social development should be guaranteed to all peoples who have lived hitherto under the power of governments devoted to a faith and purpose hostile to their own.

I speak of this, not because of any desire to exalt an abstract political principle which has always been held very dear by those who have sought to build up liberty in America, but for the same reason that I have spoken of the other conditions of peace which seem to me clearly indispensable—because I wish frankly to uncover realities. Any peace which does not recognize and accept this principle will inevitably be upset. It will not rest upon the affections or the convictions of mankind. The ferment of spirit of whole populations will fight subtly and constantly against it, and all the world will sympathize. The world can be at peace only if its life is stable, and there can be no stability where the will is in rebellion, where there is not tranquility of spirit and a sense of justice, of freedom, and of right.

So far as practicable, moreover, every great people now struggling towards a full development of its resources and of its powers should be assured a direct outlet to the great highways of the sea. Where this cannot be done by the cession of territory, it can no doubt be done by the neutralization of direct rights of way under the general guarantee which will assure the peace itself. With a right comity of arrangement no nation need be shut away from free access to the open paths of the world's commerce.

And the paths of the sea must alike in law and in fact be free. The freedom of the seas is the *sine qua non* of peace, equality, and co-operation. No doubt a somewhat radical reconsideration of many of the rules of international practice hitherto thought to be established may be necessary in order to make the seas indeed free and common in practically all circumstances for the use of mankind, but the motive for such changes is convincing and compelling. There can be no trust or intimacy between the peoples of the world without them. The free, constant, unthreatened intercourse of nations is an essential part of the process of peace and of development. It need not be difficult either to define or to secure the freedom of the seas if the governments of the world sincerely desire to come to an agreement concerning it.

It is a problem closely connected with the limitation of naval armaments and the co-operation of the navies of the world in keeping the seas at once free and safe. And the question of limiting naval armaments opens the wider and perhaps more difficult question of the limitation of armies and of all programs of military preparation. Difficult and delicate as these questions are, they must be faced with the utmost candor and decided in a spirit of real accommodation if peace is to come with healing in its wings, and come to stay. Peace cannot be had without concession and sacrifice. There can be no sense of safety and equality among the nations if great preponderating armaments are henceforth to continue here and there to be built up and maintained. The statesmen of the world must plan for peace and nations must adjust and accommodate their policy to it as they have planned for war and made ready for pitiless contest and rivalry. The question of armaments, whether on land or sea, is the most immediately and intensely practical question connected with the future fortunes of nations of mankind.

I have spoken upon these great matters without reserve and with the utmost explicitness because it has seemed to me to be necessary if the world's yearning desire for peace was anywhere to find free voice and utterance. Perhaps I am the only person in high authority amongst all the peoples of the world who is at liberty to speak and hold nothing back. I am speaking as an individual, and yet I am speaking also, of course, as the responsible head of a great government, and I feel confident that I have said what the people of the United States would wish me to say. May I not add that I hope and believe that I am in effect speaking for liberals and friends of humanity in every nation and of every program of liberty? I would fain believe that I am speaking for the silent mass of mankind everywhere who have as yet had no place or opportunity to speak their real hearts out concerning the death and ruin they see to have come already upon the persons and the homes they hold most dear.

And in holding out the expectation that the people and Government of the United States will join the other civilized nations of the world in guaranteeing the permanence of peace upon such terms as I have named I speak with the greater boldness and confidence because it is clear to every man who can think that there is in this promise no breach in either our traditions or our policy as a nation, but a fulfillment, rather, of all that we have professed or striven for.

I am proposing, as it were, that the nations should with one accord adopt the doctrine of President Monroe as the doctrine of the world: that no nation should seek to extend its polity over any other nation or people, but that every people should be left free to determine its own polity, its own way of development, unhindered, unthreatened, unafraid, the little along with the great and powerful.

I am proposing that all nations henceforth avoid entangling alliances which would draw them into competitions of power, catch them in a net of intrigue and selfish rivalry, and disturb their own affairs with influences intruded from without. There is no entangling alliance in a concert of power. When all unite to act in the same sense and with the same purpose all act in the common interest and are free to live their own lives under a common protection.

I am proposing government by the consent of the governed; that freedom of the seas which in international conference after conference representatives of the United States have urged with the eloquence of those who are the convinced disciples of liberty; and that moderation of armaments which makes of armies and navies a power for order merely, not an instrument of aggression or of selfish violence.

These are American principles, American policies. We could stand for no others. And they are also the principles and policies of forward-looking men and women everywhere, of every modern nation, of every enlightened community. They are the principles of mankind and must prevail.

THE CASE FOR
NON-ENTANGLEMENT*

BY

WILLIAM E. BORAH

[1919]

Mr. President, after Mr. Lincoln had been elected President before he assumed the duties of the office and at a time when all indications were to the effect that we would soon be in the midst of civil strife, a friend from the city of Washington wrote him for instructions. Mr. Lincoln wrote back in a single line, "Entertain no compromise; have none of it." That states the position I occupy at this time and which I have, in an humble way, occupied from the first contention in regard to this proposal.

My objections to the league have not been met by the reservations.** I desire to state wherein my objections have not been met. Let us see what our attitude will be toward Europe and what our position will be with reference to the other nations of the world after we shall have entered the league with the present reservations written therein. With all due respect to those who think that they have accomplished a different thing and challenging no man's intellectual integrity or patriotism, I do not believe the reservations have met the fundamental propositions which are involved in this contest.

When the league shall have been formed, we shall be a member of what is known as the council of the league. Our accredited representative will sit in judgment with the accredited representatives of the other members of the league to pass upon the concerns not only of our country but of all Europe and all Asia and the entire world. Our accredited representatives will be members of

---

*From the Senate debate on the ratification of the Covenant of the League of Nations on November 19, 1919. *Congressional Record*, Vol. 58, Part 9. William E. Borah (1865–1940), Republican, was United States Senator from Idaho, 1907–1940, and chairman of the Foreign Relations Committee, 1924–1932.

**EDITOR'S NOTE: This is a reference to the reservations proposed by Senator H. C. Lodge, reserving total freedom of action for the United States. Woodrow Wilson considered them as nullifying and defeating the provisions of the Covenant.

the assembly. They will sit there to represent the judgment of these 110,000,000 people—more then—just as we are accredited here to represent our constituencies. We can not send our representatives to sit in council with the representatives of the other great nations of the world with mental reservations as to what we shall do in case their judgment shall not be satisfactory to us. If we go to the council or to the assembly with any other purpose than that of complying in good faith and in absolute integrity with all upon which the council or the assembly may pass, we shall soon return to our country with our self-respect forfeited and the public opinion of the world condemnatory.

Why need you gentlemen across the aisle worry about a reservation here or there when we are sitting in the council and in the assembly and bound by every obligation in morals, which the President said was supreme above that of law, to comply with the judgment which our representative and the other representatives finally form? Shall we go there, Mr. President, to sit in judgment, and in case that judgment works for peace join with our allies, but in case it works for war withdraw our cooperation? How long would we stand as we now stand, a great Republic commanding the respect and holding the leadership of the world, if we should adopt any such course? . . .

We have said, Mr. President, that we would not send our troops abroad without the consent of Congress. Pass by now for a moment the legal proposition. If we create executive functions, the Executive will perform those functions without the authority of Congress. Pass that question by and go to the other question. Our members of the council are there. Our members of the assembly are there. Article 11* is complete, and it authorizes the

---

* EDITOR'S NOTE: Article 11 of the Covenant stipulated:

1. Any war or threat of war, whether immediately affecting any of the Members of the League or not, is hereby declared a matter of concern to the whole League, and the League shall take any action that may be deemed wise and effectual to safeguard the peace of nations. In case any such emergency should arise the Secretary-General shall on the request of any Member of the League forthwith summon a meeting of the Council.

2. It is also declared to be the friendly right of each Member of the League to bring to the attention of the Assembly or of the Council any circumstances whatever affecting international relations which threatens to disturb international peace or the good understanding between nations upon which peace depends.

league, a member of which is our representative, to deal with matters of peace and war, and the league through its council and its assembly deals with the matter, and our accredited representative joins with the others in deciding upon a certain course, which involves a question of sending troops. What will the Congress of the United States do? What right will it have left, except the bare technical right to refuse, which as a moral proposition it will not dare to exercise? Have we not been told day by day for the last nine months that the Senate of the United States, a coordinate part of the treaty-making power, should accept this league as it was written because the wise men sitting at Versailles had so written it, and has not every possible influence and every source of power in public opinion been organized and directed against the Senate to compel it to do that thing? How much stronger will be the moral compulsion upon the Congress of the United States when we ourselves have indorsed the proposition of sending our accredited representatives there to vote for us?

Ah, but you say that there must be unanimous consent, and that there is vast protection in unanimous consent.

I do not wish to speak disparagingly; but has not every division and dismemberment of every nation which has suffered dismemberment taken place by unanimous consent for the last 300 years? Did not Prussia and Austria and Russia by unanimous consent divide Poland? Did not the United States and Great Britain and Japan and Italy and France divide China and give Shantung to Japan? Was that not a unanimous decision? Close the doors upon the diplomats of Europe, let them sit in secret, give them the material to trade on, and there always will be unanimous consent.

How did Japan get unanimous consent? I want to say here, in my parting words upon this proposition, that I have no doubt the outrage upon China was quite as distasteful to the President of the United States as it is to me. But Japan said: "I will not sign your treaty unless you turn over to me Shantung, to be turned back at my discretion," and you know how Japan's discretion operates with reference to such things. And so, when we are in the league, and our accredited representatives are sitting at Geneva, and a question of great moment arises, Japan, or Russia, or Germany, or Great Britain will say, "Unless this matter is adjusted in this way I will depart from your league." It is the same thing, operating in the same way, only under a different date and under a little different circumstances.

Mr. President, if you have enough territory, if you have enough material, if you have enough subject peoples to trade upon and divide, there will be no difficulty about unanimous consent.

Do our Democratic friends ever expect any man to sit as a member of the council or as a member of the Assembly equal in intellectual power and in standing before the world with that of our representative at Versailles? Do you expect a man to sit in the council who will have made more pledges, and I shall assume made them in sincerity, for self-determination and for the rights of small peoples, than had been made by our accredited representative? And yet, what became of it? The unanimous consent was obtained nevertheless.

But take another view of it. We are sending to the council one man. That one man represents 110,000,000 people.

Here, sitting in the Senate, we have two from every State in the Union, and over in the other House we have Representatives in accordance with population, and the responsibility is spread out in accordance with our obligations to our constituency. But now we are transferring to one man the stupendous power of representing the sentiment and convictions of 110,000,000 people in tremendous questions which may involve the peace or may involve the war of the world.

However you view the question of unanimous consent, it does not protect us.

What is the result of all this? We are in the midst of all of the affairs of Europe. We have entangled ourselves with all European concerns. We have joined in alliance with all the European nations which have thus far joined the league, and all nations which may be admitted to the league. We are sitting there dabbling in their affairs and intermeddling in their concerns. In other words, Mr. President—and this comes to the question which is fundamental with me—we have forfeited and surrendered, once and for all, the great policy of "no entangling alliances" upon which the strength of this Republic has been founded for 150 years. . . .

Let us not underestimate that.   There has never been an hour
since the Venezuelan difficulty that there has not been operating
in this country, fed by domestic and foreign sources, a powerful
propaganda for the destruction of the doctrine of no entangling
alliances.

Lloyd-George is reported to have said just a few days before the
conference met at Versailles that Great Britain could give up much,
and would be willing to sacrifice much, to have America withdraw
from that policy.   That was one of the great objects of the entire
conference at Versailles, so far as the foreign representatives were
concerned.   Clemenceau and Lloyd-George and others like them
were willing to make any reasonable sacrifice which would draw
America away from her isolation and into the internal affairs and
concerns of Europe.   This league of nations, with or without
reservations, whatever else it does or does not do, does surrender
and sacrifice that policy; and once having surrendered and become
a part of the European concerns, where, my friends, are you going
to stop?

You have put in here a reservation upon the Monroe doctrine.
I think that, in so far as language could protect the Monroe doctrine, it has been protected.   But as a practical proposition, as a
working proposition, tell me candidly, as men familiar with the
history of your country and of other countries, do you think that
you can intermeddle in European affairs; and, secondly, never to
permit Europe to.

When Mr. Monroe wrote to Jefferson, he asked him his view
upon the Monroe doctrine, and Mr. Jefferson said, in substance,
our first and primary obligation should be never to interfere in
European affairs; and, secondly, never to permit Europe to interfere
in our affairs.

He understood, as every wise and practical man understands,
that if we intermeddle in her affairs, if we help to adjust her conditions, inevitably and remorselessly Europe then will be carried
into our affairs, in spite of anything you can write upon paper.

We can not protect the Monroe doctrine unless we protect the
basic principle upon which it rests, and that is the Washington
policy.   I do not care how earnestly you may endeavor to do so,
as a practical working proposition your league will come to the

United States. Will you permit me to digress long enough to read a paragraph from a great French editor upon this particular phase of the matter, Mr. Stephen Lausanne, editor of *Le Matin*, of Paris?

When the executive council of the league of nations fixes "the reasonable limits of the armament of Peru"; when it shall demand information concerning the naval program of Brazil; when it shall tell Argentina what shall be the measure of the "contribution to the armed forces to protect the signatories of the social covenant"; when it shall demand the immediate registration of the treaty between the United States and Canada at the seat of the league; it will control, whether it wills or no, the destinies of America. And when the American States shall be obliged to take a hand in every war or menace of war in Europe (art. 11), they will necessarily fall afoul of the fundamental principle laid down by Monroe, which was that Americans should never take part in a European war.

If the league takes in the world, then Europe must mix in the affairs of America; if only Europe is included, then America will violate of necessity her own doctrine by intermixing in the affairs of Europe.

If the league includes the affairs of the world, does it not include the affairs of all the world? Is there any limitation of the jurisdiction of the council or of the assembly upon the question of peace or war? Does it not have now, under the reservations, the same as it had before, the power to deal with all matters of peace or war throughout the entire world? How shall you keep from meddling in the affairs of Europe or keep Europe from meddling in the affairs of America?

Mr. President, there is another and even a more commanding reason why I shall record my vote against this treaty. It imperils what I conceive to be the underlying, the very first principles of this Republic. It is in conflict with the right of our people to govern themselves free from all restraint, legal or moral, of foreign powers. It challenges every tenet of my political faith. If this faith were one of my own contriving, if I stood here to assert principles of government of my own evolving, I might well be charged with intolerable presumption, for we all recognize the ability of those who urge a different course. But I offer in justification of my course nothing of my own save the deep and abiding reverence I have for those whose policies I humbly but most ardently support.

I claim no merit save fidelity to American principles and devotion to American ideals as they were wrought out from time to time by those who built the Republic and as they have been extended and maintained throughout these years. In opposing the treaty I do nothing more than decline to renounce and tear out of my life the sacred traditions which throughout 50 years have been translated into my whole intellectual and moral being. I will not, I can not, give up my belief that America must, not alone for the happiness of her own people, but for the moral guidance and greater contentment of the world, be permitted to live her own life. Next to the tie which binds a man to his God is the tie which binds a man to his country, and all schemes, all plans, however ambitious and fascinating they seem in their proposal, but which would embarrass or entangle and impede or shackle her sovereign will, which would compromise her freedom of action, I unhesitatingly put behind me. . . .

Senators, even in an hour so big with expectancy we should not close our eyes to the fact that democracy is something more, vastly more, than a mere form of government by which society is restrained into free and orderly life. It is a moral entity, a spiritual force, as well. And these are things which live only and alone in the atmosphere of liberty. The foundation upon which democracy rests is faith in the moral instincts of the people. Its ballot boxes, the franchise, its laws, and constitutions are but the outward manifestations of the deeper and more essential thing— a continuing trust in the moral purposes of the average man and woman. When this is lost or forfeited your outward forms, however democratic in terms, are a mockery. Force may find expression through institutions democratic in structure equal with the simple and more direct processes of a single supreme ruler. These distinguishing virtues of a real republic you can not commingle with the discordant and destructive forces of the Old World and still preserve them. You can not yoke a government whose fundamental maxim is that of liberty to a government whose first law is that of force and hope to preserve the former. These things are in eternal war, and one must ultimately destroy the other. You may still keep for a time the outward form, you may still delude yourself, as others have done in the past, with appearances and symbols, but when you shall have committed this Republic to a scheme of world control based upon force, upon the combined military force of the four great nations of the world, you will have soon destroyed the atmosphere of freedom, of confidence in the self-governing capacity of the masses, in which alone a democracy may thrive. We may become one of the four dictators of the world, but we shall no longer be master of our own spirit. And what shall it profit us as a Nation if we shall go forth to the dominion of the earth and share with others the glory of world control and lose that fine sense of confidence in the people, the soul of democracy?

Look upon the scene as it is now presented. Behold the task we are to assume, and then contemplate the method by which we are to deal with this task. Is the method such as to address itself to a Government "conceived in liberty and dedicated to the proposition that all men are created equal"? When this league, this combination, is formed four great powers representing the dominant people will rule one-half of the inhabitants of the globe as subject peoples—rule by force, and we shall be a party to the rule of force. There is no other way by which you can keep people in subjection. You must either give them independence, recognize their rights as nations to live their own life and to set up their own form of government, or you must deny them these things by force. That is the scheme, the method proposed by the league. It proposes no other. We will in time become inured to its inhuman precepts and its soulless methods, strange as this doctrine now seems to a free people. If we stay with our contract, we will come in time to declare with our associates that force—force, the creed of the Prussian military oligarchy—is after all the true foundation upon which must rest all stable governments. Korea, despoiled and bleeding at every pore; India, sweltering in ignorance and burdened with inhuman taxes after more than a hundred years of dominant rule; Egypt, trapped and robbed of her birthright; Ireland, with 700 years of sacrifice for independence—this is the task, this is the atmosphere, and this is the creed in and under which we are to keep alive our belief in the moral purposes and self-governing capacity of the people, a belief without which the Republic must disintegrate and die. The maxim of liberty will soon give way to the rule of blood and iron. We have been pleading here for our Constitution. Conform this league, it has been said, to the technical terms of our charter, and all will be well. But I declare to you that we must go further and conform to those sentiments and passions for justice and freedom which are essential to the existence of democracy. You must respect not territorial boundaries, not territorial integrity, but you must respect and preserve the sentiments and passions for justice and for freedom which God in His infinite wisdom has planted so deep in the human heart that no form of tyranny however brutal, no persecution however prolonged, can wholly uproot and kill. Respect nationality, respect justice, respect freedom, and you may have some hope of peace, but not so if you make your standard the standard of tyrants and despots, the protection of real estate regardless of how it is obtained.

Sir, we are told that this treaty means peace. Even so, I would not pay the price. Would you purchase peace at the cost of any part of our independence? We could have had peace in 1776—the price was high, but we could have had it. James Otis, Sam Adams, Hancock, and Warren were surrounded by those who urged peace and British rule. All through that long and trying struggle, particularly when the clouds of adversity lowered upon the cause, there was a cry of peace—let us have peace. We could have had peace in 1860; Lincoln was counseled by men of great influence and accredited wisdom to let our brothers—and, thank Heaven, they are brothers—depart in peace. But the tender, loving Lincoln, bending under the fearful weight of impending civil war, an apostle of peace, refused to pay the price, and a reunited country will praise his name forevermore—bless it because he refused peace at the price of national honor and national integrity. Peace upon any other basis than national independence, peace purchased at the cost of any part of our national integrity, is fit only for slaves, and even when purchased at such a price it is a delusion, for it can not last.

But your treaty does not mean peace—far, very far, from it. If we are to judge the future by the past it means war. Is there any guaranty of peace other than the guaranty which comes of the control of the war-making power by the people? Yet what great rule of democracy does the treaty leave unassailed? The people

in whose keeping alone you can safely lodge the power of peace or
war nowhere, at no time and in no place, have any voice in this
scheme for world peace. Autocracy which has bathed the world
in blood for centuries reigns supreme. Democracy is everywhere
excluded. This you say, means peace.

Can you hope for peace when love of country is disregarded in
your scheme, when the spirit of nationality is rejected, even
scoffed at? . . .

I can not get my consent to exchange the doctrine of George
Washington for the doctrine of Frederick the Great translated
into mendacious phrases of peace. I go back to that serene and
masterful soul who pointed the way to power and glory for the
new and then weak Republic, and whose teachings and admoni-
tions even in our majesty and dominance we dare not disregard. . . .

Reflect for a moment over his achievements. He led the Revolutionary Army to victory. He was the very first to suggest a union
instead of a confederacy. He presided over and counseled with
great wisdom the convention which framed the Constitution. He
guided the Government through its first perilous years. He gave
dignity and stability and honor to that which was looked upon by
the world as a passing experiment, and finally, my friends, as his
own peculiar and particular contribution to the happiness of his
countrymen and to the cause of the Republic, he gave us his great
foreign policy under which we have lived and prospered and
strengthened for nearly a century and a half. This policy is the
most sublime confirmation of his genius as a statesman. It was
then, and it now is, an indispensable part of our whole scheme of
government. It is to-day, a vital, indispensable element in our
entire plan, purpose, and mission as a nation. To abandon it is
nothing less than a betrayal of the American people. I say betrayal deliberately, in view of the suffering and the sacrifice which
will follow in the wake of such a course.

But under the stress and strain of these extraordinary days, when
strong men are being swept down by the onrushing forces of disorder and change, when the most sacred things of life, the most
cherished hopes of a Christian world seem to yield to the mad
forces of discontent—just such days as Washington passed through
when the mobs of Paris, wild with new liberty and drunk with

power, challenged the established institutions of all the world, but his steadfast soul was unshaken—under these conditions come again we are about to abandon this policy so essential to our happiness and tranquility as a people and our stability as a Government. No leader with his commanding influence and his unquailing courage stands forth to stem the current. But what no leader can or will do experience, bitter experience, and the people of this country in whose keeping, after all, thank God, is the Republic, will ultimately do. If we abandon his leadership and teachings, we will go back. We will return to this policy. Americanism shall not, can not, die. We may go back in sackcloth and ashes, but we will return to the faith of the fathers. America will live her own life. The independence of this Republic will have its defenders. Thousands have suffered and died for it and their sons and daughters are not of the breed who will be betrayed into the hands of foreigners. . . .

SOVEREIGNTY AND THE UNITED NATIONS*

BY

ARTHUR H. VANDENBERG

[1945]

Mr. President, having thus briefly summarized my affirmative approach to this subject, and recalling to the Senate that I have already discussed these mechanisms in great detail upon a previous occasion, it occurs to me that perhaps the chief service I might briefly render today would be frankly to face what seem to be some of the misgivings which still linger in some minds. Therefore, without any thought of complaining against the free expression of anybody's opinion, I want most respectfully to turn my attention very briefly to what it seemed to me was a rather complete adverse summary which recently appeared in a two-column editorial in certain important metropolitan newspapers which seemed to symbolize what I believe to be these misconceptions. I use this as my brief text because the editorial in essence seemed to be a personal challenge addressed to me. I quote from the editorial in its final summary:

> This United Nations Charter embodies Roosevelt's dream of a postwar superstate. It entails the destruction of parts of the written Constitution, without a by-your-leave to the American people. That apparently is O. K. with VANDENBERG and his cohorts.

Mr. President, I wish to say for the *Record* and with elementary consideration for my own status as, I believe, a loyal American, that this is a totally unjustified, unwarranted, and insupportable indictment of the Charter. With the greatest respect for the opinions of those who differ with me, I deny every factual word of it. This would be of no importance except as I am using the

*From the Senate debate on the Charter of the United Nations, July 23, 1945. *Congressional Record*, vol. 91, part 6. Arthur H. Vandenberg (1884–1951), Republican, was United States Senator from Michigan, 1928–1951, and delegate to many international conferences.

editorial to illustrate what I believe to be these remaining misconceptions so far as they still linger in a very small minority of our public opinion.

Mr. President, if the "United Nations Charter embodies Roosevelt's dreams of a postwar superstate," then our late President was guiltless of "dreaming" about any "superstate" at all. There is no "superstate," even remotely or by the widest indirection, in this Charter. If we have taken care of anything in writing this Charter we have scrupulously taken care of that. Such a fantastic charge defies support by any rational bill of particulars.

Now, listen. The United States retains every basic attribute of its sovereignty. We cannot be called to participate in any sort of sanctions, military or otherwise, without our own free and untrammeled consent. We cannot be taken into the World Court except at our own free option. The ultimate disposition of enemy territory which we have captured in this war is dependent solely upon our own will so far as this Charter is concerned. Our domestic questions are eliminated from the new organization's jurisdiction. Our inter-American system and the Monroe Doctrine are unimpaired in their realities. Our right of withdrawal from the new organization is absolute, and is dependent solely upon our own discretion. In a word, Mr. President, the flag stays on the dome of the Capitol.

These things, quoting the editorial, I confess are "O. K. with VANDENBERG and his cohorts." These things we toiled at San Francisco to preserve. We can effectively cooperate for peace without the loss of these things. To cooperate is not to lose our sovereignty. It is to use our sovereignty in quest of the dearest boon which the prayers of humankind pursue. I respectfully suggest that those who voice a superlative attachment to these elements of sovereignty should be the last to invite the wholly unjustified interpretation that we have surrendered the very things we have so scrupulously preserved.

So it is also with the equally irresponsible charge that the Charter "entails the destruction of parts of the written Constitution." What parts, I beg to inquire? Certainly the fact that we propose to cooperate to prevent World War III, if we can, destroys no part of our Constitution. Our Constitution is not allergic to peace.

It is not yet treason to abhor the ugly implications of war and to attempt to do something realistic about it.

Where, I ask again, do we invade our "written Constitution"? If it is meant that we "destroy" the exclusive congressional right to declare war I answer that the control of our American voice on the new Security Council is entirely and exclusively within our own congressional jurisdiction when we create this voice. The Charter does not even pretend to invade our own domestic control over this purely domestic matter. If it did it would be promptly and rightly pilloried for any such invasion.

The Charter gives us a veto on war and on any steps leading to war. The Charter could do no more. It says that our agreement covering the contribution of troops to any joint action must be approved by our own constitutional process. Does that destroy our constitutional process? To ask the question is to answer it. The Charter actually confirms our constitutional process. We shall decide for ourselves where we wish to draw the line, if any, between the constitutional authority of the President to use our armed forces in preliminary national defense action and the constitutional authority of Congress to declare war. Both Constitutional rights have existed, Mr. President, and have stood unchallenged for 150 years. We have never thought it necessary or desirable to try to set metes and bounds for each. I doubt if it is necessary or desirable now. We have but to continue the constitutional practice of a century and a half.

In our domestic statute, however, which is none of the Charter's business whatsoever—in our domestic statute creating our American delegateship to the Security Council, we can appropriately require that he shall vote for sanctions only upon instruction from the President, and that the President shall simultaneously notify the Congress. In the presence of this constant information Congress can act in any way it pleases. I repeat that this is our business, and if there be any doubt, Mr. President, that in addition to the exclusive congressional power to declare war, there is this basic constitutional military authority resident in the first instances in the President of the United States, I quote just one authority and pass on. I quote the man who is probably the favorite congressional authority upon subjects of this nature, Professor Borchard, of Yale, discussing the right and the duty of the President to protect American life, American property, and American interests anywhere in the world:

> Inasmuch as the Constitution vests in Congress the authority to declare war and does not empower Congress to direct the President to perform his constitutional duty of protecting American citizens on foreign soil, it is believed that the Executive has unlimited authority to use the armed forces of the United States for protective purposes abroad in any manner and on any occasion he considers expedient.

I believe that when the President concludes to use preliminary force, in cooperation with the Security Council, to stop a dispute before it graduates into war, he is most emphatically protecting American welfare.

So far as the Charter is concerned, it does not destroy, it does not threaten, it does not even remotely approach so much as an indirect impingement upon any portion of our written Constitution. That, too, Mr. President, if I may refer again to the personal element in the editorial from which I quote, is "Okay with VANDENBERG and his cohorts."

THE FALLACY OF COLLECTIVE SECURITY*

BY

EMERY REVES

[1945]

All the peace treaties ever signed, all the alliances ever concluded on this planet, the Covenant of the League of Nations, the
United Nations Organization, the principles of collective security,
are *identical* in their fundamental conception.   They all arbitrarily
divide the world into a number of sovereign social units, create a
status quo, and try to prevent any changes in the established order
except by unanimous consent, which makes no sense; or by force,
which makes war.

The Covenant of the League, the Dumbarton Oaks and San
Francisco documents, the notion of collective security, are all static,
Ptolemaic conceptions.   They are antidynamic and consequently
represent only barriers to peace, to life itself.   They all seek solutions on a basis which—if it existed—would leave no problems
to be solved.

Collective security without collective sovereignty is meaningless.
The insecurity of the individual as well as of groups of individuals
is the direct result of the nonexistence of law to govern their relations.   Allowing sovereign sources of law to reside, not in the
community but in the eighty-odd separate nation-states forming
that community; attempting to make their coexistence peaceful, not
by establishing institutions with sovereign power to create law
binding all members of the collectivity but by agreements and
treaties between the divided sovereign units, can never, under any
condition, create security for that collectivity.   Only a legal order
can bring security.   Consequently, without constitutional institutions to express the sovereignty of the community and to create
law for the collectivity, there can be no security for that collectivity.

* Selections from Ch. XIII of Emery Reves, *The Anatomy of Peace.*   Copyright 1945 by Emery Reves.   Reprinted by permission of Harper & Brothers,
publishers.   Emery Reves (b. 1904), publisher and author, was born in Yugoslavia and has resided in the United States since 1941.

The debate among the representatives of the nations in drafting the charter of a world organization was exclusively limited to formalities and technicalities which have absolutely no bearing upon peace and the future of mankind. All the representatives of national governments are in full agreement in rejecting the only foundation upon which a peaceful international order could be constructed.

One of the technicalities is the question of voting within a council of sovereign nations. According to the Covenant of the League, in case of an "aggression" by any sovereign member state of the League, sanctions could be taken only by unanimous consent. Naturally, this made the functioning of the inadequate League machinery—which under no conditions could have prevented major wars—utterly illusory.

No sovereign nation-state will ever freely admit that it is an aggressor, nor of its own free will, will it submit to sanctions imposed by other sovereign nations. So whenever a nation was accused by the League of aggression or threatened with sanctions, it merely tendered its resignation and left the party.

The accusing nations behaved just as hypocritically. When the consequences of such collective action were to be faced and decisions carried out against the offending nations, all the other sovereign members of the League followed the private interests of their individual nation-states. The use of force against any major power was unthinkable. That meant war.

This tragi-comic game will be repeated again and again, so long as we believe that a league or a council of sovereign nation-states can, under any circumstances, maintain peace among its members.

In a society without any system of law, no individual would ever trust a judge, a jury or a court, even if composed of the most eminent and selfless of his fellows. No individual would ever freely submit his personal freedom and fortunes to the judgment of any group of men composed of members with no higher authority than his own. No individual would ever submit of his free will, without defending himself by all means at his disposal, to interference in his life by a force, if the actions of that force had not previously been delineated and defined.

Individual members of a society are prepared to submit to one thing alone. To Law. They are ready to submit to social institutions only insofar as those institutions are the instruments of Law.

Such law is nonexistent in our inter-national life. It never did exist in inter-national relations. It has been excluded from the League of Nations and from the United Nations Organization. Under these circumstances, there can be no peace between nations.

To base "peace" on unanimous decisions of a certain number of sovereign national governments—in the present day, on the unanimous decisions of the five greatest military powers—means indulging in a daydream. It is an Alice-in-Wonderland adventure. And in seriously proposing such an organization and assuring the peoples of the earth that the five greatest military powers will—by common consent and unanimous decision—act in concert, our present leaders, our governments and diplomats are guilty of monstrous hypocrisy or else of naiveté far greater even than Alice showed in her adventures in dreamland.

History proves beyond doubt that any real danger to world peace always emanates from one of the major military powers. It is to be expected that in every situation threatening the existing order, one of the major powers will be seriously involved. It is clear that the major power will not cast its vote in any international council against its own interests. Consequently, in no major crisis will unanimous vote in the security council be obtainable. Whenever such conflicts arise, as they are bound to arise, the only course open to the others will be to close their eyes and let the events of Manchuria, Austria, Ethiopia, Spain and Czechoslovakia repeat themselves—or go to war.

But even if the nations be prepared to accept majority decisions within such a world council, the problem would remain unsolved. Majority decisions in a council of sovereign nations would be wholly unrealistic. If in a given situation, three of the major powers voted for a certain military intervention, while the other two voted against such a measure, these two powers could scarcely be pictured taking up arms and undertaking military action contrary to what they regard as their own national interests, and contrary to their votes.

So the whole debate on unanimous vote versus majority vote on issues arising in a security council of a world organization is irrelevant because in neither case could a decision on an issue involving a great power be enforced without precipitating a major war.

The conclusion to be drawn is this: The fundamental problem of regulating the relations between great powers without the permanent danger of major wars cannot be solved so long as absolute sovereign power continues to reside in the nation-states. Unless their sovereign institutions are integrated into higher institutions expressing directly the sovereignty of the community, unless the relations of their peoples are regulated by law, violent conflicts between national units are inevitable. This is not prophecy, not even an opinion, but an observable and irrefutable axiom of human society.

Just as a council of delegates and representatives of fifty sovereign cities, defending the interests of their respective municipalities, could never create a united nation, a national legal order, peaceful relations between the citizens of the fifty cities, security and freedom of the individuals living within each sovereign municipality—so the representatives and delegates of fifty sovereign nations meeting in a council and defending their own national interests, will never arrive at a satisfactory solution and settlement of any problem concerning the interrelations of the sovereign national units.

Just as peace, freedom and equality of the citizens of a nation require within their state specific institutions and authorities separate from and standing above municipal or local authorities, and the direct delegation of sovereign power by the people to these higher, national, government authorities—so peace, freedom and equality of men on this earth, between the nation-states, require specific institutions, authorities separate from and standing above national authorities, as well as the direct delegation of sovereign power by the people to these higher world government authorities, to deal with those problems of human relations that reach beyond the national state structure. . . .

Whether the application of force is an act of war or a police action depends upon one single criterion: whether or not the force is being used to execute the judgment of a court, applying established law in a concrete case.

If force is used without previously enacted law, defining clearly the principles of human conduct and the norms determining such conduct, then the use of force is arbitrary, an act of violence, war—whether the decision to resort to it be made by a national representative as a member of an international council, by a national legislative assembly, or even by national referendum.

In the charter of the new world organization, there is no provision for the creation of law regulating the relations of the nations. On the contrary, it is clearly stated that sovereign power to create law is the exclusive appanage of the individual nation-states, and that the international organization is an association of such sovereign nation-states.

There being no law to define human conduct in inter-national relations, any use of force is arbitrary, unjustified, an act of war. Such an inter-national organization may succeed in unimportant issues when force can be used by a major power or by a combination of powers against a weak and small nation. It is bound to fail whenever such use of force has to be resorted to by one power or group of powers against another power or group of powers with equal or approximately equal military strength. The application of force against a great power by a small nation in case the great power commits the aggression is, *ab ovo*, unthinkable and need not be discussed.

Such a state of affairs has absolutely nothing to do with the functioning of a police force in society. Such an organization as was the League and as the new international organization drafted at Dumbarton Oaks and San Francisco does not differ in any except external and formal aspects from the state of affairs that has always and at all times existed, without a league or any world organization.

Sovereign source of law remains scattered in *many* units. This always meant and, by the very force of things must always mean, violent conflict between these sovereign units, no matter what their relations, as long as sovereign power continues to reside in each separate unit.

Peace between the conflicting units is possible only if their relations are regulated by a higher sovereign authority embracing all of them. Once this is recognized, once developments are under way for the creation of law in international relations, then the use of force follows automatically, since real law implies its application by force.

But without previously enacted laws for international conduct, any proposal to use force is immoral and dangerous in the highest degree. It is an unforgivably false conception to believe that force without the pre-existence of law can maintain peace and prevent war, if the decision as to its application rests in the individual sovereign nation-states forming the international society, no matter which department of the sovereign nation-states may be endowed with that power. . . .

To revive the old League of Nations or to create a United Nations council on a similar basis (composed of representatives of sovereign nation-states), is an extremely simple proposition, although many people become emotional in debating the role of great powers and small powers in such a council.

The "idealists" plead for equality between great powers and small nations in the world organization, the "realists" want to give a preponderant role to the great powers, who under any circumstances would have to assume responsibility for checking aggression.

The realists who welcome the resurrection of the League of Nations under another name, with dentures in it (they say "with teeth") arrive at the peculiar conclusion that since no great power would accept military action against itself without resistance, the use of force is practicable only against small nations.

So what they really say is that the use of force against a small nation can preserve peace, but force could not be applied against a great power because that would provoke war.

According to them, the use of force against a small nation is qualitatively different from the use of force against a great power because in the first instance force brings peace, whereas in the second it brings war.

The hair-raising hypocrisy of mankind is truly astonishing. What this theory amounts to is that the theft of a loaf of bread by a poor man is an illegal act to be prosecuted, but the fraud of a millionaire banker must remain beyond the authority of law.

The assertion that the use of force against a small nation is "police power" whereas the same coercion against a great nation is not "police power" but war, is mere abracadabra. It is the result of muddled thinking, of ignorance of the meaning of the words and terms employed. It is not an attempt to shape policy according to principles; it is an attempt to justify an immoral and intolerable policy by elevating it to the level of a principle.

Force is police power when it is used to carry out the law, whether directed against a small or a great power, whether against a weak, miserable vagrant sleeping on a park bench or a strong, organized gang armed with guns who can shoot back at the police.

And force is *not* police power when it is not used to carry out law—even if it is applied by the unanimous consent of all the powers of the world against the smallest and weakest.

This great power versus small power controversy may go on forever, as it has all the characteristics of a meaningless issue that can be endlessly debated by an avalanche of words hiding particular interests and subjective feelings.

From the moral point of view, it is hard indeed to choose between great powers and small nations.

All great powers behave like gangsters. And all small nations behave like prostitutes.

They must. Under present conditions (not unlike those of the wild West), each great power mistrusts the others, must be permanently armed, keep his gun loaded and within easy reach to shoot it out with the others, if he wants to survive and keep his position. And the smaller powers who have no guns and who would never dare shoot it out with one of the big fellows, must go with those who promise them most, and in return for this protection, do whatever is demanded of them.

In the face of these realities, an organization of such sovereign nations, whether on an equal or an unequal footing, could never prevent another war. It is idealism raised to the nth degree of naiveté to believe otherwise. Such a council of sovereign units could prevent another war only if it could change human nature and make it act and react differently from the way it has been acting and reacting throughout the ages.

The national interests of the powers, large and small, do not run parallel, just as the selfish interests of individuals do not run parallel. If we want to remain on a sovereign nation-state basis, then the only chance of a somewhat longer period without war is to keep the sovereign nation-states as far apart as possible, to reduce contact between them to a minimum and not to bring them together in one organization where the conflict of their interest will only be intensified.

THE KOREAN CRISIS IN THE UNITED NATIONS

1. Excerpts from the Meeting of the Security Council, June 25, 1950.*

The Secretary-General: At midnight yesterday I was informed that a conflict appeared to have broken out in Korea. I immediately dispatched telegrams to the United Nations Commission on Korea asking for a report. This morning the reply of the Commission was received. . . .

Since November 1947 the problem of Korea has been a concern of the United Nations. In resolution 293 (IV) of 21 October 1949, the General Assembly recalled its previous declaration that there had been established a lawful government, the Government of the Republic of Korea, having effective control and jurisdiction over that part of Korea where the United Nations Temporary Commission on Korea was able to observe and consult, and in which the great majority of the people of Korea reside.

The General Assembly directed the United Nations Commission "to observe and report any developments which might lead to, or otherwise involve, military conflict in Korea" and, among other things, to "render such interim reports as it may deem appropriate to the Secretary-General for transmission to members."

The General Assembly also called upon "Member States, the Government of the Republic of Korea, and all Koreans to afford every assistance and facility to the Commission in the fulfillment of its responsibilities, and to refrain from any acts derogatory to the purposes" of the General Assembly resolution.

The report received by me from the Commission, as well as reports from other sources in Korea, make it plain that military actions have been undertaken by North Korean forces. These actions are a direct violation of the resolution of the General Assembly which had been adopted by a vote of 48 to 6 with 3 abstentions, as well as a violation of the principles of the Charter. The present situation is a serious one and is a threat to international peace. The Security Council is, in my opinion, the competent organ to deal with it. I consider it the clear duty of the Security

* From *United Nations, Security Council, Official Records*, 473rd meeting.

435

Council to take steps necessary to re-establish peace in that area.

* * *

Mr. GROSS (United States of America): At 4 o'clock in the morning of Sunday, 25 June, Korean time, armed forces from North Korea commenced an unprovoked assault against the territory of the Republic of Korea. This assault was launched by ground forces along the 38th parallel and the Ongjin, Kaesong, and Chunchon sectors, and by amphibious landings in the east coast in the vicinity of Kangnung. In addition, North Korean aircraft have attacked and strafed Kimpo airport in the outskirts of the capital city of Seoul.

The facts and a general outline of the situation have now been reported by the United Nations Commission on Korea. . . . Under these circumstances, this wholly illegal and unprovoked attack by North Korean forces, in the view of my Government, constitutes a breach of the peace and an act of aggression. This is clearly a threat to international peace and security. As such, it is of grave concern to my Government.

It is a threat which must inevitably be of grave concern to the Governments of all peace-loving and freedom-loving nations. A full-scale attack is now going forward in Korea. It is an invasion upon a State which the United Nations itself, by action of its General Assembly, has brought into being. It is armed aggression against the Government elected under United Nations supervision. Such an attack strikes at the fundamental purposes of the United Nations Charter. Such an attack openly defies the interest and authority of the United Nations. Such an attack, therefore, concerns the vital interest which all the Member nations have in the Organization. The history of the Korean problem is well known to the members of the Council. At this critical hour I shall not review that history in detail.

May I be permitted to recall just a few of the milestones in the development of the Korean situation? A Joint Commission of the United States of America and the Union of Soviet Socialist Republics sought unsuccessfully, for two years, to agree at ways and means of bringing to Korea the independence which we assumed would automatically come when Japan was defeated. This two-year deadlock prevented 38 million people in Korea from getting the independence which it was agreed was their right. My Government, thereupon, sought to hold a Four Power Conference, at which China and the United Kingdom would join the United States and the Soviet Union in seeking agreement on the independence of Korea. The Soviet Union rejected that proposal.

The United States then asked the General Assembly to consider the problem. The Soviet Union opposed that suggestion. The General Assembly in resolution 112 (II) of 14 November 1947, created the United Nations Temporary Commission on Korea. By that resolution, the General Assembly recommended the holding of elections not later than 31 March 1948 to choose representatives with whom the Commission might consult regarding the prompt attainment of freedom and independence for the Korean people. These elected representatives would constitute a national assembly and establish a national government of Korea. The General Assembly further recommended that, upon the establishment of a national government, that government should, in consultation with the Commission, constitute its own national security forces and dissolve all military or semi-military formations not included therein. The General Assembly recommended that the national government should take over the functions of government from the Military Command and from the civilian authorities of the North and South, and arrange with the occupying Powers for the complete withdrawal from Korea of their armed forces, as early as practicable and, if possible, within ninety days.

Elections were held in South Korea and the Commission observed them. A Government in South Korea was set up as a result of the elections observed by the Commission. The Commission was unable to enter North Korea because of the attitude of the Soviet Union. . . .

The United Nations Commission worked toward the United Nations objectives of the withdrawal of occupying forces from Korea, the removal of the barriers between the regions of the North and the South and the unification of that country under a representative government freely determined by its people.

In 1949, as in 1948, the Commission's efforts to attain access to North Korea, which included direct intercourse with the Northern authorities and endeavours to negotiate through the Government of the USSR, were fruitless. The Commission was unable to make progress either toward the unification of Korea or toward the reduction of barriers between the Republic of Korea and the Northern authorities. The Commission reported to the General Assembly that the border of the 38th parallel was becoming a scene of increasingly frequent exchanges of fire and armed raids, and that this constituted a serious barrier to friendly intercourse among the people of Korea.

The Commission observed the withdrawal of United States forces, which was completed on 19 June 1949. Although it signified its readiness to verify the fact of the withdrawal of the occupation forces of the Soviet Union from North Korea, the Commission received no response to its message to the USSR, and, therefore, could take no action. . . .

The United Nations Commission on Korea is presently in Seoul, and we have now received its latest report.

I have submitted a draft resolution which notes the Security Council's grave concern at the invasion of the Republic of Korea by the armed forces of North Korea. This draft resolution calls upon the authorities in the north to cease hostilities and to withdraw their armed forces to the border along the 38th parallel. It requests that the United Nations Commission on Korea observe the withdrawal of the North Korean forces to the 38th parallel and keep the Security Council informed on the implementation and execution of the resolution. The draft resolution also calls upon all Members of the United Nations to render every assistance to the United Nations in the carrying out of this resolution, and to refrain from giving assistance to the North Korean authorities. . . .

2. RESOLUTION CONCERNING THE COMPLAINT OF AGGRESSION UPON THE REPUBLIC OF KOREA. ADOPTED BY THE UNITED NATIONS SECURITY COUNCIL, JUNE 25, 1950.*

The Security Council

Recalling the finding of the General Assembly in its resolution of 21 October 1949 that the Government of the Republic of Korea is a lawfully established government "having effective control and

---

* From *Documents on American Foreign Relations,* Vol. XII, 1950, Raymond Dennett and Robert K. Turner, editors.

jurisdiction over that part of Korea where the United Nations Temporary Commission on Korea was able to observe and consult and in which the great majority of the people of Korea reside; and that this Government is based on elections which were a valid expression of the free will of the electorate of that part of Korea and which were observed by the Temporary Commission; and that this is the only such Government in Korea";

Mindful of the concern expressed by the General Assembly in its resolutions of 12 December 1948 and 21 October 1949 of the consequences which might follow unless Member States refrained from acts derogatory to the results sought to be achieved by the United Nations in bringing about the complete independence and unity of Korea; and the concern expressed that the situation described by the United Nations Commission on Korea in its report menaces the safety and well being of the Republic of Korea and of the people of Korea and might lead to open military conflict there;

Noting with grave concern the armed attack upon the Republic of Korea by forces from North Korea,

Determines that this action constitutes a breach of the peace,

I. *Calls for* the immediate cessation of hostilities; and
Calls upon the authorities of North Korea to withdraw forthwith their armed forces to the thirty-eighth parallel;

II. *Requests* the United Nations Commission on Korea

(a) To communicate its fully considered recommendations on the situation with the least possible delay;

(b) To observe the withdrawal of the North Korean forces to the thirty-eighth parallel; and

(c) To keep the Security Council informed on the execution of this resolution;

III. *Calls upon* all Members to render every assistance to the United Nations in the execution of this resolution and to refrain from giving assistance to the North Korean authorities. . . .

3. STATEMENT BY PRESIDENT TRUMAN ON THE KOREAN QUESTION, JUNE 27, 1950, 12 NOON.*

In Korea the Government forces, which were armed to prevent

---
*From Dennett and Turner, *Documents* . . . .

border raids and to preserve internal security, were attacked by invading forces from North Korea. The Security Council of the United Nations called upon the invading troops to cease hostilities and to withdraw to the 38th parallel. This they have not done, but on the contrary have pressed the attack. The Security Council called upon all members of the United Nations to render every assistance to the United Nations in the execution of this resolution. In these circumstances I have ordered United States air and sea forces to give the Korean Government troops cover and support.

The attack upon Korea makes it plain beyond all doubt that Communism has passed beyond the use of subversion to conquer independent nations and will now use armed invasion and war. It has defied the orders of the Security Council of the United Nations issued to preserve international peace and security. In these circumstances the occupation of Formosa by Communist forces would be a direct threat to the security of the pacific area and to United States forces performing their lawful and necessary functions in that area.

Accordingly I have ordered the Seventh Fleet to prevent any attack on Formosa. As a corollary of this action I am calling upon the Chinese Government on Formosa to cease all air and sea operations against the mainland. The Seventh Fleet will see that this is done. The determination of the future status of Formosa must await the restoration of security in the Pacific, a peace settlement with Japan, or consideration by the United Nations.

I have also directed that United States Forces in the Philippines be strengthened and that military assistance to the Philippine Government be accelerated.

I have similarly directed acceleration in the furnishing of military assistance to the forces of France and the Associated States in Indo China and the dispatch of a military mission to provide close working relations with those forces.

I know that all members of the United Nations will consider carefully the consequences of this latest aggression in Korea in defiance of the Charter of the United Nations. A return to the rule of force in international affairs would have far reaching effects. The United States will continue to uphold the rule of law.

I have instructed Ambassador Austin, as the representative of the United States to the Security Council, to report these steps to the Council.

4. EXCERPTS FROM THE MEETING OF THE SECURITY COUNCIL, JUNE 27, 1950, P. M.*

Mr. AUSTIN (United States of America): The United Nations finds itself confronted today with the gravest crisis in its existence. Forty-eight hours ago the Security Council, in an emergency meeting, determined that the armed invasion of the Republic of Korea by armed forces from North Korea constituted a breach of the peace. Accordingly, the Security Council called for a cessation of hostilities forthwith and the withdrawal by the North Korean authorities of their armed forces to the 38th parallel. The Security Council also requested the United Nations Commission on Korea to observe the withdrawal and to report. Finally, the Security Council called upon all Members to render every assistance to the United Nations in the execution of the resolution, and to refrain from giving assistance to the North Korean authorities.

The decision of the Security Council has been broadcast to the Korean authorities and is known to them. We now have before us the report of the United Nations Commission for Korea, which confirms our fears. It is clear that the authorities in North Korea have completely disregarded and flouted the decision of the Security Council. The armed invasion of the Republic of Korea continues. This is, in fact, an attack on the United Nations itself. The North Korean authorities have called upon the established Government of the Republic to surrender.

It is difficult to imagine a more glaring example of disregard for the United Nations and for all the principles which it represents. The most important provisions of the Charter are those outlawing aggressive war. It is precisely these provisions which the North Korean authorities have violated.

It is the plain duty of the Security Council to invoke stringent sanctions to restore international peace. The Republic of Korea has appealed to the United Nations for protection. I am happy and proud to report that the United States is prepared as a

---

* From *United Nations, Security Council, Official Records,* 474th meeting.

loyal Member of the United Nations to furnish assistance to the Republic of Korea. . . .

5. RESOLUTION CONCERNING THE COMPLAINT OF AGGRESSION UPON THE REPUBLIC OF KOREA, ADOPTED BY THE UNITED NATIONS SECURITY COUNCIL, JUNE 27, 1950.*

The Security Council,

Having determined that the armed attack upon the Republic of Korea by forces from North Korea constitutes a breach of the peace,

Having called for an immediate cessation of hostilities, and

Having called upon the authorities of North Korea to withdraw forthwith their armed forces to the 38th parallel, and

Having noted from the report of the United Nations Commission for Korea that the authorities in North Korea have neither ceased hostilities nor withdrawn their armed forces to the 38th parallel and that urgent military measures are required to restore international peace and security, and

Having noted the appeal from the Republic of Korea to the United Nations for immediate and effective steps to secure peace and security,

Recommends that the Members of the United Nations furnish such assistance to the Republic of Korea as may be necessary to repel the armed attack and to restore international peace and security in the area.

6. RESOLUTIONS ON UNITING FOR PEACE, APPROVED BY THE UNITED NATIONS GENERAL ASSEMBLY, NOVEMBER 3, 1950.**

A

The General Assembly,

Recognizing that the first two stated Purposes of the United Nations are:

"To maintain international peace and security, and to that

---

* From Dennett and Turner, *Documents* . . . .

EDITOR'S NOTE: The text is identical with the draft resolution submitted by the American delegate.

**From Dennett and Turner, *Documents* . . . .

end: to take effective collective measures for the prevention
and removal of threats to the peace, and for the suppression of
acts of aggression or other breaches of the peace, and to bring
about by peaceful means, and in conformity with the principles
of justice and international law, adjustment or settlement of
international disputes or situations which might lead to a breach
of the peace," and

"To develop friendly relations among nations based on respect for the principle of equal rights and self-determination of
peoples, and to take other appropriate measures to strengthen
universal peace,"

Reaffirming that it remains the primary duty of all Members of
the United Nations, when involved in an international dispute, to
seek settlement of such a dispute by peaceful means through the
procedures laid down in Chapter VI of the Charter, and recalling
the successful achievements of the United Nations in this regard
on a number of previous occasions,

Finding that international tension exists on a dangerous scale,

Recalling its resolution entitled "Essentials of peace," which
states that disregard of the Principles of the Charter of the United
Nations is primarily responsible for the continuance of international tension, and desiring to contribute further to the objectives of that resolution,

Reaffirming the importance of the exercise by the Security Council of its primary responsibility for the maintenance of international
peace and security, and the duty of the permanent members to seek
unanimity and to exercise restraint in the use of the veto,

Reaffirming that the initiative in negotiating the agreements for
armed forces provided for in Article 43 of the Charter belongs to
the Security Council, and desiring to ensure that, pending the conclusion of such agreements, the United Nations has at its disposal
means for maintaining international peace and security,

Conscious that failure of the Security Council to discharge its
responsibilities on behalf of all the Member States, particularly
those responsibilities referred to in the two preceding paragraphs,
does not relieve Member States of their obligations or the United
Nations of its responsibility under the Charter to maintain international peace and security,

Recognizing in particular that such failure does not deprive the General Assembly of its rights or relieve it of its responsibilities under the Charter in regard to the maintenance of international peace and security,

Recognizing that discharge by the General Assembly of its responsibilities in these respects calls for possibilities of observation which would ascertain the facts and expose aggressors; for the existence of armed forces which could be used collectively; and for the possibility of timely recommendation by the General Assembly to Members of the United Nations for collective action which, to be effective, should be prompt,

(A)

1. *Resolves* that if the Security Council, because of lack of unanimity of the permanent members, fails to exercise its primary responsibility for the maintenance of international peace and security in any case where there appears to be a threat to the peace, breach of the peace, or act of aggression, the General Assembly shall consider the matter immediately with a view to making appropriate recommendations to Members for collective measures, including in the case of a breach of the peace or act of aggression the use of armed force when necessary, to maintain or restore international peace and security. If not in session at the time, the General Assembly may meet in emergency special session within twenty-four hours of the request thereof. Such emergency special session shall be called if requested by the Security Council on the vote of any seven members, or by a majority of the Members of the United Nations;

2. *Adopts* for this purpose the amendments to its rules of procedure set forth in the annex to the present resolution.

* * *

COLLECTIVE SECURITY AND
THE WAR IN KOREA*

BY

ARNOLD WOLFERS

[1954]

The action taken by the United Nations in 1950 to halt the attack on South Korea has been heralded as the first experiment in collective security. The implication is that a radical break with the traditional foreign policy of nations has occurred; power politics, we are told, have been replaced by police action of the world community. It is quite likely that many who suffered in the Korean War on our side have been comforted by the thought that they have served the cause of law enforcement by community action, though others who believed that no vital interests of their country were at stake may have found the ordeal harder to bear. Whatever the emotional reaction, it is necessary to investigate dispassionately whether in fact a turning point in world politics was reached when the United Nations flag was unfurled in Korea. On the answer may depend what future policy we and others are entitled to expect of this country.

It may sound like quibbling to ask whether Korea was an example of "collective security." Obviously, the answer depends on the definition of the term. If one chooses to make it include every collective action undertaken for defensive purposes by a group of nations, then the Korean intervention by the United States and its associates falls under the term. Actually, it has become the habit of official spokesmen of our government to use the term in this way. For instance, they speak of NATO as a means of "collective security," although the treaty was legally justified by reference to Article 51 of the United Nations Charter, which expressly permits "collective self-defense" in cases where the universal collective security provisions of the United Nations *fail* to protect a victim of

* From the *Yale Review*, June 1954. Reprinted by permission. Arnold Wolfers (1892–1968) was Sterling Professor Emeritus at Yale University and a former director of the Johns Hopkins Washington Center of Foreign Policy Research.

aggression. But there is nothing new or revolutionary in nations aligning themselves for purposes of defense against their common national foes. Except for countries pursuing a "go it alone" policy, such conduct has been traditional among the members of multistate systems.

This is not what exponents of the principle of collective security have in mind when they urge nations to change the customary direction of their defense policy. They call upon nations to go beyond aligning themselves with each other only to meet the threats emanating from common national enemies and to embrace instead a policy of defense directed against aggression in general or, more precisely, against any aggressor anywhere. Coupled with arrangements to name the aggressor by community decision, nations—instead of reserving their power to defend or enforce their national interests—would be lined up like a police force to strike against any country, friend or foe, that had been declared an aggressor. Such a policy would constitute a radical break with tradition.

Since there are fundamental differences between these two types of collective action, with only one of them constituting a break with traditional national foreign policy, to avoid confusion and misunderstanding the two should be distinguished by the use of different labels. And since "collective security" has become the symbol for a break with power politics, it should be reserved for action that meets this test. It will be used so in this discussion, while other types of multilateral defensive action will be called "collective defense." Aside from semantics then, the problem is whether intervention in Korea represents a radical break with the traditional foreign policy of nation-states and, as a consequence, fulfils the expectations widely held for "collective security."

How serious a break with tradition the policy of collective security would be becomes evident if one considers what risks and sacrifices nations would have to incur in order to make such a policy effective and meaningful. It stands to reason that provisions and commitments for police action would add nothing to the protection that victims of aggression have enjoyed under the old system unless such victims could expect more military assistance than they would have received otherwise. The exponents of collective security have stressed this point. They have assumed that under a system of collective security such as they advocate, overwhelming force would be placed behind the law and at the disposal of a victim of attack. As in municipal affairs, therefore, the power of the police would usually suffice to deter any would-be attacker and thereby serve to maintain the peace rather than merely to punish the offender.

In order that collective security add in this way to the strength of the defense and to the chances of deterrence, it must be assumed that some nations, including one or more of the great powers, will be prepared to resort to force—that is, for all practical purposes, go to war—when, if they had not been devoted to the principle of collective security, they would have remained neutral or fought on the side of the aggressor. Instead of being allowed to reserve their military strength for the exclusive task of balancing the power of countries considered a threat to themselves or their allies, nations committed to a policy of collective security must divert their strength to struggles in remote places or, worse still, take action against friends and allies on whom reliance had been placed for defense against common foes. In extreme cases, a nation might even be called upon to defend and strengthen a foe at the expense of a friend or ally, if the latter were condemned as an aggressor.

If these should seem to be far-fetched contingencies, French experience, as well as possibilities now facing this country, prove them to be anything but theoretical. When Italy attacked Ethiopia, the French were urged in the name of collective security to participate in sanctions, if need be military sanctions, against Italy, a country which had just become a virtual ally against Germany, then considered France's number-one opponent; in the Korean War, France came under pressure to divert more of her strength to the fight with the North Koreans and Chinese aggressors at a time when she already felt too weak at home even to dare consent to German rearmament. A more dangerous situation might arise for the United States if Syngman Rhee should ever make good his threat to seek unification of his country by force. To take police action against him—or even to agree to have the Soviet bloc take such action—would run directly counter to this country's primary defense interests.

In order to be able to assert, then, that collective security has become a living reality, it is necessary to show that one or more countries have in fact proved ready to run the risks and consent to the sacrifices that this radical break with traditional defense policy presupposes. In the instance of Korea, this means inquiring whether there is evidence that such a switch to defense against aggression *per se* was made by the United States and its associates. Before doing so, it may be worth while to ask whether it is possible to conceive of incentives that might be powerful enough to induce nations to change their habits in so radical a fashion.

Those who seek to make a case for collective security, either as having become a reality or as being a practical goal for the future, argue along two lines, one more idealistic, the other more realistic. Nations, it is said, might take up arms against any aggressor anywhere simply because the crime of aggression arouses their moral indignation. The fact that there is such indignation both here and abroad is not in doubt. The desire to see perpetrators of wanton attack stopped and punished is widespread in a world that has had so much experience of brutal attack on weak and peaceful peoples. Yet, it is one thing to be indignant; another to be prepared to plunge one's country into war, though it be called police action, and to do so in an age of increasing wartime horror and destruction. Even aside from narrow nationalist preoccupations which might lessen the ardor for punitive action on behalf of the world community, there is reason to doubt whether moral indignation alone can be relied upon to carry nations into military action when no vital national interests push them in the same direction. In order to have a chance, it would rather seem as if collective security itself would have to appeal to interests of the kind traditionally considered vital to the nation.

According to the more realistic argument, such an interest is in fact at stake, though nations may still often fail to realize it. The argument rests on what has been called the principle of "indivisible peace." If aggression is allowed to go unpunished anywhere, it is said, potential aggressors will be encouraged everywhere, and as a result no nation will be secure. Instead, if any aggressor anywhere is stopped or deterred by overwhelming police power, all other potential aggressors will understand the warning and cease to constitute a threat. Thus, by a kind of detour, nations which for reasons of collective security are forced to divert strength or to weaken alignments against specific opponents gain more security in the end, even against their national foes.

This second line of argument has been called realistic because it rests on security considerations of the kind which have customarily guided national governments. But the question remains whether the long-run advantage of deterrence (which is hard to evaluate) can win out against the very real short-run risks of diversion of strength and unbalancing of power. Unless it can be shown in the case of Korea that the United States and its associates actually chose the long-run advantage at the expense of immediate security, the war in Korea cannot be called an example of collective security.

In a discussion of Korea, it might appear as if attention would have to be focused on the United Nations rather than on its members. In a sense this is true. Had no world organization such as the United Nations existed in 1950, there could have been no question of police action on behalf of the world community. Collective security presupposes that the aggressor be named and condemned by means of some recognized procedure; resort to violence in defense of the law against such an aggressor must be authorized by an organization which can claim to speak for the community. Yet no provisions, resolutions, commands, or recommendations of a world organization of sovereign nations can suffice to make collective security a reality. It can become real only by the fact of military power being employed for police purposes; the decision rests with the members who possess such military power and can use it for collective security if they will. In regard to the United Nations, the question is merely whether it did its part in inducing members of the organization to take police action on its behalf and under its auspices.

This is not the place to investigate whether the Charter of the United Nations was aimed at collective security as defined here or offered the best means of inducing countries to act in accordance with this principle. The veto provisions certainly allowed members to assume that they would never be expected to participate in police action which would seriously antagonize one or more of the major powers. Furthermore, Article 43 left the implementation of any commitment to participate in such action to subsequent negotiations which have not taken place. It is agreed, however, that when the members of the United Nations subscribed to the purpose of the organization as being "to take effective collective measures . . . for the suppression of acts of aggression," they accepted the principle of common defensive action against any aggressor anywhere. Their legal or at least moral obligation to do so whenever the competent organs of the United Nations order or recommend such action would seem to be beyond doubt, unless one were to assume that the "inherent right of self-defense" permits nations to beg out of any military action which would endanger their security. If one accepted this reservation, the Charter could not be said to create much legal embarrassment for members who wanted to avoid the risks of collective security. In the case of Korea, majorities sufficient to reach decisions both in the Security Council and in the General Assembly took all the steps for which they were competent to get police action under way.

The attack by the North Koreans occurred on June 25. On the same day, in the absence of the Soviet delegate, the Security Council determined that a breach of the peace had occurred. It called upon North Korea to withdraw its forces and proceeded to invite its members "to render every assistance to the United Nations in execution of this resolution." Some hours prior to the second meeting of the Council, on June 27, the United States Government announced that it had ordered American air and sea forces to go to the assistance of South Korea for the specific purpose of executing the June 25 resolution of the Security Council. If this was not enough to qualify American intervention as United Nations action, the Security Council identified itself with the action of the United States by voting on the same day that urgent military measures were required. The members were now called upon to furnish assistance of the kind necessary to repel the attack. From then on, the action of the United States and its associates was carried forward in the name of the United Nations, under the United Nations flag, and under a unified United Nations command set up by the United States in accordance with a resolution of the Security Council. Limited to recommendations, the United Nations continued to put what little pressure it could on its members to get them to participate or to make larger contributions; at the same time it sought to influence the United Nations command in the conduct and termination of the war, acting in this respect as a restraining factor.

Aside from this rather marginal though not unimportant role played by the United Nations itself, the character of the action in Korea must be judged by the decisions and acts of the United States and its associates. It would seem permissible, in fact, to concentrate on the conduct of the United States, because the other nations which made contributions to the defense of South Korea might conceivably have done so as friends and allies of the United States, whether this country was acting traditionally in what it considered to be its national interest and that of its friends or was conducting police action on the principle of collective security.

It is not a simple matter to discover whether or not United States intervention in Korea qualifies as collective security in the restricted sense in which the term is used here. The motivations of the chief architects of the policy are not decisive. The devotion of men like Mr. Truman and Mr. Acheson to the idea of collective security as they conceived it is not in doubt, any more than their desire to prevent the United Nations from suffering the same dismal fate which befell the League of Nations at the time of Italy's aggression against Ethiopia.

What is being asked is whether the United States, even if it believed itself to be engaging in police action in conformity with the concept of collective security, did in fact break with traditional national defense policy by accepting the kind of risks which such a break presupposes. If the aggressor had been South Korea rather than North Korea, the answer could not be in doubt. To take up arms against South Korea would have meant siding with this country's chief national enemy, the Soviet bloc, and strengthening the Communist countries at the expense of a country on which the United States could have relied as an ally in the Cold War. No more striking proof could have been given of unqualified American support for police action against any aggressor anywhere. But, the aggressor was Communist North Korea backed by the Soviet Union. It becomes necessary therefore to investigate how intervention in these circumstances looked from the point of view of American security interests as interpreted in Washington at the time.

Speaking negatively first, the United States was obviously not taking up arms against a friend or ally. On the contrary, it was setting out to stop expansion by the Soviet bloc, thus serving what had long been proclaimed to be the major goal of American foreign policy. It might be argued, however, that in extending the "containment" policy to Korea, the United States was diverting military power from Europe, which was considered the chief danger area. As the war proceeded, and American involvement exceeded all early expectations, much fear of such diversion was in fact expressed in Europe. But in this country, the opinion continued to prevail that in terms of the Cold War it would have been much more dangerous even for Europe if Communist aggression had gone unpunished in Asia. Moreover, powerful groups in Congress had long pressed for a stronger stand against Communism in Asia. Thus while the sacrifices in men and resources, borne by the American people in the course of the Korean War, were far in excess of even the most pessimistic initial expectations, they did not include the sacrifice or diversion of defensive military power from the tasks of the Cold War. Instead, the rearmament effort provoked by Communist aggression in Korea led to a multiplication of this power.

The fact that no sacrifice in terms of national protection against a major enemy was involved is not enough, however, to explain why this country should have decided to resort to military force. Except for a radical break with tradition, nations are not expected to take up arms unless there are interests which they consider vital at stake. Accordingly, the apparent absence of any vital American interest in South Korea made it seem as if devotion to collective security alone could have induced the United States to intervene. It was known that our civilian and military leaders did not consider the defense of the 38th Parallel or the preservation of a free South Korea a matter of vital strategic importance to this country, despite the fact that loss of the area to the Communists would have rendered Japan more vulnerable to attack. The Joint Chiefs of Staff had reached this decision at the time American troops were withdrawn from the territory of the Republic of Korea, long before

Secretary Acheson made his famous "perimeter" speech. It is also true that the United States was not bound by any treaty of alliance to go to the assistance of South Korea. However, this lack of what might be called a local strategic interest and the absence of any specific commitment to assist South Korea, other than that implied in the United Nations Charter, do not suffice to prove that vital interests were not at stake. The fact is that one can discern a threefold American interest of exactly the kind which, thinking along the lines of traditional power politics, governments would normally consider serious enough to justify military action or even to make it imperative.

In the first place, according to the views prevailing in both political parties at the time of the North Korean attack, any further expansion in any direction on the part of the Soviet bloc constituted a threat to American security. The "containment" policy was under attack not because it went too far in this respect but because it was thought too negative. As a matter of established policy, then, no area adjoining the Soviet Empire was held to be strategically nonvital; any addition to the territory behind the Iron Curtain would threaten to upset an already precarious world balance of power.

In the second place, the United States was vitally interested in proving to its European Allies that they could rely on American military assistance in case of a Soviet attack. NATO, this country's main bulwark against the threat from the East, was weakened by European fears of a resurgence of isolationism in this country. It was strongly felt, therefore, particularly by Secretary Acheson, that if South Korea were left at the mercy of the attacker, all of Russia's weak neighbors—and there were none but weak neighbors—would lose what confidence they had gradually gained that this country meant business when it promised to prevent further Soviet conquest.

As if this were not enough, there was a third reason for this country to be most seriously interested in not allowing a challenge by its number-one enemy to go without military response. The United States was engaged in a vast and strenuous effort to unite the entire free world in a common effort of defense against the Soviet and Communist menace. From most countries, particularly in Asia, it had not succeeded in obtaining commitments of mutual assistance of the kind customarily laid down in treaties of bilateral or multilateral alliance.   Therefore, all other non-Communist countries were committed to common defense against Communist aggression only if they could be made to accept the United Nations Charter as such a commitment.   Consequently, from the point of view of American security policy, it was of paramount importance that the United Nations be made to serve as a substitute for a formal alliance of the free world.   If there was any chance of achieving this result—and subsequent events showed how slim the chance was—it could only be done by demonstrating that under the Charter the United States considered itself committed to take up arms against the North Korean aggressor.

If it be correct, then, to assert that strong American national interests, other than an interest in collective security, pointed in the direction of intervention in Korea, certain conclusions can be drawn concerning the character of this action.   In order to avoid misconceptions, certain other conclusions which do not follow from what has been said must also be mentioned.

In the first place, because the resort to violence against North Korea served to maintain and in fact to strengthen this country's power position relative to its major national opponent, it cannot be considered the kind of break with tradition earlier defined as a prerequisite of effective collective security.   However, this does not mean that the Korean action did not represent a drastic change—or call it a break—in United States policy.   This country demonstrated its intent to stop Soviet and satellite aggression everywhere, thereby identifying its interests with those of the entire non-Communist world.   This is a far cry from earlier isolationist policies which sought national security in withdrawal from areas of conflict.   Moreover, the fact that American security interests were at stake does not prove that the Administration or the public would have considered them sufficiently vital to warrant a resort to force if defense of these interests had not coincided with the assertion of the principle of United Nations police action against aggression. Faith in this principle may at least help to explain the almost unanimous support Mr. Truman received at the start of the war.

In the second place, despite the popularity which collective security undoubtedly enjoyed in 1950 and may still enjoy, American military action against a member of the Soviet bloc cannot be taken as evidence that this country would be prepared to follow the same road in the case of an aggressor who was not a member of the Soviet bloc, or, in a particular instance, had attacked a member of that bloc. Here the national interest as traditionally understood and the interest in collective security would not coincide; instead, they might run directly counter to each other. One cannot help wondering whether the United States would resort to the same measures if at some future date a Syngman Rhee were declared the aggressor, though only the future can provide a definite answer.

It follows, then, that Korea has not established the practicability or reality of collective security in the sense in which the term is used here. Instead of being a case of nations fighting "any aggressor anywhere" and for no other purpose than to punish aggression and to deter potential aggressors, intervention in Korea was an act of collective military defense against the recognized number-one enemy of the United States and of all the countries which associated themselves with its action. If would-be aggressors have reached the same conclusion, they will not be deterred by the Korean War unless they belong to the Soviet bloc.

This is disheartening news to those who have placed their faith in deterrence through collective security, unless they should believe that aggression by non-Communist countries is out of the question anyway. Disappointment of the high hopes placed on the "first experiment in collective security" should be weighed, however, against possible advantages accruing to this country for not having committed itself by precedent to fight all aggressors everywhere.

While it will always remain a matter of controversy whether a certain commitment or course of action is or is not in the national interest, one may assume wide agreement on the proposition that in the present circumstances this country cannot afford to jeopardize seriously its ability to balance the power of the Soviet bloc. If this be so, any military action against an aggressor would run counter to the elementary rules of prudence if it threatened to tip the balance in favor of the Soviets. It need not do so in the case of every non-Communist aggressor. One can imagine cases of aggression by a non-Communist country against another non-

Communist country in which this country would have more to lose from allowing such aggression to be successful than from weakening and antagonizing the aggressor and his friends. In some instances there might be grave danger in allowing violence to continue and spread. But it needs little imagination to see how rare the cases are likely to be in which military intervention against a non-Communist country would favor this country's security position in the Cold War. One need only think of the disastrous consequences which might follow from a resort to force against, say, one of the Arab countries, or against Yugoslavia, or against a member of NATO. These consequences would be particularly grave if a large part of American military strength had to be diverted to such an operation.

A commitment to intervene would be most serious if a non-Communist country launched an attack on a member of the Soviet bloc. While it is to be hoped that this will remain a theoretical contingency, recent fears about Syngman Rhee's intentions and French fears that the West Germans might set out some day to unify their country by force, indicate why it must be taken into consideration. Police action in such instances would necessarily favor the Soviet bloc if it did not lead to Soviet expansion; it would be hard enough for the United States to remain on the sidelines while one of its erstwhile allies was being defeated by Communist "police" forces. In the present situation, in which this country and the other members of the free world are having the greatest trouble mustering enough strength for their defense against the East, how could their statesmen risk destroying what non-Communist solidarity and common defense positions now exist, even if in doing so they were serving the cause of collective security and future deterrence?

This does not answer the moral question. Some insist that it is the duty of nations to participate in police action because peace and the establishment of the rule of law in the world require that aggressors be stopped or punished. This means placing higher value on such punishment than on national self-defense whenever the two conflict. Against this view it can be argued on moral grounds that when, as today, everything the American people and most free peoples cherish, from independence to their way of life, is in grave danger of Soviet and Communist attack, precedence must be given to the defense of these values. After all even staunch supporters of collective security are apt to draw a line somewhere beyond which nations cannot be expected to go in their devotion to the cause of police action; they will not expect them to commit national suicide for the sake of serving the long-run interests of the world community.

But what about world public opinion? Will people abroad not be shocked to learn that the United States cannot be counted upon to use force against all aggressors, Communist or non-Communist, and will this not make enemies for this country? Where the public stands on this issue is a matter of conjecture. Experience during the Korean War may be revealing, however. This country was given almost unanimous and in most cases enthusiastic moral support by articulate opinion throughout the non-Communist world when it first took up arms to stop the North Koreans. Yet, when the question of taking more forceful action against Red China arose, after that country had been declared an aggressor, condemnation of any such "adventurous" or "militaristic" move was hardly less widespread. Liberal opinion—which had always been most keen to see collective security applied—was now most vigorously opposed to any extension of the war. The reason for this apparent inconsistency is not hard to discover. Punishment of an aggressor is desired but not if it means plunging the nation into a major war, in this case a world war, not even perhaps if it means gravely endangering the immediate security of the nation. "Before the great powers can join in sacrifices of blood and treasure to keep the peace in regions where they have no real interest," wrote Samuel Flagg Bemis prior to the Korean War, "a great transformation of will must take place among the peoples of the nations." This would still seem to hold true, more so, of course, where intervention runs directly counter to these "real interests." Thus, however tempting a system of collective security may appear in the abstract, its implementation in the case of aggressors of considerable military power runs into serious objections on the grounds of morality as well as of prudence.

If it is doubtful, to say the least, whether this country will intervene against any aggressor anywhere, serious disadvantages will accrue to it if the popular label of "collective security" is applied to United States foreign policy. There is first the danger of future disillusionment. There has been some already, because Red China, found guilty of aggression by the United Nations, did not receive the same punishment as North Korea, the weaker country. If the expectation takes root that American military forces will be available against any aggressor anywhere and if in some future instance this expectation is disappointed, the bitterness of the victim of an attack and its friends might have embarrassing consequences.

A second disadvantage has also been borne out by the events. If the American people are made to believe that this country involved itself in a costly and in many ways inconclusive war for no other interest than to serve the cause of collective security, is it surprising that there is resentment against other members of the United Nations who failed to live up to a principle to which they were no less committed than the United States? Such criticism of our friends and allies may be silenced if it is understood that this country in fact did have what were then considered to be very pressing national interests in stopping the North Koreans. It will also be better appreciated that some of the other members of the United Nations, including India, went quite far in backing the United Nations when, in disregard of what they believed to be their interest in neutrality, they voted to authorize the actions of the United States and its associates and to condemn the North Koreans and Chinese as aggressors.

It may be objected that if Korea has not opened the way for a universal system of collective security against all aggression, it has merely served to demonstrate once more the tragic hold that "power politics" has on the nations even of the free world. The United Nations as a security organization, it will be said, can have no place in such a world. However, such conclusions are not warranted. · The United States and its associates made good on a policy of "collective defense of the free world" carried out under the authority and control of the United Nations. While the control was weak, it nevertheless brought a restraining influence to bear on one of the world's greatest powers engaged in a bitter and costly defensive struggle. The one great contribution to the development of more lawful conditions in the world which this country can claim to have made in Korea consists therefore in its willingness to recognize the authority of the United Nations over actions which required sacrifices mainly from the American people. If some deplore the way in which the majority in the General Assembly exercised this control, believing that it would have been better for this country and the free world to have fought for victory at all costs, they give testimony thereby to the price countries may have to pay for the advantages of having collective defense operate according to the rules and with the approval of an international organization.

As to the United Nations itself, it has gained stature by the fact of having been able to be useful to the free world in its defense against Communist aggression without having to give up its universal character and its mediatory potentialities. Obviously, its role has been a more modest one than that contemplated by the exponents of collective security. Instead of being able to order the bulk of its members to fight aggressors whatever their relations to the aggressor, all the United Nations could do was to name the aggressor, to authorize and recommend action by its members, to lend its name to their action, and to seek to exert influence on the way it was carried out and terminated. This is exactly the role which would fall to the United Nations in cases in which collective self-defense was carried out under Article 51 and preceded action by the Security Council. The similarity is not accidental. If nations will resort to force only against national opponents when it accords with their national defense interests, as was true in Korea, the United Nations must limit itself to functions which are consistent with the needs of collective defense of likeminded countries. This has now been shown to be a practical and beneficial way of using an organization which, it should be added, has many important tasks to perform other than to stop or punish aggression.

THE U.S., THE U.N., AND THE MIDDLE EAST CRISIS*

BY

DWIGHT D. EISENHOWER

[1957]

I come to you again to talk about the situation in the Middle East. The future of the United Nations and peace in the Middle East may be at stake.

In the 4 months since I talked to you about the crisis in that area, the United Nations has made considerable progress in resolving some of the difficult problems. We are now, however, faced with a fateful moment as the result of the failure of Israel to withdraw its forces behind the armistice lines, as contemplated by the United Nations resolutions on this subject. . . .

When I talked to you last October, I pointed out that the United States fully realized that military action against Egypt resulted from grave and repeated provocations. But I said also that the use of military force to solve international disputes could not be reconciled with the principles and purposes of the United Nations. I added that our country could not believe that resort to force and war would for long serve the permanent interests of the attacking nations, which were Britain, France, and Israel.

So I pledged that the United States would seek through the United Nations to end the conflict. We would strive to bring about a recall of the forces of invasion and then make a renewed and earnest effort through that organization to secure justice, under international law, for all the parties concerned.

Since that time much has been achieved and many of the dangers implicit in the situation have been avoided. The Governments of Britain and France have withdrawn their forces from Egypt. Thereby they showed respect for the opinions of mankind as expressed almost unanimously by the 80 nation members of the United Nations General Assembly.

---

* From *The Department of State Bulletin*, March 11, 1957. Selections from an address to the nation made by President Eisenhower on February 20, 1957.

I want to pay tribute to the wisdom of this action of our friends and allies. They made an immense contribution to world order. Also they put the other nations of the world under a heavy obligation to see to it that these two nations do not suffer by reason of the compliance with the United Nations resolutions. . . .

We are approaching a fateful moment when either we must recognize that the United Nations is unable to restore peace in this area or the United Nations must renew with increased vigor its efforts to bring about Israeli withdrawal.

Repeated, but, so far, unsuccessful, efforts have been made to bring about a voluntary withdrawal by Israel. These efforts have been made both by the United Nations and by the United States and other member states.

Equally serious efforts have been made to bring about conditions designed to assure that, if Israel will withdraw in response to the repeated requests of the United Nations, there will then be achieved a greater security and tranquillity for that nation. This means that the United Nations would assert a determination to see that in the Middle East there will be a greater degree of justice and compliance with international law than was the case prior to the events of last October-November.

A United Nations Emergency Force, with Egypt's consent, entered that nation's territory in order to help maintain the cease-fire which the United Nations called for on November 2. . . .

Israel seeks something more. It insists on firm guarantees as a condition to withdrawing its forces of invasion.

This raises a basic question of principle. Should a nation which attacks and occupies foreign territory in the face of United Nations disapproval be allowed to impose conditions on its own withdrawal?

If we agree that armed attack can properly achieve the purposes of the assailant, then I fear we will have turned back the clock of international order. We will, in effect, have countenanced the use of force as a means of settling international differences and through this gaining national advantages.

I do not, myself, see how this could be reconciled with the Charter of the United Nations. The basic pledge of all the members of the United Nations is that they will settle their international disputes by peaceful means and will not use force against the territorial integrity of another state.

If the United Nations once admits that international disputes can be settled by using force, then we will have destroyed the very foundation of the organization and our best hope of establishing a world order. That would be a disaster for us all.

I would, I feel, be untrue to the standards of the high office to which you have chosen me if I were to lend the influence of the United States to the proposition that a nation which invades another should be permitted to exact conditions for withdrawal.

Of course, we and all the members of the United Nations ought to support justice and conformity with international law. The first article of the Charter states the purpose of the United Nations to be "the suppression of acts of aggression or other breaches of the peace, and to bring about by peaceful means, and in conformity with . . . justice and international law, adjustment or settlement of international disputes." But it is to be observed that conformity with justice and international law are to be brought about "by peaceful means."

We cannot consider that the armed invasion and occupation of another country are "peaceful means" or proper means to achieve justice and conformity with international law.

We do, however, believe that upon the suppression of the present act of aggression and breach of the peace there should be a greater effort by the United Nations and its members to secure justice and conformity with international law. Peace and justice are two sides of the same coin.

Perhaps the world community has been at fault in not having paid enough attention to this basic truth. The United States, for its part, will vigorously seek solutions of the problems of the area in accordance with justice and international law. And we shall in this great effort seek the association of other like-minded nations which realize, as we do, that peace and justice are in the long run inseparable.

But the United Nations faces immediately the problem of what to do next. If it does nothing, if it accepts the ignoring of its repeated resolutions calling for the withdrawal of invading forces, then it will have admitted failure. That failure would be a blow to the authority and influence of the United Nations in the world and to the hopes which humanity placed in the United Nations as the means of achieving peace with justice.

I do not believe that Israel's default should be ignored because the United Nations has not been able effectively to carry out its resolutions condemning the Soviet Union for its armed suppression of the people of Hungary. Perhaps this is a case where the proverb applies that two wrongs do not make a right.

No one deplores more than I the fact that the Soviet Union ignores the resolutions of the United Nations. Also no nation is more vigorous than is the United States in seeking to exert moral pressure against the Soviet Union, which by reason of its size and power, and by reason of its veto in the Security Council, is relatively impervious to other types of sanction.

The United States and other free nations are making clear by every means at their command the evil of Soviet conduct in Hungary. It would indeed be a sad day if the United States ever felt that it had to subject Israel to the same type of moral pressure as is being applied to the Soviet Union.

There can, of course, be no equating of a nation like Israel with that of the Soviet Union. The people of Israel, like those of the United States, are imbued with a religious faith and a sense of moral values. We are entitled to expect, and do expect, from such peoples of the free world a contribution to world order which unhappily we cannot expect from a nation controlled by atheistic despots.

It has been suggested that United Nations actions against Israel should not be pressed because Egypt has in the past violated the Armistice Agreement and international law. It is true that both Egypt and Israel, prior to last October, engaged in reprisals in violation of the Armistice Agreements. Egypt ignored the United Nations in exercising belligerent rights in relation to Israeli shipping in the Suez Canal and in the Gulf of Aqaba. However, such violations constitute no justification for the armed invasion of Egypt by Israel which the United Nations is now seeking to undo.

Failure to withdraw would be harmful to the long-term good of Israel. It would, in addition to its injury to the United Nations, jeopardize the prospects of the peaceful solution of the problems of the Mid-East. This could bring incalculable ills to our friends and indeed to our nation itself. . . .

The United Nations must not fail. I believe that—in the interests of peace—the United Nations has no choice but to exert pressure upon Israel to comply with the withdrawal resolutions. Of course, we still hope that the Government of Israel will see that its best immediate and long-term interests lie in compliance with the United Nations and in placing its trust in the resolutions of the United Nations and in the declaration of the United States with reference to the future.

Egypt, by accepting the six principles adopted by the Security Council last October in relation to the Suez Canal, bound itself to free and open transit through the canal without discrimination and to the principle that the operation of the canal should be insulated from the politics of any country.

We should not assume that, if Israel withdraws, Egypt will prevent Israeli shipping from using the Suez Canal or the Gulf of Aqaba. If, unhappily, Egypt does hereafter violate the Armistice Agreement or other international obligations, then this should be dealt with firmly by the society of nations.

The present moment is a grave one, but we are hopeful that reason and right will prevail. Since the events of last October-November, solid progress has been made, in conformity with the Charter of the United Nations. . . .

What I have spoken about tonight is only one step in a long process calling for patience and diligence, but at this moment it is the critical issue on which future progress depends.

It is an issue which can be solved if only we will apply the principles of the United Nations.

That is why, my fellow Americans, I know that you want the United States to continue to use its maximum influence to sustain those principles as the world's best hope for peace.

FOREIGN POLICY AND PRESIDENTIAL MORALISM*

BY

DEAN ACHESON

[1957]

The word "ideology" connotes the highly abstract and theoretical. It even suggests something un-American, or, at any rate, a long way removed from the actual conduct of our relations with foreign countries. And so it would be, if the ideology involved were not that of the President of the United States, who under our Constitution is charged with the conduct of those relations.

Let us take recent events in the Middle East as a case in point. One of the most important, but little noticed, developments of the years following the Second World War was the rapid growth and the extent of European dependence upon Middle Eastern oil as a source of energy, the essential factor in an industrial society. Under the circumstances this was a necessary dependence because there was no other practicable source for a quick expansion of the fuel supply.

But it was a dangerous dependence. The Middle East is an isthmus connecting Eurasia with Africa and leading in both directions. Through it runs the shortest water route between Europe, South Asia, and the Far East. It has long been a crossroads of power and the object of very lively Russian interest. Then, too, it is a seething caldron of unrest generated by the great Asian-African revolution against foreign control. Here are found standards of living as low as any in the world, and xenophobia which any spark can set aflame. Into this highly volatile area was introduced, under British and American auspices, Jewish immigration and the State of Israel. That did not make it a more propitious spot for nature to have placed the great resources of fossil fuel upon which Europe must, over a period of time, depend.

There is, however, one alleviating circumstance. While Europe is dependent on Middle Eastern oil, the oil-producing countries of

---

*From *The Reporter*, May 2, 1957. Reprinted by permission.

the Middle East are dependent on European markets, by far their largest paying customers. Unhappily, this latter dependence is not fully realized by the peoples of these countries and their rulers. One can easily see that any drastic change in the relative bargaining power between the Middle East and Europe would have far-reaching results.

Into this situation strode Colonel Nasser. Whether or not the humiliating withdrawal of the Aswan Dam offer precipitated his action, the Suez Canal must have offered him irresistible temptation. Egypt is, and for centuries has been, desperately poor. Its population grows at breath-taking speed. To preserve the arable land means a constant struggle with the encroaching desert. No oil or mineral resources have yet been found. Through this land of poverty Nasser saw the riches of the Middle East sail on their way to Europe. To control this artery would give him control over the lifeblood of Europe, the power to raise the economic and political price of oil—and to get his cut.

While Colonel Nasser was in a state of "letting 'I dare not' wait upon 'I would,' " his mind must have turned also to the constant assurances of this Administration to the Arab states that it would not follow what it regarded as its predecessor's attitude of partiality toward Israel. Whatever these assurances were intended to mean, what they conveyed was the conviction that the Arab states would have a much freer hand with Israel, particularly since they could count on Russian support for any action that threatened the western position.

However these considerations weighed with Colonel Nasser, in July, 1956, he seized control of the canal. He must have had some anxious moments, but they were soon relieved. Even before the committee of canal-using states met with Colonel Nasser to negotiate a regime of control, President Eisenhower had announced that force could not be used in dislodging Egypt from control. Colonel Nasser relaxed and dug in. Then followed a series of withdrawals by the United States from positions that our Allies believed they had been induced to accept as last stands. They became convinced that our government either did not understand the vital importance of their interests in the region or, understanding, found it necessary to sacrifice their interests for others that we were pursuing. They concluded that they must act to protect themselves.

At the end of October Israel struck. In a few days Colonel Nasser's military position and his prestige were shattered. Within twenty-four hours Britain and France, keeping their intentions secret from us, issued their ultimatum, and then wasted nearly a week in bombing airfields.

Their action was a grave mistake.

The Egyptian Army's confidence in Nasser was already shaken. The Anglo-French intervention was thus not only unnecessary to discredit Nasser, but in fact saved him.

The intervention was ill planned. Only a paratroop drop could hope to take the canal intact. Instead, the Egyptians used the five days of warning to block it. The intervention was weakly mounted, irresolutely pressed, and abandoned at the point that produced maximum abuse for the attempt and disdain for its failure.

The failure to consult the U.S. government, though understandable, was a fatal error. However unlikely it may have appeared that the United States and the Soviet Union would vote together against Britain and France, those countries should have realized that it was possible. When it came they were not prepared to stand up against it. Their action and ours brought near the breaking point an alliance that had been under strain for a number of years. But whatever may be said against the course taken by this government, the British and French are not the ones to say it: The U.S. government acted just as they might have expected it to act. When their attempt to present us with a *fait accompli* failed, they were in no position to complain.

But the fact remains that the sum total of all actions brought western power and prestige in the Middle East to a low ebb. Passing popularity gained by doing what Middle Eastern countries shrilly demanded should not be confused with respect and prestige.

Our government appears to have acted on a principle that Thucydides reports the Corinthian ambassadors urged upon the Athenian Assembly in justification of Corinth's expedition against Corcyra. "Every power," they said, "has a right to punish its own allies."

Our government then went on to demand and obtain, through the United Nations, the termination of the Israeli, British, and

French expeditions, the withdrawal of their forces, the reoccupation by Egypt of its bases for blockade and attack, the restoration of the canal free of cost to Egypt, and its return—all without any conditions upon or undertakings by Egypt. Colonel Nasser, defeated, humiliated, and ripe for oblivion, was given a victory unprecedented and complete.

So much for a recital of events and our government's participation in them. Let us ask now whether there were and are American interests involved here and how they fared.

President Eisenhower told us on February 20 that "the United States has no selfish ambitions or desires in this region." I fear we must disagree. We have many. But perhaps our greatest interest and desire is that the Middle East shall remain in the political and economic system of a free world and shall not be engulfed by the closed Soviet-Communist system. We desire, too, that it remain in such relationship with the rest of the free world that the fuel and sea routes essential to that world shall not be ruinously expensive, uncertain, or hazardous. Should this not be done, Europe might have to make such terms as it could. These might well be most unfavorable to the interests of the United States.

To safeguard this American position does not raise primarily a military question. True, relative military power lies in the background of most problems. But the danger here is not one of military conquest. The danger is that turmoil, hatred of the West encouraged wherever possible by Soviet agents, and unstable leaders attempting to gain position by wringing from Europe more than it can safely give may bring ruin upon all.

The first step in going at this problem must clearly be to increase our bargaining power with the Middle Eastern countries, and the first step in doing this is bringing to them a realization of the mutuality of dependence to which we have referred. Means lie ready at hand for doing this.

Temporarily the United States could provide Western Hemisphere oil and the dollars to pay for it: This could bring much illumination to oil producers in the Persian Gulf. The canal might have been left blocked by Nasser's ships: This could have given canal users like India a refreshing sense of realism. We might still start on freeing Europe from so much dependence on the canal by pipelines through non-Arab countries and by vigorous construction of large tankers. We might much more energetically hasten the day when nuclear energy could replace a substantial portion of petroleum energy, if only on a standby basis.

There are other courses of action that might induce a more understanding and reasonable attitude in Colonel Nasser—courses of action which recall Winston Churchill's admonition to the French, quoted from Thiers: "Think of it always; speak of it never."

When by our own efforts our bargaining position had been improved, a broad and imaginative economic program for the area as a whole would both be and appear to be the generous act of one in a strong position, rather than an act of appeasement from weakness.

But no such course as this has been taken; and since it has been so widely urged both in Congress and the press, one is justified in asking why not.

An answer, I suppose, is that it would cost something. Not as much, to be sure, as not doing it is likely to cost in the very near future. But in any Administration where the primacy of fiscal considerations is not doubted, maintenance deferred looks like money saved. However, I am inclined to think that this is not the basic reason.

Deeper than cost is the fact that the policy suggested lies quite outside the ideological system that seems to dominate the President's mind. Mr. Eisenhower has given us a good insight into his processes of thought by his utterances during and after the two campaigns.

In the military field one is concerned with the specific. The ultimate purposes of war are for others to concern themselves with. The soldier deals with methods, means, finite quantities, and forces. Politics involves less measurable objectives and operations. The ground under the politician's feet is boggy and unfirm.

Mr. Eisenhower at the outset of his political career sought for and found a satisfyingly firm stance in what he has continually referred to as "moral and spiritual values." These values are not more specifically defined than "Honesty, decency, fairness, service—all that sort of thing." But his attitude toward them is "deeply felt." The heart of the matter is expressed in terms of *feeling* rather than *thought*.   He feels deeply about principles and values the content of which is vague.

For this reason his actions become "crusades" or "missions." The title of his book is *Crusade in Europe*.   General Grant would have thought it odd to entitle his volume on the war in the West *Crusade on the Mississippi*.   The Republican Party under Mr. Eisenhower's leadership is engaged in a continual "crusade." Whatever his followers may think of the terminology, it gives them a desirable latitude in dealing with the infidels.   In this misty area of moral and spiritual values certain shadowy outlines dimly emerge and melt into one another.   Some of them can be identified and described.

An ebullient optimism gives expression to a boundless confidence in what Mr. Eisenhower has called man's "God-given ability to be master of his own destiny."   This is quite different from W. E. Henley's "Invictus"—"My head is bloody, but unbowed. . . . I am the master of my fate: I am the captain of my soul."   That is defiance of *Götterdämmerung*.   Mr. Eisenhower is Chanticleer causing the sun to rise.   "Remember your own power," he told an audience, "and be not dismayed, because you can do anything."

Since the values he stresses are moral and spiritual values, the power he refers to is moral power.   The only source of moral power is moral rightness, and moral power is the dominant power. Pascal, who was not a cynic, would have thought this view simpler and clearer than truth itself.   It was he who said: "Justice without power is impotent; power without justice is tyranny."

This belief in the supremacy and sole validity of moral power is reinforced by the profoundly pacifist conclusions that President Eisenhower has drawn from the development of Russian capacity for nuclear warfare.   Since the consequences of nuclear warfare might well be catastrophic beyond imagination, it is an easy step to the conclusion that all force is immoral and that its use can only be justified to meet a greater immorality—somebody else's use of force against one's own country.   Now it would be quite a valid conclusion that the deterrence of nuclear warfare is one of the highest objectives of policy.   But we must never forget that between an opponent who is prepared to use force to gain his end and one who is not prepared to use force to defend his interests—the former is usually the winner.

But, as has been said, under the President's moral philosophy force is immoral. Except when employed by others against oneself force must be opposed only by moral and political pressure. This means that it can only be effectively opposed when it is employed outside the Communist empire and by our own Allies. Soviet force used in Hungary, Indian force used in Kashmir, or Egyptian force used to conduct raids into Israel and to deny it use of the canal or the Gulf of Aqaba cannot, within the President's limitations, be *effectively* opposed because the users are immune to our moral and political pressure. But force used by our Allies, who are vulnerable to our opinion and political pressure, must yield to our moral onslaught.

Not only does the President's code demand that our Allies be made to desist from their use of force, but they must be chastened and purified of evil by being deprived of all fruits of their sin, even such security from attack or blockade as they may have obtained for themselves. All this must be destroyed as were the golden calf and the priests of Baal. Otherwise, said the President, we shall "have destroyed our best hope of establishing a world order."

If it confuses the reader that while the President is seeking to establish this moral world order, his chief lieutenant in that enterprise speaks of "the ability to get to the verge without getting into the war" as "the necessary art," let him not be dismayed. The bewilderment is widespread. Perhaps the explanation is that moral values and artistic values are not opposed but simply do not meet.

Along with this belief in moral power goes, in the President's system, a belief that earthly revelation of moral rightness is to be found in mankind in the mass. *Vox populi, vox Dei*. This is a sort of Rousseauesque notion that virtue exists in the state of nature and fades with sophistication. Since mankind in the mass is inarticulate, the conscience of mankind is embodied in the United Nations, which from time to time formulates and announces the "moral law." Here enter two new and confusing conceptions.

The first is that the men who gather in New York and who, when they left home, represented governments (and some pretty dubious ones) are transmuted en route and, on passing the portals of the glass skyscraper, embody the conscience of mankind—the conscience, for instance, of Russians, Hungarians, and Chinese. It would perhaps surprise Trujillo or Tito to know that they represent the conscience of Dominicans or Yugoslavs. Mr. Menon appears to speak with the voice of conscience on Israel, but not on Hungary or Kashmir. And Henry Cabot Lodge, Jr., when he hints at sanctions, contrary to the joint and solid position of both Republicans and Democrats in the Senate, is presumably the true voice of the conscience of his fellow countrymen, rather than the Senators.

But perhaps what we should be seeking here is not a dubious dowsing rod to find the springs of conscience but an instrument for diplomacy. "I do not regard," a most gifted contemporary has said, "the function of government as a proper field for the glorification of God." Religion is a private matter. At least the Constitution of the United States says so.

As an instrument for diplomacy the United Nations leaves a good deal to be desired. When the gold wrapping paper is taken off it, someone has said, it turns out to be a do-it-yourself set with some defective parts. Arthur Vandenberg called the Assembly "the Town Meeting of the World." Like a town meeting, it is a better place for airing complaints than for getting things done. And the Security Council, designed on the assumption of great-power unity, is rendered impotent by the cold war. Whether or not the Uniting for Peace Resolution of 1950 produced more problems than it solved, its authors fully understood that it was not a generator of policy but, at most, an instrument for its execution—and an instrument that could only be used for purposes appropriate to it.

With its present membership of eighty-one and the two-thirds rule, the General Assembly is like a Democratic Convention in the days of unit voting and the two-thirds rule. One-third of eighty-one is twenty-seven. There are twenty-eight Arab-Asian-African countries, exclusive of Israel, and ten Communist countries. Hardly the instrument to negotiate a new *status quo* in the Middle East, in which the interests of seventeen European countries and Israel are at stake.

Yet this is what is being attempted.

The second confusing conception in the President's view of the United Nations is that its Charter and pronouncements give us the "moral law." There is always a tendency for moralism to merge into legalism, for the form and words to become the substance. Jesus continually pointed this out. On one occasion he rebuked the legalism of the scribes, saying, "The sabbath was made for man, and not man for the sabbath."

The Charter becomes for Mr. Eisenhower a sacred text, whose sentences not only point but compel the way to moral rightness and the moral law. If Israel asks guarantees against attack for withdrawing her protective screen of troops, he answers, "I do not myself see how this could be reconciled with the Charter of the United Nations." Man was, as the scribes would have put it, made for the Charter or the Sabbath, as the case may be, for both are sacred.

Now it is characteristic of those who have had the good fortune to escape the study and practice of law that to them the law is—or seems to be—both simple and clear. It would not occur to them, for instance, that the plain and simple words of the Sherman Anti-Trust law do not apply to professional baseball because it is a sport and not a business, but do apply to professional football and boxing because they are both sports and businesses. A lawyer knows only too well what Longfellow meant when he wrote, "And things are not what they seem."

Mr. Eisenhower reasons that "The basic pledge of all the members of the United Nations is that they will settle their international disputes by peaceful means and will not use force against the territorial integrity of another state." Therefore, he concludes, Israel cannot be given guarantees against continued future incursions because by doing so "We will, in effect, have countenanced the use of force as a means of settling international differences. . . ."

"Two wrongs," the President admonishes us, "do not make a right." Now it is quite true that the provision against the use or threat of force is in the treaty—for that is what the Charter is—but it clearly applies both ways, to Egypt as well as to Israel. Furthermore, equally basic in the Charter is the recognition, in Article 51, of the inherent right of self-defense, a right recognized in all law.

Assuredly in our own courts if a plaintiff should ask for an injunction against a continuing trespass, which he had provoked by his own preceding trespasses, he would find that he as well as the defendant would be enjoined. For among the famous maxims of equity are these: He who seeks equity must do equity; he who comes into equity must come with clean hands; equality is equity.

Depth of feeling may be useful in the field of morals, but it is an untrustworthy substitute for clarity of thought in that of law—and even, I suggest, in that hybrid product referred to as the moral law. If we are going to talk law, let us talk good law.

I do not believe that the purpose of American policy is to carry out a "crusade" or "mission" to bring about equal justice or to "vindicate" international law. Its purpose is to protect and further the deepest and most vital interests of the United States and those states which are working toward the same end of safeguarding our common civilization. If this should require unequal treatment of other nations or the inability to satisfy the demands, even reasonable demands, of some one or more, that would be quite understandable and acceptable to me. But when I am told that we are forced to do this, where it is against our interest to do so, by a combination of phony law and fuzzy morals, I vigorously disagree.

The purpose of going into this ideological maze of moralistic legalism is not the quite unnecessary one of showing that it is bewildering, but to point out that it is tragically irrelevant to our real purposes, and both obscures them and defeats their attainment. It induces a state of mind which leads our government to say—and even worse, perhaps, to think—that the United States has no ambitions and desires in the Middle East. We do have desires. We do have interests—vitally important ones. And the idea that we are engaged on a crusade or mission to vindicate a vaguely and erroneously conceived "moral law" has led to actions which, I fear, are quite contrary to our interests.

"Be good, sweet maid, and let who can be clever" is a maxim that, perhaps unhappily, is obsolescent even in the education of young ladies. But in so far as the foreign policy of the United States is concerned, one does not have to abate one's enthusiasm for virtue to believe in the first rule of a well-known sport: Keep your head down and your eye on the ball.

VIII

STRATEGY IN THE NUCLEAR AGE

NUCLEAR WAR?*

BY

RAYMOND ARON

[1958]

When two atom bombs laid waste Hiroshima and Nagasaki in August 1945, scientists, writers, and politicians proclaimed that humanity was entering a new era, and each reverted to one of his favorite ideas.

The *optimists* saw in the diabolical weapon the promise that this time "war was going to end war"; the nuclear explosive would accomplish what had been vainly expected of gunpowder; peace would reign at last, thanks to the progress of technology, not to a universal change of heart.

The *pessimists* heralded the approach of the apocalypse. The Faustian West, carried away by a satanic impulse, would be punished for defying the gods and refusing to recognize the limits of the human condition; having divined the secrets of the atom, it possessed the sovereign capacity to destroy both itself and others; why should it suddenly find wisdom when for centuries it had sought nothing but practical knowledge and power?

The *realists,* rejecting both these extremes, left the future open. Between atomic peace and the annihilation of the species they perceived a middle way: no single weapon—however revolutionary—suffices to change human nature; political trends depend on men and societies as much as on weapons; if an atomic war is an absurd possibility for all the belligerents, it will not take place, though this does not mean that history will be exempt from the law of violence. . . .

The ten years which have elapsed since the thunderclaps of Hiroshima and Nagasaki have not enabled us to settle the argument. Today, just as ten years ago, we are equally free to imagine

* From *On War,* published by Doubleday Anchor Books. English translation, copyright 1958 by Martin, Secker and Warburg, Ltd. Reprinted by permission. Raymond Aron (b. 1905) is Professor, Faculty of Letters, of the University of Paris. His major writings include *Peace and War* and *The Opium of the Intellectuals.*

the final holocaust of civilization, the pacification of the world because of the impossibility of war ("There is no alternative to
peace," as President Eisenhower has said), or else the continuation of history as a result of the limitation of conflicts.

The defenders of each of these arguments assail the proponents
of the others with contempt. How can you possibly believe, cry the
pessimists, that men who are incapable of outlawing atomic weapons will be capable of not using the bombs they so jealously cling
to? If they are mad in peacetime, can you believe they will be sane
when war breaks out?

Come now, reply the realists, if you consider humanity insane
enough to launch an atomic war, how can you expect it to have
the wisdom to come to an agreement on the terms of a total disarmament? Does it make sense to be afraid of the thermonuclear
apocalypse and at the same time to hope for eternal peace or even
for the return by a concerted decision, to "preatomic inno-
cence"? . . .

Optimists and pessimists are concerned with the future. Only
the realists deal with the present—that is, with a world in which
two states have the means of destroying one another and are therefore condemned to suicide or coexistence. In this present which
must be measured in years, perhaps in decades, politics do not
radically change; they do not exclude violence within nations or
in the relations between states. Neither alliances nor revolutions
nor traditional armies have disappeared. Frontiers are not un-
changeable, transfers of sovereignty have not abated. More than
ever, the diplomatic field is a jungle in which "cold-blooded mon-
sters" are at grips with each other. More than ever, all possible
means are resorted to—all except one, the use of which might
well be fatal and which nevertheless profoundly influences the
course of events, just as the British fleet used to assure the freedom
of the seas, while anchored at its bases.

THE EVOLUTION OF U. S.
FOREIGN POLICY*

BY

JOHN FOSTER DULLES

[1954]

A. Speech before the Council on Foreign Relations, New York (January 12, 1954)

We need allies and collective security. Our purpose is to make these relations more effective, less costly. This can be done by placing more reliance on deterrent power, and less dependence on local defensive power. . . . We want, for ourselves and the other free nations, a maximum deterrent at a bearable cost.

Local defense will always be important. But there is no local defense which alone will contain the mighty land power of the Communist world. Local defenses must be reinforced by the further deterrent of massive retaliatory power. A potential aggressor must know that he cannot always prescribe battle conditions that suit him. Otherwise, for example, a potential aggressor, who is glutted with manpower, might be tempted to attack in confidence that resistance would be confined to manpower. He might be tempted to attack in places where his superiority was decisive.

The way to deter aggression is for the free community to be willing and able to respond vigorously at places and with means of its own choosing.

So long as our basic policy concepts were unclear, our military leaders could not be selective in building our military power. If an enemy could pick his time and place and method of warfare— and if our policy was to remain the traditional one of meeting aggression by direct and local opposition—then we needed to be ready to fight in the Arctic and in the tropics; in Asia, the Near East and in Europe; by sea, by land and by air; with old weapons and with new weapons.

---

* John Foster Dulles (1888–1959) was United States Secretary of State 1953–1959.

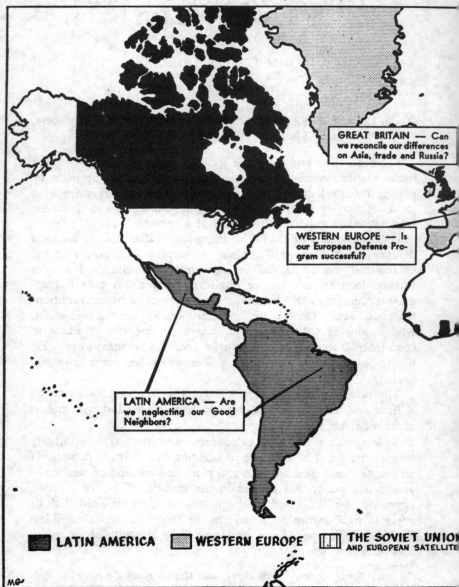

GREAT BRITAIN — Can we reconcile our differences on Asia, trade and Russia?

WESTERN EUROPE — Is our European Defense Program successful?

LATIN AMERICA — Are we neglecting our Good Neighbors?

LATIN AMERICA   WESTERN EUROPE   THE SOVIET UNION AND EUROPEAN SATELLITE

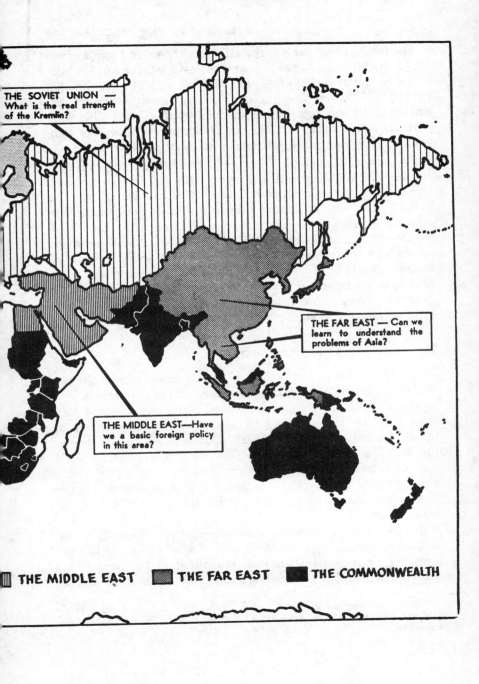

THE SOVIET UNION — What is the real strength of the Kremlin?

THE FAR EAST — Can we learn to understand the problems of Asia?

THE MIDDLE EAST—Have we a basic foreign policy in this area?

▤ THE MIDDLE EAST   ▨ THE FAR EAST   ■ THE COMMONWEALTH

The total cost of our security efforts, at home and abroad, was over $50,000,000,000 per annum, and involved, for 1953, a projected budgetary deficit of $9,000,000,000; and $11,000,000,000 for 1954. This was on top of taxes comparable to war-time taxes, and the dollar was depreciating in effective value. Our allies were similarly weighed down. This could not be continued for long without grave budgetary, economic and social consequences.

But before military planning could be changed, the President and his advisers, as represented by the National Security Council, had to take some basic policy decisions. This has been done. The basic decision was to depend primarily upon a great capacity to retaliate, instantly, by means and at places of our choosing. Now the Department of Defense and the Joint Chiefs of Staff can shape our military establishment to fit what is *our* policy, instead of having to try to be ready to meet the enemy's many choices. That permits of a selection of military means instead of a multiplication of means. As a result, it is now possible to get, and share, more basic security at less cost. . . .

B. "POLICY FOR SECURITY AND PEACE"*

. . . The events of the twentieth century, and especially the two World Wars and their aftermaths, have created an entirely new situation. In large measure the United States has inherited a responsibility for leadership which, in the past, has been shared by several nations. Today there rests upon us, to a unique degree, the threefold task of providing insurance against another world war; of demonstrating the good fruits of freedom which undermine the rule of despots by contrast; and of providing a major part of the effort required for the healthy growth of underdeveloped areas.

The Eisenhower Administration inherited security policies that had much worth. Many of these policies were bipartisan in character. They reflected a national recognition of the peril facing the civilized world, a united determination to meet it, and an

---

*Selections from an article prepared by Secretary of State John Foster Dulles for *Foreign Affairs*, April 1954. Reprinted from Department of State Press Release No. 139, March 16, 1954.

acceptance of the role of leadership thrust on us by events. We had helped to re-establish the economies of other countries shattered by the war. We had taken a major part in resisting the aggression in Korea. In the face of the Soviet threat we were engaged in rebuilding our military strength and that of other free countries.

These and like measures were costly. But they were necessary to our security. However, they partook much of an emergency character. By 1953 there was need to review our security planning and to adjust our continuing military effort to the other requirements of a well-rounded, permanent policy.

Under the conditions in which we live, it is not easy to strike a perfect balance between military and non-military efforts and to choose the type of military effort which serves us best. The essential is to recognize that there is an imperative need for a balance which holds military expenditures to a minimum consistent with safety, so that a maximum of liberty may operate as a dynamic force against despotism. That is the goal of our policy.

THE NATURE OF THE THREAT

The threat we face is not one that can be adequately dealt with on an emergency basis. It is a threat that may long persist. Our policies must be adapted to this basic fact.

The Soviet menace does not reflect the ambitions of a single ruler, and cannot be measured by his life expectancy. There is no evidence that basic Soviet policies have been changed with the passing of Stalin. . . . The Soviet Communists have always professed that they are planning for what they call "an entire historical era."

The assets behind this threat are vast. The Soviet bloc of Communist-controlled countries—a new form of imperialist colonialism—represents a vast central land mass with a population of 800,000,000. About 10,000,000 men are regularly under arms, with many more trained millions in reserve. This land force occupies a central position which permits of striking at any one of about 20 countries along a perimeter of some 20,000 miles. It is supplemented by increasing air power, equipped with atomic weapons, able to strike through northern Arctic routes which bring our industrial areas in range of quick attack.

The threat is not merely military. The Soviet rulers dispose throughout the world of the apparatus of international Communism. It operates with trained agitators and a powerful propaganda organization. It exploits every area of discontent, whether it be political discontent against "colonialism" or social discontent against economic conditions. It seeks to harass the existing order and pave the way for political coups which will install Communist-controlled regimes.

By the use of many types of manoeuvres and threats, military and political, the Soviet rulers seek gradually to divide and weaken the free nations and to make their policies appear as bankrupt by overextending them in efforts which, as Lenin put it, are "beyond their strength." Then, said Lenin, "our victory is assured." Then, said Stalin, will be the "moment for the decisive blow."

It is not easy to devise policies which will counter a danger so centralized and so vast, so varied and so sustained. It is no answer to substitute the glitter of steel for the torch of freedom.

An answer can be found by drawing on those basic concepts which have come to be regularly practised within our civic communities. There we have almost wholly given up the idea of relying primarily on house-by-house defense. Instead, primary reliance is placed upon the combining of two concepts, namely, the creation of power on a community basis and the use of that power so as to deter aggression by making it costly to an aggressor. The free nations must apply these same principles in the international sphere.

COMMUNITY DEFENSE

The cornerstone of security for the free nations must be a collective system of defense. They clearly cannot achieve security separately. No single nation can develop for itself defensive power of adequate scope and flexibility. In seeking to do so, each would become a garrison state and none would achieve security.

This is true of the United States. Without the cooperation of allies, we would not even be in a position to retaliate massively against the war industries of an attacking nation. That requires international facilities. Without them, our air striking power loses much of its deterrent power. With them, strategic air power becomes what Sir Winston Churchill called the "supreme deterrent." He credited to it the safety of Europe during recent years. But such power, while now a dominant factor, may not have the same significance forever. Furthermore, massive atomic and thermonuclear retaliation is not the kind of power which could most usefully be evoked under all circumstances.

Security for the free world depends, therefore, upon the development of collective security and community power rather than upon purely national potentials. Each nation which shares the security should contribute in accordance with its capabilities and facilities. The Inter-American Treaty of Reciprocal Assistance (Rio Pact) of 1947 set a postwar example in establishing the principle that an armed attack against one would be considered as an attack against all. The North Atlantic Treaty is based on the same principle. Its members have gone much further in organizing joint forces and facilities as a part of the integrated security system. NATO provides essential air and naval bases, to which its various members can contribute—each according to its means and capabilities. It provides the planes and ships and weapons which can use these bases. It provides so many points from which an aggressor could be harassed, in so many different ways, that he cannot prudently concentrate his forces for offense against a single victim. . . .

THE STRATEGY TO DETER AGGRESSION

The question remains: How should collective defense be organized by the free world for maximum protection at minimum cost? The heart of the problem is how to deter attack. This, we believe, requires a potential aggressor be left in no doubt that he would be certain to suffer damage outweighing any possible gains from aggression.

This result would not be assured, even by collective measures, if the free world sought to match the potential Communist forces, man for man and tank for tank, at every point where they might attack. The Soviet-Chinese bloc does not lack manpower and spends it as something that is cheap. If an aggressor knew he could always prescribe the battle conditions that suited him and engage us in struggles mainly involving manpower, aggression might be encouraged. He would be tempted to attack in places and by means where his manpower superiority was decisive and where at little cost he could impose upon us great burdens. If the free world adopted that strategy, it could bankrupt itself and not achieve security over a sustained period.

The free world must devise a better strategy for its defense, based on its own special assets. Its assets include, especially, air and naval power and atomic weapons which are now available in a wide range, suitable not only for strategic bombing but also for extensive tactical use. The free world must make imaginative use of the deterrent capabilities of these new weapons and mobilities and exploit the full potential of collective security. Properly used, they can produce defensive power able to retaliate at once and effectively against any aggression.

To deter aggression, it is important to have the flexibility and the facilities which make various responses available. In many cases, any open assault by Communist forces could only result in starting a general war. But the free world must have the means for responding effectively on a selective basis when it chooses. It must not put itself in the position where the only response open to it is general war. The essential thing is that a potential aggressor should know in advance that he can and will be made to suffer for his aggression more than he can possibly gain by it. This calls for a system in which local defensive strength is reinforced by more mobile deterrent power. The method of doing so will vary according to the character of the various areas.

Some areas are so vital that a special guard should and can be put around them. Western Europe is such an area. Its industrial plant represents so nearly the balance of industrial power in the world that an aggressor might feel that it was a good gamble to seize it—even at the risk of considerable hurt to himself. In this respect, Western Europe is exceptional. Fortunately, the West European countries have both a military tradition and a large military potential, so that through a European Defense Community, and with support by the United States and Britain, they can create an adequate defense of the Continent.

Most areas within the reach of an aggressor offer less value to him than the loss he would suffer from well-conceived retaliatory measures. Even in such areas, however, local defense will always be important. In every endangered area there should be a sufficient military establishment to maintain order against subversion and to resist other forms of indirect aggression and minor satellite aggressions. This serves the indispensable need to demonstrate a purpose to resist, and to compel any aggressor to expose his real intent by such serious fighting as will brand him before all the world and promptly bring collective measures into operation. Potential aggressors have little respect for peoples who have no will to fight for their own protection or to make the sacrifices needed to make that fighting significant. Also, they know that such peoples do not attract allies to fight for their cause. For all of these reasons, local defense is important. But in such areas the main reliance must be on the power of the free community to retaliate with great force by mobile means at places of its own choice.

A would-be aggressor will hesitate to commit aggression if he knows in advance that he thereby not only exposes those particular forces which he chooses to use for his aggression, but also deprives his other assets of "sanctuary" status. That does not mean turning every local war into a world war. It does not mean that if there is a Communist attack somewhere in Asia, atom or hydrogen bombs will necessarily be dropped on the great industrial centers of China or Russia. It does mean that the free world must maintain the collective means and be willing to use them in the way which most effectively makes aggression too risky and expensive to be tempting.

It is sometimes said that this system is inadequate because it assures an invaded country only that it will eventually be liberated and the invader punished. That observation misses the point. The point is that a prospective attacker is not likely to invade if he believes the probable hurt will outbalance the probable gain. A system which compels potential aggressors to face up to that fact indispensably supplements a local defensive system.

* * *

C. "THE STRATEGY OF COLLECTIVE SELF-DEFENSE"*

Collective security must, of course, be buttressed by military capabilities to deter armed aggression and to cope with it if it should occur. In December 1950, in an address before the American Association for the United Nations, I spoke to this problem, pointing out that, "With more than 20 nations strung along the 20,000 miles of Iron Curtain, it is not possible to build up static defensive forces which could make each nation impregnable to such a major and unpredictable assault as Russia could launch. To attempt this would be to have strength nowhere and bankruptcy everywhere." I went on to say, "Against such military power as the Soviet Union can marshal, collective security depends on capacity to counterattack against the aggressor," and I pointed to our Strategic Air Force and our stock of weapons as constituting an arsenal of retaliation.

During the ensuing years the military strategy of the free-world allies has been largely based upon our great capacity to retaliate should the Soviet Union launch a war of aggression. It is widely accepted that this strategy of deterrence has, during this period, contributed decisively to the security of the free world.

However, the United States has not been content to rely upon a peace which could be preserved only by a capacity to destroy vast segments of the human race. Such a concept is acceptable only as a last alternative. In recent years there has been no other. But the resourcefulness of those who serve our nation in the field of science and weapon engineering now shows that it is possible to alter the character of nuclear weapons. It seems now that their use need not involve vast destruction and widespread harm to humanity. Recent tests point to the possibility of possessing nuclear weapons the destructiveness and radiation effects of which can be confined substantially to predetermined targets.

In the future it may thus be feasible to place less reliance upon deterrence of vast retaliatory power. It may be possible to defend

---

* A selection from an article, "Challenge and Response in United States Policy," prepared for publication in the October 1957 issue of *Foreign Affairs* (press release 528 dated September 18). Reprinted from the Department of State *Bulletin*, October 7, 1957.

countries by nuclear weapons so mobile, or so placed, as to make military invasion with conventional forces a hazardous attempt. For example, terrain is often such that invasion routes can be decisively dominated by nuclear artillery. Thus, in contrast to the 1950 decade, it may be that by the 1960 decade the nations which are around the Sino-Soviet perimeter can possess an effective defense against full-scale conventional attack and thus confront any aggressor with the choice between failing or himself initiating nuclear war against the defending country. Thus the tables may be turned, in the sense that, instead of those who are nonaggressive having to rely upon all-out nuclear retaliatory power for their protection, would-be aggressors will be unable to count on a successful conventional aggression but must themselves weigh the consequences of invoking nuclear war.

It is precisely this evolution that Soviet diplomacy and propaganda strive most vigorously to prevent. They oppose all such experimental testing of nuclear devices as is necessary to find ways to reduce fallout and to reduce size. They seem to prefer that nuclear weapons be only the "horror" type of weapons. They apparently calculate that humanitarian instincts will prevent us from using such weapons. They know that, if Soviet conventional forces were operating in Europe, the megaton-type weapon with large fission fallout could not be used by Western forces without endangering the friendly peoples of the area. Under these conditions Sino-Soviet manpower and its conventional weapons would become the dominant military force in Eurasia. Such considerations make it important to combine the suspension of testing with other measures which will limit armament and the possibilities of surprise attack.

The Soviet Union, in its May 10, 1955, disarmament proposals, said:

> There are possibilities beyond the reach of international control for evading this control and for organizing the clandestine manufacture of atomic and hydrogen weapons, even if there is a formal agreement on international control. In such a situation the security of the States signatory to the international convention can not be guaranteed, since the possibility would be open

to a potential aggressor to accumulate stocks of atomic and hydrogen weapons for a surprise atomic attack on peace-loving states.

The foregoing is certainly true, at least as regards the use of existing stocks of fissionable material. That is why we do not seek to control existing stocks. We accept their inevitability, limiting our control proposals to newly created fissionable material that can be controlled.

The Soviet statement continued:

Until an atmosphere of trust has been created in relations between States, any agreement on the institution of international control can only serve to lull the vigilance of the peoples. It will create a false sense of security, while in reality there will be a danger of the production of atomic and hydrogen weapons and hence the threat of surprise attack and the unleashing of an atomic war with all its appalling consequences for the people.

This, again, is a true statement. Unless there are effective measures to reduce "the threat of surprise attack," whether nuclear or otherwise, it would be imprudent to interrupt the safeguarded search for methods to apply nuclear power to weapons in a manner to enlarge the possibilities of defense greatly and at the same time greatly reduce the lethal fallout factor inherent in weapons which are still in a relatively early stage of development.

As nuclear weapons come to provide greater possibilities for defense, this will require changes in military and related political strategy. So long as collective security depends almost wholly upon the deterrent of retaliatory power and the ability to wreak great destruction upon an aggressor nation, there has to be almost sole dependence upon the United States. No other nation can afford the cost of maintaining adequate deterrent power. This requires a vast arsenal of planes, weapons, and perhaps long-range missiles. These must be constantly renewed to overcome increasing defensive capabilities. This, in turn, requires vast outlay for experimentation.

However, as nuclear weapons become more tactical in character and thus more adaptable to area defense, there will inevitably be a desire on the part of those allies which are technically qualified to participate more directly in this defense and to have a greater assurance that this defensive power will in fact be used. Such factors are already leading to study of a so-called atomic weapons stockpile which could be established by the United States in the European NATO area and, as becomes appropriate, made available to NATO.

A concomitant of this problem is how to prevent the promiscuous spread of nuclear weapons throughout the world. Without safeguards, such weapons might in the future get into the hands of irresponsible dictators and be used as a form of international blackmail. The world would indeed become an unhappy place to live in if humanity had to accept an ever-present threat of this character.

We are only beginning to envisage the drastic changes in political-military relations which will be consequent upon the rapid growth of scientific knowledge and operating experience in the nuclear field. New weapons possibilities are opening up in rapid succession. Political thinking finds it difficult to keep up with that pace. And, of course, there is inevitably some interval between the thinking and the institutionalizing of the results of thinking.

The development of a common defense has meant, and will continue to mean, heavy outlays for an effective and modern United States military establishment. It has also required, and will continue to require, the United States to give military assistance and support to the military forces of those nations associated with us in collective arrangements or in special need or danger. Such assistance is in no sense to be viewed as charity. It is based on a hardheaded appraisal of our own defense needs. Without it, our own defense costs would be far greater and our security far less. The aggregate military and economic resources of the free world coalition represent the greatest and least costly insurance against war.

OUR MILITARY DEFENCE *

BY

COMMANDER SIR STEPHEN KING-HALL

[1958]

The theory of the deterrent as expounded by the free world runs as follows:

"The Russians have been told that any major act of aggression on their side, and in particular a nuclear attack by them on us, would be followed by instant and massive nuclear retaliation. If therefore the Russians wish to commit suicide this is the way to do it."

That—put I hope with fairness and moderation—is our official position. I cannot help wondering whether unofficially the free world leaders say under their breath: "We hope to goodness the Russians believe this."

Do they? [1] I hope we shall never have to find out by practical experiment. But some questions must be asked.

(*a*) Is it not true, or at any rate highly probable, that the free world will *not* be the first to drop an H-bomb? Apart from one's inner sense of what democracies do and do not do and the unlikelihood (I hope) that any H-bomb would be dropped by the U.S.A. or Britain without mutual consultation [2]—all of which takes time— the White Paper 1957 says that so far as Britain is concerned "the

---

* From *Defence in the Nuclear Age,* published by Victor Gollancz, Ltd., London, copyright 1958 by K-H Services, Ltd. Reprinted by permission. Sir Stephen King-Hall (b. 1893), founder of the Hansard Society, has written for political and historical publications. He is the author of *Communist Conspiracy* (1953).

[1] Many recent quotations could be cited from Khrushchev and Russian marshals intimating they are satisfied that, though all-out nuclear war would be highly destructive, the Soviet Union would survive and the West would not. One would expect them to *say* this sort of thing and no one can be sure whether or not their appreciation of a major nuclear war is correct or false, but my hunch is that they do believe what they say.

[2] Her Majesty's Government has received an undertaking from the U. S. that American aircraft carrying H-bombs based in East Anglia will not be used without British permission.

only safeguard against major aggression is *the power to threaten retaliation with nuclear weapons"* (italics mine). It also writes of "the initial nuclear bombardment and *counter-bombardment"* (para 24). Although it is not clearly stated who is to make the initial bombardment, I believe it unlikely that the White Paper supposes it to be ourselves. If I have misread the White Paper, and it means we are to take the initiative, what are we to make of the further statement that: "It may well be (the two bombardments) would be so crippling as to bring the war to an end within a few weeks or even days."

(*b*) If it is true or probable that we shall not initiate H-bomb war, then is there not a danger that the Russians may also reach this conclusion? If *they* are prepared to initiate it (and we take it for granted that they will not be inhibited by moral scruples), is there not a danger that they will argue something as follows: "We shall—perhaps after a conventional opening—suddenly launch a nuclear attack on the U.S.A. and the United Kingdom. In the era of Intercontinental Missiles the enemy will have a few minutes of warning that the missiles have been launched. Even today the British might have only a few minutes' warning by radar that the missiles are en route. It is inconceivable that by any method of organization in a democracy anyone can order a counter-bombardment in five minutes. If nothing happens during those minutes much of the United Kingdom will be pulverized and there may be no counter-attack or only a partial one."

In connection with this hypothesis, what arrangements do exist or could be imagined to exist in Britain to enable a counter nuclear bombardment to be launched on the sole basis of radar evidence (if radar can deal with ICBM's) that missiles ex-Russia are in the stratosphere?[1]

The only arrangement I can conceive is that *after* the nuclear missiles have fallen, some survivors in some deep shelter will endeavour to set the counter-bombardment in motion if its organi-

---

[1] According to a report presented to W.E.U. by Lord Stonehaven, M.A.: "An electronic computer used to intercept an attacking guided missile would have to perform nearly 3,000 calculations, feed the information to the defending missile and guide it to the target in a little over 2 minutes." *Manchester Guardian*, 14th October, 1957.

zation has not been destroyed. And, even should it be possible to launch a blow of revenge, what good will that do if we are already destroyed?

Does not the same argument apply to the U.S.A.–Soviet situation?

Probably not at the moment because the U.S.A. is not at present (1957) quite so open to sudden attack as is the U.K. But it will apply to the U.S.A. as soon as the ICBM is developed.

(*c*) But, granted that under (*b*) above, the Russians may lean on that argument, are they not also likely to feel that, even if they knock out Britain in the way described, there will be instant retaliation from the U.S.A.?

That is the theory but how sure are we that there is and always will be unanimity of thought between London and Washington as to when an H-bomb is to be dropped? Are we sure that each country is committed irrevocably to join the other in nuclear war irrespective of how and why each country becomes involved in hostilities? Why does the British Government keep on saying that Britain *must* have H-bombs so as to preserve its political independence *vis-à-vis* the U.S.A.?

Reflections of this nature have been engaging the attention of the leaders of the West and one of them, a very intelligent man of wide experience, has spoken out on this matter. I refer to some remarks made by Mr. Lester B. Pearson. He wrote:[1]

> "Who decides that all-out aggression has begun? Who decides when to press the button which brings about air retaliation through nuclear strategic bombing? Certainly not any NATO command or council in so far as the U.S. strategic airforce is concerned. This problem of such decisive importance remains to be solved . . . an attempt to force a solution would be unwise because it would not be likely to result in agreed and clear-cut decisions and might well result in dissensions and trouble inside the alliance."

Since the Russians can read and write as well as encircle us with artificial satellites, the above passage will be known to them. Is it

---

[1] In *Western World*, September 1957.

fanciful to suppose that Khrushchev must be thinking: "They talk about the Great Deterrent and yet they know that we know that for fear of falling out amongst themselves they dare not even try to solve the problem of who presses the button and when? I do not feel very deterred.". . .

It may help the reader, as it has certainly helped me, if I try to relate some of the reflections set forth in this chapter to a possible episode or conceivable case of aggression:

Let us suppose that there is a rising of the people in East Germany. The East German government calls for help from the Russians who exercise military force. The military forces suppressing the revolt declare that it is being organized from West Berlin (a possible truth) and that, in order to control East Berlin, they must occupy West Berlin. They advance into West Berlin with four mechanized divisions and tactical aircraft. Perhaps they put down an airborne division into West Berlin. They say to the small allied force: "Keep out of the way", or: "You had better evacuate yourselves to West Germany under safe conduct."

What happens next? Here are some possibilities. Assuming agreement between Paris, London and Washington, the allied troops in Berlin (1) retire, or (2) die to the last man. I doubt whether the Allied Commander in Berlin has precise instruction what he is to do. But would there be agreement amongst the Allies? Do not forget what Mr. Pearson has told us.

As soon as Russian troop movements are reported, the scrambled telephone talks begin between Washington–Paris–London, and, one may be sure, Bonn would expect to be consulted.

Is this a "major act of aggression"? It looks like it even though the Russians are saying: "The occupation is temporary and only to put down illegal activities against the lawful government of East Germany." Do the U.S.A. and Britain, without warning of any kind, open up a nuclear attack on Russia? I should not think so. Does the U.S.A. announce: "If West Berlin is not evacuated within 6 hours (or 12 hours) we will blast Russia?" Would the Russian reply to this be to blast the U.S.A. and Britain at zero plus 5 hours (or 11 hours) without warning?

What will people be doing in London, New York, Chicago and other large centres when this situation arises? Might there not be a panic evacuation and scenes of indescribable chaos?

Suppose the British Cabinet were simply told by the Americans (with more courtesy than we showed to them over Suez); "We tell you that we intend to have a show-down over this Berlin business. We think we can call their bluff and, if we cannot, we can hurt them more than they can hurt us." What would the Cabinet do?

Would it say to Washington: "We cannot have Britain destroyed by Intermediate Range Missiles. We are telling the Russians your nuclear bombers cannot take off from Britain and we will not drop nuclear bombs on Russia if they do not drop any on us"? Or would we say: "Britain is with you to the last heap of radio-active ashes. If you survive, remember us in the history books." I suggest we can all imagine what the French will be saying, and the Asian Dominions would certainly leave the Commonwealth without delay and loudly trumpet their neutrality.

Another guess—and I admit my guess is no better than yours—is that when the news came through that West Berlin had been seized, the Allies would seek a way out of their hideous dilemma by summoning an emergency meeting of the Security Council where Russia would exercise the veto. "Law and Order" would be restored in East Germany whilst the debate was taking place.

I will go out on a limb and risk being branded as a coward and an appeaser by saying that in the circumstances I have tried to imagine, the governments of the democratic countries will *not* risk starting up a nuclear war and that, if given a chance to express an opinion, a very small proportion of the people of the free world would decide that an illegal Russian occupation of Berlin should lead to the destruction of civilization. I fear the Russians might reach the same conclusion.

Russian action of this kind would be aggression of a serious character and, if they got away with it, they would be tempted to repeat the performance. They might, for example, if circumstances were favourable, renew their attempts to bring Greece into their orbit by a mixture of internal dissension and external Russian aid.

If the Russians got away with it in the case mentioned above, what was missing? What should we have lacked? The answer is: Adequate conventional force. If the Russians knew that in the event of their seizing West Berlin a powerful NATO conventional force would back up an ultimatum to withdraw, they might hesitate. In the last resort the NATO force, if powerful enough, could drive them out of Berlin, and lay the onus on the Russians of using nuclear weapons.

We are now back to the conception of conventional war which was becoming so destructive through traditional operational methods by 1945 that its merits were dubious, but not so destructive that it had become suicidal folly. Indeed, if looked at in a cold-blooded way and in long-term historical perspective, the destruction wrought by conventional military operations by 1945 and the miseries it inflicted on Germany forced this virile nation to re-build its cities and work so hard to live, that by 1957 their prosperity was an international embarrassment. But as things are in 1957 we have not got conventional weapons of sufficient strength to deny the capture of West Berlin to the Russians, or retake it if it were lost.

But we have got NATO and we pretend that our set-up there of conventional forces plus tactical nuclear weapons is a defence for Europe.

Let us therefore suppose that in the case we have imagined the Russians seize West Berlin and both sides declare they will not use the H-bomb.

Nevertheless it is felt in London and Washington that, if the Russians get away with this, what is the object of having NATO? Therefore a conventional war begins. This now begins to look like the limited war discussed on page 50. This school of thought would be saying in broadcasts and articles: "Do not worry too much; remember the Korean example, where in their own interests both sides observed certain conventions, viz. the U.N. forces never bombed the enemy aerodromes beyond the Yalu River because it was felt this would bring China into the war and so risk starting up a world war and probably a nuclear one, whilst the N. Koreans never bombed our ports because if they had done so we should have had to retaliate on their aerodromes in China."

This school of thought would therefore argue in the Berlin case we are discussing that there might be a limited conventional war. Unfortunately this argument is sunk on the rock of tactical nuclear weapons. The Russians might well not be the first to use nuclear weapons; they would not need to do so as their mechanized divisions poured westwards, but we have *got* to use tactical nuclear weapons from the start in order to compensate for the Russian masses.[1] We have announced officially that we shall do so. The Russian general staff would not allow its troops to be subjected to nuclear attack without retaliating in kind. The retaliation might be limited in the first instance to an atomic bomb(s) on Antwerp, one of the main bases of the NATO forces. This would call for correspondingly heavy stuff on the main Soviet bases. The enemy would then give serious consideration to getting rid of Britain with a dozen H-bombs. This would mean a full-scale nuclear war.

I have dealt with the case of the West Berlin seizure in terms of limited war in order to illustrate why those who back this theory (i.e. that the H-bomb deterrent creates a framework in which limited wars can be conducted) overlook the fact, the truly appalling fact, that tactical nuclear weapons are now conventional weapons.

---

[1] This is where the Korean analogy would break down. In Korea it was *not* militarily imperative to bomb the Chinese airfields and industries in Manchuria. But if the U.N. forces had been faced with the prospect of surrendering *en masse* or being driven into the sea by the Chinese armies are we sure that we should not have used everything we had, including nuclear weapons, to stave off this disaster? I do not see American troops being abandoned to their fate until *every* effort had been made to save them.

ON LIMITED WAR *

BY

ALAIN C. ENTHOVEN

[1963]

Military force is but one instrument in the hands of the President to be used in the struggle to keep us alive and free. It takes its place alongside diplomacy, economic policy, foreign economic and military assistance, alliances, and many other activities that contribute to our national security. Its ultimate purpose, like that of these other activities, is to enable the President, in cooperation with the leaders of other free nations, to establish and maintain a peaceful world order based on a belief in the worth and dignity of the individual, and on freedom for each person to develop his own capacities in the way he chooses. The role of military force, in the pursuit of this objective, is to prevent would-be aggressors who do not believe in freedom and human dignity from forcing free men to live under a system based on tyranny and coercion. The problem of formulation of defense policy is to select those forces which will contribute most effectively to these multiple objectives.

There are three related themes underlying and uniting our defense policies today. They are, first, deterrence of aggression; second, freedom for the President to select and apply the amount and kind of force appropriate to the threat at hand; and third, the controlled use of force. In the nuclear age, military force will be too dangerous to use if our objectives are not carefully chosen and limited at each step of a conflict, and if the force cannot be used in a controlled and deliberate way to achieve precisely the objectives being sought. To fight for unlimited objectives, or to fight in an uncontrolled way would almost surely bring on almost unlimited destruction.

* Address by Alain C. Enthoven before the Loyola University Forum for National Affairs, Los Angeles, California, February 10, 1963. Alain C. Enthoven is vice president at Litton Industries. He was formerly Deputy Assistant Secretary of Defense (Systems Analysis).

In order to give the President the freedom of action required to be able to limit appropriately the use of force, current defense policy emphasizes flexibility, options, and choice. One of its main objectives is to make available to the President a range of military responses appropriate for each threat to our security, so that he can apply force adequate to accomplish the objectives at hand without causing any unnecessary damage or loss of life, and while holding to a minimum the risk of escalation to a more destructive level of conflict.

A few years ago, there was a great deal of public debate as to whether limited war was possible. . . . Of course, total war remains possible. But, as time goes by and the size and destructive power of nuclear arsenals increase, total war between nuclear powers will, more and more, mean total destruction. It is my own opinion that with the widespread realization of this fact will come the general belief that all wars should be limited. At no time should we deliberately choose to fight an unlimited uncontrolled war. The "limited war–general war" dichotomy that has crept into our language may be harmful if it suggests that there is a kind of war that it makes sense to fight without limits, though, of course, the limits that we adopt will have to depend on the threat and on our objectives.

What this means, in practice, is that we are working to acquire a flexible, balanced defense posture giving us capabilities for the selective use of force for all kinds of conflict, from counter-insurgency and anti-guerrilla warfare through large-scale conventional (non-nuclear) warfare, through major thermonuclear war. Although the choice of the amount and kind of force to be applied in any circumstance is bound to be a difficult one, we would like to make it possible in all cases, if I may borrow a phrase from *The Mikado,* "to make the punishment fit the crime."

Keeping the use of force appropriately limited requires control. The range, speed, and destructiveness of modern weapons makes this problem both more urgent and more difficult than it has ever been before. More than ever before, this means that the President must have communication and control facilities to provide him with timely and accurate information on the course of events and to permit him to communicate his decisions in a similar manner. It also means that the military forces must be responsive to his direction, even in considerable detail. To use President Kennedy's words, "Our weapons systems must be usable in a manner permitting deliberation and discrimination as to timing, scope, and targets in response to civilian authority."

Moreover, when force is being applied, the military action must not be allowed to control events and compel the President's decisions; rather, it should be the other way around. To borrow a term from missilery, our use of military force in the cold war must be command guided, not inertially guided.

This belief may be contrasted to the view that "peace is peace and war is war," and that in war military necessity is the only valid criterion for decision. Certainly, the requirements of the military commander must be considered very seriously, both because our security requires success in whatever armed conflicts are thrust upon us and because the lives of our soldiers are involved. But still, the President must be free to weigh them against other requirements and decide what is best for the security of the United States. This principle was important before nuclear weapons; it has taken on added importance in the nuclear age.

This was one of the hard lessons of the Korean War. The United States had to re-learn to fight for limited objectives. There were reasons which the original military commander found very compelling for expanding the scope of the conflict. But in the President's judgment, to expand the conflict would have risked touching off another world war which would have left both the South Koreans and ourselves far worse off than the final outcome that actually was achieved. The President must be in a position to make and enforce such judgments. . . .

All this was summarized by President Kennedy in these words:

> Our arms must be subject to ultimate civilian control and command at all times, in war as well as peace. The basic decisions on our participation in any conflict and our response to any threat—including all decisions relating to the use of nuclear weapons, or the escalation of a small war into a large one—will be made by the regularly constituted civilian authorities.

*   *   *

How have these themes worked themselves out in the development of our defense program? One of the most important ways has been in the recent and large build-up in our conventional or non-nuclear forces.

To understand properly the importance of the build-up of non-nuclear forces, it is necessary first to understand that there is a very great difference between nuclear weapons and non-nuclear weapons. Nuclear weapons are not simply high explosives writ large. Their destructive power makes them a completely new kind of military force which must be understood and related to our national security objectives in new ways. Hiroshima was destroyed by a 20-kiloton bomb. We now have weapons a thousand times that size. . . . As well as the familiar effects of blast and heat, these weapons can cover many thousands of square miles with deadly radioactive fallout. All this is familiar.

There has been in recent years the development of small nuclear weapons having yields equivalent to a few thousand tons of TNT or less. The day will come, if it has not come already, when there will be nuclear weapons of smaller yield than the largest high explosive weapons. When that day comes, will there no longer be a distinction between nuclear and conventional weapons? Some have argued to that effect. But they are mistaken. There is and will remain an important distinction, a "firebreak" if you like, between nuclear and non-nuclear war, a recognizable qualitative distinction that both combatants can recognize and agree upon, if they want to agree upon one. And, in the nuclear age, they will have a very powerful incentive to agree upon this distinction and limitation, because if they do not, there does not appear to be another easily recognizable limitation on weapons—no other obvious "firebreak" —all the way up the destructive spectrum to large scale thermonuclear war.

Adequate conventional forces are important. It is for this reason that, in the past two years, we have increased the number of active combat-ready Army divisions from eleven to sixteen, and our active tactical air wings from sixteen to twenty-one. . . .

Moreover, it is for this reason that we are now urging our NATO allies to increase the size and effectiveness of their conventional forces. Why?

The reason strong conventional forces are required is that there are many situations in which the use of nuclear weapons would be inappropriate. For the same reasons that a sledge hammer does not make a good substitute for a fly swatter, nuclear weapons are not a good substitute for non-nuclear forces against a wide range of military threats. Even if they could be used to apply the minimum force required to achieve our objectives, their use would risk triggering escalation to a more and unnecessarily destructive level of conflict.

A nation or an alliance which maintains a strong nuclear posture combined with weak conventional forces thereby puts itself at a great disadvantage in the confrontation with another power that has both strong nuclear and strong conventional forces. This will be true no matter how strong and effective are its nuclear forces, provided that the other power maintains a secure second-strike nuclear retaliatory capability. Because nuclear war is so destructive, the use of nuclear weapons must be reserved only for the most desperate circumstances. But if the nuclears have to be reserved for vital issues, the side with the strong conventional forces is likely to be able to have its way on all issues less than vital. The side without adequate conventional forces will have no means for effective resistance in such confrontations. The side with conventional forces can use "salami-slice" tactics, or make its aggression piecemeal, in the confidence that it will be able to have its way on all but life-and-death matters. This is the kind of threat we have been facing in Berlin. The danger in piecemeal aggression is that erosion in the position of the free world over the years can end in world domination by the Communists.

Put alternatively, the President will be in a weak bargaining position indeed if he is confronted by the Communist Bloc with a choice between suicide or surrender, holocaust or humiliation. In order to resist aggression and defend our freedom, the President must have more attractive alternatives. Without conventional forces, our choice when faced with aggression may be "red or dead"; conventional forces help to deter aggression, and if deterrence fails, they can give us the opportunity to fight to stay alive and free.

Nevertheless, the build-up in our conventional forces has been costly and controversial. Two main lines of argument have been advanced against it. The first is that it weakens our nuclear resolve. In effect, it is a message to Khrushchev telling him that we are afraid or unwilling to use nuclear weapons, and that he can commit aggression against us with the expectation that we will not use them. Of course, pushed to an extreme, such an argument would say that we ought to abolish the United States Marine Corps. But the argument is defective. The important thing is not to convince an aggressor that we will use nuclear weapons. The important thing is to convince him that we will use whatever force is necessary to preserve our freedom. In many cases, that will be nonnuclear force. Sole or excessive reliance on nuclear weapons may tempt him to believe that we will not fight for less than vital issues. The danger is that each issue can be made less than vital. Aggression can be made piecemeal and in small enough pieces so that succumbing always looks attractive by comparison with thermonuclear war. Is not Berlin Khrushchev's "last territorial demand in Europe"?

In fact, reflection on the problem should convince most reasonable men that the threat of the ultimate use of nuclear weapons, if required, is much more credible to an aggressor who sees that to accomplish his objective he must first defeat a large and effective conventional force. If he succeeds in doing that, the issue at stake is likely by then to be vital for the defender.

Still, some argue that we should try to convince our adversaries that we would use nuclear weapons even in situations in which it is irrational to do so. Interestingly enough, Khrushchev himself has recently attacked this principle as a policy for the Communist Bloc, and in attacking him, the Chinese Communists have nonetheless acknowledged the enormous destructiveness of nuclear war. When it is clear that the Communists know the facts of nuclear destructiveness, it would seem foolish for us to base our strategy on the pretense that we do not. The trouble with trying to exploit "the rationality of irrationality," as theorists of bargaining and conflict call this, is that it simply is not a viable policy in the long run for a democracy, especially a democracy with allies. We must have defense policies that make sense to the American people and to our allies. Moreover, threats to blow ourselves up along with the aggressor are not likely to be credible. Rather, the most credible kind of threat is the threat that we will do what in the event will be most in our interest to do. In the case of piecemeal non-nuclear aggression, that will be to apply conventional forces.

The other main line of argument against the build-up of our conventional forces is that it will be fruitless, extremely costly, and unable to achieve the objective of adequacy because we are so badly outnumbered by the Communist hordes. These arguments, though widely believed, are not supported by the facts. Conventional military strength requires fighting men; it also requires that the men be fed, clothed, and equipped with effective weapons and other material. Equipping and supporting armies requires wealth and industrial production. The NATO allies outnumber the members of the Warsaw Pact in population, men under arms, and even foot soldiers in active army forces. In the dire straits into which mismanagement has plunged their economy, the Chinese Communists appear to be far from being able to provide modern and effective equipment from an army the size of our own. Moreover, the gross national products of the United States and its allies are more than twice the same total for the Soviet Union and its allies; in terms of industrial production, the ratio is more than two-and-one-half to one. What all of these facts suggest is that although substantial sacrifice may be involved for us and our NATO allies in equipping ourselves with adequate conventional forces, proportionally the sacrifice is much smaller for us than it is for our adversaries. Although we do need to strengthen our conventional forces somewhat, the extra costs are not large. We have already paid the entry fee into the "non-nuclear club." It is now largely a matter of making fully effective the force levels we have already agreed to provide.

A related argument has it that limiting conflicts to non-nuclear weapons puts us at a disadvantage because of our numerical inferiority, and that we need to use nuclear weapons as an equalizer in all but the smallest of armed conflicts. Leaving aside the undesirable character of the equalization they accomplish, and the unresolved question of whether the use of nuclear weapons is to our military advantage if the other side replies in kind, let me point out that our wealth and technology confer on us some important advantages in non-nuclear combat. Indeed, the effectiveness of modern non-nuclear arms is so great that they can offset substantial numerical inferiority in isolated situations in which we might be numerically inferior. The ability to produce such armaments in large quantities is a key determinant of the effectiveness of a nation's non-nuclear forces.

In summary, conventional military force is usable force. In Korea and in the Cuban crisis, we found that the non-nuclear forces were the cutting edge of our military power. We can use conventional force with a minimal risk of self-destruction. Therefore, it provides a more credible deterrent to non-nuclear aggression. As the destructiveness of nuclear war increases, and as nuclear-weapon systems become less vulnerable to sudden attack, the effectiveness of the threatened use of nuclear weapons as a substitute for conventional forces will diminish, and we will have no sensible alternative to building up our conventional forces to the point at which they can safely resist all forms of non-nuclear aggression. Our forces will be adequate if we can never be forced because of weakness to be the first to have to resort to nuclear weapons.

But if nuclear forces are not an effective substitute for adequate conventional forces, neither are conventional forces an effective substitute for adequate nuclear forces. Rather, the relationship between the two is one of complementarism. Now that the Communist Bloc is armed with nuclear weapons, we cannot successfully fight conventional wars except under the umbrella of nuclear strength. This nuclear strength is required to deter the Communists from escalating a non-nuclear conflict which is not going well for them into nuclear war, and to convince them that an act of nuclear aggression would lead to their defeat and possibly to the destruction of their society.

This, then, is the most important objective of our nuclear posture: to make thermonuclear war unlikely by deterring deliberate calculated nuclear aggression. We also seek other objectives. We want to make accidental, unpremeditated, irrational nuclear war unlikely also. And if war does occur, we want to be able to bring it to a speedy termination on military terms favorable to ourselves, and we want to do what we can to limit the damage caused to ourselves and our allies. How do we go about pursuing those objectives?

First, we attempt to deter deliberate premeditated attack by maintaining secure second-strike retaliatory capabilities—that is, force that cannot be knocked out in a surprise first blow. This means relatively invulnerable weapons systems like Minuteman, Titan, and Polaris, and secure, protected, survivable command and control facilities that will enable our national leadership to survive an attack and direct the use of retaliatory forces against any aggressor.

There is a great deal of literature and there are many approaches to the subject of deterrence. Some argue that, in the event of a nuclear attack on the alliance, we should plan to retaliate strictly against Soviet cities. Others argue that we should plan to strike back only against Soviet military forces. Still others argue for both. Some believe that we should design our posture for an irrevocable commitment to a spasm of massive retaliation. Our approach is based on options, deliberation, flexibility, and control. Rather than decide ahead of time which targets must be hit by which weapons, and then commit ourselves to it, our approach is to give the President a range of choices so that he can select the plan whose targets and timing of attacks are most appropriate to the circumstances at hand. I won't speculate here as to which nuclear response might be used in which circumstances. Nothing useful would be accomplished by doing so. But let me make three observations about this policy.

First, it is a policy of strength, not weakness. It takes superior nuclear forces to be able to ride out any kind of attack and then retain the option to destroy most of the enemies' remaining military forces, should that be appropriate. It would be a policy of weakness to commit ourselves irrevocably to a spasm of nuclear retaliation against Soviet cities.

Second, this policy requires secure forces and secure command and control. It requires weapon systems like Minuteman and Polaris that are hard and dispersed, or mobile and concealed, and that can ride out a thermonuclear attack and be held in reserve in the environment of nuclear war. . . .

Third, this approach to nuclear deterrence illustrates the principle that across the spectrum of conflict, military force is to be used with deliberation and control. There is, to be sure, a danger of breakdown of control in the environment of thermonuclear war.

But, short of complete destruction of Western society, there is no point at which it makes sense to choose to abandon control. Even when it comes to thermonuclear weapons, if your weapons are to be used to keep us alive and free, their use must be controlled.

This emphasis on control had led us, in the past two years, to emphasize the procurement of survivable, secure, redundant, and internetted command, control, and communications facilities. . . .

As well as making a major contribution to our ability to deter deliberate attack, this strengthened command structure has made an important contribution to reducing the likelihood of such unlikely eventualities as unauthorized, accidental, or other unpremeditated attacks blowing up into large-scale thermonuclear war. And, along with many other safety precautions that we have taken, it is making much less likely the possibility of accidental or unauthorized use of nuclear weapons on our side. . . .

But, despite our best efforts, a war may still occur. In these dangerous and unpredictable times, it would be foolish to base our planning on the assumption that a themonuclear war could never happen. Despite our best efforts, almost any kind of nuclear war would be an unprecedented disaster. But if such a war were thrust upon us, there are worthwhile things that could be done to mitigate its consequences. We are making preparations whose purpose is, in the event of war, to enable us to maintain a favorable military position, to bring the war to an end quickly, and to hold to a minimum the damage to ourselves and our allies. To limit the damage, we are making a combination of plans and preparations, including civil defense, active air and anti-missile defense, and an ability to destroy what we can of the enemy's offensive weapons. . . .

Beyond these physical measures, we are also opening up the option of maintaining some effective deterrence after a nuclear war begins. This was described last Spring by Secretary of Defense McNamara in an address at Ann Arbor, at the University of Michigan. In his words:

> The U.S. has come to the conclusion that to the extent feasible, basic military strategy in a possible general nuclear war should be approached in much the same way that more conventional military operations have been regarded in the past. That is to say, principal

military objectives, in the event of a nuclear war stemming from a major attack on the Alliance, should be the destruction of the enemy's military forces, not of his civilian population.

The very strength and nature of the Alliance forces make it possible for us to retain, even in the face of a massive surprise attack, sufficient reserve striking power to destroy an enemy society if driven to it. In other words, we are giving a possible opponent the strongest imaginable incentive to refrain from striking our own cities.

Doubtless, questions will arise in your minds as to whether nuclear war can and should be limited and controlled. First, can it? The answer depends on our will to make it so. With the protected weapon systems, command posts, and communications we are now acquiring, there is no technical reason why the use of nuclear weapons cannot be controlled in a nuclear war. The destructive power of their uncontrolled use should give all participants a strong incentive to find ways of avoiding it. Moreover, as both sides acquire protected forces like Minuteman and Polaris, the prospects are that neither side will be able to improve its military position by a sudden attack on the forces of the other. Then, if massive thermonuclear attack ever did make sense, it will do so no longer.

The other question is, "should we try?" The argument against trying, one that has been used against civil defense, is that it weakens the "firebreak" between nuclear and non-nuclear war. But any thermonuclear war would be such an unprecedented disaster that it is difficult to see how anything we could do to mitigate its consequences would effectively weaken the "firebreak." And the disaster of an unlimited nuclear war would be too great to permit us not to take whatever measures we can to minimize its likelihood. Moreover, the principle of controlled and limited use of military force is indivisible. If we believe in control in some circumstances and not in others, it will become more difficult to maintain it in those circumstances in which we should. An emphasis on control and limitations in the use of force is desirable across the spectrum of conflict.

I am sure that you are all concerned, as I am, about the moral problems raised by our military preparations. Is it right or wrong for us to be buying hundreds of intercontinental ballistic missiles, fighter-bomber aircraft, and equipment for many army divisions? Can we justify weapon systems and war plans that would enable us, if a nuclear war were thrust upon us, to fight back even though doing so might lead to the deaths of many millions of people? . . .

According to traditional Christian doctrine, the use of force to repress evil can be justifiable under certain conditions including the following: first, the use of force must have a reasonable chance of success. Second, if successful, it must offer a better situation than the one that would prevail in the absence of the use of force. Third, the force that is used must be proportional to the objectives being sought (or the evil being repressed). For this to be satisfied, peaceful means of redress must have failed. Fourth, the force must be used with the intention of sparing noncombatants and with a reasonable prospect of actually doing so.

It is interesting to observe that the potentially catastrophic character of thermonuclear war has forced practical decision-makers, reasoning in a secular context, to adopt a set of criteria very much like those of the traditional Christian doctrine and to apply them to the design of the military posture of the United States. Now, much more than in the recent past, our use of force is being carefully proportioned to the objectives being sought, and the objectives are being carefully limited to those which at the same time are necessary for our security and which do not pose the kind of unlimited threat to our opponents in the cold war that would drive them to unleash nuclear war. . . .

Within the broad policy of armed resistance to aggression, which is one of the alternatives open to us, and in terms of the moral criteria of the traditional Christian doctrine, I think it is fair to say that we have made considerable progress. This is not to say that we have gone as far as we can go. But it does suggest that all the moral questions are not concerned with whether or not armed resistance can be justifiable.

During the past fifteen years, a number of commentators, theologions and others, have taken the position that although in former times the traditional doctrine was valid and, under appropriate conditions, the use of armed force could be justified, now, in the atomic age, there can be no justifiable war. The argument has been made that nuclear war does not and cannot offer a reasonable

chance of bringing about a better situation than that which would
have prevailed in the absence of the use of force; that thermonuclear force, being essentially unlimited in its destructive effects,
cannot be proportioned to reasonable objectives; and that with it,
the noncombatants cannot be spared. Therefore, many argue, the
traditional doctrine is obsolete and a new doctrine must be found.
Some argue that the only morally acceptable course is to renounce
nuclear weapons; others believe that we must renounce the use of
force altogether.

I would not want to suggest that this line of thought is not based
on good and compelling reasons, even though I have not found it
convincing myself. It may prove to be the case that the danger of
escalation is so great that future limited non-nuclear wars will
bring with them an intolerable risk of massive thermonuclear
destruction. However, experience in the past fifteen years has
shown that non-nuclear wars can be kept limited and that freedom
can be defended from Communist aggression without massive
destruction.

A question to consider in one's critical thought on this problem
is whether the view that the traditional doctrine is obsolete is based
on an overemphasis on unlimited nuclear war, perhaps an identification of all armed conflict with it. An unlimited nuclear war is an
extreme on a broad spectrum of possible armed conflicts. Of
course, it is a very important extreme because of its disastrous consequences, but it is not the whole spectrum. In fact, it is only one
among many possible kinds of thermonuclear war. It can be a mistake to apply reasoning based on this extreme to all kinds of armed
resistance to aggression and injustice. I think it is important to
recognize this, for if our thinking is unclear on this point, and if
we identify any use of armed force with unlimited destruction, we
are likely unnecessarily to disarm ourselves and leave ourselves
victims of Communist aggression.

It is clear that we have elected to retain the threat of use of nuclear weapons in our own defense and that of our allies. We
thereby consciously accept the risk that we will have to use them.
Some people believe that we should reject the use of nuclear weapons. Before accepting such a judgment, one should consider carefully the full implications of such a decision. We do have world-

wide responsibilities. Many millions of people depend for their lives and freedom on our military strength. In this respect, the United States is in a very different position from any other country in the free world.

The question I would like to leave with you is whether current U.S. defense policy, which emphasizes deterrence, control, and the use of the appropriately limited amount of force, represents a good reconciliation of the traditional doctrine with the facts of life in the nuclear age? We have achieved some success with the controlled use of force. We are still alive and free today, and the missiles are out of Cuba. We are running great risks, to be sure, but would the risk be ameliorated by laying down our arms? It is tragic that nations must at times resort to armed force to resolve their differences. War is destructive and it has evil consequences. But our defense posture is being designed to make war less likely and less destructive. I am not suggesting that we can make war and violence desirable. The question is whether we have a better alternative.

I have defended our policies on the grounds that they make sense. Can they also be defended on the grounds that they are moral? Viewed with perspective, the two should be the same.

THE ROLE OF NUCLEAR DETERRENCE *

BY

BERNARD BRODIE

[1963]

Just as the "massive retaliation" doctrine characterized the main thrust of the Eisenhower administration's defense policies, so that of the Kennedy administration has been marked by persistent emphasis on very nearly the opposite theme. That theme is briefly stated as follows: although we will not voluntarily relinquish the nuclear ascendancy now enjoyed by the United States, prudent anticipation of the coming nuclear stalemate requires us to return to conventional forces for the tactical defense even of Europe.

The United States has acknowledged that it is prepared to use nuclear weapons "if necessary" for the defense of Berlin and other NATO territories, but the conception behind that "if necessary" has been responsible also for heavy pressure upon our NATO allies to make a larger contribution to the conventional capabilities of the alliance.

The new American school of thought, which exists in several variants on the part of advocates both in and out of government, possesses no label comparable in pithiness to the Dulles "massive retaliation" tag; but we shall call it here the Conventional War in Europe philosophy (CWE). . . .

After pointing out that ". . . we must continue to strengthen and modernize our tactical nuclear capabilities to deal with an attack where the opponent employs such weapons first, or any attack by conventional forces which puts Europe in danger of being overrun," Mr. McNamara went on to say: "But we must also substantially increase our non-nuclear capabilities to foreclose to our opponent the freedom of action he would otherwise have, or be-

* From *The Reporter*, May 23, 1963, copyright by The Reporter Magazine Co. Reprinted by permission. Bernard Brodie (b. 1910) is professor of political science at the University of California, Los Angeles. His most recent publication is *Escalation and the Nuclear Option*.

lieve he would have, in lesser military provocations. We must be in position to confront him at any level of provocation with an appropriate military response. The decision to employ tactical nuclear weapons should not be forced upon us simply because we have no other way to cope with a particular situation."

These words are somewhat ambiguous concerning the maximum level of Soviet non-nuclear attack that Mr. McNamara would like to see us able to oppose successfully with non-nuclear means, but additional clarification is provided later in the statement. Under Section IV, on "General Purpose Forces," he added the following:

"Although we are still a long way from achieving the non-nuclear capabilities we hope to create in Europe, we are much better off in this regard than we were two years ago. Today the NATO forces can deal with a much greater range of Soviet actions, without resorting to the use of nuclear weapons. Certainly, they can deal with any major incursion or probe. But we must continue to do everything in our power to persuade our Allies to meet their NATO force goals so that we will possess alternative capabilities for dealing with even larger Soviet attacks. And until these capabilities are achieved, the defense of Europe against an all-out Soviet attack, even if such an attack were limited to non-nuclear means, would require the use of tactical nuclear weapons on our part."

It is clear that Mr. McNamara would like to be able to meet even an "all-out" Soviet non-nuclear attack by non-nuclear means. Although in his opinion we already have the means for dealing conventionally "with any major incursion or probe," he feels that "we are still a long way from achieving the non-nuclear capabilities we hope to create in Europe." To achieve that end, he is willing "to do everything in our power to persuade our Allies" to make the required contributions.

However, on this issue as well as on several others, our major allies have for some time shown themselves markedly resistant to our persuasion. . . .

In trying to understand this attitude, one must first remember that the view our government is now advancing as the only reasonable one is the reverse of the idea that our leaders were preaching only a few years ago. It is also well known abroad that the new view is by no means accepted by the majority of senior American military officers. . . .

Though official American emphasis is on meeeting goals already agreed on, our allies are aware of the fervor behind the new concept in administration circles. It is the Germans especially who distrust the future implications of that peculiarly intense conviction —as though we had achieved a "breakthrough" in thought—and who distrust also so extraordinary a goal as having a capability for stopping by conventional means any non-nuclear attack that could be mounted even by the full field strength of the Communist bloc.

The concept is usually coupled with talk about "accidental war," that is, of Soviet miscalculations or acts of repression that would set off hostilities on a large scale but, hopefully, leave us short of the final abyss. No answer is given to the question of how much territory in Europe we should be ready to give up before deciding that we can no longer withhold nuclear weapons.

The purposes of achieving a very large conventional capability are generally given as follows:

It should discourage the enemy from thinking that our unwillingness to be the first to use nuclear weapons, or to see nuclear general war visited upon the world, gives him opportunities to achieve limited but important victories by local non-nuclear aggression. He must not suppose that he can outbid us quickly and decisively in non-nuclear strength. Making it clear that he cannot will add materially to deterrence.

If he nevertheless becomes involved through "miscalculation" in an attack on us and finds that, because of our resistance, he has applied most or all of his non-nuclear strength, he will have a chance to pause and reconsider what he is risking. If he then continues his aggression, the onus for bringing in nuclear weapons will be on him.

It may be we who want to take the diplomatic and even military initiative, and it will make all the difference in our willingness to do so if we can make some meaningful move without nuclear weapons.

There is also the conviction that at least by 1970 there will be no such thing as a meaningful superiority in strategic nuclear capabilities. Thus, the threat of strategic nuclear war as the ultimate backstop to a diplomatic position will be unavailable.

In any case the enemy is to receive the clearest warning that we will not accept a loss of territory or other comparable defeats. We remain committed to introducing nuclear weapons not only if the enemy does so but also if we find ourselves losing significantly. The aim of keeping war in Europe non-nuclear is considered terribly important, but nonetheless secondary to the aim of not losing.

We should distinguish this CWE philosophy from several other ideas which have become current of late and which I do not wish to challenge. At this date few persons professionally involved in defense doubt the need for some conventional forces for the contingencies of limited war such as might easily occur outside Europe and conceivably inside Europe as well. . . .

We should also distinguish various current doctrines of discriminate or controlled general war, especially that which not only stresses counterforce targets but which adds special and positive emphasis to sparing cities. Avoidance of city bombing, except in direct reprisal, probably has sufficient justification, apart from other obvious interests, in the elementary and familiar proposition that enemy cities have far more strategic significance as hostages than as ruins.

It is also true and important that our allies have made promises to NATO which they have not met and which, until the pertinent agreements are changed, we are justified in pressing them to fulfill. Although the commitments to these force levels were made under the explicit assumption that any outbreak of war in Europe between the Soviet bloc and the West would be almost immediately nuclear, there is no need to deprive available forces of all capability for fighting with conventional weapons.

What we shall be questioning, at least by implication, is, first, the image of the world reflected in the fervor and the zeal—and the excessive goals—behind what is up to a point a reasonable idea, and second, the evident impatience with the misgivings and contrary ideas of allies whose views are habitually dismissed on the ground that they just don't understand the basic facts of nuclear life.

CWE advocates feel, with some justice, that the United States is carrying a disproportionate share of the NATO defense burden. They argue also that American contributions to nuclear capabilities in a general war are more than adequate and should not be duplicated. They usually consider tactical nuclear capabilities in Europe dangerous and illusory. Therefore, according to them, obligations to the common defense by our European and Canadian allies can only and should only take the form of providing greater conventional capabilities.

This idea is hard to put across in Europe. . . .

The British and French governments have different ideas from ours about the value to them of independent nuclear capabilities. The French especially have long been determined to go ahead with their program regardless of American objections—partly, perhaps, because they know the United States cannot withhold from France the protective covering accorded Europe, but mostly because they are bent on rejecting the status of a satellite.

The British seem to be less concerned about nuclear dependence on the United States, and among the many who have professed willingness to give up the independent nuclear deterrent is the leader of the Labour Party, Harold Wilson. However, we should remember that many Britons who take that position do so for reasons that are not necessarily reassuring to the government of the United States. In Britain rejection of the nuclear deterrent often goes with neutralism, and certainly not often with any desire to see the reintroduction of conscription, without which Britain is not going to increase materially its contribution to conventional capabilities in Europe. The Germans, who are not yet avowedly nourishing aspirations to an independent nuclear capability, are nevertheless deeply alarmed by American emphasis on conventional-war strategies.

All these people share the view that we Americans have simply availed ourselves of our great wealth to build up the forces we thought necessary to our own defense. A good part of our defense budget has been absorbed by a large strategic nuclear capability that we have insisted on maintaining exclusively under our own national control, despite recent token gestures to the contrary. In providing protection for ourselves, we have created what in large measure protects also our European allies. They have not hitherto been asked to share the financial cost of the force that protects us all—though they have provided bases and thus shouldered some risks. It is a mistake to assume that we can now induce them to compensate us by raising additional forces which they feel they do not need and which in the French case would be at the expense of forces they insist on having.

Thus, appeals to our NATO allies to increase their military effort must be based on something more objective than the fact that we have shifted to a new strategic philosophy, especially one that must appear to them to cost more and at the same time diminish deterrence. Our insistence that it will increase deterrence is based on premises and assumptions which may be valid under some circumstances but which are certainly not unchallengeable. Our assumption that the new philosophy would demonstrate its superior merits *if* war breaks out will be weighed against the European presumption, however debatable, that the resulting stance could make it *easier* for war to break out—by appearing to push our nuclear strength into the background. Besides, our allies are deeply suspicious of alleged American efforts to get them to provide the "men-at-arms for the American nuclear knight." . . .

Those CWE advocates who urge that we should put ourselves in a position to be able to stem at least for a time a full-scale non-nuclear attack by the Soviet forces have in general advanced a startlingly modest view of the extra effort required.

Present promises to NATO would, if fulfilled, raise existing strength on the Central Front from something like twenty-four divisions to something like thirty. NATO may yet conceivably get those thirty divisions, but they are not likely to be well-equipped and full-strength divisions with adequate logistic backing. Thus, the first margin of extra effort is the difference between twenty-four lean divisions and thirty fat ones, and fat in the weaponry of conventional war.

Whatever serious studies have been made of requirements for any type of war, nuclear or non-nuclear, are naturally highly classified, but one well-informed CWE advocate offered me the probably optimistic offhand guess that the essential goals to be achieved for providing an "adequate" conventional force in Europe would require of our NATO allies about one per cent more of their respective Gross National Products than they are now contributing. And, after all, those GNPs are steadily rising.

Now, economists are accustomed to reckoning in percentages of GNP, but politicians are not. The latter think in terms of increases in existing budgets, and for a country already contributing say five per cent of its GNP to defense—which is not trivial by historical peacetime standards, and the larger allies contribute more—an increase of one per cent of GNP has more meaning as a twenty per cent increase in the defense budget.

There is another point to be considered. If estimates of Soviet ground forces have been exaggerated, it is clearly desirable to cut them down to proper size. Obviously, we want to evaluate *any* forces correctly, whether they be enemy or allied. In pointing out inherent enemy weaknesses, however, we should be careful not to gloss over our own; for example, the inherent weakness of having a force structure stemming from fifteen different nations, with an allocation of commands designed as much to accomplish political as military ends. Whatever the number of divisions available to NATO, their effectiveness must surely fall short, perhaps markedly, of being comparable to a good single-nation army having the same number of divisions.

Anyway, the substantial reduction in Russian ground forces between 1955 and 1961 was a somewhat tardy adjustment to what the Soviets considered the requirements of the nuclear age (as well as, let us add, the absence of any strong urge to conquer a nuclearly defended Western Europe). They stopped further planned cuts in 1961, apparently in response to our build-up. Experience since then suggests their readiness to move up with us to maintain their relative advantage in ground forces in Europe. . . .

As Sir Winston Churchill once wrote, concerning the planning for a particularly ill-starred offensive: "However absorbed a commander may be in the elaboration of his own thoughts, it is necessary sometimes to take the enemy into consideration." In the spinning of military theories, it is really remarkable how seldom that is done. In the present case the "enemy" should be considered under both of two guises. First, there is the shrewd opponent familiar in war-gaming rooms, blessed with a free-ranging imagination and showing no biases other than those we share with him. He is shrewd, skillful, and aggressive; he has to be, or one cannot have a challenging and interesting game. The other is the real Soviet opponent, with whom we have had prolonged experience which is available for study but which only a few people do in fact study. He is the opponent who we know has very special ways of looking at things—in other words, who has strong biases, some of which are fundamentally different from ours. This is the opponent who not infrequently blunders but who always shows a deep respect for our strength.

Concerning the CWE school's argument that the enemy will be more deterred by a strong conventional force than he would by a somewhat lesser force committed to using nuclear weapons at a relatively early stage: this can only be the war-game opponent. Certainly the argument requires some quite singular assumptions. One is that the Soviets will boldly make large forays against our nuclear power with non-nuclear arms. According to this line of reasoning, the determination of ourselves and our allies to resist clear aggression will collapse if there is any hint that tactical nuclear weapons may have to be used, and the Russians will know it. In fact, they will be so confident of our restraint that they will take what would otherwise be the most monumental risks! Actually, the question of "credibility" so effectively raised against the Dulles massive retaliation doctrine hardly applies in Europe—and we are not talking massive retaliation anyway, but tactical nuclear defense. It would probably take much persuasion on our part to shake the Soviet leaders from their apparent conviction that in the event of a substantial attack by them the nuclear weapons available to NATO forces in Europe would quickly be used. Why should we attempt to shake that conviction?

Another critical and dubious assumption is that the enemy will almost certainly refrain from using nuclear weapons if we refrain. Presumably it is "in his interest" to play the game that way—to make war locally but not to risk general war. But there is overwhelming evidence that he fears that *any* war in Europe is in great danger of escalating to general war, and that he rejects the notion that the introduction of nuclear weapons tactically makes all the difference.

Soviet military thinking continues to reject those refinements of military thought that have now become commonplace in this country—concerning, for example, distinctions between limited war and general war, between "controlled" and "uncontrolled" strategic targeting, and between nuclear and non-nuclear tactical operations. The kinds of civilian specialists who have given rise to most of the relevant ideas in this country do not even exist in the Soviet Union. The new Soviet manual of strategy written under the direction of former Chief of Staff Marshal V. Sokolovsky expresses scorn for the "modern school of American economists who consider that it is possible to juggle with nuclear warfare."

Perhaps the Soviet leaders are staging all this for our benefit, or perhaps they believe it now but will ultimately follow our lead. After all, the prospect of fighting a great land battle in Europe without nuclear weapons looked utterly bizarre to practically all Americans only a short time ago. . . .

Clearly the proposed strategy offers no inducement to the Russians to stay non-nuclear in an all-out premeditated attack with their ground forces. Proponents of the CWE philosophy repeatedly assert that we will not allow ourselves to be beaten. Since in tactical operations with nuclear weapons first use is extremely important—for example, by accomplishing the quick destruction of the opponent's supporting air forces—our determination to introduce such weapons rather than accept defeat tells the enemy if he believes us, that *he* must introduce them. It is one thing to propose an armaments restraint to which we promise to adhere, come what may, so long as the opponent does too; it is quite another to offer such restraint with the proviso that we will abandon it as soon as it clearly seems to interfere with the serious business of winning.

We are bemused, however, with the possibility of "accidental war." We feel that a conventional defense gives the opponent who lets himself slip into hostilities with us a chance to think it over. This is the concept of the "pause" for reassessment, which will enable the opponent (never ourselves, naturally) to remember the virtues of discretion. Anyway, if the enemy continues his aggression, he will proceed with it in a way calculated to win. If he refrains, it will be less our local conventional forces than our nuclear forces, strategic and tactical, that have obliged him to do so. That is exactly where we stand now and where we have stood since the beginning of NATO. What, then, will we have gained by a large conventional build-up?

The idea that the entire Russian field army could become involved in non-nuclear conflict as a result of an "accidental" outbreak of local violence is perhaps worth a place in the list of contingencies that a planner wishes to think about. But that we should consider the possibility strong enough to let it set a goal for our conventional build-up is fantastic. Anything that could properly be called "accidental war" has been extremely rare historically. What should make it more common in a nuclear age? The technical possibilities for nuclear accident are vastly outweighed by the enormous reluctance of national leaders, certainly including the Russians, to risk a war that might become nuclear.

A frequently cited scenario of accidental war has the Soviet troops putting down a major revolt in East Germany, which provokes West German troops to intervene. This implies, among other things, an ardor for intervention on the part of West German forces and a general lack of discipline all round that have yet to be demonstrated. Is the event conceivable? Of course! So are many other scenarios that follow quite different patterns. To say that something is conceivable may or may not mean that it is worth a second thought; it is hardly enough to establish that it warrants a basic shift in our strategic philosophy. In any case, why should our capacity to support an intervention, if we so desire, hinge upon our ability to fight a *large-scale* non-nuclear war? The raising of the initial level of violence is at least as much the enemy's option as ours, and it is hardly desirable to try to eliminate a consideration of our nuclear power from his reflections.

No doubt under some circumstances the Russians could not be made to feel the real determination behind our warning until they had done something to stir us to action. Something of that kind happened in Cuba. Probably too there is less chance that the demonstration will get out of control if nuclear weapons are meanwhile avoided. The idea of the "pause" is not altogether absurd. However, there is no good reason why the time for the pause should come when thirty divisions are involved rather than three, or even one. The risks may be smaller by choosing the lower threshold, because the discriminate use of small nuclear weapons can also be a powerful earnest of determination—which can have its effect *before* the opponent makes his commitment to a large-scale attack.

I see no basis in experience or logic for assuming that the increase in level of violence from one division to thirty is a less shocking and less dangerous form of escalation than the introduction of any kind of nuclear weapons. A galloping consensus has developed among some like-minded people around the entirely unfounded assumption that it is not size of conflict but use of nuclear weapons that would make all the difference. Our justified concern with the special emotions as well as the physical destruction provoked by the use of nuclear weapons has caused an unjustified depreciation of what it means to start fighting. Khrushchev indicated quite clearly last fall that where he wanted violence between the United States and the Soviet Union to stop was *before* one of our destroyers had fired a shot across the bows of a Soviet transport ship.

In view of the lessons we must draw from the Cuban crisis of 1962 concerning our position in Berlin, it is a mischievous interpretation to hold that the outcome was determined *mostly* by our local conventional superiority. If local superiority in conventional arms made all the difference, why did not Khrushchev make some face-saving retaliation in places where he was superior, as in Berlin? Many indeed predicted that he would. On the contrary, Khrushchev and Ulbricht began, on top of the abject surrender in Cuba, to be sweetly reasonable over Berlin. The significance of this seems to have been completely missed by most observers, who apparently accepted it simply as a bonus. And when the Chinese Communists castigated Khrushchev for retreating from a "paper tiger," his public reply was, "The paper tiger has nuclear teeth."

Surely all can agree that the Cuban episode demonstrated the great aversion of the present Soviet leaders to *any* direct hostilities with the United States. It indicated strongly that they fear even small outbreaks of violence between them and us, no doubt because they consider such outbreaks too likely to proceed rapidly to nuclear war. What surprised and sobered Khrushchev was our readiness to confront him. Our previous behavior had apparently led him to believe we would tolerate his installing the missiles; when he found that we were not that tolerant, he rushed to get them out—apparently unimpeded with any worries about "humiliation."

Still another assumption of the CWE school is that having greater conventional strength would permit us occasionally to take the diplomatic and military initiative where we would not dare do so if we had only nuclear weapons to work with. In the same speech at West Point on December 5, 1962, that embroiled him with the British, Dean Acheson offered the following view on "a sound plan for military defense":

"A military plan and policy which would deprive the Soviet Union of conventional superiority on its front with Western Europe requires increased production by all the allied countries, including ourselves. Such economic and military developments, should they occur, would give reality to such political policies as the reunification of Germany and more independent national lives for the East European countries. Finally, all these developments could bring such stability and balance in the relations between the Soviet Union and the Western allies that the control of armaments, including nuclear armaments, would become possible and practicable."

Later in the speech he said:

"Soviet domination of East Germany is largely based on the preponderance of Soviet conventional power on their western front. If this did not exist, Soviet intervention to support Ulbricht's authority might become increasingly impracticable."

One remembers in the 1952 elections the Republican talk of "roll-back," which only matched Acheson's earlier slogan about our need to build up our forces in order to be able to "negotiate from strength." No doubt we needed to build up our forces, but the fallacy in Acheson's slogan was the implication that he had an aggressive policy which only a lack of military support prevented him from implementing. What in fact he lacked, and what the build-up itself could not provide, was the kind of aggressive policy implied by his West Point remarks—which incidentally is to result in mutual arms control!

Since the end of the Second World War we have at no time taken or *seriously contemplated* any kind of military initiative that was not prompted by some external military aggression by the opponent. Concerning the uprisings in East Germany and in Hungary and the building of the Berlin Wall we did nothing, and our reasons could hardly have hinged on a shortage of conventional forces. In Korea we responded to a direct aggression against a protégé, and in Cuba we responded to a gambit aimed directly at ourselves.

There are many reasons why we are not more given to initiating crises where a clash of arms might be involved, but surely one is the same that caused Khrushchev to surrender in Cuba: violence between great opponents is inherently difficult to control, and it cannot be controlled unilaterally. We therefore save confrontations for the opponent's aggressions.

The most important ingredient in deterring Soviet aggression in Europe is our known readiness to oppose it. For support of this policy, our force structure has been in no important respect inappropriate. Stout hearts and a sense of Soviet methods have been and will surely continue to be more necessary than a conventional build-up.

But if war in Europe, however improbable, nevertheless does break out, what then? A future condition of stable mutual strategic deterrence (i.e., where each side deems the second-strike retaliatory capability of the other to be extremely formidable) would no doubt inhibit escalation from a limited war to a general war. But surely such a barrier against general war will not act also to prevent the use of tactical nuclear weapons in limited war. It should have exactly the opposite effect.

It is probable that the tactical use of nuclear weapons would increase the dangerousness of limited war. But who today considers any hostilities directly between the superpowers not to be anything but terribly dangerous? Who will take the first step toward war if he is so appalled at the thought of the second step, which is use of nuclear weapons? At any rate, there seems to be no empirical reason for the belief that use or non-use of tactical nuclear weapons will make all the difference between what some seem to regard as a rather safe and sane use of large-scale violence and what would be an unutterably disastrous eruption.

There are other considerations. The Germans know that not much territory can be yielded before they have yielded all of theirs. The French have pointed to our CWE philosophy as evidence, among other things, of the beginning of American withdrawal from the commitment to defend Europe even at the risk of total nuclear war. To them it confirms their foresight in aspiring for a national *force de frappe*. However wrong that deduction may be, we have needlessly given them much leverage for making it.

When charged that their philosophy looks toward making a new war in Europe resemble the Second World War, CWE advocates answer that it would be a lot better for Europeans than a tactical nuclear war—the implication being that they should jump at the chance. But most Europeans have a different way of looking at the present choice of alternatives. To contribute more men and money in order to make it possible to enjoy another Second World War strikes them, at the very least, as too much relinquishment of the nuclear deterrent. They are abundantly convinced that our staunchness and readiness to use the kind of force we already have in Europe is quite enough to keep the Russians at bay. They seem to hold the same to be true of keeping our position in West Berlin— which makes them willing to follow our lead, though we should be clear that for our non-German allies Berlin is not the best issue for inspiring them to greater sacrifice.

The Europeans, in short, want to settle for deterrence on the tactical level as well as the strategic. It is not true that they eagerly accept tactical nuclear weapons out of ignorance of the terrible implications of their use. They accept them in the same way and for the same reasons that Americans accept nuclear strategic deterrence. In fact, deterrence on the tactical level means for them exactly what deterrence on the strategic level means for us.

The more sophisticated CWE advocates have argued that tactical nuclear war in Europe would be not only terribly destructive but also militarily infeasible, because troops simply could not live in a battle environment where nuclear weapons were liberally employed. The charge of greater destructiveness would depend on the stage of violence reached, and it is far from obvious that use of a few nuclear weapons—to demonstrate readiness to use more—will force the level of violence upward rather than down.

In any case, finding tactical nuclear operations infeasible does not make large-scale conventional war in Europe feasible. Where nuclear weapons are on stand-by availability to both sides, conventional war must proceed in an extraordinarily precarious environment. Besides, if one's own armies cannot live in a nuclear environment, the chances are that neither can the enemy's. A war is not fought in order to provide a suitable battle environment for troops.

The real issues are much more political than technical. Our experience with the Russians, crowned by the Cuban episode of last October, tells us that the Soviet opponent is not ten feet tall in the moral intangibles of power—as he would have to be to do some of the bold things he does in war games. Even in the Berlin "blockade" of 1948–1949, when we failed altogether to test the Soviets' resolve to deny us access on the ground, they did not attempt to interfere with our airlift, as they could easily have done simply by jamming our Ground Controlled Approach radar system. Why should we go on postulating a kind of behavior that is radically different from what they have demonstrated over a long time? After all, the Soviet leaders have now openly broken with the Marxist-Leninist philosophy of inevitable war, avowedly on the ground that nuclear weapons do matter.

Those weapons have vastly affected the expectation of major war in Europe, and it is absurd not to make the most of that change. It is illogical to propose that the NATO powers should add substantially to their defense burdens in order to exploit a probably slim chance for moderating a possible future European war—which, however, the present dispositions make highly improbable.

It is one thing to exhort our allies to see that their contributions of forces maintain reasonable standards of efficiency, which certainly ought not to exclude a capability for limited conventional operations. It is quite another to invoke fantasies of great modern armies locked in desperate combat in Europe with never a nuclear warhead going off between them. The one attitude invites credit for our political sense as well as for our strategic thinking; the other merely discredits us in both respects.

THE ARMS RACE *

BY

ROBERT E. OSGOOD

[1965]

It is generally acknowledged that the fundamental cause of tension and war lies in the conflicting aims and special interests of states, which cause states to arm against each other. Yet it is also true that competition in armaments may aggravate tensions and help incite war. All competition for military power is bound to be provocative in so far as it threatens the security and other vital interests of adversaries. On the other hand, arms competition may also enforce caution and restraint on adversaries. The provocative effect of arms races, like other forms of international competition, should therefore be weighed against their moderating and deterrent effect.

The history of arms races demonstrates that they have been provocative (notably, the Anglo-German naval race of 1898–1912) but that, considered within the context of the whole range of international competition, they have had only a slight, indirect effect in causing war. Among the general causes of World War I the preceding arms races had much less influence than the network of alliance commitments, the nature of mobilization plans, and the confidence of statesmen and military staff officers in military victory. Furthermore, arms races have usually been self-limiting and have often exerted a deterrent or stabilizing effect. Their expense and their aggravation of tensions and insecurity have induced competing states to keep arms races limited. The ability of *status quo* powers to confront expansionist states with a disadvantageous balance of power by a continual advancement in the

---

* From *Beyond the Cold War*, edited by Robert A. Goldwin, published by Rand McNally, copyright 1963, 1965 by the Public Affairs Conference Center, The University of Chicago. Reprinted by permission. Robert E. Osgood (b. 1921) is director of the Washington Center of Foreign Policy Research and Professor of Political Science at the Johns Hopkins University School of Advanced International Studies. His publications include *Ideals and Self-Interest in America's Foreign Relations* and *Force, Order, and Justice* (with Robert W. Tucker).

quality and quantity of their arms has helped maintain peace. Thus some arms races have ended because they outlived their apparent usefulness or because political circumstances changed, and others have led to political settlements and truces. The outbreak of World War II marked the failure of deterrence not because of an arms race but because the opponents of aggression engaged in an arms race too late with too little.

The history of prenuclear arms races suggests that a prudent pursuit of countervailing power through quantitative and qualitative advances is, on balance, a moderating influence upon the continual competition for power among adversaries. This is not surprising, since the arms race has helped states to maintain their security by internal means without resorting to the unsettling territorial transfers and acquisitions, the contests for allies, and, most important, the military interventions which were common devices for achieving a favorable distribution of power in the eighteenth and nineteenth centuries.

Undoubtedly, the current US-USSR arms race has aggravated the tensions that spring from the political and ideological conflicts of the Cold War. Yet America's maintenance of vast military strength throughout a broad spectrum of continually changing technology, especially in nuclear striking power, has also been an indispensable deterrent to Soviet and Chinese military adventures. The US-USSR arms race, far from being an unlimited and increasingly provocative competition, has by reciprocal limitation settled into a dynamic equilibrium maintained by somewhat reduced expenditures and based on an approaching parity of Soviet and American capacities to devastate each other in response to a direct attack. Contrary to past expectations that a nuclear stand-off would encourage overt non-nuclear aggression, limited military actions above the level of "unconventional" or "internal" war seem securely deterred by the risk of "escalation" and some improvement in the conventional resistance capacity of the United States and its allies.

The relative limitation and stability of this arms race is fostered by three technical characteristics, which reinforce the notable caution of the participants:

(1) The extreme, virtually self-defeating destructiveness of any

war in which the nuclear powers were to use their most powerful weapons against each other, together with the prospect that these weapons *would* be used if the United States and the USSR and their allies became involved in direct combat, gives these adversaries unprecedented incentives to avoid direct combat, as long as the United States and the USSR retain a minimum capacity to inflict intolerable damage upon each other regardless of what military initiative the other might take.

(2) The maintenance by the United States and the USSR of a very great number of weapons, especially nuclear weapons, means that a given relative advance in the quantity or the offensive or defensive quality of one adversary's weapons is not likely to give him a sufficient military advantage to reduce his inhibitions against resorting to war. Beyond the minimum capacity of each side to inflict intolerable retaliatory damage upon the other, one side would have to achieve a revolutionary technological breakthrough or a tremendous quantitative superiority in order to undermine the security of the other.

(3) The fact that the US-USSR arms race is a collection of many arms races throughout a wide variety of rapidly changing weapons diminishes the chances that any single innovation or series of innovations or any numerical superiority in a particular weapon achieved by one side will upset the military balance enough to raise the incentives for war before the other side redresses the balance with its own innovations.

For these reasons the balance of deterrent over provocative effects in the current arms race seems even greater than in previous arms races. The current arms race seems inherently more stable and less prone to war than previous races (for example, the naval races before and after World War I) in which a relatively small quantitative superiority of arms could give one adversary a significant military advantage. Like previous arms races, the current one is substantially limited by the inability of either participant to gain a decisive superiority at a cost that will not jeopardize competing objectives requiring money, material, and manpower. It is true that the characteristics of some nuclear weapons have created a novel danger that warfare might result from a technical accident, the unauthorized use of weapons, or a false apprehension of sudden attack: but this danger has been reduced to minimal proportions by unilateral safeguards and the development of relatively invulnerable missiles.

On the other hand, when one thinks not of the stability and the deterrent effect of the present military equilibrium but of the consequences of warfare if, somehow, war did occur, the US-USSR arms race seems anything but beneficent. It seems, in fact, far more dangerous than any armed competition in history. This is because, by all odds, the greatest danger of the current arms race lies in the awesomely destructive weapons the race has fostered and will evidently continue to foster. The arms race may make war unlikely, but if war were to occur, it could be catastrophic. Considering the whole history of international relations, it is difficult to imagine the most powerful adversaries forever remaining in such a stable military equilibrium and indefinitely pursuing their competing interests with such caution and foresight as to avoid war with each other. It is unlikely that such a war would be significantly limited.

The current arms race also poses another novel, though more speculative, danger: the prospect that additional states will acquire nuclear and other catastrophic weapons. It now seems unlikely that any states who have not already achieved nuclear explosions will have sufficient incentive to acquire nuclear weapons in the next decade, although perhaps a dozen states have the capability. But this would be a rash prediction to make for subsequent decades if the process of nuclear diffusion is not stopped by international agreement. If India were to follow China's example, or if Israel were to decide to produce nuclear weapons, a chain effect might rapidly set in.

So far, the remarkable stability of the US-USSR arms race has depended a great deal upon several unique circumstances: There have been only two major participants, and they have enjoyed a preponderance of power in the world; both have developed a vast, diversified panoply of military power at a roughly equal pace; the defensive participant acquired nuclear weapons first and maintained nuclear superiority during the transitional period to stable parity; the leadership of both participants has been disinclined to pursue its foreign interests by military means. Under different circumstances, prospective arms races among additional nuclear powers, especially among states who are not subordinate members of the Soviet or American blocs, are likely to be far more provocative. This prospect is already unsettling to the existing nuclear powers and to the non-nuclear powers who wish to remain so. Their apprehensions may spring only from the natural distaste for changing the nuclear *status quo* on the part of those with a special interest in perpetuating it, but they may also be farsighted intimations of a period of acute international tension and disorder that would follow the end of an exclusively bilateral nuclear balance.

It is impossible to predict in detail the consequences of nuclear diffusion, because one cannot foresee exactly which nations will acquire nuclear weapons, what kinds of nuclear capabilities they will acquire, when and in what sequence and pace they will acquire them, how they will seek to exploit their capabilities in their foreign relations, or how the original nuclear powers and the remaining non-nuclear powers will react to these contingencies. Quite possibly the introduction of nuclear capabilities into some international rivalries and animosities would be stabilizing for some of the same reasons that have restrained the United States and the USSR from coming to blows, but none cannot reasonably suppose that this would be the universal effect of nuclear diffusion. More likely, a number of conditions would aggravate international conflicts and greatly increase the danger of nuclear exchanges: the uneven development of nuclear capabilities among adversaries, the incautious approach of some regimes to new-found destructive power, their lack of safeguards against unauthorized and accidental use together with the possibilities of ambiguous national responsibility for nuclear blows, the incentive for great powers to intervene preventively in small nuclear powers' conflicts, and the fragmentation of NATO—hence, the weakening of mutual defense commitments and the undermining of deterrence—under nuclear separatism.

For these reasons I reach the conclusion that the arms competition between the United States and the USSR exerts, on the whole, a stabilizing, moderating, and pacifying effect on the general competition for power that springs from the political and ideological conflicts of the Cold War, but that the kinds of weapons this competition has already produced and is likely to produce in the future and the prospect that additional states will acquire them are so dangerous to the United States and to humanity that we must seriously consider adopting any measures that might conceivably prevent or mitigate these dangers. Among such measures, disarmament has attracted ever-increasing attention in this century.

All prospective disarmament agreements, however, raise three crucial questions: (1) the question of utility: Would disarmament mitigate the dangers of the arms race without weakening national security? (2) the question of mutual acceptability: Would states see a mutual interest in disarming? (3) the question of continuity: If so, would they continue to share this interest and observe the agreement in good faith?

THE POLITICS OF NON-VIOLENCE*

PREPARED FOR THE

AMERICAN FRIENDS SERVICE COMMITTEE

[1955]

We believe there is no longer any doubt in the minds of concerned men that the American response to its world responsibility in the years since 1945 has been inadequate. Our leaders have stated time and again that the real hope of peace lies in disarmament, in developing world organization, in fundamental attacks on poverty. President Truman lifted the hopes of the world in his 1949 inaugural address with the "bold new program" that became known as Point Four. President Eisenhower followed with his celebrated disarmament speech before the American Society of Newspaper Editors and his atoms for peace address at the U.N. The note struck in these presidential utterances has been warmly echoed by the American people. Resolutions on the positive requirements of peace have poured in a steady stream from church conferences, labor and farm conventions, academic associations, women's clubs, civic and veterans' groups, and from many other points where concerned Americans assemble. . . .

But the results of their efforts are meager. The world continues to drift uncertainly on the edge of war, with each new crisis threatening to topple it over. The conditions that breed violence and the hatreds that divide men continue unchecked, despite the ebb and flow of tension at high political levels. Economic assistance programs grow smaller rather than larger and are more and more designed to meet strategic considerations instead of human need. The arms race continues unchecked and even in the midst of disarmament discussions, we proceed with vigor to plan the rearmament of Germany and Japan. . . .

---

*From "Speak Truth to Power; A Quaker Search for an Alternative to Violence," a pamphlet prepared for the American Friends Service Committee, 1955. This excerpt is not a full expression of the American Friends Service Committee's approach to world peace. Reprinted by special permission.

The tragedy of this situation is all too apparent. Though we try to congratulate ourselves on our economic prosperity, our welfare programs, and our great ideals, we are forever haunted by the spectre of nuclear power. The people of the United States are uneasily aware that carefully nurtured international hatreds and the fear that flows from bomb tests and arms races must some day erupt in violence, and that when they do, all that we love and cherish will surely be swept away. They are aware, too, that something other than military preparedness is needed to prevent disaster, and there is a sense of urgency about the search for a more adequate policy.

What is it that blocks our efforts? . . .

I

The basic reason for our failure lies in the nature of our present commitment to violence. The basic assumption upon which United States foreign policy rests is that our national interest can best be served by military preparedness against a Soviet threat on the one hand, and by constructive and world-wide economic, political, and social programs on the other. The most common image used to suggest an adequate American policy is that of a wall of military power as a shield against communism, behind which the work of democracy, in raising the level of life and educating the minds of men, can be carried on. Our material strength must provide the basis of security so that men may have a chance to grow and develop.

This is an appealing image, reflecting both our peaceful intentions and our high aspirations, but we believe it is false and illusory. We believe that whatever may have been true in the past, it is now impossible for a great nation to commit itself both to military preparedness and to carrying forward a constructive and positive program of peacemaking. We believe these two aims have become mutually exclusive, and that a willingness to resort to organized mass violence under any circumstances requires a commitment that condemns all other desires and considerations to relative ineffectiveness.

. . . Today war has its own logic, its own direction. No social institution is firmly enough based to contain it. It bends all to its needs. This is the nature of modern war. It is necessarily also the nature of preparation for war.

We suggest that American experience over the past dozen years bears out this conclusion regarding the all-engulfing nature of a commitment to military preparedness. We are not at this point in our discussion challenging the necessity for the commitment itself. We seek only to establish that it is in its nature an open-ended rather than a limited endeavor, and that it has in fact prevented us from moving in those other directions that so many agree are necessary if peace is to be won.

What then has been our experience in applying this limited restraining power? Has it been possible to act rationally and coolly to balance negative military requirements against the need for more positive and far reaching measures necessary to win the peace?

Even in a simple military sense the idea of a limited commitment to material power appears unrealistic. For it is in the nature of the situation that the limits to an armaments race are set for us by our enemy and for him by us. Here is a clear illustration of the familiar insight that by arming ourselves we do but arm our enemy. Thus in 1948 we were assured that forty-eight air wings were adequate to contain Soviet power. In July 1952 it was ninety-five; three months later, one hundred twenty-four. Recent discussion has centered around the goal of one hundred forty-three wings. It is clear that it is not what we possess, but what we fear others possess that sets the limits. Since this is also true for others, the attempt to find security in military power cannot be a matter of "thus far and no farther," but is a road that, once entered, has no end.

We have said that we would "contain" Soviet power. We have in fact *tried* to contain it. But since this would require a preponderance of force, which it has not been possible to achieve, we have failed. We have succeeded only in diverting large proportions of the economic, political, and psychological energy of both sides to non-productive and inflammatory purposes. Neither history nor our own recent experience supports the hope that the United States can make a limited commitment to military security in a world where power is concentrated in two blocs, both commanding vast resources.

Organization for modern warfare is no longer the problem of the military establishment alone. Just as the burden of war itself must now be borne by every citizen as well as every soldier, so the preparation for war must necessarily be the responsibility of the whole nation. This fact has been brought home to Americans in almost every phase of their lives. The requirements of a military posture in terms of internal security, national unity, and basic values are literally changing the character of American life.

In the first place, preparing ourselves for the eventuality of total war demands that we adopt stringent measures to insure internal security. Traditional American liberties must be sacrificed in the relentless search for subversives in our midst. Where loyalty oaths must be demanded, dissent becomes confused with disloyalty, and orthodoxy is made the badge of patriotism. Individual rights must be submerged in the interest of national security, and we have a widespread and irrational hysteria abroad in the land that strikes at the very heart of our democracy. It destroys our trust in one another, and without trust a free society cannot exist.

. . . In an age when a single bomb can destroy a city, and where secrecy may be the price of continued national existence, the pervasiveness of the subversion danger is apparent, and many a thoughtful citizen has been forced to accept the necessity of rigid security precautions. How can our old concepts of individual liberty survive under these circumstances? How indeed can a nation caught up in an atomic arms race find the calm judgment necessary to strike even a reasonable balance between freedom and security?

Secondly, as this suggests, organization for war demands the highest possible degree of national unity. If we are to be ready to act quickly and decisively in any crisis, the nation must be as nearly of one mind as possible. This need has led to the new science of "emotional engineering," the planned development of the mass mind. . . . It seems clear to us that our government, acting from the best motives, and in the interests of national security, has consciously tried to build a mass mind in America, a mind outraged by our enemies and convinced of the moral justification of our own position. . . .

It may be argued that this kind of salesmanship is necessary, but it has its price. . . . For public opinion once set in motion is not a cool moderating force. . . . Fear and hatred may be necessary to sustain a nation fighting far-off battles, but they are not emotions that can continue to be controlled. . . . War preparation now requires organizing society itself as an army, with information and control wholly in the hands of the wielders of power. Obviously, this is incompatible with democracy. We believe therefore that the commitment to violence inherent in our containment policy can only be carried out at the expense of the very democracy we seek to protect.

If it could be shown that the price that must be paid internally, in terms of vast economic outlays and the sacrifice of democratic principles, would make possible the implementation of constructive foreign policies that attack the causes of conflict, perhaps the sacrifices would be worth making. Unfortunately, the same insatiable demands of military security that dominate the domestic scene operate to inhibit constructive programs in the foreign field. Whatever we may wish to do as a nation, politically, economically, or diplomatically, must inevitably be measured in terms of its impact on national security. We believe therefore that, in the field of foreign policy, an examination of the record over the past ten years will support the conclusion that the effective implementation of constructive, long-range policies is, in fact, impossible as long as military security must also be sought. This we believe to be true in various spheres regardless of how earnestly the American people desire to move toward the positive policies that many have suggested.

1. *The impact on political policies.* One of the cornerstones of American political philosophy has always been an insistence on the right of people to choose their own governments. In pre-war years we generally supported this right of self-determination. . . . What has happened to this tradition since military containment became the central plank of our foreign policy?

A case in point is Morocco, whose demands for freedom from France have become more and more insistent in the years since 1945. But this colonial unrest has been met with repression, its leaders have been jailed, and the United Nations has been blocked from any investigation, despite the pleas of Asian and African countries. Through all this discussion and crisis, the United States has stood by, either supporting France or remaining silent. This is not because our government has been unsympathetic to the cause of Moroccan independence, but because we have other commitments which must take precedence. Our first responsibility is the North Atlantic Treaty Organization and Western European rearmament, and we could not afford to antagonize a key military partner in these enterprises. . . . We may have been convinced of the rightness of Moroccan demands, and even of the political wisdom of acceding to them, but we have found it mandatory to sacrifice these considerations on the altar of military necessity.

The same situation exists in other areas where men strive for liberation, either from colonial rule or from outworn forms of indigenous tyranny. Our sympathies are still with the oppressed. . . . Yet in country after country we find ourselves allied with those forces which stand in the way of the revolutionary changes that are demanded. . . . It may be tragic that the United States is coming to be regarded as the guardian of the *status quo* instead of the champion of the oppressed, but it appears to have no choice. Our commitment to containment requires that the price be paid. Is there any evidence of a limited commitment here? Is there any example of moral or political considerations prevailing on colonial questions except as military considerations permit? In theory, the containment concept allows for it; in practice, it has proved impossible. . . .

2. *The impact on economic policies.* Another area in which there is practically unanimous agreement among those who have studied the requirements of peace is in the field of economic policy. Underdeveloped countries must be built up. Trade barriers must be broken down. These are important ways in which poverty, disease, and unemployment can be attacked, and the basic sources of discontent and strife eliminated. But how far have we been able to move toward these goals?

United States participation in UNRRA and its sponsorship of the Marshall Plan provided a fine start, and it is unfortunate that the good effects were in both instances vitiated by the developing demands of the cold war. The international cooperative character of UNRRA, already weakened by a lack of Russian cooperation, was further damaged by the American decision in 1947 to stress bilateral arrangements, while the Marshall Plan came admittedly to be considered by both sides as an anti-communist weapon in the later years of its effective operation. Since the time of these two major recovery efforts, the first test for American economic aid has been whether or not it would strengthen the power position of the United States: Is the prospective recipient prepared to help win a possible war? Need has become a secondary criterion. Even technical assistance, once envisaged as a bold new program to lift the level of life in underdeveloped areas, has become so enmeshed in American military planning that one nation (Burma) rejected aid for fear that it would involve a commitment to American military policy, and others have been troubled by the same implication.

Fully as serious is the generally smaller size of the appropriations that Congress makes available for economic aid and technical assistance. The demands of the military are so great and the pressure against higher taxes so strong, that there are only marginal funds left over for purposes of economic development. . . . Military needs come first, and as long as they are reckoned in the tens of billions, economic assistance will continue to be reckoned in the tens of millions. . . .

The same situation exists in the field of world trade. Our government is well aware of the long-range benefits that would accrue from expanded trade—benefits that have direct bearing on world peace and stability. But again, military considerations intervene, and we are obliged to adopt a rigid policy of barring trade between East and West. Thus at many points where economic steps might be taken to correct the basic conditions that lead to violence, we find ourselves blocked by the military demands of containment.

3. *The impact on diplomacy.* Post-war diplomacy has become more and more directly related to military power. Negotiation is carried forward not to discover a *modus vivendi,* but to force acceptance of a position through the demonstration of superior power. . . . Under these conditions, great power conferences become only milestones in the cold war, and even proposals for disarmament are perverted until they become a facade behind which the great powers continue to stockpile armaments. . . . This failure

is not an accident, nor is it the result of inadequate political or military leadership. Rather it is the logical outcome of the total endeavor necessary for preparedness for modern war. . . .

* * *

In conclusion, it seems clear to us that we cannot ultimately follow the constructive policies we voice because of the nature of our commitment to violence. Military power is as corrupting to the man who possesses it as it is pitiless to its victims. It is just as devastating to its employer as it is to those who suffer under it.

"Its power of converting a man into a thing is a double one, and its application is double-edged. To the same degree, though in different fashions, those who use it and those who endure it are turned to stone."[1]

We have gone wrong here in America. We close our eyes to the meaning of the subjection of the human spirit to violence. We deceive ourselves even in our practical political judgments.

On the one hand, we want to resolve our difficulties with the Soviet Union peacefully. We want to aid the underprivileged of the world in their demand for a decent standard of life. We want to develop the United Nations as an agency of peaceful settlement and as a nascent center of world law. We want to be free of the burden of an arms race and of the terrible fear of an atomic war. We want to be free to live our lives in a manner befitting our conception of the dignity and worth of individual men.

On the other hand, we want also to find security through our ability to cause pain to others and through the phenomenal development of our nation as a society prepared to wage war.

We cannot do both.

II

We believe it is practical, and politically relevant, for men and women to move the world toward peace by individually practicing peace themselves, here and now. Each of us is both a part of the state and an individual child of God, and we are obligated to act

---

[1] Simone Weil, "The Iliad or a Poem of Force," *Politics*, Pamphlet No. 1.

responsibly in both capacities. Since we have now asserted that acting responsibly in this day involves the rejection of militarism, what is the meaning of this for us as individuals, and what is its political relevance, immediately and for the future? . . .

A personal commitment to practice peace begins with the effort to live affirmatively. Here is no simple decision to say "No" to military power and carry on business as usual in every other department of life. If we are to be respected of God and men, we cannot invoke the law of love when it comes to war if we ignore it in our relations with family, friends, and community. It is, indeed, a contradiction in terms to renounce mass violence and retain the seeds of it in our conduct toward others, for war grows directly from the accumulated prejudices, selfishness, greed, and arrogance of individual men. . . . We must, in short, so live that men will know that our faith is in man's divine potential to live nobly when nobility is expected of him.

It is, of course, impossible to express this faith, and at the same time deny it by supporting war and preparation for war. If our faith is to be in men, we cannot prepare to destroy men. Thus, we believe that the man who would practice peace must refuse to participate in war. In so far as he can, he must also refuse to profit from war, or prepare for war. A demonstration of faith in the capacity of men to respond nobly to the expectation of nobility is valid only to the extent that no limits are set on the demonstration. As long as we keep a gun within easy reach, our protestations of good will are empty. We must either have enough faith in the overcoming power of love to stake our lives and our fortunes on it, or we must seek some other basis for ultimate personal security.

These personal affirmations thus have a profound bearing on attitudes within the sphere of daily community life. They also carry implications for international attitudes. The man who dares to reject violence in his own life—unilaterally and regardless of what others do—must also be prepared to have his nation reject violence—unilaterally and regardless of what others do. . . .

We have said enough to make clear that the commitment to practice peace is an absolute commitment. The individual must be ready to trust all the way and unreservedly in man's capacity for goodness. But it does not mean that he will necessarily be called upon tomorrow or next month or next year to pay the ultimate price. For this absolute, like all other absolutes, is never wholly realized in action. The man who relies on force as his ultimate refuge and security is driven to produce a hydrogen bomb, but his absolute does not require him to drop the bomb tomorrow, or next month, or next year. Indeed, he hopes that he will never have to inflict such suffering on an enemy, just as the man who relies on non-violence hopes that he will never have to *accept* suffering from an enemy.

However, although daily living does not usually require us to demonstrate our ultimate faith, *our daily choices are made on the basis of it*. Thus, an ultimate willingness to resort to violence determines the day to day policy decisions of Americans on the national level. In certain colonial situations, for example, though we often struggle to do otherwise, in the end we support the *status quo*, because we have made an ultimate commitment to force. Only as military strategy permits are we free to advocate change. The same commitment undermines our search for a disarmament formula, for we are blocked on one side by our faith in force, and on the other by a hostile world. We have no freedom of movement, and no recourse but to pile up more arms even as we talk of disarming. We hope some day to reach agreements for universal, enforcible disarmament that will involve no risk for ourselves and no changes in our values, but the hope is dim, for the very process of rearming so poisons the climate that agreement is made ever more difficult.

We, therefore, believe that the immediate impact of a commitment to non-violence is to liberate *individuals* to act morally and responsibly on these daily problems of the world community. Herein lies its immediate political relevance. . . .

Thus in individual terms, a commitment to non-violence frees men from the painful dilemma that otherwise arises whenever the demands for justice conflict with the demands of power. This dilemma is a real one for those who must make national policy decisions in a power-centered world. . . . It is only when material power has been rejected as the basis for security that men can give both unreserved and responsible support to the claims of justice. This rejection is the essential moral and political act of our time, the initial impetus for the pioneering effort that man must make to escape disaster. . . .

Implications for the state will appear as the minority of its citizens who resolve to practice peace begins to grow. The larger the minority, and the less self-centered and self-righteous it is, the greater the impact and the greater the accommodation that will be made to it. A government which reflects the will of the people must modify and adjust Its policies in accord with the growth of opinion, and this is precisely the reason why a minority view has political relevance. . . . To cite a current example, we point to the political impact of extremist leadership in the fields of anti-communism and Asian intervention. Although it seems clear that senatorial spokesmen in both these areas represent no more than small minority viewpoints, their positions actually set the poles and pull the whole range of public discussion toward them. In short, we believe a vocal minority has an important polarizing effect that makes it politically relevant in a very practical way.

A growing pacifist minority, and the gradual modifications of national policy that it produced, would also make an impact on the international scene. Our world is a dynamic world, with men and nations altering their habits, their attitudes, and their responses as the international climate shifts and changes. The pacifist wants to recognize this fact, and build policy around its existence. He suggests, therefore, that the more a minority could succeed in modifying belligerency and encouraging restraint, the more striking and unpredictable would be the resulting mutation in international relations. . . . Beyond that is speculation, but we can venture suggestions of the broad outlines of such a full policy of international good will.

* * *

4. *The United States would get rid of its military establishment.* Various avenues might be taken to achieve this result. Many suggest that the most probable and most practical approach would be through the simple transfer of the security function to a world organization. . . .

Others less insistent on the importance of world federation suggest that disarmament would occur as the result of multilateral agreement: universal in character, enforceable in practice, and complete down to the level needed for internal policing. Both of these approaches are valid, and both could be supported by the United States in the era about which we speculate, but in the last analysis a pacifist policy would require unilateral action if agreement could not be achieved. There is no escaping the necessity to be willing to act first ourselves if we are to have solid ground for getting others to act with us.

It will be said that for a nation to consider disarming alone in an armed world is madness; but the fact that obviously stares men in the face today is that *an armed world in this age is itself madness.* To refuse any longer to labor under the delusion that it is anything else is the beginning of common sense, as it is the counsel of divine wisdom. Moreover, it is quite possible that the Soviet Union, confronted with such a change in American behavior, might startle us with a new response. At the very least, the example of a people living without the burden of militarism and offering friendship to all, would call forth the impulses of freedom that exist in all men. . . .

Nor must it be forgotten how this whole non-violent era, about which we are speculating, would be brought about. Under our democratic philosophy, it would not be created by fiat, but as the result of insistence on reconciling measures by a gradually growing pacifist minority. The writers are convinced that this process in itself would so change the climate of world opinion that no power on earth could oppose it effectively. The influence of growing programs of economic assistance, freed from the compulsions of strategy and carried forward by dedicated men and women through the operating agencies of the United Nations, would lift the heart of the world. Increasing support of the United Nations itself, as a world forum for peaceful settlement, universal in membership and inviolate of selfish national pressure, would create a new basis for an emerging world community of law. The earnest desire to negotiate differences, backed by a gradually increasing willingness to abandon our military posture, could open the way for the relaxation of tension and the achievement of disarmament. Nations which are at present hostile and threatening, would be relieved of any reason for being hostile and threatening, and would face a world opinion so warmly approving of the United States that continued hostility would be difficult to maintain.

We must, however, face the possibility that hatred has gone so far, and injustice penetrated so deeply, that even a revolutionary policy of peace could not prevent international aggression. A nation which had disarmed would not in that event abjectly surrender and let an invader run over and enslave it as is often alleged. On the contrary, it would have open to it possibilities of non-violent resistance that offer more prospects of a creative and genuinely victorious outcome than is the case with violent resistance under modern conditions. It is the nation whose reliance is upon arms that now faces the bleakest prospect in the event of international aggression; for victory in any ensuing holocaust is clearly impossible for anyone. Both "victor" and "vanquished" would dwell together in a brutalized and devastated world in which the values of democratic civilization would have been largely swept away.

Non-violent resistance, as has been demonstrated on a large scale in India, and on a smaller scale in many other places, offers greater promise of confounding and overcoming an enemy without destroying our values or our world. While there are limits to the extent to which a program of non-violent resistance can be spelled out for a nation which is quite unready to adopt it, and for a future situation whose character cannot be predicted, it is nevertheless possible to suggest the broad pattern that it would follow. The first necessity is *non-cooperation*. The population must resolutely refuse to carry out the orders of the invader. They would not run trains to transport troops. They would not operate factories to provide the invader with military supplies. They would not unload his ships. They would perform no services of any kind for him. At the same time, they would try through their words and their lives to show the meaning of a free and democratic society. Second, the population must maintain *good will* toward the individual soldier of the invading forces. However difficult this is in practice, it is clear that the effective use of non-violent resistance has always demanded that a clear distinction be drawn between hatred of an evil policy and respect for the human instrument who is caught up in its execution. Good will is the spiritual weapon of non-violence just as civil disobedience is its physical weapon. Finally, the population must be well enough disciplined to *refrain from individual acts of violence* no matter what the provocation. The whole success of the resistance depends on meeting the enemy on a level and in a manner against which he cannot retaliate effectively. He understands violence, and he is prepared to cope with it ruthlessly and drastically. He must be given no excuse to do so.

*   *   *

In summary, it is certain that whatever circumstances exist in a specific instance, any campaign of non-violent resistance will include these three elements of non-cooperation, good will, and non-violence. The technique is effective because it undermines the morale of the enemy and removes his will to conquer. When a soldier is received kindly, it is hard for him to continue to hate. When he faces no threat, it is hard for him to continue to kill. Moreover, he has no way to compel cooperation when faced with civil disobedience, and without cooperation the enemy will find his existence difficult indeed.

All of this is not to suggest that everything would proceed in idyllic fashion and that no suffering would occur in a non-violent resistance campaign. We have tried to make it clear that readiness to accept suffering—rather than inflict it on others—is the essence of the non-violent life, and that we must be prepared if called upon to pay the ultimate price. Obviously, if men are willing to spend billions of treasure and countless lives in war, they cannot dismiss the case for non-violence by saying that in a non-violent struggle people might be killed! It is equally clear that where commitment and the readiness to sacrifice are lacking, non-violent resistance cannot be effective. On the contrary, it demands greater discipline, more arduous training, and more courage than its violent counterpart. Without preparation, non-violent resistance will fail just as surely as an untrained and undisciplined army would fail in war. Not even a beginning can be made in assessing the potential of non-violent resistance as a means of national defense until a people ready to pour billions into military preparations are prepared to put some effort into research and training of a different nature. This in turn can happen only as we make a new commitment to practice peace, and recognize that the freedom worth saving is the freedom of the spirit, which can neither be protected by guns nor enslaved by tyrants.

Such is the program we would chart for the individual and for the state of which he is a part. We have not denied that it involves risk, but no policy can be formulated that does not involve risk. We have not suggested it will be easy, but only that no policy that aims at achieving peace can be easy. Finally, we have made no sweeping claims that it would work, but only that it appears to us more workable and more relevant than the barren doctrines of violence that now enslave us. We believe that it merits the consideration of thoughtful men.

III

There is a politics of time, but there is also a politics of eternity that man would ignore, but cannot. He plays with the politics of time, sees it, manipulates it, imagines it is of himself alone; but both the politics of time and of eternity are of God. Only the eye of faith perceives the relationship, for it alone glimpses the dimension of eternity. Man sees but dimly, yet enough to know the overarching Power that moves in the affairs of men. Because we are first men of faith, and only secondarily political analysts, we would speak now, finally, of the politics of eternity which has undergirded the whole. . . .

We have tried to face the hard facts; to put the case for non-violence in terms of common sense. Yet, we are aware that the man who chooses in these terms alone cannot sustain himself against the mass pressures of an age of violence. If ever truth reaches power, if ever it speaks to the individual citizen, it will not be the argument that convinces. Rather it will be his own inner sense of integrity that impels him to say, "Here I stand. Regardless of relevance or consequence, I can do no other."

This is not "reasonable": the politics of eternity is not ruled by reason alone, but by reason ennobled by right. Indeed "faith is reason grown courageous." Reason alone may dictate destroying an enemy who would destroy liberty, but conscience balks, and conscience must be heeded, for nothing in our reading of history, or in our experience of religion, persuades us that at this point conscience is wrong. We do not end violence by compounding violence, nor conquer evil by destroying the evildoer. Evil cannot overcome evil, and the end does not justify the means. Rather, we are convinced that evil means corrupt good ends; and we know with a terrible certainty demonstrated by two world wars in our time, that when we undertake to overcome evil with evil, we ourselves tend to become the evil we seek to overcome. We believe that the editors of *Life* reached a sound conclusion when, on August 20, 1945, following Hiroshima, they wrote: "Our sole safeguard against the very real danger of reversion to barbarism is the kind of morality which compels the individual conscience, be the group right or wrong. The individual conscience against the atomic bomb? Yes. There is no other way."

. . . If there is to be a religious solution to the social problem there must also be renewed in a disintegrating society the sense of community, of mutuality, of responsible brotherhood for all men everywhere. Such community is built on trust and confidence, which some will say is not possible now because the communist cannot be trusted. The politics of eternity does not require that we trust him. It requires us to love him and to trust God. Our affirmation in this day is that of John Woolman in his: "I have no cause to promote but the cause of pure universal love." We call for no calculated risk on behalf of national interest or preservation; rather for an uncalculated risk in living by the claims of the Kingdom, on behalf of the whole family of man conceived as a divine-human society.

The politics of eternity works not by might but by spirit. . . .

IX

THE STRUGGLE FOR THE
UNDERDEVELOPED COUNTRIES

POINT FOUR*

BY

HARRY S. TRUMAN

[1949]

In the coming years, our program for peace and freedom will emphasize four major courses of action.

First, we will continue to give unfaltering support to the United Nations and related agencies, and we will continue to search for ways to strengthen their authority and increase their effectiveness. We believe that the United Nations will be strengthened by the new nations which are being formed in lands now advancing toward self-government under democratic principles.

Second, we will continue our programs for world economic recovery.

This means, first of all, that we must keep our full weight behind the European Recovery Program. We are confident of the success of this major venture in world recovery. We believe that our partners in this effort will achieve the status of self-supporting nations once again.

In addition, we must carry out our plans for reducing the barriers to world trade and increasing its volume. Economic recovery and peace itself depend on increased world trade.

Third, we will strengthen freedom-loving nations against the dangers of aggression.

We are now working cut with a number of countries a joint agreement designed to strengthen the security of the North Atlantic area. Such an agreement would take the form of a collective defense arrangement within the terms of the United Nations Charter.

We have already established such a defense pact for the Western Hemisphere by the treaty of Rio de Janeiro.

The primary purpose of these agreements is to provide unmistakable proof of the joint determination of the free countries to

---

*From President Truman's Inaugural Address, January 20, 1949. Harry S. Truman (b. 1884) was President of the United States from 1945 to 1953.

resist armed attack from any quarter. Each country participating in these arrangements must contribute all it can to the common defense.

If we can make it sufficiently clear, in advance, that any armed attack affecting our national security would be met with overwhelming force, the armed attack might never occur.

I hope soon to send to the Senate a treaty respecting the North Atlantic security plan.

In addition, we will provide military advice and equipment to free nations which will cooperate with us in the maintenance of peace and security.

Fourth, we must embark on a bold new program for making the benefits of our scientific advances and industrial progress available for the improvement and growth of underdeveloped areas.

More than half the people of the world are living in conditions approaching misery. Their food is inadequate. They are victims of disease. Their economic life is primitive and stagnant. Their poverty is a handicap and a threat both to them and to more prosperous areas.

For the first time in history, humanity possesses the knowledge and the skill to relieve the suffering of these people.

The United States is preeminent among nations in the development of industrial and scientific techniques. The material resources which we can afford to use for the assistance of other peoples are limited. But our imponderable resources in technical knowledge are constantly growing and are inexhaustible.

I believe that we should make available to peace-loving peoples the benefits of our store of technical knowledge in order to help them realize their aspirations for a better life. And, in cooperation with other nations, we should foster capital investment in areas needing development.

Our aim should be to help the free peoples of the world, through their own efforts, to produce more food, more clothing, more materials for housing, and more mechanical power to lighten their burdens.

We invite other countries to pool their technological resources in this undertaking. Their contributions will be warmly welcomed.

This should be a cooperative enterprise in which all nations work together through the United Nations and its specialized agencies wherever practicable. It must be a world-wide effort for the achievement of peace, plenty, and freedom.

With the cooperation of business, private capital, agriculture, and labor in this country, this program can greatly increase the industrial activity in other nations and can raise substantially their standards of living.

Such new economic developments must be devised and controlled to benefit the peoples of the areas in which they are established. Guaranties to the investor must be balanced by guaranties in the interest of the people whose resources and whose labor go into these developments.

The old imperialism—exploitation for foreign profit—has no place in our plans. What we envisage is a program of development based on the concepts of democratic fair-dealing.

All countries, including our own, will greatly benefit from a constructive program for the better use of the world's human and natural resources. Experience shows that our commerce with other countries expands as they progress industrially and economically.

Greater production is the key to prosperity and peace. And the key to greater production is a wider and more vigorous application of modern scientific and technical knowledge.

Only by helping the least fortunate of its members to help themselves can the human family achieve the decent, satisfying life that is the right of all people.

Democracy alone can supply the vitalizing force to stir the peoples of the world into triumphant action, not only against their human oppressors, but also against their ancient enemies—hunger, misery, and despair.

On the basis of these four major courses of action we hope to help create the conditions that will lead eventually to personal freedom and happiness for all mankind. . . .

AMERICA BECOMES A "HAVE-NOT" NATION*

BY

PETER F. DRUCKER

[1956]

For the last ten years, our ventures into international economics have been the most imaginative, the most novel, and the most effective part of America's foreign policy. Now, however, they are becoming stale, obsolescent, and ineffective. The Soviet countries, by a deft shift in cold war strategy, are threatening to take the economic initiative away from us all round the world—leaving us in the sterile role of imitator and defender. Clearly it is time for a change.

Fortunately the opportunity for a change is now opening up before us. In the months just ahead, we shall have a unique chance to start on a radically new foreign economic policy—a policy which not only will satisfy the hopes of the free world, but also will fit the needs and ideals of the American people.

Our old policy was, of course, focused on "the postwar emergency." It worked· splendidly during the period when relief, repair, and rebuilding were the urgent needs. But this postwar job was finished several years ago—and since our program was originally designed for temporary emergencies, it has been continued on a patchwork basis from year to year to help meet various diplomatic and military crises as they came up. Neither Democratic nor Republican administrations have yet taken time to work out a permanent policy, *specifically designed to serve our own self-interest.*

Indeed, we have not had an *American* economic policy at all; we have had a "foreign aid program." Its unprecedented generosity fired the imagination of our own people. Abroad it rekindled

---

*From *Harper's Magazine*, April 1956. Reprinted by permission. Peter F. Drucker (b. 1909), American management consultant, has written widely on economic policy.

hope, courage, and faith in the future, in a way far more important than the immediate economic impact of our help.

But the very fact that it was a program of "foreign aid" made Congress perpetually suspicious, and built up a growing opposition to "giveaways" throughout the country. Moreover, once the first emergency was past, this emphasis on "aid" was bound to breed dissatisfaction and suspicion abroad. The friends we helped were dissatisfied because nobody likes to be cast in the role of a perennial beggar. They were suspicious because they were sure there must be some hidden motive behind such generosity—that the helping hand must be the fist of "American imperialism" in disguise.

This uneasiness—both in Congress and abroad—was well founded. A foreign policy that is purely selfish is indeed a mean policy, and will come to a mean end. But a policy entirely divorced from national self-interest is equally unsound and impermanent.

There was another flaw in the old policy. It was based on an assumption of extreme economic isolation. The Marshall Plan and Point Four program both assumed—consciously or subconsciously—that the United States is economically independent of the outside world, while the outside world is extremely dependent on the United States. This was well expressed in the slogan of a few years back: "When the United States sneezes, Europe catches pneumonia." Even today most people in this country take it for granted that, economically, "America can go it alone"—indeed, that America would be better off if there were no outside world with its clamor for American handouts.

This economic isolationism is, however, no whit less dangerous in today's world than political or military isolationism would be. Worse, it is a complete perversion of reality. In fact the outside world is daily becoming less dependent upon America; this is the meaning of the setbacks our international economic policy experienced during 1955 in Egypt, Indonesia, and Latin America. Morever, the United States is daily becoming more dependent upon the outside world—in particular, upon the raw-material producing countries.

It can be said quite bluntly that international economic relations are the Achilles' heel of the American economy. Our ability to solve the tremendous problems of our dependence on foreigners will very largely determine the rate of expansion of our economy during the next generation. For the painful truth is that our basic long-range position in the international economy is not one of strength, but one of great potential weakness.

The overriding need of the American economy will be to find a supply of raw materials to keep our industrial machine going. And a rapidly increasing amount of these raw materials will have to come from abroad.

Our own cupboard—once bountifully stuffed with raw materials—already has been emptied much more than most of us realize. The Mesabi iron range, once the world's greatest source of ore, is almost gone; and we are shipping in ore to feed our steel mills from Canada, South America, and Africa. Crude oil, which we used to export in floods, now has to be imported in increasing amounts. Other raw materials which are indispensable for our defense and our daily living—bauxite for aluminum, manganese, nickel, wood pulp, chrome, and a dozen others—all come largely from outside our borders. Within fifteen or twenty years, we may well be the major "have-not" country in the world.

To be sure, we will still supply all of our own needs in food and clothing, and most of our needs for shelter. It is also true that some other industrial nations will have to import an even larger share of their raw-material supplies than we do. But our per-capita import needs will be as large as those of any other country; and our total volume of imports probably will be as big as that of several of the great industrial countries of Western Europe lumped together. Today we have only about 10 percent of the earth's population—but we are using up about 50 per cent of the entire world output of raw materials. Obviously our standard of living—and especially our rate of growth—will become increasingly dependent on our ability to get the raw materials we need.

This of course is not a new conclusion. It was reached by the Paley Commission appointed by President Truman in 1951. But the Paley Commission seriously underrated both the speed of American economic expansion and the rate at which our demand for raw materials will grow. For instance, it expected American power needs to double within the next twenty-five years: but the Federal Power Commission—a rather conservative body, judging by its past performance—now expects our use of power by 1980 to be four times our present power consumption. Furthermore, developments of the last five years have shown that raw-material needs increase a great deal faster than production and consumption. In fact they might be said—though the statistical evidence is not altogether conclusive—to increase twice as fast.

Even more important is the fact that the Paley Commission concerned itself exclusively with U. S. requirements. It assumed that the rest of the world would remain unchanged. But raw-material demands are increasing even faster outside the United States—in the rapidly expanding industries of Western Europe, in the countries behind the Iron Curtain, and, above all, in the rapidly industrializing nations of Latin America, Australia, Asia, and Africa. In the absence of a world-wide catastrophe, we must assume that the demand for industrial raw materials outside of the United States will continue to grow faster than here, and that twenty years from now the United States will find itself in tough competition for all such imports.

How large our imports will be in ten or twenty years cannot be estimated with any accuracy. But it is reasonable to guess that, in order to double our national income within the next fifteen to twenty years—the assumption on which most economists base their forecasts and most business companies their capital investments—we will have to import the equivalent of at least a quarter of our total industrial production. We will have to pay for these imports with equivalent exports—which would mean increasing our exports four times over their present level.

This leads to four major conclusions about the basic aims of a new American economic policy.

First of all, it will have to be a policy that will make it possible for us to *increase exports* fast enough to pay our international bills. We still assume that it is the ability of foreign countries to obtain dollars that limits our exports—and nothing else. It would be safer to base our policy on the assumption that, within a decade, the dollar shortage of yesterday will have disappeared, and that our main problem will be how to earn enough foreign exchange to pay for our imports. The first goal of our new policy, therefore, must be to make the United States capable of selling in a competitive world market, and to make it possible for our potential customers to buy our goods in large volume.

The second aim must be an *expansion of raw-material production throughout the world.* Productive capacity for industrial raw materials, adequate to the world needs of tomorrow, simply does not now exist—even if the needs of the rapidly industrializing countries of the Soviet orbit are completely (and short-sightedly) left out of the calculation.

We cannot expect—as did the Paley Report by implication—that this country can obtain a very much larger share of the world's supply of industrial raw materials at the expense of our friends and allies in the Free World. This not only would be politically undesirable, since it would inevitably destroy our foreign alliances and would produce the "cannibalistic conflict of the Imperialists" on which Soviet policy banks, but it simply is not possible. In the event of a real shortage of raw materials, the supplier countries are bound to use whatever they produce for their own growing industries, rather than to stunt their own growth for the sake of the American economy.

The third goal for a permanent international economic policy must obviously be *to harmonize our own self-interest with the aspirations and interests of the peoples of the Free World.* Increasingly we will be dependent on their willingness to be closely integrated with the American economy. This cooperation cannot be forced, and it cannot be bought. It has to be earned, through a policy that clearly and imaginatively merges together the openly avowed self-interest of America and the national self-interest of our partners.

Finally such a policy must *strengthen the Free World socially and politically*—that is, it must symbolize its beliefs and values, and must express the reality of responsible American leadership.

*There is one—and only one—policy that will answer all these
requirements. That is for America to take the lead in promoting
the rapid economic growth—and especially the rapid industrial
growth—of the raw-material producing countries.*

The simplest way to illustrate this is to contrast India and
Switzerland. India—with almost 400,000,000 inhabitants and
with a fair supply of dollar exchange supplied primarily by American aid—buys less from the United States and sells less to the
United States than Switzerland. Yet Switzerland has less than
5,000,000 people and is completely independent of American aid.
In other words, it is industrial production and economic well-
being that create the need for imports, the purchasing power to
buy them, and the capacity to produce exports to pay for them.
If India could double her miserably low standard of living, both
her industrial imports and her raw-material exports might well
increase tenfold. But India can double her standard of living
only by rapid industrialization.

What is true of India is true of all the other pre-industrial
countries, which are the main sources of our raw-material.

The rapid industrialization of the countries that produce raw
materials is, therefore, the very best investment the United States
can make in its own economic future. It is, moreover, the foremost ambition of these countries themselves. And it is a job
which the United States—both because we were ourselves a "raw-
material producing country" only a few short decades ago and
because we are the leading industrial society today—should be
pre-eminently fitted to make our very own.

We have learned a good deal about economic growth these last
few years—so much that we can say now what it requires.

We do not, indeed, yet have anything that could be called an
adequate theory of economic growth; the last annual meeting of
the American Economic Association at Christmas 1955 was, in
fact, largely devoted to bemoaning the absence of any such theory.
But at least we know that the old assumptions once accepted by
both economists and businessmen were all wrong.

The essential thing is not that an economy is "backward" or

"underdeveloped," as even President Truman still assumed when he announced the Point Four program. The real point is that an economy has to have a potential of growth. (The sooner we rid our language of such terms as "backward" and "underdeveloped," the more successful our policy will be. In addition to being misleading, they are condescending to the point of insult.) Any sound policy must aim at the *economic self-development of "growth" countries.*

This is important not only because it makes possible a positive approach, instead of the "cavity-filling" and "trouble-shooting" approach of a program of "aid to underdeveloped areas." Above all it makes possible systematic planning with clear priorities—the method we have learned to use with conspicuous success in large-scale business. In fact, some of the disciplines developed in the last few years for the analysis of business decisions—such as, for instance, Operations Research and Synthesis—seem singularly applicable in diagnosing opportunities of a "growth economy."

We also know that economic development is not a slow, continuous process, but one of leap-frogging. It does not proceed step-by-step, but in "break-throughs." And it is not exclusively —maybe not even primarily—an economic process; it also involves a deep cultural and social change—a change in values, habits, knowledge, attitudes, ways of life, social ideals, and aspirations.

Most important of all, we have learned what a country needs to make these changes—with the minimum of social, political, and cultural upheaval. There are three main requirements:

(1) *A demand for investment capital* must be created. Traditional economic theory assumed that the supply of investment capital determined whether a country would grow industrially, and how fast. But we have now found that a pre-industrial country usually has more capital than investment opportunities. Capital by itself is sterile; and its lack, while painful, is rarely an absolute bar to growth. But opportunities for investment—that is, for risk-taking, productive enterprise—are economic lifeblood.

(2) *"Multiplier industries"* must be created. These are the industries that will set off economic chain reactions, thus producing industrial skill, activity, and enterprise out of all proportion

to their own size. We even know that there are four categories of such "multiplier industries" and that for maximum growth a country needs a balanced diet of all four.

There are "spectaculars," such as our Western railroads in the second half of last century, or the TVA in the thirties. In themselves, these are almost always "uneconomic," indeed wasteful; but they have a major impact because they so visibly symbolize the "new age" with its new possibilities of conquering nature, its values, and its new horizons.

There are community services—transportation facilities and power supply above all—which create an integrated economy out of fragmented and isolated districts.

There are service industries to make effective the two kinds of demand needed to move forward the wheels of an industrial economy: (a) a distribution system to create consumer demand, and (b) a credit system to create effective investment demand. For example, the revolutionary impact of a few Sears-Roebuck stores on the economic development of Mexico, Brazil, and Columbia cannot be exaggerated. By U. S. standards their total sales volume is almost negligible. Yet, these stores have put into business a host of new, home-owned and home-managed manufacturing industries. They have opened new careers and created new standards of industrial technology and industrial management. They have pushed up productivity—and with it wages and purchasing power. Finally they are forcing the entire retail system where they operate to change from selling at high profit and in low volume, to low-profit, high-volume merchandising for a homogeneous mass-market.

And—the fourth "multiplier" category—at different times and places, different manufacturing industries have a "multiplier" effect. In Monterey, Mexico—one of the fastest-growing and most modern industrial areas in this hemisphere—a brewery apparently served as the first multiplier through its demands for bottles, bottle caps, trucks, and so on. In our own Southeast, tire-making and automobile assembly seem to have had this effect of "multiplying" economic growth—an effect which was not produced at an earlier stage either by the textile industry or by the huge but economically "inert" steel mills of Birmingham, Alabama.

(3) The most important requirement of rapid industrial growth is *people*. People trained to be entrepreneurs, managers, marketers, investment and commercial bankers, engineers, geologists, and technicians of many varieties. People ready to welcome the challenge of economic change and the opportunities in it. People, above all, who are dedicated to the economic development of their country, and to high standards of honesty, competence, knowledge, and performance. What are needed beyond all else are leadership and example; and that only the right kind of people can provide.

Any policy that tries to supply money or facilities, without at the same time providing people in quantity and in quality, must inevitably fail. It may even do harm. And the people must emerge fast; the entire pre-industrial world is in a ferment—is eagerly, almost explosively, looking to economic progress as its road to salvation. If American international economic policy does not succeed in developing the trained and dedicated people whom the "growth" countries need, they will look elsewhere for the answers and for the leadership.

To a considerable extent, this is a matter of providing skills—in accounting, in industrial engineering, in metallurgy, or in management. But skills are not enough; they are not even the main thing. For the real challenge is to capture the vision and the energies of the young trained people in each country—the young people who are eager to lead and to serve, who want to do something great with their lives, and who aspire to no mean end. These men will have to learn skills, of course; for without skills dedication and zeal are futile. But they will not be satisfied with skills alone. Nor should they be. (The Communists learned this long ago; that is why they specialize in zeal.)

The extent to which industrial growth satisfies these people will decide how fast and how successfully a country grows, and also whether this growth will lead it into full membership in the Free World or toward the totalitarian abyss.

All growth countries require two things to develop the people they need. They require something that is intellectually and aesthetically satisfying: an organized body of knowledge—that is, a discipline of entrepreneurship and management. And they require social and moral principles of business conduct which a good man can respect, and on which he can build self-respect.

The main grievance which the pre-industrial world has against the Europeans is that they have failed, during their century of economic leadership, to produce native leaders who could guide the modern industrial development of their own countries. This is, at bottom, what an Indonesian means when he talks about "Western economic imperialism." It is a legitimate grievance. For such people are the only enduring resource of a society.

If our new international economic policy fails to stimulate the self-development of the kind of people needed in the growth countries, it cannot succeed. It will then be regarded—no matter how noble and unselfish our intentions, or how open our pocketbooks—as just another device of the "colonialist" and "exploiter." But if the development of trained and dedicated people is made a clear priority, then our new policy may well succeed in building a co-operative and productive world economy—the kind of economy on which our own prosperity (if not survival) increasingly depends.

Fortunately this is the one part of the job where we are somewhat ahead. Marshall Plan and Point Four—though almost by accident in the beginning—put heavy emphasis on the development of people. We called it Technical Assistance and we talked about "know-how." Yet both the foreign businessmen who came here as members of Productivity Teams, and the American businessmen who have been going abroad on Productivity Missions learned that it is not techniques and gadgets that really matter. What do matter are intellectual discipline and an ethical attitude toward the job to be done. They learned fast that the real "secret" of American economic strength is respect for human beings as the basic resource—rather than a concept of "labor" as a "cost"—and the use of people as a social, intellectual, moral, and spiritual resource, rather than as a purely economic one.

As a result every country—even those truly "underdeveloped"

countries, such as France, which are frozen in an antiquated form of European capitalism—has a fairly large number of people in business and industry who are eager, who are reaching out, who are ready to assume leadership. They are the real capital resource of the Free World; and each one is worth a regiment. This country today has hundreds, if not several thousands, of businessmen and managers who are "graduates" of Marshall Plan and Point-Four work. And there are, in every country—from India to Peru —men in native industry who have developed for themselves the knowledge, the skills, the integrity, and the dedication needed: men who can easily hold their own against our best. But these resources are no more than the "raw material." To build a "product" from them, a purposeful and imaginative American economic policy is needed.

Such a policy will first require a change in our attitude toward the international economy. Our participation in the industrial development of the growth countries would have to be regarded as an investment in our own economic future, rather than as "aid to foreigners."

It will require a long-range commitment—for ten or twenty years—not necessarily to any specific amount of money, but to the principles of the program. It will also require, however, a fair amount of money—to finance "spectaculars" such as the Aswan dam in Egypt; to provide services such as transportation, power, and irrigation projects; and to insure American investors against currency and expropriation risks. We must also recognize that rapidly industrializing countries occasionally suffer sudden economic upsets, such as the ones that trouble Turkey and Brazil today (and troubled the U. S. in 1837, 1873, and 1894). Quick short-term financial help, though in fairly small amounts, is sometimes needed to prevent such an upset stomach from turning into a wasting disease.

We shall also have to contribute American help to diagnose growth opportunities and plan economic development. We shall have to contribute knowledge, advice, technical assistance, and educational facilities. And finally we shall have to contribute people of our own.

This is to a considerable degree a job for the federal government. The government will have to raise whatever money is needed, whether in the form of loans or of grants. It will have to negotiate the agreements with foreign countries under which the policy operates. (To be effective, this has to be a truly co-operative policy, carried out in partnership with the growth countries, and separate from any program of short-range emergency relief or military alliance.)

The other industrially developed countries of the Free World— Western Europe, Japan, and Australia—should be encouraged to join in a policy that is as much in the interest of their survival as it is in ours. And as soon as growth countries emerge industrially, they should become associated as leaders with the international development program. This would make the policy truly co-operative, rather than purely American. Moreover, the experience gained and the people available in such recent growth areas as Turkey, Puerto Rico, São Paulo, or Bombay are particularly useful and should be tapped.

The government also will have to work out the conditions under which an American business investing abroad might become eligible for re-insurance against the risks of expropriation and currency devaluation. (Criteria might be, for instance: Is the investment in a growth country? Is it in an industry which is relatively new to the country and which is still, technologically or in its capital requirements, beyond the reach of local businessmen? Does it save the country several times the foreign exchange for imports that is required to service the capital investment? Is it a "multiplier" industry? Does it have an organized program for training local people within a reasonable period for managerial and technical positions?) And of course the government would also have to serve as the co-ordinator for the entire program— indeed the International Co-operation Administration would have to be made a permanent governmental agency.

But this is not a job government could, or should, do alone. A major—a very major—part of it will have to be done by the American companies operating abroad. Far too many of them still reserve their managerial and technical jobs for Americans and

Europeans—though in Latin America the oil companies, the Grace interests, and Sears are shining exceptions. Far too many also follow managerial practices in their foreign subsidiaries they would never tolerate at home.

Finally this is a job for all American business and managers (and in large measure for American labor leaders). It is a job they will find hard. The systematic knowledge of entrepreneurship and management, which they will have to exemplify and to teach, is barely in its beginning in this country, and is yet to be acquired even in its rudiments by most of our businessmen. And the social and moral principles, which they will have to practice and to convey, are still preachments for many of them.

It is a job that will require time, effort, and humility. Yet, performance of this job will decide whether the manager is worthy of the leadership role our "business society" has entrusted to him. It may also decide whether this "business society" of ours can survive.

Above all, a responsible policy, adequate to our own needs and focused on the rapid self-development of the growth countries, will require imaginative, bold leadership at the very top. In the Point Four program—and in the parallel Technical Assistance program of the United Nations—we have a foundation of experience, achievement, and dedication. In President Eisenhower's current proposal to put "foreign aid" on a long-term basis we have made the first step toward an effective policy. Prominent groups, such as the Committee for Economic Development, are demanding sharp increases in foreign aid, especially to the Near East and Asia. But much of this is still "foreign aid," still conceived as an answer to Communist pressure rather than as a basic long-range American need and self-interest.

Nine years ago, with a few quiet words spoken on a summer afternoon, George Catlett Marshall—appealing to the heads and hearts of his countrymen rather than to their pocketbooks—created a new vision for America and changed the fate of Western Europe. The danger today may be even greater. But so is the opportunity.

THE REAL PROBLEM OF UNDERDEVELOPMENT*

BY

NICOLAI KOESTNER

[1956]

Two conferences held recently are significant for the problem dealt with in this article. One was held by the FAO to discuss methods of developing food production in underdeveloped countries, the other in Washington to deal with the disposal of surplus agricultural products in certain "developed" countries.

Obviously the problems of food production and distribution vary greatly from one country to another. The study of so-called underdevelopment, though not always undertaken objectively because of prejudice and vested interests, has at least proved one thing: that more than half of the world's population is living below a subsistence level, and that the misery of the majority of these millions is increasing, in spite of all local and international efforts and in spite of the American Point Four Program. On the other hand, the surplus of agricultural produce in developed countries, artificially increased by state subsidies in one form or another, is mounting enormously.

Often forgotten or overlooked when present-day world-economic problems are under discussion is the otherwise familiar fact that today's underdeveloped countries, with a few exceptions, are all areas of very ancient civilizations, while the so-called developed countries without exception belong to relatively recent civilizations. The zone of underdevelopment starts in Spain, takes parts of the south of France, the south of Italy and the Balkans, and then extends eastwards practically without interruption all the way to the Pacific; the southern shores of the Mediterranean also are part of it. On the American continent, the areas are not so clearly defined, but they comprise the countries of ancient civilization extending from Mexico as far as Peru.

---

* From the *Swiss Review of World Affairs*, October 1956. Reprinted by permission. Nicolai Koestner (b. 1889) is counselor on economic questions to the National Bank of Egypt.

Underdevelopment in these regions is of two kinds: either these countries have become deserts or semi-deserts like Libya, Syria, Iraq, as well as parts of Spain, Dalmatia, and southern Italy, or they are tremendously overpopulated like the Nile Valley and the plains of India and China. Underdevelopment in these desert and semi-desert areas is the result of excessive exploitation of the soil because of a growing population. This process can be seen, for instance, on the Dalmatian coast, in the Balkans, and in the Western Desert of Egypt. On the coast of Dalmatia over-exploitation of the soil has laid bare the subsoil of chalk and created the well-known Karst hills. Also in the Balkans fine Alpine pastures were turned into fields, and within one generation the barren mountain sides will be visible and nothing will grow there for thousands of years. In the desert beyond Alexandria barley is still being grown, but the fields are hardly distinguishable from the desert, so miserable and few and far between are the plants. Whatever vegetation is left is being destroyed by grazing sheep and goats, so that the soil is visibly deteriorating year after year. With the growing desolation the population, too, is bound to disappear.

A classical example for soil deterioration are the salt marshes—the result of thousands of years of irrigation—now covering the countryside where the Biblical Paradise is supposed to have been. The ominous white patches in the Nile Delta, too, are signs of the same process of soil destruction by irrigation. The damming of the Nile, valuable as it was and still is considered to be, has already caused a rise in the underground water level, forcing the cotton planters to sow more densely to prevent the roots from growing too far down. For whenever the roots touch underground water the plants shed their blossoms. Thus cotton yields have not increased during this present century, though the country is now ranking among the largest consumers of mineral fertilizers per acre. The improved techniques in agriculture have been neutralized by the rising water level.

The regeneration of areas turned into deserts by man in the course of the centuries is technically feasible. Years ago, when he built the White Sea Canal, Stalin, for instance, proved that very tasty melons can be grown under glass and in artificial light in the arctic tundra—at a price. It is the high costs that prevent the settlers in Libya, the granary of Rome in the classical age, from growing wheat again. All the money spent on land reclamation, even if it were obtained free of interest, would not bring any lasting improvement, for the simple reason that production costs would be very high and the standard of living of the growers would have to be correspondingly low. The latter could only be improved by contributions from abroad, a device for which we have an outstanding example in the case of Israel. There the living standard is comparatively high, but the value of the country's imports is six times that of its exports, and the balance is made up from abroad. In neighboring semi-desert countries the standard of living is much lower, since there are no or only very small foreign contributions. Even the fabulous millions now flowing into certain Arab countries in the form of oil royalties have, until now, hardly benefited the great mass of the people. With all the available millions Iraq, for example, is making very slow progress in land reclamation. Reclaiming soil that has been soaked with salt for centuries by irrigation is a painfully slow and costly process, and capital invested in it yields very little interest.

The real breeding centers of human suffering, however, are the fertile but overpopulated valleys of the Nile, the Ganges, the Brahmaputra, the Yangtse and the Hoangho. In India the surface of arable land is approximately 300 million acres, which represents 0.8 acres per capita of a population of 360 million. Only about two thirds of this land is at present under cultivation. In the Ganges Valley (in the states of Bihar, Bengal, Uttar Pradesh) the area under cultivation nowhere passes the half-acre mark per capita. In Egypt this figure is even less, that is, a third of an acre.

All these areas have one feature already mentioned in common, besides the enormous density of population—they are the cradles of human civilization, where man has been toiling the soil for thousands of years. At the same time they bear witness to a basic economic fact underlying all economic activities of man—the law of diminishing returns in agriculture. This law was man's incentive for colonization in the past and is still responsible for migrations. It has created the underdeveloped countries which are now given advice by experts from the young and relatively thinly populated countries of the West, advice, which if followed, would only increase their misery.

It is obvious to any observer overlooking the countryside from a vantage point at the edge of the Eastern Desert in Egypt, teeming with toiling people, and comparing the small villages with their miserable huts and crowded narrow streets with the extensive ruins of an ancient city which it takes an hour to cross on a donkey's back, that in the day this city flourished the degree of urbanization must have been far higher. A migration of the people from town to country must have taken place here, and not only in Egypt, but in practically all the overpopulated agrarian countries of today. As the density of population was increasing and people were forced to obtain their livelihood from a smaller area, they were, of course, improving their agricultural techniques; but the fact remained that per family they were producing less. Less, therefore, remained as surplus to be exchanged for industrial products from the towns; requirements from the towns were gradually cut to a bare minimum, with the result that these lost their clients and consequently their population, and gradually fell into ruins. The process of adaptation went even further with the rural population. A family·rearing cattle and fowls on a very small plot of land, even if it is only for home consumption, will soon understand the basic fact which in modern scientific language is expressed in the formula that the return in calories in meat, milk and eggs is only one sixth of the calories supplied as feed. So the farmer, through force of necessity, became a vegetarian, disposed of most of his cattle and turned himself and the members of his family into beasts of burden. Since there was less and less surplus produce available, the whole civilization gradually deteriorated, the arts became crude, the sciences and literature were forgotten.

On the other hand, a vigorous urbanization took place in Western Europe during the nineteenth century. There are signs, however, that this process has come to an end, at least in Great Britain, and possibly in some other European countries. Judging from the available census figures, on the Balkans and in Egypt the proportion of the agricultural population has remained remarkably stable at slightly over 70 per cent during the same period. This seems to be the maximum figure to which it rose as a consequence of the degeneration of towns and industries in these countries. In southern Italy, too, the agricultural population now makes up 80 per cent of the total; this was certainly different when the huge temples at Pæstum were built. A country's wealth consists primarily in its surplus of agricultural output, and in this respect the Physiocrats were not as wrong as many modern economists seem to think, basing their general theories on observations made ·at the stock exchange and on Lombard Street.

From all that has been said so far it can be seen that the stage reached in economic development in the East today may, in the distant future, become the fate also of the present young Western civilizations, a fact which is often overlooked by Western experts in the East. The following statistics published in the *Annuaire Statistique de France* show the present situation regarding population and arable land in Egypt and the United States.

	Egypt		*United States*	
Total population	22	million	150	million
Agricultural population	14	million	9	million
Land under cultivation	2.5	mil. hectares	184	mil. hectares
Forests			268	mil. hectares
Under cultivation per capita	.1	hectare	1.2	hectares
Under cultivation per capita of agricultural population	1.6	hectares	20	hectares

Thus the population of the United States would have to increase a dozen times to reach the density of present-day Egypt. Is any expert so bold as to maintain that the United States, with a population of 2 billion instead of the present 160 million, would still be as "developed" a country as it is today? Western economic advisers to the Eastern peoples might well consider this. They are giving advice according to a Western pattern, suitable for an agriculture with comparatively large farms and few agricultural workers. They concentrate on tractors, improved seed, diversification and marketing problems, which are the problems of Western agriculture, but by-pass the problems of the East. The price of a tractor amounts to a two-year income of a fellah family, and to buy one would certainly mean bankruptcy. It would be more expensive to till his land by tractor than by human labor, to say nothing of the poorer quality of the tilling. And, in any case, he would hardly be able to turn the tractor on his small plot. The Egyptian fellah already possesses high quality seed, his government finances his production and he has a marketing organization which is certainly cheaper for him than the corresponding one is for the American farmer. What he lacks is land, and until this problem is solved all the other measures are poor palliatives. Therefore, the advice given recently by a well-known American agricultural expert to the European Ministers of Agriculture, "You have to increase the size of your farms: without this no real progress is possible," does not really solve the problem for the underdeveloped Eastern countries.

The experts have an easy solution for the surplus population problem when the size of the farms is to be increased—industry. In India alone, for example, more than a hundred million people, out of which about 30 million are actual workers, are to be transferred to industry. But even in the United States only some 15 million, and in Great Britain some 10 million people, are actively engaged in industry. All the same the world markets are flooded with industrial products. Obviously there is no room for additional millions in industry. It would be a miracle already if the annual increase of population—some 4 million for India—could be so placed.

One of the problems never properly tackled by the West in dealing with underdevelopment is the question of costs. Agriculture in densely populated countries in the East is very intensive, at least as far as labor is concerned. According to the law of diminishing returns a certain volume of agricultural production requires more labor in the East than in the West. If it costs the farmer more labor to produce that volume, he will obviously produce less per capita. This is the real secret of Eastern poverty. Egyptian and Chinese agriculture are—technically speaking—far in advance of the American: in both countries an acre of land produces many times more than in the United States, in Egypt at least twice as much, in the Chinese plains probably much more. But one acre has to feed about three people in Egypt and even more in China; while in the United States there are only 0.8 persons per acre, leaving out the meadows and pastures. This is why the East is poor and "backward." Its "backwardness" may often be the most rational solution of its economic problem. And when conditions permit, the East turns out to be very progressive. In Egypt, for instance, 45 metric tons of nitrogen per 1,000 ha. of agricultural land were used in 1953/54, as against 3.87 tons in the United States, and the intensive use of synthetic fertilizer was started there long before the first World War, while it is quite recent in the United States. If the fellah lives in a mud hut and his wife is harnessed together with the donkey to pull the plow, it is not because he is backward and has no use for a house with modern plumbing, but because he has only one or two acres to keep himself and his family alive. The American farmer would be no better, but probably worse off, under such circumstances.

The problem known as "underdevelopment" is a problem of land-shortage, that is, of a shortage of cheap land. In other words, it is a problem of over-population. The West has a relatively sparse agricultural population, either because the particular country in question was populated only fairly recently, as in the New World, or because a certain combination of favorable circumstances (colonies, foreign markets) not likely to occur again, permitted keeping the agricultural population low, by concentrating the surplus in industry, as in parts of Western Europe and in Japan. Farming methods in the West are either those of extensive but highly mechanized agriculture in thinly populated areas, producing little per acre but at low cost, or of intensive cultivation at high cost, subsidized by protective tariffs. Neither system is applicable to the East, where land is exceedingly scarce, population density high and facilities for export industries practically non-existent. The problem in the East is how to obtain high yields per acre at low costs. This, in view of the law of diminishing returns, cannot be achieved. The solution of the problem, therefore, is not economic but demographical.

We have a tendency to project our experiences chronologically backwards and forwards, without realizing that our actual observations cover too short a period to justify our deductions. Of course Malthusianism, that is, the thesis that population tends to grow faster than the production of the means of subsistence, has been proved wrong for certain countries during many generations. But to deduce from this that it is wrong on a world scale and that the world population will be able to produce enough even if it keeps on growing indefinitely, is quite another proposition, which has to be viewed from a far larger perspective of time.

One example may suffice to illustrate such a perspective. Supposing the increase in the population of Egypt, which during the last four years was 2.5 per cent, continues at the present rate, and supposing further that by means of the projected Aswan Dam the arable land of Egypt is increased by nearly one fourth, we find that in 107 years from now Egypt will have a population of one person per 100 square meters and in 293 years one person per every square meter! It is quite obvious that such a fantastic density is impossible and that demographical developments will have to take a different turn, long before a situation arises where there will be standing room only for the people in the Nile valley. Even on a world scale there will be standing room only for each person on dry land within about 600 years, should the present rate of increase in population not change. Thus, in any case, the world population problem is a demographical problem and not simply a question of producing more food. In spite of the present anti-Malthusian theories the increase of the world's population will have to stop sooner or later.

We should not forget that the "developed countries" are only like a beautiful oasis in the vast desert of the "underdeveloped" lands. One academic solution of the problem of underdevelopment would be a fairer distribution of the population to the world's surface. The developed countries—Europe, the United States, Canada, New Zealand, Australia—would have to receive the "hungry millions" from the East where land is scarce. The general living standard might be raised a little that way, but certainly the living standard of the developed countries would drop. With such a solution the developed countries would never agree. At present they relieve their uneasy conscience by giving a certain amount of free aid to the hungry. But this does not go a long way. Even if India were to receive only a hundred million dollars a year—an enormous sum in itself—it would amount to only 25 cents per inhabitant. Moreover, even the richest country could hardly provide such aid for any considerable length of time. So there remains only one real solution: not only must the population of the underdeveloped countries not be allowed to increase any further, but it ought to decrease if the standard of living is to be raised.

FOR A NEW FOREIGN AID CONCEPT*

BY

BARBARA WARD

[1956]

The time has clearly come to do some hard, new thinking on the whole issue of foreign aid. A full decade has passed since it began to be an annual feature of budget making in the United States— and in the British Commonwealth and indeed among the European colonial powers as well. Moreover, the suggestion has now been made by the Republican Administration that aid, in some form, should continue for at least another decade. The Colombo Plan— under which British Commonwealth countries contribute to Asian development—has had its life extended and there are successive five-year development schemes in many colonies.

One way and another, it is a safe generalization to say that over the last decade and probably for another decade to come, the Western powers are contributing about 1 per cent of their rising national incomes to help forward the development of less fortunate lands. In some years—for instance, at the height of the Marshall Plan— the American percentage has been even higher.

This vast transfer of wealth which, if sustained, could exceed $100 billion (from all Western sources) by 1966, has been undertaken, on the whole, under the spur of necessity. The Western Governments rightly believe that economic collapse is the inevitable prelude to Communist expansion. Sooner than see segment after segment of the free world slip under totalitarian control, they have put their hands in their pockets and paid up.

It cannot be said that the program has been a failure. Given the scale of economic and political disintegration caused by the last war, the advance of Communism might have been much more devastating. To give a concrete example, if India had failed to

*From *The New York Times Magazine*, March 11, 1956. Reprinted by permission. Barbara Ward (b. 1914), British economist and editor, is the author of *Policy for the West* and other works.

secure the American wheat loan during the 1951 famine, distress in the cities and resentment against internal grain hoarders would almost certainly have returned Communist Governments to power in some of the southern Indian states. These areas would then have become the beachheads—the Yenans—for further Communist advance.

Even the Chinese débâcle does not disprove the point, for the aid given was relatively small and the catastrophe had been prepared by forty years of internal upheaval and civil war and nearly a decade of enemy occupation.

Yet there are plenty of voices raised to protest that the policy has not been a success, either. There is a widespread feeling that it is not giving value for money and the feeling has been intensified by Mr. Khrushchev's junketings around Asia.

Take the example of India again. Since 1949, American gifts or grants to India have amounted to about half a billion dollars. The free gifts of steel alone—with the inclusion of the recent deal for India's railroads—have reached about 750,000 tons. Yet when the Russians announce that they will sell—not give, but sell— a million tons of steel to India, the Indian press breaks out in hosannas while all America gets is a spanking for Mr. Dulles' indiscretions over Goa. If foreign aid is a program for making friends and influencing people, it seems, in India, to be a flop.

The outlook is in some ways even less satisfactory in Burma and Indonesia. Both countries have actually refused American aid on the grounds that it would weaken their neutrality. Yet Burma's Premier U Nu is all gratitude when Russia offers to sell machinery and technical aid in return for rice—once again, the element of giving is marginal—and Indonesia is ready to receive Soviet and satellite aid in expanding its oil and rubber industries without, apparently, a qualm over neutralism.

The Russians seem to be able to get more support by selling than the West by giving. Surely there is something wrong with a program that produces such an equivocal result.

These attacks on the effectiveness of foreign aid are all the more bitter because they are relatively new. Up to last year, it was difficult to attack Western foreign aid for producing fewer results than Soviet offers, since there were no Soviet offers—save to Communist

China. The entry of Mr. Khrushchev into the field—with offers of dams and steel plants and machinery and technicians (all at a price)—has created an entirely new entry point for criticism and doubt.

Nor is it simply that political results can be compared—with disparagement for Western achievement. The whole concept of competitive aid-giving becomes increasingly distasteful. Where will it end? Are the Western powers now to dance to any tune a local Asian—or indeed African—Government chooses to play, simply because Moscow is waiting in the wings and shuffling its feet?

Senator Russell was no doubt hardly serious when he suggested that annual foreign aid programs—which no one suggests should exceed $4 billion—would "bankrupt" an America with a national income nearing $400 billion. But his uneasiness sprang from the not unreasonable fear that Mr. Khrushchev's promises and not Asia's needs could come to determine future economic assistance.

The whole effort could get out of hand and the West would find itself maneuvered into a competitive game of aid in which ever higher grants brought it ever smaller political returns. These are not irresponsible reservations. They only underline once again the need to give the whole concept of foreign aid a long, hard look.

The first point to be noted is reassuring. Russia's entry into the field of foreign aid has not undone the solid work of reconstruction already achieved in Asia with help from the West. The internal Communist party in such key areas as Burma and Malaya is very much weaker than it was, say in 1948, and a principal reason for this is the fact that there has been no disastrous collapse of local economies such as preceded the defeat of Chiang Kai-shek in China. In fact, in so far as Soviet aid helps to strengthen economic life in Asia, it can even be a factor in strengthening the present non-Communist regimes.

The initiative that the Russians appear to have gained is much more in the international arena, in the sensitive, fluctuating relations between the free world, the Communists and the uncommitted nations. This initiative is political. Indeed, it is impossible either to gauge or counter Russia's new economic policies unless one remembers that, under the Communist system, everything is subordinate to ideology, in other words, to political manipulation.

But this fact does not weaken Russia's effectiveness. On the contrary, the political slant of Communist economic policies—whether of loans or technical assistance or barter or ordinary trade—is their great strength. *Equally, the lack of any political or ideological framework is the greatest single source of weakness in the aid program undertaken by the West.*

* * *

Aid, in short, is simply part of a much wider sales talk on Communism as a method and a goal, a method of raising internal wealth and for sharing it in a cooperative world order. Soviet propaganda does not make its offers negatively—as a means of *defending* either itself or Asia against the West. The underlying theme is the collapse and decadence of capitalist imperialism. Not out of fear but out of success, generosity and confidence the new economic offers are made.

All this may make Mr. Khrushchev sound unbearably brash in Western ears. But to the new nations of Asia, it may seem more like the voice of achievement and self-respect.

In comparison with all this, our Western political approach makes a very poor showing. It is in fact overwhelmingly negative and defensive. In numberless debates in Congress, in speeches without end to Western electorates, in commentaries and articles, one theme emerges above all—that giving aid to backward areas is a painful necessity made inevitable only because they must be kept out of the Communist.camp.

Nearly every program of assistance is finally rammed through the Legislature with the techniques of Dickens' Fat Boy—"I wants to make yer flesh creep." Refuse this appropriation and Bonga-land will slip forever under the Communist yoke.

But then, by a remarkable psychological somersault, the same legislators who have grimly consented in pure self-interest to provide perhaps half the necessary funds, denounce the recipient peoples as ungrateful scoundrels who show no due appreciation of the magnificent generosity shown them (in strict preservation of Western skins). Yet is it logical to expect gratitude for steps taken openly and crudely in self-defense?

This sense that Western economic assistance is, in Western eyes, no more than a weapon in the cold war has, of course, been intensified by its close association with military aid. Not only do nations which sign on militarily receive more aid, but the balance of military and economic assistance in the general Western aid budget is heavily weighted on the military side. Yet if there is one hope more determined than any other among the peoples of Asia it is to keep out of atomic war. The Russians rarely mention war—except to rattle their own hydrogen bombs. If Soviet tanks are sent to Egypt, Colonel Nasser promises nothing. He is not pressed to take sides. No Russian envoy inveighs against Indian or Burmese neutralism. On the contrary, they are praised for being "peace-loving." Even where close Russian defense ties exist—as with China or North Korea—the economic aspects of aid are underlined, the military glossed over. Russian aid does not, therefore, appear to tie the recipient to either side in the world struggle. It appears to respect neutralism.

Many Western statesmen, on the contrary, are forever nagging at Asia on this issue. As a result, they seem for their own selfish reasons to be drawing the East toward an atomic armageddon. There can be no doubt which attitude has the great political appeal.

In all this welter of Western insistence upon self-interest and self-defense, one looks in vain for any consistent exposition of a *positive* policy of foreign aid, some general political philosophy to match the Communist confidence in world brotherhood based on Socialist production, some framework of solidarity between givers and takers of aid, some aspect of human concern beyond the narrow limits of common fear. Once or twice, a more generous Western initiative has been taken.

President Truman's original Point Four concept of aid called for a "bold new program" of shared technical progress. President Eisenhower, in one major speech, spoke of pledging the free world's resources to combating want and disease and hunger—the permanent enemies of mankind. But by no effort of imagination can these few initiatives be stretched out into a consistent, sustained expression of Western intent. The positive utterances are quite drowned in the flood of argument and debate based exclusively upon fear and defense and cold war and the Communist menace.

If the West has a positive policy, Asia has not heard of it. But it hears about Communist brotherhood and Socialist solidarity every day of the week. Is it surprising that the political impact of Soviet economic offers is heightened thereby, while the West goes on giving more but with less effect?

The urgent question now is whether the Western powers can do anything to lessen or end the ambiguities and disappointments so far attendant upon the giving of foreign aid. There are, in fact, only three alternatives—to stop giving it altogether, to put up with the political disadvantages and to continue the present program on a "cold war" basis, or to try to find the proper *political* framework for a consistent program.

The first may be ruled out, for, whatever the political disappointments of the last decade, the fact remains that Western aid can still make a crucial difference economically between stability or collapse in Asia, for collapse helps one side only—the Communists.

The second alternative is possible but very unattractive. It could lead in the end to total frustration for, if Western giving continues without corresponding political advantage, domestic pressures against the program will grow, the aid will be given ever more grudgingly, the effects will become even less advantageous—and so on in a downward spiral of resentment and ill will.

There remains the third alternative—to find a positive political philosophy of Western assistance so that the program of foreign aid may be based not solely on expediency, self-interest, Communist competitiveness or the cold war, but upon conviction and principle. Such a program should not be beyond the West's political imagination. On the contrary, it can be argued that it is a logical development of our existing social traditions in the West.

Long before the Communists appropriated it, the solidarity of mankind was a firm base of Western, Christian tradition. Today, under the shadow of the hydrogen bomb and atomic fall-out, we have at least a physical solidarity of potential destruction. And if we are "one world" in physical vulnerability, our only hope is to become one world in moral responsibility as well.

Within the national community, we have discovered, in the last century, one key to a shared sense of moral solidarity in the principle of "the general welfare"—in other words, in an agreed sharing of wealth between well-to-do and underprivileged. This technique only waits to be extended, as a matter of conviction and principle, to the world of nation-states which now make up one neighborhood in our shrinking, atomic world.

The formula devised and proved workable after the war in the United Nations Relief and Rehabilitation Administration is probably the best mechanism to express the new solidarity. One per cent of national income contributed to backward areas from the wealthy West—the percentage which they have, without planning or policy, in fact expended in the last decade—would meet world needs today and would expand further as national incomes continue to bound up around the Atlantic.

But the mechanism is less important than the conviction, accepted by electorates and by their representatives, that in the twentieth century, in a world made one by science and technology, communities claiming Christian inspiration and inheriting the humanism of Western tradition must extend their sense of solidarity beyond national frontiers. In the words of the poet, Auden, "we must love each other or die."

And, as so often happens when principle takes the place of expediency and good-will of fear, we should find that such a change of emphasis would go far to counter what is practically unsatisfactory and discouraging in our present programs. A settled policy of aid, based upon a pre-determined percentage of national resources, would make possible the long-term planning of aid which President Eisenhower has declared to be necessary for the program's full effect.

The decision to extend aid as a matter of conviction and principle removes the effort from competitive bidding in the cold war and the scale of aid would be determined not by Russian offers and cajolements but by settled Western practice. The accent on the cold war could fade because it would no longer be essential to secure appropriations under the forced draught of fear. Above all, the link with war and atomic weapons and military preparedness could be broken because the program would exist independently of any threats of aggression and would continue equal and un-shaken in times of crisis as in "a calm world and a long peace."

Such a change of emphasis might not overnight dispel the memories of centuries of Western imperialism or reassure Asia entirely on the purposes and policies of the powerful West. But in a decade or more, when time had reinforced the principle, and foreign aid had become an orderly procedure, unhurried, unquestioned and unafraid, it would be found that Asian suspicions and Western frustrations had alike given ground before the new world-wide experiment in partnership and good-will.

THE USES OF FOREIGN AID*

BY

DWIGHT D. EISENHOWER

[1957]

The common label of "foreign aid" is gravely misleading for it inspires a picture of bounty for foreign countries at the expense of our own. No misconception could be further from reality. These programs serve our own basic national and personal interests.

They do this both immediately and lastingly. In the long term, the ending or the weakening of these programs would vastly increase the risk of future war. And, in the immediate sense, it would impose upon us additional defense expenditures many times greater than the cost of mutual security today.

This evening it is my purpose to give you incontestable proof of these assertions.

We have, during this century, twice spent our blood and our treasure fighting in Europe, and twice in Asia. We fought because we saw, too late to prevent war, that our own peace and security were imperiled by the urgent danger, or the ruthless conquest, of other lands.

We have gained wisdom from that suffering. We know, and the world knows, that the American people will fight hostile and aggressive despotisms when their force is thrown against the barriers of freedom, when they seek to gain the high ground of power from which to destroy us. But we also know that to fight is the most costly way to keep America secure and free. Even an America, victorious in atomic war could scarcely escape disastrous destruction of her cities and a fearful loss of life. Victory itself could be agony.

Plainly, we must seek less tragic, less costly ways to defend ourselves. We must recognize that, whenever any country falls under the domination of communism, the strength of the free world— and of America—is by that amount weakened and communism

---

* From an address to the nation on May 21, 1957. From *The Department of State Bulletin,* June 10, 1957.

strengthened. If this process, through our neglect or indifference, should proceed unchecked, our continent would be gradually encircled. Our safety depends upon recognition of the fact that the Communist design for such encirclement must be stopped before it gains momentum, before it is again too late to save the peace.

This recognition dictates two tasks. We must maintain a common worldwide defense against the menace of international communism. And we must demonstrate and spread the blessings of liberty—to be cherished by those who enjoy these blessings, to be sought by those now denied them.

This is not a new policy nor a partisan policy. This is a policy for America that began 10 years ago when a Democratic President and a Republican Congress united in an historic declaration. They then declared that the independence and survival of two countries menaced by Communist aggression—Greece and Turkey—were so important to the security of America that we would give them military and economic aid.

That policy saved those nations. And it did so without the cost of American lives.

That policy has since been extended to all critical areas of the world. It recognizes that America cannot exist as an island of freedom in a surrounding sea of communism. It is expressed concretely by mutual security treaties embracing 42 other nations. And these treaties reflect a solemn finding by the President and by the Senate that our own peace would be endangered if any of these countries were conquered by international communism. . . .

The whole design of this defense against Communist conspiracy and encirclement cannot be with guns alone. For the freedom of nations can be menaced not only by guns but by the poverty that communism can exploit.

You cannot fight poverty with guns. You cannot satisfy hunger with deadly ammunition. Economic stability and progress, essential to any nation's peace and well-being, cannot be assured merely by the firepower of artillery or the speed of jets.

And so our mutual security programs today, at a cost of some $4 billion, are designed to meet dangers in whatever form they may appear. Thus, their key purposes are three:

First: To help friendly nations equip and support armed forces for their own and our defense.

Second: To help, in a sustained effort, less advanced countries grow in the strength that can sustain freedom as their way of life.

And third: To meet emergencies and special needs affecting our own national interest.

Examining each of these purposes briefly, I first speak of the military aspect of these programs.

This accounts for about three-fourths of their total cost—just under $3 billion. This sum serves—indeed it belongs to—our own national defense. . . .

Now let us look at mutual security on the economic front. The peril here can be just as great to us as in the military arena.

Today in many countries one billion free people, across three continents, live in lands where the average yearly income of each man is $100 or less. These lands include the 19 nations that have won their independence since World War II. Most of them are on the frontier of the Communist world, close to the pressure of Communist power. For centuries the peoples of these countries have borne a burden of poverty. Now they are resolved to hold on to political independence, to achieve the economic strength to sustain that independence, and to support rising standards of living.

In these lands no government can justly rule, or even survive, which does not reflect this resolve, which does not offer its people hope of progress. And wherever moderate government disappears, Communist extremists will extend their brand of despotic imperialism.

Our own strength would suffer severely from the loss of these lands—their people and their resources—to Communist domination. As these lands improve their own standards of living, they will be stronger allies in defense of freedom. And there will be widening opportunity for trade with them.

We seek to help these people to help themselves. We cannot export progress and security to them. Essentially, they must achieve these for themselves. But there are practical ways by which we can help, especially in the early struggles of these young nations to survive.

For one thing, they need the knowledge of skilled people—farm experts, doctors, engineers—to teach new techniques to their people. Our program of technical cooperation aims to do this. It will cost $150 million next year.

At the same time, because their inherited poverty leaves these peoples so little for saving, they need the help of some capital to begin essential investment in roads, dams, railroads, utilities—the sinews of economic strength.

Already many of these countries, like India and Pakistan, are with great difficulty devoting substantial amounts of their limited resources to this kind of long-range investment. But at this critical moment of their economic growth a relatively small amount of outside capital can fatefully decide the difference between success and failure. What is critical now is to start and to maintain momentum.

While we want and intend to see that private investors and other lending agencies supply as much as possible of this outside capital, our development assistance program under mutual security has a vital role to play. Here I am convinced that we should rely more upon loans than upon gifts. This is the sound and proper way for free allies to work together—to respect and to encourage the pride of each nation, to inspire in each nation greater zeal and sense of responsibility, to encourage thoughtful long-term planning rather than frantic emergency action.

This outlook signifies a fundamental shift of emphasis from the practice of past years. I have accordingly asked the Congress to create a development loan fund with enough capital to allow orderly and continuing operations. Only this kind of sustained operations will allow for the prudent and thoughtful use of money. Only such operations will assure priority to the most sound and necessary projects.

To assure this continuity and coherence of action, I have specifically requested for the first year $500 million already in the budget and authority for $750 million for each of the 2 succeeding years.

In this whole program, we do not seek to buy friends. We do not seek to make satellites. We do seek to help other peoples to become strong and stay free—and learn, through living in freedom, how to conquer poverty, how to know the blessings of peace and progress.

This purpose, I repeat, serves our own national interest.

It also reflects our own national character. We are stirred not only by calculations of self-interest but also by decent regard for the needs and the hopes of all our fellowmen. I am proud of this fact, as you are. None of us would wish it to be otherwise.

This is not mere sentimentality. This is the very nature of America, realistically understood and applied.

If ever we were to lose our sense of brotherhood, of kinship with all free men, we would have entered upon our Nation's period of decline. Without vision, without a quick sense of justice and compassion, no people can claim greatness.

There remains, in addition to continuing defense and economic aid, a final aspect to our mutual security programs. This entails assistance to meet various special needs, including sudden crises against which prior planning is impossible. Such crises generally demand the swiftest action.

We have seen several such examples in recent years.

In the Middle East, the freedom of Iran only 4 years ago was threatened by the rule of a government inclined toward communism. Under the courageous leadership of the Shah, the people of Iran met that danger. In their effort to restore economic stability, they received indispensable help from us. Iran remains free. And its freedom continues to prove of vital importance to our own freedom.

In our own hemisphere, Guatemala not long ago faced a similar peril, with heavy Communist infiltration into the government. Here, too, the people rose to repel this threat, but they needed—and they received—the help without which their efforts could have been in vain.

Most recently we have witnessed a like instance in the Middle East. The Kingdom of Jordan came under the sway of a succession of cabinets, each one seemingly more tolerant of Communist infiltration and subversion. King Hussein has acted swiftly and resolutely to forestall disaster, and the peril now seems checked.

Yet this victory would surely be lost without economic aid from outside Jordan. Jordan's armed forces must be paid. The nation's utilities must function. And, above all, the people must have hope.

Some necessary aid can come from neighboring Arab countries, such as Saudi Arabia, but some also must come from the United

States. For the security of Jordan means strength for all the forces of freedom in the Middle East.

Now, you have undoubtedly heard charges of waste and inefficiency in some of these programs of assistance, such as that in Iran. I do not doubt that isolated incidents could be cited to support such charges.

On this I have two convictions:

First: The remarkable truth is not that a few Americans working abroad may have been inefficient but that so many thousands of patriotic Americans have willingly and competently done their jobs in distant lands, under the most difficult conditions, often in the presence of real danger.

And second: When we speak of waste, let none of us forget that there is no waste so colossal as war itself—and these programs are totally dedicated to the prevention of that most appalling kind of waste.

All such situations—as in Iran, Guatemala, Jordan—have been tense moments in the world struggle. Each such moment has vitally touched our own national interest.

I have asked the Congress for the sum of $300 million to enable us to act, and to act swiftly, in any such moment as it may strike. Only such part of that sum will be used as is clearly needed to serve our national interest. But the history of these years surely means one thing: To give saving help at such moments is true economy on a world scale, for it can mean the saving of whole nations and the promotion of peace.

These, then, are the kinds of help and action that make up our mutual security programs, for which I have asked the Congress to appropriate less than $4 billion—one-twentieth of our national budget.

This is not a mathematical guess or an arbitrary sum. It reflects economies already achieved in some aspects of military aid. It is a reasoned figure. And, considering the issues at stake, it is a minimum figure.

I know of no more sound or necessary investment that our Nation can make. I know of no expenditure that can contribute so much, in the words of the Constitution, to our "common defense" and to securing the blessings of liberty for ourselves and our posterity.

To see all the day-to-day results of these programs in concrete terms is not always easy. They operate in distant lands whose histories, even their names, seem remote. Often the results are not swift and dramatic but gradual and steady. They operate in a way rather like police or fire protection in our own cities. When they are least in the news, they are really doing the most effective work.

We live at a time when our plainest task is to put first things first. Of all our current domestic concerns—lower taxes, bigger dams, deeper harbors, higher pensions, better housing—not one of these will matter if our Nation is put in peril. For all that we cherish and justly desire, for ourselves or for our children, the securing of peace is the first requisite.

We live in a time when the cost of peace is high. Yet the price of war is higher and is paid in different coin—with the lives of our youth and the devastation of our cities.

The road to this disaster could easily be paved with the good intentions of those blindly striving to save the money that must be spent as the price of peace.

It is no accident that those who have most intimately lived with the horrors of war are generally the most earnest supporters of these programs to secure peace.

To cripple our programs for mutual security in the false name of "economy" can mean nothing less than a weakening of our Nation.

To try to save money at the risk of such damage is neither conservative nor constructive. It is reckless. It could mean the loss of peace. It could mean the loss of freedom. It could mean the loss of both.

I know that you would not wish your Government to take such a reckless gamble. I do not intend that your Government take that gamble.

I am convinced of the necessity of these programs of mutual security—for the very safety of our Nation. For upon them critically depends all that we hold most dear—the heritage of freedom from our fathers, the peace and well-being of the sons who will come after us.

LIMITATIONS OF ECONOMIC AID *

BY

GEORGE F. KENNAN

[1958]

The demands frequently made upon us by the independent countries in part of the world seem to me to run something like this: "We," they say, "are determined to have economic development and to have it at once. For us, this is an overriding aim, an absolute requirement; and we are not much concerned about the method by which it is achieved. You in the West owe it to us to let us have your assistance and to give it to us promptly, effectively, and without conditions; otherwise we will take it from the Russians, whose experience and methods we suspect anyway to be more relevant to our problems." In response to this approach, a great many people in my own country have come to take it for granted that there is some direct relationship between programs of economic aid on the one hand and political attitudes on the other— between the amount of money we are willing to devote to economic assistance in any given year and the amount of progress we may expect to make in overcoming these troublesome states of mind I have been talking about.

This thesis, as well as the reaction to it at home, seems to me to be questionable at every point. I find myself thrown off at the very start by this absolute value attached to rapid economic development. Why all the urgency? It can well be argued that the pace of change is no less important than its nature, and that great damage can be done by altering too rapidly the sociological and cultural structure of any society, even where these alterations may be desirable in themselves. In many instances one would also like to know how this economic progress is to be related to the staggering population growth with which it is associated. Finally, many of us in America have seen too much of the incidental effects of industrialization and urbanization to be convinced that these things are absolute answers to problems anywhere, or that they could be

* From *Russia, the Atom and the West,* published by Harper & Brothers, copyright 1957, 1958 by George F. Kennan. Reprinted by permission.

worth *any* sacrifice to obtain. For these reasons I cannot fully share the basic enthusiasm on which this whole thesis is founded.

I must also reject the suggestion that our generation in the West has some sort of a cosmic guilt or obligation vis-à-vis the underdeveloped parts of the world. The fact that certain portions of the globe were developed sooner than others is one for which I, as an American of this day, cannot accept the faintest moral responsibility; nor do I see that it was particularly the fault of my American ancestors. I cannot even see that the phenomenon of colonialism was one which could be regarded as having given rise to any such state of obligation. The establishment of the colonial relationship did not represent a moral action on somebody's part; it represented a natural and inevitable response to certain demands and stimuli of the age. It was simply a stage of history. It generally took place with the agreement and connivance of people at the colonial end as well as in the mother country. Nor were the benefits derived from this relationship in any way one-sided. The Marxists claim, of course, that colonialism invariably represented a massive and cruel exploitation of the colonial peoples. I am sure that honest study would reveal this thesis to be quite fallacious. Advantages, injuries and sacrifices were incurred on both sides. Today these things are largely bygones. We will do no good by scratching around to discover whose descendants owe the most to the descendants of the other. If we are to help each other in this world, we must start with a clean slate.

I can well understand that there are instances in which it will be desirable for us from time to time to support schemes of economic development which are soundly conceived and which give promise, over the long run, of yielding greater stability and a new hopefulness for the countries concerned. I trust that we will not let such demands go unanswered when they arise. There is no fonder hope in the American breast, my own included, than that the experience we have had in developing a continent will prove relevant and helpful to others. Every American would like to see us take a useful part in solving problems of economic development elsewhere in the world. But action of this sort can be useful only if it proceeds on a sound psychological basis. If there is a general impression in the recipient countries that this aid represents the paying of some sort of a debt from us to them, then the extension of it can only sow confusion. The same is true if it is going to be interpreted as a sign of weakness on our part or of a fear that others might go over to the Communists, or if it is going to be widely attacked in the recipient countries as evidence of what the Communists have taught people to refer to as "imperialism," by which they seem to mean some sort of intricate and concealed foreign domination, the exact workings of which are never very clearly explained.

Unless such reactions can be ruled out, programs of economic aid are apt to do more harm than good psychologically; and it ought properly to be the obligation of the recipient governments and not of ourself to see that these misinterpretations do not occur. To those who come to us with requests for aid one would like to say: "You tell us first how you propose to assure that if we give you this aid it will not be interpreted among your people as a sign of weakness or fear on our part, or of a desire to dominate you."

These are not the only psychological dangers of foreign aid. There is the basic fact that any form of benevolence, if prolonged for any length of time (even in personal life this is true), comes to be taken for granted as a right and its withdrawal resented as an injury. There is the fact that any program of economic development represents a change in the terms of competition within a country and brings injury to some parties while it benefits the others. It is hard to give aid to any other country economically without its having an effect on internal political realities there— without its redounding to the benefit of one political party and the disadvantage of another.

All these considerations incline me to feel that, desirable as programs of foreign aid may sometimes be from the long-term standpoint, their immediate psychological effects are apt to be at best mixed and uncertain. For this reason, foreign aid, as a general practice, cannot be regarded as a very promising device for combating, over the short term, the psychological handicaps under which Western statesmanship now rests in Asia and Africa.

Finally, I do not think for a moment that the Soviet Union really presents the alternative people seem to think it represents to a decent relationship with the West. Moscow has its contribution

to make to what should be a common task of all the highly industrialized countries; and there is no reason why this contribution
should not be welcomed wherever it can be really helpful. But
Moscow is not exactly the bottomless horn of plenty it is often held
to be; and it is rather a pity that it has never been required to
respond all at once to the many expectations directed to it. We
ourselves should be the last, one would think, to wish to spare it
this test. The results might be both healthy and instructive.

What, then, is there to be done about these feelings of people
in Asia and Africa? Very little, I am afraid, over the short term,
except to relax, to keep our composure, to refuse to be frightened
by the Communism alternative, to refrain from doing the things
that make matters worse, and to let things come to rest, as in
the end they must, on the sense of self-interest of the peoples
concerned.

WARS OF NATIONAL LIBERATION *

BY

NIKITA S. KHRUSHCHEV

[1961]

. . . Now a word about national liberation wars. The armed struggle by the Vietnamese people or the war of the Algerian people, which is already in its 7th year, serve as the latest examples of such wars. These wars began as an uprising by the colonial peoples against their oppressors and changed into guerrilla warfare. Liberation wars will continue to exist as long as imperialism exists, as long as colonialism exists. These are revolutionary wars. Such wars are not only admissible but inevitable, since the colonialists do not grant independence voluntarily. Therefore, the peoples can attain their freedom and independence only by struggle, including armed struggle. . . .

The Algerian people, too, receive assistance from neighboring and other countries that sympathize with their peace-loving aspirations. But it is a liberation war of a people for its independence, it is a sacred war. We recognize such wars, we help and will help the peoples striving for their independence. . . .

Can such wars flare up in the future? They can. Can there be such uprisings? There can. But these are wars which are national uprisings. In other words, can conditions be created where a people will lose their patience and rise in arms? They can. What is the attitude of the Marxists toward such uprisings? A most positive one. These uprisings must not be identified with wars among states, with local wars, since in these uprisings the people are fighting for implementation of their right for self-determination, for independent social and national development. These are uprisings against rotten reactionary regimes, against the colonizers. The Communists fully support such just wars and march in the front rank with the peoples waging liberation struggles. . . .

---

* Selections from the report of N. S. Khrushchev to the Moscow Conference of Communist Parties, January 6, 1961.

A sober appraisal of the inevitable consequences of nuclear war is the indispensable condition for a persistent persuance of a policy of preventing war, and of mobilizing the masses for the solution of this task.

After all, the very appreciation of the threat of devastating war strengthens the will of the masses to struggle against war. Therefore it is essential to warn the masses of the most dangerous consequences of a new world war and, thereby, to rouse the sacred wrath of the peoples against those who are preparing this crime.

The possibility of preventing war is not something like a gift. Peace cannot be begged for; it can only be assured by active purposeful struggle. That is why we have waged and will wage such a struggle.

The entire foreign policy of the Soviet Union is directed toward the strengthening of peace. The growing might of our state has been used by us and will in the future be used not to threaten anyone, not to fan the fear of war, but to steadfastly pursue a policy of struggle against the danger of war, for the prevention of a world war. We have been and are prompted by the desire to maintain and strengthen friendly relations with all peoples in the interests of peace on the basis of the principles of peaceful coexistence.

Comrades, life itself bears out the correctness of the Leninist policy of peaceful coexistence of states with diverse social systems, consistently pursued by the Soviet Union and the other Socialist countries. Our party considers the policy of peaceful coexistence, which has been handed down to us by Lenin, to be the general line of our foreign policy. Peaceful coexistence is the high road of international relations between Socialist and capitalist countries. The consistent implementation of the policy of peaceful coexistence strengthens the position of the world Socialist system, promotes the growth of its economic might, its international prestige and influence among the people's masses, and creates for it favorable foreign-political possibilities in peaceful competition with capitalism.

GUERRILLA WARFARE IN THE UNDERDEVELOPED AREAS *

BY

W. W. ROSTOW

[1961]

. . . It does not require much imagination to understand why President Kennedy has taken the problem of guerrilla warfare seriously. When this administration came to responsibility it faced four major crises: Cuba, the Congo, Laos, and Viet-Nam. Each represented a successful Communist breaching—over the previous 2 years—of the cold-war truce lines which had emerged from the Second World War and its aftermath. In different ways each had arisen from the efforts of the international Communist movement to exploit the inherent instabilities of the underdeveloped areas of the non-Communist world, and each had a guerrilla-warfare component.

Cuba, of course, differed from the other cases. The Cuban revolution against Batista was a broad-based national insurrection. But that revolution was tragically captured from within by the Communist apparatus; and now Latin America faces the danger of Cuba's being used as the base for training, supply, and direction of guerrilla warfare in the hemisphere.

More than that, Mr. Khrushchev, in his report to the Moscow conference of Communist parties (published January 6, 1961), had explained at great length that the Communists fully support what he called wars of national liberation and would march in the front rank with the peoples waging such struggles. The military arm of Mr. Khrushchev's January 1961 doctrine is, clearly, guerrilla warfare.

Faced with these four crises, pressing in on the President from

* From an address at the United States Army Special Warfare School, Fort Bragg, N.C., June 28, 1961. Reprinted from *The Department of State Bulletin,* August 7, 1961. Walt W. Rostow (b. 1916) was special assistant to the President (1966–1969) and counselor and Chairman of the Policy Planning Council, Department of State (1961–1966).

day to day, and faced with the candidly stated position of Mr. Khrushchev, we have, indeed, begun to take the problem of guerrilla warfare seriously.

REVOLUTIONARY PROCESS IN SOUTHERN HEMISPHERE

To understand this problem, however, one must begin with the great revolutionary process that is going forward in the southern half of the world; for the guerrilla warfare problem in these regions is a product of that revolutionary process and the Communist effort and intent to exploit it.

What is happening throughout Latin America, Africa, the Middle East, and Asia is this: Old societies are changing their ways in order to create and maintain a national personality on the world scene and to bring to their peoples the benefits modern technology can offer. This process is truly revolutionary. It touches every aspect of the traditional life—economic, social, and political. The introduction of modern technology brings about not merely new methods of production but a new style of family life, new links between the villages and the cities, the beginnings of national politics, and a new relationship to the world outside.

Like all revolutions, the revolution of modernization is disturbing. Individual men are torn between the commitment to the old familiar way of life and the attractions of a modern way of life. The power of old social groups—notably the landlord, who usually dominates the traditional society—is reduced. Power moves toward those who can command the tools of modern technology, including modern weapons. Men and women in the villages and the cities, feeling that the old ways of life are shaken and that new possibilities are open to them, express old resentments and new hopes.

This is the grand arena of revolutionary change which the Communists are exploiting with great energy. They believe that their techniques of organization—based on small disciplined cadres of conspirators—are ideally suited to grasp and to hold power in these turbulent settings. They believe that the weak transitional governments that one is likely to find during this modernization process are highly vulnerable to subversion and to guerrilla warfare. And whatever Communist doctrines of historical inevitability may be, Communists know that their time to seize power in the underdeveloped areas is limited. They know that, as momentum takes hold in an underdeveloped area—and the fundamental social problems inherited from the traditional society are solved—their chances to seize power decline.

It is on the weakest nations, facing their most difficult transitional moments, that the Communists concentrate their attention. They are the scavengers of the modernization process. They believe that the techniques of political centralization under dictatorial control—and the projected image of Soviet and Chinese Communist economic progress—will persuade hesitant men, faced by great transitional problems, that the Communist model should be adopted for modernization, even at the cost of surrendering human liberty. They believe that they can exploit effectively the resentments built up in many of these areas against colonial rule and that they can associate themselves effectively with the desire of the emerging nations for independence, for status on the world scene, and for material progress.

This is a formidable program; for the history of this century teaches us that communism is not the longrun wave of the future toward which societies are naturally drawn. On the contrary. But it is one particular form of modern society to which a nation may fall prey during the transitional process. Communism is best understood as a disease of the transition to modernization. . . .

AMERICA'S PURPOSE AND STRATEGY

What is our reply to this historical conception and strategy? What is the American purpose and the American strategy? We, too, recognize that a revolutionary process is under way. We are dedicated to the proposition that this revolutionary process of modernization shall be permitted to go forward in independence, with increasing degrees of human freedom. We seek two results: first, that truly independent nations shall emerge on the world scene; and, second, that each nation will be permitted to fashion, out of its own culture and its own ambitions, the kind of modern society it wants. The same religious and philosophical beliefs which decree that we respect the uniqueness of each individual make it natural that we respect the uniqueness of each national society. Moreover, we Americans are confident that, if the independence of this process can be maintained over the coming years and decades, these societies will choose their own version of what we would recognize as a democratic, open society.

These are our commitments of policy and of faith. The United States has no interest in political satellites. Where we have military pacts we have them because governments feel directly endangered by outside military action and we are prepared to help protect their independence against such military action. But, to use Mao Tse-tung's famous phrase, we do not seek nations which "lean to one side." We seek nations which shall stand up straight. And we do so for a reason: because we are deeply confident that nations which stand up straight will protect their independence and move in their own ways and in their own time toward human freedom and political democracy.

PROTECTING INDEPENDENCE OF REVOLUTIONARY PROCESS

Thus our central task in the underdeveloped areas, as we see it, is to protect the independence of the revolutionary process now going forward. This is our mission, and it is our ultimate strength. For this is not—and cannot be—the mission of communism. And in time, through the fog of propaganda and the honest confusions of men caught up in the business of making new nations, this fundamental difference will become increasingly clear in the southern half of the world. The American interest will be served if our children live in an environment of strong, assertive, independent nations, capable, because they are strong, of assuming collective responsibility for the peace.

The diffusion of power is the basis for freedom within our own society, and we have no reason to fear it on the world scene. But this outcome would be a defeat for communism—not for Russia as a national state, but for communism. Despite all the Communist talk of aiding movements of national independence, they are driven in the end, by the nature of their system, to violate the independence of nations. Despite all the Communist talk of American imperialism, we are committed, by the nature of our system, to support the cause of national independence. And the truth will out.

The victory we seek will see no ticker tape parades down Broadway, no climactic battles, nor great American celebrations of victory. It is a victory which will take many years and decades of hard work and dedication—by many peoples—to bring about. This will not be a victory of the United States over the Soviet Union. It will not be a victory of capitalism over socialism. It will be a victory of men and nations which aim to stand up straight, over the forces which wish to entrap and to exploit their revolutionary aspirations of modernization. What this victory involves, in the end, is the assertion by nations of their right to independence and by men and women of their right to freedom as they understand it. And we deeply believe this victory will come— on both sides of the Iron Curtain.

If Americans do not seek victory in the usual sense, what do we seek? What is the national interest of the United States? Why do we Americans expend our treasure and assume the risks of modern war in this global struggle? For Americans the reward of victory will be, simply, this: It will permit American society to continue to develop along the old humane lines which go back to our birth as a nation—and which reach deeper into history than that—back to the Mediterranean roots of Western life. We are struggling to maintain an environment on the world scene which will permit our open society to survive and to flourish.

U.S. RESPONSIBILITIES

To make this vision come true places a great burden on the United States at this phase of history. The preservation of independence has many dimensions.

The United States has the primary responsibility for deterring the use of nuclear weapons in the pursuit of Communist ambitions. The United States has a major responsibility to deter the kind of overt aggression with conventional forces which was launched in June 1950 in Korea.

The United States has the primary responsibility for assisting the economies of those hard-pressed states on the periphery of the Communist bloc, which are under acute military or quasi-military pressure which they cannot bear from their own resources; for example, South Korea, Viet-Nam, Taiwan, Pakistan, Iran. The United States has a special responsibility of leadership in bringing not merely its own resources but the resources of all the free world to bear in aiding the longrun development of those nations which are serious about modernizing their economy and their social life. And, as President Kennedy has made clear, he regards no program of his administration as more important than his program for long-term economic development, dramatized, for example, by the Alliance for Progress in Latin America. Independence cannot be maintained by military measures alone. Modern societies must be built, and we are prepared to help build them.

Finally, the United States has a role to play—symbolized by your presence here and by mine—in learning to deter guerrilla warfare, if possible, and to deal with it, if necessary.

LOCAL AND INTERNATIONAL RESPONSIBILITIES

I do not need to tell you that the primary responsibility for dealing with guerrilla warfare in the underdeveloped areas cannot be American. There are many ways in which we can help—and we are searching our minds and our imaginations to learn better how to help; but a guerrilla war must be fought primarily by those on the spot. This is so for a quite particular reason. A guerrilla war is an intimate affair, fought not merely with weapons but fought in the minds of the men who live in the villages and in the hills, fought by the spirit and policy of those who run the local government. An outsider cannot, by himself, win a guerrilla war. He can help create conditions in which it can be won, and he can directly assist those prepared to fight for their independence. We are determined to help destroy this international disease; that is, guerrilla war designed, initiated, supplied, and led from outside an independent nation.

Although as leader of the free world the United States has special responsibilities which it accepts in this common venture of deterrence, it is important that the whole international community begin to accept its responsibility for dealing with this form of aggression. It is important that the world become clear in mind, for example, that the operation run from Hanoi against Viet-Nam is as clear a form of aggression as the violation of the 38th parallel by the North Korean armies in June 1950.

In my conversations with representatives of foreign governments, I am sometimes lectured that this or that government within the free world is not popular; they tell me that guerrilla warfare cannot be won unless the peoples are dissatisfied. These are, at best, half-truths. The truth is that guerrilla warfare, mounted from external bases—with rights of sanctuary—is a terrible burden to carry for any government in a society making its way toward modernization. As you know, it takes somewhere between 10 and 20 soldiers to control 1 guerrilla in an organized operation. Moreover, the guerrilla force has this advantage: its task is merely to destroy, while the government must build and protect what it is building. A guerrilla war mounted from outside a transitional nation is a crude act of international vandalism. There will be no peace in the world if the international community accepts the outcome of a guerrilla war, mounted from outside a nation, as tantamount to a free election.

The sending of men and arms across international boundaries and the direction of guerrilla war from outside a sovereign nation is aggression; and this is a fact which the whole international community must confront and whose consequent responsibilities it must accept. Without such international action those against whom aggression is mounted will be driven inevitably to seek out and engage the ultimate source of the aggression they confront.

I suspect that in the end the real meaning of the conference on Laos at Geneva will hinge on this question: It will depend on whether or not the international community is prepared to mount an International Control Commission which has the will and the capacity to control the borders it was designed to control.

LEARNING TO PREVENT GUERRILLA WARS

In facing the problem of guerrilla war, I have one observation to make as a historian. It is now fashionable—and I daresay for you it was compulsory—to read the learned works of Mao Tse-tung and Che Guevara on guerrilla warfare. This is, indeed, proper. One should read with care and without passion into the minds of one's enemies. But it is historically inaccurate and psychologically dangerous to think that these men created the strategy and tactics of guerrilla war to which we are now responding. Guerrilla warfare is not a form of military and psychological magic created by the Communists. There is no rule or parable in the Communist texts which was not known at an earlier time in history. The operation of Marion's men in relation to the Battle of Cowpens in the American Revolution was, for example, governed by rules which Mao merely echoes. Che Guevara knows nothing of this business that T. E. Lawrence did not know or was not practiced, for example, in the Peninsular Campaign during the Napoleonic wars, a century earlier. The orchestration of professional troops, militia, and guerrilla fighters is an old game whose rules can be studied and learned.

My point is that we are up against a form of warfare which is powerful and effective only when we do not put our minds clearly to work on how to deal with it. I, for one, believe that with purposeful efforts most nations which might now be susceptible to guerrilla warfare could handle their border areas in ways which would make them very unattractive to the initiation of this ugly game. We can learn to prevent the emergence of the famous sea in which Mao Tse-tung taught his men to swim. This requires, of course, not merely a proper military program of deterrence but programs of village development, communications, and indoctrination. The best way to fight a guerrilla war is to prevent it from happening. And this can be done.

Similarly, I am confident that we can deal with the kind of operation now under way in Viet-Nam. It is an extremely dangerous operation, and it could overwhelm Viet-Nam if the Vietnamese—aided by the free world—do not deal with it. But it is an unsubtle operation, by the book, based more on murder than on political or psychological appeal.

When Communists speak of wars of national liberation and of their support for "progressive forces," I think of the systematic program of assassination now going forward in which the principal victims are the health, agriculture, and education officers in the Viet-Nam villages. The Viet Cong are not trying to persuade the peasants of Viet-Nam that communism is good; they are trying to persuade them that their lives are insecure unless they cooperate with them. With resolution and confidence on all sides and with the assumption of international responsibility for the frontier problem, I believe we are going to bring this threat to the independence of Viet-Nam under control.

My view is, then, that we confront in guerrilla warfare in the underdeveloped areas a systematic attempt by the Communists to impose a serious disease on those societies attempting the transition to modernization. This attempt is a present danger in southeast Asia. It could quickly become a major danger in Africa and Latin America. I salute in particular those among you whose duty it is—along with others—to prevent that disease, if possible, and to eliminate it where it is imposed.

*   *   *

NEO-ISOLATIONISTS AND GLOBALISTS *

BY

RONALD STEEL

[1967]

The mounting pace of disorder and violence throughout the poverty-stricken states of the southern hemisphere has confronted Americans with a terrible dilemma. Should American power be used, regardless of place or circumstance, to bring about conditions which Americans believe to be morally desirable, or should that power be restrained by considerations of national interest and a tolerance for the diversity of ideologies? Have we become involved in disturbances abroad that are far beyond our vital interests and our ability to resolve—or must we, as President Johnson has said, extend our concept of freedom "to everyone, whether rich or poor, whether they agree with us or not, no matter what their race or the color of their skin"? [1]

The debate over our world role has become an urgent matter which America can no longer avoid. It is an argument between those who believe that American power and American responsibilities are limited, and those who believe that they are global; between those who see the defense of freedom as indivisible, and those who would limit our involvements to areas where our security is at stake and where we would not try to impose our ideas upon others. In the most elemental sense this is an argument about America's moral and intellectual responsibilities, and specifically about America's role in the world: whether she is, as John Kennedy said, "the watchman on the walls of world freedom," or whether, as John Quincy Adams advised, she should be the "well-wisher to the freedom and independence of all . . . [but] the champion and vindicator only of her own."

---

* From *Pax Americana,* published by Viking Press, copyright 1967 by Viking Press. Reprinted by permission. Ronald Steel is the author of several books and numerous articles critical of postwar American foreign policy.

[1] Lyndon B. Johnson, address at New York, February 23, 1966.

So far this argument has been carried on in a rather traditional vocabulary. Those who believe the nation to be overextended—militarily, intellectually, morally—are castigated as isolationists, or perhaps more charitably as neo-isolationists. Those who believe that America must intervene with her military power to prevent communist regimes from coming to power are labeled globalists. But the labeling, while convenient and perhaps unavoidable, does not do justice to either side. The so-called neo-isolationists do not want to turn the clock back to 1938 and retire to a Fortress America while the rest of the world goes up in flames. These neo-isolationists are, for the most part, convinced internationalists, supporters of foreign aid, NATO, and the Alliance for Progress. What they seek is not a denial of American responsibility but a retrenchment of American commitments to those areas which they consider vital to the national interest; more specifically, Western Europe and the western hemisphere. They believe that American military power should be used only to defend the vital strategic interests of the United States, and not to save noncommunist governments in Asia and Africa.

The globalists, on the other hand, feel that the United States has a moral as well as a national responsibility to prevent the spread of communism wherever the threat may arise. They reject the assumption of the neo-isolationists that one area of the world is more important than any other. Whereas President Kennedy declared that he was a Berliner, President Johnson more accurately reflected the globalist style by asserting that the United States is a Pacific power. The war in Vietnam is the proof of this conviction. Globalists believe that the United States is engaged in a struggle with communism that will, quite literally, determine the fate of the world. To retire from the struggle, or to refrain from using force to prevent an advance of communism, would, in this view, be ignominious. Not only would this represent a victory for a hostile ideology, but it would diminish America's stature on the world stage. Behind the appeals to a higher morality there lies a calculated consideration of national prestige. Globalists may be ideologues, but they are also confirmed believers in *Realpolitik*. The difficulty, however, occurs when the two come into conflict, when a commitment to ideology prevents a clear calculation of the national interest, or when a cynical use of power betrays basic moral principles.

This balancing of *Realpolitik* and political morality is a peculiar dilemma, but it is an American one, and it is shared equally by neo-isolationists and globalists. The former believe that calculations of national interest should determine whether or not the nation commits itself to military intervention in support of foreign governments. They would argue that only those nations whose security is crucial to our interests merit American military intervention in their support. However, because they are Americans and thus infused with a moral conception of foreign policy, they would make exceptions for certain non-strategic countries that are integral to the Western community, such as New Zealand, Israel, and Iceland. They would also argue that we should support only progressive, representative regimes that share our belief in political democracy. That such regimes are exceedingly scarce outside the Western world, even in countries that may be important to our national interest, is one of the dilemmas of the liberal neo-isolationists.

The globalists, for their part, speak movingly of the moral purpose of America as the defender of freedoms for those who are too weak to defend themselves. Yet they readily display a willingness to use American military power in such cruel ways as to make their moral imperatives appear as cynical self-justifications. "Sure of its moral purposes—surer of its own moral performance—America shall not be deterred from doing what must be done to preserve this last peace man shall ever have to win or lose," said Lyndon Johnson on June 6, 1965, as American planes strafed, bombed, and napalmed the villages of Vietnam. Behind the moral righteousness of the global interventionist lies the heavy rod of the Calvinist judge.

Thus morality and power blend in a strange combination that America's critics can look upon only as the most self-serving hypocrisy, but which all Americans will recognize as an expression of their own mixed, and often contradictory, feelings about the role of a nation engaged, in John F. Kennedy's words, "with a struggle we did not start in a world we did not make." There are no easy answers, no moral certainties, no sure rewards. There is only the reality of America's inextricable involvement in a recalcitrant world, and the gnawing fear that perhaps our great power is being dissipated uselessly, or, even worse, used in ways that diminish our worth to the world and to ourselves.

The United States is inescapably a world power, currently *the* world power, with all the responsibilities, the temptations, and the anguish that go with such overwhelming force. America did not choose to be a great power; she became a great power. She was born with great dreams and she had greatness thrust upon her. But once having achieved great power, once having had the responsibility of defending European civilization first from nazism, then from communism, the United States developed a sense of mission about the uses of her power. Just as she inadvertently picked up an empire in Europe and Asia to complement the one she had long enjoyed in Latin America, so she began to dream imperial dreams. She became absorbed not only in her own security and the defense of her closest allies from external aggression, but also in the effort to mold the world into an image conforming to her own conception of virtue.

This is, perhaps, a temptation common to many nations. But the extraordinary weight of America in the world balance transformed such an ambition from a dream into a program, albeit a rather dimly defined and only half-recognized one. American power, to a degree not fully conceived of even by the American people in whose name it is exercised, has been turned into an instrument for the pursuit of an American ideology. And that ideology is not merely the defense of the nation and its institutions, but something far more ambitious: the establishment of a world order on the American plan. It is this desire to translate American ideals into a universal political system that lies at the core of the current crisis in American diplomacy.

The nation is now experiencing a profound national debate over the uses of American power. The debate may not be phrased explicitly; its vocabulary may be vague and its frame of reference limited. But this is what the war in Vietnam is about, and what all the other interventions—those that were carried out, those that were contemplated, and those that are yet to happen—are inspired by. We cannot begin to deal with this crisis until we understand that it exists.

To raise the question of whether America should carry out unilateral military intervention in areas outside the traditional framework of American interests is not necessarily to take an isolationist position. Anyone who argued at the end of the Second World War that the United States should not suppress rebellions in Vietnam and the Congo, or maintain standing armies in Germany and Korea, would not have been considered an isolationist. He would merely have been expressing the obvious. If such a position has now come to bear tinges of isolationism, it is because we have swung so far over to the other extreme. Today our interests are universal, and so, it would seem, are our commitments. Whereas we formerly believed that American military power should be introduced only where a vital American interest was involved, we now feel that we have a moral commitment to intervene in any nation that has a communist problem.

The vision of America as the enforcer of justice and the scourge of tyrants is a noble one. It goes back, in rhetoric at least, to the early days of the republic and corresponds to the image of the United States as a standard-bearer of freedom for peoples everywhere. It was not, however, until recently that this patriotic self-image was translated into a program of action and America was declared to have a responsibility to bring her concept of democratic self-government to peoples everywhere. Woodrow Wilson thought he would bring about universal justice through a League of Nations bound to principles of morality. Franklin Roosevelt, less idealistic but wiser in the ways of nations, sought to bring about the American Century by an accord of the great powers acting in cooperation through the Security Council of the United Nations. Lyndon Johnson, however, heading a government "sure of its moral purpose," would have the United States achieve the world of justice and liberty that is every man's dream through the unilateral application of American military power.

Yet the freedom Americans are called upon to defend by the sword takes on an abstract ring when applied to societies outside the Western tradition. In the West "freedom" means the ability of men to choose, to change, and to reject the governments under which they live. To an Angolan rebel, however, it means independence from Portugal; to a Cuban revolutionary it means release from American economic control; to a Rumanian it means defiance of the Soviet Union; to white Rhodesians it means the right to dominate a black majority; to the Naga tribesman of India it means independence from the government in New Delhi; and to the peasants of Brazil's northeast it means bread and a patch of land. These are not all freedoms which it is in America's power to grant, nor even necessarily freedoms which we would value.

Yet "freedom," President Johnson tells us, "is an indivisible word." And perhaps it is, within a certain limited framework of common interests and common values, such as those shared between America and Western Europe. But if freedom is indivisible, does this mean that Americans cannot be free so long as Iraqis, Ghanaians, and Paraguayans live under repressive governments? If so, the President is proclaiming a logical absurdity, because never in the history of the world have men everywhere been free. If we know anything about freedom, we know that it is divisible; that some men live in freedom, and other men live under tyranny, and most men live in some gray area in between, where liberty and constraint are mixed in varying measure.

If freedom is divisible even in a city like Berlin, if half a city can be free and the other half under tyranny, how are we supposed to believe that the world cannot exist if freedom is not extended to "everyone, whether rich or poor, whether they agree with us or not, no matter what their race or the color of their skin"? The answer is simple: we are not supposed to believe it. This is political rhetoric, suitable for commencement addresses. In proposing such an impossibility, we can only assume, the President was speaking in allegorical terms, describing a state toward which all men should aspire—like the Kingdom of Heaven—rather than a condition which really exists.

The United States has intervened deeply in the affairs of countries where our national interests are often only remotely involved. She has done so in the name of freedom and in the struggle against communism. But we have not intervened in a good many countries where freedom is a mockery, such as Haiti, Paraguay, and Saudi Arabia; nor where it is confined to a privileged minority, such as in South Africa and Rhodesia; nor even where there was open communist aggression, such as in Tibet and Hungary. We did not intervene in these instances because the kind of freedoms that were being suppressed in the Caribbean and African dictatorships had nothing to do with our battle against communism. We did not intervene in Tibet because it was too remote and the issues were irrelevant; and we did not intervene in Hungary because we would probably have ignited a third world war. On closer inspection, therefore, it can be seen that our commitment to the defense of freedom and self-determination for all peoples, "no matter what their race or the color of their skins," depends upon whether or not communists are involved. And if communists are involved, it depends on whether we think our intervention may have some chance of success. Where our theoretical compulsion to defend freedom everywhere has come into conflict with a threat to our own national survival—as in Hungary in 1956 and in the East Berlin riots of 1953—we have shown a prudent regard for survival.

What American postwar intervention boils down to in practice is not intervention against injustice or poverty for its own sake, but intervention against communism, where we can intervene without putting ourselves in direct conflict with Russia. It is not the virtues of freedom we are primarily worried about, but the dangers of communism. Where injustice is combined with an absence of a communist problem, as in Haiti or Rhodesia, we have been indifferent to the call of our moral imperatives. Where a communist problem exists, as in Vietnam, we have found the defense of freedom to be an unshirkable obligation, even if performed on behalf of a regime which may be as indifferent to freedom as the communist one it opposes. When we decide when to honor our moral duty, the label the oppressor wears is exceedingly important.

This reluctance to become involved in the struggle against communism in instances where it is likely to trigger a sharp Russian counter-reaction is not necessarily to be criticized. Perhaps we might legitimately have intervened at Budapest, considering the moral issue at stake, although no one can reasonably criticize President Eisenhower for being unwilling to take a gamble on igniting the third world war. We have, on the other hand, certainly been right not to intervene in the unstable new countries of Africa, where Russia and China are unsuccessfully trying to outbid each other for African affections, and where any military intervention we might conceivably undertake could only rebound disastrously against us. Having had our fingers badly burned in the Congo, both we and the Russians have been reluctant to embroil ourselves in Africa's chronic troubles—and rightly so. Aside from economic and technical assistance mixed with heavy doses of forbearance, there is not much that we can do for the unstable, and still unmade, nations of Central Africa. Our guiding principles of anti-communism and self-determination have never meant very much in the context of tropical Africa, and our understandable unwillingness to act upon them in such places as South Africa and Rhodesia has revealed a deep, and often unconscious, hypocrisy in our foreign policy. As Richard Rovere has written:

> We have been trumpeting self-determination as the fundamental principle of our foreign policy for many decades now, and we have used it as our battle cry in wars in some remote corners of the earth, places in which our vital interests—by the customary economic, political, and military definitions—were no more involved than they are in Rhodesia. But we have never gone, and in all probability never will go, to war for self-determination where, as in Rhodesia, it is divorced from questions of ideology and global strategy, and is, indeed, the only important issue involved.
>
> There is a sound but rarely acknowledged reason for this: a commitment to fight for self-determination everywhere and at all times would, if honored, involve us in unending military combat on several continents, and even, conceivably, within our own boundaries. The selective application of the principle is no doubt prudent, but we have talked as though we had undertaken and were determined to fulfill a universal mission, and thus we face situations in which we can do nothing but talk and, in talking, expose our pretensions.[2]

---

[2] Richard H. Rovere, "Letter from Washington," *The New Yorker*, November 20, 1965.

Our global mission against communism, therefore, is tinged with an elementary consideration of the possible, and fortunately so. Yet this has not liberated us from the rhetoric of a diplomacy that sees freedom and communism struggling for the soul of the world. But by now it should be obvious that this is not the real issue. The communists are not going to inherit the earth, and neither are we. They are not going to do it because communism no longer means more than a nodding allegiance to some rather antiquated economic theories of Karl Marx. The various communist parties have drifted so far apart, and have been so subordinated to the more potent ideology of nationalism, that in many cases it is no longer of any great significance whether or not a nation has a nominally communist form of government. Yugoslavia is communist; so are Albania and North Korea. What benefit does the Soviet Union get out of that? Or China, for that matter? Nicaragua is anti-communist; so are Taiwan and South Korea. What good does that do us? As far as the national interest is concerned, it makes little difference what kind of ideology a government professes, so long as it does not follow policies which are hostile or dangerous. We live perfectly well with a communist Yugoslavia, and could with a communist Cuba as well, if we could swallow our hurt pride. The Russians, by the same token, live at ease with an anti-communist Norway on one side of them and an anti-communist Iran on another.

What counts is not the label a regime may choose to attach to itself, but whether it poses a threat to us or to world peace. There are some communist countries such as Yugoslavia and, according even to Konrad Adenauer, the Soviet Union itself, that are a factor for stability and peace. There are some non-communist countries, such as the Congo and South Vietnam, that are a source of instability and danger. As far as the world's peace and our own national interests are concerned, the fact that a country is communist may be less important than how much rain it gets or how many pairs of shoes it produces. It is certainly less important than the policies it follows toward its neighbors, and how capable it is of meeting the demands of its own citizens for economic justice and social equality.

Small nations along the borders of Russia and China are not

necessarily hostile to our interests because they are nominally communist. There are some communist governments that are more worthy of respect than some anti-communist governments. There are some anti-communist governments that are so unpopular with their own people that they cannot be saved. There are others which can be kept in power only by risks that are out of all proportion to the stakes involved. There are anti-communist governments that are not worth saving, regardless of how small the risks may be. And there are governments that, if the communists did take them over, would be more of a threat to the communist nations than to us. China is the classic example of a country which is a greater danger to Russia now that she is under communist control than she would have been under the control of Chiang Kai-shek.

Communism, in any case, is not taking over the world, and the reason has nothing to do with our military intervention. We intervened in Vietnam and thereby permitted the communists to seize the banner of Vietnamese nationalism against a new colonial power—that is, us. We did not intervene in Indonesia, a far more important country on any scale of power, when the communists threatened to seize control. If we had intervened militarily, it is likely that the Indonesian Communist Party would be running the government from Djakarta today, instead of having its leaders either dead or in prison. Indeed, as Singapore's anticommunist Prime Minister, Lee Kuan Yew, has said, after a bitter experience with the CIA, "If the Americans had been here, I'd have been in jail and tortured and died a commie."

The underdeveloped nations are unlikely to turn to the communists not because of the intervention of the CIA or the United States Air Force, but because they themselves have little sympathy for communism. Not a single nation which has come to independence since the Second World War has turned to communism, with the exception of Vietnam. The immunity of the new nations to communism has been remarkable. They have been, if anything, even more anti-communist than the old imperial nations of Europe. Even those which collect aid from the Soviet Union or from China do not show the slightest hesitation about jailing their own communists, outlawing the party, and expelling communist diplomats. Caught up in the ideology of nationalism, the new nations have rejected the pretensions of the communist giants along with the capitalist ones.

This does not mean that there will never be another communist government anywhere in the world. Perhaps one day there may be a communist Burma, or a communist Guatemala, or a communist Tanzania. What is important is not the label a regime chooses to pin on itself, but the policies it follows. Small communist nations in the southern hemisphere are no threat to the United States. Nor, as we should now have learned from experience, are they likely to remain the satellites of Russia or China for very long. The kind of government they choose to live under is their affair, not ours. We live perfectly comfortably with totalitarian governments of the Right; we even consider most of them allies and members of the "free world." We can learn to live with totalitarian governments of the Left as well, and let the Russians and the Chinese worry about the purity of their ideology.

If the notion that all communist governments everywhere are inherently evil and detrimental to our interests is the most pernicious myth of our foreign policy, then the second most pernicious myth is the belief that world peace depends on the maintenance of the status quo everywhere. In its basic form this myth declares that the current détente between ourselves and the Soviet Union rests upon a tacit agreement that changes in the boundary lines between the two systems—either by force or by unilateral action—are too dangerous to world peace to be tolerated. Greece and Hungary are given as examples where each side respected the existing demarcation lines: the Russians called off the Greek civil war, we refused to intervene at Budapest.

Yet this was reasonable only so long as there were in fact, as at the time of the Budapest riots, *two systems:* the communist world and ours. Any forcible change in the boundaries between the two systems could have been legitimately seen as a victory for one side or a defeat for the other. That was why President Truman intervened in Korea, and why the Russians stamped out the Budapest revolt. We could not allow South Korea to fall into their orbit, and they could not allow Hungary to fall into ours. If a loss for one side was not necessarily a victory for the other, reasonable men at least thought so at the time. There was, from the mid-1940s until the late 1950s, a bi-polar world.

But that is past history. The "communist world" does not exist any more, and neither does "ours." Therefore, to speak of boundaries and demarcation lines between the "free world" and the "communist world" is little more than cultural lag. Communist regimes may come to power in some countries and represent an actual net loss for the "international communist movement." The communist capture of China was hardly a "victory" for Russia, as Stalin had feared all along, any more than a communist Vietnam united under Ho Chi Minh would be likely to represent any kind of "victory" for China. The record has shown clearly that nationalism has triumphed over communism, even in those countries where the communists have come to power. In fact, it may well be that in certain instances (and Vietnam is probably one of them) national communism represents the best bulwark against Soviet or Chinese expansion. Cohesive, nationalistic states (whatever their political complexion) on the borders of great ones are a far more effective barrier to expansion, whether territorial or ideological, than are weak, divided ones.

Thus the idea that the détente between America and Russia rests upon a respect for "boundary lines" in the southern hemisphere is a delusion. The chaos of the underdeveloped world is a source of danger for both the super-powers, but not because a change the boundary lines in Europe by force because neither to upset the world balance. The only place the theory is still relevant is in those very few areas—notably Central Europe—where the vital interests of the great powers overlap. Neither side can change the boundary linees in Europe by force because neither America nor Russia could tolerate such a blow to her interests or her prestige. This is why the line down the center of Germany remains intact. It is also true that neither side can be allowed to upset the present military balance within the sphere of influence of the other. This was the point of the Cuban missile crisis. As we could not use Finland to set up a missile base, so the Soviets could not use Cuba for a strategic base against us. By establishing that principle, firmly but with suppleness, President Kennedy set the stage for the current détente. This détente rests on a mutual respect for the spheres of influence that are vital to the interests of the super-powers, not upon an agreement that present demarcation lines between communism and non-communism anywhere in the world shall never be changed.

To say, as many American policy-makers have been saying for the past few years, that the political status quo cannot be changed by force is to attempt to legislate stagnation into international politics. This has been tried many times in the past, but never successfully. There are always going to be people with grievances who will be forced to resort to arms to redress those grievances. That was the reason for Bunker Hill and the Bastille, for the Easter rising and the Moncada barracks. Where there are no free elections, no right of appeal, and no legal procedure for redressing grievances, then the status quo can be changed only by force. And in some countries the status quo is so intolerable to the people who live there that they will endure almost anything to change it. To dedicate American foreign policy to the perpetuation of the political status quo, except where it can be changed without violence, is to doom this nation to the role of a glorified prison warden. It would be to try to play Matternich's role on a world scale, with far greater power but with less justification and with little chance of success.

In seeking to ensure stability, we have been drawn into the suppression of progressive forces in cases where communists are, or may be, involved. Although it is not our intention to perpetuate the status quo, this has been the impact of our policy. As long as we are mesmerized by anti-communism as an ideology, it will be exceedingly difficult for us to accept the possibility that even violent changes in the political status quo in certain countries may not necessarily be hostile to our interests, or to prevent our foreign policy from being used to suppress popularly supported movements of political change. In assuming that we have an obligation to smother violent changes in the status quo by discontented groups within various countries, we are arrogating to ourselves the responsibility for being an international police power. We are doing so without anyone's consent and from no other motive than that we believe that our vision of a proper political order is valid for nations everywhere. This, whether we recognize it or not, is imperialism, and an imperial foreign policy cannot be maintained without considerable sacrifices at home and repression abroad. It is far from certain that the American people will find such a role appealing, or will support it once they realize its price.

* * *

CAN A FREE SOCIETY FIGHT A LIMITED WAR?*

BY

JOHN P. ROCHE

[1968]

As an old fashioned liberal cold warrior, I have seen and still see nothing immoral about fighting to contain aggressive totalitarianism. Suppressing my human fears, I was prepared to go to the brink with John Kennedy over Berlin and Cuba, and last year I was equally prepared to support the Israelis to the hilt had the Soviets intervened to rescue their incompetent Arab clients. In sum, just to get the record clear at the outset, I take for granted the vital role that the United States must play in helping to achieve a stable world, and I believe that South and Southeast Asia present a major challenge to stability in our generation. . . .

The basic issue in Vietnam is this: Can a free society fight a limited war? That is, a strategic war, a war without hate, a war without massive popular involvement. To put it differently, the war in Vietnam is being fought for an abstraction: American national interest in a non-totalitarian Asian future. And it is being fought by a new set of rules, rules which began to emerge during the Korean War but were forgotten in the subsequent years. It is very difficult to tell a young soldier, "Go out there and fight, perhaps die, for a good bargaining position." It is almost impossible to explain to Congressmen that Vietnam is a crucial testing ground—on one side for a brilliantly mounted "war of liberation"; on the other, for our capability to cope with (and in the future deter) such liberators. What sense, moreover, can the average American make of our offer of future economic assistance to a non-aggressive Hanoi? What, in short, has happened to the concept of "the enemy?"

As one of the early advocates of flexible response and limited

* From *The New Leader,* October 21, 1968, copyright 1968 by the American Labor Conference on International Affairs. Reprinted by permission. John P. Roche (b. 1923) is Professor of Politics at Brandeis University.

war, I have watched the defection of the liberal intellectuals with somber anguish. The record is perfectly clear: Limited war was conceived of *by liberals* as *the liberal* alternative to massive retaliation and/or isolationism. It was the liberal answer to John Foster Dulles that was to find classic formulation in the speeches of President John F. Kennedy and in Robert McNamara's spectacular reorganization of the Department of Defense. At root, the theory asserted that instead of relying on apocalyptic nuclear power to deter aggression, the United States would be capable of a flexible, measured response to the forces deployed on the other side of the hill—enough force, and no more, than was necessary to frustrate aggression. Kennedy and McNamara realized that the very character of nuclear war made any other response an all or nothing proposition; one either pushed the button or capitulated.

John Foster Dulles managed to combine verbal brinkmanship with *de facto* isolationism (the Siamese twins of Republican defense policy to this day), but to many of us liberals it seemed that American power under Eisenhower and Dulles was undergoing the death of a thousand cuts. So we assailed Dulles, called for an active foreign policy, and beat the drums for flexible response: the defense posture that did not leave the United States with the two crisis options of nuclear weapons or appeasement. . . .

We assumed, naïvely as it turned out, that the knowledge that the U.S. could transport 100,000 men 12,000 miles in 47 hours and 32 minutes (or some such logistical triumph) would itself act as a deterrent. Discussions of military strategy began to sound more and more like seminars in game theory. There was a kind of antiseptic quality permeating the atmosphere; one often had the feeling he was attending a chess match.

This, in part, was the source of many later problems. An expert chess player can at a certain point confidently tell his opponent "mate in 12 moves." Normally the opponent, if he is worth playing with, concedes and starts a new game. The atmosphere made those of us who come from the harsh training of poker decidedly uneasy. We knew that nobody has ever folded a full-house because he suspected another player of holding four of a kind. Education in these matters always costs money. In international relations it costs more than money—human lives are involved.

Vietnam has provided an agonizing education on the limitations of our theory of limited war. The worst of it is that what I believe to be the real "lessons of Vietnam" have been largely ignored on the political circuit this fall. The hustings are full of politicians solemnly intoning "No More Vietnams." But try to find out what this means. The late Senator Robert Kennedy was relatively clear. In his lexicon it merely meant "Don't support losers." . . . Assuming the winner is identifiable from the outset, this advice can be helpful.

But what is one to make of Senator Eugene McCarthy's gloss on "No More Vietnams"? It was a bit murky, but the gist of his admonition seemed to be that we should only help *good* nations. Even weak ones, for he specifically mentioned India.

Now ever since I took seriously President Kennedy's statement that we are "the watchmen on the walls of world freedom"—only to learn later from reading Arthur Schlesinger's *Bitter Heritage* that Kennedy did not really mean it—I have been reading the small print rather carefully. So when I came upon McCarthy's nomination of India as a possible substitute for Vietnam, I was, to say the least, startled. The small country of South Vietnam has swallowed up half a million American troops. Can one conceive the magnitude of the troop commitment that would be necessary to bolster India's feeble defenses? Or of the bill for the military hardware that would come due if the Indian Army were to be equipped properly?

Since I take McCarthy's intelligence for granted, his statement could only make sense if (1) he had an ironclad promise from Peking that India will not again be invaded; or (2) he was silently and surreptitiously returning to the Dulles strategy of nuclear containment. If the latter is the case, McCarthy's "No More Vietnams" formula involves the abandonment of limited war and a rejuvenation of the nuclear strike. Thus militant "liberals" are in the odd position of embracing the H-bomb as the key instrument of American policy.

The Republican position is quite simple. Richard Nixon will, of course, submit that the Democrats get the country into wars they cannot *ena*—citing Korea. This is shorthand for the proposition that the Republicans know how to deal with Communists, that President Eisenhower ended the Korean War by threatening to use nuclear weapons on the sanctuary, that limited war is a "no win" policy and a gross misuse of our incredible national power.

I believe today—as I believed in 1956—that this nuclear strategy would in the long run be disastrous for the United States. But it has the enormous political advantage of being abstract. In October 1962, we lived through the most perilous week in the history of mankind, but there was no blood on the TV screens. The "dirty little war" in Vietnam, on the other hand, is infinitely and, with TV, intimately bloody. . . . Vietnam is *war* —nuclear holocaust is a remote fantasy.

Paradoxically, the marginal character of the war in Vietnam has contributed to its political liabilities. It is not a big war; it is not, comparatively speaking, costing much—3-4 per cent of the Gross National Product compared with roughly 11 per cent for Korea— but it has no built-in support in the electorate. The President could have drummed up support by hitting the traditional chord of messianic anti-Communism, by engaging in old-style McCarthyism. . . .

But Lyndon Johnson flatly refused to whoop up yahoo chauvinism. At least half a dozen times, I have heard him say that he remembered the anti-German hysteria of World War I and the consequences of Joe McCarthy in the '50s; that he was not going to be the President "who got Americans hating." . . .

The rhetoric of limited war is in itself a major problem. Johnson was carved up by his critics for telling the troops at Camranh Bay to "bring home that coonskin." Perhaps the figure of speech could have been improved upon, but what American commander-in-chief could address his troops in the field and urge them to die, if necessary, for a stalemate? The British in the 19th century could play strategic chess with their regulars and mercenaries—invading such unlikely places as Tibet, Ethiopia, Zululand, and Afghanistan—with no repercussions at home unless (as in the First Afghan War) they lost. Once they achieved their usually limited objectives, a treaty was forthcoming and the troops pulled out. Individual families would mourn a sergeant killed in the Sixth River War, or a sepoy butchered at Kabul, but except for disasters these wars were fought outside the forum of British public opinion.

If Ho Chi Minh had permitted the war in Vietnam to remain

invisible—with only professional soldiers involved—the pattern of the 19th century might have been retained. But Ho Chi Minh has always been a problem. While we may be fighting a limited war against him, he has declared total war against us—and he has played his hand brilliantly. His central goal (learned from his experience with the French and from the lessons of Algeria) was to escalate the war in Vietnam to the point where it became *politically* unjustifiable in the United States. Put differently, he would not permit Johnson to fight an invisible war and—knowing the major tenets of the doctrine of limited war—he proceeded in 1965-68 to utilize his assets to the maximum. . . .

This commitment of PAVN (Hanoi's regulars) was a death blow to the concept of the invisible war. Airpower enthusiasts to the contrary, there is only one way to fight infantry—with other infantry. Air power provides mobile artillery, but nobody ever pacified a province with an F-4.

* * *

There have been a number of accounts by associates of the late President Kennedy to the effect that he wanted out of Vietnam too. Regrettably, these lack empirical foundation—and quoting the dead is an ancient form of historical fraud, immune to either proof or disproof. The fundamental evidence—notably his support of Secretary of State Dean Rusk and McNamara—suggests that he was unhappy about the situation in Vietnam (as who with any knowledge of the place was not?), but felt the line had to be drawn and enforced in that nation. On this basis Kennedy made the quantum jump: Disregarding the Geneva Accord of 1954 (which we had unofficially respected but never signed), he increased the number of American "advisors" from roughly 750 (as authorized at Geneva) to over 16,000. In addition, "Green Berets" were bootlegged into Vietnam under covert auspices.

This is no place to investigate the internal affairs of the Saigon government. Suffice it to say that the Diem regime, after a seemingly amazing start in the 1950s, was in deep trouble in 1962-63. Objectively viewed, Diem was in an impossible enfilade:

The Americans would not let him run an efficient dictatorship (like the one in Hanoi), and he was incapable of building effective representative government. Confronted by the chaos in Saigon, which became much worse after the fall of the Diem government in November 1963, the Americans gradually made—without really recognizing its import—a critical decision: to fight the war independently.

The basic premise, which I do not believe I have ever seen clearly articulated, was that the United States, with its massive technological assets, would directly force the Hanoi leaders to pull back their troops. We would, in other words, "punish" the Democratic Republic of Vietnam (DRV). Once Ho and his chief strategist, General Giap, knew what they were up against, they would agree "mate in 12 moves" and give up the game. This shortcut had two admirable arguments in its favor: First, we could effectively ignore the condition of the Saigon government; second, we could employ our air power assets with a relatively slight loss of American lives. The unfortunate consequence was that the South Vietnamese Armed Forces (ARVN) were treated as orphans and given essentially a spectator role in the U.S.-Hanoi competition.

Unfortunately, too, Ho and Giap were never programmed by the Pentagon's game-theorists. They were determined to prevent the United States from fighting a cut-rate war. Down the Ho Chi Minh trail came the trained regiments of the PAVN with the mission, not of defeating the United States on the ground, but of forcing the Americans to fight a ground war in full, costly visibility. To a considerable extent these soldiers were on a suicide mission, but when one appreciates that their goals were *political* rather than military the "kill-ratio" loses much of its impact. North Vietnamese Premier Pham Van Dong had announced the scenario as far back as 1962 when he told the late Bernard Fall: "Americans do not like long inconclusive wars—and this is going to be a long inconclusive war."

President Kennedy presided over the transformation of American strategic theory from massive retaliation to flexible response, but at the time of his murder (less than a month after Diem fell) the United States had only put this doctrine into action in the

Cuban missile crisis. Lyndon Johnson, then, inherited from Kennedy a strategy, a Cabinet, and a seemingly trivial conflict in Vietnam. As he went on to election in his own right in 1964, Vietnam was still on the back pages—but there was great stirring in Hanoi and PAVN engineers and support troops were busy building base camps in the Central Highlands of South Vietnam. . . .

In 1964-65, the Americans began looking for trained Vietnamese soldiers to meet Ho Chi Minh's challenge on the ground in the South; they found a poorly trained, miserably equipped, dispirited ARVN. . . . So American soldiers and Marines, instead of providing a steel frame for the training of ARVN, had to take the field themselves. There simply was no time for the necessary training. . . .

Yet military necessity, while an explanation for what has occurred over the past three years, is not an excuse. Why did Presidents Kennedy and Johnson and Secretary McNamara consistently neglect ARVN? . . .

I think the real key to ARVN's neglect was the Pentagon game-theorists' belief in their own press releases; they believed that pressure on Hanoi, "turning the screw," would lead Ho to make the logical calculation that he had more to lose than gain by continuing the conflict. Unfortunately, this was based on a complete misreading of the mind and character of a dedicated and ruthless Leninist—one who, in Koestler's phrase, is prepared to sacrifice one generation in the interest of its successor.

What Ho Chi Minh has done, to return to the main theme, is to hit the doctrine of limited war at its weakest point: domestic opinion. The Johnson Administration, hit by ground war on a scale never anticipated and by the accompanying casualty lists, tried to maintain the ground-rules of limited war. What this often amounted to was simply "hunkering up like a mule in a hailstorm" as the apocalyptics of the Left- and Right-wing spokesmen for national frustration raged throughout the land. The crux of the matter is that while any two-bit demagogue can make the eagle scream in a nice, neat "us or them" confrontation, explaining the rationale of limited war is incredibly difficult. . . .

If the "lesson of Vietnam" is that a free, democratic society cannot fight a limited war, what strategic options are still open? Must we revert to the balance of terror? Or, as some notable liberals today seem to think, can we build affluence in one country and somehow escape the broils of the outside world?

I confess that, battered as I am, I still believe that flexible response is not only a sound but a *liberal* alternative to the only other strategies I see on the horizon. And I would suggest that that those who are busy leaping up and down about Vietnam take a brief pause in their exercise to inform us precisely *how* they plan to employ American power in the interest of international stability and world order.

Except for the pacifists (and those who are pro-Hanoi), I have yet to find a critic who—when pushed back on his premises— did not end up embracing some variety of isolationism. There is nothing wicked or un-American about being an isolationist, but it is a doctrine that American liberals outgrew a quarter of a century ago. It would be tragic if a united front of Nixonites and followers of Eugene McCarthy, playing up to the understandable frustrations of the American people, undermined our commitment to limited war and returned us to the Age of Dulles. Perhaps we should recall that while limited war is nasty, for most of us resurrection would be a precondition for appreciating the strategic virtue of nuclear retaliation.

X

WHAT PRINCIPLES GUIDE AMERICAN FOREIGN POLICY?

PACIFICUS*

BY

ALEXANDER HAMILTON

[1793]

* * *

Faith and justice between nations are virtues of a nature the most necessary and sacred. They cannot be too strongly inculcated, nor too highly respected. Their obligations are absolute, their utility unquestionable; they relate to objects which, with probity and sincerity, generally admit of being brought within clear and intelligible rules.

But the same cannot be said of gratitude. It is not very often that between nations it can be pronounced with certainty that there exists a solid foundation for the sentiment; and how far it can justifiably be permitted to operate, is always a question of still greater difficulty.

The basis of gratitude is a benefit received or intended, which there was no right to claim, originating in a regard to the interest or advantage of the party on whom the benefit is, or is meant to be, conferred. If a service is rendered from views relative to the immediate interest of the party who performs it, and is productive of reciprocal advantages, there seems scarcely, in such a case, to be an adequate basis for a sentiment like that of gratitude.

The effect at least would be wholly disproportioned to the cause, if such a service ought to beget more than a disposition to render in turn a correspondent good office, founded on mutual interest and reciprocal advantage. But gratitude would require much more than this: it would exact to a certain extent even a sacrifice of the interest of the party obliged to the service of benefit of the one by whom the obligation had been conferred.

---

* The "Pacificus" article first appeared in the *Gazette of the United States* and was written in defense of Washington's Neutrality Proclamation of 1793. Alexander Hamilton (1757–1804) was Secretary of the Treasury under Washington and co-author (with Madison and Jay) of *The Federalist*.

Between individuals, occasion is not unfrequently given for the exercise of gratitude. Instances of conferring benefits from kind and benevolent dispositions or feelings toward the person benefited, without any other interest on the part of the person who renders the service, than the pleasure of doing a good action, occur every day among individuals. But among nations they perhaps never occur. It may be affirmed as a general principle, that the predominant motive of good offices from one nation to another, is the interest or advantage of the nation which performs them.

Indeed, the rule of morality in this respect is not precisely the same between nations as between individuals. The duty of making its own welfare the guide of its actions, is much stronger upon the former than upon the latter; in proportion to the greater magnitude and importance of national compared with individual happiness, and to the greater permanency of the effects of national than of individual conduct. Existing millions, and for the most part future generations, are concerned in the present measures of a government; while the consequences of the private actions of an individual ordinarily terminate with himself, or are circumscribed within a narrow compass.

Whence it follows that an individual may, on numerous occasions, meritoriously indulge the emotions of generosity and benevolence, not only without an eye to, but even at the expense of, his own interest. But a government can rarely, if at all, be justifiable in pursuing a similar course; and, if it does so, ought to confine itself within much stricter bounds.[1] Good offices which are indifferent to the interest of a nation performing them, or which are compensated by the existence or expectation of some reasonable equivalent, or which produce an essential good to the nation to which they are rendered, without real detriment to the affairs of the benefactors, prescribe perhaps the limits of national generosity or benevolence.

It is not here meant to recommend a policy absolutely selfish or

---

[1] This conclusion derives confirmation from the reflection, that under every form of government rulers are only trustees for the happiness and interest of their nation, and cannot, consistently with their trust, follow the suggestions of kindness or humanity toward others, to the prejudice of their constituents.

interested in nations; but to show, that a policy regulated by their own interest, as far as justice and good faith permit, is, and ought to be, their prevailing one; and that either to ascribe to them a different principle of action, or to deduce, from the supposition of it, arguments for a self-denying and self-sacrificing gratitude on the part of a nation which may have received from another good offices, is to misrepresent or misconceive what usually are, and ought to be, the springs of national conduct.

* * *

THE FAREWELL ADDRESS

BY

GEORGE WASHINGTON

[1796]

Observe good faith and justice towards all nations; cultivate peace and harmony with all; religion and morality enjoin this conduct; and can it be that good policy does not equally enjoin it? It will be worthy of a free, enlightened, and, at no distant period, a great nation, to give to mankind the magnanimous and too novel example of a people always guided by an exalted justice and benevolence. Who can doubt that, in the course of time and things, the fruits of such a plan would richly repay any temporary advantages that might be lost by a steady adherence to it? Can it be, that Providence has not connected the permanent felicity of a nation with its virtue? The experiment, at least, is recommended by every sentiment which ennobles human nature. Alas! is it rendered impossible by its vices?

In the execution of such a plan, nothing is more essential than that permanent, inveterate antipathies against particular nations, and passionate attachments for others, should be excluded; and that in place of them, just and amicable feelings towards all should be cultivated. The nation, which indulges towards another an habitual hatred, or an habitual fondness, is in some degree a slave. It is a slave to its animosity or to its affection, either of which is sufficient to lead it astray from its duty and its interest. Antipathy in one nation against another, disposes each more readily to offer insult and injury, to lay hold of slight causes of umbrage, and to be haughty and intractable, when accidental or trifling occasions of dispute occur.

Hence frequent collisions, obstinate, envenomed, and bloody contests. The nation, prompted by ill-will and resentment, sometimes impels to war the government, contrary to the best calculations of policy. The government sometimes participates in the national propensity, and adopts through passion what reason would reject; at other times, it makes the animosity of the nation subservient to projects of hostility instigated by pride, ambition and other sinister and pernicious motives. The peace often, and sometimes, perhaps, the liberty of nations, has been the victim.

So, likewise, a passionate attachment of one nation for another produces a variety of evils. Sympathy for the favorite nation facilitating the illusion of an imaginary common interest in cases where no real common interest exists, and infusing into one the enmities of the other, betrays the former into a participation in the quarrels and wars of the latter, without adequate inducement or justification. It leads also to concessions to the favorite nation of privileges denied to others, which is apt doubly to injure the nation making the concessions; by unnecessarily parting with what ought to have been retained; and by exciting jealousy, ill-will, and a disposition to retaliate, in the parties from whom equal privileges are withheld; and it gives to ambitious, corrupted, or deluded citizens (who devote themselves to the favorite nation) facility to betray, or sacrifice the interests of their own country, without odium, sometimes even with popularity; gilding, with the appearances of a virtuous sense of obligation, a commendable deference for public opinion, or laudable zeal for public good, the base or foolish compliances of ambition, corruption, or infatuation.

As avenues to foreign influence, in innumerable ways, such attachments are particularly alarming to the truly enlightened and independent patriot. How many opportunities do they afford to tamper with domestic factions; to practise the arts of seduction; to mislead public opinion; to influence or awe the public councils! Such an attachment of a small or weak nation, toward a great and powerful one, dooms the former to be the satellite of the latter.

Against the insidious wiles of foreign influence (I conjure you to believe me, fellow-citizens), the jealousy of a free people ought to be constantly awake; since history and experience prove, that foreign influence is one of the most baneful foes of republican government. But that jealousy, to be useful, must be impartial; else it becomes the instrument of the very influence to be avoided, instead of a defence against it. Excessive partiality for one foreign nation, and excessive dislike of another, cause those whom they actuate, to see danger only on one side; and serve to veil and even second the arts of influence on the other. Real patriots, who may resist the intrigues of the favorite, are liable to become suspected and odious; while its tools and dupes usurp the applause and confidence of the people, to surrender their interests.

The great rule of conduct for us, in regard to foreign nations, is, in extending our commercial relations, to have with them as little political connection as possible. So far as we have already formed engagements, let them be fulfilled with perfect good faith. Here let us stop.

Europe has a set of primary interests, which to us have none, or a very remote relation. Hence she must be engaged in frequent controversies, the causes of which are essentially foreign to our concerns. Hence, therefore, it must be unwise in us to implicate ourselves, by artificial ties, in the ordinary vicissitudes of her politics, or the ordinary combinations and collisions of her friendships and enmities.

Our detached and distant situation invites and enables us to pursue a different course. If we remain one people, under an efficient government, the period is not far off when we may defy material injury from external annoyance; when we may take such an attitude as will cause the neutrality we may at any time resolve upon, to be scrupulously respected; when belligerent nations, under the impossibility of making acquisitions upon us, will not lightly hazard the giving us provocation; when we may choose peace or war, as our interest, guided by justice, shall counsel.

Why forego the advantages of so peculiar a situation? Why quit our own, to stand upon foreign ground? Why, by interweaving our destiny with that of any part of Europe, entangle our peace and prosperity in the toils of European ambition, rivalship, interest, humor, or caprice?

'Tis our true policy to steer clear of permanent alliances with any portion of the foreign world; so far, I mean, as we are now at liberty to do it; for let me not be understood as capable of patronizing infidelity to existing engagements. I hold the maxim no less applicable to public than to private affairs, that honesty is always the best policy. I repeat it, therefore, let those engagements be observed in their genuine sense. But, in my opinion, it is unnecessary, and would be unwise, to extend them.

Taking care always to keep ourselves, by suitable establishments, in a respectable defensive posture, we may safely trust to temporary alliances for extraordinary emergencies.

Harmony, and a liberal intercourse with all nations, are recommended by policy, humanity, and interest. But even our commercial policy should hold an equal and impartial hand; neither seeking nor granting exclusive favors or preferences; consulting the natural course of things; diffusing and diversifying, by gentle means, the streams of commerce, but forcing nothing; establishing, with powers so disposed, in order to give trade a stable course, to define the rights of our merchants, and to enable the government to support them, conventional rules of intercourse, the best that present circumstances and mutual opinion will permit, but temporary, and liable to be, from time to time, abandoned or varied, as experience and circumstances shall dictate; constantly keeping in view, that it is folly in one nation to look for disinterested favors from another; that it must pay, with a portion of its independence, for whatever it may accept under that character; that, by such acceptance, it may place itself in the condition of having given equivalents for nominal favors, and yet of being reproached with ingratitude for not giving more. There can be no greater error than to expect to calculate upon real favors from nation to nation. It is an illusion, which experience must cure, which a just pride ought to discard.

In offering to you, my countrymen, these counsels of an old and affectionate friend, I dare not hope they will make the strong and lasting impression I could wish; that they will control the usual current of the passions, or prevent our nation from running the course which has hitherto marked the destiny of nations! But, if I may even flatter myself, that they may be productive of some partial benefit, some occasional good; that they may now and then recur to moderate the fury of party spirit; to warn against the mischiefs of foreign intrigues; to guard against the impostures of pretended patriotism; this hope will be a full recompense for the solicitude for your welfare, by which they have been dictated. . . .

THE MAINSPRINGS OF AMERICAN
FOREIGN POLICY *

BY

HANS J. MORGENTHAU

[1950]

It is often said that the foreign policy of the United States is in
need of maturing and that the American people and their government must grow up if they want to emerge victorious from the
trials of our age. It would be truer to say that this generation of
Americans must shed the illusions of their fathers and grand-
fathers and relearn the great principles of statecraft which guided
the path of the republic in its first decade and—in moralistic disguise—in the first century of its existence. The United States
offers the singular spectacle of a commonwealth whose political
wisdom did not grow slowly through the accumulation and articu-
lation of experiences. Quite to the contrary, the full flowering of
its political wisdom was coeval with its birth as an independent
nation—nay, it owed its existence and survival as an independent
nation to those extraordinary qualities of political insight, historic
perspective, and common sense which the first generation of
Americans applied to the affairs of state.

This classic age of American statecraft comes to an end with
the physical disappearance of that generation of American statesmen. The rich and varied landscape in which they had planted
all that is worthwhile in the tradition of Western political thought
was allowed to go to waste. It became a faint and baffling re-
membrance, a symbol to be worshipped rather than a source of
inspiration and a guide for action. Until very recently the American people seemed to be content to live in a political desert whose

*From *The American Political Science Review*, December 1950. Reprinted
by permission of The American Political Science Association and Hans J.
Morgenthau.

intellectual barrenness and aridity were relieved only by some sparse and neglected oases of insight and wisdom. What in that period, stretching over more than a century, went under the name of foreign policy was either improvisation in the face of an urgent problem which had to be dealt with somehow, or—and especially in our century—the invocation of some abstract moral principle in the image of which the world was to be made over. Improvisation as a substitute for foreign policy was largely successful, for in the past the margin of American and allied power to spare generally exceeded the degree to which American improvidence fell short of the demands of the hour. The invocation of abstract moral principles was in part hardly more than an innocuous pastime; for embracing everything it came to grips with nothing. In part, however, it was a magnificent instrument for marshalling public opinion in support of war and warlike policies—and for losing the peace to follow. The intoxication with moral abstractions which as a mass phenomenon started with the Spanish-American War, and which in our time has become the prevailing substitute for political thought, is indeed one of the great sources of weakness and failure in American foreign policy.

It is, however, worthy of note that underneath this political dilettantism, nourished by improvidence and a sense of moral mission, there has remained alive an almost instinctive awareness of the perennial interests of the United States. This has especially been true with regard to Europe and the Western Hemisphere; for in these regions the national interest of the United States has from the beginning been obvious and clearly defined.

I

In the Western Hemisphere we have always endeavored to preserve the unique position of the United States as a predominant power without rival. We have not been slow in recognizing that this predominance was not likely to be effectively threatened by any one American nation or combination of them, acting without support from outside the Western Hemisphere. It was, then, imperative for the United States to isolate the Western Hemisphere from the political and military policies of non-American nations.

The interference of non-American nations in the affairs of the Western Hemisphere, especially through the acquisition of territory, was the only way in which the predominance of the United States could have been challenged from within the Western Hemisphere itself. The Monroe Doctrine and the policies implementing it express that permanent national interest of the United States in the Western Hemisphere.

Since a threat to the national interest of the United States in the Western Hemisphere can come only from outside it, that is, historically from Europe, the United States has always striven to prevent the development of conditions in Europe which would be conducive to a European nation's interference in the affairs of the Western Hemisphere or to a direct attack upon the United States. Such conditions would be most likely to arise if a European nation had gained such predominance that it could afford to look across the sea for conquest without fear of being menaced at the center of its power, that is, in Europe itself. It is for this reason that the United States has consistently—the War of 1812 is the sole major exception—pursued policies aiming at the maintenance of the balance of power in Europe. It has opposed whatever European nation—be it Great Britain, France, Germany, or Russia—seemed to be likely to gain that ascendancy over its European competitors which would have jeopardized the hemispheric predominance and eventually the very independence of the United States. Conversely, it has supported whatever European nation seemed to be most likely to restore the balance of power by offering successful resistance to the would-be conqueror. While it is hard to imagine a greater contrast in the way of thinking about matters political than that which separates Alexander Hamilton from Woodrow Wilson, in this concern for the maintenance of the balance of power in Europe—for whatever different reasons—they are one. It is by virtue of this concern that the United States has intervened in both World Wars on the side of the initially weaker coalition and that its European policies have so largely paralleled those of Great Britain; for from Henry VIII to this day Great Britain has invariably pursued one single objective in Europe: the maintenance of the balance of power.

With Asia the United States has been vitally concerned only since the turn of the century, and the relation of Asia to the national interest of the United States has never been obvious or clearly defined. In consequence, the Asiatic policies of the United States have never as unequivocally expressed the permanent national interest as have the hemispheric and European ones; nor have they for that reason commanded the bipartisan support which the latter have largely enjoyed. As a further consequence, they have been subjected to moralistic influences in a measure from which the European and hemispheric policies of the United States have been largely immune. Yet beneath the confusions, reversals of policy, and moralistic generalities, which have made up the surface of our Asiatic policy since McKinley, one can detect an underlying consistency which, however vaguely, reflects the permanent interest of the United States in Asia. And this interest is again the maintenance of the balance of power. The principle that expresses it is the "open door" in China. Originally its meaning was purely commercial. However, in the measure in which other nations, especially Japan, threatened to close the door to China not only commercially, but also militarily and politically, the principle of the "open door" was interpreted to cover the territorial integrity and political independence of China not for commercial but political reasons. However unsure of itself the Asiatic policy of the United States has been, it has always assumed that the domination of China by another nation would create so great an accumulation of power as to threaten the security of the United States

II

Not only with regard to Asia, however, but wherever American foreign policy has operated, political thought has been divorced from political action. Even where our long-range policies reflect faithfully, as they do in the Americas and in Europe, the true interests of the United States, we think about them in terms which have at best but a tenuous connection with the actual character of the policies pursued. We have acted on the international scene, as all nations must, in power-political terms; we have tended to conceive of our actions in non-political, moralistic terms. This aversion to seeing problems of international politics as they are and the inclination to viewing them instead in non-political, moralistic terms can be attributed both to certain misunderstood peculiarities of the American experience in foreign affairs and to the general climate of opinion prevailing in the Western world during the better part of the nineteenth and the first decade of the twentieth centuries. Of these peculiarities of the American experience three stand out: the uniqueness of the American experiment, the actual isolation during the nineteenth century of the United States from the centers of world conflict, and the humanitarian pacifism and anti-imperialism of American ideology.

The uniqueness of the American experiment in foreign policy contains two elements: the negative one of distinctiveness from the traditional power-political quarrels of Europe and the positive one of a continental expansion which created the freest and richest nation on earth without conquest or subjugation of others.

That the severance of constitutional ties with the British crown was meant to signify the initiation of an American foreign policy distinct from what went under the name of foreign policy in Europe was a conviction common to the founders of the republic. As Washington's Farewell Address put it: "Europe has a set of primary interests, which to us have none, or a very remote relation. Hence she must be engaged in frequent controversies, the causes of which are essentially foreign to our concerns. Hence, therefore, it must be unwise in us to implicate ourselves, by artificial ties, in the ordinary vicissitudes of her politics, or the ordinary combinations and collisions of her friendships or enmities." In 1796, European politics and power politics were identical; there was no other power politics but the one engaged in by the princes of Europe. "The toils of European ambition, rivalship, interest, humor or caprice" were the only manifestations, on the international scene, of the struggle for power before the American eye. The retreat from European politics, as proclaimed by Washington, could, therefore, be taken to mean retreat from power politics as such.

The expansion of the United States up to the Spanish-American War seemed to provide conclusive proof both for the distinctiveness and moral superiority of American foreign policy. The settlement of the better part of a continent by the thirteen original states seemed to be an act of civilization rather than of conquest and as such essentially different from, and morally superior to, the imperialistic ventures, wars of conquest, and colonial acquisitions with which the history of other nations is replete. Yet it was not so much political virtue as the contiguity of the sparsely settled object of conquest with the original territory of departure, which put the mark of uniqueness upon American expansion. As was the case with Russia's simultaneous eastward expansion toward the Pacific, the United States, in order to expand, did not need to cross the oceans and fight wars of conquest in strange lands, as did the other great colonizing nations. Furthermore, the utter political, military, and numerical inferiority of the Indian opponent tended to obscure the element of power, which was less obtrusive in, but no more absent from, the continental expansion of the United States than the expansionist movements of other nations. Thus it came about that what was in actuality the fortuitous concatenation of two potent historic accidents could take on, in the popular imagination, the aspects of an ineluctable natural development, a "manifest destiny," thus confirming the uniqueness of American foreign policy in its freedom from those power-political blemishes which degrade the foreign policies of other nations.

Yet American isolation from the European tradition of power politics was more than a political program or a moralistic illusion. As concerns involvement in the political conflicts of which Europe was the center, and the commitments and risks which such involvement of necessity implies, American isolation was an established political fact until the end of the nineteenth century. The actuality of this fact was a result of deliberate choice as well as of the objective conditions of geography. Popular writers might see in the uniqueness of America's geographic position the hand of God which had unalterably prescribed the course of American expansion as well as isolation. But more responsible observers, from Washington on, have been careful to emphasize the conjunction of geographic conditions and of a foreign policy which chooses its ends in the light of geography and which uses geographic conditions to attain those ends. Washington referred to "our detached and distant situation" and asked, "Why forego the advantages of so peculiar a situation?"

From the shores of the North American continent, the citizens of the new world watched the strange spectacle of the struggle for power unfolding on the distant scenes of Europe, Africa, and Asia. Since for the better part of the nineteenth century their foreign policy enabled them to retain the role of spectators, what was actually the result of a passing historic constellation appeared to Americans as a permanent condition, self-chosen as well as naturally ordained. At worst they would continue to watch the game of power politics played by others. At best the time was close at hand when, with democracy established everywhere, the final curtain would fall and the game of power politics would no longer be played.

To aid in the achievement of this goal was conceived to be part of America's mission. Throughout the nation's history, the national destiny of the United States has been understood in anti-militaristic, libertarian terms. Where that national mission finds a nonaggressive, abstentionist formulation, as in the political philosophy of John C. Calhoun, it is conceived as the promotion of domestic liberty. Thus we may "do more to extend liberty by our example over this continent and the world generally, than would be done by a thousand victories." When the United States, in the wake of the Spanish-American War, seemed to desert this anti-imperialist and democratic ideal, William Graham Sumner restated its essence: "Expansion and imperialism are a grand onslaught on democracy . . . expansion and imperialism are at war with the best traditions, principles, and interests of the American people." Comparing the tendencies of European power politics with the ideals of the American tradition, Sumner thought with Washington that they were incompatible. Yet, as a prophet of things to come, he saw that with the conclusion of the Spanish-American War America was irrevocably committed to the same course which was engulfing Europe in revolution and war.

To understand the American mission in such selfless, humanitarian terms was the easier as the United States—in contrast to the other great powers—was generally not interested, at least outside the Western Hemisphere, in a particular advantage to be defined in terms of power or of territorial gain. Its national interest was exhausted by the preservation of its predominance in the Western Hemisphere and of the balance of power in Europe and Asia. And even this interest in general stability rather than special advantage was, as we know, not always recognized for what it was.

Yet while the foreign policy of the United States was forced, by circumstance if not by choice, to employ the methods, to shoulder the commitments, to seek the objectives, and to run the risks, from which it had thought to be permanently exempt, American political thought continued to uphold that exemption at least as an ideal—an ideal which was but temporarily beyond the reach of the American people, because of the wickedness and stupidity either of American or, preferably, of foreign statesmen. In one sense, this ideal of a free, peaceful, and prosperous world, from which popular government had banished power politics forever, was a natural outgrowth of the American experience. In another sense, this ideal expressed in a particularly eloquent and consistent fashion the general philosophy which during the better part of the nineteenth century dominated the Western world. This philosophy contains two basic propositions: that the struggle for power on the international scene is a mere accident of history, naturally associated with non-democratic government and, hence, destined to disappear with the triumph of democracy throughout the world; and that, in consequence, conflicts between democratic and non-democratic nations must be conceived not as struggles for mutual advantage in terms of power but primarily as a contest between good and evil, which can only end with the complete triumph of good and with evil being wiped off the face of the earth.

The nineteenth century developed this philosophy of international relations from its experience of domestic politics. The distinctive characteristic of this experience was the domination of the middle classes by the aristocracy. By identifying this domination with political domination of any kind, the political philosophy of the nineteenth century came to identify the opposition to aristocratic politics with hostility to any kind of politics. After the defeat of aristocratic government, the middle classes developed a system of indirect domination. They replaced the traditional division into the governing and governed classes and the military method of open violence, characteristic of aristocratic rule, with the invisible chains of economic dependence. This economic system operated through a network of seemingly equalitarian legal rules which concealed the very existence of power relations. The nineteenth century was unable to see the political nature of these legalized relations. They seemed to be essentially different from what had gone, so far, under the name of politics. Therefore, politics in its aristocratic, that is, open and violent form, was identified with politics as such. The struggle, then, for political power—in domestic as well as in international affairs—appeared to be only an historic accident, coincident with autocratic government and bound to disappear with the disappearance of autocratic government.

It is easy to see how this general climate of opinion, prevailing in the Western world, nourished similar tendencies in the American mind, grown from the specific experiences of American history. Thus it is not an accident that nowhere in the Western world was there such depth of conviction and tenacity in support of the belief that involvement in power politics is not inevitable but only a historic accident, and that nations have a choice between power politics and another kind of foreign policy conforming to moral principles and not tainted by the desire for power. Nor is it by accident that this philosophy of foreign policy found its most dedicated and eloquent spokesman in an American President, Woodrow Wilson.

III

The illusion that a nation can escape, if it only wants to, from power politics into a realm where action is guided by moral principles rather than by considerations of power, not only is deeply rooted in the American mind; it also took more than a century for this illusion to crowd out the older notion that international politics is an unending struggle for power in which the interests of individual nations must necessarily be defined in terms of power. Out of the struggle between these two opposing conceptions three types of American statesmen emerge: the realist, thinking in terms of power and represented by Alexander Hamilton; the ideological, acting in terms of power, thinking in terms of moral principles, and represented by Thomas Jefferson and John Quincy Adams; the moralist, thinking and acting in terms of moral principles and represented by Woodrow Wilson. To these three types, three periods of American foreign policy roughly correspond: the first covering the first decade of the history of the United States as an independent nation, the second covering the nineteenth century to the Spanish-American War, the third covering the half century after that war. That this division of the history of American foreign policy refers only to prevailing tendencies and does by no means preclude the operation side by side of different tendencies in the same period, will become obvious in the discussion.

It illustrates both the depth of the moralist illusion and the original strength of the opposition to it that the issue between these two opposing conceptions of foreign policy was joined at the very beginning of the history of the United States, decided in favor of the realist position, and formulated with unsurpassed simplicity and penetration by Alexander Hamilton. The memorable occasion was Washington's proclamation of neutrality in the War of the First Coalition against revolutionary France.

In 1792, the War of the First Coalition had ranged Austria, Prussia, Sardinia, Great Britain, and the United Netherlands against revolutionary France, which was tied to the United States by a treaty of alliance. On April 22, 1793, Washington issued a proclamation of neutrality, and it was in defense of that proclamation that Hamilton wrote the "Pacificus" and "Americanus" articles. Among the arguments directed against the proclamation were three derived from moral principles. Faithfulness to treaty obligations, gratitude toward a country which had lent its assistance to the colonies in their struggle for independence, and the affinity of republican institutions were cited to prove that the United States must side with France. Against these moral principles, Hamilton invoked the national interest of the United States.

* * *

Must a nation subordinate its security, its happiness, nay, its very existence to the respect for treaty obligations, to the sentiment of gratitude, to sympathy with a kindred political system? This was the question which Hamilton proposed to answer, and his answer was an unequivocal "no." Hamilton unswervingly applied one standard to the issues raised by the opposition to Washington's proclamation of neutrality: the national interest of the United States. He put the legalistic and moralistic arguments of the opposition . . . into the context of the concrete power situation in which the United States found itself on the international scene and asked: If the United States were to join France against virtually all of Europe, what risks would the United States run, what advantages could it expect, what good could it do for its ally?

IV

Considerations such as these, recognized for what they are, have guided American foreign policy but for a short period, that is, as long as the Federalists were in power. *The Federalist* and Washington's Farewell Address are their classic expression. Yet these considerations, not recognized for what they are, sometimes even rejected, have determined the great objectives of American foreign policy to this day. During the century following their brief flowering, they have by and large continued to influence policies as well, under the cover, as it were, of those moral principles with which from Jefferson onward American statesmen have liked to justify their moves on the international scene. Thus this second period witnessed a discrepancy between political thought and political action, yet a coincidence in the intended results of both. What was said of Gladstone could also have been said of Jefferson, John Quincy Adams, Theodore Roosevelt, the war policies of Wilson and Franklin D. Roosevelt: what the moral law demanded was by a felicitous coincidence always identical with what the national interest seemed to require. Political thought and political action moved on different planes, which, however, were so inclined as to merge in the end.

John Quincy Adams is the classic example of the political moralist in thought and word who cannot help being a political realist in action. . . . We are here in the presence of a statesman who had been reared in the realist tradition of the first period of American foreign policy, who had done the better part of his work of statecraft in an atmosphere saturated with Jeffersonian principles, and who had achieved the merger of these two elements of his experience into an harmonious whole. Between John Quincy Adams' moral principles and the traditional interest of the United States there was hardly ever a conflict. The moral principles were nothing but the political interests formulated in moral terms, and vice versa. They fit the interests as a glove fits a hand. Adams' great contributions to the tradition of American foreign policy, freedom of the seas, the Monroe Doctrine, and Manifest Destiny, are witness to this achievement.

The legal and moral principle of the freedom of the seas was in the hands of Adams a weapon, as it had been two centuries earlier in the hands of Grotius wielded on behalf of the Low Countries, through which an inferior naval power endeavored to safeguard its independence against Great Britain, the mistress of the seas. The Monroe Doctrine's moral postulates of anti-imperialism and mutual non-intervention were the negative conditions for the safety and enduring greatness of the United States. Their fulfillment vouchsafed the isolation of the United States from the power struggles of Europe and, through it, the continuing predominance of the United States in the Western Hemisphere. Manifest Destiny was the moral justification as well as the moral incentive for the westward expansion of the United States, the peculiar American way—foreordained by the objective conditions of American existence—of founding an empire, the "American Empire," as one of the contemporary opponents of Adams' policies put it.

V

Jefferson and John Quincy Adams stand at the beginning of the second period of American thought on foreign policy, both its most eminent representatives and the heirs of a realist tradition which continued to mould political action, while it had largely ceased to influence political thought. At the beginning of the third period, McKinley leads the United States, as a great world power, beyond the confines of the Western Hemisphere, ignorant of the bearing of this step upon the national interest and guided by moral principles which are completely divorced from the national interest. When at the end of the Spanish-American War the status of the Philippines had to be determined, McKinley expected and found no guidance in the traditional national interests of the United States. According to his own testimony, he knelt beside his bed in prayer, and in the wee hours of the morning he heard the voice of God telling him—as was to be expected —to annex the Philippines.

This period initiated by McKinley, in which moral principles no longer justify the enduring national interest as in the second, but replace it as a guide for action, finds its fulfillment in the political thought of Woodrow Wilson. Wilson's thought not only disregards the national interest, but is explicitly opposed to it on moral grounds. "It is a very perilous thing," he said in his address at Mobile on October 27, 1913,

> to determine the foreign policy of a nation in the terms of material interest. It not only is unfair to those with whom you are dealing, but it is degrading as regards your own actions. . . . We dare not turn from the principle that morality and not expediency is the thing that must guide us, and that we will never condone iniquity because it is most convenient to do so.

. . . Yet in his political actions, especially under the pressure of the First World War, Wilson could no more than Jefferson before him discount completely the national interest of the United States. Wilson's case, however, was different from Jefferson's in two respects. For one, Wilson was never able, even when the national interest of the United States was directly menaced, to conceive of the danger in other than moral terms. It was only the objective force of the national interest, which no rational man could escape, that imposed upon him as the object of his moral indignation the source of America's mortal danger. Thus in 1917 Wilson led the United States into war against Germany for the same reasons, only half-known to himself, for which Jefferson had wished and worked alternately for the victory of England and of France. Germany threatened the balance of power in Europe, and it was in order to remove that threat—and not to make the world safe for democracy—that the United States put its weight into the Allies' scale. Wilson pursued the right policy, but he pursued it for the wrong reasons.

Not only did the crusading fervor of moral reformation obliterate the awareness of the United States' traditional interest in the maintenance of the European balance of power, to be accomplished through the defeat of Germany. Wilson's moral fervor also had politically disastrous effects, for which there is no precedent in the history of the United States. Wilson's moral objective required the destruction of the Kaiser's autocracy, and this happened also to be required by the political interests of the United States. The political interests of the United States required, beyond this immediate objective of total victory, the restoration of the European balance of power, traditional guarantor of American security. Yet it was in indignation at the moral deficiencies of that very balance of power, "forever discredited," as he thought, that Wilson had asked the American people to take up arms against the Central Powers! Once military victory had put an end to the immediate threat to American security, the very logic of his moral position—let us remember that consistency is the moralist's supreme virtue—drove him toward substituting for the concrete national interest of the United States the general postulate of a brave new world where the national interest of the United States, as that of all nations, would disappear in a community of interests comprising mankind.

Consequently, Wilson considered it to be the purpose of victory not to restore a new, viable balance of power, but to make an end to it once and forever. "You know," he told the English people at Manchester on December 30, 1918, that the United States has always felt from the very beginning of her history that she must keep herself separate from any kind of connection with European politics, and I want to say very frankly to you that she is not now interested in European politics. But she is interested in the partnership of right between America and Europe. If the future had nothing for us but a new attempt to keep the world at a right poise by a balance of power, the United States would take no interest, because she will join no combination of power which is not the combination of all of us. She is not interested merely in the peace of Europe, but in the peace of the world.

Faced with the national interests of the great allied powers, Wilson had nothing to oppose or support them with but his moral principles, with the result that the neglect of the American national interest was not compensated for by the triumph of political morality. In the end Wilson had to consent to a series of uneasy compromises which were a betrayal of his moral principles—for principles can, by their very nature, not be made the object of compromise—and which satisfied nobody's national aspirations. These compromises had no relation at all to the traditional American national interest in a viable European balance of power. Thus Wilson returned from Versailles a compromised idealist, an empty-handed statesman, a discredited ally. In that triple failure lies the tragedy not only of Wilson, a great yet misguided man, but of Wilsonianism as a political doctrine as well.

Yet Wilson returned to the United States, unaware of his failure. He offered the American people what he had offered the allied nations at Paris: moral principles divorced from political reality. "The day we have left behind us," he proclaimed at Los Angeles on September 20, 1919,

was a day of balances of power. It was a day of "every nation take care of itself or make a partnership with some other nation or group of nations to hold the peace of the world steady or to dominate the weaker portions of the world." Those were the days of alliances. This project of the League of Nations is a great process of disentanglement.

VI

While before Paris and Versailles these moral principles rang true with the promise of a new and better world, they now must have sounded to many rather hollow and platitudinous. Yet what is significant for the course which American foreign policy was to take in the interwar years is not so much that the American people rejected Wilsonianism, but that they rejected it by ratifying the denial of the American tradition of foreign policy which was implicit in the political thought of Wilson. We are here indeed dealing with a tragedy not of one man, but of a political doctrine and, as far as the United States is concerned, of a political tradition. The isolationism of the interwar period could delude itself into believing that it was but the restorer of the early realist tradition of American foreign policy. Did it not, like that tradition, proclaim the self-sufficiency of the United States within the Western Hemisphere? Did it not, like that tradition, refuse to become involved in the rivalries of European nations? The isolationists of the twenties and thirties did not see what was the very essence of the policies of the Founding Fathers—that both the isolated and the preponderant position of the United States in the Western Hemisphere was not a fact of nature, and that the freedom from entanglements in European conflicts was not the result of mere abstention on the part of the United States. Both benefits were the result of political conditions outside the Western Hemisphere and of policies carefully contrived and purposefully executed in their support. For the realists of the first period, isolation was an objective of policy, which had to be striven for to be attained. For the isolationists of the interwar period, isolation was, as it were, a natural state, which only needed to be left undisturbed in order to continue forever. Conceived in such terms, it was the very negation of foreign policy.

Isolationism, then, is in its way as oblivious to political reality as is Wilsonianism—the internationalist challenge, to which it had thought to have found the American answer. In consequence, they are both strangers not only to the first, realist phase of American foreign policy, but to its whole tradition. Both refused to face political reality either in realistic or ideological terms. They refused to face it at all. Thus isolationism and Wilsonianism have more in common than their historic enmity would lead one to suspect. In a profound sense they are brothers under the skin. Both are one in maintaining that the United States has no interest in any particular political and military constellation outside the Western Hemisphere. While isolationism stops here, Wilsonianism asserts that the American national interest is nowhere in particular but everywhere, being identical with the interests of mankind itself. The political awareness of both refuses to concern itself with the concrete issues with regard to which the national interest must be asserted. Isolationism stops short of them, Wilsonianism soars beyond them. Both have but a negative relation to the national interest of the United States outside the Western Hemisphere. They are unaware of its very existence. This being so, both substitute abstract moral principles for the guidance of the national interest, derived from the actual conditions of American existence. Wilsonianism applies the illusory expectations of liberal reform to the whole world, isolationism empties the realist political principle of isolationism of all concrete political content and transforms it into the unattainable parochial ideal of automatic separation.

In view of this inner affinity between isolationism and Wilsonianism, it is not surprising that the great debate of the twenties and thirties between internationalism and isolationism was carried on primarily in moral terms. Was there a moral obligation for the United States to make its contribution to world peace by joining the League of Nations and the World Court? Was it morally incumbent upon the United States, as a democracy, to oppose Fascism in Europe and to uphold international law in Asia? Such were the questions which were raised in that debate and the answers depended upon the moral position taken. The question which was central to the national interest of the United States, that of the balance of power in Europe and Asia, was hardly ever faced squarely, and when it was, it was dismissed on moral grounds. Mr. Cordell Hull, Secretary of State of the United States from 1933-1944 and one of the most respected spokesmen of internationalism, summarizes in his *Memoirs* his attitude toward this central problem of American foreign policy in these terms:

> I was not, and am not, a believer in the idea of balance of power or spheres of influence as a means of keeping the peace. During the First World War I had made an intensive study of the system of spheres of influence and balance of power, and I was grounded to the taproots in their iniquitous consequences. The conclusions I then formed in total opposition to this system stayed with me.

When internationalism triumphed in the late thirties, it did so in the moral terms of Wilsonianism. That in this instance the moral postulates which inspired the administration of Franklin D. Roosevelt happened to coincide with the exigencies of the American national interest was again, as in the case of Jefferson and of the Wilson of 1917, due to the impact of a national emergency upon innate common sense and to the strength of a national tradition which holds in its spell the actions even of those who deny its validity in words. However, as soon as the minds of the American leaders were freed from the inescapable pressures of a primarily military nature and turned toward the political problems of the war and its aftermath, they thought and acted again as Wilson had acted under similar circumstances. That is to say, they thought and acted in moral terms, divorced from the political conditions of America's existence.

The practical results of this philosophy of international affairs, as applied to the political war and post-war problems, were, then, bound to be quite similar to those which had made the allied victory in the First World War politically meaningless. Conceived as it was as a "crusade"—to borrow from the title of General Eisenhower's book—against the evil incarnate in the Axis Powers, the purpose of the Second World War could only be the destruction of that evil, transacted through the instrumentality of "unconditional surrender." Since the threat to the Western world emanating from the Axis was conceived primarily in moral terms, it was easy to imagine that all conceivable danger was concentrated in that historic constellation of hostile powers and that with its destruction political evil itself would disappear from the world. Beyond "unconditional surrender" there was, then, a brave new world after the model of Wilson's, which would liquidate the heritage of the defeated evil, not "peace-loving" nations, and would establish an order of things where war, aggressiveness, and the struggle for power itself were to be no more. Thus Mr. Cordell Hull could declare on his return in 1943 from the Moscow Conference that the new international organization would mean the end of power politics and usher in a new era of international collaboration.   Three years later, Mr. Philip Noel-Baker, then British Minister of State, echoed Mr. Hull by stating in the House of Commons that the British Government was "determined to use the institutions of the United Nations to kill power politics, in order that by the methods of democracy, the will of the people shall prevail."

With this philosophy dominant in the West—Mr. Churchill provides almost the sole, however ineffective, exception—the strategy of the war and of the peace to follow could not help being oblivious to those considerations of the national interest which the great statesmen of the West, from Hamilton through Castlereagh, Canning and John Quincy Adams to Disraeli and Salisbury, had brought to bear upon the international problems of their day. War was no longer regarded as a means to a political end. The only end the war was to serve was total victory, which is another way of saying that the war became an end in itself. Hence, it became irrelevant how the war was won politically, as long as it was won speedily, cheaply, and totally. The thought that the war might be waged in view of a new balance of power to be established after the war, occurred in the West only to Winston Churchill—and, of course, to Joseph Stalin. The national interest of the Western nations was, then, satisfied insofar as it required the destruction of the threat to the balance of power emanating from Germany and Japan; for insofar, the moral purposes of the war happened to coincide with the national interest. However, the national interest of the Western nations was jeopardized insofar as their security required the creation of a new viable balance of power after the war.

How could statesmen who boasted that they were not "believers in the idea of balance of power"—like a scientist not believing in the law of gravity—and who were out "to kill power politics," understand the very idea of the national interest which demanded above all protection from the power of others? Thus it was with deeply and sincerely felt moral indignation that the Western world, expecting a brave new world without power politics, found itself confronted with a new and more formidable threat to its security as soon as the old one had been subdued. There was good reason for moral indignation, however misdirected this one was. That a new balance of power will rise out of the ruins of an old one and that nations with political sense will avail themselves of the opportunity to improve their position within it, is a law of politics for whose validity nobody is to blame. Yet blameworthy are those who in their moralistic disdain for the laws of politics endanger the interests of the nations which are in their care.

The history of American foreign policy since the end of the Second World War is the story of the encounter of the American mind with a new political world. That mind was weakened in its understanding of foreign policy by half a century of ever more complete intoxication with moral abstractions. Even a mind less weakened would have found it hard to face with adequate understanding and successful action the unprecedented novelty and magnitude of the new political world. American foreign policy in that period presents itself as a slow, painful, and incomplete process of emancipation from deeply ingrained error and of rediscovery of long-forgotten truths.

The fundamental error which has thwarted American foreign policy in thought and action is the antithesis of national interest and moral principles. The equation of political moralism with morality and of political realism with immorality is itself untenable. The choice is not between moral principles and the national interest, devoid of moral dignity, but between one set of moral principles, divorced from political reality, and another set of moral principles, derived from political reality. The basic fact of international politics is the absence of a society able to protect the existence, and to promote the interests, of the individual nations.

For the individual nations to take care of their own national interests is, then, a political necessity. There can be no moral duty to neglect them; for as the international society is at present constituted, the consistent neglect of the national interest can only lead to national suicide. Yet it can be shown that there exists even a positive moral duty for the individual nation to take care of its national interests.

Self-preservation for the individual as well as for societies is not only a biological and psychological necessity, but in the absence of an overriding moral obligation a moral duty as well. In the absence of an integrated international society, in particular, the attainment of a modicum of order and the realization of a minimum of moral values are predicated upon the existence of national communities capable of preserving order and realizing moral values within the limits of their power. It is obvious that such a state of affairs falls far short of that order and realized morality to which we are accustomed in national societies. The only relevant question is, however, what the practical alternative is to these imperfections of an international society based upon the national interests of its component parts. The attainable alternative is not a higher morality realized through the application of universal moral principles, but moral deterioration through either political failure or the fanaticism of political crusades. The juxtaposition of the morality of political moralism and the immorality of the national interest is mistaken. It operates with a false concept of morality, developed by national societies but unsuited to the conditions of international society. In the process of its realization, it is bound to destroy the very moral values which it is its purpose to promote. Hence, the antithesis between moral principles and the national interest is not only intellectually mistaken but also morally pernicious. A foreign policy derived from the national interest is in fact morally superior to a foreign policy inspired by universal moral principles. Albert Sorel, the Anglophobe historian of the French Revolution, well summarized the real antithesis when he said in grudging admiration of Castlereagh:

He piqued himself on principles to which he held with an

unshakable constancy, which in actual affairs could not be distinguished from obstinacy; but these principles were in no degree abstract or speculative, but were all embraced in one alone, the supremacy of English interests; they all proceeded from this high reason of state.

May as much be said by a future historian of the American foreign policy of our time!

THE AMERICAN TRADITION IN FOREIGN RELATIONS*

BY

FRANK TANNENBAUM

[1951]

A great people weathers a period of stress like that through which Americans are now living if its institutions are sound and express its deepest convictions. The American institutions, molded by time and experience, contain values that give meaning to the things we do. Time, place and fortune have wrought their own special imprint upon the American conscience and endowed our folk with an ethical bias peculiarly their own. The indefinable something we call the American outlook adds up to a philosophy of life and a political morality. But Americans are inclined to take their ethical notions for granted and busy themselves with immediate issues. They do not worry about their ideology and would not recognize the meaning of the word if used to describe their beliefs. If in the present crisis they are troubled and confused by the contradictory policies urged upon them, it is because some of their counselors speak a language alien to American experience and indifferent to the inspiration of American polity. We seem to have lost sight of the recognizable drift of our own history and of the sweep of its great energy.

This exuberant and restless power, so recognizably descriptive of the United States, has been disciplined by an equally strong moral bias which has not only canalized and contained it within bounds, but humanized it as well. How else explain this crude and boundless might, which fought two great wars 3,000 and 6,000 miles distant from its own shores, and then, at the height of its military glory—with the enemy defeated and the world helpless to resist the strength of its armies—dismantled its gathered force and returned to the pursuit of peaceful ways, asking only that the other nations of the world do the same? It has placed no

* Reprinted by special permission from *Foreign Affairs,* October 1951. Copyright by Council on Foreign Relations, New York. Frank Tannenbaum (b. 1893) has been Professor of Latin American History, Columbia University.

other people under duress and has exacted neither homage nor obeisance from the weak and the powerless, as well it might have done. Nay, more than that. It has not only denied itself any compensation for the burden and cost laid upon it by two wars, but at the end of the fighting it has offered its resources and its skill to help bind the wounds and assuage the pain that the wars had imposed upon other peoples—including the enemies it had just defeated. The Hoover Commission, in the First World War, UNRRA and the Marshall Plan at the end of the second, are but parts of the effort by the American people to make life livable again for those who had suffered in the conflict. But the story does not end there. After the First World War, Wilson became the architect of a League of Nations that would protect the weak against the strong—against ourselves in fact; and, after the Second World War, Roosevelt and Hull became the chief movers to do over again through the United Nations what had been attempted after the First World War by Wilson. To say that a people that on two such occasions behaved in this way has no philosophy of politics, no sense of direction, and no international policy is to speak the sheerest nonsense. What may be said is that the United States has never elaborated its implicit value into a conscious doctrine. This, however, is an evidence of strength and vitality. A formal ideology is an unconscious apology, a claim for validity that needs to be defended. A vigorous, spontaneous life calls for no explanation and overflows any doctrine.

The tenor of American polity, both internal and external, is clear enough if we will only look at it. If we have not looked at it in recent times, this is in part due to the distorted doctrines in which our generation and the one before it have been caught up. Many of those doctrines are not descriptive of our behavior and do not stem from American experience. We have—and here our intellectuals and teachers are perhaps more guilty than others— permitted ourselves to be beguiled by theories of economic determinism and "power politics." We have attempted to explain American foreign policy on grounds in which we really do not believe—the proof of which is that we do not act upon them. Our behavior is a standing contradiction of the theories taught us in books based upon the beliefs and practices of other peoples. And when—as happened on occasion—our government through the executive departments has behaved as if the theories of "power politics" and economic determinism were true, the American people repeatedly repudiated the policy, and forced a return to the traditional though inadequately formulated American belief that the little nations of the world have the same right to live their own life as the strong and powerful. In fact, our sympathy for the weak has always been greater than our admiration for the strong. The "big stick" formula of Theodore Roosevelt is an anomaly in our experience, was condemned by large numbers of Americans from the beginning, and formally repudiated within a few years after his death. The Reuben Clark memorandum on the Monroe Doctrine, written inside the State Department in 1928, represents the official demise of the big stick theme in American foreign policy. But even Theodore Roosevelt explained many times that he meant to strengthen the weaker states in the Caribbean rather than permanently to control them.

In short, the American people have always had a principle of foreign policy. They have had it from the very beginning. The basic motivation that has governed American relations with other states became evident during the earliest dissidence that led up to the War of Independence, was the chief cause of the Revolution itself and (to use William H. Seward's phrase) "is in reality the chief element of foreign intercourse in our history."

The controlling proposition in American foreign policy was clearly enunciated by James Madison when he said: "The fundamental principle of the Revolution was, that the colonies were coördinate members with each other and with Great Britain, of an empire united by a common executive sovereign, but not united by a common legislative sovereign. The legislative power was maintained to be as complete in each American Parliament, as in the British Parliament. . . . A denial of these principles by Great Britain, and the assertion of them by America, produced the Revolution." The "fundamental principle . . . that the colonies were coördinate members with each other and that . . . the legislative power was . . . as complete in each American Parliament, as in the British Parliament" has remained the unbroken popular theme in American foreign relations. It was this inspiration that ultimately made Rhode Island and Texas equal within the American federal union. The Pan-American system of equal states rests upon the same fundamental principle, and to this basic motivation we must ascribe the gradual evolution of the Monroe Doctrine from unilateral to multilateral policy. It explains the "hands off" injunction imposed upon European Powers in regard to the Western Hemisphere and is the reason for the non-aggressive attitude in the Monroe Doctrine. This fundamental principle was the keystone for our advocacy of the Open Door in China, as it was the justification for a continuing opposition to Japan. We accepted the challenge of a war in the Far East rather than yield the governing principle in our foreign policy.

The American commitment to the ideal of the juridical equality and moral integrity of states explains our participation in two world wars. It explains our effort to develop a League of Nations so as, in Woodrow Wilson's words, to expand ". . . the doctrine of President Monroe as the doctrine of the world . . . that every people should be left free to determine its own polity, its own way of development, unhindered, unthreatened, unafraid, the little along with the great and the powerful." In such words President Wilson was simply restating the version of the "fundamental principle" which Madison knew was the chief cause of the War of Independence. But the same motivation was also one of the chief reasons for the defeat of the League of Nations. One need but turn back to the debate in the Senate to recognize that what defeated the League of Nations was in no small degree the conviction that America's belief in the "coördinate" membership of all peoples had been repudiated. There is a peculiar consistency in this belief of ours that the little nation has the same rights as the big one. Our quarrel with Russia is upon this ground. The Truman Doctrine is a modern version of the basic propositions of President Monroe; and our defense of Korea is explainable only on the grounds that the only kind of a world the American people can comfortably live in is one in which Korea has no more right to attack and dismember Russia than Russia has to attack and dismember Korea—or Finland. We really believe that Ecuador and Haiti are coördinate with the United States, just as we believe that Poland and Bulgaria are coördinate with Russia.

To some these American notions seem impractical and foolish. Influential scholars and counselors would have us abandon them. They suggest that we cease being childish and idealistic and recognize that the national interest requires us to become disciples of Machiavelli, take our lessons from Richelieu, Bismarck or Clemenceau. The fact that Germany and Japan have committed national suicide by consistent adhesion to these doctrines seems not to dampen the eloquence of those who would persuade us to abandon the beliefs and practices by which we have lived and prospered from the beginning.

II

The United States is the oldest international society (excepting Switzerland) in existence. It is also the largest. It is composed of 48 "indestructible," "sovereign" states, greatly differing in wealth and population. How great the difference between them is can be seen by comparing Rhode Island to Texas in area, and Nevada with about 160,000 population to New York with more than 14,000,000. And yet there is no invidious distinction between them, and a Senator like Borah from a small state could be a dominant voice in the foreign policy of the United States for some 20 years. In the United States, the representative of the smallest member of the Federation can speak for the entire system without anyone being aware that he represents the least of the states. This is a profound political miracle and was made possible by our acceptance of the principle of equality. Without it, no nation based upon a federal system could have been built to span an entire continent and grow to be not merely the most powerful but perhaps the stablest political entity on the face of the earth.

The issue of juridical equality had to be settled first in the history of the United States, or this nation might never have been born. The Constitutional Convention which advised a "more perfect union" found, as had already been shown in the Continental

Congress, that the little states would not yield their juridical
equality, their equal sovereignty, or their territorial integrity.
This was the stumbling block to union. The warm debates revealed the danger of a permanent dismemberment of the newly-
born nation. Oliver Elsworth from Connecticut said on June 29,
1787: "If all the states are to exist, they must of necessity have
an equal vote in the general government. Small communities
when associating with greater can only be supported by an equality
of votes." And Luther Martin from Maryland laid it down that
"you must give each state an equal suffrage, or our business is at
an end." The course of the debates need not be reviewed here,
but the compromise—reluctantly agreed to by the large states—
adopted the older practice of Connecticut, that of an equal vote
for the political units and a popular vote for the governor. Each
state was to have two members in the Senate; representation in
the House was to be determined on the basis of population in the
states. In effect, this means that the smaller states can outvote the
larger ones in the Senate, and that in any crucial legislative issue
the states are equal, because a bill has to be passed by both houses.
It also means that in foreign relations the smaller states could
play the decisive rôle if they voted as a bloc. But they do not vote
that way. Equality has eliminated jealousy.

The extension of this principle of equality to the new states to
be carved out of the Western Territories is, next to the formation
of the union, the most important political decision in our entire
history. Without it there would have been no federal union that
spans a continent. It was recognized that in time the new states
would outnumber the original 13, it was argued that the East
would be surrendering itself into the hands of the new states, and
among other limitations it was proposed that the representatives
of the new states should never be allowed to outnumber those of
the original 13. But the principle of equality prevailed. Madison
insisted that "the Western States never would nor ought to submit
to a union which degraded them from an equal rank with other
states." The resolution adopted by the Continental Congress to
govern the admission of the new states said that new districts
"should become and ever after be and constitute a separate, free,

and sovereign state, and be admitted into the union as such, with all the privileges and immunities of those states which now compose the Union." This is what coördinate membership means. This same principle was applied to the lands that came with the Floridas, the Transcontinental Treaty, the Louisiana Purchase, and those ceded to the United States as a result of the war with Mexico. The principle was further evidenced by the agreement that no large state could be divided, and no small state united with another without its own consent.

The juridical and political equality of the "indestructible" states has made possible sharp difference of opinion over questions of interest and policy without undermining the union. What we have not quarreled about is the right of each state to its full share in a common judgment and in the formation of a common policy. And herein lies the basic issue in international relations. We forget that the United States is an international society because we do not quarrel over the right to partake in common decisions.

The principle of equal membership within the federal union ultimately eventuated in Calhoun's doctrine of a dissoluble compact between the states, and in the Civil War. The South still speaks of the War Between the States. But it also explains the even more remarkable political event of the readmission of the defeated states on a par with the victors. If the union was to survive, no other course was possible. A federal union built upon the principle of equal sovereignty is not a proper instrument for military government nor for the arbitrary denial to others of the rights and immunities which the individual states claim for themselves. The American ideal of coördinate states is in its essence anti-imperialist.

III

This is well illustrated in our relations with Latin America. The Monroe Doctrine is woven of many contradictory strands and influences, but the firm hand of John Quincy Adams, more than that of any other, shaped its final form. Two years before it was given to the world, Adams had declared that "colonial establishments cannot fulfill the great objects of governments in the just

purpose of civil society." They were, he said, "incompatible with
the essential character of our institutions"; they were "engines of
wrong," and in time it would be "the duty of the human family
to abolish them, as they are now endeavoring to abolish the slave
trade." The Monroe Doctrine, therefore, has in its background
the broad proposition, again in Adams' own words that: "The
whole system of modern colonization is an abuse of government
and it is time that it should come to an end."

Our government chose to act separately when announcing the
new policy rather than with Great Britain, as originally proposed
by Canning. But it is worth recalling that John Quincy Adams
urged the British to follow our example and recognize the independence of the Latin American nations because "upon this
ground . . . a firm and determined stand could now be jointly
taken by Great Britain and the United States in behalf of the
Independence of Nations."

President Monroe before issuing the declaration consulted Jefferson and Madison, who had preceded him in office. Jefferson
thought that it was a good occasion "of declaring our protest
against the atrocious violations of the rights of nations" begun by
Bonaparte and "now continued" by the Holy Alliance. Madison
suggested that it might encompass not merely the Western Hemisphere but Spain and Greece as well. The full significance of the
Monroe Doctrine must be read against the anti-imperialism of its
chief American sponsors. And William H. Seward, writing to
the French Government, declared that: "The practice of this Government, from its beginning, is a guarantee to all nations of the
respect of the American people for the free sovereignty of the
people in every other State."

This same theme comes, surprisingly perhaps, from Richard
Olney, famous for his boast in the Venezuelan dispute that a fiat
of the United States "is a law upon the subjects to which it confines its interposition" in this continent. He added, however, that
the Monroe Doctrine "does not contemplate any interference in
the internal affairs of any American state." And in what seems
like a reminder of the great debate in the Constitutional Convention here transferred to a debate between nations, he said that

"the United States would cherish the territorial rights of the feeblest of those states, regarding them . . . as equal to even the greatest nationalities."

It was left to Theodore Roosevelt temporarily to twist the Monroe Doctrine beyond its historical intent. He argued that, "however reluctantly," the United States might be compelled "to the exercise of an international police power" in the Caribbean area. But even Roosevelt's exuberance was modulated by the basic American tradition, and he declared that the Doctrine did not imply or carry "an assumption of superiority, and of a right to exercise some kind of protectorate" over the Latin American countries. It was during Theodore Roosevelt's administration that Elihu Root, speaking as Secretary of State, made the ever-memorable statement: "We wish for no territory except our own. . . . We deem the independence and equal rights of the smallest and weakest member of the family of nations entitled to as much respect as those of the greatest empire." And it was during Root's administration of the Department of State that the United States' delegates to the Second International Peace Conference at The Hague sought "a limitation upon the use of force" in the collection of public debts, because such a practice was inconsistent "with that respect for the independent sovereignty of other nations which is . . . the chief protection of the weak nations against the oppression of the strong." In 1915 Wilson proposed the formalization of the idea of coördinate membership in the hemisphere by a treaty which would guarantee the territorial integrity and political independence of the American nations, "so that," to use Colonel House's words, "the Monroe Doctrine may be upheld by all the American Republics instead of by the United States alone as now." Hughes, when Secretary of State, said that "our interest does not lie in controlling foreign peoples; that would be a policy of mischief and disaster," and quoted Jefferson on "the advantages of a cordial fraternalization among all American nations." While Reuben Clark in 1928 declared that "the so-called 'Roosevelt corollary' . . . is . . . not . . . justified by the terms of the Monroe Doctrine."

The Good Neighbor policy is the logical sequence to a tradition as old as our government. Bolivar's effort of 1826 to form a federation of American nations was resuscitated by Blaine when he called together a Pan American Congress in Washington in 1889. These nations, to use Blaine's words, "shall meet together on terms of absolute equality." Secretary Hull's definition of the coördinate position of the American states as consisting of "the absolute independence, the unimpaired sovereignty, the perfect equality and the political integrity of each nation large and small" has a classic finality about it. The Non-Intervention Doctrine enunciated by Franklin D. Roosevelt in Montevideo in 1933, and the series of resolutions beginning with the Havana Conference in 1940 and culminating in the Rio de Janeiro Treaty of 1947, converted the Monroe Doctrine from a unilateral to a multilateral policy. Wilson's hope, embodied in the proposed treaty of 1915, had been fulfilled. The growth of the Organization of American States extends to the Western Hemisphere the ideal of a federation of "indestructible states" upon which the United States itself is founded.

IV

The more than a century-old history of our relations with the independent countries of this hemisphere illustrates the slow and sometimes painful working out of this doctrine. When, during the Grant Administration, an attempt was made to annex Santo Domingo, Senator Sumner of Massachusetts vigorously opposed the project because: "Santo Domingo is the earliest of that independent group . . . towards which our duty is as plain as the Ten Commandments. Kindness, beneficence, assistance, aid, help, protection, all that is implied in good neighborhood—these we must give . . . their independence is as precious to them as is ours to us, and it is placed under the safeguard of natural laws which we can not violate with impunity." After the War with Spain, when the question of Cuba came up for consideration, President McKinley wrote: "I speak not of annexation, for that cannot be thought of. That by our code of morality would be criminal aggression"; and he instructed the military commander to administer the island for the benefit of the Cubans.

The controversy with Mexico, which began in 1912, when Taft was President, and continued almost unabated for 30 years through periods of great tension, ended in a peaceful settlement because the people of the United States would not destroy a nation in defense of material interests. Wilson said: "It is none of my business and none of your business how long they [the Mexicans] take in determining their form of government. It is none of my business and none of yours how they go about the business. The country is theirs, the government is theirs, the liberty, if they can get it—God speed them in getting it—is theirs, and whilst I am President nobody shall interfere with them." His statement prevailed in the end in spite of Coolidge's assertion in 1927 that, "The person and property of a citizen are a part of the general domain of the nation, even when abroad."

Theodore Roosevelt's boast, "I took the Canal," is less impressive than the fact that Panama was encouraged to set up as an equal member within the American family of nations. And after the Second World War it exercised its equality by requiring the United States to surrender, much against its will, the use of air bases which it had constructed for the defense of the Canal. In some ways the Panamanian rebellion is comparable to the secession of West Virginia during the Civil War. It is not a good instance of imperial conquest. And to appease our bad conscience we paid $25,000,000 to Colombia.

The series of interventions in the Caribbean and Central America that followed the Roosevelt Corollary are fruitful demonstrations of the workings of the American fundamental principle. The significant point to remember is that intervention is taken to be a temporary intrusion. No one believed—neither the Americans, nor the Haitians, Dominicans or Nicaraguans—that the United States was there to stay. In each case the President was placed on the defensive. The Senate appointed investigating committees, individual senators attempted to attach riders to the naval appropriation bills denying the use of public funds for the payment of the Marines in the occupied countries. The different administrations were compelled repeatedly to justify their activities before the country, and for half of the time were busy explaining that we were trying to withdraw the Marines from foreign soil. The Clark memorandum officially denied the legitimacy of the government's policy of intervention, and Hoover said in 1928 that "dominion of other people is repugnant to our ideal of human freedom," and in 1929, that "in the large sense we do not wish to be represented abroad [by Marines]." The liquidation of the policy of intervention was begun under Coolidge and Hoover and was completed by Roosevelt. The Platt Amendment, supported and opposed with so much heat, was also repudiated. The American adventure in imperialism in this hemisphere evaporated in one generation.

The one real deviation in the application of the fundamental principle in our foreign relations in this hemisphere is to be found in the annexation of Texas and the war with Mexico. Both of these events are so closely tied to the struggle for position between the slave-holding and free states that they do not really make a clear case of repudiation of the principle. The opposition to both was bitter. John Quincy Adams, "the architect of American foreign policy," signed a public manifesto opposing the annexation of Texas; Lincoln, Webster and Clay, among many others, condemned the Mexican War and the acquisition of Mexican territory. Clay said: "This is no war of defense, but one of unnecessary and of offensive aggression. It is Mexico that is defending her firesides, her castles, and her altars, not we." He then compared the war with Mexico to the partition of Poland. American historians have generally criticized the war with Mexico. H. H. Bancroft calls the war "a deliberately calculated scheme of robbery on the part of a superior power" and contemporary historians repeat Lincoln's accusation that President Polk simulated an attack by Mexico. One unhappy historian attempts a defense of the war because "every American father ought to be able to say to his boy: 'Your country never fought an unjust nor an inglorious war.'" The question has continued to trouble our conscience, and Henry L. Stimson, speaking in New York before the Council on Foreign Relations in 1931, while Secretary of State, referred back to this period as an aberration "directly attributable to the influence of slavery in this country, then at the height of its political power."

V

This same doctrine has worked its way into the Far East. After the Spanish-American War, President McKinley was sorely troubled by what we ought to do about the Philippines. He explained his decision to a delegation of the General Missionary Committee of the Methodist Episcopal Church: "I went down on my knees and prayed Almighty God for light and guidance. And one night it came to me . . . to take them all, and to educate the Filipinos, and uplift and civilize and Christianize them, and by God's grace do the very best we could by them, as our fellow-men for whom Christ also died." But this explanation failed to convince the American people. The Anti-Imperialist League declared that "the subjugation of any people is criminal aggression and open disloyalty to the distinctive principles of our government. . . . A self-governing state cannot accept sovereignty over an unwilling people." And while the President was explaining the inspiration that led him to disregard the fundamental principle of our foreign relations, one of his chief supporters in the Senate was saying that, "I do not know of anybody, from the President to his humblest follower, who is proposing by force and violence to take and hold these islands for all time to come." The bill for the annexation of the Philippines passed by a majority of one vote and that slim victory was due to the news of the rebellion of the Filipinos against the United States; it arrived the day before the vote was taken. Still the act was on our conscience. Taft, who became Governor General of the Philippines, spoke of "our little brown brothers," and implied an attitude that expressed itself by gradually including in increasing proportion Filipinos in the local administration. The Jones Act of 1916 promised the full autonomy that was given the Filipinos in 1936.

The Filipinos were saved their self-respect, the leaders of the rebellion against the United States became our chief supporters, and when the American flag was lowered and the Filipino flag raised the people of the islands spoke of *Ang Ulalin Watawat*—the orphan flag. When the crisis was upon us in 1941, instead of joining our enemies, they fought on our side. In spite of conquest,

annexation and foreign administration, the basic American belief
in coördinate membership had made itself felt in the relationship
that had grown out of the original conquest. In some ways this is
the most eloquent testimony to our inability to treat any nation
as a "subjugated" people. The episode came to an end with complete independence in 1946.

VI

The much older story of the Open Door in China led to the
tragedy of a great war and to the contemporary heartburning of
a lost cause. But what we have done in China through more than
a century is so typically American that we probably could not
have acted differently.

Our fundamental attitude toward China antedates the Open
Door Policy of Hay by nearly 70 years. In 1832, when Edward
Livingston wrote out the instructions to Edmund Roberts, our
first diplomatic agent to the Far East, he told him to inform the
rulers of those strange countries that "it is against the principles
of our nation to build forts, or make expensive establishments in
foreign countries," and "that we never make conquests, or ask
any nation to let us establish ourselves in their countries. . . ."
This statement of American policy toward China reappears over
and over again in the instructions from the Secretary of State to
our representatives in China. Caleb Cushing asked our Minister
to make it clear to the Chinese that they need stand in no apprehension of territorial ambition on our part. W. L. Macy informed
Robert M. McLean, who had urged our joining Great Britain and
France in a more aggressive policy, that there was "no hope that
such authority could be obtained from Congress." Lewis Cass
told our Minister that "this country, you will constantly bear in
mind, is not at war with China, nor does it seek to enter that empire for any other purpose than those of lawful commerce. . . .
You will, therefore, not fail to let it be known to the Chinese
authorities that we are not a party to the . . . hostilities and have
no intention to interfere in their political concerns." Hay's well-
known statement of 1900 that our policy is one "which may bring
about permanent safety and peace to China, preserve Chinese

territorial and administrative entity," is but a logical sequence to what had originally been stated in 1832.

The only major deviation in a century-long policy toward China is to be found under the administration of Theodore Roosevelt, who made so many others as well in American relations to the world. In the Taft-Katsura memorandum of July 1905, Japan was given a free hand in Korea, and the Root-Takahira Agreement of November 1908 "suggests," to use Professor S. F. Bemis' words, "that Roosevelt was preparing to give to Japan a free hand in Manchuria as he had done already in Korea." It is worth noting that both of these were executive agreements and were not submitted to the Senate for confirmation. But Taft, when he became President, sought to safeguard China against further depredations. He suggested a loan to China for the purchase of the Manchuria Railroad, as "perhaps the most effective way to preserve the undisturbed enjoyment by China of all political rights in Manchuria."

President Wilson opposed the International Consortium. Within two weeks after he took office—on March 18, 1913—he made the far-reaching public statement which reasserted the traditional position of the American people toward China: "The conditions of the loan seem to us to touch very nearly the administrative independence of China itself. . . . Our interests are those of the Open Door—a door of friendship and mutual advantage. This is the only door we care to enter." And Bryan in 1915 told the Japanese that "the United States cannot recognize any agreement or undertaking between the Governments of Japan and China, impairing the political or territorial integrity of the Republic of China, or the . . . Open Door policy."

The Nine-Power Treaty of 1922 brought the principles so long maintained by the United States into a formal international agreement of the signatory Powers, including Japan, Great Britain and France. Those Powers agreed: "To respect the sovereignty, the independence, and the territorial and administrative integrity of China; to provide the fullest and most unembarrassed opportunity to China to develop and maintain for herself an effective and stable government."

To Japan, however, the Nine-Power Treaty, the Pact of Paris and the Kellogg-Briand Pact were in the nature of plausible sentiments uttered to satisfy the mood of the moment. As others have done and still do, she made the profound mistake of assuming that we could not really mean what we said. And when she saw the opportunity—when the Western World was distraught by the economic and political difficulties of the Great Depression, when the League of Nations was a council divided, when the United States and Great Britain had both permitted their navies to fall below even the permitted strength under the Washington Naval Treaties—she attacked Manchuria.

China was weak, the United States was pacifist and isolationist, and Great Britain could not and would not fight alone against Japan in defense of China. The United States protested, Secretary Stimson reminded Japan of her signatures to the Nine-Power Treaty and the Kellogg-Briand Pact, but the Japanese pursued their fateful adventures, regardless of the judgment of the world.

On January 7, 1932, the American Secretary of State announced the now famous Stimson Doctrine that the United States does not "intend to recognize any treaty or agreement . . . which may impair . , . the sovereignty, the independence, or the territorial and administrative integrity of the Republic of China . . . or the Open Door policy. . . ." America gave her adherence to the Lytton Commission's report which condemned Japanese actions in China. Japan walked out of the League. In 1940-41 the old story was drawing to a dramatic close. We had frozen Japanese assets and had placed an embargo against oil shipments. Japan had occupied most of China and had invaded French Indo-China. On November 20, 1941, the Japanese Ambassador handed a note to Secretary Hull containing the conditions of peace for the Pacific. Japan promised to withdraw from French Indo-China in return for the lifting of the embargo, removal of the order freezing Japanese assets, and restoration of normal commercial relations. Those were the things Japan asked from the United States as a condition of peace. They seemed very simple and realistic. Surely they would serve the national interest of Japan and would not injure that of the United States. But Secretary Hull and the

American people thought otherwise. The American Secretary of State replied on November 26, 1941. The reply was as follows: "The Government of the United States and the Government of Japan, being both solicitous for the peace of the Pacific, affirm that their national policies are directed toward lasting and extensive peace throughout the Pacific area, that they have no territorial designs in that area, that they have no intention of threatening other countries or of using military force aggressively against any neighboring nation, and that . . . they will actively support the following fundamental principles . . . : (1) The principle of inviolability of territorial integrity and sovereignty of each and all nations.   (2) The principle of non-interference in the internal affairs of other countries.   (3) The principle of equality, including equality of commercial opportunity and treatment.   (4) The principle of reliance upon international coöperation . . . and pacific settlement of controversies . . . and that the Government of Japan will withdraw all military, naval, air, and police forces from China and from Indo-China."

Japan's answer was Pearl Harbor, December 7. And so the climax had come. The statement made by Hull in November 1941 is not unlike the first one made by Livingston in January 1832. Roosevelt and Hull fulfilled an original American commitment: the pledge that we would not be a party to the destruction of another nation.

Why were we so idealistic as to insist upon the affirmation of national integrity at a moment when the "wave of the future" seemed so overwhelming? Our acceptance of the Japanese challenge involved us in mortal danger and the staggering military expenditure that no possible benefits from an Open Door policy would have justified. Our investments in China in 1914 were smaller than those of England, Japan, Russia, France or Germany, and in 1931 they were only about equal to those of France, representing only 2.8 percent of our investments abroad; our exports and imports to and from China hovered between one and two percent of our international trade. To argue that we accepted so dangerous a challenge in order to defend so small a material interest is a conclusion which could only be drawn in an age when economic determinism is the great obsession. When the Japanese offered us peace in the Far East, after they had already occupied most of China and a large part of French Indo-China, we refused. They even agreed to evacuate Indo-China if we would but recognize their conquest in China and Manchuria. We declined. Because of economic interests? No. Because Roosevelt and Hull, speaking for the American people, recognized that no settlement which compromised Chinese political independence and territorial integrity would be acceptable to our sense of justice or consistent with our basic tradition. No American President could have satisfied the Japanese demands without risking repudiation, not merely by the opposition, but by his own party as well.

The fundamental principle of the coördinate state ruled this decision as it has most others in our foreign policy from the beginning.

VII

This attitude does not imply any special virtue on our part. It has not saved us from serious errors in dealing with other nations, and it has not endowed us with any special grace in cultivating the good will and friendship of foreign people. On the contrary, our record for irritating our friends by saying the wrong things in the worst way is well above the average. Our good intentions are a small excuse for the unwelcomed preachments we like to indulge in, and the "holier than thou" tone which we often adopt does not add to our persuasiveness in the world of diplomacy. Nor is our record for coöperation, even by our own standards, by any means above reproach. But our failings are within a consistent historical tradition that leads back directly 150 years— and indirectly much further. The policy derives from the assumption that security rests upon coöperation, that coöperation is possible only among equals, that equality eliminates the basic reason for political disruption because those equal politically are coördinate in dignity and in rank.

The doctrines of "power politics" now being preached by such persuasive scholars as Professor Hans J. Morgenthau of the University of Chicago are a denial of this tradition and a repudiation of the lessons of American experience. The advice offered is exactly that which has ruined half of the nations of the world. Historically these doctrines have always led to war, and often to national suicide. The new school of *Realpolitik* advances its arguments for a settlement with the Soviets on the basis of "spheres of influence," and in terms of the "national interest." The "national interest" is a beguiling phrase: everyone desires to advance the interests of his country. But what country, concretely, is to be sacrificed in the power deal which would determine the *quid pro quo?* Which national interests do not count? Intellectuals abroad who urge upon us this "return to diplomacy" (as the fashionable slogan goes) should be sure of one thing— that we will not bargain away the independence of any other nation.

Fortunately, with all our errors and misjudgments, Americans have never successfully been persuaded that in foreign policy might makes right, or that Machiavelli was a great moral teacher or even a good guide for an understanding of human motives. Our repudiation of "power politics" in this sense of the term does not mean that we do not believe that policy must not be backed by strength, or that we do not possess strength. Germany and Japan can testify to that. When Dean Acheson speaks of a "position of strength" he means strength to resist aggression. To assume that this position is mere sentimentalism and utopianism is to miss the basic point of American history. We are a strong nation because we are an "indestructible union" of weak states. The very essence of American international relations rests upon the idea of coöperative relationship.

The United States entered the First World War because we were convinced that we could not abide a world dominated by such brutal disregard of the rights of other nations as imperial Germany displayed. The German attack upon Belgium was seen by the American people with absolute horror. Here was a little peaceful nation bound by treaty to remain neutral, cultivating its fields and following in quiet its own affairs, suddenly destroyed without a declaration of war, without cause and in complete repudiation of a solemn treaty. The declaration that the treaty was a scrap of paper merely confirmed the callousness of the German Government. The burning of the library of Louvain, the unrestricted submarine warfare, the braggadocio, and the contempt for the small and the weak all confirmed the American people in the belief that the German régime was a present danger to all nations. And we went to war not to increase our power, not to expand our territory, not for aggrandizement, but to end such practices. That was the meaning of the Fourteen Points; that too was the purpose of the League of Nations. And paradoxically that too was one of the major reasons why the League was defeated. One needs but read the debates in the Senate to recognize that the bitter feeling that turned on Wilson stemmed in part from disillusionment at a peace which repudiated the moral purpose that had taken us into the war.

Our entrance into the Second World War was no less an expression of the great tradition. The surrender at Munich had made it seem that there was no moral principle left in Europe that was worth defending. The spheres of influence settlement at Munich was a yielding of the basic principle of national integrity and political equality for which we had gone into the First World War and crossed the ocean a million strong to maintain. It would have been infinitely easier for the American people to have joined Great Britain in war if she had in 1938 thrown herself against Hitler on the grounds that she would not be a party to the destruction of an independent nation. When Britain became the small bastion that resisted destruction by the evil reborn in Hitler, the attitude of the American people changed. In 1939 when Roosevelt, who clearly saw the meaning of the Nazi threat, had addressed himself to Hitler and Mussolini to exact from them the terms of a possible peace, he spelled out the old American tradition in favor of the security of the independent nation by listing separately all of the nations within the possible reach of the European dictators. Again when in 1940 Russia occupied the Baltic countries, Sumner Welles reasserted the old tradition on the grounds that the very basis of our civilization rested upon the respect for the little nations. This same doctrine of the equality, freedom and independence of the small nation along with the great reappeared in the Atlantic Charter and gave the Second World War the meaning that the First World War had had. Those ideals reappear in the Moscow Declaration, in the statements issued after the Teheran Conference, and are embodied in the Charter of the United Nations: "The organization is based upon the principle of the sovereign equality of all its members." These same principles reappear in President Truman's speech on the fundamentals of American foreign policy delivered in October 1947, "We shall not recognize any government imposed upon any nation by the force of any foreign power"; and in the Truman Doctrine the same old proposition is reasserted. It is implied in the North Atlantic Treaty and in the national defense assistance policy. The fundamental principle of the coördinate state with which our history as a nation began has remained a continuing philosophy of international relations to the present.

No swing away from it lasts long. The deviation in some of the Yalta agreements has, characteristically, met bitter and continuous opposition. The announcement that the United States had asked for three votes in the General Assembly to offset Russia's demand for three votes was made on March 29, 1945, and repudiated April 3: a major policy reversal in five days. The Great Power veto has been widely criticized in America from the beginning. It since has lost much of its effect by the transfer to the Assembly of issues that could be blocked by the Russian veto. The fact that that transfer of jurisdiction was made in an effort to protect the sovereignty of an independent nation—Korea—is eloquent testimony to the soundness of the American tradition. The provisions for permanent membership of certain Powers in the Security Council seem to Americans just as unreasonable as it would have been for the Constitutional Convention to have named the states of New York, Pennsylvania, Massachusetts and Virginia as the great states of the Union with special power and privileges —a proposition which was indeed made and rejected. One may predict that if the United Nations is to survive it will in time adopt, perhaps in stages, the proposition of "coördinate" membership in the fullest sense. On this point the lesson of American experience is plain, for, as we have noted, the American Federal

Union and the Pan-American system have grown stronger with the years: the principle of equality, by providing an equal opportunity to participate in a decision which affects all members, removes the fundamental obstacle to international coöperation. International security can stem only from the loyal coöperation of people associated in the enterprise of peaceful existence in a recalcitrant universe. Power derived from conquest, exploitation and abuse is insecure precisely because it is unjust. There is neither an alternative nor a substitute for the strength that comes with union. But a true union depends upon voluntary adhesion, only possible among those possessed of equal dignity.

It would be good for the world, and for ourselves, to be clear about the concrete significance of this tradition at the present moment. Americans want peace with Russia, but will not buy it at the expense of other nations. The American tradition has no room for a settlement which would divide the world into spheres of influence. It has no room for the sacrifice to Russia of any nation, small or large, for the sake of securing an abatement of the "cold" war or for the sake of avoiding a hot one. The only kind of peace acceptable to it is one based on collective security—again, the principle of the coördinate membership of all states in the family of nations. Much misunderstanding would be avoided if, in their reasoning about us, our friends began with that simple fact.

The enormous energy of the United States has been disciplined by the ethical conception of political equality, and harnessed to the ideal of collective security resting upon a federation of coordinate states. These are the grounds of our difference with Russia. We are not quarreling over economic interests, political doctrines or her internal policies, even if we do not like them. We cannot accept Russia's denial of the coördinate character of other states. We do not believe in the Big Five, the Big Three or the Big Two. The day the Soviet Union learns, if it can, to accept its neighbors as of equal rank with itself, the world will be united again and the Iron Curtain will melt into thin air. Our quarrel is not about Russia, but about her contempt for the independent sovereignty of other nations.

THE NATIONAL INTEREST*

BY

CHARLES B. MARSHALL

[1952]

My assignment calls for me to relate the national interest to the problems of the United States in the present world situation. Let me comment first on that phrase, "the national interest."

Only a few years ago the economic interpretation of virtually everything was in vogue. Writers of considerable repute were fobbing off the significance of the national interest as a factor in foreign policy, interpreting it as merely a facade to conceal special interests and to deceive the public. The return of the phrase to respectable parlance, indicating the recognition of a valid national interest paramount over particular interests, is a gain for straight thinking.

Often a decision in foreign policy is inseparable from the question of the domestic consequences of the decision. It is necessary in such an instance to recognize that our national destiny in a world of many nations is more important than the domestic group interests affected by the decision. In settling questions of conflict between the necessities of national security and group interests, the idea of national interest is valid and essential. The phrase, moreover, indicates a step away from the utopianism beclouding too much the discussion of international affairs in the sequel to both World War I and World War II.

Nations do have interests. In some instances their interests coincide with the interests of other nations. Sometimes interests of different nations harmonize without coinciding. Sometimes they differ, but not incompatibly. Sometimes they are mutually exclusive. Out of these variations comes the real nature of international life. It is useless to try to ignore this by talk about global

---

*From the Department of State *Bulletin*, May 5, 1952. This article is derived from an address made before the American Academy of Political and Social Science, on April 18, 1952. Charles B. Marshall (b. 1908), was a member of the Policy Planning Staff of the Department of State.

harmony and the universal state. Such talk, while edifying to those who like it, only hinders—it does not help—the handling of world problems.

So it is good to hear people talk about international problems again in terms of national interests rather than in the abstractions of world government and world law. Indeed, it would be a blessed thing if all differences among nations could be translated into differences of interest alone and not differences of basic purpose and principle. It is unselfish to compromise on interests. It is unseemly to compromise on one's principles.

Here I myself stray off into utopianism of another sort. The world is nowhere near that stage of adjustment where all national differences can be dealt with as solely differences of interest, and the coming of that day is too remote for prediction.

I have said enough in praise of the idea of national interest. Now let me say some things in criticism. The usefulness and significance of the phrase are limited. It begs more questions than it answers. In appraising the significance of the national interest, I must distinguish between instances in which the decision turns on weighing our world position as a Nation against the claims of particular domestic interests and instances in which the issue lies simply between lines of action in the foreign field.

I know of no case of the latter character in which the settlement of an issue of our national policy in the line of responsibility would have been facilitated by injecting the question: Shall we or shall we not try to serve the national interest?

The question in the arena of responsibility in handling an issue involving foreign policy alone is not whether, but how, to serve the national interest. That involves the question of what is the national interest in a particular situation. The question of serving the national interest is always a subtle and complex one in real situations.

I am sure all of the following things are clearly in our national interest: To avoid war; to preserve our institutions; to have strong allies; to avoid inflation; to have a prosperous civilian economy; to find common grounds on which to stand with the various nations which have newly come to responsibility; to preserve our access to strategic waterways and vital raw materials; and to protect the property and safety of our nationals abroad. I could extend this list by dozens of items.

Now any matter of foreign policy pertaining only to the realization of one of those items would not present an issue at all. No one would have to work his brains overtime on it. No series of exhaustive meetings would have to be held. No protracted debate about the nuances and contradictions would be necessary. In such an instance the policy decision would crystallize spontaneously.

In any practical question presenting a real issue the national interest has several aspects. Indeed, there are many national interests, not just one. The difficulties arise in the conflict of one interest with another; for example, in the clash of the interest in peace with the interest in preserving national institutions, in the clash of the interest in having a strong defense with the interest in having a strong civilian economy, or in the clash of the interest in preserving access to a waterway with the interest in eliciting the adherence of another country to one's cause.

I trust I have made my point of the inconclusiveness of the national interest as a guide in any particular policy problem. Beyond that, I believe the concept of national interest is inadequate and misleading even as a broad concept on which to found a policy.

It seems to me that a more appropriate guiding principle is the idea of responsibility. This is a very different sort of idea. I want to take the rest of my time in talking about the contrast between national interest and responsibility and examining the idea of responsibility as it enlightens our present problems.

First I want to discuss our special role in the world today.

The great political issues of our time revolve around rival approaches to the handling of the problems growing out of such circumstances peculiar to modern times as the massing of peoples —their expanded numbers and their increased concentration; the sharpening of the clash between cultures due largely to awakened consciousness of the disparities in well-being between peoples in relation to the advance or lag of production techniques, and the destructiveness of modern war due both to the concentration of industry and population and to the greater inherent efficacy of modern weapons—their huge lethal power and the capability for distance and stealth in attack.

One approach would exploit these circumstances for the purpose of widening the scope and strengthening the foundations of a monopoly of political power. The other approach seeks to compose clashes of interest and to work out patterns of accommodation.

The legitimate question of politics is not how to eliminate conflict of interest—a utopian concept—but how to organize society so that conflicts can be adjusted rather than fought out. This difference in approach is brought to bear both within and among nations. The lines of difference are intertwined and subtle, for the lines along which great issues form are never as sharp as a razor. Insofar as the issue has crystallized among nations, however, the Soviet Union stands clearly as the champion of the first approach.

Internal political circumstances cast the Soviet Union in that role. It is ruled by tyrants, who reached the seat of power through conspiracy and, having achieved power, have not dared risk their hold on it by resort to a valid procedure of consent. They have remained conspirators after becoming governors, combining the usages of conspiracy with the prerogatives of the state. Both at home and in the world at large, the conspiracy that walks like a state requires tension and conflict to maintain its grip. In the service of this purpose it employs a doctrine emphasizing the patterns of conflict—class war, subversion, and the like.

This rule is established over a great range, commanding great resources in people and materials. Huge military forces at its disposal are deployed in positions bearing on northern and central Europe, the eastern Mediterranean, the Middle East, Southeast Asia, the Republic of Korea, and Japan. The Soviet Union has auxiliaries in the form of embryonic governments under the guise of domestic political groups in territories beyond its imperium. The Soviet power is such that no combination of nations adequate to cope with it is conceivable without the support and participation of the United States.

The United States thus finds itself in the position of leadership among peoples which prefer to work out a method of handling the problems of our times alternative to the pattern offered by the Soviet and which are impeded in this effort by the fact of Soviet opposition.

A failure to exercise this leadership would almost certainly result in a world power situation endangering the survival of our constitutional values. These are the values expressed in the Preamble of our Constitution. I do not doubt that you know them all, but let me enumerate them anyway.

The first is the perfection of our Union, the concept of a nation with steadily growing public values.

Second comes the idea of justice—of power subjected to standards superior to the mere attainment of the ends of power.

Third in the enumeration is domestic tranquility, conveying the idea of a nation at peace with itself, a nation where issues can be decided by reason, by discussion, and by compromise.

Then we come to the common defense—the protection of the nation from penetration from the outside.

The idea of the general welfare is another of the values set forth. It embodies the idea of a government which serves and is not master, which is accountable to all of its people as contrasted to a government which serves the exclusive interest of a dominant group.

Finally, we have the blessings of liberty—the situation in which each person can make choices for himself, regarding his life, the life of his children, his religion, and his thoughts.

The fundamental and enduring purpose of our foreign policy is to maintain in the world circumstances favorable to the continued vitality of these values in the United States.

I want to stress the novelty in the American consciousness of the responsibilities which the present world situation imposes. Our power, whence come our responsibilities, has three main foundations: position, political strength, and economic resourcefulness. The circumstances surrounding the development of each of these were such as to conceal their eventual implications. The diffusion of power among several nations of great magnitude provided the relatively stable and protective situation which enabled the Americans to move onward from an Atlantic beachhead to become a continental Nation, singular among the great powers in that it lies in both the Northern and Western Hemispheres, faces on both the Atlantic and the Pacific, and stretches from the tropics to the Arctic. The same circumstances enabled the Americans to preserve and mature a Government based upon stipulated principles of accountability and freedom. Their purpose in doing this was purely domestic. The strength of the Government thus established is one of the great political facts of our time, important for all the globe. The Americans developed a fecund agriculture and productive industry, without equal, through the expansion of an internal market. That circumstance concealed from them the eventual world importance that American economic strength would have.

Some 60 years ago Lord Bryce described the United States as living "in a world of peace" and as "safe from attack, safe even from menace." Such was the national situation in the historic past, when the United States was a remote and intermittent factor in the ratios of world power and when Americans were concerned almost exclusively with the problems of their own national development. Lord Bryce added: "For the present at least—it may not always be so—America sails upon a summer sea."

Within a lifetime the summer sea vanished. The world frontiers closed. Two world wars were fought. Germany and Japan were eclipsed in defeat. Other great powers suffered relative declines. Patterns of empire were sundered. Many erstwhile dependencies attained sovereignty. Revolutionary communism established a power base. Two nations emerged into positions of primary magnitude—the United States as one and the Soviet adversary, the other.

So great an accession of responsibility in so brief a span has placed great moral tests on this Nation. One difficulty rises from the sense, as expressed recently by former Chancellor Robert M. Hutchins of the University of Chicago, that "this country has been thrust against its will into a position of world leadership." True, no referendum on the issue whether or not to be a nation of such wide responsibilities was ever held. The choice was made unconsciously in many decisions of our past. We were thrust ahead not against but by our wills. The choice is nonetheless binding for having been made in unawareness of the consequences.

Here we have a paradox—an accession to great power accompanied by a sense of deprivation of freedom. We feel that paradox in another way. In our historic past we viewed our role as that of standing normally aloof from the power balance whose benefits we enjoyed. At most we would entertain the idea of throwing in our weight only momentarily to reestablish the balance whenever it might break down in general war.

We regarded our role as like that of a pedestrian who might choose to vary his solitary walks by intermittently riding with others, without foreclosing himself from choosing to walk alone again. Now that is changed. Our power makes our interposition essential to the preserving of the causes with which our interests lie. We must go along with others if we are to keep others with whom to go along. Our power is the basis of our essentiality, and our essentiality compels us to replace our historic sense of freedom by a new consciousness of responsibility. While losing a sense of freedom, we lose also a sense of effectiveness.

In the era when we stood normally aloof from the balance of power, our decision to become a world factor for a season had drastic and immediate results in redressing the balance. Now, by having become permanently involved in preserving the balance, we are no longer vouchsafed the opportunity to alter the situation dramatically and radically by sudden action.

This involvement leaves for us the exacting course of seeking a solution in the long pull through persistent effort to make the best of the situation stage by stage in the knowledge that such is the only way of making the situation better.

Let us look for a moment at the foreign policy which this situation imposes. It gives us no promise of arrival at some calculable moment at which we can say that all our troubles are behind us, that everything henceforth will be tidy and easy, and that we have crossed the one last river.

I said this to a group of Texans with whom I was discussing our national policy recently. One of them asked me whether I actually thought coexistence with the Soviet Union was possible.

That is a curious question. It makes a matter of speculation out of something known to be true. Coexistence with the Soviet Union is not simply possible; it is a fact. Coexistence with a great power that tries to lead a double life as state and as conspirator is vexatious for sure, but it is preferable to the tragedy of general war and its sequel, whichever side might win. Our policy seeks to avoid the tragedy of war, to abate the difficulties of coexistence by correcting the circumstances affording special advantage to the adversary, and to work with other nations as best we can to guide international life toward the patterns of conduct preferable to us.

This policy, often called the policy of containment, is sometimes criticized as if it aimed for a protracted, static confrontation—a sort of perpetually frozen *status quo*. Such perpetual equilibrium is foreign to the processes of history. The policy is based upon no assumption of arresting change. It rests rather upon the assumption that the factors of position, population, talents, resources, and moral values redound to the ultimate advantage of the side of our interests, and that, in the long pull, it will be the adversary who must adjust his purposes.

This is not a foregone conclusion. What we and our friends do will be an essential factor in determining the outcome. This is no cause for disquiet. History presents no foregone conclusions. I know of no way to formulate a policy that will absolve us from the subsequent necessity of exercising resolution and restraint and paying the costs, whatever they may be.

The policy works along three general lines. The first is to make coexistance more tolerable. This calls for improving our armed strength and that of the nations standing with us and combining them more effectively through a system of alliances; for helping the depleted and dislocated economies of our friends to regain a healthy level of activity; for helping the economically lagging countries to improve their production methods; and for widening the area of peace by bringing the former enemy countries, Japan and Western Germany, back into collaboration with other countries.

The second line is to prevent serious deterioration in the conditions of coexistence by avoiding losses in areas of sharp political conflict.

The third general line relates to the development of international usages and institutions of responsibility as instruments of free collaboration among nations instead of the collaboration by intimidation offered by the adversary.

To succeed in these endeavors will require the collaboration of others. They will not work along with us on the basis solely of our national interest. The collaboration must be founded on an identity among their interests and ours. The primary responsibility for discovering and developing that identity of interests is ours, because we are in the position of greatest strength. This is not a simple responsibility. It is irksome and expensive and contains no easy formula for complete success in a stipulated interval.

The policy of responsibility lacks the simplicity—here I use the word "simplicity" in the sense of Proverbs 1:22—of the counsel of unlimited violence, a counsel based on the fallacy of trying to reduce all problems of power to the limits of the problems of force. The policy lacks the utopian tidiness of the dream of solution by world government. It lacks the traditional ring of the counsel of solution by default, by which I mean the idea of confining our security to this hemisphere—a counsel put forth by some claiming the mantle of statesmanship even though the formula on which it rests contains a fallacy recognizable to any school boy familiar with solid geometry. The fallacy inheres in this: Two points on the same sphere can never be farther than a hemisphere apart; hence the whole world lies in the same hemisphere with us.

The policy based on the principle of responsibility lacks the crisp appeal of a phrase like "the national interest." It involves this paradox—that we can serve our national interest in these times only by a policy which transcends our national interest. This is the meaning of responsibility.

No nation could ask more of history than the privilege of coming to great responsibility. To satisfy our American professions of the values of competition, we have at hand one of the most exacting contests in ideas ever experienced. To test our faith in freedom, we have abundant opportunity to make choices of action that will profoundly affect the course of human affairs. To test our devotion to values, we have the opportunity not simply to proclaim them but actually to support them by gifts and deeds and perseverance.

This juncture in our experience is not comforting for those who take the utopian approach to international problems—those who remind one of Kipling's lines:

> Thinking of beautiful things we know;
> Dreaming of deeds that we mean to do,
> All complete, in a minute or two—
> Something noble, and grand and good,
> Won by merely wishing we could.

I recall the words opening one of Christina Rossetti's poems:

> Does the road lead uphill all the way?
> Yes, to the very end.

That is the road which a great and responsible nation must tread. It is an uphill road all the way. For Americans who do not mind walking that kind of a road, this is not a time for misgiving but a great time in which to live.

THE AMERICAN EXAMPLE *

BY

J. WILLIAM FULBRIGHT

[1966]

Rich and powerful though our country is, it is not rich or powerful enough to shape the course of world history in a constructive or desired direction solely by the impact of its power and policy. Inevitably and demonstrably, our major impact on the world is not in what we do but in what we are. For all their worldwide influence, our aid and our diplomacy are only the shadow of America; the real America—and the real American influence—are something else. They are the way our people live, our tastes and games, our products and preferences, the way we treat each other, the way we govern ourselves, the ideas about man and man's relations with other men that took root and flowered in the American soil.

History testifies to this. A hundred years ago England was dominant in the world, just as America is today. Now England is no longer dominant; her great fleets have vanished from the seas and only fragments remain of the mighty British Empire. What survives? The legacy of hatred survives—hatred of the West and its arrogant imperialism, hatred of the condescension and the exploitation, hatred of the betrayal abroad of the democracy that Englishmen practiced at home. And the ideas survive— the ideas of liberty and tolerance and fair play to which Englishmen were giving meaning and reality at home while acting on different principles in the Empire. In retrospect, it seems clear that England's lasting and constructive impact on modern India, for example, springs not from the way she ruled in India but, despite that, from the way she was ruling England at the same time.

Possessed as they are of a genuine philanthropic impulse, many Americans feel that it would be selfish and exclusive, elitist and isolationist, to deny the world the potential benefits of our great

---

* From *The Arrogance of Power,* published by Random House, copyright 1966, by J. William Fulbright. Reprinted by permission.

wealth and power, and to restrict ourselves to a largely exemplary role.

It is true that our wealth and power can be, and sometimes are, beneficial to foreign nations, but they can also be, and often are, immensely damaging and disruptive. Experience—ours and that of others—strongly suggests that the disruptive impact predominates, that, when big nations act upon small nations, they tend to do them more harm than good. This is not necessarily for lack of good intentions; it is rather for lack of knowledge. Most men simply do not know what is best for other men, and when they pretend to know or genuinely try to find out, they usually end up taking what they believe to be best for themselves as that which is best for others.

Conceding this regrettable trait of human nature, we practice democracy among ourselves, restricting the freedom of individuals to impose their wills upon other individuals, restricting the state as well, and channeling such coercion as is socially necessary through community institutions. We do not restrict the scope of Government because we wish to deny individuals the benefits of its wealth and power; we restrict our Government because we wish to protect individuals from its capacity for tyranny.

If it is wisdom to restrict the power of men over men within our society, is it not wisdom to do the same in our foreign relations? If we cannot count on the benevolence of an all-powerful Government toward its own people, whose needs and characteristics it knows something about and toward whom it is surely well disposed, how can we count on the benevolence of an all-powerful America toward peoples of whom we know very little? Clearly, we cannot, and, until such time as we are willing to offer our help through community institutions such as the United Nations and the World Bank, I think that, in limiting our commitments to small nations, we are doing more to spare them disruption than we are to deny them benefits.

Mr. President, I might add that it has struck me as rather inconsistent that some of my friends who are most devoted to the rights of the States in domestic affairs are, at the same time, very determined to project our Nation's power into the affairs of peoples abroad.

Wisdom consists as much in knowing what you cannot do as in knowing what you can do. If we knew and were able to acknowledge the limits of our own capacity, we would be likely, more often than we do, to let nature take its course in one place and another, not because it is sure or even likely to take a good course but because, whatever nature's course may be, tampering with it in ignorance will almost surely make it worse.

We used, in the old days, to have this kind of wisdom and we also knew, almost instinctively, that what we made of ourselves and of our own society was far more likely to have a lasting and beneficial impact on the world than anything we might do in our foreign relations. We were content, as they say, to let conduct serve as an unspoken sermon. We knew that it was the freedom and seemingly unlimited opportunity, the energy and marvelous creativity of our diverse population, rather than the romantic non-sense of "manifest destiny," that made the name of America a symbol of hope to people all over the world.

We knew these things until events beyond our control carried us irrevocably into the world and its fearful problems. We recog-nized thereupon, as we had to, that some of our traditional ideas would no longer serve us, that we could no longer, for example, regard our power as something outside of the scales of the world balance of power, and that, therefore, we could no longer remain neutral from the major conflicts of the major nations.

But, as so often happens when ideas are being revised, we threw out some valid ideas with the obsolete ones. Recognizing that we could not help but be involved in many of the world's crises, we came to suppose that we had to be involved in every crisis that came along, and so we began to lose the understanding of our own limitations.

Recognizing that we could not help but maintain an active for-eign policy, we came to suppose that whatever we hoped to ac-complish in the world would be accomplished by acts of foreign policy, and, this—as we thought—being true, that foreign policy must without exception be given precedence over domestic needs; and so we began to lose our historical understanding of the power of the American example.

The loss is manifest in Vietnam. There at last we have embraced the ideas that are so alien to our experience—the idea that our wisdom is as great as our power, and the idea that our lasting impact on the world can be determined by the way we fight a war rather than by the way we run our country. These are the principal and most ominous effects of the war—the betrayal of ideas which have served America well, and the great moral crisis which that betrayal has set loose among our people and their leaders.

The crisis will not soon be resolved, nor can its outcome be predicted. It may culminate, as I hope it will, in a reassertion of the traditional values, in a renewed awareness of the creative power of the American example. Or it may culminate in our becoming an empire of the traditional kind, ordained to rule for a time over an empty system of power and then to fade or fall, leaving, like its predecessors, a legacy of dust.

AMERICA'S WORLD RESPONSIBILITY *

BY

IRVING KRISTOL

[1968]

Everyone is to some extent aware that American foreign policy, after this trauma, will never again be the same. But too many people seem to be content to leave it at this, under the impression that, the recent past having been so awful, the future—whatever its shape or form—can only represent an improvement. There is, it seems to me, a shocking lack of recognition of the fact that the debacle in Vietnam initiates a major *crisis* in American foreign policy—and perhaps in world history too.

Thus, there are many people who have concluded rather smugly that, from now on, a chastened United States will be more reluctant to exercise a roving commission as "policeman of the world." The conclusion itself is indisputable: any future Administration will be most hesitant about entering into a new military commitment overseas, and will even think twice before moving to honor an old one.

Still, the fact remains that the moving force behind American foreign policy in these last two decades has been something more than mere presumption or "the arrogance of power." For the world *needs* a measure of policing—the world *does* rely on American power, does count on American power, does look to American power for the preservation of a decent level of international law and order. . . .

One can only wonder what the situation in Central Africa would be today if we had not helped establish stability of a kind in the Belgian Congo, an area of no direct concern—economic or military—to us. We intervened there because most of the world

* From *The New York Times Magazine,* May 12, 1968, copyright by *The New York Times.* Reprinted by permission. Irving Kristol is co-editor of *The Public Interest* and Henry R. Luce Professor of Urban Values at New York University.

thought it was our responsibility to do so—we had the ships, the planes, the men and the money, too.

Power breeds responsibilities, in international affairs as in domestic—or even private. To dodge or disclaim these responsibilities is one form of the abuse of power. If, after Vietnam, the nations of the world become persuaded that we cannot be counted upon to do the kind of "policeman's" work the world's foremost power has hitherto performed, throughout most of history, we shall unquestionably witness an alarming upsurge in national delinquency and international disorder everywhere. Nor shall we remain unaffected, in our chrome-plated American fortress. Let me propose an example of how drastically we might indeed be affected—one which has received surprisingly little attention.

I happen to think that the Administration's "domino theory" is a perfectly correct description of what an American defeat (as against a settlement that falls short of victory for either side) will lead to. But let us assume that I'm wrong and that the nations of Southeast Asia will remain uncoerced, unintimidated and unsubverted by a Communist Vietnam, allied or not with a Communist China. There still remains the question of how India is going to react to a situation in which the sole and unrivaled Great Power in Asia is a nuclear-armed China. Can anyone doubt that—dominoes or no dominoes—the immediate consequence of an American withdrawal from Asia will be India's arming itself with nuclear weapons?

Even now, the Indian Government is balking at signing the nonproliferation agreement, so laboriously negotiated by the United States and Russia, because it is skeptical of the willingness or ability of these two powers to protect her from nuclear blackmail on the part of China. Should the United States cease being an Asian military power—as is now being urged by so many—this skepticism will turn into certitude. India will then start arming itself with nuclear weapons—it has had the technical capacity to do so for some time now. And if India proceeds, can Pakistan be far behind? How do we contemplate a world in which India and Pakistan glower at each other, their fingers curled around nuclear triggers? *That* is the kind of thing which has been at stake in Vietnam. . . .

It is exceedingly strange that so many people who have a sincere and passionate concern over the Bomb should be oblivious to the fact that we live in a nuclear age. . . . It is a world which, without "policing," will almost certainly blow itself to bits.

It is because this reality of world politics is so blithely ignored or passed over that I find much of the present controversy over American foreign policy so unreal. Will the United States go isolationist or neo-isolationist as a result of Vietnam, as some fear and others hope? But what can "going isolationist" mean, in today's world? There is no special American atmosphere; the air we breathe can be radioactively polluted by the actions of men, thousands of miles away, contesting issues in which, strictly speaking, we have no kind of national interest. What it comes down to, indeed, is that in the nuclear age no Great Power can responsibly define its national interest in "strictly speaking" terms.

I also find only a little less unreal the notion that the United States should be strictly selective in its international commitments —avoiding all cases where we are likely to get more deeply involved than we have determined beforehand we are willing to be. Things just do not work that way. "Strictly selective" commitments are as much an anachronism as a "strictly speaking" national interest. Like any policeman, a Great Power can remain prudently aloof from various imbroglios. A policeman on the beat can turn his eyes away from family quarrels, no matter how bitter and noisy, from petty bookmaking, no matter how flagrant. But if the family quarrel should become a street riot, or petty bookmaking be taken over by a syndicate, he has no choice but to intervene. Similarly, the United States need not—and does not— meddle in everything happening all over the globe. But to try to catalogue our commitments to suit our convenience is really not within our power. It may be recalled that Dean Acheson did precisely that with regard to South Korea; that "non-commitment" quickly turned into a major war for us.

Besides, the truth of the matter is that, because we are a Great Power, we are a "committed" nation without knowing what our commitments precisely are. Our commitments are necessarily defined, to a considerable extent, by circumstance and contingency. What, for instance, is the exact nature and extent of our commitment to the survival of the State of Israel? I don't know; the United States Government doesn't know, either; nor do the Governments of Israel, Egypt or the Soviet Union. What we will do to insure Israel's survival will depend on the kind of trouble it is in; it will also depend on the kind of trouble *we* are in, at the particular moment. This state of affairs will offend only the prissily tidy-minded. A precise and public definition of our commitment might, at some point, force us to choose between a nuclear war with the Soviet Union or China and a humiliating capitulation. The fewer such public definitions of our commitments we burden ourselves with, the better off we are.

*   *   *

Above all, I find unreal the idea, so popular on the liberal-left, that our troubles arise from something called "the cold war," and especially from a dogmatic opposition to anything carrying the odor of something called "Communism." True, some leading figures in American life—mainly in the Republican party, so far as I can see—talk this way. And it is unquestionably true that one major aim of American foreign policy is to establish or sustain a friendly and hospitable world environment.

But this last aim is shared by *all* Great Powers; it is attached to the very meaning of the term "Great Power." And the Administration has not been carrying on any kind of doctrinaire, ideological crusade against Communism, wherever and whenever. We are, for instance, scrupulously refraining from intervening in the present anti-Soviet and anti-Communist turmoil in Eastern Europe; we are not even *saying* very much about it. And there are quite a few of the new nations in Africa that have pro-Communist regimes without the Administration's even seeming to take any anxious notice of the fact.

Indeed the "cold war," properly speaking, is no longer a terribly significant fact of international life. Our conflict with the Soviet Union by now has few ideological overtones; during the last Middle East crisis, neither we nor the Soviet Union talked very much about "Communism" or "capitalism," except in a purely routine and ritualistic way. Our conflict with the Soviet Union today is much more a traditional struggle between Great Powers, in the 19th-century sense, with each protagonist trying to tilt the balance of power in its own direction. Were the Communist party of the Soviet Union to be replaced tomorrow by a Romanov Czar, this conflict would endure, and probably in much the same way.

The same is not yet true of China—but I suspect it soon will be. . . . Though we know little about the inner turmoil now taking place within China's political system, it is reasonable to suppose that the eventual upshot will be the emergence of a China which—like the U.S.S.R.—will be more interested in extending its national power than in selflessly propagating any ideology.

But there's the rub, precisely. For, in the nuclear age, there have emerged certain ground rules governing the *modus operandi* and the *modus vivendi* of Great Powers. The keystone of this system of rules is the assumption that no Great Power will attempt to revise the status quo by the use of force and violence—either directly or through a surrogate. It can use money, propaganda or various means of persuasion and intimidation, covert and overt, to tilt the balance of power in its favor. But it cannot use force—for such use of force brings with it the prospect of a military confrontation between Great Powers, and such a confrontation in turn immediately raises the possibility of a nuclear holocaust.

This is what the doctrine of "containment" has come to mean. It is not a peculiarly American doctrine, and certainly not an intrinsically anti-Communist one, since the Soviet Union in practice also subscribes to it. It is, to be sure, a relatively conservative doctrine, since it insists that the pattern of world power change gradually, subtly, as unobtrusively as possible. But when a world walks on explosive eggshells, as ours has been doing for nearly two decades now, there is no alternative to such conservatism.

APPENDIX

THE CHARTER
OF THE UNITED NATIONS

WE the peoples of the United Nations determined to save succeeding generations from the scourge of war, which twice in our lifetime has brought untold sorrow to mankind, and

to reaffirm faith in fundamental human rights, in the dignity and worth of the human person, in the equal rights of men and women and of nations large and small, and

to establish conditions under which justice and respect for the obligations arising from treaties and other sources of international law can be maintained, and

to promote social progress and better standards of life in larger freedom,

and for these ends to practice tolerance and live together in peace with one another as good neighbors, and

to unite our strength to maintain international peace and security, and

to ensure, by the acceptance of principles and the institution of methods, that armed force shall not be used, save in the common interest, and

to employ international machinery for the promotion of the economic and social advancement of all peoples,

have resolved to combine our efforts to accomplish these aims.

Accordingly, our respective Governments, through representatives assembled in the city of San Francisco, who have exhibited their full powers found to be in good and due form, have agreed to the present Charter of the United Nations and do hereby establish an international organization to be known as the United Nations.

CHAPTER I: PURPOSES AND PRINCIPLES

ARTICLE 1

The Purposes of the United Nations are:

1. To maintain international peace and security, and to that end: to take effective collective measures for the prevention and removal of threats to the peace, and for the suppression of acts of aggression or other breaches of the peace, and to bring about by peaceful means, and in conformity with the principles of justice and international law, adjustment or settlement of international disputes or situations which might lead to a breach of the peace;

2. To develop friendly relations among nations based on respect for the principle of equal rights and self-determination of peoples, and to take other appropriate measures to strengthen universal peace;

3. To achieve international cooperation in solving international problems of an economic, social, cultural, or humanitarian character, and in promoting and encouraging respect for human rights and for fundamental freedoms for all without distinction as to race, sex, language, or religion; and

4. To be a center for harmonizing the actions of nations in the attainment of these common ends.

ARTICLE 2

The Organization and its Members, in pursuit of the Purposes stated in Article 1, shall act in accordance with the following Principles.

1. The Organization is based on the principle of the sovereign equality of all its Members.

2. All Members, in order to ensure to all of them the rights and benefits resulting from membership, shall fulfill in good faith the obligations assumed by them in accordance with the present Charter.

3. All Members shall settle their international disputes by peaceful means in such a manner that international peace and security, and justice, are not endangered.

4. All Members shall refrain in their international relations from the threat or use of force against the territorial integrity or

political independence of any state, or in any other manner inconsistent with the Purposes of the United Nations.

5. All Members shall give the United Nations every assistance in any action it takes in accordance with the present Charter, and shall refrain from giving assistance to any state against which the United Nations is taking preventive or enforcement action.

6. The Organization shall ensure that states which are not Members of the United Nations act in accordance with these Principles so far as may be necessary for the maintenance of international peace and security.

7. Nothing contained in the present Charter shall authorize the United Nations to intervene in matters which are essentially within the domestic jurisdiction of any state or shall require the Members to submit such matters to settlement under the present Charter; but this principle shall not prejudice the application of enforcement measures under Chapter VII.

CHAPTER II: MEMBERSHIP

ARTICLE 3

The original Members of the United Nations shall be the states which, having participated in the United Nations Conference on International Organization at San Francisco, or having previously signed the Declaration by United Nations of January 1, 1942, sign the present Charter and ratify it in accordance with Article 110.

ARTICLE 4

1. Membership in the United Nations is open to all other peace-loving states which accept the obligations contained in the present Charter and, in the judgment of the Organization, are able and willing to carry out these obligations.

2. The admission of any such state to membership in the United Nations will be effected by a decision of the General Assembly upon the recommendation of the Security Council.

ARTICLE 5

A member of the United Nations against which preventive or enforcement action has been taken by the Security Council may be suspended from the exercise of the rights and privileges of membership by the General Assembly upon the recommendation of the Security Council. The exercise of these rights and privileges may be restored by the Security Council.

ARTICLE 6

A Member of the United Nations which has persistently violated the Principles contained in the present Charter may be expelled from the Organization by the General Assembly upon the recommendation of the Security Council.

CHAPTER III: ORGANS

ARTICLE 7

1. There are established as the principal organs of the United Nations: a General Assembly, a Security Council, an Economic and Social Council, a Trusteeship Council, an International Court of Justice, and a Secretariat.

2. Such subsidiary organs as may be found necessary may be established in accordance with the present Charter.

ARTICLE 8

The United Nations shall place no restrictions on the eligibility of men and women to participate in any capacity and under conditions of equality in its principal and subsidiary organs.

CHAPTER IV: THE GENERAL ASSEMBLY

COMPOSITION

ARTICLE 9

1. The General Assembly shall consist of all the Members of the United Nations.

2. Each member shall have not more than five representatives in the General Assembly.

FUNCTIONS AND POWERS

ARTICLE 10

The General Assembly may discuss any questions or any matters within the scope of the present Charter or relating to the powers and functions of any organs provided for in the present Charter, and, except as provided in Article 12, may make recommendations to the Members of the United Nations or to the Security Council or to both on any such questions or matters.

ARTICLE 11

1. The General Assembly may consider the general principles of cooperation in the maintenance of international peace and security, including the principles governing disarmament and the regulation of armaments, and may make recommendations with regard to such principles to the Members or to the Security Council or to both.

2. The General Assembly may discuss any questions relating to the maintenance of international peace and security brought before it by any Member of the United Nations, or by the Security Council, or by a state which is not a Member of the United Nations in accordance with Article 35, paragraph 2, and, except as provided in Article 12, may make recommendations with regard to any such questions to the state or states concerned or to the Security Council or to both. Any such question on which action is necessary shall be referred to the Security Council by the General Assembly either before or after discussion.

3. The General Assembly may call the attention of the Security Council to situations which are likely to endanger international peace and security.

4. The powers of the General Assembly set forth in this Article shall not limit the general scope of Article 10.

ARTICLE 12

1. While the Security Council is exercising in respect of any dispute or situation the functions assigned to it in the present Charter, the General Assembly shall not make any recommendations

with regard to that dispute or situation unless the Security Council so requests.

2. The Secretary-General, with the consent of the Security Council, shall notify the General Assembly at each session of any matters relative to the maintenance of international peace and security which are being dealt with by the Security Council and shall similarly notify the General Assembly, or the Members of the United Nations if the General Assembly is not in session, immediately the Security Council ceases to deal with such matters.

ARTICLE 13

1. The General Assembly shall initiate studies and make recommendations for the purpose of:

a. promoting international cooperation in the political field and encouraging the progressive development of international law and its codification;

b. promoting international cooperation in the economic, social, cultural, educational, and health fields, and assisting in the realization of human rights and fundamental freedoms for all without distinction as to race, sex, language, or religion.

2. The further responsibilities, functions, and powers of the General Assembly with respect to matters mentioned in paragraph 1 (*b*) above are set forth in Chapters IX and X.

ARTICLE 14

Subject to the provisions of Article 12, the General Assembly may recommend measures for the peaceful adjustment of any situation, regardless of origin, which it deems likely to impair the general welfare or friendly relations among nations, including situations resulting from a violation of the provisions of the present Charter setting forth the Purposes and Principles of the United Nations.

ARTICLE 15

1. The General Assembly shall receive and consider annual and special reports from the Security Council; these reports shall include an account of the measures that the Security Council has decided upon or taken to maintain international peace and security.

2. The General Assembly shall receive and consider reports from the other organs of the United Nations.

ARTICLE 16

The General Assembly shall perform such functions with respect to the international trusteeship system as are assigned to it under Chapters XII and XIII, including the approval of the trusteeship agreements for areas not designated as strategic.

ARTICLE 17

1. The General Assembly shall consider and approve the budget of the Organization.

2. The expenses of the Organization shall be borne by the Members as apportioned by the General Assembly.

3. The General Assembly shall consider and approve any financial and budgetary arrangements with specialized agencies referred to in Article 57 and shall examine the administrative budgets of such specialized agencies with a view to making recommendations to the agencies concerned.

VOTING

ARTICLE 18

1. Each member of the General Assembly shall have one vote.

2. Decisions of the General Assembly on important questions shall be made by a two-thirds majority of the members present and voting. These questions shall include: recommendations with respect to the maintenance of international peace and security, the election of the non-permanent members of the Security Council, the election of the members of the Economic and Social Council, the election of members of the Trusteeship Council in accordance with paragraph 1 (c) of Article 86, the admission of new Members to the United Nations, the suspension of the rights and privileges of membership, the expulsion of Members, questions relating to the operation of the trusteeship system, and budgetary questions.

3. Decisions on other questions, including the determination of additional categories of questions to be decided by a two-thirds

majority, shall be made by a majority of the members present and voting.

ARTICLE 19

A Member of the United Nations which is in arrears in the payment of its financial contributions to the Organization shall have no vote in the General Assembly if the amount of its arrears equals or exceeds the amount of the contributions due from it for the preceding two full years. The General Assembly may, nevertheless, permit such a Member to vote if it is satisfied that the failure to pay is due to conditions beyond the control of the Member.

PROCEDURE

ARTICLE 20

The General Assembly shall meet in regular annual sessions and in such special sessions as occasion may require. Special sessions shall be convoked by the Secretary-General at the request of the Security Council or of a majority of the Members of the United Nations.

ARTICLE 21

The General Assembly shall adopt its own rules of procedure. It shall elect its President for each session.

ARTICLE 22

The General Assembly may establish such subsidiary organs as it deems necessary for the performance of its functions.

CHAPTER V: THE SECURITY COUNCIL

COMPOSITION

ARTICLE 23

1. The Security Council shall consist of eleven Members of the United Nations. The Republic of China, France, the Union of Soviet Socialist Republics, the United Kingdom of Great Britain and Northern Ireland, and the United States of America shall be

permanent members of the Security Council. The General Assembly shall elect six other Members of the United Nations to be non-permanent members of the Security Council, due regard being specially paid, in the first instance to the contribution of Members of the United Nations to the maintenance of international peace and security and to the other purposes of the Organization, and also to equitable geographical distribution.

2. The non-permanent members of the Security Council shall be elected for a term of two years. In the first election of the non-permanent members, however, three shall be chosen for a term of one year. A retiring member shall not be eligible for immediate re-election.

3. Each member of the Security Council shall have one representative.

FUNCTIONS AND POWERS

ARTICLE 24

1. In order to ensure prompt and effective action by the United Nations, its Members confer on the Security Council primary responsibility for the maintenance of international peace and security, and agree that in carrying out its duties under this responsibility the Security Council acts on their behalf.

2. In discharging these duties the Security Council shall act in accordance with the Purposes and Principles of the United Nations. The specific powers granted to the Security Council for the discharge of these duties are laid down in Chapters VI, VII, VIII, and XII.

3. The Security Council shall submit annual and, when necessary, special reports to the General Assembly for its consideration.

ARTICLE 25

The Members of the United Nations agree to accept and carry out the decisions of the Security Council in accordance with the present Charter.

ARTICLE 26

In order to promote the establishment and maintenance of international peace and security with the least diversion for armaments of the world's human and economic resources, the Security Council shall be responsible for formulating, with the assistance of the Military Staff Committee referred to in Article 47, plans to be submitted to the Members of the United Nations for the establishment of a system for the regulation of armaments.

VOTING

ARTICLE 27

1. Each member of the Security Council shall have one vote.

2. Decisions of the Security Council on procedural matters shall be made by an affirmative vote of seven members.

3. Decisions of the Security Council on all other matters shall be made by an affirmative vote of seven members including the concurring votes of the permanent members; provided that, in decisions under Chapter VI, and under paragraph 3 of Article 52, a party to a dispute shall abstain from voting.

PROCEDURE

ARTICLE 28

1. The Security Council shall be so organized as to be able to function continuously. Each member of the Security Council shall for this purpose be represented at all times at the seat of the Organization.

2. The Security Council shall hold periodic meetings at which each of its members may, if it so desires, be represented by a member of the government or by some other specially designated representative.

3. The Security Council may hold meetings at such places other than the seat of the Organization as in its judgment will best facilitate its work.

ARTICLE 29

The Security Council may establish such subsidiary organs as it deems necessary for the performance of its functions.

Article 30

The Security Council shall adopt its own rules of procedure, including the method of selecting its President.

Article 31

Any Member of the United Nations which is not a member of the Security Council may participate, without vote, in the discussion of any question brought before the Security Council whenever the latter considers that the interests of that Member are specially affected.

Article 32

Any Member of the United Nations which is not a member of the Security Council or any state which is not a Member of the United Nations, if it is a party to a dispute under consideration by the Security Council, shall be invited to participate, without vote, in the discussion relating to the dispute. The Security Council shall lay down such conditions as it deems just for the participation of a state which is not a Member of the United Nations.

CHAPTER VI: PACIFIC SETTLEMENT OF DISPUTES

Article 33

1. The parties to any dispute, the continuance of which is likely to endanger the maintenance of international peace and security, shall, first of all, seek a solution by negotiation, enquiry, mediation, conciliation, arbitration, judicial settlement, resort to regional agencies or arrangements, or other peaceful means of their own choice.

2. The Security Council shall, when it deems necessary, call upon the parties to settle their dispute by such means.

Article 34

The Security Council may investigate any dispute, or any situation which might lead to international friction or give rise to a dispute, in order to determine whether the continuance of the dispute or situation is likely to endanger the maintenance of international peace and security.

ARTICLE 35

1.   Any Member of the United Nations may bring any dispute, or any situation of the nature referred to in Article 34, to the attention of the Security Council or of the General Assembly.

2.   A state which is not a Member of the United Nations may bring to the attention of the Security Council or of the General Assembly any dispute to which it is a party if it accepts in advance, for the purposes of the dispute, the obligations of pacific settlement provided in the present Charter.

3.   The proceedings of the General Assembly in respect of matters brought to its attention under this Article will be subject to the provisions of Articles 11 and 12.

ARTICLE 36

1.   The Security Council may, at any stage of a dispute of the nature referred to in Article 33 or of a situation of like nature, recommend appropriate procedures or methods of adjustment.

2.   The Security Council should take into consideration any procedures for the settlement of the dispute which have already been adopted by the parties.

3.   In making recommendations under this Article the Security Council should also take into consideration that legal disputes should as a general rule be referred by the parties to the International Court of Justice in accordance with the provisions of the Statute of the Court.

ARTICLE 37

1.   Should the parties to a dispute of the nature referred to in Article 33 fail to settle it by the means indicated in that Article, they shall refer it to the Security Council.

2.   If the Security Council deems that the continuance of the dispute is in fact likely to endanger the maintenance of international peace and security, it shall decide whether to take action under Article 36 or to recommend such terms of settlement as it may consider appropriate.

ARTICLE 38

Without prejudice to the provisions of Articles 33 to 37, the

Security Council may, if all the parties to any dispute so request, make recommendations to the parties with a view to a pacific settlement of the dispute.

CHAPTER VII: ACTION WITH RESPECT TO THREATS TO THE PEACE, BREACHES OF THE PEACE, AND ACTS OF AGGRESSION

ARTICLE 39

The Security Council shall determine the existence of any threat to the peace, breach of the peace, or act of aggression and shall make recommendations, or decide what measures shall be taken in accordance with Articles 41 and 42, to maintain or restore international peace and security.

ARTICLE 40

In order to prevent an aggravation of the situation, the Security Council may, before making the recommendations or deciding upon the measures provided for in Article 39, call upon the parties concerned to comply with such provisional measures as it deems necessary or desirable. Such provisional measures shall be without prejudice to the rights, claims, or position of the parties concerned. The Security Council shall duly take account of failure to comply with such provisional measures.

ARTICLE 41

The Security Council may decide what measures not involving the use of armed force are to be employed to give effect to its decisions, and it may call upon the Members of the United Nations to apply such measures. These may include complete or partial interruption of economic relations and of rail, sea, air, postal, telegraphic, radio, and other means of communication, and the severance of diplomatic relations.

ARTICLE 42

Should the Security Council consider that measures provided for in Article 41 would be inadequate or have proved to be inadequate, it may take such action by air, sea, or land forces as may be necessary to maintain or restore international peace and security. Such action may include demonstrations, blockade, and other operations by air, sea, or land forces of Members of the United Nations.

ARTICLE 43

1. All Members of the United Nations, in order to contribute to the maintenance of international peace and security, undertake to make available to the Security Council, on its call and in accordance with a special agreement or agreements, armed forces, assistance, and facilities, including rights of passage, necessary for the purpose of maintaining international peace and security.

2. Such agreement or agreements shall govern the numbers and types of forces, their degree of readiness and general location, and the nature of the facilities and assistance to be provided.

3. The agreement or agreements shall be negotiated as soon as possible on the initiative of the Security Council. They shall be concluded between the Security Council and Members or between the Security Council and groups of Members and shall be subject to ratification by the signatory states in accordance with their respective constitutional processes.

ARTICLE 44

When the Security Council has decided to use force it shall, before calling upon a Member not represented on it to provide armed forces in fulfillment of the obligations assumed under Article 43, invite that Member, if the Member so desires, to participate in the decisions of the Security Council concerning the employment of contingents of that Member's armed forces.

ARTICLE 45

. In order to enable the United Nations to take urgent military measures, Members shall hold immediately available national air-force contingents for combined international enforcement action. The strength and degree of readiness of these contingents and plans for their combined action shall be determined, within the limits laid down in the special agreement or agreements referred to in Article 43, by the Security Council with the assistance of the Military Staff Committee.

ARTICLE 46

Plans for the application of armed force shall be made by the Security Council with the assistance of the Military Staff Committee.

ARTICLE 47

1. There shall be established a Military Staff Committee to advise and assist the Security Council on all questions relating to the Security Council's military requirements for the maintenance of international peace and security, the employment and command of forces placed at its disposal, the regulation of armaments, and possible disarmament.

2. The Military Staff Committee shall consist of the Chiefs of Staff of the permanent members of the Security Council or their representatives. Any Member of the United Nations not permanently represented on the Committee shall be invited by the Committee to be associated with it when the efficient discharge of the Committee's responsibilities requires the participation of that Member in its work.

3. The Military Staff Committee shall be responsible under the Security Council for the strategic direction of any armed forces placed at the disposal of the Security Council. Questions relating to the command of such forces shall be worked out subsequently.

4. The Military Staff Committee, with the authorization of the Security Council and after consultation with appropriate regional agencies, may establish regional subcommittees.

ARTICLE 48

1. The action required to carry out the decisions of the Security Council for the maintenance of international peace and security shall be taken by all the Members of the United Nations or by some of them, as the Security Council may determine.

2. Such decisions shall be carried out by the Members of the United Nations directly and through their action in the appropriate international agencies of which they are members.

ARTICLE 49

The Members of the United Nations shall join in affording mutual assistance in carrying out the measures decided upon by the Security Council.

ARTICLE 50

If preventive or enforcement measures against any state are taken by the Security Council, any other state, whether a Member of the United Nations or not, which finds itself confronted with special economic problems arising from the carrying out of those measures shall have the right to consult the Security Council with regard to a solution of those problems.

ARTICLE 51

Nothing in the present Charter shall impair the inherent right of individual or collective self-defense if an armed attack occurs against a Member of the United Nations, until the Security Council has taken the measures necessary to maintain international peace and security. Measures taken by Members in the exercise of this right of self-defense shall be immediately reported to the Security Council and shall not in any way affect the authority and responsibility of the Security Council under the present Charter to take at any time such action as it deems necessary in order to maintain or restore international peace and security.

CHAPTER VIII: REGIONAL ARRANGEMENTS

ARTICLE 52

1. Nothing in the present Charter precludes the existence of regional arrangements or agencies for dealing with such matters relating to the maintenance of international peace and security as are appropriate for regional action, provided that such arrangements or agencies and their activities are consistent with the Purposes and Principles of the United Nations.

2. The Members of the United Nations entering into such arrangements or constituting such agencies shall make every effort to

achieve pacific settlement of local disputes through such regional arrangements or by such regional agencies before referring them to the Security Council.

3. The Security Council shall encourage the development of pacific settlement of local disputes through such regional arrangements or by such regional agencies either on the initiative of the states concerned or by reference from the Security Council.

4. This Article in no way impairs the application of Articles 34 and 35.

ARTICLE 53

1. The Security Council shall, where appropriate, utilize such regional arrangements or agencies for enforcement action under its authority. But no enforcement action shall be taken under regional arrangements or by regional agencies without the authorization of the Security Council, with the exception of measures against any enemy state, as defined in paragraph 2 of this Article, provided for pursuant to Article 107 or in regional arrangements directed against renewal of aggressive policy on the part of any such state, until such time as the Organization may, on request of the Governments concerned, be charged with the responsibility for preventing further aggression by such a state.

2. The term enemy state as used in paragraph 1 of this Article applies to any state which during the Second World War has been an enemy of any signatory of the present Charter.

ARTICLE 54

The Security Council shall at all times be kept fully informed of activities undertaken or in contemplation under regional arrangements or by regional agencies for the maintenance of international peace and security.

* * *